THE WRITINGS OF JULIAN OF NORWICH

EDITED BY

Nicholas Watson and
Jacqueline Jenkins

THE PENNSYLVANIA STATE UNIVERSITY PRESS | UNIVERSITY PARK, PENNSYLVANIA

THE WRITINGS OF JULIAN OF NORWICH

A Vision Showed to a Devout Woman

AND

A Revelation of Love

Library of Congress Cataloging-in-Publication Data

The writings of Julian of Norwich :
A vision showed to a devout woman and A revelation of love /
edited by Nicholas Watson and Jacqueline Jenkins.
   p.   cm. — (Brepols medieval women series)
Includes bibliographical references.
ISBN 0-271-02547-6 (alk. paper)
1. Julian, of Norwich, b. 1343.
2. Mysticism—England—History—Middle Ages, 500–1500.
I. Watson, Nicholas.
II. Jenkins, Jacqueline.
III. Julian, of Norwich, b. 1343. Revelations of divine love.
IV. Series.

BV4832.3.W75 2005
242—dc22
2005010832

The Pennsylvania State University Press is a member
of the Association of American University Presses.

This book is dedicated
to the memories of two grandmothers

DR. MARY WATSON (NÉE GRIFFITHS)
1898–1993
medical missionary
England (Norwich), China (Kunming-Yunnanfu),
England (Bromley, Chinnor)

❧

MRS. FLORENCE JENKINS (NÉE CAIRNS)
1911–2000
Canada (Bancroft, Ontario)

CONTENTS

PREFACE

Julian of Norwich (ca. 1343–after 1416) was a contemporary of Geoffrey Chaucer, William Langland, John Wyclif, and Margery Kempe, her younger counterpart, and is the earliest known woman writer of English. This last fact alone would make her worth reading, but in practice the reputation of her two surviving works, *A Vision Showed to a Devout Woman* and its greatly expanded revision, *A Revelation of Love,* is built less on their historical significance than on their conceptual sophistication, their prose, and the urgency to many of what they have to say. Long neglected outside a small circle, Julian has been studied with increasing excitement over the last hundred years, and by readers outside the academy as least as much as by students and scholars. Since the 1970s, in particular, a flood of translations, excerpts, academic studies, and spiritual reflections on her thought, along with five editions, has washed into print, and her rebuilt cell in a tiny Norwich church has become a regular stop on devout bus tours. Although she describes herself as "a simple creature unletterde" and is still sometimes thought of as no more than the saintly optimist who said "alle shalle be wele," she is now widely recognized as one of the great speculative theologians of the Middle Ages: an intellectual whose rare ability to pay simultaneous attention to what is true in an abstract sense and to what humans need to be true in a material one gives her writing extraordinary tension and energy. She remains, however, a difficult thinker: partly for the intricacy with which she thinks through and with the text of her revelation; partly for the complexity of her modelings of God and the soul; partly for the elusiveness and allusiveness of her language. Readers, including scholarly readers, often resort to translations to understand her.

This book presents a new edition of the writings of Julian of Norwich in Middle English: an edition that aims to make possible the serious reading and study of her thought no translation can provide and to do so not only for students and scholars of Middle English but for those with little or no previous experience with the language. Julian states that she writes for "mine evenchristen," or fellow Christians, "that they might alle see and know the same that I sawe" (*Rev.* 8.22–23). In late-fourteenth-century Norwich, "evenchristen" nominally meant everyone, but this edition will have many readers who adhere to religions other than Christianity, or to none. Nevertheless, the editors have tried to take more seriously than others the force and ambition of the words "alle" and "same," with their call not only to make her thought widely available but to do so as deeply and in as much detail as possible.

The main features of the edition are as follows:

- Separate texts of both Julian's works, *A Vision Showed to a Devout Woman* and *A Revelation of Love,* with modern punctuation, paragraphing, and partly regularized spelling, all based on new transcriptions of the manuscripts and original editorial policies and arguments.
- A second, analytic edition of *A Vision* printed underneath the text of *A Revelation,* with varying typefaces and other symbols to show what was left out, changed, or added as the earlier work was expanded into the later one.
- Facing-page explanatory notes, with translations of difficult words and phrases, cross-references to other parts of the text, citations of biblical and other sources, and brief comments on structure and argument when these are not immediately clear.
- Textual endnotes that fully explain the editorial decisions involved in establishing the texts.
- An appendix of records relating to Julian and her writings, including the earliest series of excerpts from *A Revelation,* three wills bequeathing her money, an excerpt about her from *The Book of Margery Kempe,* and several extracts from seventeenth-century works that either use or attack her thought. (These last derive from or attack the English Catholic milieu in which the only surviving manuscripts of *A Revelation* were copied, probably by nuns living in exile in Belgium and France, and out of which the earliest printed edition of the work was produced.)
- A bibliography of editions, translations, scholarly studies, and other works.
- An introduction describing what is known about Julian's life, early reputation, and the history of her reception and including both a detailed account of the edition and a guide to its use.

Not part of the edition as it stands are an account of the theology and composition history of *A Vision* and *A Revelation;* a comparative study of their style, content, and language; an analysis of their English and European historical contexts; and a sustained argument as to their modern significance. These topics are to be covered in a companion volume, *The Lowest Part of Our Need: A Guide to Julian of Norwich.*

From a scholarly point of view, the most distinctive feature of the edition may be its treatment of the evidence provided by the manuscripts of *A Vision* and especially *A Revelation.* Middle English editions habitually retain the spellings of their base manuscript and only emend that manuscript when its readings make no sense. Despite the fact that both complete manuscripts of *A Revelation* are from the seventeenth century, earlier editions of Julian's writings follow suit. This edition is at once more interventionist and more speculative, drawing on several kinds of evidence—the evidence not only of the *Revelation* manuscripts themselves but also of the work's tissue of internal allusions and the readings provided by *A Vision*—to establish a hybrid text that differs in many details from its predecessors. Not only does it take hundreds of readings from manuscripts other than the base manuscript; to facilitate reading, it regularizes and modernizes many spellings, although it also aims to retain enough of the spelling system of the original to convey the flavor of the manuscript's Middle English. For readers who are not concerned with textual matters, the result should be experienced simply as a gain in the lucidity and balance of Julian's prose. For Middle English scholars, the edition is intended both as a hypothesis and as a challenge to the assumptions the field habitually brings to the business of editing.

ACKNOWLEDGMENTS

This edition began life more than a decade ago as part of a project funded by the Social Sciences and Humanities Research Council of Canada and owes the council a very real debt. We could not have seen the manuscripts, met with one another, or hired research assistants without their help. We thank them, as well as the universities that provided us with institutional homes and further funding: the University of Western Ontario, the University of Calgary, and Harvard University.

We thank the British Library, the Bibliothèque nationale, and the Westminster Cathedral Treasury for permission to consult and quote from their manuscripts and early printed books. We also thank the English Benedictine convent communities of Stanbrook Abbey, Worcestershire, and St. Mary's Abbey, Colwich, Staffordshire, both in England, for providing us with information about the seventeenth-century manuscripts we discuss in the Appendix, and for their permission to include extracts from them in this edition. In particular, we would like to thank Sr. Margaret Truran, OSB, archivist at Stanbrook Abbey, for her kind assistance and for sharing information about her own research with us. We also thank The Julian Centre at Saint Julian's, Conesford, Norwich, for their hospitality, and for their generosity in opening their archives to us.

Several people have worked with us as collaborators, research assistants, or consultants. Among the first, we thank Hugh Kempster for letting us use his work on the Westminster Manuscript and Amy Appleford for taking responsibility for the bibliography. Among the second, we again thank Amy Appleford, as well as Allyson Foster, Ayn Becze, Amy Britton, and Kristen Warder, all of whom worked on various stages of the project. We also thank Glenn Mielke, who acted as our consultant on page layout, and the readers for Penn State Press, Bella Millett and Roger Ellis, for their careful analysis of the manuscript and thoughtful suggestions, most of which we followed. Among those who have given less formal kinds of help, we thank Jocelyn Wogan-Browne, who helped make our most difficult decisions; Michael Sargent, for early encouragement; Marleen Cré, for copies of her two outstandingly useful theses; Will Robins, whose careful frankness much sharpened our theorizing of our editorial position; Barbara Newman, for some excellent specific suggestions; and the students in our graduate classes at Harvard and Calgary, where we test-drove the edition. Finally, we thank Penn State Press for undertaking this complex project and committing their talent and resources to it. In particular, we owe a deep debt to Keith Monley, our

XII   ACKNOWLEDGMENTS

copy editor, not only for the hundreds of hours he worked, with all his wonted precision, on our manuscript but also for his insistence on understanding the project so deeply. To an extent that he and its editors alone can fully appreciate, this is a far better book because of him. We are also deeply grateful to Peter Potter, editor-in-chief of Penn State Press, not only for his good advice but for his faith in the project over all too many years, as it grew and grew, and as deadline after deadline passed in profound scholarly silence.

INTRODUCTION

Part One: On Julian and Her Writings

1. *A VISION* AND *A REVELATION*

"Julian of Norwich" is the only name we have for the author of two closely linked works called *A Vision Showed to a Devoute Woman* and *A Revelation of Love* and written in a northeastern dialect of Middle English sometime between the mid-1370s and Julian's death more than forty years later.[1] Both are first-person accounts of the same visionary experience, which the works represent as the climax of a near-fatal illness Julian suffered when she was thirty. In the form in which the works enact it for us, this experience is at once intensely focused and strangely fragmentary. A sculpted image of Christ's head, fixed to a crucifix held before Julian as she lies dying, begins to bleed, while a medley of visionary thoughts and images shimmer in the background, some hardly more than shadows or guesses at absences. Scenes from Christ's Passion play out "in the face of the crucifixe," on an ascending scale of horror (*Vis.* 2.26). After enduring for an endless instant the compassion caused by these sights, Julian is rewarded by seeing Christ, still on his sculpted cross, come suddenly back to life. Then he makes a mysterious promise, not just to her but to everyone, that "sinne is behovelye [fitting] . . . Botte [but] alle shalle be wele, and alle maner of thinge shalle be wele" (*Vis.* 13.45, 61). Out of her excited dismay come more visions. Two feature demons, who taunt her for not believing her revelation when she wakes up for a few hours to the everyday and finds herself still sick. The revelation ends with Christ sitting enthroned in the human soul, promising her that all she has seen and heard is true.

A Vision is a wonderfully crafted scene-by-scene account of this experience, which in the form we now have it may have been finished in the middle of the 1380s, a full fifteen years after the revelation (according to the date given in *A Revelation*) took place.[2] In it, Julian presents herself mainly as a participant, not an interpreter, who at first understands her experience simply as a sequence of events. Since the revelation is broken up into multiple layers and levels, this exposition by narration has the effect of emphasizing the otherworldly obscurity of its logic. *A Vision* depicts the scene at Julian's sickbed, the progress of her disease, and her first reactions to her revelation, as she suffers with Christ, worries at the unpredictable comings and goings of his

---

1. *A Vision Shewed be the Goodenes of God to a Devoute Woman* and *A Revelation of Love that Jhesu Christ, Our Endles Blisse, Made in Sixteen Shewinges.* Citations to *A Vision* and *A Revelation* are by section and chapter number, followed by line numbers, respectively.

2. Nicholas Watson, "The Composition of Julian of Norwich's *Revelation of Love,*" *Speculum* 68 (1993): 637–83.

presence, rejoices in his resurrection, asks him about the meaning of sin, and begins to be answered with some initially unbelievable new ideas about the place of sin in God's love. The whole work stays close to the historical present of the single day during which the revelation is said to have happened, leaving little room for elaboration. In its more discursive later sections especially, discussions of theological ideas can be so brief as to be obscure, taking wing for a few sentences before being suddenly cut off, as though more had been thought or drafted than was allowed into the final copy. Bold, movingly written, and full of interest though it is, coherent though it is about the "comforthe" it claims God wants to offer its readers (*Vis.* 6.7), *A Vision* still labors under the weight of all it has wanted to say and, for whatever reason, cannot.

Altogether more ambitious, *A Revelation* is a full-scale expansion and rewriting of *A Vision* that may not have been begun until the middle of the 1390s and may have been finished any-time between then and Julian's death, after 1416. *A Revelation* is more than four times the length of *A Vision* and shows deep respect for the words and ideas of its predecessor even as it transforms them into something new: a specu-lative argument, only dimly visible in *A Vision,* about the being and nature of God, human-kind, and creation. According to *A Revelation,* the engines of transformation were two second-ary revelations of 1388 and 1393, which together enabled Julian to resolve her puzzlement at the significance of the original revelation. In the first, Julian learned that "love," and nothing else, "was his mening" (*Rev.* 86.14); in the sec-ond, she was told that, in reenvisioning the rev-elation as this message of love, she needed to focus especially on an episode she claims to have left out of *A Vision* because she did not understand it. In this dim, hardly remembered glimpse of a truth, a servant, asked to do work for his lord, sets out with such zeal to get his job

done that he trips, falls, and ends up on the ground, "groning and moning" in pain at his hurt and shame at his failure (*Rev.* 51.250–51). Far from being angry at him, however, his lord pities him and promises to reward him more than he would have done if he had not fallen. It seems that, in falling, the servant has not failed but mysteriously performed the work he was given.

Working its every detail with fierce inten-sity, *A Revelation* turns this simple exemplum into the starting-point of an argument of great complexity and optimism that reconstrues the nature of human sin and goodness from the ground up in bold, speculative leaps. Like the servant's fall (which signifies both Adam's Fall and Christ's Incarnation, here versions of the same event), sin is a product of inexperience, not perversion, and does not even affect the entirety of the soul, only its lower part, or "sen-sualite." There remains a higher, unfallen part of the soul, the "substance," hidden with God (the lord in the exemplum) and longing to be reunited with the sensuality. God is a father, endlessly pleased with his children. He is a mother, too, always willing to help and, if need be, discipline them. In the Passion, then, Christ our mother, "falling" into Mary's womb, came to the aid of the sensuality, to comfort it; and he comforts it again in giving Julian her revelation, which reenacts the Passion to show its true meaning: "alle shalle be wele" (*Rev.* 27.10). This promise tantalizingly suggests that all humanity will gain salvation, a thought whose daring causes anxiety in *A Vision.* But the revelation shows that God wants some things kept hidden so that humans can remain at their work of hopeful suffering, and the resolution of this promise is left to the "privy conceyles" of Christ (*Rev.* 30.12). Presenting Julian now not only as participant in her vision but as its cocreator and most rigorous and qualified interpreter—even as her understanding of the revelation becomes ever more preoccupied with the limits of her own, and of all human, understanding—*A Revelation* repeatedly circles round these and other themes and images, as it seeks to proclaim God's message of comfort and ruminates on the knowability, and the far deeper unknowability, of truth.

A Vision, the earliest writing in English we know to be by a woman, can profitably be read as an essay in the genre of personal meditation associated with Anselm of Canterbury, although in its later stages it becomes increasingly involved in another genre, that of the "remedy against sin." Like even the most learned of Anselm's meditations, it, too, is less concerned with ideas than it is intent to give birth to words that will be "gretly stirrande [stirring] to alle thaye [those] that desires to be Cristes loverse" (*Vis.* Rubric 3–4). Fixated on Christ's Passion and the desire for union with his suffering through the medium of the gaze (Julian's, Christ's, the reader's), much of *A Vision* would not seem strange to anyone, medieval or modern, familiar with the affective theology and rhetoric cultivated by Anselm and his successors, or the language of spiritual comfort found in works like *Ancrene Wisse* or William Flete's *Remedy Against the Troubles of Temptations.* Despite its intellectualism, the work even bears traces of that most emotive outgrowth of Anselmian meditation, the Middle English soliloquies for enclosed women—with passionate names like *The Love Rune, The Wooing of Our Lord* and *A Talking of the Love of God*—and clearer signs of two affective Continental texts in the Franciscan tradition: James of Milan's meditative compendium, *Stimulus amoris* (translated into English as *The Prickynge of Love*) and Johannes de Caulibus's life of Christ, *Meditationes vitae Christi* (translated as *The Privity of the Passion*). *A Vision* also has close affinities with earlier visionary writings, including writings associated with other visionary women, which similarly balance the devotional and the theological. English readers seem to have begun showing deep interest in this Continental tradition of visionary texts only late in the fourteenth century. Yet at least two of them—Elizabeth of Hungary's *Revelations* and Bridget of Sweden's *Liber celestis*—would have been known to Julian or members of her circle and could have provided models or precedents for *A Vision.*[3]

By contrast—and despite the eclectic way it borrows from religious manuals, biblical commentary, and other genres—*A Revelation* is a work with no real precedent: a speculative vernacular theology, not modeled on earlier texts but structured as a prolonged investigation into the divine, whose prophetic goal is to birth a new understanding of human living in the world and of the nature of God in his interactions with the world, not just for theologians but for everyone. *A Revelation,* too, has its affinities with meditations, remedies, and other visionary writings. But its only peers are a small heterogeneous group of works of similar ambition that (with the exception of the last mentioned) Julian is unlikely to have known: Mechtild of Magdeburg's *Das fließende Licht der Gottheit* (*The Flowing Light of the Godhead*), Dante Alighieri's *Commedia* (*Divine Comedy*), John of Morigny's *Liber visionum* (*Book of Visions*), and William Langland's *Piers Plowman.* Outstanding even in this company for the intensity of its determination to reimagine Christian thought in its entirety, not as a system of ideas but as an answer to human need, *A Revelation* is one of the most inventive, intellectually

3. Rosalynn Voaden, ed., *Prophets Abroad: The Reception of Continental Holy Women in Late-Medieval England* (Cambridge: D. S. Brewer, 1996); Roger Ellis, "'Flores ad Fabricandum . . . Coronam': An Investigation into the Uses of the Revelations of St. Bridget of Sweden in Fifteenth-Century England," *Medium Aevum* 51 (1982): 163–86.

consumed, and consuming literary projects of the European Middle Ages.

2. A FRAGMENTARY BIOGRAPHY

Who, other than an unforgettably thoughtful, persistent, supple narrative voice, was "Julian of Norwich"? Unfortunately, this question can for the most part only be answered with guesses and conjectures, for we do not know either of the crucial pieces of information that might enable us to identify her, or at least her family, in the historical records: her name at birth and the date of her death. According to the date of her revelation and her age at the time, given in *A Revelation* (chaps. 2–3), we can assume she was born in 1342–43 and thus that, as a young child, she lived through the Black Death. From her level of education, social connections in later life, love of courtly language, and from the underlying dialect of her works, we can guess that she grew up in or near Norwich, in affluent circumstances. We are told that her revelation (variously dated in the manuscripts May 8 and May 13, 1373) took place as she lay on her sickbed, attended by her priest, mother, and others (*Rev.*, chap. 3; *Vis.*, secs. 2, 10). *A Vision* gives an intimate account of the slow dying of her body. The import of both her books is that the revelation and the charge it laid on her was the summit of her life, from which all else sloped steeply away.

Her profession and state of life at the time of the revelation is not known, although there is a strong possibility she was a nun at the Benedictine convent at Carrow, a mile from the church of St. Julian's, Conesford, in Norwich, where she was later enclosed as an anchoress. In recent years a certain pressure has been placed on the scanty evidence to suggest she was an "ordinary laywoman," perhaps married and a mother.[4] But the references to mothering and pregnancy in *A Revelation* are theological, not autobiographical, and the presence of Julian's mother in *A Vision*'s version of the sickbed scene and the absence of references to "sisters" may testify only to the close ties between late medieval English religious houses and their communities. Julian's cell was in the gift of the Carrow nuns, most of them members of prominent local families, and Carrow is a likely place for Julian to have received what must have been her thorough early education. Her reported response to the beginning of the revelation—as she repeats over and over again the exclamation "Benedicite dominus!"—recalls the greeting formula used between Benedictine monks and nuns, by which the junior religious says, "Benedicite" (Bless me), and the senior replies, "Dominus te benedicat" (May the Lord bless you) (*Vis.* 3.15). During the revelation, Christ thanks Julian "of thy service and of thy travaile [labor] and namly [especially] in thy youth," as though she had consecrated herself to God in childhood or early adulthood, at a moment in both works full of evocations of the literature of professional virginity (*Vis.* 8.53–54; *Rev.*, chap. 14). The religiosity of nuns and devout laywomen may not have differed a great deal, and it is possible that Christ is congratulating Julian on a less formal commitment than religious profession, such as the one implied by the "thre graces" she asks for at the outset (*Vis.* 1.1). But a straightforward reading of this passage in light of other fragments of evidence makes it likely she was a nun.[5]

---

4. Benedicta Ward makes the best case for Julian as a laywoman. See "Julian the Solitary," in *Julian Reconsidered*, Fairacres Publications 106, ed. Kenneth Leech and Benedicta Ward (Oxford: SLG Press, 1988).

5. On Carrow and female monasticism in Norwich and East Anglia, see Roberta Gilchrist and Marilyn Oliva, *Religious Women in Medieval East Anglia: History and Archaeology, c.1100–1540* (Norwich: Centre of East Anglian Studies, University of East Anglia, 1993); Marilyn Oliva, *The Convent and the Community in Late Medieval England: Female Monasteries in the Diocese of Norwich, 1350–1540* (Woodbridge, Suffolk: Boydell Press, 1998); Norman P. Tanner, *The Church in Late Medieval Norwich, 1370–1532*, Studies and Texts 66 (Toronto: Pontifical Institute of Mediaeval Studies, 1984).

That Julian had decided on the theoretically more rigorous life of the anchorite sometime before she was fifty we know, not only from the opening rubric of *A Vision* and the closing rubric in the Paris manuscript of *A Revelation* (which refer to her respectively as "recluse" and as "anacorite" of Norwich) but from the evidence of surviving wills, which record several bequests made to her between 1393/94 and 1416. Roger Reed, rector of St. Michael's, Coslany, Norwich, gave two shillings when he died in 1393/94; Thomas Emund, a chantry priest in Aylesham, Norfolk, gave twelve pence in 1404/5, as well as eight pence to a certain "Sarah, living with her"; John Plumpton, a Norfolk merchant, gave forty pence in 1414 to "le ankeres in ecclesia sancti Juliani de Conesford in Norwice" (the anchoress in the church of St. Julian's, Conesford, in Norwich), as well as bequests to her serving maid and to her former maid, Alice, perhaps a certain "Alice the hermit"; Isabel Ufford, an aristocratic nun at the great house of Campsey in Suffolk and daughter of the Earl of Warwick, gave the sum of twenty shillings to "Julian recluz a Norwich" in 1416, when Julian was into her seventies.[6] Apart from confirming that she spent more than two decades in her cell, these wills also say something about her local reputation and her wide (and lofty) social and religious connections. So, it has been argued, do the increasing number of bequests that begin to be made to other Norwich anchorites, men and women, in the wake of these gifts to Julian, after a long period from which we have little evidence of hermits and anchorites living in the city. Perhaps Julian's fame and influence helped to spearhead a revival of the anchoritic life in the area.[7]

As an anchorite, Julian followed the ancient tradition of living as an independent religious person, under the obedience, not of an abbess, but only of God: a tradition that proudly understood itself to embody the earliest form of religious profession, deriving from the fourth-century desert hermits of Egypt whose sayings make up *The Lives of the Fathers* and the *Conferences* of John Cassian. Her immediate guide to her profession, however, was more likely *Ancrene Wisse*, a thirteenth-century discussion of the duties and meanings of the anchoritic life that tells of the need to shut out the fearful nearness of the world outside the cell, in prose whose intricate beauty rivals that of *A Vision* and *A Revelation* themselves.[8] *Ancrene Wisse* imagines anchorites as solitary women practicing a routine of austere reflectiveness in an inner version of the physical desert that was home to their forebears. But anchorites actually lived in villages or cities, their cells attached to churches that were often anything but isolated, ministering and ministered to by the community.[9] The solitude *Ancrene Wisse* ascribes to them is metaphoric, not physical: far from living in isolation, anchorites were public figures, performing every Christian's need for detachment from the world and inner solitude before God. Julian's cell, in a busy neighborhood of one of England's largest cities, must have left her far more exposed to the world than she would have been as a nun. Norwich was a regional center in the

---

6. The surviving wills are translated and discussed in section B of the Appendix.

7. Tanner, *Church in Late Medieval Norwich.*

8. Robert Hasenfratz, ed., *Ancrene Wisse* (Kalamazoo, Mich.: Published for TEAMS in association with the University of Rochester by Medieval Institute Publications, Western Michigan University, 1998); Anne Savage and Nicholas Watson, trans. and eds., *Anchoritic Spirituality: "Ancrene Wisse" and Associated Works,* Classics of Western Spirituality (New York: Paulist Press, 1991).

9. Ann K. Warren, *Anchorites and Their Patrons in Medieval England* (Berkeley and Los Angeles: University of California Press, 1985); Paulette L'Hermite-Leclercq, "La réclusion volontaire au Moyen Âge: Une institution religieuse spécialement féminine," in *La condición de la mujer en la Edad Media* (Madrid: Universidad Complutense, 1986), 136–54.

late Middle Ages, linked commercially to the Netherlands, northern Germany, and the Baltic, as it was linked intellectually, through its monasteries and other institutions, to Cambridge University, as well as Oxford.[10] Not surprisingly, *A Vision* and *A Revelation* shuttle to and fro between the solitude of the visionary, Julian, her passionate identification with her "evenchristen" (fellow Christians), and her learned awareness of formal theology and institutional faith. In so doing, they traverse a conceptual version of the ground Julian occupied herself in her years as an anchorite: between self and community, God, church, and world.

Our one direct, and seductively pleasing, account of Julian's public reputation is found in *The Book of Margery Kempe,* that other major visionary work by an East Anglian woman of the period. In a careful early chapter, the *Book* recounts a visit Margery made to "Jelyan" to consult her about her own visionary experiences, perhaps in 1413, when Julian was seventy.[11] Margery meets Julian after talking to the vicar of St. Stephen's, Richard Caister (later in the *Book* to be venerated as a saint), and the Carmelite friar William Southfield, who recommend her as "expert." The *Book* has Margery spending days at Julian's cell, "comownyng [communing] in the lofe [love] of owyr lord," and gives Julian a well-informed speech, reminiscent of the ending of *A Vision*, about the need to avoid doubt by trusting what the holy spirit sends. This scene paints an idealized picture of a visionary anchorite, a senior specialist, in action, passing on what she has learned of God to one of her "evenchristen" in the world. Although Margery's life never follows Julian's

pattern, in the rest of the *Book* Julian's words prove to be a talisman to her younger contemporary, whose experiences both threaten and reinforce this early lesson of trust, amid the confusion of a world Margery herself declines to leave. Symbolically separated from this confusion, Julian's words can still reach out to it and, by comprehending it, occasionally help to still it.

3. A VISIONARY AUTHOR

The *Book*'s profusion reminds us that a main reason for our ignorance of Julian's life is that her writings are silent about it. The *Book* is full of names, times, places, reading lists, and other details: a mode of presentation thematically appropriate to its heroine's busy career as laywoman. The frugality of *A Vision* and especially *A Revelation* with regard to personal detail is similarly appropriate to Julian's career as anchorite: a profession into which she would have entered via a ceremony in which a bishop, taking away her old name to give her a new one—the male name of her church's patron saint, probably Julian the Hospitaler—walled her into her cell while reciting the Office of the Dead.[12]

The works are almost as reticent about Julian's intellectual biography. Truer than many visionary writings to the logic of their genre, which attends to what can be known through a chosen individual's experience, rather than through the authoritative teachings of others, they say almost nothing directly about their intellectual affiliations. They cite no book except the Bible. When *A Revelation* refers to teachings other than its own on specific topics, it lumps

---

10. Tanner, *Church in Late Medieval Norwich;* John P. H. Clark, "Late Fourteenth-Century Cambridge Theology and the English Contemplative Tradition," in *The Medieval Mystical Tradition in England,* ed. Marion Glasscoe, vol. 5 (Cambridge: D. S. Brewer, 1992).

11. Transcribed and discussed in section C of the Appendix.

12. For ceremonies of enclosure, see Warren, *Anchorites and Their Patrons.* It is not certain if St. Julian's, Conesford, is dedicated to Julian the Hospitaler or Julian of Toledo.

them together under the general term "the faith." They mention no people by name, except for Jesus, Mary, and a small group of saints: Mary Magdalene, Peter, Paul, Cecilia, Dionysius, and John of Beverley. Apart from cameo appearances by "the person my curette" and the "religious person" who is the first to believe in her revelation (*Vis.* 2.20, *Rev.* 66.12), they are, in particular, silent about any of the teachers from whom Julian must have learned. This is rare among the women's visionary writings of the period, which usually give much notice to priests or other educated men, often in the role of amanuenses.[13] Constantly pushing away all specific reference to the world and its facts to focus on the single burning fact of revelation, the signature phrase of both works, used to introduce the most abstruse material, is "I saw." Bodily visions, "ghostly" (spiritual) visions, visions part the one, part the other; understandings arising from any of these visions or from conversation with Christ; interpretations of the entire revelation developed over dozens of chapters: all are mediated to us through Julian's open eye. *A Revelation,* much concerned with the passage of time between the first experience of the vision and the moment of writing, introduces more recent layers of reflection with "I understood." Yet even here it is Julian, enacting both the visionary's and the anchorite's symbolic solitude in the presence of God, who thinks, discovers and, over and over again, still simply "sees."[14]

At first reading, then, it can seem as if the cell in which both works may have been written has kept all the insights they explore isolated from the outside world in order to expose them to a single, shadowless visionary glare. Yet even

though the works in one sense present themselves as nothing but revelation, and present the revelation as unified in meaning, if multiple in manifestation, their presentation of the Julian who sees this multiplicity and intuits this unity is not single, but double. In *A Vision,* and more in *A Revelation,* the figures of Julian the participant in her revelation and Julian its interpreter have discernibly different functions: one existing to ground the two works' thought in the confusing textures of lived experience, the other to elucidate the experience's general claims, meanings, and implications. The pull between these functions, and their mutual dependence, complicates *A Vision*'s and *A Revelation*'s enactment of the anchorite's symbolic solitude before God, keeping the works humanly and intellectually engaged with the world.

In both *A Vision* and *A Revelation,* the revelation is bestowed on a figure who desires God but lacks the skills that would help her find out divine truths by bookish means. In *A Vision,* the participant is "a devoute woman" with whom the older, narrating Julian associates herself as "a woman, lewed [uneducated], febille, and freylle," who insists she cannot be a "techere" (*Vis.* Rubric 1, 6.35–37). In *A Revelation,* the self-abasement has been much toned down, and all explicit reference to Julian's gender has gone, but otherwise the participant is the same: "a simple creature unletterde" (*Rev.* 2.1). These self-characterizations are more than gestures of modesty. In the visionary genre it is such individuals, helpless in their untutored createdness, not the educated, who experience visions: chosen individuals, to be sure, but more importantly representatives of everyone. Even a learned literary vision, like *Piers Plowman,* has the "doted daffe" (silly fool)

13. Catherine M. Mooney, ed., *Gendered Voices: Medieval Saints and Their Interpreters* (Philadelphia: University of Pennsylvania Press, 1999).

14. Nicholas Watson, "The Trinitarian Hermeneutic in Julian of Norwich's *Revelation of Love,*" in *Julian of Norwich: A Book of Essays,* Garland Medieval Casebook 21, ed. Sandra J. McEntire (New York: Garland, 1998), 61–90.

Will for protagonist, in tribute to the poem's visionary demonstration that "the foolishness of God is wiser than men" (1 Cor. 1:25).[15] In Christian thought Christ, who emptied himself to become human, "taking the form of a servant," has a mysterious affinity with the humble (Phil. 2:7).[16] As Julian sees his painted wooden head bleed at the outset of her vision, she marvels "that he that is so reverent and so dreadful [awe-inspiring] will be so homely [intimate] with a sinful creature liveing in this wretched flesh." Yet she knows she can use her creaturely simplicity to make demands of him, daring the needy, ignorant questions that lure him into answer: "A, good lorde, how might alle be wele for the gret harme that is come by sinne to thy creatures?" (*Rev.* 4.15–16, 29.2–3).

To make the revelation happen, then, Julian the participant, or "creature," as this figure will be called from here on, must be presumptuously trusting and receptive, asking "lewed" questions out of personal need. But to fulfill the revelation's ambition to be put to use, Julian the interpreter must be represented as educated, through the long process of its unfolding, into a specialist capable of justifying it, expounding it, and making it public. Only thus can the singular experience of the creature be revealed as exemplary of a wider human need and a larger divine truth. "Alle that I saye of myselfe, I meene in the persone of alle mine evencristene [fellow Christians]" (*Vis.* 6.1). To carry out this mandate, Julian the interpreter must assume the authoritative role many women's visionary writings give to clerics. In *A Vision,* this state of affairs only begins to emerge in the final sections. *A Revelation* announces it from the start with its magisterial subdivision of the "revelation of love that Jhesu Christ . . . made" into "sixteen shewinges,"

of which the first is the "ground" of the whole (*Rev.* 1.1–2, 1.6). As Jesus' head bleeds, the interpreter intervenes again, to lay down a hermeneutic rule whose aim is the vast extension of the revelation's scope: "Wher Jhesu appireth the blessed trinity is understand, as to my sight" (*Rev.* 4.11–12). From here on, everything said about the human Jesus is also true of the divine Trinity. This intervention in turn pushes *A Revelation* toward learned theological subjects and genres. Its patterns of exposition and argument become reminiscent of biblical exegesis or the syllogistic reasoning taught in medieval universities. Despite its scrupulosity in noting when the revelation does not cover a given topic, the work as a whole comes to have the air of a general vernacular exposition of the faith, careful to cover the essential topics of Christian theology, with a lucidity that recalls Julian's Cambridge-educated contemporary, the Augustinian canon Walter Hilton, in his *Scale of Perfection.* In its second half, engaged with the exemplum of the lord and the servant, *A Revelation* moves well beyond anything medieval pastoral theology considered essential, to reflect on what becomes a major theme, the nature of the "oning" (union) between the soul and God. As the work expounds a new model of the human soul (divided into substance and sensuality), its solution to the controversial problem of how creature and creator can be imagined as one without violating their distinctness finally turns on the most academically subtle shift in word order: "For I saw full sekerly [very surely] that oure substance is in God. And also I saw that in our sensualite God is" (*Rev.* 55.19–21). Despite being grounded in the needy questions of creatures, at its farthest reach *A Revelation* aims not only to be learned but to engage, and convince, the learned.

---

15. William Langland, *The Vision of Piers Plowman: A Critical Edition of the B-Text Based on Trinity College Cambridge ms B.15.17,* ed. A. V. C. Schmidt, 2nd ed. (London: Dent, 1995), 1.140.

16. David Aers and Lynn Staley, *Powers of the Holy: Religion, Politics, and Gender in Late Medieval English Culture* (University Park: Pennsylvania State University Press, 1996).

The intellectual complexity of much of *A Revelation* can create such a sharp contrast between Julian the interpreter and the creature who provides her raw material that the work can begin to seem abstracted from the revelation that gave it birth: a clerical superstructure cut off from its foundation in experience, or the ruminations of the anchorite as she moves further and further into herself and away from the world. Yet by using the visionary "I saw" to describe both kinds of activity, experiencing and interpreting, the work actually produces a less schematic and more sinuous effect: something like a relationship of mutual care between the interpreter and the creature, in which neither forgets her final identity with the other—much as the soul's substance and its sensuality remain united, in *A Revelation*'s account of them, by their very knowledge of their unity. The interpreter honors the memory of the experience given to the creature, learnedly lingering on its every nuance; and in turn, the creature infuses the most abstract of the interpreter's analyses of that experience with creaturely desire. Any of the longer expositions in *A Revelation* show the interpreter's habit of arguing inductively, setting out logical proofs whose premises are grounded in desire, or mingling logic and desire in those series of parallel assertions connected by "for": a word that evokes the "therefore" of argument but also the "now see this" of revelation. Often the interpreter's "I saw" is not separable from the creature's; the difference between experience and interpretation is never absolute. But even when interpreter and creature are farthest apart in their ways of perceiving truth, they are in symbiosis: "And whan oure good lorde . . . saide this worde—'Wilte thou see her [Mary]?'—I answered and saide: 'Ye good lorde, gramercy [thank you]. Ye good lorde, if it be thy wille.'

Oftentimes I preyde this, and I wend [expected] to have seen her in bodely likenes. But I saw her not so. And Jhesu in that worde [statement] shewed me a gostly [spiritual] sight of her" (*Rev.* 25.18–21, also *Vis.* 13.7–12). Here the interpreter, finding truth "in that worde" (in the fact Jesus offers to show Julian his mother, rather than in the offer itself), neither explains away nor overrides the creature's baffled desire, but resolves this desire and, in so doing, completes a moment of revelation: through its failure to lead to a "bodely" sight, a "worde" becomes a "gostly sight." If the interpreter represents a learned ability to explain divine meaning, the creature's naively literal desire for a sight of Mary thus comes to represent the human need for that meaning: the need to see the woman who gave birth to the world's salvation. It is by countless similar acts of engagement and understanding on the creature's behalf that the interpreter wins her right to add her own "I saw." And it is by keeping Julian in the double role of one who desires and one who understands that *A Revelation* and *A Vision,* despite their lack of particularity, bridge the gulf, not only between God and self, but between the cell and the world.

None of this helps us decide how to think about *A Vision*'s and *A Revelation*'s two versions of Julian in even general biographical terms, and not just for the familiar reason that both are literary personae, not actual figures, but for the knottier one that this is only partly true. Along with other women of her time debarred from receiving an advanced formal education, Julian likely did think of herself as "a simple creature unletterde," a self-definition she put to such positive use.[17] At the same time, even if we cannot always be sure what specific reading fed the well-informed arguments and intricate rhetoric of *A Revelation,* it is not (by any definition)

---

17. Felicity Riddy, "'Women Talking About the Things of God': A Late Medieval Sub-Culture," in *Women and Literature in Britain, 1150–1500,* ed. Carol M. Meale, Cambridge Studies in Medieval Literature 17 (Cambridge: Cambridge University Press, 1996), 104–27.

"unletterde" work. Not only does it show knowledge, besides intuitive understanding, of late medieval theology. Its intense awareness of the theological implications of certain words and grammatical structures can only be the result of formal study of language. We are left with two not clearly separated but not easily coherent images of Julian, neither of which can be wholly a construct.

Perhaps the "unletterde" creature was Julian the nun, the learned interpreter Julian the anchorite, now become "expert" enough to minister, through *A Revelation,* to the world, as she is said to have ministered to Margery.[18] Perhaps, since Julian as an anchorite lived close to many learned men and their libraries and must have made churchmen believe urgently in her revelation (or she could hardly have become an anchorite), *A Revelation* is the result of a specially designed course of study.[19] Perhaps the works involved more extensive participation by learned men or others.[20] We will never know. Written under a name and profession that symbolized separation from the world, the works have been carefully put together so as to conceal the worldly history of their composition.

❦

Part Two:
On Readers of Julian's Writings

1. LOVERS OF GOD: 1400–1450

As is true with most Middle English writings, the early history of the circulation of *A Vision* and *A Revelation* is a matter of speculation. Yet it is still possible to guess at the attitudes toward the works passed on by Julian's immediate circle (the women and men who knew her and her revelation, independent of her writing), sometimes centuries before the surviving copies were made: the single manuscript of *A Vision* (Additional), the two complete seventeenth-century manuscripts (Paris, Sloane), and the fifteenth-century series of excerpts of *A Revelation* (Westminster).[21] For besides implying a good deal about how readings of Julian's works evolved after her death, these copies also preserve traces of the earliest copies in which the works were presented for public circulation.[22]

Additional, a mid-fifteenth-century manuscript, contains a rubric written in 1413, which names Julian the recluse as participant in a vision: "[H]ere es a vision, shewed be the goodenes of God to a devoute woman. And hir name es Julyan that is recluse atte Norwyche and yitt is onn lyfe, anno domini 1413" (*Vis.* Rubric 1–2; see note 83). Paris, probably an early-seventeenth-century manuscript, closely modeled on a medieval exemplar, ends with a Latin rubric likely written soon after Julian's death, which gives the same minimal personal information but makes her the author of a *liber* (an original and authoritative work): "Explicit liber revelationum Juliane anacorite Norwiche, cuius anime propicietur Deus" (Here ends the book of the revelations of Julian, anchorite of Norwich, in whose soul may God be pleased) (*Rev.* 86.24–25). Here, Julian the interpreter, not the creature, is to the fore. Backing up this

---

18. For the topos of the "unlettered nun," see Jocelyn Wogan-Browne, Nicholas Watson, Andrew Taylor, and Ruth Evans, eds., *The Idea of the Vernacular: An Anthology of Middle English Literary Theory, 1280–1520* (University Park: Pennsylvania State University Press, 1999), 2.7–9.

19. This is the position effectively taken by Edmund Colledge and James Walsh in their edition, *A Book of Showings to the Anchoress Julian of Norwich,* 2 vols., Studies and Texts 35 (Toronto: Pontifical Institute of Mediaeval Studies, 1978).

20. As suggested by Felicity Riddy, "Julian of Norwich and Self-Textualization," in *Editing Women,* ed. Ann M. Hutchison (Toronto: University of Toronto Press, 1998), 101–24.

21. London, British Library MS Additional 37790; Paris, Bibliothèque Nationale MS Fonds Anglais 40; London, British Library MS Sloane 2499; Westminster Cathedral Treasury MS 4.

22. Formal descriptions of the manuscripts are in Colledge and Walsh, *Book of Showings;* see also Marion Glasscoe, "Visions and Revisions: A Further Look at the Manuscripts of Julian of Norwich," *Studies in Bibliography* 42 (1989): 103–20, and Part Three below. Attempts to date them are to be treated with caution; those given here are deliberately imprecise.

acknowledgment of *A Revelation*'s theological importance, the exemplar—assuming it was laid out the same way as Paris—was carefully punctuated and rubricated, with numbered chapters, and divine sayings written in red ink, just as scriptural quotations are sometimes written in other kinds of text. More significant, it presented the work, not in its original local dialect, but in a version of the East Midland dialect that by 1420 was becoming standard for the copying of works intended for wider circulation. The fifteenth-century compilation, also written in an East Midland dialect, copied into Westminster around 1500, takes this process in a different direction by placing excerpts of *A Revelation* alongside passages drawn from works by or associated with Walter Hilton, the most nationally respected of Middle English religious writers.[23] Most elaborate, the copy from which the seventeenth-century Sloane manuscript was made, probably written in Julian's dialect, omits all reference to her name, profession, and place of origin (carrying out *A Revelation*'s program of anonymity), but adds a series of headings to each chapter and a closing rubric (which again calls the work a "book"). Both headings and rubric are so pertinent that they seem likely to originate from Julian's immediate circle:

> I pray almyty God that this booke com not but to the hands of them [may only come into the hands of those] that will be his faithfull lovers, and to those that will submitt them to the feith of holy church, and obey the holesom [wholesome] understondyng and teching of the men that be of vertuous life, sadde [mature] age, and profound lernyng. For this revelation is hey [high] divinitye and hey wisdam, wherfore it may not dwelle with him that is thrall to synne and to the devill. And beware thou take not on [one] thing after thy affection [desire] and liking and leve another, for that is the condition of an heretique.

But take everything with other. And truly understonden, all is according to holy scripture and growndid in the same; and that Jhesus, our very love, light, and truth shall shew to all clen soules that with mekenes aske perseverantly this wisdom of hym.[24]

Couched in cautionary terms, this rubric makes the most explicit claims for *A Revelation* found in the manuscripts, presenting the work as a systematic theology, any statement of which has to be read in its total context, and demanding high standards of would-be readers. Read one-sidedly, the work is dangerous; "taken" properly, it contains a revelation of "hey divinitye and hey wisdam" that has the power to leave the page and "dwelle" with the reader. Although the copy behind Sloane may have been intended mainly for readers local to Norwich, the weightiness of this rubric and the formal care taken to produce chapter headings indicate the firmest conviction of *A Revelation*'s importance.

Not all these phenomena need go back to the very earliest manuscripts, and it is well to remember that we know neither how many copies there were between Additional, Westminster, Paris, and Sloane and the earliest copies of *A Vision* and *A Revelation* nor what happened to the texts and their manuscript presentation in the process of transmission. But what might we still deduce from these traces of the early distribution of Julian's works? A very few Middle English religious writings, such as *The Scale of Perfection,* seem to have been selected as suitable for broad public distribution and were widely copied by members of the Carthusian order and others, coming down to us in numbers of carefully rubricated and relatively uniform manuscripts (and sometimes early printed editions). Despite signs that copies were prepared for distribution beyond East Anglia, their variation in dialect and format

---

23. For a more detailed discussion, see section A of the Appendix.
24. See the textual notes to Chapter 86 of *A Revelation* for the entire rubric.

suggests that *A Vision* and *A Revelation* were not, as it turned out, distributed in this systematic manner, even though it may have been intended that they be so. Nor were they promoted in the same way as another celebrated group of works, the writings of Continental visionaries such as Bridget of Sweden or Catherine of Siena, whose popularity was partly an effect of their authors' reputations as holy women and which circulated in a variety of forms, almost always attached to the names of their saintly authors.[25] Very much of a piece with the tenor of her writings, this is a thought-provoking act of restraint on the part of Julian and her circle.

A plausible model for their early distribution is implied, rather, by *The Book of Margery Kempe,* in the early chapters of which Margery is passed from hand to hand, in Lynn, Norwich, York, and elsewhere, between members of an informal group of priests, monks, anchorites, and laypeople whom the *Book* calls "our Lord's lovers" or "God's servants." These individuals have no more in common than that they share an outlook sympathetic to devotional and visionary experience, as well as a discernible dislike of ecclesiastical formalism. A few members of the Lynn clerisy and laity belong to this group, and provide Margery with local support. But on her travels around England, she knows where to find others, perhaps (although Christ gets the credit) through ties of friendship, going back to university days, between clerics in Lynn and their opposite numbers in other centers. *A Vision* and *A Revelation* could well have circulated by parallel methods and among similar people: passed from hand to hand through an informal countrywide network of similarly

minded people. Indeed, Julian may have self-consciously written as a member of "the lovers of God," a phrase she uses, in various forms, of the devout, of potential readers, and of herself. *A Vision* calls the souls gathered in contemplation of the passion "Cristes loverse" and "his trewe loverse" (*Vis.* Rubric 4, 1.14–15); *A Revelation* repeatedly describes Christ's initial audience in the revelation in somewhat exclusive terms, as "his tru lovers," "his lovers in erth," "his servantes and his lovers" (*Rev.* 18.8, 36.9, 61.10–11); the Sloane rubric consigns copies of *A Revelation* to "his faithfull lovers."[26] Julian's works share attitudes with the *Book* that imply they were written in a similar milieu: an intense focus on Christ's passion, which the devout can experience directly; a desire to work out the most optimistic possible salvation theology; and a grounding of that theology, not only in the incarnation and passion, but in God's oldest relationship with humankind, as creator. It may well be that the *Book* should even be considered a theological response to Julian's writings.[27] Perhaps *A Vision* and *A Revelation* derive from the same irregular community of "lovers of God"— a community that cut across institutional, as well as geographical, boundaries—finding its first readers in Norwich before being adapted for and distributed to regions where Julian's name was not known and her dialect not spoken.

2. MONKS AND NUNS: 1450–1670

By some such network, Julian and her first readers sought to fulfill God's desire to have his message of love "knowen more than it is" (*Rev.* 86.6–7), distributed as widely as its potential for being misread allowed. Yet evidence of actual readers

---

25. Voaden, *Prophets Abroad.*

26. The phrase "lovers of God" is also found in several works by Richard Rolle (d. 1349) and other vernacular texts, such as *The Holy Book Gratia Dei* and *A Ladder of Four Rungs.* The submission to "God's love" implied in the phrase may have distinguished those who so named themselves from reformists who spoke of "God's law," the Bible. Some of these reformers also had group names for themselves: "true men," "known men," and "true preachers" were names used by the radicals called Lollards by their enemies. See Anne Hudson, "A Lollard Sect Vocabulary?" in *Lollards and Their Books* (London: Hambledon, 1985), 165–80. It is unclear whether the "lovers of God" were as tight-knit a group as this parallel might imply.

27. Lynn Staley, *Margery Kempe's Dissenting Fictions* (University Park: Pennsylvania State University Press, 1994).

remains sparse well into the seventeenth century, and these readers were not the mix of individual laypeople and religious whom the *Book*
suggests constituted the "lovers of God" but,
rather, seem mostly to have lived in monasteries. This might not be true in the case of the
readers of Westminster, which has left no clear
indications of its audience.[28] But the Additional
manuscript, which preserves *A Vision* as part of
a large collection, was copied by a Carthusian
from the northeast, probably for the use of
members of his order.[29] And Paris and Sloane,
the complete manuscripts of *A Revelation,* were
owned by, and probably copied in, English
Benedictine convents in seventeenth-century
France: the convents of Our Lady of Consolation in Cambrai and its daughter house Our
Lady of Good Hope in Paris, from which we
also have two records of responses to *A Revelation* and which likely provided the copy text of
Serenus Cressy's printed edition of 1670. Even
in Julian's lifetime, conditions were becoming
difficult for writing and distributing speculative
vernacular works like hers, and in the sixteenth
century the upheavals of the Reformation and
Counter-Reformation made matters worse.[30]
The survival rate of medieval books is so low
that it is hard to be sure, but the impression the
manuscripts make is that Julian's "book of revelations" did not reach either as large or as broad
a readership as she desired.

What these manuscripts do suggest is,
on the one hand, continuing, engaged, varied
attention on the part of those who had access to
her works and, on the other, a gradual harden-
ing into fixed form, not so much of Julian's
thought as of Julian herself, as she recedes into
history and is presented less and less as a religious intellectual, more and more as a "simple
creature" and medieval English Catholic holy
woman. The Additional manuscript places *A
Vision* in the middle of a group of contemplative works of ascending degrees of difficulty
(and, to fifteenth-century English readers, unfamiliarity), between translations of Richard
Rolle's *Incendium amoris* and *Emendatio vitae*
(both well known) on one side and of Jan van
Ruusbroec's *Sparkling Stone* and Marguerite
Porete's *Mirror of Simple Souls* (neither much
known in England) on the other. *A Vision* is the
only major work in the manuscript originally
written in Middle English, the only work identified with a woman (the translator of the *Mirror* assumes the author to be male), and the
only visionary text. Its inclusion pays the work
the compliment of noticing its theological and
hermeneutic implications; its placement treats
it as a bridge between the sensory language of
Rolle and the emphasis on the unsayability of
the divine in the Continental works.[31] In Westminster, on the other hand, excerpts from *A
Revelation* are used not as a bridge but as a cul-
mination, whose aim is to take the compilation
beyond Hilton's theorizing into a direct, though
still analytic, account of the experiences at
which he points. The anonymous "I" or "she" of
the Julian excerpts is the embodiment of the
devout person evoked by the psalmist at the

---

28. See Hugh Kempster, "A Question of Audience: The Westminster Text and Fifteenth-Century Reception of
Julian of Norwich," in *Julian of Norwich,* ed. McEntire, 257–90.

29. Margaret Laing locates the Additional scribe in Grantham, Lincs. See her "Linguistic Profiles and Textual Criticism: The Translations by Richard Misyn of Rolle's *Incendium Amoris* and *Emendatio Vitae*," in *Middle English Dialectology: Essays on Some Principles and Problems,* ed. Margaret Laing (Aberdeen: Aberdeen University Press, 1989), 188–203.

30. James Simpson, *Reform and Cultural Revolution: 1350–1547,* Oxford English Literary History 2 (Oxford:
Oxford University Press, 2002); Nicholas Watson, "Censorship and Cultural Change in Late Medieval England: Ver-
nacular Theology, the Oxford Translation Debate, and Arundel's Constitutions of 1409," *Speculum* 70 (1995): 822–64;
Jennifer Summit, *Lost Property: The Woman Writer and English Literary History, 1380–1589* (Chicago: University of
Chicago Press, 2000).

31. See Marleen Cré, "Vernacular Mysticism in the Charterhouse: An Analysis of BL MS Additional 37790 in Its
Religious and Literary Context" (Diss., University of Fribourg, 2001). (Revised version forthcoming as volume 10 of
The Medieval Translator [Turnhout: Brepols].)

outset of the compilation, who "utterly for-saketh himselfe and sekyth helpe of God, put-ting all his truste in hym." But she is also the perfected and self-aware soul in the passage from book 2 of *The Scale of Perfection* just before the Julian excerpts begin, as she "begyn-nyth . . . to perseyve a lytil of the prevytees [secrets] of the blessed trynyte. It may, wel inough [enough], for the lyght of grace goeth before. And therfor the soule shall not erre as long as she holdith her with [keeps herself close to] that lyght."[32] If the full version of *A Revela-tion* differs from Hilton on many matters, the informed visionary in the excerpts selected here, compounded of Julian the experiencing creature and Julian the analysing interpreter, convincingly speaks the same language.[33]

For all the respect they show her, the fifteenth-century manuscripts juxtapose Julian's words and the words of others with a familiarity born of closeness in time, finding no need to treat her thought as unique and taking no spe-cial interest in her as an individual. By contrast, the seventeenth-century manuscripts, both of them probably copied by nuns determined to retain an identity as English Catholics, treat *A Revelation* with the reverence reserved for a her-itage that is precious partly because it has so nearly been lost.[34] Indeed, it is to this preserva-tionist attitude, and the care it engendered in the Paris and Sloane scribes to reproduce the now

obscure language of their exemplars, that we owe the work's survival in something like origi-nal shape. In Paris, perhaps the older of the two, reverence partly takes visual form in the scribe's attempt to reproduce the look of a medieval book: lined pages, paragraph markers, running titles in red, blue chapter initials, medievalizing calligraphy, and something not too far from fif-teenth-century orthography. It has recently been argued that the paper on which the Paris manu-script is written (which carries watermarks sug-gestive of production in the 1580s) was made too early for the Cambrai community (founded in 1623) to have been responsible for it.[35] But we know from Augustine Baker's *Life and Death of Dame Margaret Gascoigne* (written in the 1630s) that Cambrai, from soon after its foundation, owned an "old manuscript book of [Julian's] Revelations," a manuscript that (from the frag-mentary quotation Baker goes on to give) was clearly similar to Paris and may have been its immediate exemplar, and it remains as likely that Paris represents an act of preservationist devotion on the part of the Cambrai com-munity or its daughter house.[36] In Sloane—a much plainer manuscript perhaps written by Clementina Cary, founder of the English Bene-dictine convent in Paris—reverence takes the form of careful preservation of the exemplar's probably Norwich dialect, accompanied by marginal translations of many unfamiliar words

---

32. Quotations adapted from Marleen Cré, "Westminster Cathedral Treasury MS 4: A Fifteenth-Century Spiritual Compilation" (M.Phil. diss., University of Edinburgh, 1997); punctuation and capitalization modernized. The text is also discussed and modernized in Edmund Colledge and James Walsh, eds., *Of the Knowledge of Ourselves and of God: A Fifteenth-Century Florilegium* (London: Mowbrays, 1961).

33. For further discussion, see section A of the Appendix.

34. On the Paris/Cambrai nuns, see Benedictines of Stanbrook, *In a Great Tradition: Tribute to Dame Laurentia McLachlan, Abbess of Stanbrook* (New York: Harper, 1956), 3–45.

35. See Anna Maria Reynolds and Julia Bolton Holloway, eds., *Julian of Norwich: Showing of Love,* Biblioteche e archivi 8 (Florence: Sismel, Edizioni del Galluzzo, 2001), 121–42.

36. The passage from Baker's *Life and Death of Dame Margaret Gascoigne* is first noticed in Margaret Truran, "Spirituality: Fr. Baker's Legacy," in *Lamspringe: An English Abbey in Germany, 1643–1803,* ed. Anselm Cramer, OSB (York: Ampleforth Abbey, 2004), 83–96. For a transcription of the full passage, see the headnote to section D of the Appendix. Paris looks very different from other Cambrai or Paris manuscripts, to this extent lending credence to Reynolds and Holloway's suggestion that it originated earlier and elsewhere (though not to their insistence on a Brid-gettine provenance). But unless Paris itself is Baker's "old manuscript book," which seems unlikely (it can hardly have been "old" in the 1630s), it is likely to be a Cambrai or Paris copy of that "old" (i.e., medieval) book.

by different readers, and an introductory rubric that, with poignant inaccuracy, describes the work as "Revelations to one who could not read a letter."[37] Knowing that the work fails to conform to the contemplative theology set in place during the Counter-Reformation, the scribe protectively interprets the description of Julian as "simple creature unletterde" by invoking a form of the Renaissance view that all early texts are primitive.

Paris and Sloane are too meticulous to indicate much about how the nuns actually read Julian, except that they did so with care and with a remarkable level of concern both to preserve and to understand her Middle English. However, two other fragments of *A Revelation* reveal that, besides the historical veneration the nuns showed these ancient Catholic words, preserved in a mother tongue now given over to the reformers, they saw special continuities between Julian's experience and their own. One fragment is in a treatise by the young Cambrai nun Margaret Gascoigne, writing in the 1630s, who uses a sentence from the work as the basis for a meditation on her devotional life: "Thou hast saide, O Lorde, to a deere child of thine, 'Lette me alone, my deare worthy childe, intende (or attende) to me, I am inough to thee; rejoice in thy Saviour and Salvation' (this was spoken to Julian the Ankress of Norwich, as appeareth by the booke of her revelations.) This o Lorde I reade and thinke on with great joie, and cannot but take it as spoken allso to me." The sentence is from *A Revelation,* Chapter 36 (lines 39–40), where Christ is imagined speaking it to Julian or the reader every time "we by oure foly turne us to the beholding of the reproved" (*Rev.* 36.37–38), becoming preoccupied with the doctrine of damnation or the fate of individual souls. Partly (though not wholly) detaching it from its context, Gascoigne takes

the sentence apart phrase by phrase and applies it to her soliloquizing self's own experience: "Thou therein biddest me 'lette thee alone'; to which I can not but answere and readilie yealde and submitte my selfe, sayeng; 'O yes, my Lorde'; for what doe I desire more then to lett thee alone in all things." In earlier sections of her treatise, Gascoigne repeatedly returns to a sentence near the beginning of *A Revelation,* to which Christ's "I am inough to thee" alludes and which her meditator uses as a bulwark against the terrible fear of divine justice and wrath: "thou art inough to me," a clause of the brief soliloquy, "God, of thy goodnes geve me thyselfe" at the end of *A Revelation,* Chapter 5 (lines 31–33). Gascoigne's gradual acceptance of Christ's promise to Julian as also applying to her suggests both her increasing trust in the reality of divine mercy and her belief in the divine origin of Julian's book. Augustine Baker, who edited this treatise, prefacing it with an account of its author's life and early death, notes that, on her deathbed, Gascoigne imitated Julian's sickbed experience, after a fashion, by having Christ's promise to Julian "written at and underneath the Crucifix, that remained there before her, and which she regarded with her eyes during her sickness and till her death." In this reported scene, Julian's optimistic Christ speaks words of comfort across two and a half centuries, to a dying woman still beset by the uncertainties of a theologically gloomier age.[38]

The other, rather different fragment is a set of passages from the twelfth and thirteenth revelations, copied in partly modernized form by an unknown Cambrai nun in the so-called Upholland Anthology, under the interesting heading "Saint Julian." Here again is a focus on material that can apply personally to the scribe. Yet the emphasis on passages about the meanings of

---

37. The handwriting is tentatively identified by Colledge and Walsh, *Book of Showings,* 8. On the dialect of Sloane, see page 37 and note 88 below.

38. For a full transcription and discussion, see section D of the Appendix.

Christ's promise that "all manner of thing shall be well," and the attempt to understand the passages in detail by combining the original wording with close paraphrase, also suggest an interest in the prophetic implications of Julian's thought. Like Gascoigne, this nun believes that Christ spoke words to Julian and that these words have special force for her: "For full well our lord loveth People that shall bee saved. That is to say gods servants," she writes.[39] Unlike Gascoigne, she focuses attention on one of the most densely interpretive and theologically audacious moments in *A Revelation*.

Augustine Baker, the famous spiritual director to the Cambrai and Paris nuns, may have had a role in procuring the medieval manuscripts copied by the Sloane and (possibly) Paris scribes.[40] A surviving letter written by him to the collector Sir Robert Cotton on behalf of the nuns asks for "such bookes as you please, either manuscript or printed, being in English, conteining contemplation, saints' lives, or other devotions." Although the letter states that the nuns already owned some books, perhaps the antecedents of either Sloane or Paris were loans or gifts from the Cotton library.[41] But while it has been claimed he modernized the excerpts copied into the Upholland Anthology, Baker himself took more interest in Julian's contemporaries, Walter Hilton and the anonymous author of *The Cloud of Unknowing*, than he did in *A Revelation*.[42]

It was his friend and executor, Serenus Cressy, royal chaplain at the court of Charles II, who in 1670 did what the nuns did not have the financial resources to do, produce a printed edition of *A Revelation*.[43] Probably based on Paris, and with marginal translations of obsolete words, the edition was financed by abbot John Gascoigne (whose sister was abbess of Cambrai) and dedicated to Lady Blount (mother of Clementina Cary). In its thorough personalization of *A Revelation*, this edition, which was read for over two centuries, is the most important document in the history of the work's reception and of perceptions of its author, fixing the image of Julian for centuries to come.

Cressy's introductory material describes *A Revelation* as an account of Julian the creature's experience, rather than a work of interpretive theology, and as a conduit both of that experience and of Julian herself to the devout reader.[44] The title page to the xvi *Revelations of Divine Love* names its author as "a Devout Servant of our Lord, called MOTHER JULIANA, an Anchorete of NORWICH: Who lived in the Dayes of KING EDWARD the Third," using an honorific normally reserved for abbesses and giving Julian's name as that of the early virgin martyr Juliana (not the male saint Julian the Hospitaler), while also linking her with English royalty. An "Epistle Dedicatory" to the book invites Lady Blount, "who will not be induced to the perusing of it by

---

39. See section D of the Appendix. The Upholland Anthology here quotes *Rev.* 28.3–4.

40. Luke Bell and Hywel Wyn Owen, "The Upholland Anthology: An Augustine Baker Manuscript," *Downside Review* 107 (1989): 274–92.

41. Placid Spearitt, "The Survival of Mediaeval Spirituality Among the English Exiled Black Monks," *American Benedictine Review* 25 (1974): 287–309. The letter, dated 1629, is reproduced in *Memorials of Father Augustine Baker and Other Documents Relating to the English Benedictines,* Catholic Record Society 33, ed. Justin McCann and Hugh Connolly (London: Catholic Record Society, 1933), 280–81. It is just possible that Cotton responded soon enough for one of his manuscripts to become the "old manuscript book of [Julian's] Revelations" read by Gascoigne in the Cambrai library before her death in 1636. If so, it was either returned to Cotton (possibly with the medieval antecedent to the Sloane manuscript), and subsequently perished in the 1736 Cotton library fire, or was kept at the Cambrai or Paris convent, only to be confiscated and dispersed, with much of the rest of both libraries, during the French Revolution.

42. Baker makes extensive use of the *Scale* in his posthumous *Holy Wisdom* (compiled from his works by Serenus Cressy) and wrote a commentary on the *Cloud*. See *Holy Wisdom; or, Directions for the Prayer of Contemplation* (Wheathampstead, Hertfordshire: Anthony Clarke Books, 1972).

43. For Cressy's career, see references in section E of the Appendix.

44. Transcribed in full in section E of the Appendix.

Curiosity, or a desire to learn strange things," to admit the author, "a Person of your own Sex," into her closet, "where at your Devout Retirements, you will enjoy her Saint-like Conversation." *A Revelation* thus offers its dedicatee an encounter, not with ideas ("Curiosity," "strange things"), but with the words, feelings, and felt presence of a long dead but knowable woman anxious to describe "the Wonders of our *Lords* Love to *Her*." After justifying Cressy's retention of Middle English (translation "*would have been a prejudice to the agreeable simplicity of the Stile*"), an address "To the Reader" describes Julian's by now defunct profession of anchorite, portraying it nostalgically as a life of complete separation from the world, and analyses the modes of her revelation. Then the reader is ready to follow Julian, not into theological exploration, but into "*affectuous, operative* Contemplation *of the meer* Nothingness *of* Creatures, *of the inconceivable* ugliness *of* Sin, *of the infinite* tenderness *and* indefectibility *of* God's Love *to his* Elect, *and of the* Omnipotency *of* Divine Grace *working in them*."

This presentation of *A Revelation* as a spur to personal contemplation, which makes a principle of the practice followed by Gascoigne and Constable, is a comprehensible adaptation of the work to its new context and readers, one that carefully limits the claims made for it and cloaks Cressy's nervous awareness of its sophistication under talk of "agreeable simplicity" of style. As we have noted, it is also based on a real feature of the work, its focus on the creature and her reactions to what she sees. Yet there is also much this presentation ignores, from the radicalism of the work's theology (it is actually sin *A Revelation* describes as "Nothingness," not "Creatures") to its urgent sense of the situation of all souls, not just the "Elect," before God, and

its suppression of the "devoute woman" of *A Vision* in favor of an anonymous speaker who, as creature and interpreter, represents everyone. We owe Cressy, as we owe the Paris and Sloane scribes, a very great debt for keeping all of Julian's text in circulation, and in Middle English. All the same, in the introductory matter to this edition, *A Revelation* first becomes in detail the very thing it tries so hard not to be but has for the most part remained: a vehicle for readers to think about its so carefully inscrutable author. Saint, mother, daughter, child, and intimate companion: "Julian of Norwich" has been born.

3. MYSTICISM AND SPIRITUALITY: 1670–2000

Cressy's edition would have been read mainly in English monasteries and convents on the Continent and by members of the tightly-knit group of Catholic families that helped sustain these institutions. It is probably from these same convents that there also survive two eighteenth-century manuscripts of *A Revelation*: a careful, elegantly produced semi-modernization of Sloane, perhaps a Cambrai or Paris production, and a neatly handwritten copy of Cressy's edition.[45] Until well into the twentieth century, even Cressy's personalized "Julian" was too idiosyncratic to attract the broader Roman Catholic readership, who were officially encouraged to read and venerate a very few other women mystical thinkers, from Teresa of Avila in the late sixteenth century to Thérèse of Lisieux in the nineteenth (both of whom are now officially "Doctors of the Church"). At the same time, as a devotee of Mary, associated with Roman Catholic intellectuals like Cressy and Baker, Julian was unlikely to draw notice either from Anglican divines like William Law and Jeremy Taylor, who would have found much to

---

45. London, British Library MS Sloane 3705; London, British Library MS Stow 42. Reynolds and Holloway, *Showing of Love,* xv, offer a more complex transmission history, but we see no reason to disagree with Colledge and Walsh, *Book of Showings,* and Glasscoe, "Visions and Revisions."

interest them in her thought, or among esotericists like William Blake, who would have approved of her visionary means of communicating with the divine and might have provided her with a different reading tradition. It is true that soon after publication Cressy's edition was lambasted by the Bishop of Worcester, Edward Stillingfleet, for publicizing "the blasphemous and senseless tittle tattle" of a "*Hysterical* Gossip," in a sustained attack on Julian and other medieval women visionaries that is most suggestive of Anglican anxieties about the encroaching influence of Roman Catholicism in the Restoration court.[46] Yet there is no evidence that Julian's work ever gained a positive reputation outside the Roman Catholic church or that she was known to the seventeenth- and eighteenth-century English women prophets to whom similar epithets were applied.[47] She has an entry (clearly inspired by Cressy) in the Protestant Pierre Poiret's *Bibliotheca Mysticorum Selecta* of 1708 (the first time she is categorized as a "mystic"): "*Julianae,* Matris Anachoretae, Revelationes de amore Dei. *Anglice.* Theodacticae, profundae, ecstaticae." (The divinely inspired, profound, ecstatic *Revelations of the Love of God* in English by Mother Julian, anchoress.) Here again, Julian the experiencer of God, not Julian the theologian, is to the fore.[48] By the mid–nineteenth century, she had attracted mild interest from the Transcendentalists: Henry Thoreau appears to have read her, perhaps in G. H. Parker's 1843 reissue of Cressy's edition. But for the most part, before the second half of the nineteenth century, her reputation did not cross the great gulf that separated Roman Catholic from Reformed.[49]

Although three nineteenth-century modernizations of *A Revelation* (two based on Cressy, one on Sloane) did something to change this situation, it finally broke down only in the first years of the twentieth century, with the broad emergence of interest (among Christians of many denominations and others) in what came to be called "spirituality."[50] This ostensibly nondogmatic and experience-based way of thinking about religion ran parallel with the development of experimental psychology on the one hand and the rise of modern occultism on the other, sharing characteristics (despite the disclaimers issued by its advocates) with both.[51] It was only in the wake of this movement— once Grace Warrack's modernization of the Sloane text of *A Revelation* had been noticed by one of the movement's most influential scholars, Evelyn Underhill—that Julian (now, thanks to Warrack, under the courtly names "Lady" and "Dame" Julian) at last began to be as widely read as she apparently desired: first (from the 1920s) among Anglicans, Episcopalians, and English-speaking Catholics; then (during the 1970s) among academic medievalists, especially in English departments; and now among Christians of all sorts and general readers, especially those who espouse the New Age.

---

46. Stillingfleet's attack and the ensuing controversy is transcribed in section E of the Appendix.

47. Diane Watt, *Secretaries of God: Women Prophets in Late Medieval and Early Modern England* (Cambridge: D. S. Brewer, 1997); Phyllis Mack, *Visionary Women: Ecstatic Prophecy in Seventeenth-Century England* (Berkeley and Los Angeles: University of California Press, 1992).

48. On the word "mystic," see Michel de Certeau, *Mystic Fable* [*Fable mystique*], trans. Michael B. Smith (Chicago: University of Chicago Press, 1992).

49. T. A. Birrell, "English Catholic Mystics in Non-Catholic Circles," *Downside Review* 94 (1976): 60–81, 99–117, and 213–31, which includes an extremely useful survey of responses to Julian from the sixteenth through the nineteenth centuries.

50. Alexandra Barratt, "How Many Children Had Julian of Norwich? Editions, Translations, and Versions of Her Revelations," in *Vox Mystica: Essays on Medieval Mysticism,* ed. Anne Clark Bartlett et al. (Cambridge: D. S. Brewer, 1995).

51. Bernard McGinn, *The Presence of God: A History of Western Christian Mysticism,* vol. 1, *The Foundations of Mysticism* (New York: Crossroad, 1991), app.; Nicholas Watson, "The Middle English Mystics," in *The Cambridge History of Medieval English Literature,* ed. David Wallace (Cambridge: Cambridge University Press, 1998), 539–65.

Underhill's great study, *Mysticism: A Study in the Nature and Development of Man's Spiritual Consciousness* (1911), offered readers doubtful of Catholic Christianity a map of mystical literature that was both more accessible than the technical discussions favored by Catholic scholarship and less skeptical than its most distinguished predecessor, William James's *Varieties of Religious Experience* (1902). Irenic in aim, and presenting the history of spirituality as a history of heroes whose experiences of the absolute have assisted humanity's slow evolution toward higher states, *Mysticism* helped to create a canon of spiritual geniuses and a widespread understanding of these "mystics" as artists of the transcendent, whose influence is still felt. Since it is organized around a structure foreign to *A Revelation*, that of the stage-by-stage ascent to the absolute, the book cannot much more than glance at "Lady Julian," who appears only in an early chapter (Chapter 4) in a guise that still carries the firm imprint of Cressy: a "simple and deeply human Englishwoman" whose intimate descriptions of the Trinity "carry with them a conviction of her own direct and personal apprehension of the theological truth she struggles to describe." But Underhill had taken enough notice of Julian to attract others, including a charismatic friend, Charles Williams, another believer in the identity of the artist and the mystic.[52] For Williams, who was connected to Anglo-Catholic and esoteric groups in London and knew C. S. Lewis and T. S. Eliot, Julian was a medieval writer second in importance only to Dante. Williams included thirty excerpts from her work in his anthologies *The Passion of Christ* and *The New Christian Year* (1939, 1941) and gave the famous statement "All shall be well" prominent place in the act of redemption that ends his first novel, *War in Heaven* (1930).

Lewis read Julian around 1940, with feelings sufficiently mixed that even his later works (much influenced as they are by Williams) do not reveal her traces; to this day, she still has few readers among Lewis's evangelical admirers.[53] The High Church Anglican Eliot, however, treats her as an important figure both of Englishness and of transcendence at the end of his poem *Little Gidding,* the last of *Four Quartets,* published in 1943, a year after the church of St. Julian's, Conesford, was destroyed in one of the bombing raids to which the poem alludes.[54] Here, Julian's words, which seem to come to him from the deep past of the language—once again they are "And all shall be well and / All manner of thing shall be well"—gesture toward a redemption of time in the deep future, when "the fire and the rose are one." This fusion of religious belief, art, devotion to place, and attachment to the past has parallels in a third Julian-inspired ending, that of H. F. M. Prescott's novel about the dissolution of the monasteries, *The Man on a Donkey* (1952). An idiot-savant

---

52. Underhill's appreciation of Julian grew in the years after *Mysticism*. Her *Mystic Way* (London: Dent, 1913) mentions Julian on ten occasions, and *The Essentials of Mysticism and Other Essays* (London: Dent, 1920) has a whole chapter on Julian (183–98). A more perceptive, although perhaps less influential, early Anglican study of Julian was that by William Ralph Inge in *Studies in English Mystics* (London: Murray, 1905), 49–79, which combines a tendency to use diminutives for *A Revelation* ("this little book") and a gallant sentimentalizing of its author, somewhat reminiscent of Cressy, with a clear articulation of Julian's difficult doctrine of the soul's "substance."

53. John Lawlor, *C. S. Lewis: Memories and Reflections* (Dallas, Tex.: Spence Publishing Co., 1998), reproduces pages of Lewis's copy of *A Revelation,* with his marginal comments.

54. Appeals to rebuild the church on the grounds that it had housed the famous anchorite began as early as 1943, and Eliot could have known of the raid from the *Eastern Daily News* soon after it happened. Restoration was complete by 1953, with a new chapel standing in for Julian's cell, which was destroyed at the Reformation (possibly because of its associations?) but of which the foundations survived. The "cell," which connects to the church via a small window and Romanesque arch salvaged from another building and looks out on a garden, not, as it used to, on a street, is an interesting example of High Anglican medievalism, all cool lines and tranquillity.

serving woman named Malle is making boats out of an old book left ransacked by the reformers. Shocked by this final act of destruction, Sir Gilbert Dawe, priest, sees the pages "not yet folded into boats," lying "in a bright litter at his feet." "He looked down and read upon one the words: 'It is true, that sin is the cause of all this pain; but all shall be well, and all manner of thing shall be well.'" Another reads "'What? wouldest thou wit thy Lord's meaning in this thing? Wit it well: Love was his meaning.'" As the paper boats go "dipping and dancing away towards the sea," Julian's words again offer an "in-folding," as the chaos that brought the post-Reformation English world into being is resolved into what Prescott calls "The End and the Beginning."[55]

In these literary appropriations of fragments of *A Revelation,* Julian turns spiritual artist while remaining both a symbol of a lost past and a seer, whose words are powerful partly because so few of them are known. Between the 1960s and the 1980s, this latest incarnation of Julian the creature became important to an ever wider range of people, both throughout the English-speaking world and elsewhere: with the publication of Clifton Wolters's Penguin Classic paraphrase of *A Revelation* in 1966, besides translations into German, French, Spanish, Italian, Dutch, and Finnish; the celebration of the sexcentenary of Julian's revelation in Norwich in 1973, twenty years after the rebuilding of St. Julian's, Conesford, in her honor;[56] and the dissemination of devotional biographies and

sets of translated excerpts for use in meditation and prayer. In 1987, the American poet Denise Levertov published a sequence, "The Showings: Lady Julian of Norwich 1342–1416," in which Julian is seen as an artist in her being more than her writing, as the saint of the hazelnut "held safe / in God's pierced palm," she whose faith might sustain the lives of doubting moderns: "you . . . clung like an acrobat, by your teeth, fiercely, / to a cobweb-thin high-wire, your certainty / of infinite mercy."[57] Ten years earlier, in *Holy the Firm* (1977), the novelist Annie Dillard was at first more skeptical, reincarnating Julian as the seven-year-old Julie Norwich, whose face is burnt off in a plane crash: a casual interruption to the quiet of the Pacific coast paradise— where the narrator, a novelist and teacher of creative writing, is living in anchoritic seclusion—the pain of which is part of the "scandal of particularity, by which God burgeons up or showers down into the shabbiest of occasions."[58] Yet the vision of the baptism of Christ this event generates in the narrator—"Water beads on his shoulders. I see the water in balls as heavy as planets. . . . I deepen into a drop and see all that time contains" (67)—and the affirmation of a theology of transcendent immanence and immanent transcendence that grows out of this are expressed in terms of the same need to make art out of Julian as is found in Levertov's poems. We are not surprised when, at the end of the novella, the narrator subsumes Julian into herself: "I'll be the nun for you," she says: "I am now" (76).

---

55. Williams, Eliot, and Prescott all allude to *Rev.* 27, Prescott also to *Rev.* 86.

56. The sexcentenary celebration was an ecumenical event held at the cathedral, with supporting exhibition and procession to the shrine; Anglicans, Roman Catholics, Methodists, and others in attendance; and a little less of the infighting between Evangelical and High Church Anglicans over Julian's "Catholicity" than took place in the wake of the rededication service, twenty years earlier. The Julian shrine, a busy place that includes a library and a hostelry, has a helpful collection of press cuttings.

57. Published in Denise Levertov, *Breathing the Water* (New York: New Directions, 1987).

58. Annie Dillard, *Holy the Firm* (New York: Harper & Row, 1988 [orig. pub. 1977]), 54. See *Rev.* 6.25–26: "Forto the goodnes of God is the highest prayer, and it cometh downe to us, to the lowest party of our need." *Holy the Firm* is full of such reminiscences. The crash occurs on November 19 (36), at the opposite end of the year from Julian's revelation in May.

Only Iris Murdoch, in *Nuns and Soldiers* (1980), resists making Julian, here figured as the former nun Anne, into an explicit image of the artist. Yet even here Anne's revelation of Christ—with his "strangely elongated head and a strange pallor, the pallor of something which had been long deprived of light, a shadowed leaf, a deep sea fish, a grub inside a fruit"[59]—stirs uncomfortable longings in the novel, moving the author to separate Anne from her closed-minded set of London bohemians by sending her to the New World, as a community of Poor Clares in Chicago offers her a home. This exotic, washed-out, but beautiful Christ, his mouth "thoughtful and tender," his eyes "large and remarkably luminous" (297), holds a stone in his hand, not the hazelnut Anne expects. He has no wounds on his body, and he speaks not through Anne to the world but to Anne against the reality of any general truth, especially the truth she most deeply associates with him, that of the redemptive value of pain: "Are you really so sentimental? Art thou well paid that ever suffered I passion for thee?" (299).[60] Yet pain is there in the revelation itself. The burn mark on Anne's hand where she touches him persists, and even her revelation's opposition to suffering is presented by Christ as a truth she can decide to refuse: "'You must do it all yourself, you know'" (297). Try as it may,

the novel can no more assimilate the revelation than Anne the nun can assimilate it or her friends her. Her departure from England, "elliptical grey stone" in hand and faith in "at any rate her Christ" intact (505), leaves the soldiers in possession of the field, all imagination beyond the pulsing of talk, friendship, sex, marriage, and the social round gone with her. Even as it rescues Anne from the Old World of the novel or exiles her to the new one the novel never visits, *Nuns and Soldiers* confirms Julian's significance, not only for devout readers of Levertov or Dillard but for Murdoch and the secular intellectuals who form Murdoch's most important audience.[61]

Today, with more translations and a host of little books in circulation, Julian remains an iconic figure: her name borrowed for a movement for silent meditation (the Anglican Church's highly successful "Julian groups"); her writings plundered for their most evocative images and musical moments (drops of blood like herring scales, the creation as hazelnut, God in a point, that ubiquitous "all shall be well"); her sculpted and glazed image gazing down from several surfaces in Norwich cathedral; her cell a stop on many a devout bus tour; her presence on the Web a strange mix of the scholarly, the devout, and the mythological ("Fun Facts: Julian of Norwich obviously loved cats"). She has inspired

---

59. Iris Murdoch, *Nuns and Soldiers* (Harmondsworth, Middlesex: Penguin Books, 1987 [orig. pub. 1980]), 295. Compare *Rev.* 7.20–23 on the sight of Christ's blood: "Thes thre thinges cam to my minde in the time: pelettes, for the roundhede in the coming oute of the blode; the scale of herring, for the roundhede in the spreding; the droppes of the evesing of a house, for the plentuoushede unnumerable."

60. Compare *Rev.* 22.1–4: "Then saide oure good lorde, asking: 'Arte thou well apaid that I suffered for thee?' I saide: 'Ye, good lorde, gramercy. . . .' Then saide Jhesu, our good lord: 'If thou arte apaide, I am apaide. It is a joy, a blisse, an endlesse liking to me that ever I sufferd passion for the.'" As the spellings and word order show, Murdoch's Jesus is quoting, or misquoting, from Warrack's modernization of the Sloane manuscript.

61. The ending of the novel again evokes Julian's vision of the blood, as Anne watches snow falling in the dark of a London street: "The big flakes came into view, moving, weaving, crowding, descending slowly in a great hypnotic silence. . . . It reminded her of something, which perhaps she had seen in a picture or in a dream. It looked like the heavens spread out in glory, totally unrolled before the face of God, countless, limitless, eternally beautiful, the universe in majesty proclaiming the presence and the goodness of its Creator" (512). Compare *Rev.* 7.10–14, 23–24: "The gret droppes of blode felle downe fro under the garlonde like pelottes, seming as it had comen oute of the veines. And in the coming oute they were browne rede, for the blode was full thicke. And in the spreding abrode they were bright rede. And when it came at the browes, ther they vanished. . . . This shewing was quick and lively, and hidous and dredfulle, and swete and lovely."

poetry, paintings, plays, musical compositions, and a novel.[62] With Hildegard of Bingen, Teresa of Avila, and other women visionaries, she has become an important symbol for Christian feminists. She has lent her name to a religious order of women and men in the United States, the Episcopalian Order of Julian of Norwich (founded in 1982). True, despite Murdoch, her reputation has not flourished so vigorously in the secular world, including the secular academy: she still makes only sporadic appearances in English literary survey courses and has only recently found a place in the *Norton Anthology of English Literature.* Yet in many powerful, if sometimes indistinct, forms, "Julian Lives On," as A. M. Allchin notes in a small book sold by the Julian Shrine, *Enfolded in Love: Daily Readings with Julian of Norwich* (1980). A century into her modern reception history, her name— the name we have for her—is known by more people than that of any other medieval English writer except Chaucer.

Missing in much (though not all) this creative and devotional material, and even in much of the scholarship on Julian, is the figure of Julian the interpreter. Twentieth-century Roman Catholic study of Julian, which might seem to have been best placed to recognize the significance of this figure, was initially held back by her sudden success among non-Catholics, by a general tendency (until at least the 1970s) to treat most writing in the vernacular as popular and devotional, and even more by the neoscholastic distrust of "mystical phenomena" (from

revelation to levitation) with which the church countered secular society's new enthusiasm for spirituality. After the excommunication and early death of George Tyrrell, a leading Catholic modernist whose controversial views on hell and salvation owed much to Julian and whose disastrous fall from favor was a direct result of those views,[63] the first twentieth-century Catholic scholars to write about her, such as David Knowles, were understandably cautious in their appreciation, still assuming, with Cressy, that their task was the analysis of Julian's experience.[64] The first book-length study, by Paul Molinari, published in 1958, followed suit. Although subtitled *The Teaching of a Fourteenth-Century English Mystic,* the book is actually a "scientific" inquiry into the authenticity of Julian's revelation (that is, its origins in the divine supernatural) and as such examines the biographical traces left by *A Vision* and *A Revelation,* using the severely rationalist methodology of the canonization process. Here, medical analysis of Julian's illness and psychoanalysis of her state, before and after, rub shoulders with the medieval science of the "discernment of spirits," while the arguments of *A Revelation,* once they enter, are important mostly as they point to Julian's conformity with a modern version of Catholic orthodoxy. Although the creature is presented as herself a devout rationalist, the role of the interpreter goes largely unexplored.[65]

It was not until twenty years after Molinari's book that Edmund Colledge and James Walsh published their extraordinary two-volume edition

---

62. For a selection, see section 6 of the Bibliography.

63. George Tyrrell introduced an edition of XVI *Revelations of Divine Love Shewed to Mother Juliana of Norwich 1373* (London, 1902; 2nd ed., London: Kegan Paul, Trench, Trübner & Co., 1920) (a modernization of Cressy), having championed her as a theological liberal in two controversial articles: "The Relation of Theology to Devotion" (*The Month,* 1899) and "A Perverted Devotion" (*Weekly Review,* 1899), both reprinted in *Essays on Faith and Immortality,* ed. Maude Petre (London: Longmans, 1914). (Maude Petre also had a long-considered interest in Julian.) For the importance of these articles to the fate of the Catholic modernist movement and the negative attention they drew in Rome, see Nicholas Sagovsky, *"On God's Side": A Life of George Tyrrell* (Oxford: Clarendon Press, 1990).

64. David Knowles, *The English Mystics* (London: Burns, Oates & Washbourne, 1927), and idem, *The English Mystical Tradition* (New York: Harper, 1965).

65. Paul Molinari, *Julian of Norwich: The Teaching of a Fourteenth-Century English Mystic* (London: Longmans, 1958). Published the same year, Conrad Pepler's *English Religious Heritage* (London: Blackfriars, 1958) does deal with Julian as a mystical theologian (see 305–71), although in a somewhat ahistorical way.

of Julian, *A Book of Showings to the Anchoress Julian of Norwich* (1978).[66] Building on Molinari's defense of the visionary authenticity of Julian the creature, Colledge and Walsh devoted themselves to the reinvention of Julian the interpreter, claiming for her a deep knowledge of the Latin Bible and a familiarity with patristics, mystical theology, and vernacular literature. Their notes suggest more than a thousand allusions to a wide array of writers and as many examples of fifty formal rhetorical figures; even their list of her biblical citations is seven hundred items long. Taking small interest in the desires of Julian the creature, Colledge and Walsh understand Julian as a systematic theologian, laying out arguments about the objective being of God that inevitably coincide with the rational structure of Catholic faith; their introduction translates these arguments at length into the technical language of Catholic Trinitarian theology to prove the point. As for the creature's claim to be "unletterde," this is a mere humility topos: "So far from being the simple, untutored devotee miraculously endowed by the Spirit," they argue, "she had laboured long and hard to equip herself to speak to the Church with the Church's authentic voice."[67] For Colledge and Walsh, Julian is a learned Catholic doctor, reinterpreting the divine and human wisdom of the past in the light of a present revelation for the benefit of the future.[68]

Colledge and Walsh's account of Julian is such a radical departure from most of its predecessors and is so firmly situated within its intellectual Catholicity that it could not expect to find unqualified acceptance or understanding from readers who were not Catholic theologians—indeed, theologians of the specific generation that straddled the Second Vatican Council. Apart from its unqualified assimilation of Julian's thought to a specific contemporary orthodoxy, its particular claims can also be questionable: it is hard to know what to make, for example, of a majority of the allusions to the Bible or other writings it proposes. Furthermore, by the time *A Book of Showings* was published, an alternative edition and model of Julian as a thinker was already available. Two years earlier, Marion Glasscoe's edition of *A Revelation* (1976)—the first modern edition of either of Julian's works in Middle English, aimed not at theologians but at students of literature—pictured her in startlingly different terms, giving the most intelligent account yet written of the role of the desiring creature: as an early experimenter with the resources of the English language, whose prose "point[s] to an author thinking aloud rather than polishing preformulated ideas," so that "the reader is involved in a primary mental process."[69] Colledge and Walsh's theological and rationalist version of Julian thus at once found itself in uneasy negotiation with Glasscoe's literary and affective one, as even the punctuation of the two editions pulls the reader in opposite directions.[70] Colledge and Walsh's edition remains by far the most significant account of Julian's writings since the seventeenth century, both for its rediscovery of her intellectual ambition and for its powerful sense of her importance as a medieval theologian who, as Rowan Williams puts it, "in terms of what

---

66. The edition began as an outgrowth of a thesis edition by Anna Maria Reynolds (1956), now published in much altered form as Reynolds and Holloway, *Showing of Love.*

67. Colledge and Walsh, *Book of Showings,* 196.

68. Colledge and Walsh also published a translation, *Julian of Norwich: Showings* (New York: Paulist Press, 1978), as the first and still the flagship volume in the important Classics of Western Spirituality series, having sold in the vicinity of a hundred thousand copies.

69. Marion Glasscoe, ed., *A Revelation of Love,* Exeter Medieval Texts (Exeter: University of Exeter Press, 1976; reprint, 1993), xvi.

70. The negotiation can be followed in the proceedings of a series of conferences organized by Marion Glasscoe and more recently by E. A. Jones, *The Medieval Mystical Tradition in England,* 7 vols. (Exeter: University of Exeter Press, 1980, 1982; Cambridge: D. S. Brewer, 1984, 1987, 1992, 1999, 2004).

her theology *makes possible* for Christian perception ... deserves to stand with the greatest theological prophets of the Church's history."[71] Indebted as many of these studies are to Glasscoe, the many essays and books on Julian's thought published in the last two decades—a period in which she has been read with increasing intensity within the academy, as within the church—would not be imaginable without their edition's assertion of her intellectual stature.[72] At the same time, the gulf between Colledge and Walsh's presentation of *A Revelation* as a work of learned, formally argued theology and Glasscoe's account of it as a record, rather, of a thought process suggests that neither edition quite succeeds in capturing the specific texture of her writing. The elusive relationship between re-creation and interpretation, desire and argument, experience and theology, imaged here as the relation between Julian the creature and Julian the interpreter, has not even now been adequately articulated.

❦

Part Three:
On Editing Julian's Writings

1. EDITING IN PRINCIPLE

Given her contemporary role as saintly icon and spiritual comforter, most reading of Julian is understandably in excerpt and in translation. Yet despite the publication over the last thirty years of several editions of her writings, readers not familiar with Middle English often turn to one of the complete translations even for serious study. This has something to do with the editions, which are designed either for the academic library or the classroom and reproduce many of the oddities found in the manuscripts; more to do with the difficulty of Julian's prose in any form, translated or not; and most to do with the look of Middle English itself, its unfamiliar words, pronunciation, and spellings. Unlike modernization—Warrack's strategy of writing out Middle English in modern spelling—which creates an illusory sense of familiarity with the language, translation at least admits the differences between Middle and Modern English, offering the reader what can be an expert witness to the meanings of the text for which it substitutes, and it serves some works well. Yet as Cressy and the nuns who copied *A Revelation* in the seventeenth century saw (even if Cressy hid his perception under the phrase "agreeable simplicity"), any careful reading of writing like Julian's has to be in Middle English, the language in which her thinking is incarnated as fully as the Christ of her revelation is incarnated in the flesh. This is not an idle analogy.[73] Julian's thought is difficult in any language, but the differences between medieval and modern English have less to do with this than the cultural shifts that divide her conception of what written English does from our own. More like modern lyric poetry than prose,

---

71. *The Wound of Knowledge: Christian Spirituality from the New Testament to St. John of the Cross* (London: Darton, Longman & Todd, 1979), 143 (italics in original).

72. For theological studies see, e.g., Joan M. Nuth, *Wisdom's Daughter: The Theology of Julian of Norwich* (New York: Crossroad, 1991); Grace M. Jantzen, *Power, Gender, and Christian Mysticism,* Cambridge Studies in Ideology and Religion 8 (Cambridge: Cambridge University Press, 1995); Frederick Christian Bauerschmidt, *Julian of Norwich and the Mystical Body Politic of Christ* (Notre Dame, Ind.: University of Notre Dame Press, 1999); Kerrie Hide, *Gifted Origins to Graced Fulfilment: The Soteriology of Julian of Norwich* (Collegeville, Minn.: Liturgical Press, 2001). (Jantzen's book is of special interest as the most serious attempt made so far to integrate a study of Julian's thought within wider contemporary theological conversations.) The most important book-length historical and literary studies of the last fifteen years are Denise Nowakowski Baker, *Julian of Norwich's "Showings": From Vision to Book* (Princeton, N.J.: Princeton University Press, 1994); Aers and Staley, *Powers of the Holy*; Christopher Abbott, *Julian of Norwich: Autobiography and Theology* (Cambridge: D. S. Brewer, 1999).

73. Nicholas Watson, "Conceptions of the Word: The Mother Tongue and the Incarnation of God," *New Medieval Literatures* 1 (1997): 85–124.

Julian's writing still feels the tug of the oral (as Glasscoe suggests), needing to be read in the mouth as well as with the eye, and with a sense of her thought as performance as well as argument. Like many writers from a culture dominated by speech, she uses language full of gesture, motion, and evocations of the material: evocations too rich to be paraphrased and too integral to her ideas to be construed as imagery. For all its superficial unfamiliarity, the look and sound of Middle English provide a clearer avenue than translation or modernization into the strangeness of the language as this is molded in Julian's hands, a strangeness essential to understanding her and that translation can only destroy as it tames:

> Rev. 5.19–24 [*Middle English*] This little thing that is made, methought it might have fallen to nought for littlenes. Of this nedeth us to have knowinge, that us liketh to nought all thing that is made, for to love and have God that is unmade. For this is the cause why we be not all in ease of hart and of soule: for we seeke heer rest in this thing that is so little, wher no reste is in, and we know not our God, that is al mighty, all wise, and all good. For he is very reste.

> [*Modernized Spelling*] This little thing that is made, methought it might have fallen to nought for littleness. Of this needeth us to have knowing, that us liketh to nought all thing that is made, for to love and have God that is unmade. For this is the cause why we be not all in ease of heart and of soul: for we seek here rest in this thing that is so little, where no rest is in, and we know not our God, that is all mighty, all wise, and all good. For he is very rest.

> [*Translation*] This little thing which is created seemed to me as if it could have fallen into nothing because of its littleness. We need to have knowledge of this, so that we may delight in despising as nothing everything created, so as to love and have uncreated God. For this is the reason why our hearts and souls are not in perfect ease, because here we seek rest in this thing which is so little, in which there is no rest, and we do not know our God who is almighty, all wise and all good, for he is true rest.[74]

If modernization tends here to produce a slight sense of clarification in the short term, long passages in this format are hypnotic, making the thought seem vaguer than it is and lulling the reader into thinking that all the words on the page carry the same meanings they do today. Translation avoids this problem, but at the cost of overspecificity as to the meaning of key words: Colledge and Walsh here offer a just-plausible path through the perils of the verb "nought" by rendering it "despising as nothing," but neither this phrase nor any of the possible alternatives—"diminish," "deny," "annihilate," and "reduce to nothing" among them—is necessarily right, and "despise" is not normally part of Julian's lexicon, or her ethics. The meanings of "nought" for Julian have to be understood gradually, through assimilation of the word in its many contexts. No less seriously, Colledge and Walsh's use of the Latinate "create" for "make" and the abstract noun "knowledge" for the participle "knowing" also produces a distancing effect, and the rhythm, rhetorical force, and sound of the passage are all but wrecked: "rest in this thing" no longer balances "no reste is in"; "littlenes," "liketh," and "love" no longer allude to each other through alliteration; "for" no longer has its extraordinary Middle English flexibility.

However committed this edition is to making serious study of Julian's writings possible even for readers with no knowledge of Middle English, it thus cannot take the easy route of

---

74. Colledge and Walsh, *Julian of Norwich: Showings*, 183–84.

excessive modernization, or even that of modern translation in parallel with a Middle English text. Instead, it must focus on realizing as lucidly and fully as possible the power and nuance of the Middle English prose, offering texts from which only the incidental problems arising from the manuscript copies, such as certain spelling irregularities, have been smoothed away, while providing glosses, paraphrases, and other points of entry into comprehension and exploration. Perhaps the most productive of these points of entry is the analytic version of *A Vision*, which runs underneath the text of *A Revelation* in our edition, with all the information it can yield to careful study about how Julian and her circle thought of the details of her argument in *A Vision* while working on its expansion and revision.

Very real difficulties must remain, and there is, in particular, no way to make reading Middle English as *fast* as reading modern—just as there is almost no way to make extended study of *A Vision* and *A Revelation* as slowly ruminative, as aware of the nuance and physicality of the language, as medieval vocalized reading, in private or public, is likely to have been.[75] But the difficulties should at least be interesting ones, for they are not only the products of our situation as readers of a language that is partly foreign, or even of the formal complexity of Julian's thought, but also of the linguistic situation in which her prose was from the beginning situated. While the intended audience for her writings is clearly "alle mine evencristene" (all my fellow Christians), a phrase that in the context of late medieval Norwich should be taken to imply everyone, their use of a local dialect of Middle English to communicate with this audience inevitably generates a tension between the local and the universal found in many late medieval vernacular texts (*Vis.* 6.1). To address "alle mine evencristene" in English in the late Middle Ages was to think of this vernacular, at least by comparison with the clerical language, Latin, as a kind of universal language: one that held inside its informal grammatical uses and the constant "thingness" of its word choices the thoughts and feelings of the vast unlettered majority. But to address such an audience in *writing,* and to use that writing to attempt a theologically ambitious argument with conceptual precision, was equally to make Latin learning a constant and inevitable reference point: a source of ideas, doctrines, words, and authority. For all the great richness of thirteenth- and fourteenth-century theological thought in English, Anglo-Norman, French, German, Dutch, Italian, Catalan, and other languages, Latin remained, and would long remain, the most important source of formal thought and terminology for all other languages, a bridge between vernacular languages, and a language of appeal in the event of criticism or controversy: in short, a universal language in its own right, not because everyone spoke or read it, but because it was spoken and read by the educated everywhere.[76]

Insofar as *A Vision* and *A Revelation* were intended to signify abstract truths in a clear way for educated readers, the two works were thus committed to a degree of translatability into Latin, since these readers would by definition interpret them partly through correspondences between vernacular and Latin terms and structures, as well as through their membership in a vernacular speech community. But because the terms and structures of the two works were in any case already informed by Latin, they were

75. Joyce Coleman, *Public Reading and the Reading Public in Late Medieval England and France,* Cambridge Studies in Medieval Literature 26 (Cambridge: Cambridge University Press, 1996).

76. Fiona Somerset and Nicholas Watson, eds., *The Vulgar Tongue: Medieval and Postmedieval Vernacularity* (University Park: Pennsylvania State University Press, 2003). See especially Sara S. Poor, "Mechthild von Magdeburg: Gender and the 'Unlearned Tongue'" (57–80).

also committed to being, in a certain sense, translations themselves, full of words and syntactic structures that were not in regular spoken use and that carried, especially for less-educated readers, some of the weight and distance of Latin; for the full penetration of English by Latin that is such an important feature both of modern prose and of modern formal speech had not yet occurred. Straddling two linguistic worlds in this way, even the earliest readers of the works, educated or not, must have found them in some respects alien and in many respects difficult—as we do ourselves. Perhaps our situation as readers, sometimes drawn in by the poetry of what feels like our own language, sometimes forced to puzzle through unfamiliar constructions and translate them as best we may, is not as different as we might think it to be from that of Julian's contemporaries.

2. EDITING IN THEORY

Previous editions of *A Revelation* follow closely one or the other, or both separately, of the two main witnesses to the text, Sloane and Paris, both of them late copies, or copies of copies, in traditions of representing the work that go back to the fifteenth century. Advocates of Sloane (such as Glasscoe and Georgia Ronan Crampton, editor of a second student edition) argue that the dialect of this text is close to Julian's dialect and that Paris was modernized by its scribe. Advocates of Paris (notably Colledge and Walsh) argue that, whatever *A Revelation*'s original dialect, Paris does a better job of preserving the rhetorical and logical structures of Julian's prose. Although editions of Sloane make some use of Paris and vice versa, all are wary of any attempt to synthesize the evidence provided by these manuscripts, or by either the

Westminster excerpts of *A Revelation* or the Additional manuscript of *A Vision*. In recent years, the belief has grown up that each manuscript offers a separate reading of *A Revelation,* each with its own agenda: a belief that finds logical expression in Reynolds and Holloway's edition, *A Showing of Love,* in which each of the manuscripts is transcribed separately.[77]

To edit a medieval work like *A Revelation* from a single manuscript, rather than use all the manuscript evidence to create a synthetic edition that aspires to be superior in some respect to any of the surviving manuscripts, has two clear advantages. First, the result represents something that actually exists—albeit, in this case, a manuscript made around two hundred years after the work was completed. Second, making such an edition does not involve difficult guesses about how the work was written and whether it ever existed in a definitive form or was instead distributed in customized versions, each of independent interest. Synthetic editions often have to make such guesses, since their purpose is usually to get "behind" the existing manuscripts, using the evidence of the manuscript readings to reconstruct a text that is closer either to the text of the manuscript from which all surviving copies derive, to the earliest text in circulation, or to the elusive authorial holograph itself. In the case of a work that was never intended to take a definitive form, this enterprise is more likely to blur the work than to clarify it.

Some scholars, indeed, argue that the idea of the "definitive form" of a work is foreign to medieval manuscript culture, where all works were more or less fluid, subject to what Paul Zumthor has influentially called *mouvance.* Zumthor argues that, since medieval works so

---

77. Glasscoe, *Revelation of Love;* Georgia Ronan Crampton, *The Shewings of Julian of Norwich,* Middle English Text Series (Kalamazoo, Mich.: TEAMS in association with the University of Rochester by Medieval Institute Publications, Western Michigan University, 1994); Colledge and Walsh, *Book of Showings;* Reynolds and Holloway, *Showing of Love;* Barratt, "How Many Children Had Julian of Norwich?"; Riddy, "Julian of Norwich and Self-Textualization." Hypertext would be another natural end result of this line of thought.

often shifted shape as they were copied by scribes with different interests and aims, and so often survive in a multitude of versions, we should go so far as to consider the "text" of a medieval work, not as any single version of it, however close to what its author probably wrote, but as the sum of all the manuscript copies: a claim that makes each manuscript copy of a work an equally authentic partial instantiation of the larger "whole work." For Bernard Cerquiglini, writing "in praise of the variant," this means celebrating all the variant readings provided by the manuscripts as tokens of the creative instability of meaning in play in a culture whose notion of the author (before printing, the rise of humanist scholarship, copyright, and indeed systematic censorship) is so different from our own. For Bella Millett, editing *Ancrene Wisse,* it means acknowledging that each of the manuscripts of this guide to anchoritic living shaped the lives of real readers, as the work was intended to do, and that the task of a critical edition is not to reconstruct a lost original but to take one carefully chosen manuscript as a place from which to survey the tradition as a whole. For Tim Machan, it means respecting the historical conditions under which medieval writing took place, in which vernacular works were seldom regarded as having a status that demanded their preservation in definitive form.[78]

Despite their different emphases, all these ideas of editing share with one another a respect for the individual manuscript copy of a work as object and for the ways in which changes in the forms of a work might reflect the changing circumstances under which it circulated.[79] As Part Two of this Introduction shows in the case of Julian's writings, these are important matters for analysis of a work with a complex reception history. While *A Vision* must be edited more or less as it stands in the Additional manuscript, this book, however, operates on a different set of assumptions about editing *A Revelation.* In the case of this work, we argue, a synthetic approach to the manuscript evidence results in a more intellectually sophisticated representation of the text than the choice of either complete manuscript. In some respects, indeed, this representation has a strong claim to approximate the definitive form of the work—the form *A Revelation* was in when it was considered finished—more closely than any single-manuscript edition. Even if practical works like *Ancrene Wisse,* or the anonymous romances Machan takes as a paradigm, were indeed considered to be collective property, never fixed in shape and adapted to new circumstances every time they were copied, there were other kinds of medieval work that did aspire to, even if they did not easily attain, a definitive form. These include not only the poetry of protohumanists such as Dante and Chaucer, who modeled themselves on the Latin *auctores* like Virgil and Ovid, but other intellectually complex works, aware of the balance of their arguments and their need to be read as a whole. A strong proprietorial sense of the rights or genius of the author is not the only source of an ideal of textual fixity: strong responsibility to the material or the reader can be another. Thus the prologue to *The Cloud of Unknowing,* a work Julian could have known,

---

78. Paul Zumthor, *Toward a Medieval Poetics,* trans. Philip Bennett (Minneapolis: University of Minnesota Press, 1992); Bernard Cerquiglini, *In Praise of the Variant: A Critical History of Philology,* trans. Betsy Wing (Baltimore: Johns Hopkins University Press, 1999); Bella Millett, "*Mouvance* and the Medieval Author: Re-editing *Ancrene Wisse,*" in *Late-Medieval Religious Texts and Their Transmission,* ed. A. J. Minnis (Cambridge: D. S. Brewer, 1994), 9–20; Tim Machan, *Textual Criticism and Middle English Texts* (Charlottesville: University Press of Virginia, 1994).

79. They also share respect for individual copies with traditional Middle English editing, often more intent on gleaning philological information than on the works themselves. Millett's and Machan's formulations do not quite admit the extent to which editing of single manuscripts can also arise out of, and express, indifference to the work and its cultural context.

charges all who engage with it "to take hem [them] time to rede it, speke it, write [copy] it, or here it al over. For paraventure [perhaps] ther is som mater [topic] therin, in the beginning or in the middel, the whiche is hanging and not fully declared ther it stondeth [where it occurs]—and yif [if] it be not there, it is sone after or elles in the ende. Wherefore yif a man saw o [one] mater and not another, paraventure he might lightly be led into errour." Carefully anonymous though it is, speaking, rather, "by the autorite of charite," the *Cloud* here seeks to limit the forms in which it circulates, especially to prevent itself from being copied in extract, on the grounds that "errour" (a serious intellectual sin) will likely result from partial copying or reading.[80] Clearly this work was understood to be in definitive form by its hidden author when its prologue was written. As we saw, the Sloane manuscript of *A Revelation* closes with a rubric to similar effect, which instructs readers to "take everything with other," since it is "the condition of an heretique" to indulge in partial readings (see page 11 above). This statement suggests that the writer of the rubric considered *A Revelation* to have attained (at the hands of a hidden author who cedes authority to her material, telling readers to "behold God," not her [*Rev.* 8.35]) a completeness of expression similar to that assumed of itself by the *Cloud*. Nor is this surprising, seeing that the work begins with a careful articulation of its structure (divided into sixteen revelations) found in other treatises of the period, including the *Cloud;* that this opening statement asserts the unity of the revelation and the work, claiming that the whole is "groundide and oned" in the first revelation; that the work is even more intricately argued than the *Cloud,* always within the framework of the sixteen revelations; and that, even as it declares itself endlessly incomplete—beginning

its final chapter with the paradoxical "This boke is begonne by Goddes gifte and his grace, but it is not yet performed, as to my sight"—the work ends with a witty meditation on ending: "In oure making we had beginning, but the love wherin he made us was in him fro without beginning, in which love we have oure beginning. And alle this shalle we see in God withouten ende" (*Rev.* 86.1–2, 20–23).

Even though it has so often been excerpted in modern times, *A Revelation* does not present itself primarily as a resource for others to adapt as they wish, but as an authoritative account of a divine intervention in the world: an intervention the work carefully dates, itemizes, and explores. As such, it may never have attained quite a definitive form in practice: for example, it is conceivable (to invent a hypothetical scenario) that, just after the work was completed, it existed in a "working copy," written in the hand of Julian or her scribe and containing cancellations, rewritings, and occasional slips or infelicities, and a "fair copy," made by a professional scribe, to be used as an exemplar, which corrected the mistakes in the working copy but introduced new mistakes (and even deliberate changes) in the process. Here, the "definitive form" of the work would have existed somewhere between the two copies, an ideal version of both in the mind of Julian and others intimately involved in the composition and copying process. Yet while such a situation might lead to awkwardness for later editors (if, to spin the scenario further, copies were made from both the fair copy and the working copy, so that both textual traditions had a more or less equal, but nonetheless different, claim to authenticity), the notion that the work aspires to definitive form remains and deserves serious consideration in deciding what editorial methodology to follow.

---

80. Cited from Wogan-Browne et al., *Idea of the Vernacular,* excerpt 3.3. See elsewhere in this volume for discussion of medieval views of authorship and textual integrity.

In weighing this decision, a synthetic approach that takes all the manuscript evidence into account has two advantages, one of practice, one of principle. The advantage of practice is twofold. First, the three manuscripts of *A Revelation* (Paris, Sloane, Westminster) are all careful examples of traditions of copying the work that are neither so closely related nor so different as to make detailed comparison unworkable. (The textual evidence is consonant with a tight pattern of circulation, with the existing manuscripts implying the prior existence of between six and twelve earlier manuscripts, though there will have been others in circulation, not directly related to the three survivors.) Paris and Sloane are differentiated by dialect and presentation, as well as by several hundred readings that are not dialect related: some of these the result of conscious decision making on the part of a scribe somewhere in the tradition (Sloane's shortening of Chapter 2, Paris's frequent use of "she" for the soul); many the result of the normal wear and tear of copying (word order shifted, lines missed, exemplars misread). As Hugh Kempster shows, Westminster is differentiated from both the Paris and Sloane traditions, sharing readings otherwise unique to each and with unique readings of its own, but again a careful witness to the parts of the work it excerpts. Although it is sometimes impossible to decide between readings, in many instances such a decision can be made, even when different readings make equal sense. A synthetic edition is in a position to take these decisions and so produce a clearer, more consistent text.[81]

Second, while editors of *A Revelation* suffer under the apparent disadvantage that all their manuscripts are late, they do have one unusual advantage, in the shape of the parallel existence, in one manuscript, of *A Vision,* on which *A Revelation* is closely based for much of its length. Because it seems that *A Revelation*'s alterations to *A Vision* typically took the form of additions and cancellations, rather than rewriting—one's impression is that *A Revelation* began life in the margins of a copy of *A Vision,* expanding gradually into pasted-in slips of parchment or paper, then leaves, then entire quires—readings from the Additional manuscript of *A Vision* are potentially deeply useful in mediating differences between Paris, Sloane, and, where relevant, Westminster, for in theory the *Revelation* manuscript whose reading coincides with Additional may well be the right one. These manuscripts can also be used to resolve problems with the Additional text of *A Vision* (see sections 3.3a and 3.3b below).

The advantage of principle, as George Kane and his collaborators argued through their great, controversial edition of *Piers Plowman,* is that a synthetic edition of a work that aspires to a definitive form allows its editors, in building their text, to use their detailed experience of the aesthetic and intellectual principles on which a work is based.[82] Like the editor of an anonymous romance or pastoral treatise, who understands the fluidity of textual *mouvance* to be an inherent characteristic of the genre with which he or she is engaged, they can edit a work as they believe the work asks to be edited. To apply a work's own implied principles to its editing is admittedly an interpretive process, more art than science, and the result needs to be understood as a reading of the work, a hypothesis about its definitive form: it cannot, by its nature, be "definitive" itself. What the result can be (so far as the manuscript evidence allows) is consistent and clearly focused, presenting a text

---

81. Hugh Kempster, ed., "Julian of Norwich: The Westminster Text of *A Revelation of Love,*" *Mystics Quarterly* 23 (1997): 177–245. See further section 3.3c below.

82. George Kane, E. Talbot Donaldson, George Russell, eds., *Piers Plowman: The Three Versions,* 3 vols. (London: Althone Press, 1960, 1975, 1997), a fundamental reference-point for this edition.

whose features are more than usually integrated and whose attention to textual detail is more than usually intense. Since it must perforce be self-conscious about its own agenda, it can also be transparent, giving readers the means to test, and perhaps improve on, its hypothesis.

Whatever the advantages of a synthetic edition of Julian's writings may be, there is a natural reluctance to think of an edition as the constructed thing it is: not a "copy of an original" but a hypothetical model, in which some textual details are given more weight than others and the one sure thing is that the model's attempt to approximate the definitive form of *A Vision* and *A Revelation* will remain an approximation. Some readers may wonder if the result is not as heavily mediated as a translation. Others will know that it is not, but will be sharply aware of the linguistic hybridity that results from using manuscripts written in more than one dialect, and of the limits even this aspect of our edition puts on its claims to approximate the definitive form, in particular, of *A Revelation.*

But there is another way to think about the artificiality inherent in an edition like this: as a sign of the distance that lies between the works and their modern readers and the inevitable incompleteness of the attempt to think across that distance. In her contemporary form as saint and cultural icon, Julian the creature seems to speak directly through the translated snippets of her prose, "fulle many comfortabille wordes" (as the opening of *A Vision* puts it) by means of which comes a sense of her presence to those able to receive it. The Christian intellectual, Julian the interpreter, is not to be apprehended thus. *A Vision* and *A Revelation,* probably always difficult even to those "lovers of God" who most nearly shared in the works' thought-worlds, are now much more so, to the point that even details of wording can be a matter for theorizing and dispute. If there is anything "comfortabille" here—anything to ameliorate

our recognition of loss as we struggle to reconstruct her thought—it must somehow lie within the fact of distance itself. For Julian's writings are themselves an incomplete attempt to think across a distance, one not of time and culture but of transcendence, and their coherence is achieved only by the precision of her acknowledgment of the limits of what can be known: the light of faith (all that can be known), she concludes, "is mesured discretly, nedfully stonding to us in the night" (is measured with discretion, standing beside us as we need it in the night) (*Rev.* 83.13). A strong resonance vibrates between our incompletable attempts to interpret aright and hers.

3. EDITING IN PRACTICE

From the viewpoint of textual criticism, our editions of *A Vision* and *A Revelation* can be seen as a line-by-line answer to the following questions: (1) What is the relationship between *A Vision* and *A Revelation*? (2) What is the relationship between the Additional manuscript of *A Vision* (**A**), the definitive form of *A Vision,* and the definitive form of *A Revelation*? (3) What is the character of the manuscripts of *A Revelation*—Paris (**P**), Sloane (**s**), and Westminster (**w**); what is their relationship; and what relationship does each have to the definitive form of *A Revelation*? (4) How far is it possible to emend our text of *A Vision* on the basis of manuscripts of *A Revelation,* and vice versa, or find internal criteria for deciding between manuscript readings? None of these questions stands alone: questions about the manuscripts make presuppositions about the definitive form of the works, while questions about the definitive form of the works make presuppositions about the manuscripts. Here, however, we address these questions in order, on the way to the choice of a "base manuscript" of *A Revelation* (the manuscript whose readings are preferred unless there is reason to emend them)

and decisions regarding treatment of that manuscript in editing it.[83]

a) The Relationship Between *A Vision* and *A Revelation*

Like most Julian scholars (the sole modern
exception is Julia Bolton Holloway), we assume
that the manuscripts preserve two texts, *A Vision*
and *A Revelation,* the second of which is a large-
scale amplification of the first.[84] We cannot dis-
count the possibility that *A Revelation* actually
amplifies, not *A Vision,* but a lost intermediate
text, or the possibility that other accounts
of Julian's experience formed the basis for *A
Vision;* indeed, both works show signs of having
been written and rewritten in stages, as one
would expect with anything composed over a
long period of time. But we also cannot see any
way to reconstruct these compositional processes clearly enough to hypothesize the existence of separate recensions or editions of
either text, or to improve on the standard view
that *A Revelation,* more or less as we have it, is
closely based on *A Vision,* more or less as we
have it.

Despite Holloway's suggestion that *A Vision*
is an abbreviated later version of *A Revelation,*
we also see no reason to question the traditional
chronology. *A Revelation* is not only more
assured, densely written, and rhetorically elaborate than *A Vision,* especially in its use of triple
and quadruple patterns of clauses to allude
to the divine Trinity or the Trinity and divine
unity; as the analytic version of *A Vision* that
runs underneath our text of *A Revelation* shows,
A Revelation is often effectively a commentary
on *A Vision,* layering "the inwarde lerning that I

have understonde therein sithen" on top of a
simpler original structure (*Rev.* 51.65).

This layering accounts, for example, both
for *A Revelation*'s new subdivision of Julian's
experience into sixteen particular revelations
(Chapter 1) and for the firm grasp of this experience's structure that is found in *A Revelation*'s
first long addition to *A Vision:*

> And in the same shewing, sodeinly the trinity ful-
> filled my hart most of joy [with the utmost joy].
> And so I understode it shall be in heaven without
> end, to all that shall come ther. For the trinity is
> God, God is the trinity. The trinity is our maker,
> the trinity is our keper, the trinity is our everlast-
> ing lover, the trinity is our endlesse joy and our
> blisse, by our lord Jesu Christ and in our lord
> Jesu Christ. And this was shewed in the first sight
> and in all. For wher Jhesu appireth [appears] the
> blessed trinity is understand [understood], as to
> my sight. (*Rev.* 4.6–12)

No such generalizations about structure and
meaning are found in *A Vision;* nor does that
work bear any traces of the hermeneutic principle outlined here ("wher Jhesu appireth the
blessed trinity is understand"). While phrases
such as "I understode" or "I understande" do
occur in *A Vision,* the language of understanding, usually suggesting a stage of comprehension
beyond "I saw," is used ubiquitously throughout
A Revelation as a signal that the earlier text is
being supplemented:

> This shewing was geven, as to my understanding,
> to lerne [teach] our soule wisely to cleve [cleave]
> to the goodnes of God. (6.1–2)

---

83. In the following sections (as above in section 2.1), quotations from Julian's writings in discussions of the
manuscripts (A, P, S, W) follow manuscript spelling (except that, as in the textual notes, thorn, yogh, and *u/v* and *i/j*
variation are normalized) but in most cases the word division, capitalization, and punctuation of the edition. Quotations from Julian's writings in discussions of the versions (*A Vision* and *A Revelation*) follow the spelling, word division, capitalization, and punctuation of the edition. For convenience, all references are given to the edition, rather than
to folio numbers in the manuscripts.

84. Reynolds and Holloway, *Showing of Love,* given wide currency by Holloway's website: http://www.umilta.net/
julian.html. Holloway cites the opening rubric of *A Vision* (on which, see below) as evidence the work was written in
1413, describing it as a careful rewriting of *A Revelation* in the wake of Arundel's *Constitutions,* of 1409.

And to lerne us this, as to my understanding, our good lorde shewed our lady, Sent Mary, in the same time. (7.1–2)

One time my understanding was led downe into the sea grounde. (10.16)

A Revelation also indicates passages added to *A Vision* with the phrase "in the same time" (e.g., "And in that same time, the custome of our prayer was brought to my mind"); with self-conscious references to one of the numbered revelations as "this vision" (e.g., "Theyse be two workinges that may be seen in this vision"); or by repeating a phrase from *A Vision* that requires further explanation in the manner of a commentary: "And I saw truly that nothing is done by happe ne by aventure, but alle by the foreseing wisdom of God. *If it be hap or aventure in the sight of man, our blindhede and our unforsight is the cause*" (italics indicate the passage new to *A Revelation*) (*Rev.* 6.2–3, 10.71, 11.5–7). A close look at the relationship between *A Vision* and *A Revelation* as revealed by the analytic version of *A Vision,* at the foot of the text of *A Revelation,* should convince anyone that *A Revelation* is a rewriting of *A Vision* that amplifies it on systematic lines.

b) The Additional Manuscript, *A Vision,* and *A Revelation*

The basic nature of the relationship of *A Vision* to *A Revelation* is thus not in question. But how well does ᴀ preserve the definitive form of *A Vision*? At best, ᴀ (a mid-fifteenth-century manuscript) is a copy of a copy of Julian's original text, for its opening rubric, with its reference to the year 1413, derives from an earlier copy of the work already perhaps twenty-five years later than the work itself. Given the fluidity (*mouvance*) of many medieval religious works, which might be substantially rewritten

in the process of copying, ᴀ might arguably differ greatly from the form *A Vision* was in when it became the basis for *A Revelation:* ᴀ's scribe having rewritten passages, cut phrases, sentences, or entire episodes, or even introduced passages from *A Revelation* into this copy of *A Vision*. Even the notion that *A Vision* had a definitive form at all is open to question, for we do not know if the work was ever officially released into circulation. Indeed, there are signs that the last few pages of the work were written later than the rest, perhaps out of dissatisfaction with the original ending, suggesting that it may never have assumed quite a final shape in Julian's mind.[85]

Certainty is not possible, but some observations are worth making. First, despite any unease one might feel about ᴀ's text of *A Vision,* the work as preserved reads well, shows a consistency of language and tone, and has no obvious cracks in it. It is carefully written and corrected in a manner that suggests concern to reproduce its exemplar closely. Even the informality of the final sections may be a sign that the scribe of ᴀ was unwilling to improve on the exemplar. Second, immediately before these last sections, ᴀ preserves a passage, not found in manuscripts of *A Revelation,* that reads like a peroration, written before the final few sections were planned. Like the ending of *A Revelation,* the passage plays with the idea of ending, though here sin, not love, has the last word:

A, wriched synne! Whate ert thowe? Thowe er nought [you are nothing]. For I sawe that God is alle thynge: I sawe nought the [I did not see you]. And when I sawe that God hase made alle thynge, I sawe the nought. And when I sawe that God is in alle thynge, I sawe the nought. And when I sawe that God does alle thynge that is done, lesse and mare, I sawe the nought. And when I sawe oure lorde Jhesu sitt in oure saule so wyrschipfully,

85. Watson, "Composition," suggests *A Vision* once ended halfway through its Section 23. These paragraphs repeat and build on that argument.

and luff and lyke and rewle and yeme [love and take pleasure in and rule and govern] alle that he has made, I sawe nought the. And thus I am sekyr [certain] that thowe erte nought. And alle tha that luffes the [all those who love you] and lykes the and folowes the and wilfully [deliberately] endes in the, I am sekyr thay schalle be brought to nought with the, and endleslye confownded. God schelde [shield] us alle fra the. Amen par charite. (*Vis.* 23.23–31)

Even if Julian eventually rejected this passage, its self-conscious virtuosity is hardly the sign of a work in draft that did not aspire to a definitive form and was never intended for circulation.

Third, there is no evidence for what is uglily termed "lateral contamination" between A's text of *A Vision* and *A Revelation*: no evidence, that is, that the scribe of A, or his or her exemplar, modified *A Vision* using a manuscript of *A Revelation* or that any scribe of a *Revelation* manuscript did the same thing the other way around. Admittedly, such evidence can be hard to come by in the absence of an obvious textual problem shared by A and one or more manuscripts of *A Revelation*, one possible sign of this kind of cross-fertilization.[86] But it is hard to see how anyone copying *A Vision* could have consulted *A Revelation* without becoming swamped by its additions. Here we have worked on the hypothesis that such consultations are not part of the textual history of A. Right or wrong, this

hypothesis provides a powerful tool for assessing the textual situation of *A Vision* and *A Revelation*. For if the surviving text of *A Vision* and the surviving texts of *A Revelation* are independent—if A's text of *A Vision* derives from the work's definitive form without introducing readings from *A Revelation;* and if P, S, and W's texts of *A Revelation* derive from that work's definitive form without introducing readings from *A Vision*—then, inter alia, this greatly increases our knowledge of *A Vision* and its manuscript, A. For on this hypothesis, the relation between our texts of *A Revelation* and our text of *A Vision* can provide evidence both about the accuracy of A's copy of *A Vision* and about the work's status during the period it was used to write *A Revelation*.

The textual notes and the analytic version of *A Vision* present the detailed results of this analysis. Even as it rewrites the earlier work in large and small ways, *A Revelation* shows an attitude bordering on veneration for most aspects of *A Vision,* except for those portions of the work that might be termed commentary, rather than visionary narrative. Passages of *A Vision* that do not appear in *A Revelation* and that we thus have inferred were deliberately omitted (printed in **bold** in the analytic version) are clustered in Sections 6 (Julian's apologia), 19 (on the nature of prayer), 23, and 25 (on the meaning of the revelation as a whole). But elsewhere most of what is omitted is apologia

---

86. Along just these lines, Frances Beer proposes that a repeated sentence in A does show mutual influence ("lateral contamination") between the textual traditions. See her *Julian of Norwich's Revelations of Divine Love: The Shorter Version, from BL Add. MS 37790,* Middle English Texts 8 (Heidelberg: Carl Winter Universitätsverlag, 1978). A reads: "mervelande with grete reverence that he wolde be borne of hir that was a sympille creature of his makynge. For this was hir mervelynge: that he that was hir makere walde be borne of hir that was a sympille creature of his makynge" (*Vision* 4.25–27 and textual note). S omits the second sentence entirely; P, followed by W, substitutes "that was made" for its last six words: "For this was her marvayling, that he that was her maker would be borne of her that was made" (*Rev.* 4.30–31). Beer suggests that P/W and S find different means to rationalize a problem in a common exemplar, which must either have been introduced into the *Revelation* textual tradition from the *Vision* textual tradition or vice versa. Colledge and Walsh agree (*Book of Showings,* 19). However, there are cleaner interpretations. Here, we assume that P/W's reading is right (it is both logical and of a piece with Julian's incremental rhetoric); that S's omission of the sentence is consistent with its tendency to abbreviate, especially in the early chapters (it responds, not to a mistakenly repeated sentence but to the wordiness of the argument); and that A's repetition is an example of dittography (writing the same phrase in the exemplar twice, in this case because the immediate context is confusing).

(1, 13), autobiographical detail (10), and theological observation (13, 15). Outside these passages, which account for less than 10 percent
of the *Vision* text, there are minor differences
in wording between all texts of *A Revelation*
and that of *A Vision,* probably the product of
"scribal variation": the leeway even careful
Middle English scribes gave themselves to
vary word order, substitute synonyms for one
another, and translate texts into their own
dialect. Setting this level of variation aside,
however, it seems clear that *A Revelation* does
not take much interest in small-scale rewriting
of *A Vision.* Less than 5 percent of *A Vision* (in
italics in the analytic version) reappear rewritten but recognizable in *A Revelation,* while
more than 80 percent of *A Vision* is reproduced
verbatim.[87]

Assuming that the two textual traditions are
independent, then, the parallels between parts
of *A Revelation* and A's text of *A Vision* offer
evidence, first, that *A Vision* was considered finished and worthy of the respect *A Revelation*
shows it and, second, that A is a good copy of
the definitive form of *A Vision* (the form, we
presume, that was used for *A Revelation*). In
theory, A might still contain a shorter or a
longer version of *A Vision* than existed when *A
Revelation* was built around it; only the consistency of the relationship between the works
suggests otherwise. There is also no sure way to
judge when variations in detail between the two
works are scribal, when authorial (judgments
that could affect the percentage of the analytic
version in italics, and hence one's picture of
the process of revision). But in broad outline,
A Revelation confirms the impression that A is
a careful and competent representation of *A
Vision* and that Julian and her scribes shared a

common respect for *A Vision,* as in some sense
an unsuperseded account of an act of divine
revelation.

c) The Text of *A Revelation* in Paris, Sloane, and Westminster

This argument—that A is a good copy of the
definitive form of *A Vision,* textually independent of *A Revelation*—has major implications for
how we assess the character and accuracy of
Paris, Sloane, and Westminster. Any passage of
A largely identical with the same passage in the
manuscripts of *A Revelation,* according to this
argument, is likely close to the definitive form
of *A Vision.* Just so the other way around: any
passage in the manuscripts of *A Revelation*
largely identical with A is likely close to the
definitive form of *A Revelation.* But since *A
Revelation* survives in three (for most of its
length, two) witnesses, whose readings often
differ in detail, we can also use A in another
way: to help decide which of P, S, and W has the
reading closest to the definitive form of *A Revelation.* Most of the time, this should be the
reading P, S, or W shares with A. Admittedly, different stories can always be told about how a
reading came into being: stories involving, for
example, the possibility of "convergent error"
(the same mistake made, randomly or in
response to common confusion, in A and P, S,
or W) or of indecision between readings in the
"archetype" of P, S, and W (the hypothetical
copy from which surviving copies derive),so
that readings that were meant to be canceled are
ambiguously preserved. Such problems are discussed later. But in general terms, at least, the
relationship between A and each manuscript
copy of *A Revelation* can tell us a good deal
about the character of that copy and the trust

---

87. There is some circularity in this account of *A Revelation*'s close relation with *A Vision,* since our synthetic edition of *A Revelation* is constructed so as to enhance this closeness as far as the manuscript evidence allows (see section
3.3d below). However, the percentages in this paragraph are only slightly lower if one compares A's text of *A Vision*
with P or S, rather than with our edition.

we can repose in its readings. We can also derive information from a more conventional comparison of the *Revelation* manuscripts with one another.

Previous editors of *A Revelation* are agreed (*a*) that s provides a copy of the work likely to be dialectally closer to what Julian wrote than p; (*b*) that a number of passages in s are more compact than those in p, sometimes by a single word, a phrase, or a clause, and occasionally a sentence; (*c*) that readings in p often parallel readings in w.[88] On the other hand, there is no agreement about (*a*) the character of p's language, especially to what extent it modernizes; (*b*) the character of the differences between p and s, specifically whether p is a "wordy" (perhaps even a theologically improved) text or s a "cut" one; (*c*) the manner in which w should be fitted into the jigsaw puzzle made by p and s. Recently, however, the status of w has been discussed in detail by Hugh Kempster, who argues convincingly that w should be seen as independent of both the p and s textual traditions.[89] This is of great interest for editors of *A Revelation,* since it gives w's readings weight of their own. The other main disagreements remain.

As to the matter of language: as is often noted, the theory that *A Vision* and *A Revelation* were written in the same dialect (a dialect located in or near Norwich) is borne out not only by the solidly northeastern dialect of a and the northern East Anglian dialect of s, but also by occasional northernisms in p: for example, p's triple use of "mekylle," instead of its usual "much" (*Rev.* 40.32, 42.12, 67.6).[90] A whole set of words and forms in p regularly differ from those words and forms in a, s, and occasionally w. The fact that, in most cases, these words and

forms irregularly retain the reading preferred by a and s (as in the case of "mekylle") suggests that p is a product of a systematic, though not quite thorough, process of translation into its current dialect, a version of fifteenth-century East Midlands Standard English. Considering also the northernisms in a/s, we thus agree with Glasscoe and others that characteristics of p like those described below imply that an ancestor of p (we think not the immediate ancestor) regularly shared the forms preferred in a/s, whose forms are therefore closer to the original dialect of *A Revelation:*

a/s's northern form of the present participle, which ends in "-and" (e.g., "wakand," "wakande"), is always the southern "-ing" in p ("waking," "wakynge"). The p scribe can misunderstand the infinitive ending "-yn" (e.g., "trekelyn" [trickle]) as "-ing" (textual note to *Rev.* 4.1; see also the note to 75.16–17, where s does the same).

a/s's characteristic use of the suffix "-hede," usually to make a noun out of an adjective (e.g., "roundhede" = "roundness"), is often rendered as "-ness" in p. But it is also retained (see, e.g., 7.15–23, where p has "feyerhede," "livelyhede," "plentuoushede," and "roundhede," as well as "roundnesse"). (w also adopts the "-hede" ending, e.g., "lytyllhed" [at *Rev.* 5.11]; perhaps Julian used both forms.)

a/s's "sekyr/siker" is regularly rendered as "suer" (a spelling of "sure"), "sikerly" as "suerly"/"verily," "sekirnesse" as "suernesse"/"feythfulnesse" in p (e.g., 15.2, 72.26; compare w's "sure"). But the word is sometimes retained in the forms "seker," "sekerest," "sekerly" (e.g., 41.2; 60.13; 65.3–12, 20).

---

88. Glasscoe, "Visions and Revisions," provides a helpful summary. On the dialect of s, see Hoyt S. Greeson, "Glossary to British Library Sloane 2499," in Reynolds and Holloway, *Showing of Love,* 627–42, which locates the dialect in northern East Anglia (thus in or near Norwich).

89. Kempster, "Julian of Norwich: The Westminster Text."

90. Laing, "Linguistic Profiles"; Greeson, "Glossary to British Library Sloane 2499."

A/S's "sothelye/sothly" is regularly rendered as "truly"/"verely" in P (e.g., S/W's "sothfastly" at 41.20 is "verely" in P). But it is sometimes retained in the forms "soth," "sothnes," "sothly," "sothfastly" (e.g., 33.3; 50.22; 78.14; 82.6, 25, 26). (Julian likely used all three of "sothly," "verily," and "truly" in her writings, but did not regard them as the synonyms they become in P.)

A/S's "blisful"/"blisfulle" is regularly rendered "blessydfulle" in P (compare W's use of "blessed"). But it is sometimes retained (e.g., 49.28, 51.269, 72.18).

S's "woning" is generally rendered as "dwelling" in P (e.g., 68.13, 27; but see 52.31, 55.27).

Other, more ambiguous instances, involving less common words, appear in the textual notes.

Along with these seeming instances of irregularly executed dialect translation are moments where the P scribe misinterprets the sense of a word or a grammatical structure: for example, "yemeth" (rules) as "yevyth" (gives) at 68.8, although at 1.48 it has correctly rendered the word as "comannding"; or the apparent misreading of S's use of the present participle to denote a state of being, as in "thus may we see, enjoyand," in which the P scribe apparently understands "enjoyand" as a reversal of the correct word order and renders it "and enjoye" (30.9). In other instances the P scribe makes changes that affect the sense: one is the unique preference in P for the feminine pronoun in describing the soul (e.g., 10.65, 49.36); another is its rendering of A/S's "nowting"/"nowted" (annihilation/annihilated) as "trybulation"/"trobelyd" (27.12, 14), though it also retains "noughtyng" (e.g., 28.19). Not all these instances need point to P as translator; some of S's usages are not attested in the other manuscripts: for example, "clepe"/"cleped" (14.4; 56.17, 18), where A/P/W have "call"/"called"; or "underfong" (= "receive") (2.19, 14.22, 41.29), where A and sometimes P have "undertake." But S's usage is more often in agreement with A than is P's.

There is thus much to be said for following many of Sloane's word choices, which tend to be more consistent than Paris's, are generally northeastern in character, and are often supported by Additional, sometimes by Westminster, and sometimes by irregular forms in Paris. On the other hand, we see little evidence for the assumption that many of P's word choices are modernizations into seventeenth-century English rather than translations from one Middle English dialect into another.[91] With a few exceptions, P's language is late Middle English, not Early Modern; its relative familiarity to modern readers (a familiarity that does not extend to its spellings) is due to the Midlands dialect's ancestral relationship to Modern English.

In matters of diction, the analysis clearly favors S's readings over those of P, to the point that, at this stage, S seems the natural base manuscript to use in editing A Revelation. However, we get a different picture when we consider other aspects of these manuscripts. Not only is P often a fuller text than S, the logic of its arguments clearer, its rhetorical figures more balanced, but its readings are usually endorsed by W and, most important, with the exception of the linguistic differences just described, by A. It has often been noted that P is longer than S, especially in the earlier chapters, but proponents of S take this as a sign of expansion in P, rather than abbreviation in S. Readers used to S (almost all modern readers who have come to know A Revelation through any edition other than Colledge and Walsh's) are in danger of responding to P as wordy through force of habit.

---

91. See, e.g., Glasscoe's presentation of P in her edition, A Revelation of Love.

However, on many occasions, ᴘ's greater length is likely attributable, not to wordiness on its part, but rather to truncation on s's part.

i) Eyeskip (the scribal tendency to miss a line or more of an exemplar after confusing a word or phrase for a similar one lower down the page). Eyeskip is a regular feature of s. For example, s misses out the italicized words in the following passage of ᴘ (ᴀ is identical) because of eyeskip between two instances of the phrase "that sight": "I beheld with avysement, seeyng and knowyng *in that syght that he doth alle that is done. I merveyled in that* syght with a softe drede" (11.2–4). Again, where ᴀ reads "In this, oure lorde brought unto my mynde and schewyd me a perte of the fendys malyce, and fully his unmyght. And, for that, he schewyd me that the passyonn of hym is overcomynge of the fende," ᴘ retains almost the identical wording, whereas s misses a line (in italics) because of eyeskip between the two examples of "shewed": "In this, our lord shewed *a parte of the feendes malyce, and fully hys unmyght, for he shewed* that the passion of hym is the ovyrcomyng of the feende" (*Vis.* 8.33–35, *Rev.* 13.6–7). (The differences between ᴀ and ᴘ here may also be scribal; there are two other instances of eyeskip in s in this chapter, 13.23–24, 13.36–37.) Sometimes, the fact that a line has been skipped in s can be established partly with the help of w. For example, although the following passage of ᴘ is not in ᴀ, it occurs verbatim in w. However, s once again omits the italicized words, this time misled by the repetition of the phrase "wisdom and truth" into skipping between "God" and the synonym "maker": "the hyghe wysdom and truth that she had in beholdyng of her maker. *This wysdom and truth made her to beholde hyr God* so gret, so hygh, so myghty, and so good" (7.2–4). In short, the absence of almost thirty lines from s that are present in ᴘ is likely the result of eyeskip (see also, e.g., 32.21–24, 34.3–4, 42.49, 46.2–3, 56.17–18), and enough of these

cases produce unintelligible readings of s, or find ᴘ's reading endorsed by ᴀ or w, to indicate that this is a regular feature of s, introduced by the s scribe herself or an earlier copyist. (There are eight instances of eyeskip in ᴘ: 13.15–16, 25.24–25, 27.15–16, 52.64–66, 59.14–15, 75.7–8, 86.8–9, 86.14–15.)

ii) Possibly deliberate truncation of passages. Some of s's other abbreviations seem deliberate. One example is its slimmed-down version of Chapter 2. Where ᴘ for the most part closely follows ᴀ, s omits whole clauses and sentences, sometimes reintroducing their main idea in another place, almost as if the chapter had been written down from memory, or as if a scribe had found the deliberate structure of Julian's exposition irritating. Thus, for ᴘ's brief "The secund was bodilie sicknes" (almost identical in ᴀ), s reads "The secund was bodily sekenesse in youth at thirty yeeres of age," but then at the end of the chapter omits another sentence ᴘ shares with ᴀ: "This sicknes I desyred in my jowth, that I might have it when I ware xxxth yeare olde" (*Rev.* 2.4, 31–32). Abbreviation for its own sake seems to be the point here, as it is in other early chapters where s's readings are briefer than those of ᴀ/ᴘ:

> ᴀ: "For methought it myght be welle that I schulde, be the suffyrannce of God and with his kepynge be temptyd of fendys or I dyede" (*Vis.* 3.19–21).
> ᴘ: "For methought it might well be that I should, by the sufferance of God and with his keping, be tempted of fiendes before I should die" (*Rev.* 4.18–20).
> s: "For methowte by the sufferance of God I should be tempted of fends or I dyed."
> ᴀ: "And I undyrstode of bodelye thyrste that the bodye hadde of faylynge of moystere" (*Vis.* 10.15–16).
> ᴘ: "And I understode by the bodyly thurste that the body had feylng of moyster" (*Rev.* 17.4).

s: "the which I understode was causid of failyng of moysture."

(See also 5.3–6, where A, P, and W all differ only in detail, but s is again substantially abbreviated.)

These kinds of abbreviation seem unlikely to be emendations by the s scribe, given her apparently punctilious retention of the dialect of her exemplar and other features. They suggest (as does other evidence) that between s and the carefully laid-out and correct early copy from which derived its chapter headings and closing rubric intervened a copy that was less scrupulously made.

iii) Deliberate or casual omission of phrases. A and W confirm the omission of a number of phrases in s that are present in P (italicized passages below are omitted in s):

> A: "And this same tyme that I sawe this bodyly syght" (*Vis.* 4.1).
> P: "In this same tyme *that I saw this sight of the head bleidyng*" (*Rev.* 5.1).

> P (followed by W): "he shewyd to my understandyng in part the blyssydfulle godhede, *as farforth as he wolde that tyme*" (*Rev.* 24.7–8; *A Vision* is semi-independent at this point; see 13.1–6).

iv) Reconstruction of corrupted passages. s sometimes has rhetorically convincing readings that differ from A/P. Glasscoe cites these as evidence of s's theological depth,[92] but they can also be read as the result of a scribe's attempt to make sense of errors in the exemplar:

> A: "For methought alle that tyme that I hadd lyeve here so lytille and so schorte in the regarde of endeles blysse. I thought thus: 'Goode lorde, maye my lyevynge be no langere to thy worschippe?'" (*Vis.* 2.10–13).

P: "For mythought all that tyme that I had leved heer so litle and so shorte in regard of that endlesse blesse. I thought: 'Good lord, may my levyng no longar be to thy worshippe?'" (*Rev.* 3.10–12).

Here, s has "in reward of that endlesse blesse," but then inserts the clause "I thought nothing" and introduces the following sentence with "Wherefore." Given the agreement between A and P, this beautiful reading is best understood as a response to a mistaken repetition of the phrase "I thought" in s's exemplar.

> A: "And yit is this reverente drede and luffe nought bathe ane, bot thay er twa" (*Vis.* 25.15–16).
> P: "And, though, this reverent drede and love be nott both in oone, but it are two" (*Rev.* 74.23–24).

Here, s has "And thow this reverent drede and love be," but then inserts the words "not partid asundre, yet thei are" before proceeding. It seems that a scribe has here understood "thow" to mean "although" (rather than "nonetheless"), and again found a way to make sense of the sentence by adding several words. (See also the complicated case of *Rev.* 5.15–16.)

By comparing P and s with A, and where relevant W, it becomes clear that P's "wordiness" is, in most instances, concern for accuracy and that s's tendency to cut to the chase of a sentence or passage is unlikely to represent the wording in the definitive form of *A Revelation*. Colledge and Walsh's portrayal of Julian as a highly formal prose writer, who where possible proceeds deliberately from point to point and who has a conscious concern for rhetorical and logical balance, seems broadly right. These characteristics of Julian's prose are much better preserved in P than in s.

To summarize: s is a copy of *A Revelation* more or less in Julian's dialect. However, while it

---

92. Glasscoe, "Visions and Revisions."

remains a careful copy, somewhere in the history of its text are scribes who (in the early chapters) abbreviated material deliberately, sometimes left material out accidentally, and had to reconstruct readings whose sense had been lost. P, on the other hand, is the product of a careful, probably fifteenth-century dialect translation, which produced a text that appears (from comparison with A and W) to have been transmitted, on the whole, with fussy attention to detail.

This situation leaves editors in search of a base manuscript with a choice between linguistic consistency and argumentative clarity that, if their aim is to produce an edition that makes synthetic use of all the available evidence, could go either way. It would certainly be possible to use S as a base, translating readings imported from W and P into its dialect and using those readings to reconstruct the fuller form of *A Revelation* that seems better represented in P. The main difficulty with doing this is the more tortuous textual history behind S, which makes for difficult judgments about the particular pressures at work at any given moment in the text. Using P as a base has the advantage that it wears its character as a dialect translation openly and (despite occasional idiosyncrasies) treats with considerable consistency the words it translates and even the few forms it apparently misunderstands. Since P also tends to have more intellectually and rhetorically rigorous readings, it makes the better base manuscript for an edition of *A Revelation* one of whose goals is to emphasize the sophistication and complexity of Julian the visionary interpreter. However, many dialectal or untranslated forms seem important to the thought of *A Revelation*—the participle "oning," often translated in P as the abstract noun "union"; "sothly," as distinct from "verely"; and "wonninge" (being at home), subtly different from "dwelling" (staying somewhere)— and also to its music; moreover, many of these forms are shared by S and A. The case can thus be made for a synthetic edition that imports considerable numbers of readings from A and S into its

representation of P in order to restore some of the vocabulary and other linguistic features of Julian's original dialect, as well as to take advantage of the clearest readings available and to facilitate comparison between *A Vision* and *A Revelation*. As noted, such an edition is a hybrid, lacking the philological sensitivity other editions would insist on, although more than making up for this, we claim, in its responsiveness to the texture of *A Revelation*'s prose and the nuances of its argument. This is the edition we offer here.

d) Principles of Emendation

As should be clear, the main grounds on which we have decided between readings is comparison of Additional with Paris, Sloane, and on occasion Westminster. Often, agreement between A and P against S, or A and S against P, is enough to decide a reading. The situation is more difficult when P and S agree against A, even in passages where *A Revelation* is closely similar to *A Vision*, because it is possible that *A Revelation* is at this point revising *A Vision,* or that neither P nor S retains the original wording of *A Revelation,* or that A does not retain the original wording of *A Vision.* In these cases, we have left both A and P/S readings unchanged, unless there were other reasons not to do so. (Here and in all other cases, we have been more cautious in emending A than P/S, since it represents our sole witness to the text of *A Vision,* although the textual notes include a number of conjectural emendations we have chosen not to adopt into our text.) In passages where W is also in play, the logic is more complicated, and here we have often decided on a case-by-case basis. W's witness is precious, but since the manuscript contains only about one-tenth of *A Revelation,* it is often hard to know how much weight to give its readings, and again caution is in order here. Finally, since three-quarters of *A Revelation* has no equivalent in *A Vision,* for these stretches of text we have had to evolve principles from sections where both works are running parallel to mediate between readings.

The main principles are these: First, as base manuscript, P takes precedence unless there is reason to change its readings. Second, after analysis of Julian's vocabulary as represented in A/S, the clearest reason for making such a change is apparent deviation in P from Julian's original dialect. Words we have retranslated, usually following S, include most of the words and forms discussed above: "blisseful" (from "blessydfulle"), "seker" (from "suer"), "sothly" (from "truly" or "verily"), the suffix "-hede" (from "-nesse"). On several grounds we have also retranslated rarer words and forms: if these appear in A; if they appear irregularly in P; if S's reading is backed by W. However, we have not attempted retranslation of many grammatical forms—for example, retaining P's "-ing" for the present participle, despite A/S's common use of "-ande"—and we have not adopted a word only on dialectal grounds (e.g., we read "call," with P, rather than "clepe," with S).

These principles place much weight on the relationship between A and P/S/W. However, we have also emended P's text of *A Revelation* (and, occasionally, A's text of *A Vision*) according to another, unrelated but important principle: a principle of internal coherence. Julian's writing is not only highly organized; especially in *A Revelation,* it is lucid and self-referential, interpreting the creature's experience from a series of different perspectives, from which arguments are developed incrementally. For example, large stretches of the second half of the work concern no one moment of experience but "all the revelations" (see, e.g., *Rev.*, Chapters 44–50, 73–85), often citing one or more revelations in support of its argument, in language meant to evoke earlier discussions. The words spoken by Christ are especially often repeated and elaborated upon. Much of this second half (from Chapter 51 to Chapter 63) is also a sustained discussion of the exemplum of the lord and the servant, in which many terms, details, and ideas recur. Close familiarity with Julian's

writing expands one's sense of how passages of exposition depend on cross-reference with earlier or later passages. Of course, Julian need not quote herself, or even Christ, verbatim, but often the mechanics of allusion itself demand that she keep more or less the same vocabulary and sentence structure. It is thus possible, especially if S or W provides some support, to emend P on the basis of these cross-references:

P's version of *Rev.* 1.48–49, a summary of the sixteenth revelation, has Christ "rewlyng and comannding [S "geveand"] all thinges." The reference is to *Rev.* 68.7–8, "he rulyth and yevyth [S "gemeth," A "yemes"] heven and erth." Both S and P substitute "give"/"geve" for the unfamiliar "geme"/"yeme" on some occasions, and on other occasions get the word right, S transcribing it correctly, P substituting a synonym. Hence in *Rev.* 1.48–49, S's "geveand," a mistake, and P's "comannding," a translation ("yeme" means "command" or "rule"). We adopt the readings "yeming" and "yemeth."

Rev. 60.36 refers the reader back to the "ix revelation" (P) or the "ninth" (S), but the words Julian is quoting are from the tenth revelation. We adopt the reading "tenth." As edited below, Chapter 79 of *A Revelation* includes the sentences: "But he wille that we hastely entende to him. For he stondeth alle alone, and abideth us continually, swemefully, and moningly, tille when we come" (79.30–32). "Swemefully" and "moningly" here are from S, P reading "monyng and mornyng," avoiding use of the word "sweme," as it usually, but not invariably, does. The phrase "the monyng and the mornyng" is used in both P and S at 82.1, giving P's reading here some support, though it is the soul, not Christ, who mourns. At 29.1 P and S both read "generally, swemly, and mournyngly," while at 71.6–8 the "chere of passion" Christ showed during his sufferings is described as "mornyng and swemfulle." These passages, especially the second, seem to us to provide the probable model for the phrasing here.

To emend on the basis of "internal coherence" is also to take Julian's ideas and arguments seriously. This can be challenging when the differences between the manuscripts lead to different theological conclusions, for here author, scribes, and editors all have an intellectual stake. P is sometimes charged with improving Julian theologically, and in a few instances this charge seems justified:

P, 8.26–27, reads "For that day that man or woman dyeth is he demyde *particulerly* as he schal be withoughte ende." "Particulerly," not in A/S, refers to the late medieval distinction between the particular judgment, which takes place at a person's death, and the general judgment, which takes place at the end of time. Given A/S's omission of the word, we treat it as an addition in P.

P, 40.33–34, reads "For a kynd soule hatyth no payne but synne"; S reads "For a kynde soule hath no helle but synne." S continues the logic of the previous sentence (which in P, followed by S, reads "And to me was shewed none harder helle than synne"); P evades the implication that hell is only a state of mind. Here we mostly adopt S's reading, though we read "hateth" with P (see *Rev.* 76.5–6).

Elsewhere, however, it appears to be S that is making the theological improvements:

P, 51.115–16, reads "The joy and the blysse was *of the fallyng* of his deerwurthy son"; the italicized phrase is not in S. P explores an idea crucial to the exemplum of the lord and the servant: that "[w]hen Adam felle Godes sonne fell" (185–86). S avoids the implication of a fallen God.

P, 60.39–41, reads "Thys feyer, lovely worde, 'moder,' it is so swete and so kynde in itselfe that it may not verely be seyde of none, ne to none, but of hym and to hym that is very mother of lyfe and of alle." W is similar. S reads "This fair lovely word moder, it is so swete and so kynd of the self that it may ne verily be seid of none but of him, and to hir that is very moder of hym and of all." We understand the S scribe or a predecessor to be reincluding Mary in a discussion of spiritual motherhood where the context suggests she has no place: she thus alters "him" to "hir," and "life" to "hym."

An edition of Julian that takes her theology seriously must present both sides of the case, in instances such as these, but it must also try to decide between them. To some extent, the editorial principle of the *difficilior lectio* is a guide here: the long-standing editorial theory that the reading most likely to be correct is the "strongest," that is, the least rhetorically and conceptually conventional.

As an interpretive, hybrid edition whose editors have sought out the most lucid readings from the available manuscripts and used principles of internal coherence and rhetorical balance as evidence, this edition becomes part of the interpretive tradition of Julian's writings. The evidence on which we have based our interpretation is fragmentary and difficult, not least because manuscripts do not, in the end, quite tell a coherent story. Even if P, S, and W are divided from the definitive form of *A Revelation* by as few as three intervening copies, the scribes who made those copies will have worked to different levels of accuracy and different ideas of what constituted a "good copy": some intervening at the dialectal or intellectual level; some leaving out lines or shorter passages; some trying to fix the problems their predecessors created. By the very nature of the evidence, the attempt made here to wrestle the most compelling texts of *A Vision* and *A Revelation* out of the manuscripts that are the end results of this process is guaranteed to be an uncertain success, an intricate hypothesis whose detailed accuracy is, by the nature of the case, impossible to confirm or deny. However, if this edition does no more than focus a new intensity of attention on what, phrase by phrase and sentence by sentence, *A Vision* and *A Revelation* set out to mean, it will have served a useful purpose.

🙟

Part Four: On Using This Edition

1. READING THE TEXTS:
A VISION AND *A REVELATION*

a) Spelling

The previous section outlines the criteria by which this edition emends its base manuscripts, Additional and especially Paris, at the level of word and phrasing, as it produces its hypothetical reconstruction of the "definitive form" of Julian's works, *A Vision Showed to a Devout Woman* and *A Revelation of Love*. But the base manuscripts have also undergone other editorial changes. Many editors of Middle English impose modern punctuation, word division, capitalization, and paragraphing on the texts they edit, and silently expand the abbreviations used by scribes. It is also relatively common for editors to normalize the now unfamiliar characters thorn (*þ*) and yogh (*ȝ*) as *th* and *y, gh,* or *-s,* and to rationalize the scribal variation between *u* and *v,* and *i* and *j,* in accordance with modern English conventions. These practices are followed in all the Middle English edited or quoted in this volume, including both the quotations directly from the manuscripts in the previous section (see note 83) and the textual notes (see section 2a below) and the conservatively edited excerpts in the appendix. But in the editions of *A Vision* and *A Revelation* themselves, the base manuscripts also undergo a series of further modernizations to their orthography to make Julian's writings more accessible to modern readers, a particular preoccupation of this

book: relatively cautious modernizations in the case of *A Vision,* where the edition is based on a single manuscript copied within half a century of Julian's lifetime; somewhat more drastic ones in the case of *A Revelation,* where the edition is based on a manuscript copied perhaps as much as two centuries after her death and takes very careful note of two other manuscripts of the work, one of them even later.

The clearest way to present these editorial changes and their effect, and to detail the specifically orthographic changes involved, is by giving an example of how they operate in practice in each work. Figure 1, on the next page, compares a passage from Section 2 of *A Vision,* transcribed as it appears in the Additional manuscript, folios 97v–98r (see plates 1–2 on pages 46–47) with the same passage as it appears in our edition. In the transcription (figure 1a) scribal abbreviations are expanded in italics rather than reproduced, except the abbreviation for "and," which is transcribed "&"; subpuncted deletions are transcribed as ~~struck out~~; insertions above the line are placed between two vertical lines ||; the note /*fol. 98r*/ indicates the folio break. In the passage as it appears in the edition (figure 1b), apart from the changes to punctuation (discussed in section 1b below), the non-orthographic changes to the text consist of four words or phrases marked to direct the reader to explanatory textual notes (see section 2a below). These changes involve, in two cases, our own importation of a reading from the *Revelation* manuscripts ("lange" becomes "langere," "that myght" becomes "that I might") and, in the two others, corrections in the manuscript itself (substitution of "hadd" for "wolde," where the corrector then failed to change "lyeve" to "lyevede" as the grammar requires; insertion of "I" into the phrase "And was an*n*swerde"). Besides these emendations and corrections (whose principles are outlined in Part Three above), and in addition to the standard orthographic normalizations

[FIGURE 1A]   British Library MS Additional 37790, fols. 97v–98r

Ande when I was thryttye wyntere Alde and a halfe god sente me A bodelye syekenes in the whilke I laye thre dayes and thre nyghttes and on the ferthe nyght I toke alle my ryghttynges of haly kyrke And wenyd nought tylle haue lyffede tylle daye · And aftyr this y langourede furthe two dayes & two nyghttes & on the thyrde nyght · I wenede ofte tymes to hafe passede and so wenyd thaye that were abowte me Botte in this I was ryght sarye & lothe thouʒt for to dye botte for nothynge that was /fol. 98r/ in Erthe that me lykede to lyeve fore nor for nothynge That I was aferde fore for I tristyd in god botte it was fore I walde hafe lyevede to have lovede god better and lange tyme that myght be the grace of that lyevynge have the more knowynge and lovynge of god in the blysse of hevene · ffor me thought alle the tyme that I ~~wolde~~/hadd/ lyeve here so lytille and so schorte in the regarde of endeles blysse I thouʒt thus · Goode lorde maye my lyevynge be no langere to thy worschippe And /I/ was annswerde in my resone and be the felynges of my paynes that I schulde dye · And I asentyd fully with alle the wille of mye herte to be atte god ys wille

[FIGURE 1B]   *A Vision Showed to a Devout Woman,* 2.1–15

SECTION 2

Ande when I was thrittye wintere alde and a halfe, God sente me a bodelye syekenes in the whilke I laye thre dayes and thre nightes, and on the ferthe night I toke alle my rightinges of haly kyrke, and wened nought tille have liffede tille daye. And after this I langourede furthe two dayes and two nightes, and on the thirde night I wenede ofte times to hafe passede, and so wened thaye that were aboute me. Botte in this I was right sarye and lothe thought for to die, botte for nothinge that was /fol. 98r/ in erthe that me likede to lyeve fore, nor for nothinge that I was aferde fore, for I tristed in God. Botte it was fore I walde hafe lyevede to have lovede God better and langere° time, that I might,° be the grace of that lyevinge, have the more knowinge and lovinge of God in the blisse of hevene. For methought alle the time that I had lyevede° here so litille and so shorte in the regarde of endeles blisse. I thought thus: "Goode lorde, maye my lyevinge be no langere to thy worshippe?" And I was answerde° in my resone and be the felinges of my paines that I shulde die, and I asented fully with alle the wille of mye herte to be atte Godes wille.

5

10

15

and regularizations just mentioned, the following principles of normalization, in accordance with modern English spelling conventions, apply to the spelling and orthography of *A Vision:*

• *sch* is normalized to *sh:* "schorte" becomes "shorte," "worschippe" becomes "worshippe," "schulde" becomes "shulde"

• *y* is normalized to *i:* the first-person pronoun "y" becomes "I," and "ryght" becomes "right," although "kyrke" remains as is, since "kirke" is not necessarily more recognizable in standard modern English. Where appropriate, *i* is also normalized to *y:* for example, the occasional spellings "bodelie" and "hali" (neither represented here) become "bodelye" and "haly"

• -*yd* is normalized to -*ed:* "wenyd" becomes "wened," "tristyd" becomes "tristed," and "asentyd" becomes "asented"; elsewhere *ys/-ys* is also normalized to *es/-es* (so that "ryste" becomes "reste," "techys" becomes "teches" etc.) and *yr* to *er* (so that "undyrstode" becomes "understode")

• double consonants are normalized to single: "ryghttynges" becomes "rightinges," "an*n*swerde" becomes "answerde"—except when eliminating the double consonant would change the phonetic value of the vowel according to modern English spelling conventions: "litille" remains "litille" because, in modern English, the second *i* of "litile" would be long; see also "worschippe," which becomes "worshippe" not "worshipe"

The same principle is in operation for double vowels, although the only example in the passage above concerns the semivowel *w*, where "abowte" becomes "aboute" (*w* is retained when the situation is more ambiguous, as with "trewth" and "trowthe"). Elsewhere in *A Vision,* "eelde" becomes "elde" (1.35), "eende" becomes "ende" (7.16), "loove" becomes "love" (4.3), "soo" becomes "so" (6.36), and, as in the passage above, medial *w* (literally, double *u*) becomes a single *u* when modern English spelling demands it. Finally, although the passage above gives no example, the suffix -*cion* is normalized to -*tion*, *ci/ti* variation is normalized in a few other situations (for example, "pacience" becomes "patience"), while certain words (both the many versions of "plentyuouse" and "mykylle" and occasional individual words such as "condystyon" or "leued") have their spelling modified on an ad hoc basis. Yogh occasionally disappears altogether, as in the word "ȝif," which becomes "if." These normalizations leave some strange-looking spellings, such as "syekenes," but aim to reduce their number so they become easier to assimilate.

The second example compares a passage from Chapter 10 of *A Revelation of Love,* transcribed from the Paris manuscript, folios 23r–v (see plates 3–4 on pages 50–51), with the same passage as it appears in our edition (figure 2, page 48). The manuscript transcription here (figure 2a) follows the same conventions as were used in figure 1a. In the edited version (figure 2b), several words or phrases not found in the manuscript transcription are again marked by the textual note marker °, indicating that Paris is here being emended from Sloane and/or Westminster (or, in the case of "by discretion," emended conjecturally without manuscript authority); the most complicated of these is "fulle hende, homely, and curteise," which reads "fulle homely curteyse" in Paris. One word, "blissefully," is marked with the symbol for a global emendation with no textual note,• (see section 2a below). With regard to the spelling of the passage, all normalizations applied to *A Vision* are also made here: double consonants and vowels become single; *y* becomes *i* or vice versa; -*yd*, *ys/-ys*, *yr/-yr* become -*ed*, *es/-es*, *er/-er*; *sch* becomes *sh*; -*cion* becomes -*tion* and other examples of *ci/ti* variation are regularized, all in accordance with modern English spelling conventions. In addition: normalization of *y*, the Paris scribe's favorite vowel, has been extended as follows:

• In some words and word groups where Paris uses *ey* and *ay* interchangeably, *ey* as well as *ay* have both been amended to *ai:* thus "veyne" in the passage above becomes "vaine." Elsewhere in the text, some spellings are normalized, such as "payne/peyne" to "paine," while others are not: "seyd," for example, is normalized to "said," whereas "seyeth" remains "seyeth," since the *y* here is apparently consonantal, giving the word two syllables where the spelling "saith" would give it only one.

So that I myght in the sekenes take alle my Ryghtynges of haly
kyrke wenande my selfe. That I schulde dye and that alle creature
that sawe me myght wene the same. ffor I wolde hafe no comforth
of no flesshlye nothere erthelye lyfe. In this sekenes I desyrede to hafe
alle manere of paynes bodelye & gastelye that I schulde hafe zyf I sch
ulde dye. alle the dredes & tepestes of feyndys & alle maner of payre
paynes of the owte passynge of the sawlle. for I hope that it myzt
be to me a spede when I schulde dye. ffor I desyrede sone to be with my
god. This two desyres of the passyon and of the sekenes. I desyrede
thame with a condicon for me thought that it passede the comene
courz of prayers and therfore I sayde. lorde thowe wote whate I wi
lde zyf it be thy wille that I hafe it grawnte it me And zyf it be
nouzt thy wille goode lorde be nought dysplesede for I wille nought
botte as thowe wille. This sekenes desyrede I yn my thought þat
y myght hafe it whene I were threttye zere elde. ffor the thride
I harde A man telle of haly kyrke of the storye of Saynte Ce
cylle. In the whilke schewynge I vndyrstede that sche hadde thre
wowndys with A swerde In the nekke with the whilke sche py
nede to the dede. By the styrrynge of this I conseyfede a myghty
desyre & prayande ovre lorde god that he wolde grawnte me thre
wowndys in my lyfe tyme that es to saye the wowndys of cotryon
the wonde of compassyon the wounde of wyffulle langgynge to god
ryght as I askede the othere two with a condysyon. I askyd the thyrde
with owtyn any codystyon. This two desyres before sayde passed
fro my mynde And the thyrde dwellyd cotynuelye.

And when I was thryttye wyntere alde and A halfe god
sente me A bodelye sykenes in the whilke I laye thre dayes
and thre nyghttes and on the ferthe nyght I toke alle my
ryghttynges of haly kyrke And wenyd nought to hafe lyffede
tylle daye. And aftyr this y langourede furthe two dayes & two
nyghttes & on the thyrde nyght. I wenede ofte tymes to hafe passe
de and so wenyd thaye that were aboute me. Botte in this I was
ryght sarye & lothe thouzt for to dye. Botte for nothynge that was

PLATE 1. British Library MS Additional 37790, fol. 97v

in Erthe that me hyrede to hyere fore nor for nothynge That I was
aferde fore for I tristyd in god botte it was fore I walde hafe hyrede
to hafe lofede god better and lange tyme that myght be the grace
of that lyfynge hafe the more knowynge and lofynge of god in
the blysse of hevene. ffor me thought alle the tyme that I [had] wolde hy
be here so lytille and so schorte in the regarde of endeles blysse I thouzt
thus. Goode lorde maye my lyfynge be no langere to thy worschippe
And was answerde in my resone and be the felynges of my paynes
that I schulde dye. And I asentyd fully with alle the wille of mye
herte to be atte god ys wille thus I endurede tille daye and by than
was my bodye dede fra the myddys downwarde as to my felynge
than was I styrrede to sette [be] uppe ryghttes lenande with clothes to
my heede forto hafe the mare fredome of my herte to be atte goddes
wille and thynkynge on hym whilys my lyfe walde laste and thay
that were with me sente for the person my curette to be atte my
ne endynge he come and a childe with hym and brought a crosse &
be thane I hadde sette myne eyen. And myght nouzt speke the per
sone sette the crosse before my face and sayde dowztu. I hafe brought
the the ymage of thy savioure loke there opon & coforthe the yere
with in reverence of hym that dyede for the & me. me thouzt pan
that y was welle for myne eyen ware sette upwarde into hevene
whethyr I trustede for to come. Botte nevere the lesse I assendyd to
sette myne eyen in the face of the crucyfixe zif y myght for to endu
re the lange in to the tyme of myn endynge. ffor me thought I myzt
langyr endure to loke evyn forthe than uppe ryght Aftyr this my
syght by ganne to fayle and it was alle dyrke abowte me in the cha
nmbyr and myrke as it hadde bene nyght safe in the ymage of
the crosse they helde a comon lyght And I wyste nevere howe alle
that was besyde the crosse was hidghe to me as zyf it hadde bene
my kylle occupyede with fendys Aftyr this the over partye of my
bodye beganne to dye as to my felynge myne handdys felle downe
on aythere syde And also for unpowere my heede satylde downe

PLATE 2. British Library MS Additional 37790, fol. 97r

[FIGURE 2A]   Bibliothèque Nationale MS Fonds Anglais 40, fols. 23r–v

¶ Theyse be two workyng*es* that may be seen in this vision. that one is sekyng. the other is beholdyng. the Sekyng is comyn that ech sowle may haue. *with* his grace. and owyth to haue Dyscrecion and techyng of holy church. it is gods will that we haue. iij. thynges in our Sekyng of his ȝefte. ¶ The furst is that we seke wyllfully and besyly *witho*uȝte slowth. as it may be /*fol. 23v*/ *with* his grace. gladly and merely. *with*out vnresonable hevynesse and veyne sorow. ¶ The seconde ðat we abyde hym stedfastely for his loue *witho*uȝte groȝyng and stryvyng agaynst hym in to our lyvys ende for it shall last but a whyle. ¶ The. iij is. that we truste in hym myghtely of fulle and tru feyth. ffor it is his wylle ðat we know that he shall aper sodenly and blyssydefully to all his lovers. ¶ ffor his workyng is prevy and he wille be perceyved and his aperyng shalle be swete sodeyn. And he wylle be trustyd for he is fulle homely curteyse blessyd mott he be.

[FIGURE 2B]   *A Revelation of Love*, 10.70–82

Theyse be two workinges that may be seen in this vision. That one is seking, the other is beholding. The seking is comen: that, ech soule may have with his grace, and oweth to have, by discretion° and teching of holy church. It is Gods will that we have three thinges in our seking of his gifte. The furst is that we seke wilfully and besily withoute slouth, as it may be /*fol. 23v*/ with his grace, gladly and merely without unskilfulle° hevinesse and vaine sorow. The seconde is° that we abide him stedfastely for his love, withoute gruching° and striving against him, into our lives ende, for it shall last but a while. The third is that we truste in him mightely, of fulle seker° faith. For it is his wille that we know that he shall aper sodenly and blissefully• to all his lovers. For his working is prevy, and he wille be perceived, and his apering shalle be swithe° sodeyn. And he wille be trowed,° for he is fulle hende, homely, and curteise.° Blessed mot he be!

75

80

• On the other hand, *y* is sometimes preferred to P's *i* or *ie,* for example, where medial *i* is consonantal (as in the case of "praied," which becomes "prayed"), or where *-ie* is used as an alternative to *-ey* or *-y* (as in the case of "bodie," which becomes "body").

Sometimes words are normalized simply because their spelling is so awkward or inconsistent that they are unnecessarily difficult to read. On such occasions we construct a spelling from elsewhere in the manuscript, from another manuscript, or, if we must, from what is known of Middle English spelling practices in general (e.g., *c* is very occasionally transposed to *s* where that aids in correct pronunciation of the word). In general, though, we have tried to normalize spellings in groups.

Normalizing as we do on a larger scale than is usual in Middle English editing, some degree of orthographic consistency is inevitably lost in this edition of *A Revelation* (from which, as a result, it is often not possible to reconstruct manuscript spellings, as one generally can from our edition of *A Vision*). Even the degree of modernization cannot very well remain constant. In order to produce a text that is clear enough for the general reader yet still responsive in as many respects as possible to the manuscript from which the text derives, some aspects of manuscript orthography have to be treated with more caution than others, or else the look and sound of Middle English become attenuated. Readers who know the Paris manuscript from Colledge and Walsh's edition may either feel we have gone too far or, to the extent that they find that edition's scrupulous representation of Paris's orthography baffling, not far enough. Finding the correct compromise between authenticity and clarity is inevitably an indefinite and subjective process.

b) Punctuation and Capitalization

The manuscripts offer no clear or consistent system for punctuating the texts. As is common in many medieval and renaissance texts, scribal punctuation tends to reflect rhetorical delivery, rather than modern notions of sentence structure or organization, with the result that different manuscripts punctuate the same passages in different ways.[93] A conservative (or "diplomatic") edition can reproduce all the scribal punctuating marks and capital letters of a given manuscript, and it would be tempting to edit the Paris manuscript of *A Revelation* in particular in this way, since its system of punctuation and paragraphing is unusually detailed. But the needs of modern, usually silent reading are different, and the punctuation adopted here instead draws attention to Julian's prose as a vehicle, above all, of argument, articulating her often ambiguous syntactic structure in whatever ways seems best to express the logic of her thought. (There are usually other possibilities and they often produce different emphases,

some of them well worth exploring.) Readers of this volume should thus remember that here—as in most editions, even when this goes unremarked—the system of punctuation is neither original (either to the base manuscript or to any other early instantiation of the work) nor disinterested. Figures 1b and 2b offer several cases in point.

Our practice with capitalization is different. Middle English makes much more sparing use of capitalization than modern, preferring "god" to "God," "passion" to "Passion," and so on. Modern conventions have become somewhat vexed, as a reaction against such practices as capitalizing the first letter of "He" when the subject is the deity, and at present a wide variety of conventions can be found in different publications. With the exception of "God," "Christ," and "Saint," each of which we begin with a capital, our texts follow the conventions of our manuscripts.

2. READING THE TEXTUAL NOTES, SIDENOTES, AND APPENDIX

a) Textual Notes

Both *A Vision Showed to a Devout Woman* and *A Revelation of Love* have lengthy and sometimes discursive textual notes. These do two things: provide information about the wording of passages in the different manuscripts and justify the wording (the "readings") of our edition, especially when the edition has emended the manuscript on which it is based (Additional or Paris)—a particularly important matter in this unusually interventionist edition. The information in these notes can be useful in thinking through the logic of Julian's thought and the shape of her rhetoric in detail, whether or not

---

93. See D. C. Greetham, *Textual Scholarship: An Introduction* (New York: Garland, 1994); M. B. Parkes, *Pause and Effect: An Introduction to the History of Punctuation in the West* (Berkeley and Los Angeles: University of California Press, 1993).

23

The theent Chapter

And how a sowle shall haue her
in his beholding he shall teach hym
selfe. and that is most worshippe to
hym and most profyght to the sowle.
and most receyved of mekenesse and
vertue wt the grace and ledyng of ye
holy gost. ffor a sowle that only pre=
refynyth hym to god wt very truste.
eyther in sekyng or in beholdyng. it
is the most worshippe that he may do
as to my syght. Theyse be two
workyngs that may be seen in this
vision. that one is sekyng. the other
is beholdyng. the sekyng is comyn
that ech sowle may haue. wt his grace.
And owyth to haue Dyscrecion and
techyng of holy church. it is gods
will that we haue. iij. thynges in
our sekyng of his zefte. The
furst is that we seke wylfully and
besyly wonzte slowth. as it may be
wt

PLATE 3. Bibliothèque Nationale MS Fonds Anglais 40, fol. 23r

The seconde reuelation

wt his grace . gladly and merely . wout
vnresonable heuynesse and veyne
sorow ⁊ ☙ The seconde ẏ we abyde
hym stedfastely for his loue wouʒte
grochyng and stryuyng agaynst hym
in to our lyuys ende for it shall last
but a whyle ⁊ ☙ The · iij is . that
we truste in hym myghtely of fulle
and trw feyth . ffor it is his wille ꝥ
we know that he shall aper sodenly and
blyssydfully to all his lovers ☙ ffor
his workyng is prevy and he wille be
pereeyued and his aperyng shalle be
swete sodeyn . And he wylle be trustyd
for he is fulle homely curteyse blessyd
most he be . ‖ —— ‖ ——— ‖

The third reuelation . the 4i e̅

And after this I saw Chapter
god in a poynte . that is to say
in my vnderstandyng . by which
syght I saw . that he is in althyng .
I beheld wt avysement . seeyng and

knowyng

[FIGURE 3A] *A Vision Showed to a Devout Woman,* Section 4

SECTION 4

And this same time that I sawe this bodily sight, oure lorde shewed me a gastelye sight of his hamly° lovinge. I sawe that he es to us alle thinge that is goode and comfortabille to oure helpe. He es oure clethinge, that° for love wappes us and windes us, halses us and alle becloses us,° hinges aboute us for tender love, that he maye nevere leve us. And so in this sight I sawe sothelye that he is alle thinge that is goode, as to mine understandinge.   5

And in this, he shewed me a litille thinge the quantite of a haselle nutte, lygande in the palme of my hande, and, to my understandinge, that it was as rounde as any balle. I lokede theropon, and thought: "Whate maye this be?" And I was answerde generaly thus: "It is alle that is made." I merveylede howe that it might laste, for   10 methought it might falle sodaynlye to nought for litille. And I was answerde in mine understandinge: "It lastes and ever shalle, for God loves it. And so hath alle thinge the beinge thorowe the love of God."

[FIGURE 3B] Textual notes, *A Vision Showed to a Devout Woman,* Section 4

[SECTION 4] 2 **hamly** A initially read "anly," but the corrector added an initial *h* and an extra minim to the *n* above the line. "Anly" would mean "solitary" or "unique" • 3 **clethinge, that** from P/S: A reads "clethynge" only, making "love" the subject of the rest of the sentence • 4 **becloses us** from P/S: A reads "beteches us us" • 8 **that it was as rounde** P/S omit "that," a word that complicates the syntax in A and may be a mistake

---

one ends up agreeing with all the choices made by the editors. Figures 3–4 (above and above-right) again offer two examples, in which the notes to the relevant passages have been placed immediately under the material to which they refer (rather than, as in the edition as a whole, after the texts). In figures 3a and 4a, which contain passages from *A Vision* and *A Revelation* respectively, the presence of textual notes is marked according to the following conventions:

• The degree sign [°] in the text is used, first, to signal editorial emendations to the base manuscript (A or P), second, to signal corrections made in the manuscripts themselves. (Some of the very frequent minor corrections in P are not recorded.)
• This sign is not always placed immediately after the emended or corrected word itself, but at the end of the phrase quoted at the beginning of the relevant textual note (the "lemma," i.e., the word or phrase from the edited text on which the note comments). Thus, in the first phrase of the passage from *A Revelation* (figure 4a), "With a glad chere," the emended word is "glad" but the degree sign appears after "chere."
• In the case of *A Revelation* only, a dot sign [•] is used to signal certain words and forms that are emended so often, and in such a regular way, that they do not require a textual note to explain them after the first instance in which the emendation occurs. This class of emendation, which involves reimporting s's East Anglian vocabulary back into P's more standardized Middle English, is used in the case of the following words and forms:

blissed/blisseful/blissefully (see textual note to *Rev.* 1.24)

[FIGURE 4A] *A Revelation of Love,* Chapter 24 (Revelation 10)

AND THE TWENTY-FOURTH CHAPTER

With a glad chere° oure good lorde loked into his side and behelde, enjoyenge.° And with his swete loking he led forth the understanding of his creature by the same wound into his sid, within. And ther he shewed a fair, delectable° place, and large inow for alle mankinde that shalle be saved to rest° in pees and in love. And therwith he */fol. 46v/* brought to minde his dereworthy blode and his precious water which he let poure all out° for love. And with the swete beholding he shewed his blissful• hart even° cloven on two. And with this swete enjoyeng° he shewed to my understanding in part the blessed° godhede, as farforth as he wolde that time, strengthing the pour soule for to understande as it may be saide: that is to mene, the endlesse love that was without beginning, and is, and shal be ever.

5

10

[FIGURE 4B] Textual notes, *A Revelation of Love,* Chapter 24 (Revelation 10)

[CHAPTER 24] The text of Chapter 24 is based on P, collated with S, A, and W, which excerpts the entire chapter • S has the rubric "The Tenth Revelation is that our lord Jesus shewith in love his blissid herte cloven in two, enjoyand. Twenty-Fourth Chapter" • 1 **With a glad chere** from S/W: P reads "Wyth a good chere" • 1 **enjoyenge** from S/W: P reads "with joy." The scribe seems to have found this absolute use of the participle awkward • 3 **delectable** from S/W: P reads "and delectable" • 4 **to rest** from S/W: P reads "and rest" • 6 **poure all out** from S/W: P reads "poure out" • 7 **even** from S/W: not in P • 7 **this swete enjoyeng** from S/W: P reads "hys enjoyeng" • 8 **blessed** from S/W: P reads "blyssydfulle" • 8 **as farforth as he wolde that time** not in S • 9 **strengthing the pour soule** S reads "steryng than the pure soule"

mekille (see textual note to *Rev.* 3.27)

seker/sekerly/sekernesse (see textual note to *Rev.* 1.41)

-hede (see textual note to *Rev.* 7.19)

• textual notes are otherwise not marked. Thus neither the note to *Vis.* 4.8 **that it was as rounde** and *Rev.* 24.8 **as farforth as he wolde that time** is signaled with a marker in the text, since neither affects the text or represents a correction in the manuscript

The notes to *A Revelation* (figure 4b) include major differences ("substantive variants") between the Paris (P), Sloane (S), and Westminster (W) manuscripts, as well as corroborative or otherwise notable readings from the Additional (A) manuscript of *A Vision,* whether or not our edited text has incorporated the wording of these other manuscripts. It is

thus possible to track the decisions made to retain the readings of the base manuscript (P), as well as the decisions made to prefer other readings. "Minor" differences, not noted, include spelling differences (P and S spell the majority of words differently) and small changes in word order, as well as inclusion or omission of certain function words ("and," "or") where this does not affect sense, and minor variations in ceremonial titles ("lady", "saint," "lord").

The notes to *A Vision* (figure 3b) are simpler, including only emendations to the text and a few instances where emendation is tempting but the manuscript reading has been retained (as in the note to 4.8). With only a single manuscript of this work, emendations are necessarily fewer: we are cautious about using readings from manuscripts of *A Revelation* unless there is very good reason to do so. Most of the major differences between A and the three *Revelation* manuscripts are likely the result of the rewriting that produced *A Revelation* out of *A Vision,* and many of the minor variations are also, at least arguably, in the same category. These minor variations can best be tracked by using the analytic version of *A Vision* that runs at the foot of the corresponding pages of *A Revelation* (see section 3 below, "Reading the Analytic Version of *A Vision*").

Each note takes the same form.

- line number within the chapter or section
- lemma in **bold face** (a word or phrase from the edition, following the edition's capitalization, spelling, and punctuation)
- comment

When the note provides the rationale for emending the base manuscript (that is, for including in our edition of *A Vision* or *A Revelation* a word or phrase not originally in A or P, respectively), the comment provides the following information:

- identification of the manuscript or combination of manuscripts from which the word or phrase in the lemma comes
- citation of the word or phrase from the base manuscript that has been excluded from or emended in the edited text; these citations follow the spellings of the manuscripts from which they come, except that thorn, yogh, and variation between *u* and *v* and *i* and *j* are regularized; where two manuscripts, for example P/S, share the same reading, the spellings are those of the first one listed
- if appropriate, an explanation of the decision taken

The second note in figure 4b thus reads "1 **enjoyenge** from s/w: P reads 'with joy.' The scribe seems to have found this absolute use of the participle awkward." The structure "from X/Y: Z reads" is formulaic, repeated on innumerable occasions through the notes.

b) Sidenotes

The sidenotes on the facing page of the editions of *A Vision* and *A Revelation* provide word, phrase, or sentence translations ("glosses") and discussions of matters that call for comment ("annotations"). Focusing primarily on details of meaning, their main goal is to clarify the structure of the two works and the complicated processes by which revelation becomes argument. So far as possible, they thus draw readers inward, back to the texts, rather than outward, toward exploration of their wider historical and intellectual significance—or, indeed, toward scholarship on the text, which informs the sidenotes but is not acknowledged or discussed there.[94] Sidenotes to *A Vision* and *A Revelation* are usually, but not invariably, identical when the two works are identical; differences may reflect differences in spelling between the works, only one of which sometimes requires a gloss, or the different contexts of common passages, which are sometimes in service to different arguments. Just as they do not comment on the scholarship, the sidenotes do not comment on specifically textual difficulties.

The glosses are eclectic, sometimes offering word-for-word, sometimes sense-for-sense translations: often rendering the Middle English by the modern English cognate word or phrase but as often choosing idioms for similarity of effect

---

94. Apart from previous editions, especially that of Colledge and Walsh (to which they owe a considerable debt), the sidenotes draw especially on articles by Anna Maria Reynolds and Annie Sutherland, and a thesis by Amy Appleford. See Reynolds, "Some Literary Influences in the *Revelations* of Julian of Norwich"; Annie Sutherland, "'Oure Feyth Is Groundyd in Goddes Worde'—Julian of Norwich and the Bible," in *The Medieval Mystical Tradition in England: Exeter Symposium 7,* ed. E. A. Jones (Cambridge: D. S. Brewer, 2004), 1–20; Amy Appleford, "Learning to Die: Affectivity, Community, and Death in Late Medieval English Writing" (Ph.D. diss., University of Western Ontario, 2004).

rather than strict verbal equivalence. Their presence in an edition that insists on the impossibility of translating or modernizing Julian's Middle English is, of course, paradoxical, and although they do a lot of work for the reader, they should not be taken too literally. Their preference for straightforward readings of the original does reflect the editors' belief that *A Vision* and *A Revelation* are very often argumentative before they are lyrical. Yet their tendency to reduce verbal ambiguity—as when they attach adjectives and adverbs to specific nouns and verbs when the original leaves their affiliations uncertain, or give clear readings of passages that are obviously obscure—is mainly a practicality. As with the editorial punctuation, they should emphatically be understood as starting-points for investigation into the meaning of passages, not as conclusions. Since readers may begin anywhere in either text and since contexts vary, difficult words tend to be glossed repeatedly and not always in the same way. Concerned only with the particular idiolects of *A Vision* and *A Revelation,* the glosses do not provide etymological or dialectal information, for which readers should consult the *Middle English Dictionary*. Glosses are distinguished from annotations by beginning with a lowercase letter: "**shewed** revealed" (*Rev.* 2.1), as distinct from "**For the third** The third desire is less idiosyncratic than the others . . ." (*Rev.* 2.33). Yet annotations often comment closely on the language of a passage, providing paraphrases that are almost equivalent to translations.

When they are not engaged in direct exposition of argument, the annotations offer several kinds of information: cross-references within the text (especially important in *A Revelation,* which is highly self-referential, especially in its later phases); short definitions of theological terms or concepts, with a minimum of historical background; explanations of ideas and allusions that the argument of *A Vision* or *A Revelation*

assumes readers will understand; and citations of clearly relevant biblical passages and analogous passages of works contemporary with Julian or likely known to her. Since the analytic version of *A Vision* already offers extensive information about the relationship between the versions, the sidenotes exclude commentary on this important matter, on the assumption that, however intricate the relationship between the two works may be, a reading of either one of them needs to approach that work as an integrated whole.

Unusual among Middle English editions—which commonly prefer Jerome's Latin Vulgate, since this was the version in use in fourteenth-century England—this edition cites the Bible from the Revised Standard Version, giving cross-references to the language or numbering system of the Vulgate only when these are important. The RSV is the most readable of the translations deriving from the early-seventeenth-century Authorized Version; retaining much of the sonority and rhetorical balance of that version, its language seems to us to offer a bridge between Julian's Middle English and the present. Also unusual among editions of medieval theological works, this edition finds its analogues to Julian's thought, not in the writings of the Church Fathers or of medieval monastic and scholastic theologians, but rather in a carefully selected group of thirteenth- and fourteenth-century vernacular theologies in Middle English and occasionally Anglo-Norman French. Julian may have known Augustine, Cassian, Gregory, Bernard, and even Thomas Aquinas directly—since, in common with most visionary writers, she seldom cites sources, it is hard to be sure—but her reading of them would have been deeply imbued with language and assumptions drawn from the sophisticated vernacular milieu in which she lived and wrote. The language and thought of *A Vision* and *A Revelation* constantly evoke this milieu, sometimes drawing on particular texts, sometimes echoing commonplaces, but always speaking with (as it were) a theological accent specific to their place and time, mingling popular and formal religious thought in a mode particular to vernacular writing (see the discussion of the vernacular in "Editing in Principle," section 3.1 above). If the Fathers often occupy the hinterland of Julian's thought, along with apocryphal works such as *The Gospel of Nicodemus* and *The Vision of Paul* and the lives of the saints, closer to home are five great early works known to every English religious writer of her time: Honorius of Autun's theological dialogue *Elucidarium* (here quoted in the Anglo-Norman verse version, *La lumere as lais* by Pierre D'Abernon); two "rules" for religious people, *Ancrene Wisse* and Edmund of Abingdon's *Speculum ecclesie* (here quoted in a Middle English version, *The Mirror of Holy Church*); Robert Grosseteste's theological romance *Le château d'amour;* and that vast poetic treatise on the Last Things, *The Pricke of Conscience.* Closer still are works by Julian's immediate predecessors and contemporaries: including Continental writers such as Johannes de Caulibus (whose *Meditationes vitae Christi* is here quoted in a Middle English version, *The Privity of the Passion*), James of Milan (whose *Stimulus amoris* is quoted in a Middle English version, *The Prickynge of Love*), and Bridget of Sweden; and a number of contemporary English writers: the hermits Richard Rolle and William Flete; the canon Walter Hilton; the anonymous author of *The Chastising of God's Children;* and perhaps the poet William Langland, author of *Piers Plowman.* Citations from these and other works in the sidenotes do not necessarily imply a claim for Julian's direct knowledge or use of them, any more than the absence of a work (such as most of those attributed to the author of *The Cloud of Unknowing*) implies a claim that Julian did not know or use it: like much else, a detailed account of Julian's theological affiliations, vernacular, scholastic,

and patristic, must wait for the companion volume. The purpose of the citations is rather to throw light on Julian's thought, either by showing how it is paralleled in a contemporary text or, conversely, by pointing to its differences from standard teaching. Citations modernize the spellings of the editions from which they are taken following the same conventions used in the edition of *A Vision*, with occasional simplification of individual words on an ad hoc basis; they modify capitalization and punctuation as necessary. Difficult words or phrases are glossed in square brackets within the citation.

3. READING THE ANALYTIC VERSION OF *A VISION*

The "analytic version" of *A Vision* is printed at the foot of the corresponding pages of *A Revelation* as a guide to the relationship between the two works and the process of revision that turns the former into the latter. As explained below, different typefaces and selected symbols aim to show not only where *A Revelation* adds material but also where it keeps it unchanged, revises it, or omits it:

- passages of the two works that are identical or nearly identical (except for spelling variations and minor, "non-substantive" differences of wording) are printed in regular typeface
- passages or words unique to *A Vision* are printed **in bold**
- passages or words that are clearly related but not identical in *A Vision* and *A Revelation* are printed *in italics,* if, in the opinion of the editors, the differences between the versions may be "substantive": that is, if they could plausibly be explained as a product of authorial revision, rather than minor scribal variation
- placement of short passages in *A Revelation* that do not occur in *A Vision*—words, phrases, and clauses up to the length of a short sentence—is signaled by a bold double dagger,

or diesis, ‡; again, minor differences of wording are not necessarily signaled

- placement of longer passages in *A Revelation*
  that do not occur in *A Vision* is signaled by
  a brief reference between diagonal slashes:
  /*Rev. 1.1–2.2*/
- section and line references to *A Vision* are given
  at the beginning of each page and wherever *A
  Revelation* presents material in a different order

These symbols and typographies do not offer an
objective analysis of the relationship between *A
Vision* and *A Revelation* but rather an interpretation. This is obviously so each time the analytic *Vision* represents relatively small verbal
differences between the texts—whether the editors have opted for the italics and dieses that signify authorial revision or have retained a regular
typeface in order to signify scribal variation—
for in either case not only is a specific editorial
judgment being exercised, but a whole set of
assumptions about how medieval works are
written, copied, and revised is in play. Interpretation is also present in other cases: for example,
where a given passage of *A Vision* can plausibly
be represented either as revised or as abandoned
by *A Revelation*; or in many instances where the
relationship between the versions can be analyzed in more than one way. Nonetheless, keeping these caveats in mind, reading *A Vision* and
A Revelation against each other through the
analytic *Vision* offers a good deal of information
both about each text individually and about the
process of revision. Figure 5 (page 58) shows a
representative example.

Editorial decisions about how to represent
the relationship between these passages begin
with the third word of the passage from *A
Vision*, "this," not present in *A Revelation* but
not printed in bold because this variation seems
to us a minor, rather than a substantive, variation. Other examples of what the editors consider minor variation in the passage include
"withoute" in the second sentence (not present

in *A Revelation*); the variation later in that sentence between "this worde" in *A Vision* and
"these wordes" in *A Revelation;* and the differences between "overcominge of the fende" and
"to paine and to shame" in *A Vision* and "the
overcoming of the feende" and "to shame and
paine" in *A Revelation*. Noting all such variations
would lead to an excessive cluttering of the
analytic *Vision* and a loss of focus on the more
important differences between it and its revision. So would an attempt to categorize substantive differences between the texts too
closely. In the first sentence, the italicized *"langere"* is understood as revised into the phrase
"him a conveniable time" in *A Revelation,* despite
the fact that a more elaborate solution—the
inclusion of a diesis to represent *A Revelation*'s
"him"—might seem to offer more precise
information. Other italicized phrases are not
necessarily less elaborate than their alternatives
but offer a particular reading of the situation.
Again in the first sentence, the italicized *"alle
that was therein,"* which in *A Revelation* becomes
"all the understanding that was therin," could
equally be represented as "alle ‡ that was therein";
italics draw attention to the rethinking of the
entire phrase involved in the incorporation of
the term "understanding." The analytic symbols
and typographies offer, in short, a starting-
point for a comparative study of the works and
should not be seen as attempting to fix any single view of their relationship into place.

So far as the comparative reading of *A Vision*
and *A Revelation* made available by the analytic
Vision is concerned, this is not the place to ana-
lyze this passage in detail, but several things
stand out, starting with how similar the two
versions of it are: *A Revelation*'s continuing
trust in the earlier account of Julian's experience is here, as through most of the text, much
in evidence. The one systematic difference
between the works is *A Revelation*'s avoidance
of *A Vision*'s very frequent first-person references: on four occasions simply by the deletion

[FIGURE 5] *A Revelation of Love,* Chapter 13 (Revelation 5)

The Fifth Revelation
THE THIRTEENTH CHAPTER

And after, or God° shewed any wordes, he sufferde me to beholde him a conveniable time, and all that I had seen, and all the understanding that was therin, as the simpilnes of the soule might take it. /fol. 27r/ Then he, without voys and opening of lippes, formed in my soule these wordes: "Herewith is the feende overcome." This worde saide our lorde mening his blessed passion, as he shewed before. In this, our lord shewed a parte of the feendes malice, and fully his unmight, for he shewed that the passion of him is the overcoming of the feende. God shewed that the feend hath nowe the same malice that he had before the incarnation, and also sore he traveyleth, and as continually he seeth that all soules of salvation eskape him worshipfully, by the vertue of his precious passion. And that is his sorow, and full evil is he attemed,° for all that God suffereth him to do turneth us to joy and him to shame and paine. And he /fol. 27v/ hath as mekille• sorow when God geveth him leve to werke as when he worketh not. And that is for he may never do as ille as he wolde, for his might is alle lokked in Gods hande. But in God may be no wrath, as to my sight. For our good lorde—endlessly having regard to his awne worshippe and to the profite of all them that shal be saved—with might and right he withstondeth the reproved, the which of malice and of shrewdnes besye them to contrary and do against Goddes will.

   5

   10

   15

[VIS. 8.29–41] And after this, or° God shewed **me** any wordes,° he sufferde me to behalde *langere,* and alle that I hadde seene, and *alle that was therein* ‡. And than *was,* withouten voice and withoute openinge of lippes, formede in my saule this worde: "Herewith is the feende overcomen." This worde saide oure lorde menande° his ‡ passion, as he shewed **me** before. In this, oure lorde **brought unto my minde and** shewed **me** a perte of the fendes malice, and fully his unmight. *And, for that,* he shewed **me** that the passion of him is overcominge of the fende. God shewed **me** that he hase nowe the same malice that he had before the incarnation, and als sare he travailes, and als continuelye he sees that *alle chosene saules* escapes him worshipfullye ‡. And that es alle his sorowe ‡. For alle that God suffers him to° do turnes us° to joye and him to paine and to shame. And he has als mekille sorowe when God giffes him leve to wyrke as when he werkes nought. And that es for he maye nevere do als ille as he wolde, for his might es alle lokene in Goddes hande. /Rev. 13.14–18/

---

of "me" in *A Revelation,* on a fifth by the additional excision of a whole phrase, *A Vision's* "brought unto my minde and." References to the activities of Christ, on the other hand, tend to be made more direct, for example by shifting the second sentence from the passive to the active voice. Other minor shifts increase the passage's precision ("langere" becomes "a conveniable time") or worry over the language of predestination ("alle chosene saules" becomes "all soules of salvation"). The additions in *A Revelation* do several things whose purpose is not readily obvious from a brief extract, but their heightened awareness of the need for theological precision is especially striking: "by the vertue of his precious passion," for example, insists on the role of the Passion in the salvation of the elect. The longer addition at the end, on the other hand, works more as an anticipation of a theme *A Revelation* explores in detail later, and its tentativeness here is marked by the return of one of those repressed first-person pronouns: the claim that "in God may be no wrath" is qualified by the phrase "as to my sight."

A few of the substantive, as well as the minor, differences between the passages might be understood as scribal, not authorial. *A Revelation* often adds references to "understanding," but the absence of the phrase "the understanding" in *A Vision*'s "alle that was therein" could be the result of a scribal omission, not an authorial expansion in *A Revelation; A Vision*'s awkward sentence opening "And, for that," is perhaps actively suspect. In the larger context of both works, however, most changes here, even details, have all the appearance of system, suggesting that explicit policies and rethinkings, not scribal slips of the pen, were responsible.

The analytic *Vision* should not be thought of as necessary for understanding *A Revelation*, which was clearly envisaged as a separate text and, for the most part, asks to be read as one. But insofar as it presents a detailed and, it would seem, reasonably accurate picture of a process of revision in progress, it has the potential to take us further into both *A Vision* and *A Revelation*, in much the same way as do the textual notes. For while the texts offered by this edition represent *A Vision* and *A Revelation* in as polished and lucid a form as the evidence will bear, both kinds of apparatus act as reminders of the processes by which their meanings are made and remade, both during the initial period of their composition and subsequently, by scribes and editors. Reflection on these processes can only increase a reader's sense of what is at stake in the two works.

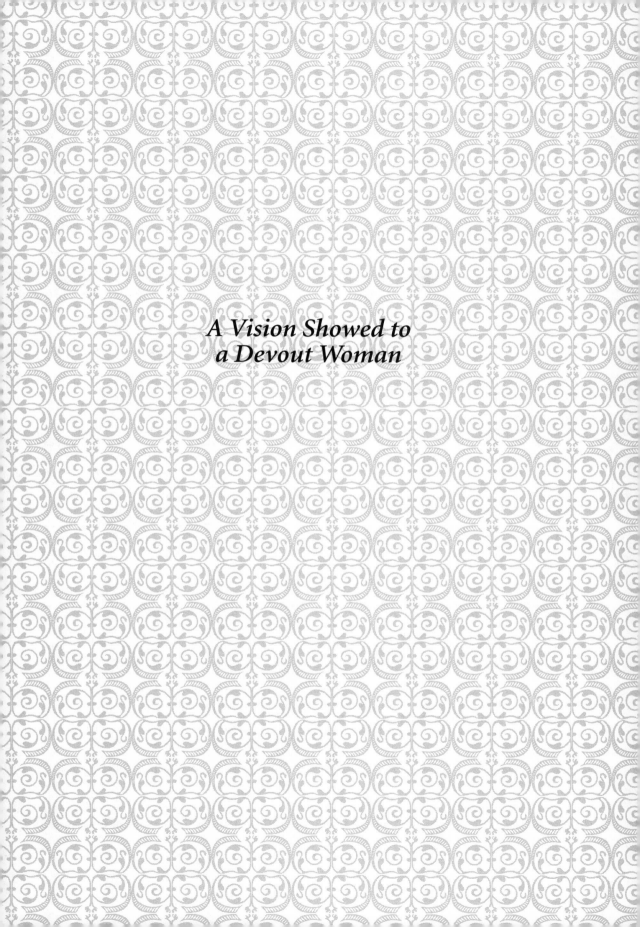

A Vision Showed to
a Devout Woman

[RUBRIC] 1–4 **Here es a vision . . . loverse** The second sentence must date from a copy of *A Vision* made in 1413. The rest, including the reference to Julian as anonymous "devoute woman," could be earlier • 1 **shewed be . . . God** revealed by the goodness of God. "Be" (by) can also mean "about" • 2 **that is recluse** who is enclosed. "Recluse" is from Latin *reclusus* (enclosed) • 2 **yit is on life** is still alive • 2 **anno domini 1413** in the year of our Lord 1413. Although *A Vision* does not date the revelation it recounts, as visions often do, the scribe provides a date, a name, and a place, tying the text to history • 3–4 **In the whilke . . . loverse** in which vision are very many comforting and greatly stirring words for all those who desire to be Christ's lovers. "Comfortabille" and "stirrande" are key words, "comfort" and variants appearing forty times in *A Vision*, "stir" and variants more than twenty. They outline a double agenda for the work: to bring peace and to impel to action

[SECTION 1] 1 **be** by • 1–2 **minde of Cristes passion** intense recollection of Christ's Passion. Although Julian takes it in idiosyncratic directions, this was a common desire among the late medieval devout: to submerge the self in the details of Christ's suffering, scene by scene from his arrest to his death. *The Privity of the Passion* promises readers: "I trowe [believe] fully that whoso wolde besy hime [would occupy himself] with all his herte and all his minde and umbethinke him of [think about] this glorius passione . . . it sulde [would] bring him and chaunge him into a new state of lifinge" (prologue, in Horstmann, *Yorkshire Writers* [henceforth cited as *YW*], 1:198) • 2 **syekenes** sickness • 2 **thrid** third • 2–3 **of Goddes gifte** through God's gift • 4 **come to my minde** which came to my mind. Literally, "having come," the first of a number of Latinate constructions in *A Vision* • 4 **methought** it seemed to me • 5 **yitte** yet • 5 **mare** more • 6 **I wolde . . . time** I wanted to have been present at that time • 6–7 **Mary Maudeleyne . . . loverse** Mary Magdalene was present at the Crucifixion (John 19:25). Medieval writers often take her love for Christ as exemplary for all the devout, especially women. On "Cristes loverse," see page 12 in the Introduction • 7 **might have sene bodilye** could have seen physically. Rather than merely in her imagination • 9–10 **Notwithstandinge . . . teches** despite the fact that I believed soberly in all the sufferings of Christ, in the form holy church shows and teaches them. Most fourteenth-century churches had wall paintings or stained glass depicting the sequence of events that make up the Passion narrative • 10–12 **the paintinges of crucifexes . . . reche** the paintings of crucifixes that are made in the likeness of Christ's Passion by the grace of God according to the teaching of holy church, so far as human intelligence can envisage them. Decorated crucifixes, ubiquitous in late medieval English churches and public spaces, were under attack from reformers in the

1380s, who objected to their lavishness and the practice of venerating them • 13 **bodilye sight** physical sight. A vision, conceptualized here as an actual experience of an event, rather than a mere meditation. See 7.1–3 • 13 **more knawinge** greater understanding • 14 **compassion of oure ladye** compassion of the Virgin Mary. If Mary Magdalene's suffering is most like that of the devout believer, the suffering of Christ's mother most resembles that of Christ • 15 **that were belevande . . . sithene** who believed in his suffering at that time and since • 15–16 **I wolde . . . thame** I wished I had been one of them. Other late medieval women visionaries, including Bridget of Sweden and Margery Kempe, experienced visionary presence at the Crucifixion • 16–17 **Othere sight . . . none** I never asked for any other sight or revelation from God • 17 **tille atte** until • 17 **were departed** would be separated • 17–18 **trayste sothfastlye . . . safe** trusted confidently that I would be saved. An essential attitude for the devout to maintain according to many Middle English religious works. William Flete's *Remedy Against the Troubles of Temptations* considers doubt of the certainty of one's own salvation a temptation to despair, and instructs: "Truste fully that by his goodnes he will save you and bringe you to everlastinge joye whan he seeth best time, for he hath bought you full dere with his precious blode and painefull deth" (chap. 4, *YW* 2:112). Certainty of salvation is a major theme of the second half of *A Vision* • 18 **this was my meninge** this was my intention. The formal prose here suggests that the request for this "grace" itself has the formality of a pledge • 18–19 **for I wolde after . . . have** because I wanted afterward . . . to have • 19 **more trewe minde in** more faithful recollection of • 20 **For the seconde** as to the second desire • 20 **come . . . with contrition** which came into my mind with sorrow for sin. The word "contrition" marks this second desire as penitential in character • 20–21 **frelye withouten any sekinge** freely, without my searching for it. It is emphasized that this unusual second desire originated from outside Julian, as a gift of grace • 21 **wilfulle desire** urgent desire • 22 **so harde as to the dede** so harsh it would bring me to the point of death • 23 **my rightinges of halye kyrke** my rites of holy church. The last rites included a final confession, absolution, and extreme unction (anointment of the dying person with holy oil), essential preparations for making a good death • 23 **wenande** expecting • 24–25 **I wolde hafe . . . life** I did not want to preserve any of the comfort of bodily or earthly living • 26 **bodelye and gastelye** physical and spiritual • 26 **that I shulde have . . . die** that I would have if I were actually dying • 27 **dredes . . . feyndes** dreads and agitations caused by fiends. Expected occurrences at a medieval deathbed • 27-28 **safe . . . saule** except for the soul's passing from the body • 28–29 **hoped that it might . . . die** hoped this experience might be of assistance to me when I was really dying • 29 **I desirede sone . . . God** A pious desire for death different from the urgent desire for sickness

/fol. 97r/

H*ere° es a vision, shewed be the goodenes of God to a devoute woman. And hir name es Julian, that is recluse atte Norwiche and yit is on life, anno domini 1413. In the whilke vision er fulle many comfortabille wordes and gretly stirrande to alle thaye that desires to be Cristes loverse.*

SECTION 1

I° desirede thre graces be the gifte of God. The first was to have minde of Cristes° passion. The seconde was bodelye syekenes. And the thrid was to have of Goddes gifte thre woundes.

For the firste, come to my minde with devotion: methought I hadde grete felinge in the passion of Criste, botte yitte I desirede to have mare, be the grace of God. 5
Methought I wolde have bene that time with Mary Maudeleyne and with othere that were Cristes loverse, that I might have sene bodilye the passion of oure lorde that he sufferede for me, that I might have sufferede with him as othere did that loved him. Notwithstandinge that I leeved sadlye alle the peynes of Criste as halye kyrke shewes and teches, and also the paintinges of crucifexes that er made be the 10
grace of God aftere the techinge of haly kyrke to the liknes of Cristes passion, als farfurthe as manes witte maye reche—noughtwithstondinge alle this trewe beleve, I desirede a bodilye sight, wharein I might have more knawinge of bodelye paines of oure lorde oure savioure, and of the compassion of oure ladye, and of alle his trewe loverse that were belevande his paines that time and sithene. For I wolde have beene 15
one of thame and suffrede with thame. Othere sight of Gode ne shewinge desirede I nevere none tille atte the saule were departed frome the bodye, for I trayste sothfastlye that I shulde be safe. And this was my meninge: for I wolde after, because of that shewinge, have the more trewe minde in the passion of Criste.

For the seconde, come to my minde with contrition, frelye withouten any 20
sekinge: a wilfulle desire to hafe of Goddes gifte a bodelye syekenes. And I wolde that this bodilye syekenes might have beene so harde as to the dede, */fol. 97v/* so that I might in the sekenes take alle my rightinges of halye kyrke, wenande myselfe that I shulde die, and that alle creatures that sawe me might wene the same. For I wolde hafe no comforth of no fleshlye nothere erthelye life. In this sekenes I desirede to 25
hafe alle manere of paines, bodelye and gastelye, that I shulde have if I shulde die, alle the dredes and tempestes of feyndes, and alle manere of othere° paines, safe° of the outepassinge of the saule, for I hoped° that it might be to me a spede when I shulde die. For I desirede sone to be with my God.

31 it passede . . . prayers [these desires] went beyond the usual practice in praying. Visions were held in low esteem by many specialists of the spiritual life. In book 1.10 of his *Scale of Perfection* (1380s), Hilton writes that "visiones or revelatiouns . . . aren not verily contemplation," even if they can have a "secundrye" place. Julian's request for illness has no immediate known parallels • **32 thowe woote whate I wolde** you know what I want • **33–34 I wille nought . . . wille** I do not want it except as you want it. Perhaps an echo of Christ at Gethsemane in Matt. 26:39: "My Father, if it be possible, let this cup pass from me; nevertheless, not as I will, but as thou wilt" • **34 in my youth** Seems to refer to the time when Julian made her requests, not to her thirtieth year, when she hoped they would be fulfilled • **35 in threttye yeere elde** in my thirtieth year of age. The age when Christ was said to have begun his ministry • **36 For the thirde** The third desire is less idiosyncratic than the others, crystallizing them into a publicly acceptable mode of devotion. Hence it can be asked "withouten any condition" (line 42) • **36 a man telle of halye kyrke** a man of holy church tell • **36 the storye of Sainte Cecille** the history of Saint Cecilia. A virgin martyr of the early church, whose probably apocryphal story is told in *The Golden Legend* and Chaucer's *Second Nun's Tale,* Cecilia, a highborn Roman, is a powerful preacher, evangelist, and lover of God • **37–38 thre woundes . . . nekke** three sword wounds in the neck. In *The Golden Legend,* Cecilia is killed with a sword, but her executioner fails to dispatch her with three blows, and she preaches for three days before dying • **38 pinede to the dede** suffered to death • **38 stirringe** inspiration • **40–41 contrition . . . compassion . . . wilfulle langinge to God** sorrow for sin, compassion for Christ's suffering, active longing toward God. Apparently an original interpretation of Cecilia's sword wounds. "Contrition" here corresponds to the second desire, line 20–21; "compassion" to the first, lines 4–9; "wilfulle langinge," perhaps, to the tenfold repetition of the word "desire" in this first section • **42 This** these • **43 passed fro my minde** passed out of my mind. Forgotten after they were made, the first two desires are never explicitly recalled in the course of the revelation, despite their shaping role

[SECTION 2] **1 alde** old • **1–2 bodelye syekenes** physical sickness. See 1.21 • **2–5 thre dayes. . . . two dayes . . . thirde night** The days and nights here are hard to count. Probably a "day" is to be taken as beginning on the previous evening (as would be the case in a liturgical calender), so that the "thre dayes and . . . nightes" are actually counted as three nights and days, and the "ferthe night" is thus also the first night of the "two dayes and two nightes." If so, the "thirde night" begins the sixth day of Julian's sickness, the day on which her revelation takes place, lasting from morning until the evening, with a break in the middle, though demonic temptations continue into the seventh morning (21.21–22, 23.18–19). The sickness thus takes up a calender week, here symbolically

divided into two periods of three days, paralleling the three days of Christ's Passion. The association between sickness and revelation was well established in the visionary tradition. After a long illness, the Monk of Eynsham's visions take place in a state of rapture that begins on the morning of Good Friday and lasts until the compline before Easter, during the whole of which time the crucifix in the abbey church bleeds (*The Revelation of the Monk of Eynsham,* chaps. 2–4) • **2 ferthe** fourth • **3 rightinges of haly kyrke** rites of holy church. See sidenote to 1.25 • **3–4 wened nought . . . daye** did not expect to live until day. Hence Julian's reception of the last rites • **4 langourede furthe** went on languishing • **5–6 thaye that were aboute me** those who were around me. The deathbed is a communal center, as Julian's friends wait with her for the end. At 7.14 and 8.48–52, she speaks to those around her as her "evencristene," the fellow Christians for whom her revelation is intended • **6 right sarye** very sorry • **6 lothe thought for to die** thought it was hateful to die. Julian's earlier desire "sone to be with my God" has "passed fro [her] minde" (1.29, 43). Her deep hatred of death here is one of the "gastelye paines" she asks for in 1.25–28 • **7 that me likede to lyeve fore** that I wanted to live for • **8 aferde fore** frightened of • **8 tristed** trusted. See 1.17–18 • **8 walde hafe lyevede** wanted to have lived • **9–10 be the grace of that lyevinge** by the grace further living would bring me. The logic here, which the Middle English poem *Pearl* goes to lengths to deny, is that long life gives more opportunities for good works, which lead to greater heavenly reward. *Vis.* 8.53–54 also assumes this cumulative idea of reward, again associated with Julian's early life. See also 17.15–21 • **11 methought** it seemed to me • **11 so litille and so shorte** The language here is reminiscent of Job 14:1, the first of the lessons in the Office of the Dead: "Man that is born of a woman is of few days, and full of trouble." See also Job 7:16: "Let me alone, for my days are a breath" • **11–12 in the regarde of** by comparison with • **14 asented fully** fully consented • **14–15 to be atte Godes wille** In her extremity, Julian's fundamental obligation is to honor the clause of the Lord's Prayer, "thy will be done" • **16–17 fra the middes downwarde** from the waist downward • **17 was I stirrede . . . upperightes** I was moved to be sat upright • **17–18 lenande with clothes to my hede** leaning back, my head supported by cloths • **18 for to have . . . herte** The shift in Julian's physical posture temporarily eases what seems to be a constriction in the chest • **19 thinkinge** Probably the infinitive "thinken," not the participle "thinking" • **20 the person my curette** the parson, my curate. In Middle English, a "person" is usually a parish priest, while "curette" refers to anyone in religious orders responsible for the "cure" of souls. Although Julian has already taken her "rightinges of haly kyrke" (line 3) earlier, when it was first supposed she was dying, her parson returns to fulfill his responsibility to ease her passing from the world • **21 be thane** by then • **21 sette mine eyen** fixed my eyes

This two desires of the passion and of the seekenes, I desirede thame with a   30
condition. For methought that it passede the comene course of prayers. And
therfore I saide: "Lorde, thowe woote whate I wolde. If it be thy wille that I have it,
graunte it me. And if it be nought thy wille, goode lorde, be nought displesede, for I
wille nought botte as thowe wille." This sekenes desirede I in my youth,° that I might
have it whene I were in threttye° yeere elde.   35

For the thirde, I harde a man telle of halye kyrke of the storye of Sainte Cecille,
in the whilke shewinge I understode that she hadde thre woundes with a swerde in
the nekke, with the whilke she pinede to the dede. By the stirringe of this, I
conseyvede a mighty desire, prayande oure lorde God that he wolde graunte me thre
woundes in my life time: that es to saye, the wounde° of contrition, the wounde of   40
compassion, and° the wounde of wilfulle langinge to God. Right as I askede the
othere two with a condition, so° I asked the thirde withouten any condition. This
two desires before saide passed fro my minde, and the thirde dwelled continuelye.

SECTION 2

Ande when I was thrittye wintere alde and a halfe, God sente me a bodelye
syekenes in the whilke I laye thre dayes and thre nightes, and on the ferthe
night I toke alle my rightinges of haly kyrke, and wened nought tille have liffede tille
daye. And after this I langourede furthe two dayes and two nightes, and on the
thirde night I wenede ofte times to hafe passede, and so wened thaye that were   5
aboute me. Botte in this I was right sarye and lothe thought for to die, botte for
nothinge that was /fol. 98r/ in erthe that me likede to lyeve fore, nor for nothinge
that I was aferde fore, for I tristed in God. Botte it was fore I walde hafe lyevede to
have lovede God better and langere° time, that I might,° be the grace of that
lyevinge, have the more knowinge and lovinge of God in the blisse of hevene. For   10
methought alle the time that I had lyevede° here so litille and so shorte in the
regarde of endeles blisse. I thought thus: "Goode lorde, maye my lyevinge be no
langere to thy worshippe?" And I was answerde° in my resone and be the felinges of
my paines that I shulde die, and I asented fully with alle the wille of mye herte to be
atte Godes wille.   15

Thus I endurede tille daye, and by than was my bodye dede fra the middes
downwarde, as to my felinge. Than was I stirrede to be sette° upperightes, lenande
with clothes to my hede, for to have the mare fredome of my herte to be atte Goddes
wille, and thinkinge on him whiles my life walde laste. And thay that were with me
sente for the person my curette to be atte mine endinge. He come, and a childe with   20
him, and brought a crosse, and be thane I hadde sette mine eyen and might nought

22 **The persone sette . . . face** The dying were supposed to gaze at the cross during their final agony. The priest "sets" a cross in front of Julian, initiating a public ritual that interrupts her private "setting" of her eyes. A crucifix was typically an effigy, perhaps painted, of Christ on the cross, arms outspread, head slightly to one side, body twisted, with one ankle laid over the other and a single nail transfixing both • 22–23 **I have brought the the image** I have brought you the image • 25 **mine eyen ware sette upwarde** Julian has adopted a typical devotional posture, with eyes upward and hands folded (see lines 33–35) • 27 **endure the langer . . . endinge** endure it longer toward the moment of my death • 28 **evenforthe** straight ahead • 29 **it was alle dyrke aboute me** it was completely dark around me. In fact, dawn has broken (line 16) • 30 **mirke** murky • 30–31 **there helde . . . light** there remained a natural light. All Julian's "bodely sights" (see 3.6) take place inside the narrow circle of clarity her tunnel vision leaves her • 31 **wiste nevere howe** never knew how. *A Vision* does not attribute this "comon light" to a miracle, although "wiste nevere howe" creates an atmosphere of suspense • 31 **Alle . . . beside the crosse** everything other than the cross • 32 **huglye** ugly • 32 **mekille occupiede with fendes** greatly infested with fiends. Demons are an important presence in much of the revelation. See 1.27, 10.51–53, 21.20–31, 23.1–22 • 33 **overe partye** upper part • 33–35 **Mine handes . . . on side** my hands fell down on either side, and also my head sagged down onto one side from weakness. Julian's posture here, as she lies across her bed with the cross before her eyes, closely resembles that of the crucified Christ • 35 **maste** most • 36 **wende I sothelye . . . dede** I truly imagined I was at the moment of death • 37 **sodeynlye** suddenly. A recurrent word in this part of *A Vision*, suggesting direct intervention by God. See 3.1, 10 • 37 **hole** whole • 37 **namelye** especially • 39 **a prive wyrkinge of God** a mysterious work of God • 39 **nought of kinde** not a work of nature • 39–40 **yitte be . . . ese** yet despite feeling this easing • 40 **I trystede . . . shulde lyeve** I did not gain any more hope that I was going to live • 41 **ne fulle ese to me** not entirely an easement for me • 41–42 **I hadde levere . . . worlde** I would rather have been delivered from this world. The consonance of "lever" and "deliverede" stresses Julian's desire at this point to slide quietly from the world • 42 **wilfulle thereto** willing for death

[SECTION 3] 1 **the seconde wounde** The wound of compassion (1.40–41), although the language here is more like that of the first desire, in 1.4–19. The wound is dealt Julian throughout Sections 3–12 • 2–3 **walde fulfille . . . felinge** would choose to fill my body with intense recollection and feeling • 4 **langinge to God** longing for God. The third wound asked for in 1.41 • 6–7 **in this . . . shewinge of God** in making this wish I never desired a bodily vision or any kind of divine revelation. Julian's first desire is not generating the revelation that is about to begin, even if the revelation is given partly in answer to that desire. *The Chastising of God's Children,* adapting the words of Bridget's confessor, Alphonse of Pecha, stresses that a true visionary must not have "a sodeyn wit for fantesye" (a mind that leaps to the fantastic) but rather a "sad [sober] knowing," as someone who "hath longe continued in gostly liveng" (174–75): much the impression this passage sets out to make • 7 **kinde saule** natural soul. Any living soul • 8 **wolde become man dedlye** wished to become a mortal human • 9 **lyevande in dedlye bodye** while still alive in my mortal body. Julian desires a brief extension of her life "in dedlye bodye" to suffer with Jesus as a "man dedlye" by thinking of his death as she dies • 10 **And in this . . . I sawe** "In this" is used more than fifty times in *A Vision* to suggest a movement inward from one state of perception to another, as sight follows sight. "I sawe" is used even more often, sixty-five times, to describe any kind of perception, from a bodily sight to a mental intuition or a realization • 10–11 **rede blode trekille . . . livelye** red blood trickle down from under the garland, all hot, freshly, plentifully, and vividly. The crown of thorns on the head of the image of the crucified Christ mentioned in 2.20–27, which animates and magnifies itself as the vision begins. This sight underlies all the "ghostly sights" in the first five sections of *A Vision* • 12 **thyrstede on his blessede hede** thrust on his blessed head. After his trial by Pontius Pilate. See Matt. 27:27–31. The language resembles that of *The Privity:* "They . . . toke a garlande of sharp thornes in stede of a corowne and threste [thrust it] one his hede. . . . Beholde his blissede face all rinnande [running] with rede blode!" ("Ad primam," *YW* 1:203–4) • 13–14 **I conseyvede . . . withouten any meen** I realized truly and powerfully that it was Christ himself who showed it, without any intermediary. In *The Chastising,* the "thridde tokene to knowe a vision" is true occurs when a visionary "feelith in his soule a sodeyne gostly thing springing with an inwarde feeling, and a knowing of soothfastnesse [truth]" (179)

speke. The persone sette the crosse before my face, and saide: "Doughter, I have
brought the the image of thy savioure. Loke thereopon, and comforthe the
therewith in reverence of him that diede for the and me." Methought than that I was
welle, for mine eyen ware sette upwarde into hevene, whether I trustede for to come.   25
Botte neverethelesse I assended to sette mine eyen in the face of the crucifixe, if I
might, for to endure the langer into the time of min endinge. For methought I
might langer endure to loke evenforthe than upperight.

After this my sight begane to faile, and it was alle dyrke aboute me in the
chaumber, and mirke as it hadde bene night, save in the image of the crosse there   30
helde a comon light, and I wiste nevere howe. Alle that was beside the crosse was
huglye to me, as if it hadde bene mekille occupiede with fendes.

After this the overe partye of my bodye begane to die, as to my felinge. Mine
handes felle downe on aythere side, and also for unpowere my hede satylde downe
/fol. 98v/ on side. The maste paine that I feled was shortnes of winde and failing of   35
life. Than wende I sothelye to hafe bene atte the pointe of dede. And in this,
sodeynlye alle my paine was away fro me and I was alle hole, and namelye in the
overe partye of my bodye, as evere I was before or after. I merveylede of this change,
for methought it was a prive° wyrkinge of God, and nought of kinde. And yitte be
the felinge of this ese I trystede nevere the mare that I shulde lyeve, ne the felinge of   40
this ese was ne fulle ese to me. For methought I hadde levere have bene deliverede of
this worlde, for my herte was wilfulle thereto.

SECTION 3

And sodeynlye come unto my minde that I shulde desire the seconde wounde
of oure lordes gifte and of his grace: that he walde fulfille my bodye with
minde and felinge° of his blessede passion, as I hadde before prayede. For I wolde
that his paines ware my paines, with compassion and afterwarde langinge to God.
Thus thought me that I might, with his grace, have his woundes that I hadde before   5
desirede. But in this I desirede nevere ne bodely sight ne no manere shewinge of
God, botte compassion, as methought that a kinde saule might have with oure lorde
Jhesu, that for love wolde become man dedlye. With him I desirede to suffere,
lyevande in dedlye bodye, as God wolde giffe me grace.

And in this, sodaynlye I sawe the rede blode trekille downe fro under the   10
garlande alle hate, freshlye, plentefully, and livelye, right as methought that it was in
that time that the garlonde of thornes was thyrstede on his blessede hede. Right so,
both God and man, the same sufferde for me. I conseyvede treulye and mightelye
that it was himselfe that shewed it me, withouten any meen. And than I saide:

15 **Benedicite dominus!** bless Lord! The Latin of this formula is not grammatical, but it is used elsewhere and is modeled on the greeting between two Benedictines, in which the junior asks for, and the senior offers, blessing. See page 4 of the Introduction. Repetition might cause "dominus" to be heard as a vocative, "domine," so that the phrase would be felt to mean "bless me, O Lord!" • 16 **astonned** astonished • 16–17 **wolde be so homlye** should desire to be so intimate. "Homely" also means "simple," "plain," "direct"—all words with social connotations: to treat people in a "homely" way is to treat them as equals • 18 **I tokede it for that time** at that time I supposed • 18 **of his curtayse love** "Curtayse" has overtones of "courtly," "polite," and "generous" and is balanced between "reverent dread" and "homeliness" • 20 **be the sufferrance . . . kepinge** by God's permission and with his protection • 21 **tempted of fendes or I diede** tempted by fiends before I died. Julian still has no awareness that she is at the beginning of a revelation • 22 **I sawe in min understandinge** Only the human Jesus, not the divine Christ (his "godhede"), suffers on the cross. Christ is thus intellectually, not physically, present in the bleeding of Jesus' head • 23 **alle creatures . . . safe** all living people who were to be saved. Anticipates Section 6 in its immediate incorporation of "alle creatures" into the revelation as potential witnesses and beneficiaries

[SECTION 4] 1–2 **bodily sight . . . gastelye sight** physical vision . . . spiritual vision. A common distinction. "Bodily sight" corresponds to what *The Chastising,* following Augustine's influential taxonomy of visions, calls "corporal vision . . . whanne any bodily thing by the gift of God is shewid to a mans bodily sight whiche other men seen nat." "Gastelye sight" is close to "intellectual vision, whanne no body ne image ne figure is seen, but . . . the insight of the soule . . . is clierly fastned in unbodily substaunce with a soothfast knowing [is lucidly joined in its spiritual substance with true knowledge]" (169–70). See 7.1–7. This account of "gastelye sightes" associated with Christ's blood lasts until the end of the section • 2 **hamly lovinge** intimate loving. The word "hamly," already used in 3.17, acts as the point of contact between this "gastelye sight" and the "bodily" sight of Christ's blood in the previous section • 3 **clethinge** clothing • 3–4 **wappes us and windes us** wraps us and winds about us • 4 **halses us . . . aboute us** embraces us and wholly encloses us, hangs about us. Although this is a "gastelye sight," these words evoke the sinuous figure of Christ's body on the cross represented in many late medieval texts, images, and crucifixes (see 2.22). *Speculum devotorum*

adapts the words of Bernard to describe "howe the lovely lordes hede hangede downwarde as it were to kisse, his armes spredde on brode as to be halsede" (226) • 7–13 **And in this . . . the love of God** See *The Scale* 2.33: "Sooth it is that oure lord is withinne alle creatures, not on that manere as a kirnel is hid withinne the shale of a note [shell of a nut], or as a litil bodily thinge is hid and holden withinne another mikil [kept within a bigger one]. But he is withinne alle creatures as holdinge [maintaining] and kepinge hem [them] in here [their] beinge." See also Wisd. of Sol. 11:22–25: "The whole world before thee is like a speck that tips the scales, and like a drop of morning dew . . . thou lovest all things that exist. . . . How would anything have endured if thou hadst not willed it?" • 7 **quantite** size • 7 **haselle nutte** hazelnut. An image of littleness, compactness, fragility, toughness, fertility, "hamly lovinge"; perhaps also, despite *The Scale,* an evocation of the idea that meaning is hidden inside appearances like a kernel inside a nut • 7 **lygande** lying • 8–9 **that it was as rounde . . . balle** As written, this clause depends on "shewed": "he shewed . . . that" • 10 **generaly** By intuition, not by a particular speaker • 11 **it might falle . . . litille** it was so little it could have collapsed suddenly into nothingness • 11–12 **answerde in mine understandinge** See 7.1–3 and 8.30–32 for this mode of revelation • 12–13 **so hath alle thinge . . . God** so has everything its existence through the love of God. The belief that the creation is kept in being at each moment by love is crucial to Julian's theology of creation • 16 **the makere, the lovere, the kepere** The "parties" of the "haselle nutte" mean nothing to Julian except insofar as they make her think of their source, the Trinity: "makere" (Father), "kepere" (Son), "lovere" (Spirit) • 16 **substantiallye aned to him** united in substance to God • 17 **varray** true • 18 **festenede** fastened. Language evocative of the Crucifixion, here of Christ's body "festenede" to the cross. Compare lines 3–5 • 18 **right nought** nothing at all • 19 **wha** who • 19–20 **he has made . . . restored** he has created and joyfully redeemed me for this purpose • 21–22 **gastelye . . . lyekenes** spiritually, but in physical form. Similar to Augustine's intermediate category of vision in *The Chastising,* "spiritual vision or imaginatif, whan a man . . . seeth images and figures of diverse thinges, but no bodies, by shewing or revelation of God" (169) • 22–23 **in the stature . . . conceivede** at the stage of growth she was in when she conceived. Mary is around fifteen in medieval accounts of the Annunciation, the scene described here • 24–25 **beholdinge . . . hire God** contemplation with which she looked upon her God • 25 **mervelande** marveling

"Benedicite dominus!" This I saide reverentlye in my meninge, with a mighty voice.   15
And fulle gretlye I was astonned, for wondere and merveyle that I had, that he wolde
be so homlye° with a sinfulle creature lyevande in this wreched fleshe.°

/fol. 99r/ Thus I tokede it for that time that oure lorde Jhesu, of his curtayse love,
walde shewe me comforthe before the time of my temptation. For methought it
might be welle that I shulde, be the sufferance of God and with his kepinge, be   20
tempted of fendes or I diede. With this sight of his blissede passion, with the
godhede that I sawe° in min understandinge, I sawe that this was strengh enoughe
to me—ye, unto alle creatures lyevande that shulde be safe—againes alle the feendes
of helle and againes alle gostelye enmies.

SECTION 4

And this same time that I sawe this bodily sight, oure lorde shewed me a
gastelye sight of his hamly° lovinge. I sawe that he es to us alle thinge that is
goode and comfortabille to oure helpe. He es oure clethinge, that° for love wappes
us and windes us, halses us and alle becloses us,° hinges aboute us for tender love,
that he maye nevere leve us. And so in this sight I sawe sothelye that he is alle thinge   5
that is goode, as to mine understandinge.

And in this, he shewed me a litille thinge the quantite of a haselle nutte, lygande
in the palme of my hande, and, to my understandinge, that it was as rounde as any
balle. I lokede theropon, and thought: "Whate maye this be?" And I was answerde
generaly thus: "It is alle that is made." I merveylede howe that it might laste, for   10
methought it might falle sodaynlye to nought for litille. And I was answerde in mine
understandinge: "It lastes and ever shalle, for God loves it. And so hath alle thinge
the beinge thorowe the love of God."

In this litille thinge I sawe thre parties: the firste is that God made it,° the
seconde is that he loves it, the thirde is that God kepes it. Botte whate is that to me?   15
Sothelye, the makere, the lovere, the kepere. For to I am substantiallye aned to him I
may nevere have full reste° ne varray blisse: that is to saye, that /fol. 99v/ I be so
festenede to him that thare be right nought that is made betwyxe my God and me.
And wha shalle do this dede? Sothlye himselfe, be his mercye and his grace, for he
has made me thereto and blisfullye restored.   20

In this, God brought oure ladye to mine understandinge. I sawe hir gastelye in
bodilye lyekenes, a simpille maidene and a meeke, yonge of age, in the stature that
sho was when sho conceivede. Also God shewed me in parte the wisdom and the
trowthe of hir saule, wharein I understode the° reverente beholdinge that she
behelde hire° God, that is hir makere, mervelande with grete reverence that he wolde   25

27 **hir that was made** her who was created. "Made" (created) puns on "handemaidene" (line 30) and "maiden" (virgin). The phrase parallels "alle that is made" in line 10 • 28 **knawande** knowing • 29–30 **"Lo me here, Goddes handemaidene"** See Luke 1:38 • 30 **sothfastlye** truly • 30–31 **sho is mare . . . fulhede** Mary's humility paradoxically demonstrates her "fulhede" • 33 **that es benethe . . . Marye** Of less "worthines and fulhede" than she. The passage may allude to depictions of Mary as the "woman clothed with the sun, with the moon under her feet," in Rev. 12:1, in which she is represented standing on a globe • 34–35 **Methought . . . for litille** A near repetition of the passage at line 11 • 36 **thre noughtes** three zeros. This first "nought" is the nothingness of the creation without God the creator. The second is sin (described as a "nought" in 8.16 and 23.23–31), as well as the "noughting" of the devil Christ and Julian jointly celebrate in 8.42–44. The third is Christ's "noughtinge," the humiliation or effacement of his death, described in 13.45–51 • 37–44 **Of this nedes . . . reste us in him** The language of this passage is close to that in Rolle's *Form of Living*: "The fifte asking [your fifth question] was in what state men may maste [most] lufe God. I answer: in wilk state sa it be that men er in maste rest of body and saule [in whatever state it may be in which people are in most physical and spiritual rest], and leest occupied with any nedes or bisines of this worlde. For the thoght of the lufe of Jhesu Criste, and of the joy that lastes ay, sekes rest withouten, that it be noght letted with comers and gangers [comers and goers] and occupation of worldely things . . . And namely al that lufes contemplatife lif, thay seke rest in body and in saule." (chap. 10, *YW* 1:44–45) • 37–39 **Of this nedes . . . that es unmade** every man and woman who wants to live in a contemplative way needs to know this about the first nought, so that it pleases him to reject everything that is created, in order to have the love of God, who is uncreated. The very thing that God keeps from falling to "nought" needs to be "noughted." To "lyeve contemplatifelye" is to turn from the world and set one's mind on God • 38 **him like** Impersonal constructions like this are a regular feature of the work's style • 40–41 **thaye that . . . warldlye wele** those who are deliberately caught up in earthly endeavors and forever seek worldly well-being. These are "active" Christians, who do not wish to "lyeve contemplatifelye." The language here is suggestive of the "besines" of mercantile Norwich, whose trade connections

extended through Europe and from one of whose families Julian may have come. See page 4 of the Introduction • 41 **er nought all in ese . . . saule** are not completely comfortable in heart and in soul. A notably mild comment: worldly Christians, especially those who seek "warldlye wele," might well be understood to have no "ese" at all by contemplative writers such as Rolle • 41 **seekes here reste** look here for rest. "Here" could also mean "their," but see *Rev.* 5.22 • 42 **whare no reste is in** in which there is no rest • 43–46 **God wille be knawen . . . made** This passage echoes the famous opening of Augustine's *Confessions:* "Thou hast made us for thyself and restless is our heart until it comes to rest in thee." In *The Scale* 1.43, Hilton, echoing Augustine, describes how the fallen soul "seketh his reste in creatures, now fro oon to another [shifting from one to another], and never may finde ful reste, for he hath lost him in whom is ful reste" • 44–45 **suffices nought to us** is not enough for us • 45–46 **to it be noghthed . . . made** until it is freed from all things that are created • 46 **When he is noughthid** Now it is the soul, not the created order, that must be "noughthid"

[SECTION 5] 2 **plentyouse bledinge of the hede** plentiful bleeding from the head. See 3.10–17 • 3 **Benedicite dominus!** See 3.15 • 4 **In this . . . sex thinges** Summarizes what are taken as the central moments of revelation to this point, beginning with the "bodilye sight," then moving to the "gastelye sightes" by way of the vision of Mary, seen "gastelye in bodilye lyekenes" (4.21–22). "This firste shewinge" seems to suggest a numbering system for the revelations in *A Vision,* but there are no hints of this elsewhere in the work • 5 **The furste** See 3.10–17 • 5 **takens** symbols. In medieval iconography, the crown of thorns, the cross, and the pillar to which Christ was bound were all regarded as "tokens" of his Passion, detachable from the narrative of the Passion as objects of meditation in their own right, just as they are seen in *A Vision* • 7 **The seconde** See 4.21–32 • 7 **dereworthy** precious • 8 **The thirde** See 4.14–20, understood as an actual revelation of the "blisfulle godhede" • 10–12 **The ferthe . . . makere** See 4.7–11, 33–35 • 10–11 **wele I woote . . . goode** I know well that heaven and earth and all that is created is vast and beautiful and broad and good. A reaction against 4.36–47 and its account of creation as "noughte" • 12 **for I sawe itte** that I saw it be borne of hir that was a simpille creature of his makinge. For this was hir mervelinge: that he that was hir makere walde be borne of hir that was made.° And this wisdome and trowthe, knawande° the gretnes of hir makere and the litellehede of hirselfe that is made, made hir for to° saye mekelye to the angelle Gabrielle: "Lo me here, Goddes handemaidene." In this sight I sawe sothfastlye that sho is mare than alle that God made benethe hir in worthines and in fulhede. For abovene hir is nothinge that is made botte the blissede manhede of Criste.

30

This litille thinge that es made that es benethe oure ladye Saint Marye, God shewed it unto me als litille as it hadde beene a haselle notte. Methought it might hafe fallene for litille.

35

In this blissede revelation God shewed me thre noughtes, of whilke noughtes this is the firste that was shewed me. Of this nedes ilke man and woman to hafe knawinge that desires to lyeve contemplatifelye, that him like to nought alle thinge that es made for to hafe the love of God that es unmade. For this es the cause why thaye that er occupiede wilfullye in erthelye besines, and evermare sekes warldlye wele, er nought all in ese° in herte and in saule: for thaye love and seekes here reste in this thinge that is so litille, whare no reste is in, and knawes nought God, that es alle mighty, alle wise, and alle goode. For he is verraye reste. God wille be knawen, and him likes that /fol. 100r/ we reste us in him. For alle that ar benethe him suffices nought to us. And this is the cause why that na saule is restede to it be noghthed of alle that es made. When he is noughthid for love to hafe him that is alle that is goode, than es he abylle to resayve gostlye reste.

40

45

SECTION 5

And in that time that oure lorde shewed this that I have nowe saide in gastelye° sight, I saw° the bodilye sight lastande of the plentyouse bledinge of the hede. And als longe as I sawe that sight I saide often times: "Benedicite dominus!"

In this firste shewinge of oure lorde I sawe sex thinges in mine understandinge.

The furste is the° takens of his blisfulle passion and the plenteous shedinge of his precious blode.

5

The seconde is the maidene, that she is his dereworthy modere.

The thirde is the blisfulle godhede that ever was and es and ever shalle be: alle mighty, alle wisdome, and alle love.

The ferthe is alle thinge that he has made. For wele I woote that heven and erth and alle that is made° is mekille and faire and large and goode. Botte the cause why it shewed° so litille to my sight was for I sawe itte in the presence of him that es makere. For to a saule that sees the makere of alle thinge, alle that es made semes° fulle litille.

10

14 **The fifte** See 4.11–13 • 16 **The sexte** See 4.1–6 • 19 **behalde** contemplate • 19 **stinted** ceased • 19 **dwelled** remained • 20 **abade** waited • 20 **with reverente drede** Compare Mary's "reverente beholdinge" at the Annunciation, 4.24–26. See Section 25 for more on this "drede" • 20 **joyande in that I sawe** rejoicing in what I saw • 21 **durste** dared • 21 **for to see mare** to see more. Julian's earlier sense that her experience is a prelude to her death, in 3.18–21, is here represented as beginning to shift • 21 **langer time** for a longer time

[SECTION 6] 1 **I meene . . . evencristene** I mean to be interpreted as referring to all my fellow Christians. Exegetes often referred to passages of the Bible as voiced "in the person" of a certain group. References to Julian in *A Vision* are to be interpreted according to the same principle • 2 **lernede in . . . he meenes so** taught by our Lord's spiritual revelation that he means so • 3 **counsayles yowe** advise you. "Counsayle" is what equals or friends offer each other: see lines 35–36 • 4–5 **leve the beholdinge . . . unto** stop dwelling on the wretched, sinful creature to whom it was shown. A fierce plea for the anonymity of Julian's voice • 6–7 **walde shewe . . . vision** wished to reveal this vision publicly • 8 **edification** moral improvement. This somewhat formal word for self-improvement (which joins the equally official "profit" and "counsayles"), with its implied reference to building (it derives from *edificare*, to build), is appropriate to a section concerned with *A Vision*'s relation to the Christian community • 11 **For the shewinge . . . better** I am not good merely because of the revelation unless I love God the better for it. This antielitism marks a return to the careful modesty of 3.6–9. *The Chastising*, adapting Alphonse, states that a true visionary can be known by "whether he hath any presumption of his visions, or maketh any bost of hem with veinglorye, or holdith himsilf the more of reputatioun, or hath any other men in dispite or indignation" (174). Elsewhere it notes "that visions . . . proven nat a man or woman holy or parfite" (182) • 11–12 **so may and so shulde ilke man do** so can and so should everyone do. That is, love God the better • 12 **sees it . . . trewe meninge** sees and hears

the revelation with goodwill and sincere intention. An instruction on how to read *A Vision* in the manner described in lines 9–10, "as Jhesu hadde shewed it yowe," the sentence is also an implied warning to those who do not have "good wille and trewe meninge." *The Cloud of Unknowing* similarly forbids the book to be shown to any readers who do not wish to follow its contemplative path "in a trewe wille and by an hole entent" (2) • 15 **as we ar alle ane** because we are all one • 15 **sekere** certain • 19 **if I loke . . . myselfe** if I regard myself only as a single individual. "Singularity" is usually a negative term in Middle English, suggesting an inappropriate and prideful self-separation from others, a vice any visionary would be warned against. *The Form* lists "singulere wit" and "vaine glory" as two of the special temptations the devil sends "when he sees a man or a woman . . . turne haly [wholly] to God" (chap. 1, *YW* 1:5) • 20 **in generalle** in relation to everyone else • 20 **anehede of charite** the unity of charity • 20–21 **For in this anehede . . . safe** The sentence is a little personification allegory, in which a character called Life takes a stand inside Unity of Charity. Compare the way all Christendom awaits the apocalypse inside the barn Unity at the end of Langland's *Piers Plowman* (B 20) • 21–28 **For God . . . loves alle** A proof of the previous sentence and a defense of the "general." Salvation depends on "anehede of charite" with the saved, who constitute the unity of all. The "anehede" of those in charity is the exact opposite of the claim to be "singuler" that visionaries might be tempted, inappropriately, to make • 21–22 **God is alle that is goode** All but identical to 5.16: "God is alle thing that is goode" • 23 **departe his love fra** should separate his love from • 23–24 **he loves right nought** he loves nothing at all. *Pore Caitif*, building on 1 John 4:7–8, notes that "he that kepith not this love to his neighbore holdith non heest [does not keep any commandment] of God. For he that kepith not charite brekith alle Goddis heestes . . . and he that hatith ony man hatith Crist" (87) • 26 **mankinde that shalle be safe** humankind who will be saved • 26 **comprehende** included

The fifte es that he has made alle thinge that is made for love. And thorowe the
same love it is kepede and ever shalle be withouten ende, as it is before saide. 15

The sexte es that God is alle thinge that is goode. And the goodenes that° alle
thinge has is he.

And alle this° oure lorde shewed me in the first sight, and gafe me space and
time to behalde it. And the bodily sight stinted, and the gastely sight dwelled in
mine understandinge. And I abade with reverente drede, joyande in that I sawe, and 20
desirande as I durste for to see mare, if it ware his wille, or the same langer time.

SECTION 6

Alle that I saye° of myselfe, I meene in the persone of alle° mine evencristene,
for I am lernede in the gastelye shewinge of oure lorde that he meenes so. And
therfore I praye yowe alle for Goddes sake, and counsayles yowe for youre awne
profit, that ye leve the behaldinge of the wrechid, /fol. 100v/ sinfulle creature° that it°
was shewed unto, and that ye mightlye, wiselye, lovandlye, and mekelye behalde 5
God, that of his curtays love and of his endles goodnes walde shewe generalye this
vision in comforthe of us alle. And ye that heres and sees this vision and this
techinge that is of Jhesu Criste to edification of youre saule, it is Goddes wille and
my desire° that ye take it with als grete joye and likinge as Jhesu hadde shewed it
yowe as he did to me. 10

For the shewinge I am not goode but if I love God the better, and so may and so
shulde ilke man do that sees it and heres it with goode wille and trewe meninge.
And so is my desire that it shulde be to everilke manne the same profitte that I
desirede to myselfe, and therto was stirred of God in the firste time when I sawe itte,
for it is comon° and generale, as we ar alle ane. And I am sekere I sawe it for the 15
profitte of many oder. For sothly it was nought shewed unto me for that God loves
me bettere thane the leste saule that is in grace. For I am sekere thare is fulle many
that nevere hadde shewinge ne sight botte of the comon techinge of haly kyrke that
loves God better than I. For if I loke singulerlye to myselfe, I am right nought. Botte
in generalle, I am in anehede of charite with alle mine evencristende. For in this 20
anehede of charite standes the life of alle mankinde that shalle be safe. For God is
alle that is goode, and God has made alle that is made, and God loves alle that he has
made. And if anye man or woman departe his love fra any of his evencristen he loves
right nought, for he loves nought alle. And so that time he is nought safe, for he es
nought in pees. And he that generaly loves his evencristen, he loves alle that es. For 25
in mankinde that shalle be safe is comprehende alle that is: alle that is made and the

27 **For in manne . . . alle** A reference to a key theme in Julian's writings, the "mutual indwelling" in which God and humankind are each seen as "enclosed" in the other. The theme recurs in Section 22, where Christ is seen dwelling in the human soul • 29–30 **I mene . . . even-cristene** I speak here as a representative of my fellow Christians • 30–32 **the more I love . . . that is God** the more I love in this manner of loving while I am in this life, the closer I come to the bliss I shall have in heaven without end: that is God. Heaven in Middle English texts such as *The Pricke of Conscience* is both a place of redeemed community and one of communion between the individual soul and God • 33 **behaldes it thus** thinks about it in this way. Alludes back to the plea to "leve the behaldinge" of Julian as she narrates her revelation • 33 **trewly taught** The revelation will not yield even its doctrinal truth to someone who insists on adulating Julian rather than reading in the way just described • 34 **if him nede comforthe** if he should need comfort. Presumably comfort for having no "shewinge ne sight botte of the comon techinge of haly kyrke" (line 18) • 35 **take it so** understand it • 35 **techere** Someone formally expounding doctrine as a *magister*, rather than merely passing on what she has seen and heard. Every Christian had the duty to teach others by way of "counsayle" (line 3) and to testify to the truth, but matters of doctrine were to be left to professionals • 36–37 **lewed, febille, and freylle** uneducated, feeble, and frail. Julian strategically adopts a standard medieval view of "woman" as lacking the strength and understanding to initiate new ideas but for the same reason especially receptive vehicles of revelation. To deny that Julian is a "techere" is also to assert that what is contained in *A Vision* is the teachings of Christ, the "soverayne techare." Such a formulation leaves room for the work to contain doctrinal insights as well as testimony • 37 **wate** know • 37 **I hafe it of the shewinge** I have derived it from the revelation • 38 **sothelye** truly • 38 **charite stirres me . . . it** A common medieval justification for writing a religious work, here linking the reader with the "even-cristene" around Julian's bed in 7.8–10 • 38–40 **I wolde . . . of God** I wish God were known and my fellow Christians helped, as I would like to be myself, toward greater hatred of sin and love for God • 40 **leve** believe • 41 **sine** since • 42–43 **in the same matere . . . after** in the continuation of the account. The "matere" of Julian's

book (from Latin *materia*, subject matter) is her revelation, which is said here to include within itself the instruction "that it be knawen." No such explicit direction to Julian to publicize or record her experience appears in the revelation as described in *A Vision,* but see 7.8–11 • 43 **welle and trewlye taken** properly and faithfully understood • 44 **dose so** do so • 44–45 **lette yowe nought** do not interfere with you • 45–46 **I speke of thame . . . nothere** *A Vision* is not a general statement about humankind's relationship with God but instead concerns only members of that unknowable body, the saved: the double negative "no nothere," nobody else, reinforcing this point. Here, as elsewhere in *A Vision,* the phrase "thame that shalle be safe" cuts across the universalizing logic of the surrounding passage, with its insistence on the "generalle" meaning of the revelation and heavy use of the word "alle" • 46–49 **Bot in alle thinge . . . halye kyrke** According to *The Chastising,* a vision can be judged by whether it is "enclined to ony errour of holy chirche, of the feith, or ony wondir or newe thing" (176) • 46 **lyeve** believe • 47 **I behelde it as ane** I perceived the revelation and the teaching of holy church as the same • 48–49 **stones me . . . techinge** amazes ("stuns") me or keeps me from the true teaching

[SECTION 7] 1 **in thre parties** in three modes. See 4.1–2 for the first and third of these • 2 **worde . . . understandinge** See 4.11–13 and especially 8.29–32 • 3–4 **Botte the gastelye sight . . . wolde** but I do not know how, nor have I the power, to declare the spiritual visions as explicitly or as completely as I would wish. The auxiliaries "can," "may," and "would" each relate to one of the faculties of the mind: memory, reason, and will. These parallel the "powers" associated with the persons of the Trinity. See 4.16 • 5 **shalle** Here retains some of its earlier sense of "must." See 13.61 • 6 **so motte it be** so must it be. The gap between *A Vision* and the truths it tells must be bridged • 8 **mekille stirrede . . . evencristene** very much moved in charity toward my fellow Christians. The need to disseminate the revelation among "evencristene" is implied by its deathbed setting, with Julian's friends gathered around • 10–11 **in generalle and nathinge in specialle** in general and in no way merely for individual understanding. The revelation is more than merely the personal act of divine comfort Julian at first supposed it to be • 11 **maste** most

makere of alle. For in manne is God, and so in man is alle. And he that thus
generalye loves alle his evencristene, he loves alle. And he that loves thus, he is safe.

And thus wille I love, and thus I love, and thus I am safe. For I mene in the
person of mine evencristene. And the more I love of this lovinge whiles I am here, 30
the mare I am like to the blisse that I /fol. 101r/ shalle° have in hevene withouten
ende: that is God, that of his endeles love wolde become oure brothere and suffer for
us. And I am sekere that he that behaldes it thus he shalle be trewly taught and
mightelye comforthtede, if° him nede comforthe.

Botte God forbede that ye shulde saye or take it so that I am a techere. For I 35
meene nought so, no I mente nevere so. For I am a woman, lewed, febille, and
freylle. Botte I wate wele, this that I saye I hafe it of the shewinge of him that es°
soverayne techare. Botte sothelye charite stirres me to telle yowe it. For I wolde God
ware knawen and min evencristene spede, as I wolde be myselfe, to the mare hatinge
of sinne and lovinge of God. Botte for I am a woman shulde I therfore leve that I 40
shulde nought telle yowe the goodenes of God, sine that I sawe in that same time
that it is his wille° that it be knawen? And that shalle ye welle see in the same matere
that folowes after, if° itte be welle and trewlye taken.

Thane shalle ye sone forgette me that am a wreche, and dose so that I lette yowe
nought, and behalde Jhesu that is techare of alle. I speke of thame that shalle be safe, 45
for in this time God shewed me no nothere. Bot in alle thinge I lyeve as haly kyrke
techis. For in alle this° blissede shewinge of oure lorde I behelde it as ane in God
sight. And I understode never nathinge therein that stones me ne lettes me of the
trewe techinge of halye kyrke.

SECTION 7

Alle this blissede techinge of oure lorde God was shewed to me in thre parties:
that is, be bodilye sight, and be worde formede in mine understandinge, and
be gastelye sight. Botte the gastelye sight I maye nought ne can nought shewe it unto
yowe als oponlye and als fullye as I wolde. Botte I truste in oure lorde God
allemighty that he shalle, of his goodnes and for youre love, make yowe to take it 5
mare gastelye and mare swetly than I can or maye telle it yowe. And so motte it be,
for we are alle one in love.

And in alle this I was mekille stirrede in charite to mine evencristene, that thaye
might alle see and knawe the same that I sawe, for I walde that it ware comforthe to
thame /fol. 101v/ alle, as it es to me. For this sight was shewed in generalle and 10
nathinge in specialle. Of alle that I° sawe, this was the maste comforthe to me: that

12 hamlye intimate • **12–13 likinge and syekernes** delight and confidence • **14 the folke ... with me** Julian's companions are here treated as representatives of her "evencristene" • **14 It es todaye domesdaye with me** today is judgment day for me. This remark, though it follows the expectations of the deathbed scene in progress, seems at odds with the revelation just described, which makes no allusion to judgment • **15 wenede** expected • **15–16 that daye ... withouten ende** on the day that a man or a woman dies he is judged as he shall be without end. Recalls the teaching, commonly but not universally held in Julian's day, that the individual is judged by God at death, rather than at Judgment Day, and that this judgment remains fixed for eternity • **17 prise** price • **17–18 hafe minde** recollect • **18 in ensampille be me** in the example offered by me. Unable to convey her revelation, Julian offers to her fellows her death as an example of life's brevity

[SECTION 8] **1 I sawe ... the crucifixe** As with the revelation of Christ's blood, this "bodely sight" effects a single transformation of the cross that has been placed before Julian's eyes. Scenes of humiliation from Christ's trial appear on the image of Christ's head, which is "the face of the crucifixe." The first of a set of short revelatory moments linked by "after this" • **2–3 despise ... buffetinge** contempt, spitting, soiling, and buffeting. The torments Jesus is said to have suffered after trial by the Sanhedrin: "They lede him into theire chapeterehous and examende him straitly [closely] ... they ... despisede him and spitte in his faire face, they hillide his eyen and bobbed him [shrouded his eyes and hit him]" (*The Privity*, prologue, *YW* 1:201, based largely on Matt. 26:67). In *The Privity* and the Gospels, these torments take place before the crowning of thorns evoked in 3.10–12 • **4 langoures** long agonies • **4 ma** more • **4 ofte changinge of coloure** frequent changes of color. The torments are seen as changes of color on Jesus' face • **5 a time** at one time • **5 closede** covered • **5 dry blode** Not the fresh blood seen earlier • **5–6 bodilye and hevelye and derkelye** physically and sorrowfully and obscurely. The revelation shows the bloody effects of blows but nobody delivering them, as though the blindfold over Christ's eyes during this scene in Luke 22:64, where Christ is taunted with "Who is it that struck you?" obscured Julian's vision also. In late medieval church roof bosses, the scene is also disturbingly fragmentary, the tormenters sometimes depicted merely as a spitting mouth or a slapping hand with no bodies attached • **7 if God walde ... he shulde** if God wanted to show me more he would do so • **7–8 botte ... him**

but I needed no light except him • **9 God in a pointe** Has an evocative, if inarticulate, relationship with the vision of the hazelnut in Section 4. A "point" is also a subdivision in an argument and a punctuation mark, meanings reflected in the scholastic cast of phrases like "me behovede nedes graunte" (line 14) • **9–10 by whilke sight I sawe** The use of "sawe" here makes the perception "that he es in alle thinge" as much part of the revelation as the sight of "God in a pointe" that precipitates it • **10 with visemente** with close attention • **10–11 wittande and knawande** understanding and knowing. The two words are to be read as synonyms, a common Middle English stylistic device • **11–12 with a softe drede** with a gentle awe • **12 "Whate es sinne?"** This question haunts the whole of *A Vision*. See especially 23.23–31 • **13–14 Nor nathinge ... God** nor is anything done by chance or accident, but by the endless foresight of the wisdom of God • **14 me behovede nedes graunte** I am obliged to concede. The language of logic or dialectic, used to announce a conclusion that, given the fact of sin, might seem unexpected • **16 seker** sure • **16–17 sinne is nought ... shewed me** sin is nothing, for in all this, sin was not shown me. The argument depends on the use of "nought" both as a noun ("nothing") and as a simple negative ("not") • **19 nakedlye be the selfe** nakedly, as it is in itself. See 13.45–51 • **20 plenteouslye** plentifully • **20 hate** hot • **21 as I sawe before** See 3.10–12 • **22 in the semes of scourginge** in a representation of the scourging. Unless "seming" is from "seam" (groove or wound), in which case the phrase means "through the wounds caused by the scourging." Christ is tied to a pillar and scourged with "sharp knotty scourges," sometimes said to be tipped with lead (*The Privity*, "Ad primam," *YW* 1:203), before his crowning with thorns. See Matt. 27:26 • **23 if it hadde ... time** if it had actually been that plentiful at that time • **23–24 it shulde hafe made ... blode** it would have covered the bed completely in blood • **24 passede on aboute** overflowed around it • **24–28 God has made waterse ... oure kinde** Despite the cruelty and sorrow of Christ's scourging, this brief meditation on the divine plenitude is detached from the narrative moment that gave birth to it. Rolle's *Meditations on the Passion* also compares Christ's tormented body to a set of beautiful things: a net, a dovecot, a book, a meadow "ful of swete flouris and holsum herbis" (*YW* 1:96–97) • **24–25 waterse plenteouse in erthe** See Ps. 65:9–10 (Vulgate 64:10–11): "Thou visitest the earth and waterest it, thou greatly enrichest it; the river of God is full of water. ... Thou waterest its furrows abundantly"

oure lorde es so hamlye and so curtayse. And this maste filled° me with likinge and syekernes in saule.

Than saide I to the folke that were with me: "It es todaye domesdaye with me." And this I saide for I wenede to hafe died. For that daye that man or woman dies is   15
he demed as he shalle be withouten ende. This I saide for I walde thaye loved God mare and sette the lesse prise be the vanite of the worlde, for to make thame to hafe minde that this life es shorte, as thaye might se in ensampille be me. For in alle this time I wenede to hafe died.

SECTION 8

And after this, I sawe with bodely sight the face of the crucifixe that hange before me, in whilke I behelde continuely a party of his passion: despite, spittinge, sowlinge° of his bodye, and buffetinge in his blisfulle face, and manye langoures and paines, ma than I can telle, and ofte changinge of coloure, and alle his blissede face a time closede in dry blode. This I sawe bodilye and hevelye and   5
derkelye, and I desired mare bodelye light to hafe sene more clerelye. And I was answerde in my resone that if God walde shewe me mare he shulde, botte me neded na light botte him.

And after this, I sawe God in a pointe—that es, in mine understandinge—by whilke sight I sawe that he es in alle thinge. I behelde with visemente, wittande and   10
knawande in that sight that he dose alle that es done. I merveylede in this sight with a softe drede, and thought: "Whate es sinne?" For I sawe trulye that God dothe alle thinge, be it nevere so litille. Nor nathinge es done be happe ne be eventure, botte be the endeles° forluke of the wisdome of God. Wharefore me behovede nedes graunte that alle thinge that es done es wele done, for our lord God doth all.° And I was   15
seker that God dose na sinne. Therfore it semed to me that sinne is nought, for in alle this, sinne° was nought shewed me. And I walde no lenger mervelle of this, botte behalde oure lorde, whate he wolde shewe me. And in another time God shewed me whate sine es nakedlye be the selfe, as I shalle telle afterwarde.°

And after this I sawe, behaldande, the bodye plenteouslye bledande, hate and   20
freshlye and lifelye, right as I sawe before in the hede. And this was shewed°
/fol. 102r/ me in the semes of scourginge. And this ranne so plenteouslye to my sight that methought, if it hadde bene so in kinde for that time, it shulde hafe made the bedde alle on blode, and hafe passede on aboute. God has made waterse plenteouse in erthe to oure service, and to oure bodilye ese, for tender love that he has to us.   25
Botte it likes him better that we take fullye his blessede blode to washe us with of

27 **likoure** liquid. Perhaps in the sense "medicine," with an allusion to Communion wine • 27 **him likes . . . giffe us** pleases him as much to give us • 28 **of oure kinde** shares our human nature • 29 **or** before • 29 **sufferde** allowed • 30 **langere** longer • 30–31 **than was . . . lippes** The mode of revelation called "worde formede in mine understandinge" (7.2). These words are evidently not heard physically but in some sense also differ from the general words Julian hears in her understanding, e.g., at 4.9–10. *The Chastising* quotes Gregory as saying: "Whanne [God] spekith to us by himsilf, thanne is the hert enformed and taught of his worde, withoute any worde or sillable . . . also the speche of God inward to us is rather made or do [made or performed] thanne herd" (172). Christ's words in *A Vision* are similar, but do assume precise verbal form. See 22.20–21 • 32 **Herewith is the feende overcomen** by this (blood) is the devil overcome. See 22.25–29 for the structural significance of these words • 32 **menande** referring to • 34 **perte** part • 34 **fully his unmight** the whole of his impotence • 34 **for that** in addition to that • 35 **the passion of him** the Passion of our Lord • 36–37 **als sare he travailes** he works just as hard • 37–38 **als continuelye . . . worshipfullye** he sees just as unfailingly that all chosen souls honorably escape him • 39 **turnes us to joye** turns to joy for us • 39 **als mekille** as much • 40 **giffes him leve to wyrke** allows him to act • 40 **that es for** that is because • 41 **his might . . . hande** his power is completely locked in God's hand. According to *The Gospel of Nicodemus*, Christ chained Satan during the harrowing of hell. See also Rev. 20:1–3: "Then I saw an angel coming down from heaven, holding in his hand the key of the bottomless pit and a great chain. And he seized the dragon, that ancient serpent, who is the Devil and Satan, and bound him for a thousand years, and threw him into the pit" • 42 **scorne his malice . . . him** scorn the devil's malice and deride him • 43 **laugh** laughed • 43–44 **that were aboute me** who were standing around me • 44 **was likinge to me** gave me pleasure • 44 **wolde** wished • 46 **Botte I sawe nought Criste laugh** Medieval lives of Christ note that the Gospels never describe the "man of sorrows" as laughing • 46–47 **in comfortinge of us** to comfort ourselves • 48 **saddehete**

state of seriousness • 48 **saide** Julian again tries to communicate her revelation to her "evencristene," this time offering an interpretation of the words she has just heard. See 7.14 • 48–49 **game, scorne, and arneste** play, scorn, and seriousness • 51 **be his dede** by his death • 52 **ful erneste** very seriously • 52 **sadde travaile** hard labor • 54 **namly in thy youth** especially in your youth. A commendation either of Julian's life of devotion before the revelation or, perhaps, of the three youthful requests to God described in Section 1

[SECTION 9] 1 **thre degrees of blisse** Middle English writings such as *The Pricke* often follow Anselm's categorization of the joys of heaven into seven spiritual and seven physical "dowries," which overlap with, and likely underlie, the list of "blisses" here • 1 **ilke** each • 2 **wilfullye** consciously • 2 **in any degree** in any state of life. Probably alludes to the "three spiritual estates" of virgins, widows, and spouses, who are often taken to receive amounts of "blisse" that correspond to the yield of the fruitful seed in the parable of the sower (Matt. 13:3–8). Working out from this parable, *Holy Maidenhood* states that "marriage brings forth her fruit thirtyfold in heaven, widowhood sixtyfold," while "virginity, with a hundredfold, outdoes both" • 3 **wyrshipfulle thankinge** See Matt. 25:21: "Well done, good and faithful servant . . . enter into the joy of your master." According to *The Pricke*, "Thare [in heaven] es mare worshepe and honoure / Than ever had king here or emparoure" (7827–28) • 3 **he shalle resayfe** the soul shall receive • 4 **when he es . . . paine** At death or after passing through purgatory • 5 **him thinke it filles him** it seems to the soul it (this first degree of bliss) fills him up. *The Pricke* likens heavenly joy to a bowl so full of water it "na mare [no more] water within may hald" (8049) • 5 **though** even if • 5–7 **For methought . . . servede God** for it seemed to me that all the pain and labor that could be suffered by everyone who has ever lived could not have merited the thanks that even one person shall receive who has willingly served God. Heaven is often described through tropes of inexpressibility. Compare the attempt to describe the extent of Christ's pain in 11.6–10

sinne, for thare is no likoure that es made that him likes so welle to giffe us. For it is so plenteouse and of oure kinde.

And after this, or° God shewed me any wordes,° he sufferde me to behalde langere, and alle that I hadde seene, and alle that was therein. And than was, withouten voice and withoute openinge of lippes, formede in my saule this worde: "Herewith is the feende overcomen." This worde saide oure lorde menande° his passion, as he shewed me before. In this, oure lorde brought unto my minde and shewed me a perte of the fendes malice, and fully his unmight. And, for that, he shewed me that the passion of him is overcominge of the fende. God shewed me that he hase nowe the same malice that he had before the incarnation, and als sare he travailes, and als continuelye he sees that alle chosene saules eschapes him worshipfullye. And that es alle his sorowe. For alle that God suffers him to° do turnes us° to joye and him to paine and to shame. And he has als mekille sorowe when God giffes him leve to wyrke as when he werkes nought. And that es for he maye nevere do als ille as he wolde, for his might es alle lokene in Goddes hande.

Also I sawe oure lorde scorne his malice and nought him, and he wille that we do the same. For this sight, I laugh mightelye, and that made tham to laugh that were aboute me, and thare laughinge was likinge to me. I thought I wolde mine evencristene hadde sene as I sawe. Than shulde thaye alle hafe laughen with me. Botte I sawe nought Criste laugh. Neverthelesse him likes that we laugh in comfortinge of us and enjoyande° in God for the feende is overcomen.

And after this, I felle into a saddehete, and saide: "I see° thre thinges: game, scorne, and arneste. I see game, that the feende is overcomen. And I see scorne, /fol. 102v/ that God scornes him, and he shalle be scornede. And I see arneste, that he es overcomen be the passion of oure lorde Jhesu Criste, and be his dede that was done ful erneste and with sadde travaile."

After this, oure lorde saide: "I thanke the of thy service and of thy travaile and namly in thy youth."

SECTION 9

God shewed me thre degrees of blisse that ilke saule shalle hafe in hevene that wilfullye hase served God in any degree here in erthe.

The firste is the wyrshipfulle thankinge of oure lorde God that he shalle resayfe when he es deliverede fro paine. This thanke is so highe and so wyrshipfulle that him thinke it filles him, though thare ware no mare blis. For methought that alle the paine and travaile that might be sufferde of alle liffande men might nought hafe° deservede the thanke that a man shalle hafe that wilfullye has servede God.

30

35

40

45

50

5

8–9 **alle the blissede creatures . . . thankinge** *The Pricke*, following Anselm, notes that the saved will see one another's joys and rejoice: "Thare salle ilk ane many thousandes se / In sere joyes, als himself salle be [there each one of them will see many thousand people in various joys, as he himself will be]" (8623–24) • 9–10 **he makes . . . knawen** God makes a person's service known to all who are in heaven • 11 **als new ande als likande** as freshly and as pleasingly • 11 **es resayvede** is received • 12 **so shalle it laste withouten ende** *The Pricke* lists the sixth spiritual dowry as security: "For thay salle be thare siker and certaine / To have endeles joy, and nevermare paine" (8559–60) • 12–13 **I sawe that . . . to me** I saw that this was said and shown to me in a good and sweet way. By Christ's words to Julian in 8.53–54 • 14 **rewarded for his . . . time** Compare 2.8–10 • 14–16 **namelye . . . wonderlye thanked** This elevation of youthful devotion evokes the account of the young virgins who sing before the throne of God and "follow the Lamb wherever he goes" in Rev. 14:1–4, a passage central to the medieval virginity tradition, as well as to the Middle English poem *Pearl* • 14 **namelye** especially • 15 **passande** surpassingly • 16 **wonderlye** wondrously • 17 **shewed . . . in my saule** manifested a sensation of supreme spiritual delight in my soul • 18 **sekernesse** certainty • 18 **mightlye festnede** made powerfully secure • 20 **shulde hafe greved me** could have injured me • 21 **turnede and lefte to myselfe** The mood darkens, partly in preparation for the Passion sequence in Section 10. The alternation of ease and difficulty, a common feature of accounts of the "service and . . . travaile" of religious living (8.53), is what *The Chastising*, following *Ancrene Wisse*, calls "the pley of love": "The pley of love is joye and sorwe, the whiche two comen sundry times oon aftir another, by the presence and absence of him that is oure love" (99). See also *The Scale* 2.41 • 22 **irkesumnesse** loathing • 22–23 **unnethes . . . to lyeve** I had scarcely enough patience to stay alive • 23–24 **hope, faithe, and charite** The three theological virtues that form the basis of Christian living. See 1 Cor. 13:13: "So faith, hope, love abide, these three; but the greatest of these is love" • 24 **in trowthe . . . in felinge** The dichotomy between truth or faith and feeling was traditional. At times of spiritual difficulty, faith must be trusted, not feeling • 25 **anone** soon • 26 **syekernesse** certainty • 27 **dissesede me** made me uneasy • 29 **tane . . . tothere** one . . . other • 29 **diverse** various • 30 **sithes** times • 30 **with Paule** See Rom. 8:38–39: "I am sure that neither death, nor life, nor angels . . . nor anything else in all creation, will be able to separate us from the love of God in Christ Jesus our Lord" • 31 **departe me fro** separate me from • 31–32 **with Sainte Peter** A conflation of two appeals to Christ on the Sea of Galilee, only one spoken by Peter: Matt. 8:25 and 14:30 • 33–45 **This vision was shewed . . . lovere and kepare** In a manner that may seem to belie *A Vision*'s claim that Julian is not a "techere" (6.35), this passage moves well beyond the content of the "shewing." The passage anticipates the more direct instruction of the second half of the work, and its use of literature in the "remedy" genre, such as Flete's *Remedy* • 33 **to lere me atte** to teach me in • 35 **wille that we knowe** wants us to know • 35–36 **he kepes us . . . wo** he keeps us always equally secure, in well-being and in woe • 37–38 **And towhethere, sinne . . . cause** and yet, sin is not the reason. The main claim of this passage, as the next sentence makes clear. Contrast *The Chastising*, which is closer to Middle English religious writing in general in advocating the opposite attitude toward the "hevinesse" of Christ's absence: "I counceile every man to rette it to his owne defaute [to consider it his own fault] that grace is withdrawe" (111) • 38–39 **wherefore I shulde . . . myselfe** in such a way that I ought to be left to myself • 40 **suffers us in wa** allows us to be in misery • 42 **passande** transitory • 43 **folowe** pay attention to • 44 **sodaynlye** quickly • 44 **passe over** get over them

For the seconde: that alle the blissede creatures that er in hevene shalle see that
worshipfulle thankinge of oure lorde God. And he makes his service to alle that er in
heven knawen.   10

And for the thirde: that als new ande als likande as it es resayvede that time,
right so shalle it laste withouten ende. I sawe that goodelye and swetlye was this
saide and shewed to me: that the age of everilk man° shalle be knawen in heven and
rewarded for his wilfulle service and for his time. And namelye the age of thame that
wilfullye and frelye offers thare youth unto God, es passande rewardede and   15
wonderlye thanked.

And after this, oure lorde shewed me a soverayne, gastelye likinge in my saule. In
this likinge, I was fulfilled of everlastande sekernesse, mightlye festnede withouten
any drede. This felinge was so gladde to me and so goodly that I was° in pees, in ese,
and in reste, so that there was nothinge in erthe that shulde hafe greved me.   20

This lasted botte a while, and I was turnede and lefte to myselfe in hevines and
werinesse of myselfe and irkesumnesse of my life, that unnethes I couthe hafe
patience to lyeve. Thare was none ese ne na comforthe to my felinge, botte hope,
faithe, and charite, and this I hadde in trowthe, botte fulle litille in felinge.

And anone after, God gafe me againe the comfort and /fol. 103r/ the reste in   25
saule: likinge and syekernesse so blisfulle and so mighty that no drede, no sorowe,
no paine bodilye no gastelye that might be sufferde shulde have dissesede me. And
than the paine shewed againe to my felinge, and than the joye and than the likinge,
and than the tane and nowe the tothere, diverse times, I suppose aboute twentye
sithes. And in the time of joye, I might hafe saide with Paule: "Nathinge shalle   30
departe me fro the charite of Criste." And in paine, I might hafe saide with Sainte
Peter: "Lorde, save me, I perishe."

This vision was shewed me to lere me atte my understandinge that it es
nedefulle to ilke man to feele on this wise: sumtime to be in comforthe, and
sumtime to faile and be lefte to himselfe. God wille that we knowe that he kepes us 35
evere like seker, in wele and in wo, and als mekille loves us in wo as in wele. And
sumtime, for the profitte of his saule, a man es lefte to himselfe. And towhethere,
sinne es nought the cause. For in this time, I sinnede nought wherefore I shulde be
lefte to myselfe, ne also I deservede nought to hafe this blisfulle felinge. Botte frelye
God giffes wele when him likes, and suffers us° in wa sumtime, and bothe es of love. 40
For it is Godes wille that we halde us in comforthe with alle oure might. For blis es
lastande withouten ende, and pain es passande, and shalle be brought to nought.
Therefore it es nought Goddes wille that we folowe the felinges of paine in
sorowinge and in mourninge for thaim,° botte sodaynlye passe over and halde us in
endelesse likinge that es God allemighty, oure lovere and kepare.   45

[SECTION 10] 1 **nere his dyinge** near the time of his death. In this section, Julian's youthful request to have "sene bodilye the passion of oure lorde" (1.7) reaches its climax. Again, the focus on a single detail, here the drying of Christ's body, is fierce. If the sight of the blood flowing from Christ in 3.10–17 and 8.20–28 is surprisingly joyful, here the sight of dryness is associated with absence and pain • 2 **swete** sweet • 2 **pale dyinge** the pallor of death • 2 **sithen** afterward • 2 **dede** deathly • 3 **langourande** languishing • 3–4 **than turnede . . . mare blewe** then turned more deathly blue; and afterward still more blue • 4 **turnede mare deepe dede** became more deeply dead • 5 **als farfurthe as** insofar as • 5–6 **namelye in the lippes** especially in the lips. The wounds in Christ's hands, feet, and side, and the crown of thorns on his head, were often separate objects of contemplation in Passion meditation, with prayers directed toward each. Not only are Christ's lips an addition to these standard "tokens" of the Passion; visionary contemplation here focuses, not on the lips themselves, but on the process they undergo as Christ dies. The object of contemplation is generally static. Here, the lips are seen in time • 6 **thare I sawe** where I saw • 6 **thaye** those lips • 7 **freshlye . . . likande** fresh and ruddy, lively and delicious. In Bridget's *Liber celestis,* Mary describes Christ's lips, when he was a young man, as "thike anogh and redyse [very thick and ruddy]" (4.70) • 8 **the nese claungede** the nose withered • 9 **lange pininge** long torment • 9 **as he hadde . . . dede** as if he had been dead seven nights. The number of nights Julian has lain sick. See 2.1–6 • 10 **maste** most • 12 **dryhede** state of dryness • 12–13 **"I thriste"** See John 19:28 • 13 **doubille thirste** A standard interpretation of Christ's words. See *The Privity:* "For thof [although] it were so that him thristede for the hele of manes soule, nevertheles in sothefastnes him thristede bodily; and that was no wonder, for thurghe sheddinge of his preciouse blode so habundandly . . . he was all inwardly drye and thristy" ("Meditatione of None," *YW* 1:207) • 14 **gastelye thirste** spiritual thirst • 15 **als I shalle saye efterwarde** See 15.11–19 • 15 **of bodelye thirste** concerning the bodily thirst • 17–20 **The blissed bodye . . . paines** the blessed body dried alone a long time, with the wrenching of the nails and the settling of the head and the weight of the body, with the blowing of the wind on the outside, which dried him more and tormented him with cold more than my heart can think—and other pains. Grammatically incoherent, the sentence breaks down under its own intensity • 19 **blawinge of winde** Not a standard detail in accounts of the Passion, although *The Privity* notes that "the wedire was colde" ("Ad primam," *YW* 1:203). A cold east wind from the North Sea might have been a feature of many Good Fridays in fourteenth-century Norwich • 21–22 **Swilke paines . . . tolde** such pains I saw that everything that I can tell or say is too little, for it cannot be told • 22–23 **feele in him . . . Jhesu**

See Phil. 2:5: "Have this mind among yourselves, which is yours in Christ Jesus," the first words of Paul's meditation on the self-humiliation (or kenosis) of Christ in his Incarnation and suffering death. See 11.12–13 • 23 **This shewinge . . . fulle of paines** An equivalence between Christ's Passion and the devout Christian's compassion, a common aim of meditation and the basis of Julian's first desire, is achieved. In *The Pryckinge of Love,* the meditator's focus on Christ's pain guarantees "that thou shalt be wounded with his woundes and over-helte [overcome] with peynes of his passioun" (15) • 24 **I wate wele . . . anes** I know well he suffered only once. See Heb. 10:10: "And by [God's] will we have been sanctified through the offering of the body of Jesus Christ once for all" • 24 **botte as he walde shewe it me** except insofar as he wished to show me it. Julian acknowledges she is seeing a representation of the Passion, not the Passion itself • 25 **as I hadde desirede before** See Section 1 • 26–28 **My modere . . . my sorowe** This brief return to Julian's sickbed reinforces the parallel between her and Christ made in Section 2, especially its account of her posture, lines 33–36. Here, the moment of her near death coincides with the moment of his. Julian's mother stands in for Mary, whose grief is described in lines 38–43 and whose presence at the Crucifixion is often said to increase Christ's pains. Rolle's *Meditations* states that "the sorewe that heo [she] made and the mykel dool [great grief] agregged manifold [multiplied many times] alle thin [Christ's] othere peines" (*YW* 1:86) • 26 **that stode emanges othere** who stood among the others • 27 **lokke min eyen** shut my eyes. This ritual is still performed as soon as possible after a death • 27–28 **had bene dede . . . diede** that I had been dead for a while or had just died • 28 **mekille** greatly • 29 **I wolde nought hafe been letted** I did not want to be hindered from seeing Christ's suffering • 30 **towhethere** nevertheless. Despite the intensity of Julian's empathetic pain • 31 **I knewe ful litille . . . I asked** See Matt. 20:22, Jesus' answer to the mother of James and John: "You do not know what you are asking. Are you able to drink the cup that I am to drink?" • 32–33 **Es any paine . . . paine?** See Lam. 1:12: "Look and see if there is any sorrow like my sorrow". A version of a commonly asked question, whether Christ's pain was worse than hell: "Thenne may sum mon [person] seyen that the sorwe that he suffrede for us on the crois was grettere then the peine of helle is," as Edmund of Abingdon's *Mirror of Holy Church* has it ("Contemplation biforen Midday," *YW* 1:256). Unlike *The Mirror,* which accepts the question, *A Vision* stresses the difference in kind between these pains • 33 **dispaire** The worst pain because by definition eternal. According to *The Pricke,* the damned "ay [always] dwelle" in despair "withouten hope of mercy," since they realize the truth of Job's words: "For in hell . . . es na redemptioune" (7234–351) • 34 **gastelye paine** spiritual suffering. Empathy, for Julian, is a physical phenomenon

SECTION 10

After this, Criste shewed me a partye of his passione nere his dyinge. I sawe that swete face as it ware drye and bludyelesse with pale dyinge; sithen mare dede° pale, langourande; and than turnede more dede to the blewe; and sithene mare blewe, as the fleshe turnede mare deepe dede. For alle the paines that Criste sufferde in his bodye shewed to me in the blissede face, als farfurthe as I sawe it, and namelye in the lippes, thare I sawe this foure colourse—thaye that I sawe beforehande freshlye and ruddy,° liflye and likande to my sight. This /fol. 103v/ was a hevy change, to see this deepe dyinge. And also the nese claungede° and dried to my sight. This lange pininge semede to me as he hadde bene a sevennight dede, allewaye sufferande paine. And methought the dryinge of Cristes fleshe was the maste paine of his passion and the laste.

And in this dryhede was brought to my minde this worde that Criste saide: "I thriste." For I sawe in Criste a doubille thirste: ane bodilye, ane othere gastelye. This worde was shewed to° me for the bodilye thirste, and for the gastelye thirste was shewed to me als I shalle saye efterwarde. And I understode of bodelye thirste that the bodye hadde failinge° of moistere, for the blessede fleshe and banes ware lefte allane withouten blode and moistere. The blissed bodye driede allane° lange time, with wringinge of the nailes and paysinge of the hede° and weight of the bodye, with blawinge of winde fra withouten that dried mare, and pined him with calde mare, than min herte can thinke, and alle othere paines.

Swilke paines I sawe that alle es to litelle that I can telle or saye, for it maye nought be tolde. Botte ilke saule, aftere the sayinge of Sainte Paule, shulde "feele in him that in Criste Jhesu." This shewinge of Criste paines filled me fulle of paines. For I wate wele he suffrede nought botte anes, botte as he walde shewe it me and fille me with minde, as I hadde desirede before.

My modere, that stode emanges othere and behelde me, lifted uppe hir hande before me face to lokke min eyen. For she wened I had bene dede or els I hadde diede. And this encresed mekille my sorowe. For noughtwithstandinge alle my paines, I wolde nought hafe been letted for love that I hadde in him. And towhethere, in alle this time of Cristes presence, I feled no paine botte for Cristes paines. Than thought me, I knewe ful litille° whate paine it was that I asked, for methought that my paines passede any bodilye dede. I thought: "Es any paine in helle like this paine?" And I was answerde in my resone that "dispaire is mare, for that es gastelye paine. Bot bodilye paine es nane mare than this. Howe might my paine be more° than to see him that es alle my life, alle my blis, and alle mye

36 **sothfastlye** truly • 36–37 **so mekille aboven myselfe . . . diede bodilye** so much more than myself that it seemed to me it would have been a great relief for me to have physically died. See *Meditations:* "The minde of that mater I wolde were my deth" (*YW* 1:91) • 38 **the compassion of . . . Marye** Mary's presence at the foot of the cross made her the first, as well as the best-informed, person to experience the Passion, and as such an object of identification and veneration • 39 **sho** she • 39 **anede** united • 40 **mekillehede** magnitude • 41 **alle his trewe lovers** See 1.6–7: both Mary Magdalene and the company of Christ's lovers she represents, those who through meditation or vision are at the scene of the Passion "that time" • 42 **awne** own • 44 **aninge** cause of union ("one-ing") • 44 **betwyx** between • 45 **alle creatures** all created beings • 46–47 **thaye that knewe him nought . . . time** Refers to the eclipse and the earthquake that, in Luke 23:44–45 and Matt. 27:45, 51, follow the death of Jesus. In *Liber celestis,* Mary describes how, "in the deing [death] of my son, all thinges were turbled [troubled]. . . . All the elementes were disesed. The son and the mone withdrawen [withdrew] ther light in tokening of [as a sign of] compassion, the erth tremlid, the stones braste [burst open]" (6.11). Langland's *Piers Plowman* B evokes the scene in a single line: "The day for drede withdrough and derk bicam the sonne" (18.60) • 49 **for failinge . . . alle creatures** because of the failure of the comfort given by [or to] all created things • 50 **walde hafe . . . crosse** wanted to look away from the cross. Julian has been looking at the cross since 2.26–28 • 50 **durste** dared • 51 **wiste** knew • 51 **seker and safe** safe and sound • 52–53 **na syekernesse . . . feendes** no safety, but the ugliness of the fiends. The demons cluster around both Julian's deathbed and the dying figure of Christ • 53 **profer** proposition • 53–54 **as if it hadde beene frendelye** as if it were friendly. The status of the "profer" is never clarified, though the phrasing here suggests a sinister source for the words that follow • 54 **isaide** said • 54 **Luke uppe** look up. As Julian is looking up in 2.24–25, before lowering her eyes to the cross • 56 **might hafe desesed me** could have given me trouble • 56 **othere me behoved . . . answere** I must either look up or else answer • 57 **Naye, I may nought!** Julian's change of mind is not explained, although it seems connected not only with her desire to suffer with Christ but with her desire to live beyond her experience of dying—with both the first two "desires" described in Section 1. Fidelity to the sufferings of the human Jesus is often prized in medieval women's writings: see *The Book of Margery Kempe,* chaps. 35–37, on Margery's devotion to Christ's humanity and reluctance to undergo mystical marriage to the godhead. When Julian denies her revelation in Section 21, her devastation leads to an episode of demonic temptation to despair • 57 **For thowe erte mine heven** *The Scale* 2.33 begins an account of the contemplative's sight of heaven with "What is hevene to a resonable soule? Sothly, not ellis but Jhesu God" • 58 **For I hadde lever . . . to domesdaye** for I would rather have been in that pain until Judgment Day. A formulation that links Julian's pain with the pains of purgatory, which cease on the Day of Judgment • 59–60 **he that bonde me so sare** he who bound me so tight. The image is erotic. In Chaucer's *Troilus and Criseyde* 3.1358, Troilus asks Criseyde: "How koude ye withouten bond me binde?" Here, however, the bonds are mutual. As part 7 of *Ancrene Wisse* makes clear, when it comes to love, Christ is as bound to humanity as humanity is to him: "Love binds our Lord, so that he cannot do anything except with love's leave" (198)

[SECTION 11] 1 **chese** chose • 1 **wham I saw onlye in paine** The conflation of pain and heaven here is profoundly contradictory. According to *The Pricke,* life in heaven is defined by "hele and liking" (health and pleasure) and the absence of "ivel" and "paine" (8011–12). "Paine," on the other hand, is a synonym for "hell" • 2 **no nothere** no other • 2–3 **whilke . . . thare** who will be my joy when I am in heaven • 3 **ever beene a comforthe to me** The only reference in *A Vision* to the longterm effect of the revelation on Julian • 3 **chesed** chose • 4 **lerninge** lesson • 5 **anly** only • 6 **langoure** languish • 6–7 **aninge . . . might** unification with the divinity of Christ for love gave strength to his humanity to suffer more than anyone could, or than everyone put together could. The next sentence resolves the ambiguity • 7–8 **I mene . . . suffer** I do not only ("anly") mean more pain by himself ("anly") than all humans were capable of suffering. Christ's suffering exceeds all historical suffering in practice, as well as theory. Compare *The Mirror:* "Theigh alle the seknesses and alle the serwes [sorrows] of this world were in o [one] monnes body . . . hit were not but litel, or as nought, to regard of [it would not be more than a little, or nothing, by comparison with] the serwe that he suffrede for us in on houre of the day" ("Contemplation biforen Midday," *YW* 1:256)

/fol. 104r/ joye suffer?" Here° feled I sothfastlye that I lovede Criste so mekille aboven myselfe that methought it hadde beene a grete ese to me to hafe diede bodilye.

Herein I sawe in partye the compassion of oure ladye, Sainte Marye. For Criste and sho ware so anede in love that the gretnesse of hir love was the cause of the mekillehede of hir paine. For so mekille as sho loved him mare than alle othere, her paine passed alle othere. And so alle his disciples and alle his trewe lovers sufferde paines mare than thare awne bodelye dying. For I am seker, be min awne felinge, that the leste of thame luffed him° mare than thaye did thamselfe.

Here I sawe a° grete aninge betwyx Criste and us. For when he was in paine, we ware in paine, and alle creatures that might suffer paine sufferde with him. And thaye that knewe him nought, this was thare paine: that alle creatures, sone and the mone, withdrewe thare service and so ware thaye alle lefte in sorowe for the time. And thus thaye that loved him sufferde paine for luffe, and thay that luffed him nought sufferde paine for failinge of comforthe of alle° creatures.

In this time I walde hafe loked beside the crosse, botte I durste nought, for I wiste wele whiles I luked upon the crosse I was seker and safe. Therfore I walde nought assente to putte my saule in perille, for beside the crosse was na syekernesse,° botte uglinesse of feendes. Than hadde I a profer in my resone, as if it hadde beene frendelye, isaide to me: "Luke uppe to heven to his fadere." Than sawe I wele, with the faithe that I feled, that thare ware nathinge betwyx the crosse and heven that might hafe desesed me, and othere me behoved loke uppe or els answere. I answerde and saide: "Naye, I may nought! For thowe erte mine heven." This I saide for I walde nought. For I hadde lever hafe bene in that paine to domesdaye, than hafe comen to hevene otherewise than be him. For I wiste wele, he that bonde me so sare° shulde unbinde me when he walde.

40

45

50

55

60

SECTION 11

Thus chese I Jhesu for my heven, wham I saw° onlye in paine at that time. Me likede no nothere hevene */fol. 104v/* than Jhesu, whilke shalle be my blisse when I am thare. And this has ever beene a comforthe to me, that I chesed Jhesu to my hevene in alle time of passion and of sorowe. And that has beene a lerninge to me, that I shulde evermare do so, and chese anly him to my heven in wele and in wa.

5

And thus sawe I my lorde Jhesu langoure lange time. For the aninge of the godhede for love gafe strenght to the manhede to suffer mare than alle men might. I mene nought anly mare paine anly than alle men might suffer, bot also° that he sufferde mare paine than alle men that ever was, fra the firste beginninge to the laste daye. No tonge maye telle, ne herte fully thinke, the paines that oure savioure

10

11 **haffande rewarde to** taking account of • 12 **dede** death • 12 **dispittous** pitiless • 13 **fulliest noghthede . . . dispiside** most fully humiliated and most utterly despised. See Phil. 2:6–8, a statement of Christ's self-humiliation through Incarnation and Passion: "Though he was in the form of God, [he] . . . emptied himself, taking the form of a servant. . . . And being found in human form he humbled himself and became obedient unto death, even death on a cross" • 14 **als fare** as far • 15 **a dede done in a time** a single deed done at a single time • 17 **sodaynlye** Again, this word announces visionary transformation. See 2.37, 3.1 • 17 **me behaldande . . . crosse** as I looked into the same cross. Even the following joyful scene is played out in "the face of the crucifixe" (8.1) • 17–18 **he chanchede into blisfulle chere** his face transformed into an expression of joy. A change that completes the story of the Passion by alluding to the Resurrection • 19–20 **Whate . . . grefe?** what does any part of your pain or your sorrow matter?

[SECTION 12] 1 **Arte thou wele paide** are you fully satisfied • 2 **Gramercy** "grant merci," great thanks • 2 **blissed mut thowe be** may you be blessed • 4–5 **For if I might . . . walde suffer** The liturgy for Good Friday contains the words: "What more should I do for you and have not done?" See Isa. 5:4; also the lyric "Woefully Arrayed," where Christ on the cross laments, "What might I suffer more / Then I have sufferde, man, for thee?" • 7 **thre hevens** Compare Paul's vision of the third heaven in 2 Cor. 12:2–4: "I know a man in Christ who fourteen years ago was caught up to the third heaven—whether in the body or out of the body I do not know, God knows. . . . and he heard things that cannot be told." The "thre hevens" emerge from the three words "joye," "blisse," and "likinge" spoken by Jesus in lines 3–4, though they are anticipated by 10.57: "thowe erte mine heven" • 7 **I was gretlye merveylede** I was greatly astonished • 8 **alle of the blessed manhede** "Of," always a difficult word in Middle English, seems to mean both "for" and "consisting of" • 9 **the firste heven** For the second and third heavens, see lines 32–35 • 10 **shewed Criste me his fadere** Christ showed me his Father • 10 **bot in na bodelye liknesse** Makes it clear that the revelation does not represent the persons of the Trinity visually • 10 **properte** character • 11 **wyrkinge** activity • 11–12 **that he giffes mede . . . Criste** that he gives reward to his Son, Jesus Christ. See Phil. 2:9–10: "God has highly exalted him and bestowed on him the name which is above every name, that at the name of Jesus every knee should bow, in heaven and on earth and under the earth" • 12–13 **his fadere might haffe . . . bettere** his Father could have given him no reward that could have pleased him more. Initially, it seems as if the reward is the Father's gift and the gift is the Son's joy at the reward, but by line 17 the gift has become more specific: "we er his mede" • 16 **aboute oure salvation** concerning our salvation • 16 **nought anely his thurgh byinge** not only his through buying. Economic language was and is basic to discussion of the "redemption." Christ has "bought" the human race back from sin and owns them • 17 **curtayse gifte of his fadere** The underlying image switches to the courtly register, and the language of gift and reward, not purchase. Having been bought by Christ, humankind is given him again by his Father as a reward ("mede") for his service. Humans owe Christ a double allegiance. From Philippians, the underlying biblical source shifts to Hebrews 1–2, where Christ, "when he had made purification for sins, . . . sat down at the right hand of the Majesty on high," all things "in subjection under his feet" (1:3, 2:8) • 17–18 **We ere his blisse . . . crowne** Humankind here replaces the crown of thorns that, in Section 3, causes the shedding of Jesus' blood. See Heb. 2:7: "Thou hast crowned him with glory and honour" • 18–19 **settes atte nought** considers as nothing • 19 **dede** death • 19–22 **And in this wordes . . . done it** An attempt to define the infinitude of Christ's love by the infinitude of his willingness to undergo suffering. In *Liber celestis* the devil speaks to Christ about Bridget: "If it were possibil, thou wald moste gladly suffir in ilke of thy membres [in each of your limbs] swilke one pain spiritually [a spiritual version of each pain] as thu suffird ones in all the membris [in all your limbs] upon the cross, or thou wald forgo her [before you would give her up]" (1.34). A *Vision* similarly imagines Christ suffering again, but for each one of the saved, rather than for a specially precious individual • 20–22 **I sawe sothly . . . alle** I saw truly that if he could die so often that he could die once for every person who will be saved, in the way he died once for everyone. See Rom. 6:10: "he died to sin, once for all" • 22 **to** until • 23 **sette it atte nought for luff** out of love reckon it as nothing • 23 **for alle thinke . . . litille** for it all seems to him only little. Recalls the hazelnut image of 4.7–13. "Alle" and "litille" could be taken as abstract nouns: "for infinity seems to him like littleness" • 23–24 **in regarde of** by comparison with • 24 **wele sobarly** very seriously

sufferde for us, haffande rewarde to the worthines of the hyest, worshipfulle kinge
and to the shamefulle, dispittous, and painfulle dede. For he that was hieste and
worthiest was fulliest noghthede and witterliest dispiside. Botte the love that made
him to suffere alle this, it passes als fare alle his pains as heven es aboven erthe. For
the paines was a dede done in a time be the wyrkinge of love. Botte luffe was   15
withouten beginninge, and es, and evere shalle be withouten any ende.

   And sodaynlye, me behaldande in the same crosse, he chanchede into blisfulle
chere. The chaunginge of his chere changed mine, and I was alle gladde and mery as
it was possibille. Than brought oure lorde merelye to my minde: "Whate es any
pointe of thy paine or of thy grefe?" And I was fulle merye.   20

<h2 style="text-align:center">SECTION 12</h2>

Than saide oure lorde, askande: "Arte thou wele paide that I sufferde for the?"
"Ya, goode lorde," quod I, "Gramercy goode lorde, blissed mut thowe be!" "If
thowe be payede," quod oure lorde, "I am payede. It es a joye and a blisse and ane
endlesse likinge to me that ever I sufferde passion for the. For if I might suffer mare,
I walde suffer."   5

   In this felinge, mine understandinge was lifted uppe into heven, and thare I sawe
thre hevens. Of the whilke sight I was gretlye merveylede, and /fol. 105r/ thought: "I
sawe thre hevens, and alle of the blessed manhede of Criste. And nane is mare, nane
is lesse, nane is hiare, nane is lawere, botte evene like in blisse." For the firste heven,
shewed Criste me his fadere, bot in na bodelye liknesse botte in his properte and in   10
his wyrkinge.° The wyrkinge of the fadere it is this: that he giffes mede tille his sone
Jhesu Criste. This gifte and this mede is so blisfulle to Jhesu that his fadere° might
haffe giffene na mede that might hafe likede him bettere.

   For the firste heven, that is blissinge of the fadere, shewed to me as a heven, and
it was fulle blisfulle. For he is fulle blissede with alle the dedes that he has done   15
aboute oure salvation, wharefore we ere nought anely his thurgh byinge, botte also
be the curtayse gifte of his fadere. We ere his blisse, we er his mede, we er his
wyrshippe, we er his crowne. This that I saye is so grete blisse to Jhesu that he settes
atte nought his travaile and his harde passion, and cruelle and shamefulle dede. And
in this wordes—"if I might suffer mare, I walde suffer mare"—I sawe sothly that if   20
he might die als ofte als fore everilke man anes that shalle be safe as he died° anes for
alle, love shulde never late him hafe reste to he hadde done it. And when he hadde
done it, he walde sette it atte nought for luff, for alle thinke° him botte litille in
regarde of his love. And that shewed he me wele sobarly, sayande this worde: "If I
might suffere mare." He saide nought, "if it ware nedfulle to suffer mare," botte, "if I   25

26–27 and he might . . . walde if he could suffer more, he would want to suffer more • **29–31 I sawe a fulle blisse . . . done** Only perfect suffering could have given Christ perfect bliss • **30 shulde . . . done fulle** would not have been fully accomplished. "Done fulle" recalls Christ's last words on the cross in John 19:30. See *The Privity:* "The sexte worde was whene he saide: 'It es all done,' as who say: 'Fader, the obedience that thou bad me do [commanded me to do], I have fulfillede it; and yit, if thare be any more that ye will that I do, I am redy to fulfill it'" ("Meditatione of None," *YW* 1:207) • **31 And in this thre wordes** See lines 3–4 • **33 plesance of the fadere** delight of the Father. See line 14 (where the word is "blissinge") • **33 wirshippe of the sone** honoring of the Son. See lines 17–18: "we er his wyrshippe" • **35–36 Jhesu wille . . . of oure salvation** Jesus wants us to pay heed to the joy that is in the blessed Trinity over our salvation • **36 like als mekille** take as much pleasure. As do the persons of the Trinity • **37–38 Erte . . . payed?** See line 1 • **38 Be the tothere worde** it was also showed by the other word. The syntax is informal • **38–39 he shewed me the understandinge** Of "Erte thow wele payed?" • **40 I aske . . . paye the** I ask nothing else for my labor except that I might satisfy you • **40 Plentyouslye** plenteously • **41–42 Thinke also . . . for the** also think intelligently about the magnitude of this phrase: "that I ever suffered the Passion for you." See line 4. The only clause in Christ's speech not to have been expounded to this point. The injunction to "thinke" briefly makes readers colleagues in the exposition of the revelation • **42–43 in that worde was . . . salvation** in that phrase was revealed an elevated knowledge of the love and the pleasure that he had in our salvation

[SECTION 13] **1 loked** looked • **1 into his side** The wound in Christ's side made by a spear in John 19:34. According to the fifteenth-century *Treatise of Ghostly Battle*, building on this verse, "his side was openede and his herte clovene a-two [sliced in two] with a sharpe spere and . . . he shadde [shed] oute both bloode and water . . . yef he had hade [if he had had] more bloode, more he wolde have yevene for mannes soule to the fadere of hevene" (*YW* 2:426) • **2 loved the** loved you • **2 as if he hadde saide** The speech that follows, a paraphrase of Christ's

words "Lo, how I loved the," analyzes the words by putting a commentary on them into Christ's mouth. A technique derived from medieval biblical exegesis, this method of analytic paraphrase has the effect of blurring the distinction between text and commentary, revelation and exposition. The speech also echoes Christ's words to Thomas after the resurrection: "Put your finger here, and see my hands; and put out your hand, and place it in my side; do not be faithless, but believing" (John 20:27) • **2–3 if thow . . . godhede** even if you cannot contemplate my divinity. Julian has seen even heaven as "the blessed manhede of Criste" (12.8) and has decided against contemplating the Father directly (10.53–60) • **3 lette open my side** let my side be opened • **4 clovene in twa** cloven in two. The image of the Sacred Heart, from which the healing liquids of blood and water flowed • **4 lette oute . . . tharein** let out all the blood and water that was in it • **4–5 this likes me . . . the** this gives me pleasure, and I desire that it do the same for you • **7–8 the right side . . . oure ladye stode** In late medieval painting and sculpture Mary is usually depicted on the right side of the cross, from Christ's perspective, while the apostle John stands on the left. The portable crucifix in which Julian is seeing the revelation would not include either figure • **9 Wille thowe see hir?** do you want to see her? **9 gramercy** "grant merci," great thanks • **10 wened** expected • **10 to haffe sene here** to have seen her • **11–12 Jhesu in that worde . . . hire** in the statement "Do you want to see her?" Jesus showed me a spiritual sight of her. The words themselves generate the sight. Apart from the demonic temptations of Sections 22–23, there are no further "bodily sights" in the revelation • **12 before sene hire** See 4.21–32 • **12 here** her • **13 hye . . . aboven alle creatures** Cycles of paintings and sculptures of the life of Mary end with her Assumption and coronation, the scenes evoked here • **14 alle tha that likes . . . in hire** all those who delight in him must delight in her. "Like" is a more intimate word in this context than "love" and alludes punningly back to "likenes" (line 10) • **16–17 in that worde . . . giffen me** in that word that Jesus said— "Do you want to see her?"—it seemed to me I had the greatest delight he could have given me

might suffer mare." For though it be nought nedefulle and he might suffer mare, mare he walde.

This dede and this werke aboute oure salvation was als wele as he might ordayne it, it was done als wyrshipfullye as Criste might do it. And in this, I sawe a fulle blisse in Criste, botte this blisse shulde nought hafe bene done fulle if it might any bettere hafe bene done than it was done. And in this thre wordes—"It is a joye, a blisse, and ane endeles likinge to me"—ware shewed to me thre hevens, as thus: for the joye, I understode the plesance of the fadere; for the blisse, the wirshippe of the sone; and for the endeles likinge, the haly gaste. The fadere is plesed, the sone is worshipped, the haly gaste likes. Jhesu wille that we take heede to this blisse that is in the blissedfulle trinite of oure salvation, and that we like als mekille, /fol. 105v/ with his grace, whiles we er here. And this was shewed me in this worde: "Erte thow wele payed?" Be the tothere worde that Criste saide—"if thowe be payed, I am paid"—he shewed me the understandinge, as if he had saide: "It is joye and likinge enough to me, and I aske nought els for my travaile botte that I might paye the." Plentyouslye and fully was this shewed to me. Thinke also wiselye of the gretnesse of this worde: "That ever I suffred passion for the." For in that worde was a hye knawinge of luffe and of likinge that he hadde in oure salvation.

30

35

40

SECTION 13

Fulle merelye and gladlye oure lorde loked into his side and behelde, and saide this worde—"Lo, how I loved the"—as if he° hadde saide: "My childe, if thow kan nought loke in my godhede, see here howe I lette open my side, and my herte be clovene in twa, and lette oute blude and watere alle that was tharein. And this likes me, and so wille I that it do the." This shewed oure lorde me to make us gladde and mery.

5

And with the same chere and mirthe he loked downe on the right side, and brought to my minde whare oure ladye stode in the time of his passion, and saide: "Wille thowe see hir?" And I answerde and saide: "Ya goode lorde, gramercy, if it be thy wille." Ofte times I prayed it, and wened to haffe sene here in bodely likenes. Botte I sawe hir nought so. And Jhesu in that worde shewed me a gastelye sight of hire. Right as I hadde before sene hire litille and simpille, right so he shewed here than hye and nobille and gloriouse and plesante to him aboven alle creatures. And so he wille that it be knawen that alle tha that likes in him shulde like in hire, and in the likinge that he hase in hire and sho in him.

10

15

And in that worde that Jhesu saide—"Wille thowe see hire?"—methought I hadde the maste likinge that he might hafe giffen me, with the gastelye shewinge

18 **nothinge in specialle** nothing individually. The phrase also occurs in 7.11 and 16.20, 25–26 • 19 **in thre times** on three occasions: 4.21–32, 10.38–43, 13.7–21 • 20 **consayved** conceived • 22–24 **And efter this . . . by contemplation** The glorification of Mary now gives way to that of Jesus, as the contemplation of Mary is seen as no more than a stage on the way to the contemplation of God. The careful limits placed on Mary's role in the revelation, where she is briefly glimpsed at three moments in her life—one reverent, one sorrowing, one joyful (lines 19–21)—before being transcended in contemplation of God, resemble the limits Julian places on her own role in 6.2–7, where she asks readers to "leve the behaldinge" of herself "and mekelye behalde God." The Christ who announces himself in the lines that follow is once again the Christ of Phil. 2:9–11, the passage from which the devotion to the Holy Name of Jesus derives. See 12.11–12 • 22 **shewed him** manifested himself • 23 **lerede** taught • 23 **ilke saule contemplatife** every contemplative soul. Every soul seriously engaged in a life of spiritual contemplation. See 4.37–39 • 23–24 **to whilke . . . God** to whom it is given to look at and seek God • 24 **shalle se . . . contemplation** shall see her and pass beyond her to the contemplation of God • 25 **hamelye . . . life** intimate and courtly and full of bliss and true life. These epithets could apply either to the "techinge" or to "Jhesu" • 26 **I it am** I am the one. Despite the emphasis on Mary in lines 18–21, Jesus' words of wooing leave little room for devotion to anyone other than himself. The aggressively masculine Jesus of *Ancrene Wisse*, part 7, is likely a model: "Am I not the fairest one? Am I not the richest king? Am I not the highest born?" (194). However, "I it am" (not "I am he") goes out of its way not to emphasize this Jesus' maleness • 27 **that thowe serves** whom you serve • 27 **that thowe langes** for whom you long • 28 **that thowe menes** to whom your intention is directed • 29 **preches the** preaches to you • 29 **that shewed me are** who showed myself before • 29–30 **I declare nought** I will not expound • 30 **botte for ilke man** but let every person • 30 **efter** after • 30 **giffes** gives • 31 **resayfe** receive • 31 **in oure lordes meninge** according to our Lord's intention • 32 **And efter** and after that. Although this phrase occurs in midsection, according to the divisions in the manuscript, it initiates an important new phase of *A Vision*, calling to mind Julian's state before the revelation began and developing new theological arguments. Later moments that step outside the revelation in this same way seem to have similar structural importance. See 19.1–16, 20.1–6. Perhaps this section was originally divided in two here • 32–33 **langinge . . . to him before** the longing I had for him before the time of the revelation. "Wilfulle langinge" is the third of the "thre woundes" for which Julian asks in 1.38–41. This new phase of the revelation opens by returning Julian to her somber starting point • 33 **nathinge letted me bot sin** nothing prevented me but sin. Perhaps a digest of the meaning of the first phase of

the revelation • 33–34 **so I behelde . . . alle** this I saw to be generally true of us all • 34–35 **hafe bene clene . . . as he made us** have been as pure and as like our Lord as he made us • 36 **why . . . letted** why, by the great, foreseeing wisdom of God, sin was not prevented. In Pierre D'Abernon's translation of Honorius's *Elucidarium, La lumere as lais*, the lay voice also asks: "Why would God create humankind when he knew it would sin?" and "Why did God allow humankind to be tempted?" (*pur quei suffri Deu tempter humme?* [70]). *Piers Plowman* B has "heighe men" asking the latter question with "crabbede wordes: / 'Why wolde oure saveour suffre swich a worm in his blisse, / That biwiled the woman and the wye [man] after?'" (10.106–8) • 37 **alle shulde hafe bene wele** all would have been well or must have been well. The phrase is picked up by Christ in line 61 and again by Julian in 14.3 • 38–39 **This stirringe . . . of fulle grete pride** this thought was much to be repudiated, and [yet] I mourned and sorrowed over it without reason or moderation with very great pride • 40–44 **I saye nought . . . life** These two sentences gloss the phrase "enfourmede me of alle that me neded," dispelling any idea that the revelation might contain all the teaching needed for salvation and so allow the teachings of holy church to be discarded. This flurry of explanation is a sure sign that the next moment of revelation is of special importance to the work. See 6.46–49 for a similar statement • 40–41 **na mare techinge** no more teaching • 41 **with the shewinge of this** besides the manifestation of this truth • 41 **hase lefte me to haly kyrke** has left me in the care of holy church • 42 **freele** frail • 42–43 **wilfully submittes me** willingly submit myself • 45 **behovelye** necessary or fitting, also good or opportune. The sole adjectival use in *A Vision*, though as an impersonal verb, in the forms "behoves" and "behoved/e," the word is common. See 8.14, where the word means "was necessary," although the word "nedes" is brought in to make this clear; elsewhere the word can mark a stage in an argument, announce a custom, express satisfaction at a good fit with something. The statement "Sinne is behovelye" may echo words from the Easter liturgy, where the Fall is invoked in words of paradoxical joy: "O happy fault, O necessary sin of Adam!" (*O felix culpa, O necessarium peccatum Ade*). If so, "behovelye" might be considered a translation of both *felix* and *necessarium* • 46–47 **shamefulle dispite . . . noghtinge** shameful contempt and the absolute humiliation. Refers not only to Christ's sufferings during his lifetime but to the "noghtinge" of the Incarnation. See 4.36–47 • 48 **alle the paines . . . bodelye** all the physical and spiritual pains and sufferings of all his creatures. "Sinne" in this formulation includes all creaturely suffering • 49 **in party noghted** partly negated • 49 **shulde be** ought to be • 49 **to we be** until we are • 50–51 **of oure awne dedely fleshe** of our own mortal flesh • 51 **inwarde affections** inner impulses • 53 **toch moment** • 53 **redely** easily • 54 **afferde** afraid

that he gafe me of hire. For oure lorde shewed me nothinge in specialle botte oure
lady Sainte Marye. And here he shewed me in thre times: the firste was as she
consayved; the seconde was as sho were in hire sorowes undere the crosse; and the   20
thrid as sho is nowe, in likinge, wirshippe, /fol. 106r/ and joye.

   And efter this, oure lorde shewed him to me mare glorified as to my sight than I
sawe him before. And in this was I lerede that ilke saule contemplatife to whilke es
giffen to luke and seke God shalle se hire and passe unto God by contemplation.

   And efter this techinge, hamelye, curtayse, and blisfulle and verray life, ofte   25
times oure lorde Jhesu saide to me: "I it am that is hiaste. I it am that thowe luffes. I
it am that thowe likes. I it am that thowe serves. I it am that thowe langes. I it am
that thowe desires. I it am that thowe menes. I it am that is alle. I it am that haly
kyrke preches the and teches the. I it am that shewed me are to the." Thies wordes I
declare nought, botte for ilke man, efter the grace that God giffes him in   30
understandinge and lovinge, resayfe tham in oure lordes meninge.

   And efter, oure lorde brought unto my minde the langinge that I hadde to him
before. And I sawe that nathinge letted me bot sin. And so I behelde generallye in us
alle, and methought: "If sin hadde nought bene, we shulde alle hafe bene clene and
like to oure lorde as he made us." And thus in my folye before this time, ofte I   35
wondrede why, be the grete forseande wisdome of God, sin was nought letted. For
than thought me that alle shulde hafe bene wele.

   This stirringe was mekille to forsayke, and mourninge and sorowe I made
therfore withouten resone and discretion of fulle grete pride. Neverthelesse Jhesu in
this vision enfourmede me of alle that me neded. I saye nought that me nedes na   40
mare techinge. For oure lorde, with the shewinge of this, hase lefte me to haly kyrke;
and I am hungery and thirstye and nedy and sinfulle and freele, and wilfully
submittes me to the techinge of haly kyrke, with alle mine evencristen, into the ende
of my life.

   He answerde be this worde and saide: "Sinne is behovelye." In this worde "sinne,"   45
our lorde brought to my minde generallye alle that is nought goode: the shamefulle
dispite and the utter noghtinge that he bare for us in this life and in his dyinge, and
alle the paines and passions of alle his creatures, gastelye and bodelye. For we ere alle
in party noghted, and we shulde be noghted, folowande oure maister Jhesu, to we be
fulle purgede: that is to say, to we be fully /fol. 106v/ noghted of oure awne dedely   50
fleshe, and of alle oure inwarde affections° whilke ere nought goode.

   And the behaldinge of this, with alle the paines that ever ware or ever shalle be,
alle° this was shewed me in a toch and redely passed overe into comforth. For oure
goode lorde God walde noght that the saule ware afferde of this uglye sight. Botte I

55–56 **I lefe . . . cause of** I believe it has no kind of actuality, nor any share of existence, nor could it be apprehended were it not for the pain it causes. This theme is introduced in 8.9–19. Although it sounds daring, this is a theological commonplace: far from being an active principle, sin is merely "a lackinge of love and of light . . . a wantinge of God [some manuscripts read 'good']," as Hilton puts it in *The Scale* 1.53 • 57 **For it purges** Sin is defined only in relation to its positive effects • 58–59 **alle this** all the effects of sin • 59 **and so is his blissed wille** and this (that his Passion comfort us) is his blessed will • 59–60 **to alle that shalle be safe** to all who will be saved. See 6.45 for the first use of this phrase ("I speke of thame that shalle be safe"), which qualifies what might otherwise be the explicit universalism of parts of *A Vision* • 60 **be his wordes** by his words • 61 **Botte alle shalle be wele** but all will be well or must be well. "Shall" implies necessity at least as strongly as futurity, as Christ's distinction between "shalle" and "wille" in 15.1–10 shows. "Alle," used more than 250 times in *A Vision,* already has resonances derived from the visions of the hazelnut ("alle that is made") and God in a point ("God doth all") in 4.10, 8.15, the second of which asks, "Whate es sinne?" "Alle shalle be wele" dominates the arguments and insights of Sections 13–18, and its importance is confirmed by its repetition at the end of the revelation, 22.36 • 62 **na to nane** nor to anyone • 64 **sen** since • 65 **compassion of us . . . sinne** compassion for us by reason of sin. A reason that is still hidden at this stage of *A Vision,* and that to some extent remains so • 65–66 **right as . . . like** just as . . . in the same way • 66 **before** See Section 10 • 67 **in party** in part • 68 **ilke kinde compassione . . . evencristene** every natural feeling of compassion that someone has for his fellow Christians. A main theme of the following section

[SECTION 14] 1 **Bot in this I stode** but at this point I stood still or dug my feet in • 1 **behaldande . . . mournande** contemplating widely, anxiously, and mournfully. *A Vision* regularly uses participles as adverbs, as here with "mournande" • 2 **in my meninge** in my intention. Julian does not speak aloud • 3 **the grete harme . . . creatures** the great damage that has come to your creation because of sin. *La lumere* devotes several questions and answers to this damage, under headings like "Whether humankind can know how things would

have been if it had never sinned" (79–84) • 4 **as I durste** so far as I dared • 4 **mare open declaringe** more explicit exposition • 4–5 **wharewith . . . this** through which I could feel easier about this • 6 **Adames sinne was the maste harme** Adam's sin was the greatest harm. Christ puts a face to Julian's word "harme" in line 3. *La lumere* likewise responds to questioning on sin by describing the gravity of eating the apple and the process by which "the sin of Adam [*le pecché Adam*] passes to all those engendered from him" (75–76, 85–87) • 7–8 **this is openly knawen . . . erthe** this is known publicly by the whole of holy church on earth. An endorsement of standard teaching on sin. Underneath Julian's question in lines 2–3 lies doubt about whether that teaching can be correct • 9 **lered** taught • 9 **I shulde behalde the gloriouse asethe** I should see the glorious Atonement. The "asethe" is Christ's Passion: in *A Treatise of Ghostly Battle,* Christ makes "aseeth to the fader in hevene for the gilt of mankinde" (*YW* 2:421). Julian is promised that she will see the full efficacy of the "asethe" in heaven: perhaps in the form described in *The Pricke* (5271–302), in which all the "tokens" of the Passion, including the cross, are displayed in the sky at the Day of Judgment to encourage the blessed and reprove the sinful • 10 **asethmakinge** act of reparation • 13 **take hede to this** pay attention to this message • 13 **sen** since • 13 **the maste harme** the greatest harm. The harm caused by Adam's sin • 14 **therby** from this fact • 15 **He gaffe me understandinge** he gave me to understand. This formulation leaves it unclear how this teaching is conveyed. Replacement of the usual "I saw" with "understanding" signals a shift of mode in *A Vision* away from moment-by-moment exposition of a revelation and toward explicit didacticism • 15 **twa parties** two categories of truth. Continues Christ's answer to Julian's anxious question in lines 2–3 • 15–16 **The ta . . . oure salvation** one category is our savior and our salvation. Knowledge of Christ and of the moral, ritual, societal, and theological truths pertinent to human living and dying • 16–17 **open . . . plentious** explicit and lucid and lovely and easy and plentiful. "Plentuouse" is earlier used of Christ's blood. See 8.20–28 • 18 **comprehended** included • 18–20 **Hereto . . . the same grace** to this category of truth we are bound and led by God and taught and counseled by the Holy Spirit within and, through the same grace, by holy church without • 20 **enjoyande** rejoicing • 20 **for** because

sawe noght sinne. Fore I lefe it has na manere of substance, na partye of beinge, na it   55
might nought be knawen bot be the paines that it is cause of. And this paine, it is
sumthinge, as to my sight, for a time. For it purges us and makes us to knawe
oureselfe and aske mercy. For the passion of oure lorde is comforth to us againes alle
this, and so is his blissed wille. And for the tender love that our goode lorde hath° to
alle that shalle be safe, he comfortes redely and swetlye be his wordes, and says: 60
"Botte alle shalle be wele, and alle maner of thinge shalle be wele." Thies wordes
ware shewed wele tenderlye, shewande na manere° of blame to me, na to nane that
shalle be safe. Than were it a grete unkindenesse of me to blame or wonder of God
for my sinnes, sen he blames not me for sinne.

Thus I sawe howe Criste has compassion of us for the cause of sinne. And right   65
as I was before with the passion of Criste fulfilled with paine and compassion, like in
this I was in party filled with compassion° of alle min evencristene. And than sawe I
that ilke kinde compassione that man hase of his evencristene with charite, that it is
Criste in him.

SECTION 14

Bot in this I stode,° behaldande generallye, drerelye, and mournande, sayande
thus to oure lorde in my meninge with fulle grete drede: "A, goode lorde, howe
might alle be wele for the grete harme that is comon by sinne to thy creatures?"
And I desired as I durste to hafe sum mare open declaringe wharewith I might be
hesed in this. And to this oure blissede lorde answerde fulle mekelye and with fulle   5
lovelye chere, and shewed me that Adames sinne was the maste harme that ever was
done or ever shalle to the warldes ende. And also he shewed me that this is openly
knawen° in alle haly kyrke in erthe.

Forthermare he lered me that I shulde behalde the gloriouse asethe. For this
aseth-makinge is mare plesande to the blissede godhede and mare wyrshipfulle to   10
mannes salvation withoutene comparison than ever was the sinne of Adam
harmfulle. Thane /fol. 107r/ menes oure blissede lorde° thus in this techinge, that we
shulde take hede to this: "For sen I hafe made wele the maste harme, it is my wille
that thowe knawe therby that I shalle make wele alle that is the lesse."

He gaffe me understandinge of twa parties. The ta party is oure saviour and   15
oure salvation. This blissed party is open and clere and faire and light and
plentious. For alle mankinde that is of goode wille or that shalle be es
comprehended in this partye. Hereto ere we bidden of God and drawen and
consayled and lered inwardlye be the haly gaste and outwarde by haly kyrke by the
same grace. In this wille oure lorde that we be occupied, enjoyande in him for he   20

21 **take of this** partake of this category of truth • 22 **mare spede** greater benefit • 23 **Oure parte is oure lorde** Perhaps from Ps. 119:57 (Vulgate 118): "The Lord is my portion" • 24 **tother** other • 24 **spared** locked away • 24–25 **beside oure salvation** irrelevant to our salvation • 25 **prive consayles** secret counsel. The term is political, not religious, referring to the king's inner circle or to confidential matters of state. In Chaucer's *Man of Law's Tale,* the sultan sends for his "privee conseil" to consult them about his marriage (II [B] 204). The expected word here would be "privetes," which often means "heavenly secrets," as in *The Scale* when the apostle John is "raveshid by love into contemplation of Goddis privetees" (1.17) • 26–27 **it langes to . . . councelle** it is proper to God's royal lordship to hold his secret counsels peacefully, and it is proper to his servants, out of obedience and reverence, not to desire to know his counsels • 28 **for that sum creatures . . . therin** because some people make themselves so anxious about them [God's "prive consayles"] • 28 **seker** certain • 29 **wiste howe mekille** knew how greatly • 29 **for to lefe it** to leave it alone • 30 **wille nathinge witte** desire to know nothing • 30 **bot that** except what • 31 **there charite . . . lorde** their love and desire is ruled according to the will of our Lord. The blessed have nothing to do with speculation. According to *The Pricke,* although wisdom is the first spiritual dowry or joy of the blessed, who "salle knaw and se / Alle that was, and es, and yit salle be," this wisdom is still limited to "that God vouches safe / That any creature knawing may have" (what God allows any creature to have knowledge of) (8187–206) • 32 **awe . . . thame** ought we to desire to be like them • 32–33 **nathinge wille ne desire** neither will nor desire anything • 33–34 **For we er . . . meninge** for from God's perspective we are all the same • 34–35 **we shalle . . . Jhesu** we should only rejoice in our blessed savior, Jesus. This sounds conclusive, but, characteristically, the next section complicates the discussion

[SECTION 15] 2 **sayande** speaking • 2 **comfortabelye** comfortingly • 2 **on this wise** in this way • 2–3 **may . . . can . . . wille . . . shalle** The auxiliary verbs refer, respectively, to God's power to make well ("may"), his wisdom ("can"), his will ("wille"), and his intention ("shalle"). Compare Flete's *Remedy:* "Nothinge to him is impossible. . . . Thinke ferthermore that his might and power may do all, that his wisdome can, and his goodnes wil.

And therfore truste fully that by his goodnes he will save you" (chap. 4, *YW* 2:112) • 4–10 **There he says . . . trinite** The auxiliary verbs correspond to the properties associated with the persons of the Trinity: power (the Father), wisdom (the Son), love (the Holy Spirit). The unity of the Trinity is then deduced from "shalle" (intention), and humanity's participation in God from "thowe shalle se thyselfe" • 8 **thre persones in a trewthe** three persons in one truth. All three persons of the Trinity agree on the truth of "alle shalle be wele." Alludes to the creedal formulation "three persons in one God" • 9 **aninge** uniting • 9 **sayfe** saved • 11 **in this five wordes . . . pees** in fulfilling these five promises God will be immersed in rest and in peace. The "wordes" are fulfilled at the end of time, after the Last Judgment. God's "closing" by the soul is the theme of the final moment of the revelation, Section 22 • 11–12 **has the gastely thirst of Criste ane ende** the spiritual thirst of Christ shall have an end. Refers back to 10.13–15. In *Piers Plowman* B 18.368–70, Christ also anticipates that his thirst for souls can be slaked only at the Judgment: "I faught so, me thursteth yet, for mannes soule sake; / May no drinke me moiste, ne my thurst slake, / Til the vendage [harvest] falle in the vale of Josaphat," that is, as the dead rise up on the Last Day • 12 **luff-langinge** love-longing. Christ cannot suffer lack, but he does suffer "love-longing," the emotion of the lover not yet united with the beloved in Song 2:5 and 5:8: "For I languish for love" (our translation; RSV: "am sick with love") • 13 **to we see . . . domesdaye** until we see that sight (promised at lines 8–10) at the Judgment • 14 **ere yit here . . . the daye** are still in this life and will continue to be until the Last Day. See Matt. 16:28: "Some standing here . . . will not taste death before they see the Son of man coming in his kingdom" • 15 **falinge** failing • 16 **haelye** wholly • 16–17 **shewinge of compassion** The revelation shown in Sections 13–17. See especially 13.65–69 • 17 **that shalle sese atte domesdaye** compassion will cease at the Day of Judgment. Along with Christ's thirst and all his promises, as they come to fulfillment • 17 **reuthe** pity • 19 **suffers nought the ende . . . beste tym** does not allow the end of the world to happen until the best time. According to Hilton, *The Scale* 2.4, this delay in completing the work of salvation "unto the laste day" is "for this skile [reason]: our lord Jhesu of his mercy hath ordained a certain nombre of soulis to salvation" and waits for that number to be fulfilled

enjoyes in us. And the mare plentyouslye that we take of this, with reverence and mekenesse, the mare we deserve thanke of him and the mare spede to oureselfe. And thus maye we saye, enjoyande: "Oure parte is oure lorde."

The tother parte is spared fra us and hidde: that is to saye, alle that is beside oure salvation. For this is oure lordes prive consayles, and it langes to the ryalle lordeship   25
of God for to have his prive consayles° in pees, and it langes to his servantes for obedience and reverence nought to wille witte his councelle. Oure lorde has pite and compassion of us, for that sum creatures makes tham so besy therin. And I am seker if we wiste howe mekille we shulde plese him and ese oureselfe for to lefe it, we walde. The saintes in heven wille nathinge witte bot that oure lorde wille shewe   30
thame, and also there charite and ther desire is rewled efter the wille of oure lorde. And thus awe we to willene to be like to thame.° And than shalle we nathinge wille ne desire botte the wille of oure lorde, as thaye do.° For we er alle ane in Goddes meninge. And here was I lered that we shalle anely enjoye in oure blissid saviour Jhesu, and trist in him for alle thinge.   35

SECTION 15

And thus oure goode lorde answerde to alle the questions and doutes that I might make, sayande fulle comfortabelye on this wise: "I may make alle thinge wele, I can make alle thinge wele, I wille make alle thinge wele, and I shalle make alle thinge wele.° And thowe shalle se it° thyselfe that alle thinge shalle be wele." There he says he "maye," I understande for the fadere; and there he says he "can," I   5
understande for the sone; and ther he says /fol. 107v/ "I wille," I understande for the haly gaste; and there he says "I shalle," I undirstande for the unite of the blissede trinite, thre persones in a trewthe. And there he says "thowe shalle se thyselfe," I understande the aninge of alle mankinde that shalle be sayfe into the blisfulle trinite.   10

And in this five wordes God wille be closed in reste and in pees. And thus has the gastely thirst of Criste ane ende. For this is the gastely thirste: the luff-langinge that lastes° and ever shalle to we see that sight atte domesdaye. For we that shalle be safe, and shalle be Cristes joye and his blisse, ere yit here and shalle be unto the daye. Therefore this is the thirste: the falinge of his blisse, that he has us nought in him als   15
haelye as he shalle thane haffe. Alle this was shewed me in the shewinge of compassion, for that shalle sese atte domesdaye. Thus he hath reuthe and compassion of us, and he has langinge to hafe us, botte his wisdome and his love suffers nought the ende to come to the beste tym.

20 **wordes** clauses • 20 **"I may make . . . wele"** Understand "etcetera" after "wele" • 21–22 **a mighty comforthe . . . come** a great comfort deriving from all the works of our Lord that are yet to come. Hints at a resolution of the problem of sin in the future • 24 **hafe grete rewarde** pay close attention • 24–25 **he wille . . . shalle do** by it ["alle the dedes that he has done"] he wants us to know everything he is going to do. The Day of Judgment is often presented as a time of justice and fear, when Christ returns in wrath to condemn the wicked. According to *The Pricke:* "Alle sal haf gret drede that day, / Bath gude and ille [both the good and the evil], als we here clerks say. / Thar sal be nouther aungel na man / That thay ne sal tremble for drede than [then]" (5368–71). Christ's manifestation of love for humankind in the past, as seen in the revelations described in Sections 2–12, refocuses this picture • 27 **twa manerse** two manners • 27 **ane, I am wele payed . . . noght** one, I am well satisfied that I do not know it. The future tense of "shall" shows that the meaning of "alle shalle be wele" belongs within the category of God's "prive consayles" (14.24–27). "Wele payed" and "gladde and mery" (lines 27–28) also allude to the scene of Christ's "chaunginge of . . . chere" in 11.17–12.5, where Julian is "gladde and mery" even before she is asked "arte thou wele paide?" The joy in that representation of "the dedes that he has done" (line 24) anticipates the joy that is to come at the Day of Judgment • 30 **botte as it langes** except so far as it is relevant

[SECTION 16] 1 **plesance** pleasure • 2 **takes** accept • 2–3 **the prechinge . . . haly kyrke** The topic follows from the last sentence of Section 15: "And that is the techinge of haly kyrke." See also 6 and 13.40–44 on the need to accept the church's teaching and on the adequacy of that teaching, despite the importance attributed to the revelation. Hilton similarly writes of how most souls do no more than "liven mekely in the trouthe of holy chirche" and are nonetheless saved by the church's prayers (*The Scale* 2.10). Lines 1–11 of this section seem designed to reassure readers in this category that their way of life is legitimate and that *A Vision* is merely a practical adjunct to that way of life, rather than a piece of threateningly abstruse theological speculation • 3 **For he is haly kyrke** See 1 Cor. 12:12, 27: "For just as the body is one and has many members, and all the members of the body, though many, are one body, so it is with Christ. . . . Now you are the body of Christ and individually members of

it." In sacramental theology, the church is the body of Christ, affirming this every time its members consume that body at the Mass. To submit to the church is thus to obey the injunctions to "hafe grete rewarde to alle the dedes that he has done" and to leave "oure lordes prive consayles" to him (15.24, 14.25–27) • 3 **grounde** foundation • 4–5 **the mede . . . travailles** the reward for which each true soul labors • 6–7 **And I am seker . . . God** and I am certain that all those who seek in this way (through "the prechinge and the techinge of haly kyrke") will prosper, for they seek God • 8–11 **Alle this that I hafe . . . shalle be wele** Defining *A Vision* in pastoral terms, as a contribution to the spiritual literature of comfort, this passage addresses the work to "men and women" who take "the prechinge and the techinge of haly kyrke" in lines 1–3, despite its visionary genre and truth claims. The passage alludes back to the revelation of "God in a pointe" in 8.9–17, with its perception that God "dose alle that es done," and forward to various passages, especially the denunciation of sin in 23.23–31 • 13 **I desired . . . with hire** I wanted to know, about a certain person whom I loved, how it would turn out for her. Prophetic information about the living or the dead was often part of visionary experience, as Julian's expectations here suggest. Margery Kempe is shown "hy revelations . . . of many soules, sum for to ben saved and sum for to ben dampned," even though she attempts to refuse them (*Book* 1.59) • 14 **I letted myselfe** I stood in my own way • 15 **a frendfulle meen** a friendly intermediary. Perhaps an angelic or saintly voice • 15 **Take it generally** understand the revelation to be about general truths • 16 **as he shewes it to the** in the form in which he shows it to you. Rather than try to pull the revelation in her own direction • 16 **mare** more • 17 **specialle** particular • 18 **therwith** with that • 18 **to knawe** for us to understand • 19 **like in** take pleasure in • 19 **anythinge in specialle** Special or particular truths thus prove to fall into the category of "oure lordes prive consayles" (14.25) • 19–20 **do wisely . . . techinge** act wisely in accordance with this teaching • 20 **nought be glad . . . specialle** not be glad on account of anything specific. Julian has sought the gladness of "specialle" knowledge of the eternal destiny of her friend or relative, the "certaine person" • 20 **desesed** made anxious. For this word, see 10.56 • 22 **I shulde sinne** I must or would sin • 22 **for likinge** because of the pleasure • 23 **entendid nought redely** did not pay immediate attention

And in thies same five wordes before saide—"I may make alle thinge wele"—I   20
understande a mighty comforthe of alle the werkes of oure lorde that ere for to
come. For right as the blissed trinite made alle thinge of nought, right so the same
blissed trinite shalle make wele alle that es nought wele. It is Goddes wille that we
hafe grete rewarde to alle the dedes that he has done. For he wille that we knawe
thereby alle that he shalle do. And that shewed he me in this worde that he saide: 25
"And thowe shalle see thyselfe that alle manere of thinge shalle be wele."

    This I understande in twa manerse: ane, I am wele payed that I wate it noght;
anothere, I am gladde and mery for I shalle witte it. It is Goddes wille that we witte
that alle shalle be wele in generalle. Botte it is nought Goddes wille that we shulde
witte it nowe, botte as it langes to us for the time. And that is the techinge of haly   30
kyrke.

SECTION 16

God shewed me fulle grete plesance that he has in alle men and women that
mightelye and mekelye and wyrshipfullye takes the prechinge and the
techinge of haly kyrke. For he is haly kyrke. For he is the grounde, he is the
substance, /fol. 108r/ he is the techinge, he is the techare, he is the ende, he is the
mede° wharefore ilke trewe saule travailles. And this is knawen° and shalle be   5
knawen to ilke saule to whame the haly gaste declares it. And I am seker that alle tho
that sekes thus shalle spede, for thay seke God.

    Alle this that I hafe nowe saide, and mare that I shalle saye efter, es comforthinge
againe sinne. For first, when I sawe that God does alle that es done, I sawe nought
sinne. And than sawe I that alle is wele. Bot when God shewed me sinne, than saide   10
he: "Alle shalle be wele."

    And when God allemightye hadde shewed me plentyouslye and fully of his
goodnesse, I desired of a certaine person that I loved howe it shulde be with hire.
And in this desire I letted myselfe, for I was noght taught in this time. And than was
I answerde in my reson, als it ware be a frendfulle meen:° "Take it generally, and   15
behalde the curtaysy of thy lorde God as he shewes it to the. For it is mare
worshippe to God to behalde him in alle than in any specialle thinge." I assented,
and therwith I lered that it is mare wyrshippe to God to knawe alle thinge in
generalle than to like in anythinge in specialle. And if I shulde do wisely efter this
techinge, I shulde nought be glad for nathinge in specialle, na desesed for na manere   20
of thinge, for alle shalle be wele.

    God brought to my minde that I shulde sinne. And for likinge that I hadde in
behaldinge of him, I entendid nought redely to that shewinge. And oure lorde fulle

24 **abayde to I walde entende** waited until I was prepared to pay attention

[SECTION 17] 1 **If alle oure lorde** although our Lord •
1 **I shulde sinne** See 16.22 • 1 **be me allayn . . . alle** the
revelation that I individually must sin must be interpreted to apply to everyone • 2 **I consayved a softe
drede** I experienced a quiet fear • 2–3 **I kepe the fulle
sekerly** I protect you in complete security. The final
statement made in this phase of the revelation, although
it reverberates through the whole of Sections 17–18 and
beyond • 3–4 **gastely kepinge** spiritual protection •
5 **right so . . . shewed to me** just so was the comfort
revealed to me. As meant for all, not just Julian • 7 **alle
a saule** all a single soul. God's dealings with Julian's soul
imply his dealings with all • 8–11 **And in ilke . . . blissed
trinite** and in each soul that will be saved is a principle
of goodness (or godliness) that never consented to sin
and never will. For just as there is a bestial will in the
lower part of the soul that cannot will anything good,
even so there is a good (or godly) will in the higher part
that cannot will anything evil (any more than can the
persons of the blessed Trinity), but always good.
"Bestely" here may be merely a synonym for "impure,"
but the human soul was thought to include an "animal
soul," whose mode was instinctive rather than rational
or ethical; "goodely" may be a spelling of "godly," the
word used in the parallel passage of *A Revelation*: the
two words often appear interchangeable in Middle English. The claim for the absolute goodness of the soul
made here is one of *A Vision*'s few declarations of a theological doctrine, related in some sense to Christ's
promise "I kepe the fulle sekerly." *The Remedy* has a similar passage on the devout soul's resistance to sin: "Every
man and woman hath two willes, a good will and an
evil. The evil will cometh of sensualite, the whiche is
ever inclininge downwarde to sinne. And the good will
cometh of grace, which alweye stireth the soule upwarde
to all goodnes. . . . Though ye . . . be enclined to sensualite, yet ye do it not, ne consent therto, but it is the sensualite that doth it in you. And your good will abideth in
you still unbroken" (chap. 5, *YW* 2:114) • 11–14 **And this
shewed . . . face** Julian "sees" the essential purity of part
of the soul "in" the fact that God loves the saved
"als wele" now as he will in heaven • 12 **in the holehed
of luffe** by means of the wholeness of the love. If there
were no good will in the soul in this life, God's love for
us now would not be the same as his love for the saved •
15 **sin is na shame . . . man** sin is not a cause of humiliation but does a person honor. A paradox derived from "I
kepe the fulle sekerly" that is almost as startling as the

doctrine of the "goodely wille" in lines 8–14. *The Pricke*
8297–364, following Anselm, argues that the saved in
heaven remember their sins without shame: "Na mare
than Petre now has shame / Of that, that he forsoke our
Lord by name; / Or Mary Maudelayne now has of hir
sin / That sho [she] som time delited in" (8333–36). This
passage's introduction of the idea of sin as "wirshippe"
takes this argument a significant step further • 16–17 **than
com verrayly to my minde** then came truly to my
mind • 17 **David . . . the Maudelayn** All these holy figures sinned: David with Bathsheba (2 Sam. 11–12), Peter
by denying Christ (Matt. 26:69–75), Paul by persecuting
Christians before his conversion (Acts 8–9, under the
name Saul), Thomas (supposed founder of the Nestorian church in India) by doubting the Resurrection
(John 20:19–29), Mary Magdalene (according to tradition) by an early life as a prostitute (Luke 7:36–50) •
17–18 **howe thaye er knawen . . . wirshippe** how they are
known by the earthly church so that their sins con-
tribute to their honor. Good comes from all the sins
mentioned, while the legends of these sinner saints in
collections like the *South English Legendary* contributes
to their earthly reputation • 18–19 **it is to tham no shame**
Compare *The Pricke* 8333–36, cited in the sidenote to line
15 above • 19 **thare** in heaven • 20 **takeninge** significance • 21 **theder** there, to heaven • 22 **Sin is the
sharpeste scourge** The notion that sin does the sinner
honor in heaven is immediately qualified by discussion
of the damage sin does, as penitential language takes
the place of the language of remedy and comfort •
22 **whilke** which • 23 **forbettes** beats down. "For" is an
intensifier • 23 **forbrekes tham** breaks them to pieces •
23–24 **noghtes thamselfe** reduces them to nothing •
24–25 **sa fareforth . . . into helle** so much that it seems to
him he is only worthy to sink, as it were, into hell •
25 **contrition** sorrow for sin. One of the wounds Julian
prays for at the outset, in 1.40 • 25 **touching** inspiration • 26 **bitternesse** bitterness of sin • 27 **hile** heal •
27 **quiken** revive • 27 **turned** converted • 28–29 **wilfully . . . shame** The characteristics of true confession in
part 5 of *Ancrene Wisse* include all these items: "Confession must be accusing, bitter with sorrow . . . naked . . .
full of shame . . . true and willing" (159–60) • 28 **nakedlye** plainly • 29–30 **defouled . . . God** defiled the lovely
image of God in his soul. A common understanding of
sin. *The Scale* 1.52 claims that an image of sin replaces
the image of God (see Gen. 1:27) in the fallen soul •
30–31 **Than he takes . . . haly kyrke** then, as enjoined by
his confessor, he performs the penance that is grounded
in holy church for every sin. Confessors consulted lists
of penances to be imposed for sins

curtayslye abayde to I walde entende. And than oure lorde brought to minde with
my sinnes the sinne of alle mine evencristen, alle in generalle and nathinge in   25
specialle.

SECTION 17

If alle oure lorde shewed me that I shulde sinne, be me allayn I understode alle. In
this, I consayved a softe drede. And to this oure lorde answerde me thus: "I kepe
the fulle sekerly." This worde was saide to me with mare love and sekernes of gastely
kepinge than I can or maye telle. For as it was be- /fol. 108v/ fore shewed to me that I
shulde sinne, right so was the comfort shewed to me: sekernesse of kepinge for alle   5
mine evencristen. What may make me mare to luff mine evencristen° than to see in
God that he loves alle that shalle be safe, as it ware alle a saule?

And in ilke saule that shalle be sayfe is a goodely wille that never assented to
sinne, na never shalle. For as ther is a bestely wille in the nethere party that maye
wille na goode, so is thare a goodely wille in the over partye that maye wille nane   10
eville, botte ever goode, na mare than the persones of the blissed trinite. And this
shewed oure lorde me in the holehed of luffe that we stande in, in his sight:° ya, that
he luffes us nowe als wele whiles we ere here as he shalle do when we ere thare
before his blissed face.

Also God shewed me that sin is na shame, bot wirshippe to man. For in this   15
sight min understandinge was lifted up into heven, and than com verrayly to my
minde David, Peter and Paule, Thomas of Inde and the Maudelayn: howe thaye er
knawen in the kyrke of erth with thare sinnes to thayre wirshippe. And it is to tham
no shame that thay hafe sinned, no mare it is in the blisse of heven. For thare, the
takeninge of sinne is turned into wirshippe. Right so oure lorde God shewed me   20
tham in ensampille of alle othere that shalle cum theder.

Sin is the sharpeste scourge that any chosen saule maye be bette with, whilke
scourge it alle forbettes man and woman, and alle forbrekes tham, and noghtes
thamselfe° in thare awne sight, sa fareforth that him thinke that he is noght worthy
bot as it ware to sinke into helle. Botte when contrition takes him be the touchinge   25
of the haly gaste, than turnes the bitternesse° into hope of Goddes mercye. And than
beginnes his woundes to hile and the saule to quiken, turned in to the life of haly
kyrke. The haly gaste leddes him to confession, wilfully to shewe his sinnes, nakedlye
and trewly, with grete sorowe and grete shame that he hase swa defouled the faire
image of God. Than he takes penance for ilke a sine, enjeuned be his domesman,   30
that is grounded in haly kyrke be the techinge of the haly gaste.

32 **Be this medicin . . . heled** every sinful soul must be healed by this medicine. Pastoral texts such as *Ancrene Wisse* often describe remedies for sin as medicines • 33 **dedely in the selfe** mortal in their effect on the self. Penitential theory distinguished venial and mortal sin, the first punished in purgatory, the second (if unrepented) in hell • 33 **Though he be heled** if he ("everilke sinfulle saule") is healed • 34 **nought** not at all • 34 **on contrarye wise** in the opposite way • 34–35 **as it es punished here** to the same extent that it is punished in this life • 36–37 **that wille . . . his travaile** who desires that nobody who comes there should lose his labor • 37 **mede** reward • 40 **ilke kinde saule** every natural soul • 40–41 **the lathere es him for to sinne** the more unwilling he is to sin

[SECTION 18] 1–3 **if thowe be stirred . . . enmy** Despite 17.39–41. See Rom. 6.1–2: "Are we to continue in sin that grace may abound? By no means!" In *The Remedy*, after describing the power of the divine mercy, Flete adds a similar warning: "God forbede . . . that ony creature be the more . . . bolde to sinne wilfully [on purpose]. For in so moche [because] the mercy of God is so large [generous] we ought to be the more besy and diligent to love and praise him" (chap. 4, *YW* 2:113) • 1 **Sen this is sothe** since this is true • 2 **mare mede** greater reward • 2 **dispice** despise • 4 **to he be amended** until he has done penance • 4 **as of dedely sinne** as for a mortal sin • 4–5 **For if . . . sinne** for if (on the one hand) all the pain in hell and purgatory and on earth—including death and other pains—were laid before me and (on the other hand) sin. A hyperbolic statement designed to shock the reader out of the complacency the previous sections may have induced • 6 **lever chese** rather choose • 6–7 **so mekille for to hate** so much to be hated • 7 **maye be likened . . . sin** cannot be compared to any pain that is not sin. Sin is categorically different from everything else in the universe and can be "likened" only to itself • 8–9 **Sinne es . . . no liking** sin is neither a deed nor a pleasure. Partly modeled on 8.11–19, in which "God dothe alle thinge," so that sin cannot be a "deed." That sin also cannot be a "liking" is reinforced by the next sentence, which makes it synonymous with "paine" • 9 **cheses wilfully** deliberately chooses • 9 **sinne—that is, paine** sin—that is, torment. "Paine" could mean either suffering in general or eternal damnation • 9 **as fore his God** in preference to his God • 9–10 **atte the ende he hase right nought** at the end he has absolutely nothing. "Right nought" again alludes to 8.16, "sinne is nought" • 10 **herdeste helle** worst kind of hell • 11 **botte in sinne** except in a state of sin • 12 **mighty . . . witty . . . willy** powerful, wise, desiring. The properties of the Trinity: power, wisdom, love. The whole Trinity joins in the salvation of humankind.

See 15.4–10 • 13 **grounde of alle . . . men** the foundation of all the laws of Christian people. Christ is the basis of the "new law" that, in Christian belief, supersedes the "old law" God gave the Jews • 13–14 **do goode againes eville** do good in return for evil. See Matt. 5:38–48, a passage that explicitly contrasts the old law and the new. See also Luke 6:27: "Love your enemies, do good to those who hate you." Having taught this lesson, Christ can be trusted to follow it himself • 14 **he es himselfe this charite** See 1 John 4:8 and 16: "God is love." Much of this chapter is relevant here, as earlier in Section 6 • 14–15 **does to us . . . to do** does to us as he teaches us to do to others. See Matt. 7:12: "So whatever you wish that men would do to you, do so to them; for this is the law and the prophets" • 15–16 **anehede of endeles luffe . . . evencristen** the unity of eternal love for ourselves and for our fellow Christians. See 6.19–21 • 16–17 **Na mare . . . evencristen** no more than Christ's love for us is broken because of our sin, no more does he desire that our love for ourselves or for our fellow Christians be broken. Knowledge of sin is not to lead to despair or hatred of others • 18 **botte nakedlye hate sinne . . . loves it** but we should openly hate sin and endlessly love the soul just as God loves it. *The Scale* 1.65 stresses the difficulty of keeping this distinction clear: "It is a greet maistrye [feat] for a man to kunne love [know how to love] his evencristene in charite and wisely hate the sinne of him and love the man" • 19 **that "he kepes us fulle sekerlye."** See 17.2–3

[SECTION 19] 1 **shewed me for prayers** gave me a revelation concerning prayers. The new topic follows from the emphasis on the constructive role of sin in Sections 17–18. Lines 1–11 outline traditional positions on prayer, amplifying Julian's experience and endorsing church teaching; lines 12–16 describe a problem in prayer; and the rest of the section shows how the revelation addresses that problem • 1 **conditions** characteristics • 1–2 **tham that prayes** those who pray • 2 **after that . . . myselfe** according to how I have felt myself • 2–4 **Ane es . . . wirshippe** one characteristic is that they do not wish to pray for just anything that could come to pass, but only for that thing that is God's will and brings him honor. *Contemplations of the Love and Dread of God* likewise instructs: "Put all thy will into Goddes will, in the ende of thy prayer desiringe evermore . . . his will to be fulfilled and nothinge thy will" (chap. U, "What Profit Is in Prayer," *YW* 2:93). See Julian's prayer in 1.32–34 • 4 **sette tham . . . continually** set themselves powerfully and continuously. The treatise *Pore Caitif* describes one of the eight "needful things" in prayer as "abiding in preyer: that no man stinte to preye [stop praying] . . . but be he [but let him be] fervent and perseveraunt" (95)

Be this medicin behoves everilke sinfulle saule be heled, and namlye of sinnes that ere dedely in the selfe. */fol. 109r/* Though he be heled, his woundes er sene before God nought as woundes bot as wyrshippes. And so on contrarye wise, as it es punished here with sorowe and with penance, it shalle be rewarded in heven be the curtayse love of oure lorde God alle mightye, that wille that nane that comes thare lese his travaile. That mede that we salle resayfe thare salle nought be litelle, bot it shalle be hy, gloriouse, and wirshipfulle. And so shalle alle shame turne into wyrshippe and into mare joye. And I am sekere be min awne felinge, the mare that ilke kinde saule sees this in the kinde and curtayse love of God, the lathere es him for to sinne.

SECTION 18

Bot if thowe be stirred to saye or to thinke, "Sen this is sothe, than ware it goode for to sinne for to hafe the mare mede," beware of this stirringe and dispice it, for it is of the enmy. For whate saule that wilfully takes this stirringe, he maye never be safe to he be amended as of dedely sinne. For if it ware laide before me, alle the paine that is in helle and in purgatorye and in erth—dede and othere—and sinne, I had lever chese alle that paine than sinne. For sinne is so vile and so mekille for to hate that it maye be likened to na paine whilke paine es nought sin. For alle thinge is goode botte sinne, and nathinge is wikked botte sinne. Sinne es nowthere deed no liking. Botte when a saule cheses wilfully sinne—that is, paine—as fore his God, atte the ende he hase right nought. That paine thinke me the herdeste helle, for he hase nought his God: in alle paines a saule may hafe God botte in sinne.

And als mighty and als witty as God is for to safe man, als willy he is. For Criste himselfe is grounde of alle the lawe of cristen men, and he has taught us to do goode againes eville. Here may we see that he es himselfe this charite, and does to us as he teches us to do. For he wille that we be like to him in anehede of endeles luffe to oureselfe and to oure evencristen. Na mare than his love es broken to us for oure sinne, na mare wille he that oure love be broken to oureselfe ne to oure evencristen, botte nakedlye hate sinne, and endeleslye love the saule as God loves it. For this worde that God saide es ane endelesse comforth: that "he kepes us fulle sekerlye."°

SECTION 19

After this, oure lorde shewed me for° prayers. I sawe two conditions in tham that prayes, after that I hafe feled in myselfe. Ane */fol. 109v/* es, thaye wille nought praye for nathinge that may be, botte that thinge that es Goddes wille and his wirshippe. Anothere is that thay sette tham mightelye and continuely to beseke that

6 in this . . . the same in this revelation our Lord taught me what holy church taught me • **7 faith, hope, and charite** The theological virtues. See 1 Cor. 13.13 • **7 in this** in the state of faith, hope, and charity • **8 Pater noster, Ave, and Crede** the Lord's Prayer, the Hail Mary, and the Creed. The three prayers all Christians were supposed to know • **9 fore alle oure evencristen . . . men** for all our fellow Christians and for every kind of person. Prayer extends outward both to all Christian people and to the whole world. Margery Kempe sometimes prayed an hour each for her own sins, for "the sinne of the pepil . . . for the soules in purgatory . . . for hem in mischefe, in poverte, er in any disese . . . for Jewes, Sarasines, and alle fals heretikes" (*Book* 1.57) • **9 that Godes wille es** that God's will be done. A paraphrase of "thy will be done," the most fundamental of all the petitions in the Lord's Prayer, to which all prayer can be reduced. See 2.18–19 • **11 awe . . . oureselfe** ought to desire for ourselves • **12 ofttimes . . . nought fulle** often our trust is not complete. *Pore Caitif* describes "ful trist and stidfast hope in him that me preyeth to" as the seventh "needful thing" in prayer, quoting James 1:5–8: "He that doutith is liik the flood of the see" (95) • **12 sekare** sure • **13 as us thinke for oure unworthinesse** on account of our unworthiness, as we think • **13–14 fore we fele right nought** because we feel nothing at all • **14 als barayne and als drye** as barren and as dry. See 21.4 • **15 And thus . . . waykenesse** and so, as we imagine, our foolishness is the reason for our weakness. Subjectively, it seems that the weakness of prayer is caused by "foly," here synonymous with "unworthinesse" (line 13) • **17 sodaynlye** suddenly • **17 mightely and lifely** powerfully and vividly • **18 comfortande** comforting • **18 waykenesse in prayers** The key phrase of this section. See line 28 • **18–19 I am . . . besekinge** I am the foundation of your prayer • **19 sene** next • **20 and thowe beseke it!** and you ask for it! • **21 in the firste reson** in the first clause of Christ's promise. Analysis of the passage divides it into six "resons," or clauses • **23 thare . . . thare** where . . . there • **26 sobere undertakinge** serious rebuke. The next sentence explains why • **26–27 For we tryste . . . shulde do** for we do not trust as powerfully as we ought to do. Given the "sobere undertakinge" that guarantees that prayer will be answered • **27–29 For the**

cause . . . prayers for the intention of the aforementioned "reasons" (the six clauses of Christ's promise) is to make us powerful against weakness in our prayers • **30 therto** to prayer • **31 For he wille . . . hafe oure prayere** for he wants us to be certain that we will obtain our prayer. According to *The Mirror*, "We shul haven foure thinges in orison [prayer]," all taught by the first clause of the Lord's Prayer: "Parfit love anentes him that we preyeth to [perfect love toward him to whom we are praying]; and certeyn hope to haven [obtain] that we asken; and studefast [steadfast] beleeve in whom that we hopen [in the one we trust]; and sothfast mekenes [true humility]" ("Sevene Preyeres of the Pater Noster," *YW* 1:252) • **32 Prayer pleses man with himselfe** prayer makes a person pleased with himself. The first of the two reasons why "prayer pleses God" (lines 31–32) • **33 strife and travaile** struggle and labor • **33 Prayer anes the saule to God** prayer unites the soul to God. The second of the two reasons • **34 be ever like . . . substance** is always in the likeness of God in its essential nature and substance. This view of the state of the fallen soul is related to Section 17's notion of the "goodely wille" • **34–35 unlike in condition** unlike God in its actual state • **35 thurgh sin of mannes party** because of sin on humanity's side. "Ceesing of sinne and leving to do yvel" is the first "needful thing" in prayer in *Pore Caitif*: "For medicin helith not while the arwhed [arrowhead] is in the fleish" (93) • **35–36 Than makes prayer . . . as God wille** prayer makes the soul like God when the soul wills as God wills. The Lord's Prayer's "thy will be done" is thus the soul's union with God • **37 tryste** trust • **38 For alle thinge . . . prayed it** for everything that is done would still be done even if we never prayed it. This important assertion perhaps follows from the assertion in 8.11–19 that "God doth alle thinge," combined with the promise "I kepe the fulle sekerly" in 17.2–3 • **39 partiners of** partners in. A "partiner" is an accomplice in an action or a member of an association • **40 therfore he stirres . . . do** for this reason (to make us partners with him) he moves us to pray for what he wants us to do • **40 for whate** for which • **41 that we hafe of his gifte** which we have because he gives them to us • **42 And thou beseke it!** See 19.20

thinge that es his wille and his wirshippe. And that es as I hafe understandide be the   5
techinge of haly kyrke. For in this oure lorde lered me the same: to hafe of Goddes
gifte faith, hope, and charite, and kepe us therein to oure lives ende. And in this we
say Pater noster, Ave, and Crede with devotion, as God wille giffe it. And thus we
praye fore alle oure evencristen and for alle manere of men, that Godes° wille es. For
we walde that alle maner of men and women ware in the same vertu and grace that   10
we awe to desire to oureselfe.

    Botte yit in alle this ofttimes oure triste is nought fulle. For we ere nought sekare
that God almighty heres us, as us thinke for oure unworthinesse, and fore we fele
right nought. Fore we ere als barayne and als drye oftimes efter oure prayers as we
ware before. And thus, in oure felinge, oure foly es cause of oure waykenesse. For   15
thus hafe I felede in myselfe.

    And alle this brought oure lorde sodaynlye to my minde, and mightely and lifely,
and comfortande me againes this maner of waykenesse in prayers, and saide: "I am
grounde of thy besekinge. First it is my wille that thowe hafe it, and sene I make the
to will it, and sene I make the to beseke it—and thowe beseke it!° Howe shulde it   20
than be that thowe shulde nought hafe thy besekinge?" And thus in the firste reson,
with the thre that folows eftere, oure lorde shewed a mighty comfort. And the
fifth°—thare he says, "And thowe beseke it!"°—thare he shewes fulle grete plesance
and endelese mede that he wille giffe us for oure besekinge. And in the sixth°
reson—thare he sais, "Howe shulde it than be that thowe shulde noght hafe thy   25
besekinge?"—thare he shewes a sobere undertakinge. For we tryste nought als
mightelye als we shulde do. Thus wille oure lorde that we bath praye and triste. For
the cause of the resones beforsaide is to make us mighty againes waiknesse in oure
prayers.

    For it is Goddis wille that we pray, and therto he stirres us in thies wordes   30
beforsaide. For he wille that we be sekere to hafe oure prayere. For prayer pleses
God. Prayer pleses man with himselfe, and makes him sobure and meke that
beforehand /fol. 110r/ was in strife and travaile. Prayer anes the saule to God. For
though the saule be ever like God in kinde and in substance, it is oft unlike in
condition, thurgh sin of mannes party. Than makes prayer the saule like unto God   35
when the saule wille as God wille, and than es it like to God in condition as it es in
kinde. And thus he teches us to pray and mightely tryste that we shalle hafe that we
praye fore. For alle thinge that es done shulde be done though we never prayed it.
Botte the luff of God es so mekille that he haldes us partiners of his goode deede.

    And therfore he stirres us to praye that him likes to do, for whate prayere or   40
goode wille, that we hafe of his gifte, he wille rewarde us and gife us endelese mede.
And this was shewed me in this worde: "And thou beseke it!" In this worde, God

43 **so . . . so** such . . . such • 43 **plesance** See 19.23 • 43–44 **as if he ware mekille behaldene to us** as if he were much indebted to us • 44 **alle if it es he** although it is he • 44–45 **And for that . . . as if he saide** and because we diligently ask him to do the thing he wants to do, it is as if he were saying • 47 **makes prayere accorde** prayer reconciles. This phrase, "makes accorde," often used in political contexts, signals a gradual shift in the section from the topic of prayer to that of the state of the sinful soul. See lines 56–66 • 48 **hamelye with God** intimate with God. Like Julian in the revelation. See 3.16–17 • 50 **to hafe allewaye this welle . . . for comforth** to have this always well in my mind for comfort. It is just possible that "welle" here is the noun "well"—so that the clause means "to have this always in my mind for comfort, like a well"—only no similar imagery appears elsewhere in *A Vision,* and it is unclear why Julian, during the course of her revelation, would think of the needlessness of prayer as a "well" • 51 **we hafe that we desire** we have what we desire • 51, 52 **nedes us** we need • 52–53 **for failinge . . . to Jhesu** because of our weakness and to prepare ourselves for Jesus. According to *The Chastising,* in its treatment of the "play" of Christ's presence and absence, "in his absence we bien al cold and drye . . . the wreched saule sodanly is chaunged and made ful hevy and ful of sorwe and care" (98) • 53 **tempted, trubled** Feelings stirred up by "false drede," according to 25.22–23 • 53 **lefte to itselfe** See 9.21 • 53–54 **be unreste** by distress. See 4:43: "For he is verraye reste" • 54 **himselfe** itself • 54 **souple** compliant • 54 **boxsom** obedient • 55 **Bot he . . . souple to him** but by no kind of prayer does the soul make God compliant to him. In theory, Middle English writers on prayer would have agreed with this, but in practice only an argument like the one made here gives clear justification for such a view. *Pore Caitif* notes comfortably that God "wol heere hise frendis and graunte hem al resonable thing that they asken of him" (92) • 55 **ylike** alike • 56–57 **unmightye . . . unwise . . . unluffande** weak . . . foolish . . . unable to love. All the

powers of the soul are occluded by sin • 57–58 **The maste mischefe . . . alle this** the greatest trouble he has is his blindness, because he does not perceive all of this. *The Remedy* notes that many "cannot nor will not in time of temptation se or perceive" comfort, "but have a dredefulnes and a sorines [fear and depression] in themselfe" (chap. 6, *YW* 2:116) • 58 **the hale luffe** all the love • 59 **ever is ane** is always the same • 59 **sight to himselfe** a sight of himself • 59–60 **And than wenes . . . sinne** and then he imagines that God is angry with him on account of his sin. Rather than at the sin, as is really the case. According to *Pore Caitif,* "God hatith . . . nothing but sinne and wickidnesse: nethir soule ne body, ne non othir thing that man hath" (87) • 60–61 **than is he stirred . . . wrathe of God** then is he moved to sorrow for sin and, through confession and other good works, to quench the anger of God • 61–62 **unto the time he finde** until he finds • 63 **soth true** • 63 **in the sight of saule** from the soul's perspective • 64 **turnede into the behaldinge of the saule** turned so that he contemplates the soul. Rather than the soul's sinfulness • 68 **custumabille** customary • 68 **be the techinge** according to the teaching

[SECTION 20] 1–6 **Before this time . . . beselye lange** The longing for death described here is a common feature of meditative writing from Paul on. See Phil. 1:23: "My desire is to depart and be with Christ, for that is far better" • 1–2 **desired of Goddes gifte . . . warlde** desired to be delivered from the world by God's gift. See 1.29: "I desirede sone to be with my God" • 2 **for I shulde** so that I would • 3 **hope sikerlye** confidently hope • 4 **wa** woe • 4 **here** on earth • 4 **wele** happiness • 4 **blissede beinge** blessed existence • 4 **if** even if • 4 **thare** in heaven • 6 **to mourne . . . lange** to mourn and anxiously desire. Compare Julian's state as she questions the meaning of sin in 13.38–39 • 8 **fra** from • 8 **dissese** discomfort • 9 **to thy mede** as your reward

shewed me so grete plesance and so grete likinge as if he ware mekille behaldene to
us for ilke goode dede that we do, alle if it es he that does it. And for that we beseke
besily to do that thinge that him likes, as if he saide: "Whate might thowe plese me   45
mare than to bisike bisily, wisely, and wilfullye to do that thinge that I wille do?"

 And thus makes prayere accorde betwix God and mannes saule. For whate time
that mannes saule es hamelye with God, him nedes nought to praye, botte behalde
reverentlye whate he says. For in alle this time that this was shewed me I was noght
stirred to praye, botte to hafe allewaye this welle in my minde for comforth: that   50
when we see God we hafe that we desire, and than nedes us nought to praye. Botte
when we se nought God, than nedes us to pray for failinge and for habelinge of
oureselfe to Jhesu. For when a saule es tempted, trubled, and lefte to itselfe be
unreste, than es it time to pray and to make himselfe souple° and boxsom to God.
Bot he be na maner of prayer° makes God souple to him. For he is ever ylike in love.   55
Botte in the time that man is in sinne, he is so unmightye, so unwise, and so
unluffande that he can nought love God ne himselfe. The maste mischefe that he
hase es blindnesse, for he sees nought alle this. Than the hale luffe of God
allemighty, that ever is ane, giffes him sight /fol. 110v/ to himselfe. And than wenes he
that God ware wrathe with him for his sinne. And than is he stirred to contrition   60
and be confession and othere goode dedes to slake the wrathe of God, unto the time
he finde a reste in saule and softnesse in conscience. And than him thinke that God
hase forgiffen his sinnes, and it es soth. And than is God, in the sight of saule,
turnede into the behaldinge of the saule, as if it had bene in paine or in preson,
sayande thus: "I am gladde that thowe erte comen to reste, for I hafe ever loved the   65
and nowe loves the, and thowe me."

 And thus with prayers as I hafe before saide, and with othere goode werkes that
ere custumabille° be the techinge of haly kyrke, is the saule aned to God.

SECTION 20

Before this time I hadde ofte grete langinge, and desired of Goddes gifte to be
delivered of this warlde and of this life, for I shulde be with my God in blisse
whare I hope sikerlye thurgh his mercye to be withouten ende. For oftetimes I
behelde the wa that is here and the wele and the blissede beinge thare. And if thare
hadde bene na pain in erthe bot the absence of oure lorde God, methought sumtime   5
it ware mare than I might bere. And this made me to mourne and beselye lange.

 Than God saide to me for patience and for sufferance thus: "Sudanly thowe
shalle be takene fra alle thy paine, fra alle thy sicknesse,° fra alle thy dissese, and fra
alle thy wa. And thowe shalle comen up aboven, and thowe shalle hafe me to thy mede,

10 **fulfillede** filled full • 10–12 **thowe shalle never hafe . . . withouten ende** you shall never have any kind of pain, any kind of sickness, any kind of displeasure, any frustration of your desire, but always joy and eternal bliss. The many double negatives here ("never . . . na . . . na . . . na . . . na . . .") increase the forcefulness of the promise. *The Pricke* writes similarly of the "dowries," or joys, of the saved: "The fift blis, als clerkes wate [know] wele, / Es hele [health] that the saved bodyse salle fele, / Withouten seknes or grevaunce, / Or angre, or paine, or penaunce"; "And what-swa [whatever] thay wille think in thought, / Alle salle be at thair wille thare wroght [everything shall be done as they want it]"; "The sevend blis es joy parfite. . . . For thare salle be mare sere joyes [there will be more different joys] than / Than ever couth noumbre erthly man [than anyone on earth could count]" (8007–10; 8493–94; 8601, 8615–16) • 12–13 **Whate shulde . . . awhile** why then should it grieve you to be patient for a while • 13 **my wirshippe** for my honor • 14 **reson** clause • 14–15 **God rewardes . . . time** God rewards people for the patience that they exercise in waiting on God's desire during their lifetime • 15–17 **man lengthes . . . passing** people stretch their patience out over the whole time they are alive, because of their ignorance about the time of their death. This and the next sentences are full of commonplaces. In Rolle's *Form*, the second of four things the contemplative must keep in mind is "uncertente of oure ending. For we wate [know] never when we sal die, ne whare we sal die, ne how we sal die, ne whider we sal ga [where we will go] when we er dede. And . . . God wil that this be uncertain til us: for he will that we be ay redy to die" (chap. 4, *YW* 1:19) • 18 **overe** during • 18–19 **God wille . . . taken** Rolle writes: "God . . . wol that we be ever redy to dey" • 19 **atte the pointe to be taken** at the point of being taken from this world • 19–20 **For alle this life . . . bot a pointe** for all this life in this suffering that we have here is no more than an instant. In *The Form*, the first of the four things the contemplative must keep in mind is: "The mesur of thy lif here, that sa short es that unnethis es it oght [that it is scarcely anything]. For we live bot in a point, that es the leste thing that may be. And sothely [truly] oure life es les [is less] than a point, if we liken it to the life that lastes ay [eternally]" (chap. 4, *YW* 1:19) Contrast 8.8, where "pointe" primarily means "point in space" • 22 **therfore** this is why • 23 **sen** since • 23 **take** understand • 23 **behestes** commands • 24 **als largelye and als mightelye** as comprehensively and powerfully • 25 **oure abidinge and oure desese** the lingering and distress of our lives • 25–26 **als lightelye as we may take tham** as cheerfully as we are able to take them. Continues the teaching of Section 19 on the need to move beyond sorrow and anxiety to ease and rest • 26–27 **the lesse price . . . luff** the less we set store by them, out of love. This clause parallels the previous one,

rather than opposes it • 29–30 **In this blissed revelation . . . he is chosene** After the several references to "thame that shalle be safe" (e.g., 6.45), which is possible to read as arguing a strongly predestinarian position, it is stated here that the chosen soul is anyone who chooses God. The soul's choice has also been emphasized in 18.9–10, in the account of the soul who "cheses wilfully sinne—that is, paine—as fore his God," but in this context of comfort the need is to assert the equal efficacy of the opposite choice • 31 **als sekere in tryste . . . heven** as certain in our trust of the bliss of heaven. See 1.17–18 • 32 **in sekernesse . . . thare** in certainty when we are there. "Sekernesse" is another "dowry" of the blessed, according to *The Pricke*: "For thay salle be thare siker and certaine / To have endeles joy, and nevermare paine" (8559–60) • 33–34 **the bettere likes him** the better it pleases him • 34–35 **For I am seker . . . done for me** for I am confident that if there had been nobody else except me who was to be saved, God would have done all he has done just for me. The obverse of the work's frequent injunctions not to understand the revelation or its teaching as for a specific individual. A remedy against anxiety and despair, as lines 38–45 make clear. See Section 7, where the principle is established • 37 **for him** for that person alone • 38 **thinke me** I think • 38–39 **nought drede bot him** fear nothing except him • 40 **loken in oure frendes hande** locked in our friend's hand. A near repetition of 8.41. See Rev. 20:1–2. The weakness of the devil is one of the remedies against despair in *The Chastising*: "The fiende is so fieble of himself that he hath no power to overcome a mans soule, but a man wil himself [unless a person himself wants it so]" (153) • 40 **wate sekerly this** knows this for sure • 41–42 **alle othere dredes . . . imaginations** attribute all other kinds of fear to the passions and bodily disease and fantasies. *The Chastising* describes the many fears to which contemplatives are subject, including the fear that Christ's Passion will not be efficacious in one's own case. Those "travelid in imaginatiouns [attacked by fantasies] and thoughtis of predestinatioun and of the prescience of God [divine foreknowledge of the soul's damnation]" are most inclined to despair (156) • 42–44 **And therfore . . . that he feles** and so if someone should be in so much pain, in so much woe, and in so much anxiety that it seems to him he can think about absolutely nothing except the state he is in or what he is feeling. Anticipates, and forgives in advance, Julian's confused behavior in Section 21 • 45 **passe lightlye overe** move cheerfully on • 45 **God wille be knawen** God wants to be known. Alludes to 4.43–46: "God wille be knawen, and him likes that we reste us in him. For alle that ar benethe him suffices nought to us. And this is the cause why that na saule is restede to it be noghthed of alle that es made"

and thowe shalle be fulfillede of joye and blisse. And thowe shalle never hafe na   10
maner of paine, na maner of sekenes, na maner of mislikinge, na wantinge of wille,
botte ever joye and blisse withouten ende. Whate shulde it than greve the to suffer
awhile, sen it is my wille and my wirshippe?"

Also in this reson, "Sudanly thou shalle be taken," I sawe how God rewardes man
of the patience that he has in abidinge of Goddes wille in his time, and that man   15
lengthes his patience overe the time of his liffinge, for unknawinge of his time of
passinge. This is a grete profitte. For if a man knewe his time, he shulde noght hafe
patience overe that time. Also God wille that whiles the saule es in the bodye, that it
semen to itselfe that it es ever atte the pointe to be taken. For alle this /fol. 111r/ life in
this langoure that we hafe here is bot a pointe, and when we ere takene sodaynly   20
oute of paine into blisse it shalle be nought.

And therfore saide oure lorde: "Whate shulde it than greve the to suffere a while,
sen it is my wille and my wyrshippe?" It is Goddes wille that we take his behestes
and his confortinges als largelye and als mightelye as we maye take thame. And also
he wille that we take oure abidinge and oure desese als lightelye as we may take   25
tham, and sette tham atte nought. For the lightlyere we take tham, the lesse price we
sette be tham for luff, the lesse paine salle we hafe in the felinge of tham, and the
mare thanke we shalle hafe for them.

In this blissed revelation I was trewly taught that whate man or woman wilfully
cheses God in this° life, he may be sekere that he is chosene. Kepe this treulye, for   30
sothly it is Godes wille that we be als sekere in tryste of the blis in heven whiles we
ere here as we shulle° be in sekernesse when we ere thare. And ever the mare likinge
and the joye that we take in this sekernesse, with reverence and mekenes, the bettere
likes him. For I am seker if thare hadde nane ben bot I that shulde be safe, God
wolde hafe done alle that he hase done for me. And so shulde ilke saule thinke in   35
knawinge of his lovere, forgettande, if he might, alle creatures, and thinkande that
God hase done for him alle that he hase done.

And this thinke me shulde stirre a saule for to luff and like him, and nought
drede bot him. For it is his wille that we witte that alle the might of oure enmye is
loken in oure frendes hande. And therfore a saule that wate sekerly this shalle   40
nought drede botte him that he loves, and alle othere dredes sette tham emange
passions and bodelye sekenesse and imaginations. And therfore, if a man be in so
mekille paine, in so mekille wa, and in so mekille deseses, that him thinke that he
can thinke right nought bot that that he es in or that he feles, als sone as he maye,
passe lightlye overe and sette it atte nought. And why? For God wille be knawen. For   45

46 we shulde hafe patience The main object of this moment of revelation, according to line 7 • **48 in thies wordes** See lines 12–13 • **48 greve** upset

[SECTION 21] **1 felle to myselfe** collapsed into myself • **2 understandande** realizing • **2 that I shulde life** that I was going to live • **2–3 as a wrech . . . feled** tossed and complained like a wretch, for the physical pain I was feeling • **3 irksumnes** annoyance • **4 als barane and drye** as barren and dry. The terms are elsewhere used in the context of prayer. See 19.14 • **5 for fallinge to . . . felinge** for giving way to my sufferings and losing my spiritual perception • **6–10 Than com . . . my reklessenes** Julian's denial of Christ here is treated as a serious sin in the rest of *A Vision*, and certainly this scene has little in common with the decorum of *The Chastising*, where the visionary submits experiences "lowely to the doom of his gostly fadir [humbly to the judgment of his spiritual father], or of other discreet and sad gostly livers [careful and serious spiritual persons], for drede of illusion" (174). As described, however, Julian's revelation passes even the severe tests suggested by *The Scale*. Although doubtful "whether ther be ony" true visionary "livande in erthe [living on earth]," *The Scale* admits the possibility of an experience that "though it be so that it stonyeth [amazes] thee in the first biginninge, nevertheles aftirward it turneth and quikeneth thin herte to more desire of vertues and encreseth thy love more bothe to God and to thin evenecristen; also, it maketh thee more meke in thyn owen sight" (1.11) • **6 religiouse person** a member of a religious order. Probably a friar or canon • **7 enterlye** sincerely • **7–8 The crosse . . . faste** See 3.10–17, 5.1–2 • **8 my bedde feete** foot of my bed • **8 it bled faste** it bled heavily • **9 wex alle sadde and mervelande** grew all serious and wondering • **9 onane** straightaway • **9 sare** sorely • **10 sadlye** seriously • **10 leste** least • **11 that says**

na mare therto who says no more about it • **13 walde haffe bene shrifen** would have liked to take confession • **14 Howe shulde a preste leve me?** how is a priest going to believe me? Even though a "religiouse person" just has. The confusion and difficulty of bringing the revelation back into the world begins at once • **14–15 This I leved . . . sawe him** I truly believed the revelation during the time in which I saw him • **16 fule** fool • **17 wrich** wretch • **17 unkindnes** unnaturalness • **17–18 for folye of . . . paine** out of folly caused by feeling a little bodily suffering. "Folye" is similar in nuance to "reklessenes" in line 10. See 19.15 • **20 of myselfe** by myself • **20 herein** in this state • **21 tristande in his mercye** trusting in God's mercy. *A Vision* presents Julian as taking the advice of the previous two sections, which recommend an attitude of trust during even the worst confusions of the soul. See especially 20.42–45 • **22–23 sette him in my throte** took me by the throat. The physicality of the demonic assault in this passage is in accord with late medieval understandings of the devil's power to afflict the body through disease and illusion. According to *The Chastising*, holy men since antiquity have been "chastised sodeynly with bodily infirmitees and sumtime grevously travelid with illusions of wikked spirites" (164) • **23 walde hafe** wanted to • **24 unnethes hadde I my life** I was scarcely alive • **25 persones** people • **26 onane** soon • **26 come** came • **27 foule stinke** Smoke, smells, and heat traditionally accompany demons. *The Pricke* lists "filthe and stink" as the third pain of hell, caused by fire, brimstone, and pitch (6683–94) • **27 Benedicite dominus!** bless Lord! See 3.15 for this ungrammatical cry • **27–28 Is alle . . . here?** is everything here on fire? • **28 I wened** I supposed • **28 it hadde bene** it was • **28 shulde hafe brenned** was going to burn • **29 feled any stinke** noticed any smell • **30 wiste I wele** knew I well • **31 tempest me** torment me

if we knewe him and luffed him, we shulde hafe /fol. 111v/ patience and be in grete
reste, and it shulde be likinge to us, alle that he does. And this shewed oure lorde me
in thies wordes that he saide: "Whate shulde it than greve the to suffer a while, sen it
is my wille and my wirshippe?"

And here was ane ende of alle that oure lorde shewed me that daye.   50

SECTION 21

And efter this sone I felle to myselfe and into my bodelye seknes,
understandande that I shulde life, and as a wrech hevyed° and mourned° for
the bodely paines that I feled, and thought grete irksumnes that I shulde langere
liffe. And I was als barane and drye as if I hadde never had comforth before bot
litille, for fallinge to my paines and failinge of gastelye felinge.   5

Than com a religiouse person to me and asked me howe I farde, and I saide that
I hadde° raved that daye. And he laughed loude and enterlye. And I saide: "The
crosse that stode atte my bedde feete, it bled faste." And with this worde, the person
that I spake to wex alle sadde and mervelande, and onane I was sare ashamed for my
reklessenes. And I thought thus: "This man takes it sadlye the leste worde that I   10
might saye, that says na mare therto."

And when I sawe that he toke it so sadelye and with so grete reverence, I wex
right gretly ashamed, and walde haffe bene shrifen. Bot I couth telle it na preste.
For I thoght: "Howe shulde a preste leve me? I leved nought oure lorde God." This I
leved sothfastlye for the time that I sawe him, and so was than my wille and my   15
meninge ever for to do withouten ende. Bot as a fule I lette it passe fro my minde.
Lo, I, wrich! This was a grete sinne and a grete unkindnes, that I, for folye of felinge
of a litille bodelye paine, so unwiselye lefte for the time the comforth of alle this
blissede shewinge of oure lorde God.

Here maye ye see whate I am of myselfe. Botte herein walde nought oure   20
curtayse lorde leve me. And I laye stille tille night, tristande in his mercye, and than I
begane to slepe. And in my slepe, atte the beginninge, methought the fende sette
him in my throte and walde hafe strangelede me, botte he might nought. Than I
woke oute of my slepe, and unnethes hadde I my life.

The persones that ware with me behelde me and wette my temples, and my   25
herte began to comforth. And onane a litelle smoke come in atte the dore with a
grete hete /fol. 112r/ and a foule stinke. I saide: "Benedicite dominus! Is alle on fire
that is here?" And I wened it hadde bene a bodely fire that shulde hafe brenned us to
dede. I asked tham that ware with me if thaye feled any stinke. Thay saide "naye,"
thay feled nane. I saide: "Blissede be God!" For than wiste I wele it was the fende was   30
comen to tempest me.

32 **onane** soon • 32 **I tuke . . . shewed me** I recollected what our Lord had showed me • 33 **for I holde it as bathe ane** for I reckon both of them are the same • 34 **al sone** very quickly • 34 **brought to gret reste and pees** The state God rejoices in when the soul attains it in 19.63–66

[SECTION 22] 1 **lefte I stille wakande** I was left still awake • 1 **gastely eyen** spiritual eyes • 2 **in middes** in the middle • 2–4 **I sawe my saule . . . cite** The city in the soul resembles the New Jerusalem of Rev. 21:1–27, as represented in art and poems such as *Pearl* or *The Pricke,* where the vision of God "es mast joy" of the city of heaven, a city so "large and wide" it has space for all the saved, all of whom can nonetheless clearly see "the face of God allemighty" (9207–31). In the section as a whole, the city is taken to be a figure for both the individual soul and the collective souls of "alle that shalle be safe" • 2–3 **swa large as it ware** as expansive as if it were • 3 **be the conditions . . . therin** judging by the fittings I saw in it • 4 **wirshipfulle cite** honorable city • 4 **sittes oure lorde Jhesu** In *The Book of Margery Kempe* 1.86, the Trinity and the whole court of heaven come to sit in Margery's soul. In *Piers Plowman* B 5.605–7, Piers tells the pilgrims that, if they search diligently for truth, they will eventually find him in their own hearts: "Thou shalt see in thiselve Truthe sitte in thin herte, / In a cheyne of charite, as thou a child were [as if you were a child], / To suffren him and segge nought ayein thi sires wille [to submit to him and to say nothing against your lord's will]" • 4–5 **verraye God and verray man** true God and true human. The God who is "closed in reste and in pees" in the human soul at the end of time (see 15.11) is the incarnate Christ • 5 **a faire persone and of large stature** See Mary's account of Christ's beauty and size in Bridget's *Liber celestis,* where he is "so fare in visage [so beautiful of face] that ilka man [everyone] that saw it had likinge tharein," and "large of persone, noght fleshely bot bony" (4.70) • 6 **cledde solemplye in wyr-shippes** solemnly clad in honors. Christ wears the badges of his triumphant suffering and the "mede" given him by the Father (12.9–12) • 6 **sittes . . . even right** sits squarely in the middle of the soul. "Even right" also has an ethical connotation, "impartially" or "justly" • 7 **yemes** governs • 9 **instrumente or besines** assistance or work. Christ rules creation directly, without intermediaries or effort • 9 **my saule . . . godhede** my soul is joyfully possessed by the godhead. The faculties of the soul are "occupied" by the persons of the Trinity in whose image they were created • 10 **sufferayn might** sovereign power. God the Father • 11 **remove** leave • 12 **haymelieste hame** most intimate home • 12 **likinge** pleasure • 14 **whiles we ere here** while we are in this life • 15 **spede** profit • 15–16 **And the saule . . . behaldene** and contemplation transforms the soul who contemplates in this way into the image of that which is contemplated. See 2 Cor. 3:18: "And we all, with unveiled face, beholding the glory of the Lord, are being changed into his likeness from one degree of glory to another" • 16 **anes in reste and in pees** unites the soul to God in rest and in peace. See 15.1–11 • 17 **that I sawe him sitte** Rather than assume any other posture • 17–18 **the behaldinge . . . dwellinge** the perception of this sitting revealed to me the certainty that he would stay forever. "Sekernesse" has been central to *A Vision* since 17.2–3: "I kepe the fulle sekerly" • 18–19 **I knewe . . . before** I knew truly that it was he who had shown me everything that happened before. This knowledge precedes Christ's words in lines 22–24, which in a sense do no more than make public what, it is said here, Julian had already understood. Christ's occupancy of the soul, and the fact that "I sawe him sitte" (line 17), in themselves refute her reckless claim to have been "raving" (21.6–7). Christ has, from the beginning, been in full command not only of the revelation but, from his seat in Julian's soul, of her apprehension of it • 20 **behalden . . . avisement** contemplated this with full deliberation. A deliberation paralleled by the length of this section's buildup to Christ's words that follow • 20–21 **shewed oure lorde me wordes** our Lord revealed words to me • 21–22 **as he hadde done before** See 8.30–32, where Christ speaks in the same fashion • 22 **Witte it welle** know it well • 22 **it was na ravinge** it was no madness. See 21.6–7 • 23 **take it, and leve it** accept it, and believe it • 23 **kepe the therto** hold yourself to it • 24–28 **This laste wordes . . . overcomen** Christ's last words confirm the revelation not only by what they say but by the formal beauty of their allusion to his first words. The repetition of "overcome" brings the revelation full circle. The intricate circular structure of *Pearl* has an analogous function • 24–25 **for lerninge . . . sikernes** to teach me absolute and complete certainty • 25–26 **the firste worde** See 8.30–32 • 28 **trewe comforthe** The main purpose of the revelation, according to Rubric 3, 6.7, 16.8–9 • 29 **generalle to** generally applicable to. See 6.1–7 • 29 **alle mine evencristen** Despite the fact that "thow" in "Thow shalle nought be overcomen" is singular • 29 **and so is Goddes wille** and such is God's will • 30 **sharpely** fiercely

And onane I tuke tha that oure lorde hadde shewed me on the same daye, with
alle the faith of haly kyrke—for I holde it as bathe ane—and fled therto as to my
comfort. And al sone alle vanished awaye, and I was brought to gret reste and pees,
withoutene seknes of bodye or drede of conscience.   35

SECTION 22

Bot than lefte I stille wakande, and than oure lorde openede my gastely eyen and
shewed me my saule in middes of my herte. I sawe my saule swa large as it
ware a kingdome, and be the conditions that I sawe therin, methought it was a
wirshipfulle cite. In middes of this cite sittes oure lorde Jhesu, verraye God and
verray man: a faire persone and of large stature, wyrshipfulle, hiest lorde. And I sawe   5
him cledde solemplye in wyrshippes. He sittes in the saule even right in pees and
reste, and he rewles and yemes heven and erth and alle that is. The manhede with
the godhede sittis in reste; and the godhede rewles and yemes withouten any
instrumente or besines. And my saule is° blisfullye occupied with the godhede: that
is, sufferayn might, sufferayne wisdome, sufferayne goodnesse.   10

The place that Jhesu takes in oure saule he shalle never remove it withouten
ende, for in us is his haymelieste hame and maste likinge to him to dwelle in. This
was a delectabille sight and a restefulle, for it is so in trowth withouten ende. And
the behaldinge of this whiles we ere here es fulle plesande to God, and fulle grete
spede to us. And the saule that thus behaldes, it makes it like to him that is   15
behaldene, and anes in reste and in pees. And this was a singulere joye and a blis to
me that I sawe him sitte, for the behaldinge of this sittinge shewed to me sikernes of
his endelesse dwellinge. And I knewe sothfastly that it was he that shewed me
/fol. 112v/ alle before.

And when I hadde behalden this with fulle avisement, than shewed oure lorde   20
me wordes fulle mekelye, withouten voice and withouten openinge of lippes, as he
hadde done before, and saide fulle soberlye: "Witte it welle, it was na ravinge that
thowe sawe today. Botte take it, and leve it, and kepe the° therto, and thowe shalle
nought be overcomen." This laste wordes ware saide to me for lerninge of fulle trewe
sikernes, that it is our lorde Jhesu that shewed me alle. For right as in the firste   25
worde that oure lorde shewed me, menande his blissed passion—"Herewith is the
fende overcomen"—right so he saide in the laste worde, with fulle trewe sikernesse:
"Thow shalle nought be overcomen." And this lerninge and this trewe comforthe, it
es generalle to alle mine evencristen, as I haffe before saide, and so is Goddes wille.

And this worde, "Thowe shalle nought be overcomen," was saide fulle sharpely   30
and fulle mightely for sekernes and comforth againe alle tribulations that maye

32 **He saide nought** For this mode of exposition by means of what is not said, see 12.25–26 • 32 **tempested** tormented • 33 **travailed** wearied • 33 **desesed** distressed • 34 **take hede of** pay attention to • 36 **alle shalle be wele** See 13.61 • 37 **alle was close** everything was finished. The end of the revelation. Compare 20.50

[SECTION 23] 1 **com** came • 1 **with his heete . . . stinke** See 21.26–27 • 1–2 **made me fulle besye** kept me very busy. As described in lines 11–17. "Besy" and "besines" are used often in this section. The word "besy" sometimes has negative connotations in Middle English religious writing and elsewhere in *A Vision* (see 14.27–28), but Julian's "besines" is justified by that of her tempters • 2–3 **the bodely heete also . . . travailous** the physical heat equally frightening and exhausting. "Bodely heete" might seem like a reference to fever, but "body" is used several times in this passage to convey the disgusting physicality of the demons, and the phrase probably refers to the same diabolical heat mentioned in line 1 • 3 **harde** heard • 3 **bodely jangelinge** audible squabbling • 3–4 **as it hadde bene of two bodies** as if it had been between two bodies. "Bodies," not "persons" or "creatures," terms that would dignify the demonic presence • 4 **bathe** both • 4 **jangled at anes** squabbled at the same time • 4–5 **as if thay had haldene. . . . besines** as if they were conducting a parliament with much energy. The devil's "besines" parodies Julian's (line 2). A "parliamente" is a meeting to decide something: here, perhaps, Julian's eternal destiny • 7 **triste besely** trusted energetically • 7–9 **comforthede . . . travailede** comforted my soul by speaking aloud, as I would have done for any other who had been in similar difficulty. Talking to herself to drown out the mutterings of the demons, Julian follows a course of action suggested in *The Remedy*, which recommends that the tempted person "strength himselfe and be mery [cheerful], though it be ayenst his herte [not in accordance with how he feels], and drede nothinge the fendes malice" (chap. 6, *YW* 2:116) • 9–10 **Methought this besines . . . besenes** A curious remark, since the entire account has consisted of "likning" the temptation to "bodely besenes." It evokes the inverted ineffability of the scene, as far below words and metaphors as the divine is above them • 11–12 **before**

that time See 2.22–28 • 12–13 **my tunge . . . haly kyrke** I occupied my tongue with talk of Christ's Passion and rehearsal of the faith of holy church. Standard remedies in temptation, meant to awaken faith, hope, charity. *The Remedy* notes that if "the fende cometh and tempteth a soule fiersly like a dragon," the tempted "creature" should "strength himselfe saddely in the passion of almighty God and arme him with that holy passion" (chap. 4, *YW* 2:112) • 13 **festende** fastened. Julian is attempting to recapture the experience she describes in 9.17–20 • 14 **menande** thinking this • 14–15 **Thowe hase nowe grete besines** now you have to make a big effort • 15 **Walde . . . sinne** if from now on you could always be as busy to keep yourself from sin • 16 **trowe** believe • 16–17 **ware I safe . . . saule** if I were safe from sin, I would be completely safe from all the devils of hell and enemies of my soul. *The Remedy* argues that "somtime . . . the fende tempteth and travailleth a rightwise soule so sharply that it is . . . driven to dispaire. And yet all that time, though the soule perceive it not, it dwelleth still in the drede and love of God. . . . for our lorde . . . arrecteth [attributes] not to the soule that sinne which himselfe suffreth the fende to werke in the soule without the consente . . . of the said selfe soule" (chap. 1, *YW* 2:107) • 19 **prime dayes** early morning • 19 **onane** after a while • 20 **I scorned thame** See 8.42–47 • 21–22 **therewith is the fende overcomen** See 8.32 • 23–31 **A, wriched sinne! . . . Amen par charite** Perhaps originally intended as the peroration of *A Vision*, coming as it does immediately after the final moment of revelation, this set piece is a formal "scorning" of the devil, anticipated by Julian's laughter at him in 8.42–47. Although it proclaims sin nothing, it still presents sin in a light different from and more damaging than that which plays over some sections of the work, especially Sections 13–17, where "sin is na shame, bot wirshippe to man" (17.15) • 23 **Thowe er nought** you are nothing. The meaning of "nought" in this passage shifts between "not," "nothing," and "nothingness," as it has earlier, in Section 8 • 23–24 **God is alle thinge** See 8.9–10 • 24 **God hase made alle thinge** See 4.7–13 • 26 **God does alle thinge** See 8.14–15 • 27 **when I sawe . . . oure saule** See 22.1–10 • 28 **like** take pleasure in • 28 **yeme** govern • 29 **alle tha that luffes the** all those who love you

com. He saide nought, "Thowe salle not° be tempested, thowe shalle not be travailed, thowe shalle not be desesed," bot he saide, "Thowe shalle nought be overcomen." God wille that we take hede of his worde, and that we be ever mighty in sekernesse, in wele and in wa. For he luffes us and likes us, and so wille he that we 35 luff him and like him and mightely triste in him, and alle shalle be wele. And sone efter alle was close, and I sawe na mare.

SECTION 23

After this, the fende com againe with his heete and with his stinke, and made me fulle besye. The stinke was so vile and so painfulle, and the bodely heete also dredfulle and travailous. And also I harde a bodely jangelinge and a speche, as it hadde bene of two bodies, and bathe to my thinkinge jangled at anes, as if thay had haldene a parliamente with grete besines. And alle was softe mutteringe, and I 5 understode nought whate thay saide. Botte alle this was to stirre me to dispaire, as methought. And I triste besely in God and comforthede my saule with bodely speche, as I shulde hafe done to anothere person than myselfe that hadde so bene travailede. Methought this besines might nought be /fol. 113r/ likned to na bodely besenes. 10

My bodelye eyen I sette on the same crosse that I hadde sene comforth in before that time, my tunge I occupied with speche of Cristes passion and rehersinge of the faith of haly kyrke, and my herte I festende on God with alle the triste and alle the might that was in me. And I thought to myselfe, menande: "Thowe hase nowe grete besines. Walde thowe nowe fra this time evermare be so besy to kepe the fro sinne, 15 this ware a soferayne and a goode occupation. For I trowe sothlye, ware I safe fra sinne, I ware fulle saife fra alle the fendes of helle and enmyse of my saule."

And thus thay occupied me alle the night and on the morn tille it was aboute prime dayes. And than onane thay ware alle gane and passed, and there lefte nathinge bot stinke, and that lasted stille a while. And I scorned thame, and thus was 20 I delivered of tham be the vertu of Cristes passion. For "tharewith is the fende overcomen," as Criste saide before to me.

A, wriched sinne! Whate ert thowe? Thowe er nought. For I sawe that God is alle thinge: I sawe nought the. And when I sawe that God hase made alle thinge, I sawe the nought. And when I sawe that God is in alle thinge, I sawe the nought. And 25 when I sawe that God does alle thinge that is done, lesse and mare, I sawe the nought. And when I sawe oure lorde Jhesu sit in oure saule so wyrshipfully, and luff and like and rewle and yeme alle that he has made, I sawe nought the. And thus I am seker that thowe erte nought. And alle tha that luffes the and likes the and folowes

31 **shelde us alle** shield us all • 31 **Amen par charite**
amen for the sake of love. A standard ending for a prayer
or literary text • 32 **whate wrechednesse is I wille saye** I
want to describe the nature of misery. The following difficult passage, the first of what might be considered a
series of footnotes or addenda to *A Vision*, concerns the
relation between evil, pain, and the condition of being
in the world. In this passage, "wrechednesse" means variously "sin," "suffering," "impermanence," and "the
entire world." The question-and-answer format resembles that of *La lumere*, but rather than expound a vice or
a virtue, the passage takes the category "wrechednesse"
precisely because it lies in the middle, confusingly sometimes a good, sometimes an evil • 32 **lernede** taught •
32 **be the shewinge of God** by God's revelation. The
rest of *A Vision* continues to draw lessons from the revelation as a whole, rather than expound individual
moments • 33 **gastelye blindehede** spiritual blindness •
34 **in the firste sinne** through original sin • 34 **folowes
of that wrechednesse** follows from that act of wretchedness • 34–35 **passions and paines** A second subdivision
of "wrechednesse" • 35–36 **alle that es in erth . . . nought
goode** everything that is not good on earth or in another
place. "Othere place" is one of *A Vision*'s few allusions to
hell and purgatory • 36 **of this** following from this •
36 **Whate er we?** in what sense are we good or bad? •
37 **departed fra us** separated from us • 39 **Whate is
alle . . . us?** what is the status of everything on earth that
separates us from God? Here the entire creation is close
to being labeled "wrichednes" • 39–40 **in that that it
serves us** insofar as it serves us • 41 **otherewise than thus**
in any other way than with full awareness of this. Setting
the heart on earthly goods turns them into evils • 42 **if
any be swilke** if anyone is like this. Compare 18.9–11,
where choice of sin is choice of pain, and so fundamen-
tally incomprehensible • 44 **by frelty or unkunninge** by
weakness or stupidity • 45–46 **he falles nought . . . alle
his wille** he does not truly fall, for he will powerfully rise
up again and contemplate God, whom he loves with all
his will. The trinity of the powers of the soul—might,
wisdom, and love—are hidden in the language of this
passage (see 7.2–4), which also alludes to the doctrine of
the "goodely wille" (17.8–14). It may also allude to a verse
sometimes used to distinguish mortal from venial sins
(see 17.32–33), Prov. 24.16: "for a righteous man falls
seven times [some medieval Bibles add "in a day"], and
rises again" • 46–47 **God has made him. . . . sinnere**
God has caused himself to be loved by the man or the
woman who has been a sinner. This sentence (even

emended, as here) is obscure, but its general implication
is that God has brought about the situation in which all
who love him are former sinners: the implication being
that despite their sins, people may love him confidently •
49 **be thre parties** in three modes • 49–50 **as I hafe
saide before** See 7.1–7. Signals a structural parallel
between the opening sequence of *A Vision* and this
coda • 51–53 **For the bodely sight . . . me thame** Julian
claims to have represented both the first two kinds of
vision with fullness and precision. "Trewlye" is often
used to describe paintings or images that are faithful
depictions of what they represent. "I hafe saide tham
right" insists that Julian has reproduced the specific
words spoken by Christ in the revelation • 53 **somdele**
some part

[SECTION 24] 1 **twa maners of sekenes** two kinds of
sickness • 1–2 **of whilke . . . amended** of which he wants
us to be cured • 2 **tone** one • 2 **inpatience** impatience.
Contemplations has a chapter on patience that begins by
noting: "Charite, whiche is moder and keper of vertues,
is lost ful often by inpatience" (chap. Y, "How Thou Shalt
Be Patient," *YW* 2:98) • 2 **travaille** labor • 3 **tothere**
other • 3 **dispaire or doutefulle drede** despair or doubting fear • 3 **as I shalle saye efterwarde** See 25.11–13 •
4 **thiese twa er it that** these are the two that • 4 **travailes
us and tempestes us** See 22.32–33 • 4–5 **as by that . . . me**
according to what our Lord showed me. "Inpatience" is
a theme in Section 9, "dispaire" especially in 23.1–9 •
5 **maste lefe to him** and it is most pleasing to him •
5–7 **I speke of swilke . . . aboute us** Lovers of God are
more inclined to impatience and despair than others,
presumably because of their intense awareness of sin.
Much of this coda appears to be addressed to this more
particularized readership • 6 **disposes tham** set themselves • 7 **Than . . . sinnes** then these two are secret sins.
Despair is a preoccupation of Flete's *Remedy* and of *The
Chastising*, associated in both with temptation to intellectual doubt and with self-recrimination, as it is in Sections 21 and 23 here. Impatience is conventionally linked
to the rigors of the religious life. Patience is the subject
of a short tract in *Pore Caitif* (taken from Rolle's *Emendatio vitae*), which follows immediately after the tract
on the "perfect" life of the contemplative. It is also the
implied subject of parts 3 and 4 of *Ancrene Wisse*, as of
any treatment of temptation, sin, and tribulation •
7 **maste besye aboute us** most energetic around us.
Impatience and despair are briefly personified, as
though they were demons • 8 **knawen** recognized

the and wilfully endes in the, I am seker thay shalle be brought to nought with the,   30
and endleslye confounded. God shelde us alle fra the. Amen par charite.

And whate wrechednesse is I wille saye, as I am lernede be the shewinge of God.
Wrechednesse es alle thinge that is nought goode: the gastelye blindehede that we
falle into in the firste sinne, and alle that folowes of that wrechednesse, passions and
paines, gastelye or bodely; and alle that es in erth or in othere place whilke es   35
nought goode. And than may be asked of this: "Whate er we?" /fol. 113v/ And I answere
to this: if alle ware departed fra us that is nought goode, we shulde be goode. When
wrechidnesse is departed fra us, God and the saule is alle ane, and God and man alle
ane. "Whate is alle in erthe that twinnes us?" I answere and saye: in that that it serves
us, it is goode; and in that that it shalle perish, it is° wrichednes; and in that that a   40
man settes his herte theropon otherewise than thus, it is sinne. And for that time
that man or woman loves sinne, if any be swilke, he is in paine that passes alle
paines. And when he loves nought sinne, botte hates it and luffes God, alle is wele.
And he that trewlye does thus, though he sin sumtime by frelty or unkunninge in
his wille, he falles nought, for he wille mightely rise againe and behalde God wham   45
he loves in alle his wille. God has made him° to be loved of him or hire that has bene
a sinnere. Bot ever he loves, and ever he langes to hafe oure luffe. And when we
mightelye and wisely luffe Jhesu, we er in pees.

Alle the blissede techinge of oure lorde God was shewed to me be thre parties as
I hafe saide before: that es to saye, be bodely sight,° and be worde formed in min   50
understandinge, and by gastelye sight. For the bodely sight, I haffe saide as I sawe, als
trewlye as I can. And for the wordes fourmed, I hafe saide tham right as oure lorde
shewed me thame. And for the gastely sight, I hafe saide somdele, bot I maye never
fully telle it. And therfore of this gastely sight I am stirred to say more, as God wille
gife me grace.   55

SECTION 24

God shewed me twa maners of sekenes that we hafe, of whilke he wille that we
be amended. The tone es inpatience, for we bere our travaille and oure paine
hevely. The tothere is dispaire or° doutefulle drede, as I shalle saye efterwarde. And
thiese twa er it that moste travailes us and tempestes us, as by that oure lorde
shewed me, and maste lefe to him that thiese be amendede. I speke of swilke   5
/fol. 114r/ men and women that for Goddes love hates sinne and disposes tham to do
Goddes wille. Than ere thiese twa prive sinnes, and maste besye aboute us.
Therefore it is Goddes wille that thay be knawen, and than shalle we refuse them, as
we do othere sinnes.

10–11 **fulle mekelye oure lorde shewed . . . for love** See Sections 10–12 • 11 **hafes** has • 12 **in ensampille** by way of example • 13–14 **cause why . . . tham** the reason we are exercised about them (i.e., "oure paines") • 14 **unknawenge of luffe** ignorance of love. The love that underlies "oure paines" and that *A Vision* seeks to elucidate in order to provide a remedy for "inpacience" and "dispaire," as the next lines explain • 15 **alle even in properte** completely equal in their natures • 16 **moste nere** closest • 17–19 **For many men . . . stinte** See 4.16 for the properties of the Trinity, 15.4–10 for the auxiliary verbs used here • 17 **leves** believe • 19 **thar thay stinte** at that belief they baulk • 20 **lettis** hinders • 21 **by the ordinance of holye kyrke** according to the rules established by holy church. Through contrition, confession, and satisfaction • 21–22 **yit there dwelles . . . sinnes before done** there still remains a fear that incites them to contemplation of themselves and their earlier sins. According to *The Remedy*, too, the devil "many times bringeth into their mindes [the minds of contemplatives] againe the sinnes that they before had done and were confessed of" (chap. 7, *YW* 2:117) • 23–24 **this drede . . . waykenesse** they take this fear for humility, but this is an ugly blindness and a weakness • 24 **we can it nought dispise** we are incapable of despising it. Being ignorant of its sinfulness • 24 **sodaynly** immediately • 25 **of the enmy** from the enemy • 26 **againe** against • 28 **sekernesse** confidence • 28–29 **For luffe . . . meke to us** for God's love makes his power and his wisdom very humble before us. God's majesty is mediated through his homeliness • 29–30 **for time we repente us** at the time we repent

[SECTION 25] 1 **foure maner of dredes** four kinds of fear. The four fears described here are similar to those in other Middle English texts, such as *Contemplations* (which lists three; see chap. C, "What Is Drede," *YW* 2:76–77), though the schema adopted here seems specific to this work • 1–2 **One is drede of afray . . . frelty** one is the fear of attack (or alarm), which comes over one suddenly out of vulnerability. *Ancrene Wisse* offers the example of fear caused by someone's shouting "Fire! Fire!" (136) • 3 **swilke odere paine** other similar pains • 4 **taken** received • 5 **drede of paine** fear of suffering. This is similar to the "servile fear" or "drede of servage," fear of God's punishment, described in *Contemplations* (chap. C, "What Is Drede," *YW* 2:76): the same fear a text like *The Pricke* sets out to arouse with its evocations of hell and judgment. Lines 7–8 emphasize how in this state it is punishment itself, more than God, that is feared • 5 **wakned** wakened • 6 **harde in slepe of sin** fast asleep in sin. Jonah's sleep during a storm at sea, as described in the Middle English poem *Patience*, provides the model for this traditional image • 6 **resayfe** receive • 7 **to he hafe geten** until he has acquired • 7 **bodely dede** bodily death • 9 **antre** gateway. See Prov. 1:7: "The fear of the Lord is the beginning of knowledge" • 9–10 **ables . . . contrition** enables him to experience sorrow for sin • 10 **be the blisfulle touchinge** by the blessed inspiration • 11 **doutfulle drede** doubting fear. Doubt as to the reality of God's forgiveness • 11–12 **be litille . . . knawen** would not be anything much if it was recognized • 12 **spice** taste. "Spice" (Latin *species*) was thought etymologically related to "spes" (hope), so the phrase "spice of dispaire" is an oxymoron • 13 **hafe tham departed fro us** have them separated from us • 13 **with trewe knawinge** by a true recognition

And thus fulle mekelye oure lorde shewed me the pacience that he hadde in his 10
harde passion, and also the joye and the likinge that he hafes of that passion for love.
And this° he shewed me in ensampille that we shulde gladlye and esely bere oure
paines, for that es grete plesinge to him and endelesse profitte to us. And cause why
we ere travailed with tham is for unknawenge° of luffe.

Though the persones in the blissede trinite be alle even in properte, luffe was 15
moste shewed to me, that it is moste nere to us alle. And of° this knawinge er we
moste blinde. For many men and women leves that God is allemighty and may do
alle, and that he is alle wisdome and can do alle. Botte that he is alle love and wille
do alle, thar thay stinte.

And this unknawinge it is that most lettis Goddes luffers. For when thay begin to 20
hate sinne, and to amende tham by the ordinance of holye kyrke, yit there dwelles a
drede that stirres tham to behaldinge of thamselfe and of ther sinnes before done.
And this drede thay take for a mekenesse, bot this is a foulle blindehede and a
waykenesse. And we can it nought dispise, for if we knewe it we° shulde sodaynly
dispice it, as we do ane othere sinne that we knawe, for it comes of the enmy and it 25
is againe the trewthe.

For of alle the propertees of the blissed trinite, it is Goddes wille that we hafe
moste sekernesse in likinge and luffe. For luffe makes might and wisdome fulle
meke to us. For right as be the curtasye of God he forgettes oure sinne for time we
repente us, right so wille he that we foregette oure sinne, and alle oure hevinesse, 30
and alle oure doutefulle dredes. */fol. 114v/*

SECTION 25

Fore I saw foure maner of dredes. One is drede of afray, that comes to a man
sodanly be frelty. This drede is good, for it helpes to purge a man, as does
bodely seknes or swilke odere paine that is nought sinne. For alle swilke paines
helpes man, if thay be patiently taken.

The secunde is drede of paine, wharby a man is stirred and wakned fro slepe of 5
sin. For man that is harde in slepe of sin, he is nought able for the time to resayfe the
soft comfort of the haly gaste, to he hafe geten this drede of paine of bodely dede
and of the fire of purgatory. And this drede stirres him to seke comfort and mercy
of God. And thus this drede helpes him as ane antre, and ables him to hafe
contrition be the blisfulle touchinge° of the haly gaste. 10

The thirde is a doutfulle drede. For though it be litille in the selfe and it ware
knawen, it is a spice of dispaire. For I am seker that alle doutefulle dredes God hates,
and he wille that we hafe tham departed fro us with trewe knawinge of luffe.°

14 **reverente drede** reverent fear. Respect or awe. Similar to the "frendely drede" described in *Contemplations*: "Whan a man dredeth the longe abidinge here for grete desire that he hath to be with God" (chap. C, "What Is Drede," *YW* 2:76). Exemplified in Mary's reaction to the Annunciation in 4.21–32 • 15 **softe** easy • 15 **mekille-hede** greatness • 16 **nought bathe ane** not both the same • 16–17 **thay . . . wyrkinge** they are different in their nature and in how they are expressed • 17 **nowthere** neither • 19–20 **Alle dredes . . . not so trewe** A surprising turn to the argument, since "drede of afray" and "drede of paine," just described as good things in themselves, are now categorized with "doutfulle drede" as "not so trewe." *Contemplations*, on the other hand, argues that "drede of servage," its equivalent of "drede of paine," "may be . . . proufitable," and proceeds to show how (chap. C, "What Is Drede," *YW* 2:77). The next passage provides some nuancing of the categories • 19 **pro-ferde** offered. See 10.53 for an equally sinister use of this word • 20 **undere the coloure of halines** disguised as holiness. A phrase often used in relation to hypocrisy or diabolic temptation. Hilton writes: "Thou shalt not resieve non opinioun, ne fantasye, ne singuler conceit under colour of more holinesse, as summe don that aren not wise" (*The Scale* 1.21) • 20–21 **hereby . . . whilke is whilke** in this way they can be known and discerned which is which • 22 **softes** softens • 25 **wikked**

spiritte . . . goode angelle See 2 Cor. 11:14: "Even Satan disguises himself as an angel of light." The verse is often used in discussions of the spiritual life, in relation both to visionary experience and to any serious temptation. In *The Form*, Rolle writes: "Also, umwhile [sometimes] the fende temptes men and women that er solitary by tham ane [by themselves] on a quaint [strange] maner and a sotell: he transfigurs him in the liknes of an aungel of light, and apers till tham, and sayes that he es ane [one] of Goddes aungels comen to comforth tham; and swa [so] he deceives foles" (chap. 2, *YW* 1:12). For medieval contemplatives, discernment or "discretion of spirits" was a fundamental responsibility, and *A Vision* appropriately ends by invoking one of the key texts of discretion literature, reassuring readers that its own message of "pees" (line 30) guarantees its divine source • 26 **ille spirit** evil spirit • 26 **coloure** appearance • 27 **daliance** manners • 27 **wirkinge** behavior • 28 **lettes** obstructs • 29 **lefes** leaves • 29 **comones** converses • 31 **oure spede** to our benefit • 31 **knawe tham thus ysundure** tell them (i.e., the kinds of fear) apart in this way • 32 **sekere** confident • 32 **pesabile** peaceful • 32 **ristefulle** restful • 33–34 **of the same . . . to oureselfe** he wants us to be in the same relation to ourselves as he is to us • 35 **Explicit Juliane de Norwich** here ends Julian of Norwich

The fourthe is reverente drede. For thare is na drede that pleses him in us bot
reverente drede, and that is fulle swete and softe for mekillehede of luffe. And yit is   15
this reverente drede and luffe nought bathe ane, bot thay er twa in properte and in
wyrkinge, and nowthere of tham may be hadde withouten othere. Therfore I am
sekere, he that luffes, he dredes, though he fele bot litille.

Alle dredes othere than reverente dredes that er proferde to us, though thay
come undere the coloure of halines, thay ere not so trewe. And hereby may thaye be   20
knawen and discerned whilke is whilke: for this reverente drede, the mare it is
hadde, the mare it softes and comfortes and pleses and restes, and the false drede it
travailes and tempestes and trubles.

Than is this the remedye, to knawe tham bath and refuse the° fals, righte as we
walde do a wikked spiritte that shewed him in liknes of a goode angelle. For right as   25
ane ille spirit, though he com undere the coloure and the liknes of a goode
angelle—his daliance and his wirkinge though he shewe never so faire—first he
travailes and tempestes° and trubles the person that he spekes with, and lettes him
and lefes /fol. 115r/ him alle in unreste. And the mare that he comones with him, the
mare he travailes him, and the farthere is he fra pees. Therfore it is Goddes wille and   30
oure spede that we knawe tham thus ysundure.

For God wille ever that we be sekere in luffe, and pesabile and ristefulle as he is
to us. And right so of the same condition as he is to us, so wille he that we be to
oureselfe, and to oure evencristen. Amen.

Explicit Juliane de Norwich.   35

A Revelation
of Love

[CHAPTER 1] 1 **a revelation of love** "Revelation" was a new word in English in the 1380s, when it began displacing the older "shewing." The word refers both to visionary experience and to biblical prophecy. Unlike a "vision," which can have good or evil sources, a "revelation" is assumed to be divine in origin. In *A Revelation,* the word designates (1) the whole work, (2) the whole revelation, (3) the numbered revelations. The word "love" occurs more than four hundred times during the work • 1–2 **sixteen shewinges** sixteen manifestations. Many Middle English works begin with a list of chapters, but here the emphasis is on the structure of the revelation, not the book. "Shewinge" occurs more than a hundred times in *A Revelation,* and there are almost four hundred examples of the verb "shew." "Shewinge" refers sometimes to the numbered revelations but usually to a specific detail "shewed" by God and seen by Julian • 3 **the first** See Chapters 4–9 • 3 **of his precious . . . thornes** about his precious crowning with thorns • 4 **comprehended and specified** The vocabulary is learned and up-to-date: both words are recorded only from the 1380s on. The use of synonymous doublets here is a common feature of late Middle English prose, especially translations. Although the nuances of word meaning are unusually important in *A Revelation,* elsewhere in this opening chapter are at least three: "shewinges and techinges," "groundide and oned," "doeth and worketh" (lines 5, 6–7, 11) • 4 **the blessed trinity** See 4.6–12 • 5 **oning . . . mans soule** See 9.7–14 • 6–7 **be groundide and oned** are founded and brought together. See 6.54–58. The phrase aligns the first revelation with the foundation of the liberal arts, grammar, often described as the "ground" of learning as a whole. "Ground" can also mean "axiom," the foundation of an argument • 8 **The secunde** See Chapter 10 • 8 **in tokening of** as a representation of. For "token," see 8.4 • 8 **deerworthy** precious • 10 **The third** See Chapter 11 •

10 **mighty . . . wisdom . . . love** Traditional attributes of God the Father, Son, and Holy Spirit respectively. See 11.45 • 10–11 **right also verily . . . right also verily** just as truly . . . just as truly • 11 **doeth and worketh** does and performs • 12 **that is done** that are done. Middle English is not so concerned with grammatical agreement as modern written English • 13 **The fourth** See Chapter 12 • 13 **skorging** scourging • 15 **The fifth** See Chapter 13 • 16 **The sixth** See Chapter 14 • 16 **worshipful thanking . . . God** our Lord God's reverential gratitude • 18 **The seventh** See Chapter 15 • 18 **oftentimes feeling . . . woe** a recurrent sensation of joy in alternation with misery • 19 **gracious touching and lightning** grace-given illumination and inspiration • 19 **sekernes of** confidence in • 20 **heavenes and irkehede** heaviness and disgust • 20 **fleshely living** living in the body • 20 **ghostely** spiritual • 21 **also sekerly** as surely • 23 **The eighth** See Chapters 16–21 • 23 **cruel drying** The drying of Christ's body on the cross: the climax of the revelation's account of the Passion • 24 **The ninth** See Chapters 22–23 • 24 **liking** pleasure • 24 **of the hard passion** about the harsh passion • 25 **ruefull** pitiful • 27 **The tenth** See Chapter 24 • 27–28 **his blissful hart . . . enjoying** his blessed heart, split quite in two, rejoicing • 29 **The eleventh** See Chapter 25 • 29 **ghostly shewing** spiritual revelation. For this term, see 9.24–28 • 30 **The twelfth** See Chapter 26 • 31 **The thirteenth** See Chapters 27–40. The description of the revelation that follows is at once selective and partially inaccurate, with no exact correspondences between several of its details and the chapters themselves • 32 **noblete . . . making** nobility of his creation of all things • 33 **excellence of manes making** excellence of humanity's creation. There is no direct discussion of this in the thirteenth revelation • 34 **asseeth** Atonement. See 29.9 • 34 **all our blame** all our guilt

This is a revelation of love that Jhesu Christ, our endles blisse, made in sixteen shewinges.

Of which the first is of his precious crowning of thornes. And therin was comprehended° and specified the blessed trinity, with the incarnation and the oning° betweene God and mans soule, with many fair shewinges and techinges of endelesse wisdom and love, in which all the shewinges that foloweth be groundide and oned.° 5

The secunde is of the discoloring of his fair face, in tokening of his deerworthy passion.

The third is that our lord God, al mighty, all wisdom, and all love, right also 10 verily as he hath made all thinges that is, right also verily he doeth and worketh all thinges that is done.

The fourth is skorging of his tender body, with plentuous sheding of his precious */fol. 1v/* bloud.

The fifth is that the feende is overcome by the precious passion of Christ. 15

The sixth is the worshipful thanking of our lord God, in which he rewardeth all his blessed servantes in heaven.

The seventh is oftentimes feeling of wele and of woe. Feeling of wele is gracious touching and lightning, with true sekernes of endlesse joy. The feeling of wo is of temptation by heavenes and irkehede° of our fleshely living, with ghostely 20 understanding that we be kept also sekerly° in love in wo as in wele, by the goodnes of God.

The eighth is the last paines of Christ, and his cruel drying.°

The ninth is of the liking which is in the blisseful° trinity of the hard passion of Christ after his rueful dying, in which joy and liking he will that we be in solace and 25 */fol. 2r/* mirth with him tille that we come to the fullehede° in heaven.

The tenth is our lord Jhesu sheweth by love his blisseful° hart even cloven on two, enjoying.°

The eleventh is an high ghostly shewing of his deerworthy mother.

The twelfth is that our lord God is all sovereyn being. 30

The thirteenth is that our lord God will that we have great regarde to all the deedes which he hath done in the great noblete of all thing making; and of the excellence of manes making, the which is above all his workes; and of the precious asseeth° that he hath made for mans sinne, turning all our blame into endlesse worshippe. Than meaneth he thus: "Behold and see, for by the same might, wisdom, 35

38 **kepe us in** maintain ourselves within • 38 **willing to wite** wanting to know • 39 **privities** secrets. See 30.10–21 • 39 **not but . . . to us** except as it concerns us • 40 **The fourteenth** See Chapters 41–43. Missing from Chapter 1's outline of this part of *A Revelation* is any description of the long sequence of chapters from 44 to 63, at the center of which is the exemplum of the lord and the servant in Chapter 51. These chapters, many of which state that they expound "all the revelations," were evidently considered too abstracted from the experience on which *A Revelation* is based to be included here • 40 **ground of our beseking** foundation of our prayer. See 41.8 • 40 **Heerin** in this revelation • 41 **one is rightful . . . seker trust** one is true prayer, the other is certain trust. Nearly identical to 41.2 • 42 **be alike large** be equally generous. See 42.11 • 42 **liketh him** pleases him • 44 **The fifteenth** See Chapters 64–65 • 44 **sodeynly be taken** See 64.9. This sentence as a whole paraphrases Christ's speech in Chapter 64 • 46 **meed** reward • 46 **forto** also • 47 **The sixteenth** See Chapters 66–68 • 48 **wonneth** lives • 48 **rewling and yeming** ruling and governing • 49 **us mightly . . . saving** powerfully and wisely saving us • 50 **enemy** the devil

[CHAPTER 2] 1 **shewed** revealed • 1 **a simple creature unletterde** a simple, unlearned person. See pages 6–10 in the Introduction. "Creature" is used seventy times in *A Revelation* to designate a person: Julian herself, as visionary and narrator when the word is singular; all humans when plural. A gender-neutral term, the word keeps the reader's attention focused on the dependence of humankind on their creator • 1–2 **deadly flesh** mortal flesh • 2–3 **Which creature . . . giftes** which person had previously asked for three gifts • 3 **mind of the passion** intense recollection of Christ's Passion. Although Julian takes it in idiosyncratic directions, this was a common desire among the late medieval devout: to submerge the self in the details of Christ's suffering, scene by scene from his arrest to his death. *The Privity of the Passion* promises readers: "I trowe [believe] fully that whoso wolde besy hime [would occupy himself] with all his herte and all his minde and umbethinke him of [think about] this glorius passione . . . it sulde [would] bring him and chaunge him into a new state of lifinge" (prologue, in Horstmann, *Yorkshire Writers* [henceforth cited as *YW*], 1:198) • 4 **of Godes gifte** through God's gift • 5 **For the first** as to the first desire • 5 **come to my minde** which came to my mind. Literally, "having come to my mind," the first of a number of Latinate constructions in *A Revelation* • 5 **methought** it seemed to me • 5–6 **sumdeele feeling in** some measure of inner feeling for • 7 **I woulde . . . time** I wanted to have been present at that time. Time is a major preoccupation in *A Revelation,* the word itself occurring on more than two hundred occasions • 7–8 **Mary Magdaleyne . . . lovers** Mary Magdalene was present at the Crucifixion (John 19:25). Medieval writers often take her love as exemplary for all the devout, especially women. On "Christus lovers," see pages 10–12 of the Introduction • 8 **might have seen bodily** could have seen physically. Rather than merely in her imagination

and goodnes that I have done all this, by the same might, wisdom, /fol. 2v/ and goodnes I shall make well all that is not well, and thou shalt see it." And in this he will that we kepe us in the faith and truth of holy church, not willing to wite his privities, not but as it longeth to us in this life.

The fourteenth is that our lord God is ground of our beseking. Heerin was seen   40
two fair properties: that one is rightful prayer, that other is seker° trust, which he will both be alike° large. And thus our prayer liketh him, and he of his goodnes fulfilleth it.

The fifteenth is that we shall° sodeynly be taken from all our paine and from all our wo, and of his goodnes we shall come uppe above, wher we shall have our lord   45
Jesu to our meed and, forto, be fulfilled of joy° and blisse in heaven.

The sixteenth is that the blisseful° trinity our maker, in Christ /fol. 3r/ Jesu our saviour, endlesly wonneth° in our soule, worshipfully rewling and yeming° all thinges, us mightly and wisely saving and keping for love. And we shall not be overcome of our enemy.   50

THE SECUNDE CHAPTER

This revelation was shewed° to a simple creature unletterde, living in deadly flesh, the yer of our lord 1373, the thirteenth day of May. Which creature desired before thre giftes by the grace of God. The first was mind of the passion. The secund was bodily sicknes. The thurde was to have of Godes gifte thre woundes.

For the first, come to my minde with devotion:° methought I had sumdeele   5
feeling in the passion of Christ, but yet I desired to have more, by the /fol. 3v/ grace of God. Methought I woulde have ben that time with Mary° Magdaleyne and with other that were Christus lovers, that I might have seen bodily the passion that our

---

[vis. RUBRIC, 1.1–7] /Rev. 1.1–2.2/ /fol. 97r/ **Here° es a vision, shewed be the goodenes of God to a devoute woman. And hir name es Julian, that is recluse atte Norwiche and yit is on life, anno domini 1413. In the whilke vision er fulle many comfortabille wordes and gretly stirrande to alle thaye that desires to be Cristes loverse.**

I° desirede thre graces be the gifte of God. The first was to have minde of Cristes° passion. The seconde was bodelye syekenes. And the thrid was to have of Goddes gifte thre woundes.

For the firste, come to my minde with devotion: methought I hadde *grete* felinge in the passion of Criste, botte yitte I desirede to have mare, be the grace of God. Methought I wolde have bene that time with Mary Maudeleyne and with othere that were Cristes loverse, that I might have sene bodilye the passion of oure

10 **bodely sight** physical sight. A vision, conceptualized here as an actual experience of an event, rather than a mere meditation. See 9.24–28 • 10 **more knowinge** greater understanding • 11 **compassion of our lady** compassion of the Virgin Mary. If Mary Magdalene's suffering is most like that of the devout believer, the suffering of Christ's mother most resembles that of Christ • 12–13 **I would . . . them** I wished I had been one of them. Other late medieval women visionaries, including Bridget of Sweden and Margery Kempe, experienced visionary presence at the Crucifixion • 13–14 **Other sight . . . none** I never asked for any other sight or revelation from God • 14 **were deperted** would be separated • 14 **I beleved to be saved** I believed myself to be saved. An essential attitude for the devout to maintain according to many Middle English religious works. William Flete's *Remedy Against the Troubles of Temptations* considers doubt of the certainty of one's own salvation a temptation to despair, and instructs: "Truste fully that by his goodnes he will save you and bringe you to everlastinge joye when he seeth best time, for he hath bought you full dere with his precious blode and painefull deth" (chap. 4, *YW* 2:112) • 15 **This was my meaning** this was my intention. The formal prose here suggests that the request for this "gifte" itself has the formality of a pledge • 15–16 **for I would after . . . have** because I wanted afterward . . . to have • 16 **more true mind in** more faithful recollection of • 17 **For the secunde** as to the second desire • 17 **come . . . with contrition** which came into my mind with sorrow for sin. The word "contrition" marks this second desire as penitential in character • 17 **frely without any seking** freely, without my searching for it. It is emphasized that this unusual second desire originated from outside Julian, as a gift of grace • 18 **wilful desire** urgent desire • 18–19 **were so hard . . . death** would be so harsh it would bring me to the point of death • 19–20 **undertake . . . holy church** receive all my rites of holy church. The last rites included a final confession, absolution, and extreme unction (anointment of the dying person with holy oil), essential preparations for making a good death • 20 **wening** expecting • 21 **I would . . . erthely life** I did not want to preserve any of the comfort of bodily or earthly living • 22 **bodily and ghostly** physical and spiritual • 22–23 **that I should have . . . die** that I would have if I were actually dying • 23 **dredes and tempests of fiendes** dreads and agitations caused by fiends. Expected occurrences at a medieval deathbed • 24 **save . . . the soule** except for the soul's passing from the body. This "outpassing" is evoked in 64.24–36 • 24 **this ment I** this was my intention. See line 15

lord suffered for me, that I might have suffered with him as other did that loved
him. And therfore I desired a bodely sight, wherin I might have more knowinge° of   10
the bodily paines° of our saviour, and of the compassion of our lady, and of all his
true lovers that were living that time and saw his paines. For I would have be one of
them and have suffered with them. Other sight nor shewing of God desired I never
none til whan the soule were deperted from the body, for I beleved to be saved by
the marcy of God. This was my meaning: for I would after, because of that shewing,   15
have the more true /fol. 4r/ mind in the passion of Christ.

  For the secunde, come° to my mind with contrition, frely without any seking: a
wilful desire to have of Gods gifte a bodily sicknes. I would that that sicknes were so
hard as to the death, that I might in that sicknes undertake° all my rightes of holy
church,° myselfe wening that I should die,° and that all creatures might suppose the   20
same that saw me. For I would have no maner of comforte of fleshly ne erthely life.
In this sicknes° I desired to have all maner of paines, bodily and ghostly, that I
should have if I should die,° all the dredes and tempests° of fiendes, and all maner
of other paines, save the outpassing of the soule. And this ment I: for I would be
purged by the mercy of God, and after live more to the worshippe /fol. 4v/ of God   25

<hr />

[vis. 1.7–28] lorde that he sufferede for me, that I might have sufferede with him as othere did that loved him. **Notwithstandinge that I leeved sadlye alle the peynes of Criste
as halye kyrke shewes and teches, and also the paintinges of crucifexes that er made be
the grace of God aftere the techinge of haly kyrke to the liknes of Cristes passion, als
farfurthe as manes witte maye reche—noughtwithstondinge alle this trewe beleve, ‡**
I desirede a bodilye sight, wharein I might have more knawinge of bodelye paines of oure
lorde oure savioure, and of the compassion of oure ladye, and of alle his trewe loverse
that were *belevande his paines that time and sithene.* For I wolde have beene one of thame
and suffrede with thame. Othere sight of Gode ne shewinge desirede I nevere none tille
atte the saule were departed frome the bodye, *for I trayste sothfastlye that I shulde be safe.*
And this was my meninge: for I wolde after, because of that shewinge, have the more
trewe minde in the passion of Criste.

  For the seconde, come to my minde with contrition, frelye withouten any sekinge: a
wilfulle desire to hafe of Goddes gifte a bodelye syekenes. And I wolde that this bodilye
syekenes might have beene so harde as to the dede, /fol. 97v/ so that I might in the
sekenes take alle my rightinges of halye kyrke, wenande myselfe that I shulde die, and
that alle creatures that sawe me might *wene* the same. For I wolde hafe no comforth of
no fleshlye nothere erthelye life. In this sekenes I desirede to hafe alle manere of paines,
bodelye and gastelye, that I shulde have if I shulde die, alle the dredes and tempestes of
feyndes, and alle manere of othere° paines, safe° of the outepassinge of the saule,
/Rev. 2.24–26/

26 **hoped that it might . . . die** hoped this experience might be of assistance to me when I was really dying • 27 **I desired to be soone . . . maker** A pious desire for death different from the urgent desire for sickness • 28 **twey** two • 28 **of the passion** concerning the Passion • 28–29 **was with a condition** were made with one condition • 29 **not the commune use of prayer** not the usual practice in praying. Visions were held in low esteem by many specialists of the spiritual life. In book 1.10 of his *Scale of Perfection* (1380s), Walter Hilton writes that "visiones or revelatiouns . . . aren not verily contemplation," even if they can have a "secundarye" place. Julian's request for illness has no immediate known parallels • 30 **thou wotest what I would** you know what I want • 31 **I will not . . . wilt** I do not want it except as you want it. Perhaps an echo of Christ at Gethsemane in Matt. 26:39: "My Father, if it be possible, let this cup pass from me; nevertheless, not as I will, but as thou wilt" • 32 **in my youth** Seems to refer to the time when Julian made her requests, not to her thirtieth year, when she hoped they would be fulfilled • 32 **thirtieth yeare olde** in my thirtieth year. The age at which Christ was said to have begun his ministry • 33 **For the third** The third desire is less idiosyncratic than the others, crystallizing them into a publicly acceptable mode of devotion. Hence it can be asked "without any condition" (line 37) • 34 **in my life** during my lifetime • 34–36 **very contrition . . . kind compassion . . . wilful longing to God** true sorrow for sin, natural compassion for Christ's suffering, active longing toward God. "Contrition" here corresponds to the second desire, line 17; "compassion" to the first, lines 5–6; "wilful longing," perhaps, to the twelvefold repetition of the word "desire" in this chapter.

"Compassion" is "kind," natural, because Christ's Incarnation makes him one with humankind, as a result of which all can join in his suffering, as his fleshly relatives, or "kin," by com-passion • 36 **twayne** two • 37 **mightly** mightily • 37–38 **passid from my mind** passed out of my mind. Forgotten after they were made, the first two desires are never explicitly recalled in the course of the revelation, despite their shaping role

[CHAPTER 3] 2–4 **three days . . . two days . . . third night** The days and nights here are hard to count. Probably a "day" is to be taken as beginning on the previous evening (as would be the case in a liturgical calender), so that the "three days and . . . nightes" are actually counted as three nights and days, and the "fourth night" is thus also the first night of the "two days and two nightes." If so, the "third night" begins the sixth day of Julian's sickness, the day on which her revelation takes place, lasting from morning until the evening, with a break in the middle around noon, though demonic temptations continue into the seventh morning (65.31–67.21). The sickness thus takes up a calender week, here symbolically divided into two periods of three days, paralleling the three days of Christ's Passion. The association between sickness and revelation was well established in the visionary tradition. After a long illness, the Monk of Eynsham's visions take place in a state of rapture that begins on the morning of Good Friday and lasts until the compline before Easter, during the whole of which time the crucifix in the abbey church bleeds (*The Revelation of the Monk of Eynsham,* chaps. 2–4) • 2–3 **all my rightes of holy church** See sidenote to 2.19–20 • 3 **wened** expected • 3 **liven** lived

because of that sicknes, for I hoped that it might be to me a spede when I shuld die.° For I desired to be soone with my God and maker.

These twey desires of the passion and of the sicknes that I desired of him was with a condition. For methought this was not the commune use of prayer. Therfor I said: "Lord, thou wotest° what I would. If it be thy wille that I have it, grant it me.° And if it be not thy will, good lord, be not displesed, for I will not but as thou wilt." This sicknes I desired in my youth, that I might have it when I ware thirtieth yeare olde.

For the third, by the grace of God and teching of holy church, I conceived a mighty desire to receive thre woundes in my life: that is to say, the wound of very contrition, the wound of kind */fol. 5r/* compassion, and the wound of wilful longing to God. Right as I asked the other twayne with a condition, so asked I this third mightly without any condition. These twayne desires before said passid from my mind, and the third dwellid continually.

THE THIRD CHAPTER

And when I was thirty yere old and a halfe, God sent me a bodily sicknes in the which I ley three days and three nightes, and on the fourth night I toke all my rightes of holy church, and wened° not to have liven till day. And after this I

[*VIS.* 1.28–43] for I hoped° that it might be to me a spede when I shulde die. For I desirede sone to be with my God ‡.

This two desires of the passion and of the seekenes, *I desirede thame* with a condition. For methought that *it passede the comene course* of prayers. And therfore I saide: "Lorde, thowe woote whate I wolde. If it be thy wille that I have it, graunte it me. And if it be nought thy wille, goode lorde, be nought displesede, for I wille nought botte as thowe wille." This sekenes desirede I in my youth,° that I might have it whene I were in threttye° yeere elde.

For the thirde, **I harde a man telle of halye kyrke of the storye of Sainte Cecille, in the whilke shewinge I understode that she hadde thre woundes with a swerde in the nekke, with the whilke she pinede to the dede. By the stirringe of this,** ‡ I conseyvede a mighty desire, *prayande oure lorde God that he wolde graunte me thre woundes in my life time:* that es to saye, the wounde° of ‡ contrition, the wounde of ‡ compassion, and° the wounde of wilfulle langinge to God. Right as I askede the othere two with a condition, so° I asked the thirde ‡ withouten any condition. This two desires before saide passed fro my minde, and the thirde dwelled continuelye.

[*VIS.* 2.1–4] Ande when I was thrittye *wintere* alde and a halfe, God sente me a bodelye syekenes in the whilke I laye thre dayes and thre nightes, and on the ferthe night I toke alle my rightinges of haly kyrke, and wened nought tille have liffede tille daye. And after this I

4 **langorid forth** went on languishing • 5 **they that were with me** The deathbed is a communal center, as Julian's friends wait with her for the end. At 8.24–25 and 13.29–33, she speaks to those around her as her "even-cristen," the fellow Christians for whom her revelation is intended • 5–6 **great louthsomnes to die** great hatred of dying. Julian's earlier desire "to be soone with my God and maker" has "passid from [her] mind" (2.27, 37–38). Her deep hatred of death here is one of the "gostly paines" she asks for in 2.22–24 • 6 **that me liked to live for** that I wanted to live for • 7 **ne** nor • 8–9 **by the grace of that living** by the grace further living would bring me. The logic here, which the Middle English poem *Pearl* goes to lengths to deny, is that long life gives more opportunities for good works, which lead to greater heavenly reward. *Rev.* 14.23–30 also seems to assume this cumulative idea of reward, again associated with Julian's early life. Its place in the theology of *A Revelation* as a whole is unclear, although see Chapter 38 • 10 **methought** it seemed to me • 10 **heer** here, in the present life • 10 **so litle and so shorte** The language here is reminiscent of Job 14:1, the first of the lessons in the medieval Office of the Dead: "Man that is born of a woman is of few days, and full of trouble." See also Job 7:16: "Let me alone, for my days are a breath" • 10–11 **in regard of** by comparison with • 13 **ascented fully** fully

consented • 13 **to be at Gods will** In her extremity, Julian's fundamental obligation is to honor the clause of the Lord's Prayer, "thy will be done" • 14–15 **from the middes downward** from the waist downward • 15 **was I stered** I was moved • 15–16 **underlening with helpe** leaning, supported from below • 16 **for to have . . . hart** The shift in Julian's physical posture temporarily eases what seems to be a constriction in her chest • 17 **curate** priest. In Middle English, "curate" refers to anyone in religious orders responsible for the "cure" of souls, often a parish priest. Although Julian has already taken her "rightes of holy church" (line 3) earlier, when it was first supposed she was dying, her curate returns to fulfill his responsibility to ease her passing from the world • 18 **by then he cam** by the time he came • 18 **set up my eyen** fixed my eyes • 18–19 **He set the crosse** The dying were supposed to gaze at the cross during their final agony. The priest "sets" a cross in front of Julian, initiating a public ritual that interrupts her private "setting" of her eyes. A crucifix was typically an effigy, perhaps painted, of Christ on the cross, arms outspread, head slightly to one side, body twisted, with one ankle laid over the other and a single nail transfixing both • 20 **therwith** with it • 21 **uprightward** pointing upward. Julian has adopted a typical devotional posture

langorid forth° two days and two nightes, and on the third night I wened oftentimes
to have passed, and so wened they that were with me. And yet in this I felt a great   5
louthsomnes to die, but for nothing that was in earth that me liked° to live for,
/fol. 5v/ ne for no paine that I was afraid of, for I trusted in God of his mercy. But it
was for I would have lived to have loved God better and longer time, that I might, by
the grace of that living, have the more knowing and loving of God in the blisse of
heaven. For methought all that time that I had lived heer so litle and so shorte in   10
regard of that endlesse blesse. I thought: "Good lord, may my living no longar be to
thy worshippe?" And I understode in my reason and by the feeling of my paines that
I should die, and I ascented fully with all the will of min hart to be at Gods will.

   Thus I indured till day, and by then was my body dead from the middes
downward, as to my feeling. Then was I stered° to be set upright, underlening with   15
helpe,° for to have the more /fol. 6r/ fredom of my hart to be at Gods will, and
thinke° on God while my life would° laste. My curate was sent for to be at my
ending, and by then° he cam I had set up my eyen and might not speake. He set
the crosse before my face, and said: "I have brought thee the° image of thy saviour.
Looke therupon and comfort thee therwith." Methought I was well, for my eyen   20
were° set uprightward° into heaven, where I trusted to come by the mercy of God.

[VIS. 2.4–25] langourede furthe two dayes and two nightes, and on the thirde night I
wenede ofte times to hafe passede, and so wened thaye that were aboute me. *Botte in this
I was right sarye and lothe thought for to die,* botte for nothinge that was /fol. 98r/ in erthe
that me likede to lyeve fore, nor for *nothinge* that I was aferde fore, for I tristed in God ‡.
Botte it was fore I walde hafe lyevede to have lovede God better and langere° time, that I
might,° be the grace of that lyevinge, have the more knowinge and lovinge of God in the
blisse of hevene. For methought alle the time that I had lyevede° here so litille and so
shorte in the regarde of endeles blisse. I thought thus: "Goode lorde, maye my lyevinge
be no langere to thy worshippe?" And I *was answerde°* in my resone and be the felinges of
my paines that I shulde die, and I asented fully with alle the wille of mye herte to be atte
Godes wille.

   Thus I endurede tille daye, and by than was my bodye dede fra the middes downwarde, as to my felinge. Than was I stirrede to be sette° upperightes, *lenande with clothes
to my hede,* for to have the mare fredome of my herte to be atte Goddes wille, and
thinkinge on him whiles my life walde laste. *And thay that were with me sente for the
person my curette* to be atte mine endinge. **He come, and a childe with him, and brought
a crosse,** and be thane I hadde sette mine eyen and might nought speke. *The persone*
sette the crosse before my face, and saide: "**Doughter,** I have brought the the image of
thy savioure. Loke thereopon, and comforthe the therewith **in reverence of him that
diede for the and me.**" Methought than that I was welle, for mine eyen ware sette
upwarde into hevene, whether I trustede for to come ‡.

23 **might longar dure** might longer endure • 23 **even-forth** straight ahead • 24 **it was alle darke aboute me** In fact, dawn has broken (line 14) • 25–26 **wherin held . . . light** in which remained a natural light. All Julian's "bodely sights" (see 2.10) take place inside the narrow circle of clarity her tunnel vision leaves her • 26 **wiste not how** knew not how. *A Revelation* does not attribute this "comon light" to a miracle, although "wiste not how" creates an atmosphere of suspense • 26 **All . . . beseid the crosse** everything other than the cross • 26 **oglye** ugly • 27 **mekille occupied with fiendes** greatly infested with fiends. Demons are an important presence in much of the revelation. See especially Chapters 19, 67, 69 • 28 **over part** upper part • 28–29 **so farforth that . . . feeling** so much that I had scarcely any sensation left • 29–30 **wened I sothly . . . passed** I truly imagined I was dying • 30 **sodenly** suddenly. A recurrent word in this part of the work, suggesting direct intervention by God.

See lines 32, 36, and 4.1, 6 • 31 **hole** whole • 31 **namely** especially • 32 **prevy working** mysterious work • 33 **not of kind** not a work of nature • 33 **yet by . . . ease** yet despite feeling this easing • 33–34 **I trusted never . . . lived** I did not gain any more hope that I was going to live • 34 **no full ease to me** not entirely an easement for me • 34–35 **I had lever . . . world** I would rather have been delivered from this world. The consonance of "lever" and "delivred" stresses Julian's desire at this point to slide quietly from the world • 35 **wilfully set therto** willingly fixed on death • 36 **the second wound** The wound of compassion (2.35), although the language here is closer to that of the first desire, in 2.5–16. The wound is dealt Julian throughout Chapters 4–20 • 37–38 **mind and feeling of** recollection of and feeling toward • 39 **langing to God** longing for God. The third wound asked for in 2.33–36

But nevertheles I ascented to set my eyen in the face of the crucifixe, if I might, and so I dide, for methought I might longar dure to looke evenforth then right up.

After this my sight began to faile, and it was alle darke° aboute me in the chamber as if it had ben night, save in the image of the crosse, wherin held a comon light, and I wiste not /fol. 6v/ how. All that was beseid the crosse was oglye and ferful to me, as if° it had ben mekille° occupied with fiendes.

After this the over part of my body began to die, so farforth that unneth I had any feeling. My most paine was shortnes of winde and failing of life.° Then wened I sothly° to have passed. And in this, sodenly all my paine was taken from me and I was as hole, and namely in the over parte of my body, as ever I was befor. I merveyled of this sodeyn change, for methought that it was a prevy working of God, and not of kind. And yet by the° feeling of this ease I trusted never the more to have lived, ne the feeling of this ease was no full ease to me. For methought I had lever have ben delivred of this world, for my hart was wilfully set therto.

Then cam sodenly to my mind /fol. 7r/ that I should desire the second wound of our lordes gifte and of his grace: that my body might be fulfilled with mind and feeling of his blessed passion, as I had before prayed. For I would that his paines were my paines, with compassion and afterward langing to God. Thus thought me

25

30

35

[VIS. 2.26–42] Botte neverethelesse I assended to sette mine eyen in the face of the cruci-fixe, if I might, **for to endure the langer into the time of min endinge ‡**. For methought I might langer endure to loke evenforthe than upperight.

After this my sight begane to faile, and it was alle dyrke aboute me in the chaumber, **and mirke** as it hadde bene night, save in the image of the crosse there helde a comon light, and I wiste nevere howe. Alle that was beside the crosse was huglye ‡ to me, as if it hadde bene mekille occupiede with fendes.

After this the overe partye of my bodye begane to die, *as to my felinge.* **Mine handes felle downe on aythere side, and also for unpowere my hede satylde downe** /fol. 98v/ **on side.** *The maste paine that I feled* was shortnes of winde and failinge of life. Than wende I sothelye to hafe *bene atte the pointe of dede.* And in this, sodeynlye alle my paine was *awaye* fro me and I was *alle* hole, and namelye in the overe partye of my bodye, as evere I was before **or after**. I merveylede of this ‡ change, for methought it was a prive° wyrkinge of God, and nought of kinde. And yitte be the felinge of this ese I trystede nevere the mare that I shulde lyeve, ne the felinge of this ese was ne fulle ese to me. For methought I hadde levere have bene deliverede of this worlde, for my herte was wilfulle thereto.

[VIS. 3.1–5] And sodeynlye come unto my minde that I shulde desire the seconde wounde of oure lordes gifte and of his grace: that he walde fulfille my bodye with minde and felinge° of his blessede passion, as I hadde before prayede. For I wolde that his paines ware my paines, with compassion and afterwarde langinge to God. Thus thought me

41 **no maner shewing of God** any kind of divine revelation. Julian's first desire is not generating the revelation that is about to begin, even if the revelation is given partly in answer to that desire. *The Chastising of God's Children,* adapting the words of Bridget's confessor, Alphonse of Pecha, stresses that a true visionary must not have "a sodeyn wit for fantesye" (a mind that leaps to the fantastic) but rather a "sad [sober] knowing," as someone who "hath longe continued in gostly liveng" (174–75): much the impression this passage sets out to make. As 2.13 implies, "shewing" indicates a more elevated mode of experience than the "bodily sight" Julian has desired • 42 **kind soule** natural soul. Any living soul • 42–43 **would become a deadly man** wished to become a mortal human • 43 **living in my deadly body** while still alive in my mortal body. Julian desires a brief extension of her life "in my deadly body" to suffer with Jesus as "a deadly man" by thinking of his death as she dies

[CHAPTER 4] 1 **And in this . . . I saw** In the state described at the end of Chapter 3. The phrase "in this" is used a hundred and fifty times in *A Revelation* to describe a movement inward from one state of perception to another, as sight follows sight. "I saw" is used a hundred and sixty times, to describe any kind of perception, from a bodily sight to a mental intuition or a realization—although in these last two cases its place is sometimes taken by the more intellectual "I understood" • 1–2 **red bloud trekile . . . lively** red blood trickle down from under the garland, hot and freshly, plentifully and vividly. The crown of thorns on the head of the image of the crucified Christ mentioned in 3.18–19, which animates and magnifies itself as the vision begins. This sight underlies all the "ghostly sights" in the first revelation • 3 **pressed on his blessed head** After his trial by Pontius Pilate. See Matt. 27:27–31. The language resembles that in *The Privity*: "They . . . toke a garlande of sharpe thornes in stede of a corowne and threste [thrust it] one his hede. . . . Beholde his blissede face all rinnande [running] with rede blode!" ("Ad primam," *YW* 1:203–4) • 3–4 **Right so . . . sufferd for me** Best read as an exclamation • 4–5 **I conceived . . . without any**

meane I realized truly and powerfully that it was Christ himself who showed it, without any intermediary. In *The Chastising,* the "thridde tokene to knowe a vision" is true occurs when a visionary "feelith in his soule a sodeine gostly thing springing with an inwarde feeling, and a knowing of soothfastnesse [truth]" (179) • 6 **the trinity fulfilled . . . joy** the Trinity filled my heart with the utmost joy. Not only is the sight of the bleeding cross "shewed" by God directly, Julian's response is given her by the Trinity. "Joy" is a response both to the blood itself, which is clearly first seen as an emblem of life, rather than death ("hote and freshely, plentuously and lively," line 2), and to the fact of revelation • 7–8 **the trinity is God** Late medieval Christian catechism insisted especially on the two mysteries that distinguish Christianity from its neighbors, Judaism and Islam: the doctrine of the Incarnation, alluded to in lines 1–5, and that of the Trinity, affirmed here. The first revelation, the "ground" of the revelation as a whole according to 1.6–7, thus begins by grounding itself in the fundamentals of the faith • 8–9 **maker . . . keper . . . lover . . . blisse** Another allusion to the "powers" of the three persons of the Trinity (see 1.10), this time followed by a fourth power, "joy and . . . blisse," which represents the unity of the three persons of the godhead, as well as the response they evoke in human souls • 9 **by** through • 11 **wher Jhesu appireth . . . understand** where Jesus appears in the revelation, the blessed Trinity is understood. This hermeneutic principle, that references to Jesus also allude to the Trinity, is in operation throughout the work, allowing a revelation much of which seems only to concern the human person of Christ to be interpreted as applying equally to his divinity. In *A Revelation* not only is Jesus God; God is Jesus • 13 **Benedicite dominus!** bless Lord! The Latin of this formula is not grammatical, but it is used elsewhere and is modeled on the greeting between two Benedictines, in which the junior asks for, and the senior offers, blessing. See page 4 of the Introduction. Repetition might cause "dominus" to be heard as a vocative, "domine," so that the phrase would be felt to mean "bless me, O Lord!" • 14 **astonned** astonished

that I might, with his grace, have the woundes that I had before desired.° But in this 40
I desired never no bodily sight ne no maner shewing of God, but compassion, as
methought that a kind soule might have with our lord Jesu, that for love would
become a deadly man. With him I desired to suffer, living in my deadly body, as God
would give me grace.

∞∞∞∞∞∞∞∞∞∞∞∞∞∞∞∞∞∞

The First Revelation
THE FOURTH CHAPTER

And in this, sodenly I saw the red bloud trekile° downe from under the
garlande, hote and freshely, /fol. 7v/ plentuously and lively, right as it was in
the time that the garland of thornes was pressed on his blessed head. Right so, both
God and man, the same that sufferd for me. I conceived truly and mightly that it
was himselfe that shewed it me, without any meane. 5

And in the same shewing, sodeinly the trinity fulfilled my hart most of joy. And
so I understode it shall be in heaven without end, to all that shall come ther. For the
trinity is God, God is the trinity. The trinity is our maker, the trinity is our keper,
the trinity is our everlasting lover, the trinity is our endlesse joy and our blisse, by
our lord Jesu Christ and in our lord Jesu Christ. And this was shewed in the first 10
sight and in all. For wher Jhesu appireth the blessed trinity is understand, as to
my sight.

And I said: "Benedicite dominus!" This I said for /fol. 8r/ reverence in my
mening, with a mighty voice. And full greatly was I astonned, for wonder and

---

[VIS. 3.5–16] that I might, with his grace, have *his* woundes that I hadde before desirede.
But in this I desirede nevere ne bodely sight ne no manere shewinge of God, botte compassion, as methought that a kinde saule might have with oure lorde Jhesu, that for love
wolde become man dedlye. With him I desirede to suffere, lyevande in dedlye bodye, as
God wolde giffe me grace.

And in this, sodaynlye I sawe the rede blode trekille downe fro under the garlande
alle hate, freshlye, plentefully, and livelye, right as **methought that** it was in that time that
the garlonde of thornes was *thyrstede* on his blessede hede. Right so, both God and man,
the same sufferde for me. I conseyvede treulye and mightelye that it was himselfe that
shewed it me, withouten any meen. /Rev. 4.6–12/

And than I saide: "Benedicite dominus!" This I saide reverentlye in my meninge,
with a mighty voice. And fulle gretlye I was astonned, for wondere and

15 **so reverent and so dreadful** so worthy of respect and so awe-inspiring • 15 **will be so homely** wants to be so intimate. "Homely" also means "simple," "plain," "direct"—all words with social connotations: to treat people in a "homely" way is to treat them as equals. God's wish to be "homely" with humankind is a key idea in *A Revelation,* and variants of the word are used nearly thirty times in the work • 17 **I toke it for that time** at that time I supposed • 17 **of his curteys love** "Curteyse" has overtones of "courtly," "polite," and "generous" and is balanced between "reverent dread" and "homeliness." For the distinction between "curtesye" and "homelyhed," see 77.42–45 • 19 **by the sufferance . . . keping** by God's permission and with his protection • 19–20 **tempted of fiendes . . . died** Julian still has no awareness that she is at the beginning of a revelation • 20–21 **I saw in my understanding** As becomes clear in 23.23–28, only the human Jesus, not the divine Christ (his "godhead"), suffers on the cross. Christ is thus intellectually, not physically, present in the bleeding of Jesus' head • 21–22 **all creaturs . . . saved** all living people who were to be saved. Anticipates Chapters 8–9 in its immediate incorporation of "all creaturs" into the revelation as potential witnesses and beneficiaries • 25 **ghostly . . . likenes** spiritually, but in physical form. An intermediate form of vision, not mentioned in 9.24–28, this is similar to the second of three kinds of vision described in *The Chastising,* following Augustine's influential taxonomy, as "spiritual vision or imaginatif, whan a man . . . seeth images and figures of diverse thinges, but no bodies, by shewing or revelation of God" (169). See 5.1–2 • 25–26 **a little waxen . . . childe** grown a little taller than a child • 26 **in the stature . . . conceivede** at the stage of growth she was in when she conceived. Mary is around fifteen in medieval accounts of the Annunciation • 28 **beholding . . . her God** contemplation with which she looked upon her God • 28–29 **marvayling with great reverence** Mary's reverent marveling parallels Julian's "wonder and marvayle" in lines 14–15, suggesting a wider parallel between Annunciation and revelation, as both in different senses bring Christ to birth in the world. Julian's "Benedicite dominus!" (line 13) also foreshadows Mary's "Lo me here, Gods handmaiden," spoken to Gabriel, in lines 32–33. Chapter 3 of the learned fifteenth-century life of Christ *Speculum devotorum* similarly links the Annunciation with the topic of visionary experience, arguing in words derived from Catherine of Siena's *Dialogo* that Mary's "drede" at the angel's appearance and the "mekenes" his words engendered in her were guarantees of the authenticity of her experience • 30–31 **her that was made** her who was created. "Made" (created) puns on "handmaiden" (line 33) and "maiden" (virgin) • 32 **littlehead** smallness • 32–33 **Lo me here, Gods handmaiden** See Luke 1:38 • 33 **sothly** truly • 33–34 **she is more . . . fullhead** Mary's humility paradoxically demonstrates her "fullhead"

marvayle that I had, that he that is so reverent and so dreadful will be so homely 15
with a sinful creature liveing in this wretched flesh.

Thus I toke it for that time that our lord Jhesu, of his curteys love, would shewe
me comfort before the time of my temptation. For methought it might well be that I
should, by the sufferance of God and with his keping, be tempted of fiendes before
I died.° With this sight of his blessed passion, with the godhead that I saw in my 20
understanding, I knew well that it was strength inough to me—ye, and to all
creaturs living that should be saved—against all the fiendes of hell and against
all ghostely enemies.

In this, he brought our lady Saint Mary to my understanding. /fol. 8v/ I saw her
ghostly in bodily likenes, a simple maiden and a meeke, yong of age, a little waxen 25
above a childe, in the stature as she was when she conceivede. Also God shewed me
in part the wisdom and the truth of her soule, wherin I understode the reverent
beholding that she beheld her God, that is her maker, marvayling with great
reverence that he would be borne of her that was a° simple creature of his making.
For this was her marvayling: that he that was her maker would be borne of her that 30
was made. And this wisdome and truth, knowing the greatnes of her maker and the
littlehead of herselfe that is made, made her to say full meekely to Gabriel: "Lo me
here, Gods handmaiden." In this sight I did understand sothly° that she is more then

---

[VIS. 3.16–24] merveyle that I had, that he ‡ wolde be so homlye° with a sinfulle creature
lyevande in this wreched fleshe.°

/fol. 99r/ Thus I tokede it for that time that oure lorde Jhesu, of his curtayse love, walde
shewe me comforthe before the time of my temptation. For methought it might be welle
that I shulde, be the sufferance of God and with his kepinge, be tempted of fendes or I
diede. With this sight of his blissede passion, with the godhede that I sawe° in min understandinge, I *sawe* that this was strengh enoughe to me—ye, unto alle creatures lyevande
that shulde be safe—againes alle the feendes of helle and againes alle gostelye enmies.

[VIS. 4.21–31] In this, God brought oure ladye to mine understandinge. I sawe hir gastelye in bodilye lyekenes, a simpille maidene and a meeke, yonge of age, ‡ in the stature
that sho was when sho conceivede. Also God shewed me in parte the wisdom and the
trowthe of hir saule, wharein I understode the° reverente beholdinge that she behelde
hire° God, that is hir makere, mervelande with grete reverence that he wolde be borne of
hir that was a simpille creature of his makinge. For this was hir mervelinge: that he that
was hir makere walde be borne of hir that was made.° And this wisdome and trowthe,
knawande° the gretnes of hir makere and the litellehede of hirselfe that is made, made
hir for to° saye mekelye to the angelle Gabrielle: "Lo me here, Goddes handemaidene." In
this sight I *sawe* sothfastlye that sho is mare than

[CHAPTER 5] **2 ghostly sight** spiritual vision. The sentence alludes to the common distinction between physical and spiritual vision. The first corresponds to what *The Chastising*, following Augustine's influential taxonomy of visions, calls "corporal vision . . . whanne any bodily thing by the gift of God is shewid to a mans bodily sight whiche other men seen nat." "Ghostly sight" is close to "intellectual vision, whanne no body ne image ne figure is seen, but . . . the insight of the soule . . . is clierly fastned in unbodily substaunce with a soothfast knowing [is lucidly joined in its spiritual substance with true knowledge]" (169–70). The account of the "ghostly sights" associated with the sight of Christ's blood lasts until 7.8 • **2 homely loving** intimate loving. The word "homely," already used in 4.15, acts as the point of contact between this "ghostly sight" and the "bodily" sight of Christ's blood • **3–4 wrappeth us and windeth us** wraps us and winds about us • **4 halseth us and all becloseth us** embraces us and wholly encloses us. Although this is a "ghostly sight," these words evoke the sinuous figure of Christ's body on the cross represented in many late medieval texts, images, and crucifixes. *Speculum devotorum* adapts the words of Bernard to describe "howe the lovely lordes hede hangede downwarde as it were to kisse, his armes spredde on brode as to be halsede" (226) • **7–13 And in this . . . God** See *The Scale* 2.33: "Sooth it is that oure lord is withinne alle creatures, not on that manere as a kirnel is hid withinne the shale of a note [shell of a nut], or as a litil bodily thing is hid and holden withinne another mikil [kept within a bigger one]. But he is withinne alle creatures as holdinge [maintaining] and kepinge hem [them] in here [their] beinge." See also Wisd. of Sol. 11:22–25: "The whole world before thee is like a speck that tips the scales, and like a drop of morning dew . . . thou lovest all things that exist. . . . How would anything have endured if thou hadst not willed it?" • **7 quantity** size • **7 haselnot** hazelnut. An image of littleness, compactness, fragility, toughness, fertility, "homely loving"; perhaps also, despite *The Scale*, an evocation of the idea that meaning is hidden inside appearances like a kernel inside a nut • **8 as me semide** as it seemed to me • **9 eye of my understanding** Julian's "spiritual eye," since this is a "ghostly sight" • **10 answered generally** By intuition, not by a particular speaker. See 9.24–25, 13.3–5 • **11 it might sodenly . . . littlenes** it was so little it could have collapsed suddenly into nothingness • **12–13 so hath all thing . . . God** so has everything its existence through the love of God. The belief that the creation is kept in being at each moment by love is crucial to Julian's theology of creation. See, e.g., 49.8–14, where it is used to argue against the existence of anger in God • **14 propreties** characteristics • **16 the maker, the keper, the lover** The "propreties" of the "haselnot" mean nothing to Julian except insofar as they make her think of their source, the Trinity: "maker" (Father), "keper" (Son), and "lover" (Holy Spirit) • **16 substantially oned to him** united in substance to God. The phrase develops great complexity in the course of *A Revelation*, especially in Chapters 53–58

all that God made beneth her in worthines° and in fullhead. For above /fol. 9r/ her is
nothing that is made but the blessed manhood of Christ, as to my sight.   35

THE FIFTH CHAPTER

In this same time that I saw this sight of the head bleeding, our good lord shewed
a ghostly sight of his homely loving. I saw that he is to us all thing that is good
and comfortable to our helpe. He is oure clothing, that for love wrappeth us and
windeth us, halseth us and all becloseth us, hangeth about us for tender love, that
he may never leeve us. And so in this sight I saw that he is all thing that is good, as   5
to my understanding.

And in this, he shewed a little thing the quantity of an haselnot, lying in the
palme of my hand as me semide, and it was as rounde as any° balle. I looked theran
with the eye of my understanding, and thought: "What may this be?" And it was
answered generally thus: /fol. 9v/ "It is all that is made." I marvayled how it might   10
laste, for methought it might sodenly have fallen° to nought for littlenes. And I was
answered in my understanding: "It lasteth and ever shall, for God loveth it. And so
hath all thing being by the love of God."

In this little thing I saw three propreties: the first is that God made it, the secund
is° that God loveth it, the thirde is° that God kepeth it. But what is that to me?   15
Sothly, the maker, the keper, the lover.° For till I am substantially oned° to him

---

[VIS. 4.31–32] alle that God made benethe hir in worthines and in fulhede. For abovene
hir is nothinge that is made botte the blissede manhede of Criste ‡.

[VIS. 4.1–16] And this same time that I sawe *this bodily sight,* oure lorde shewed **me** a gastelye sight of his hamly° lovinge. I sawe that he es to us alle thinge that is goode and comfortabille to oure helpe. He es oure clethinge, that° for love wappes us and windes us, halses us
and alle becloses us,° hinges aboute us for tender love, that he maye nevere leve us. And so
in this sight I sawe **sothelye** that he is alle thinge that is goode, as to mine understandinge.

And in this, he shewed **me** a litille thinge the quantite of a haselle nutte, lygande in the
palme of my hande, *and, to my understandinge, that* it was as rounde as any balle. I lokede
theropon ‡, and thought: "Whate maye this be?" And *I* was answerde generaly thus: "It is
alle that is made." I merveylede howe that it might laste, for methought it might falle
sodaynlye to nought for litille. And I was answerde in mine understandinge: "It lastes and
ever shalle, for God loves it. And so hath alle thinge the beinge thorowe the love of God."

In this litille thinge I sawe thre parties: the firste is that God made it,° the seconde is
that he loves it, the thirde is that God kepes it. Botte whate is that to me? Sothelye, the
makere, *the lovere, the kepere.* For to I am substantiallye aned to him

17 **very** true • 17 **fastned** Language evocative of the Crucifixion, here of Christ's body "fastened" to the cross. Compare lines 3–4 and see 15.2 • 18 **right nought** nothing at all • 19–20 **This little thing . . . littlenes** A near repetition of the passage at lines 10–11 • 20–25 **Of this nedeth . . . rest us in him** The language of this passage is close to that in Rolle's *Form of Living:* "The fifte asking [your fifth question] was in what state men may maste [most] lufe God. I answer: in wilk state sa it be that men er in maste rest of body and saule [in whatever state it may be in which people are in most physical and spiritual rest], and leest occupied with any nedes or bisines of this worlde. For the thoght of the lufe of Jhesu Criste, and of the joy that lastes ay, sekes rest withouten, that it be noght letted with comers and gangers [comers and goers] and occupation of worldely things . . . And namely al that lufes contemplatife lif, thay seke rest in body and in saule." (chap. 10, *YW* 1:44–45) • 20–21 **Of this nedeth . . . unmade** we need to know this about it: it benefits us to reject everything that is created, in order to love and have God, who is uncreated. Although the syntax is not quite clear (see page 25 of the Introduction), "this" is presumably "this little thing that is made." The very thing that God keeps from falling to "nought" needs to be "noughted" • 24 **him liketh** it pleases him. An impersonal construction, a regular feature of the work's style. See, e.g., 1.42 • 25 **suffiseth not to us** is not adequate for us • 26 **till it is noughted . . . made** until it is freed from all things that are created. The passage echoes the famous opening of Augustine's *Confessions:* "Thou hast made us for thyself and restless is our heart until it comes to rest in thee." In *The Scale* 1.43, Hilton, echoing Augustine, describes how the fallen soul "seketh his reste in creatures, now fro oon to another [shifting

from one to another], and never may finde ful reste, for he hath lost him in whom is ful reste" • 26–27 **wilfully noughted** deliberately effaced or made nothing. Now it is the soul, not the created order, that must be "noughted" • 28–29 **sely soule** innocent soul • 29 **nakedly, plainly, and homely** simply, plainly, and intimately. The first two of these qualities of the "sely soule's" approach to God resemble the qualities pastoral theologians often enjoined on those going to confession. *Ancrene Wisse* is only one of many works to insist that confession be "naked and plain" (pt. 5) • 29 **kinde yerning** natural longing • 30 **touching** prompting. A prompting seen as "kinde," natural, even as it includes the spiritual, despite the fact that, a few lines earlier, people have been described as "seek[ing] heer rest in this thing that is so little, wher no reste is in." What constitutes "kinde" behavior, and God's role in reminding the soul of its "kinde," is explored in detail in Chapters 52–63 • 30–31 **as by the understanding . . . shewing** according to the understanding that I have received in this revelation. This clause introduces a speech by the soul that is extrapolated from the "shewing" of the creation as nut but that lines 33–35 then treat as though it were part of the original revelation. *Rev.* 51.65 calls this mode of revelation, often formally introduced by the word "understanding," "the inwarde lerning that I have understonde [in the revelation] sithen [since it occurred]" • 33 **ever me wanteth** I will always desire • 34 **full lovesum** very comforting • 34 **full neer touche** are most intimately linked with • 35 **comprehendeth** includes. See 1.4 • 36 **overpasseth without end** eternally transcends them. God's goodness is not limited to or defined by his creatures and his works • 36 **endlesshead** the source of eternity

I may never have full reste ne very blisse: that is to say, that I be so fastned to him
that ther be right nought that is made betweene my God and me.

This little thing that is made, methought it might have fallen to nought for
littlenes. Of this nedeth us to have knowinge,° that us liketh to nought° all thing that
is made, for to love /fol. 10r/ and have God that is unmade.° For this is the cause why
we be not all in ease of hart and of soule: for we seeke heer rest in this thing that is
so little, wher no reste is in, and we know not our God, that is al mighty, all wise,
and all good. For he is very reste. God will be knowen, and him liketh that we rest us
in him. For all that is beneth him suffiseth not to us. And this is the cause why that
no soule is rested° till it is noughted of all thinges that is made. When he° is wilfully
noughted for love to have him that is all, then is he° able to receive ghostly reste.

And also our good lord shewed that it is full great plesance to him that a sely
soule come to him nakedly,° plainly, and homely. For this is the kinde yerning° of
the soule by the touching of the holy ghost, as by the understanding that I have in
this shewing: /fol. 10v/ "God, of thy goodnes geve me thyselfe. For thou art inough to
me, and I may aske nothing that is lesse that may be full worshippe to thee. And if I
aske anything that is lesse, ever me wanteth. But only in thee I have all." And these
wordes, "God, of thy goodnes,"° be full lovesum to the soule, and full neer touche°
the will of our lord. For his goodnes comprehendeth° all his creaturs and all his
blessed workes and overpasseth° without end. For he is the endlesshead, and he hath

20

25

30

35

[VIS. 4.16–20] I may nevere have full reste° ne varray blisse: that is to saye, that /fol. 99v/
I be so festenede to him that thare be right nought that is made betwyxe my God and
me. **And wha shalle do this dede? Sothlye himselfe, be his mercye and his grace, for he
has made me thereto and blisfullye restored.**

[VIS. 4.33–47] This litille thinge that es made **that es benethe oure ladye Saint Marye,
God shewed it unto me als litille as it hadde beene a haselle notte.** Methought it might
hafe fallene ‡ for litille.

**In this blissede revelation God shewed me thre noughtes, of whilke noughtes this is
the firste that was shewed me.** Of this nedes *ilke man and woman* to hafe knawinge **that
desires to lyeve contemplatifelye,** that *him* like to nought alle thinge that es made for to
hafe the love of God that es unmade. For this es the cause why *thaye that er occupiede wilfullye in erthelye besines, and evermare sekes warldlye wele, er* nought all in ese° in herte
and in saule: for *thaye love and sekes* here reste in this thinge that is so litille, whare no
reste is in, and knawes nought God, that es alle mighty, alle wise, and alle goode. For he
is verraye reste. God wille be knawen, and him likes that /fol. 100r/ we reste us in him.
For alle that ar benethe him suffices nought to us. And this is the cause why that na saule
is restede to it be noghthed of alle that es made. When he is ‡ noughthid for love to hafe
him that is alle **that is goode,** than es he abylle to resayve gostlye reste. /Rev. 5.28–7.8/

[CHAPTER 6] 1–2 **This shewing . . . God** The "ghostly sight" of the creation as hazelnut produces a meditation one step further removed from the "bodily sight" of the blood in Chapter 4. The sentence "God, of thy goodnes geve me thyselfe," spoken by the soul in 5.31, is the agent of generation • 1 **lerne** teach • 2 **cleve** cleave • 3–4 **how that we use . . . meanes** how we tend, through ignorance of love, to invent many mediators. That is, Christians tend to pray to God through his attributes or the saints rather than directly, as the soul does in 5.31–33 • 4–5 **more very delite** a truer pleasure • 7 **For if we make . . . litle** for even if we invoke all of these mediators, our invocation is inadequate • 8 **But in his goodnes . . . nought** but in his goodness is the entire wholeness [of God], and nothing at all is lacking from it. In its rejection of "meanes," *A Revelation* is here close to the attitude inculcated by *The Cloud of Unknowing,* which similarly instructs its readers to "lift . . . up thin herte unto God with a meek stering of love, and mene God that mad thee and bought thee and that graciously hath clepid [called] thee to this werk, and reseive [receive] none other thought of God" (28) • 9–10 **We pray . . . holy flesh** we pray to God through his holy flesh. Liturgical and private prayers often invoke Christ by his body, blood, Passion, death. Rolle's *Meditations* includes many such invocations: "Swete lord Jhesu Crist, I thanke the of peynes that thou soffred for us and for the swete blod that thou bledde for us. . . . I prey the and byseke the as my dere lord, that swete blood that thou bledde so largely for me, may be ful remissioun for my soule" (*YW* 1:84) • 12 **of all this** as a result of all these • 13 **that him bare** who bore him • 16 **special saintes** patron saints. Saints to whom one was linked by day of birth, name, or place • 17 **frenship** patronage. It was the responsibility of a "special sainte" to offer aid when asked • 19–24 **For God . . . goodnes of all** This passage states a position almost opposite to the one just articulated: a mode of exposition by thesis and antithesis characteristic of *A Revelation,* although this is an extreme example. The church's prayers, after all, often invoke "meanes" • 19 **full faire and fele** very fair and many • 20–21 **kinde . . .**

maiden human nature he received from the Virgin • 22–24 **Wherfor . . . goodnes of all** The hinge sentence between the two parts of the chapter • 25–26 **Forto . . . need** From being the sole necessary "meanes" for praying to God, "goodnes" now becomes the prayer of God himself, descending to minister to human need in a repetition of Christ's descent to earth at the Incarnation. This passage is reminiscent of Langland's *Piers Plowman* B 1.148, 154, where love, the "triacle [medicine] of hevene," cannot rest till it has "eten his fille" of "erthe" • 26 **It quickeneth . . . bringeth it on life** God's goodness quickens our soul and brings it to life • 27 **waxe . . . vertu** As the human child grows. See 55.26–31 • 29 **verely** truly • 29 **beclosede** enclosed • 29–31 **A man goeth . . . honestly** A difficult passage, the key to which is the meaning of the word "soule." If this word is "soul," the passage metaphorically describes either birth or death. However, in the context of the vocabulary of the rest of the passage, "soule" is probably a spelling of "saule"/ "sawlee" (French *saulee*), food or meal, a common word in late Middle English. The "purse" is then the bowel, and "nescessery" excretion, while "upperight" stresses the difference between humankind and four-legged animals, just as the most animal of human functions is about to be invoked. "A person walks upright and the food he has eaten is closed as though in a very beautiful drawstring purse. And when it is time for him to excrete, the purse is opened up and closed again very cleanly." Divine "goodnes" is present even in this basic process. Anticipates the portrayal of God as a mother in Chapters 55–62 • 32 **wher he seith** In lines 25–26. God's goodness comes down to "our need" not only in sublime and spiritual ways, but also in humble ones: he comes down even to a person's "nescessery," taking care of the "saule" as he does of the "soule" • 33 **he hath no dispite . . . made** he has no contempt for what he created. Penitential literature, meditating on the vileness of the flesh, sometimes encouraged an attitude of contempt for bodily functions, describing the body itself as a *vas stercorum,* a bag of shit, a phrase used in *Ancrene Wisse,* part 4, and elsewhere

made° us only to himselfe and restored us by his precious passion, and ever kepeth us in his blessed love. And all this is of his goodnes.

THE SIXTH CHAPTER

This shewing was geven, as to my understanding,° to lerne our soule wisely to cleve to the goodnes of God. And in that same time, the custome of our prayer was brought to my mind: how /*fol. 11r*/ that we use, for unknowing of love, to make meny meanes. Then saw I sothly° that it is more worship to God, and more very delite, that we faithfully pray to himselfe of his goodnes and cleve therto by his grace, with true understanding and stedfast beleve, then if we made all the meanes that hart may thinke. For if we make all these meanes, it is to litle and not ful worshippe to God. But in his goodnes is all the hole, and ther faileth right nought.

For thus as I shall say cam to my mind in the same time. We pray to God for his holy flesh and for his precious bloud, his holy passion, his dereworthy death and worshipful woundes: and° all the blessed kindnes and the endlesse life that we have of all this, it is of his goodnes.° And we pray him for his sweete mothers love /*fol. 11v*/ that him bare:° and all the helpe that we have of her, it is of his goodnes. And we pray for his holy crosse that he died on: and all the helpe and all the vertu that we have of that crosse, it is of his goodnes. And on the same wise, all the helpe that we have of special saintes, and of all the blessed company of heaven, the dereworthy love and the holy endles frenshipe that we have of them, it is of his goodnes.

For God of his goodnes hath ordained meanes to helpe us° full faire and fele.° Of which the chiefe and principal meane is the blessed kinde that he toke of the maiden, with all the meanes that gone° before and come after, which belong° to our redemption and to our endles salvation. Wherfor it pleaseth him that we seke him and /*fol. 12r*/ worshippe him by meanes, understanding and knowing that he is the goodnes of all.

Forto the goodnes of God is the highest prayer, and it cometh downe to us, to the lowest party of our need. It quickeneth° our soule and bringeth it on life,° and maketh° it to waxe in grace and in vertu. It is nerest in kinde and rediest in grace. For it is the same grace that the soule seketh and ever shalle, tille we knowe oure God verely, that hath us all in himselfe beclosede. A man goeth upperight, and the soule of his body is sparede as a purse fulle fair. And whan it is time of his nescessery, it is openede and sparede ayen fulle honestly. And that it is he that doeth this, it is shewed ther wher he seith: "He cometh downe to us, to the lowest parte of oure nede." For he hath no dispite of that he made, /*fol. 12v*/ ne he hath no disdaine

5

10

15

20

25

30

34 **that . . . longeth in kinde** that is proper to our body in its natural state • 36 **harte in the bowke** heart in the chest. The old-fashioned word "bowke," from Old English "buc," body or carcass, is evidently chosen here in preference to "body" for its associations with the densely corporeal. The word is elsewhere used for the bodies of animals, or human bodies hewn about on the field of battle • 37 **cladde . . . goodnes of God** See 5.3: "He is oure clothing" • 38 **were away** wear away. At death, the end of the natural cycle whose beginning is invoked in line 26 • 39 **more nere . . . without any likenes** closer to us without any comparison. Divine goodness is incomparably closer to human selfhood than is the body to its clothing, the flesh to the skin, etc. • 40 **with all the mightes** with all its powers • 41 **cleving to his goodnes** Returns to the language of lines 1–2 and of 5.31–33 • 41 **it pleseth most God** this most pleases God. "Cleving to his goodnes" • 42 **soneste spedeth** is most quickly useful • 43 **overpasseth . . . creatures** transcends the knowledge of all created beings • 44 **wit** know • 44 **mekille** greatly • 46–47 **stande in gostly beholding . . . marveling** See Mary's similar "beholding" in 4.27–28, as she contemplates the incarnation of the "goodnes of God" (line 25) • 48–49 **therfore we may aske . . . all that we wille** By this point in the chapter, it is hardly relevant whether one chooses to use "meanes" to pray to God, so pervasive is his "goodnes" • 49 **kindely wille** See "kinde yerning" at *Rev.* 5.29. The human need for God is as natural as God's concern to minister to "the simplest office that to oure body longeth in kinde"

(line 34) • 50 **never blin of willing** never cease from wanting • 54 **herefore** therefore • 54 **lesson of love** See the opening and close of *A Revelation,* 1.1 and 86.13–17 • 56 **the beholding . . . maker** contemplating and loving the creator • 56–57 **seme lest . . . sight** seem least in his view of himself. Contemplating the creator is a more effective way to humility than the contempt for the world initially implied by the vision of creation as mere "haselnot" in 5.7 • 57 **reverent drede** reverent fear. See 7.5, where the phrase is applied to Mary • 58 **evencristen** fellow Christians. First use of this key word. See 8.31–37

[CHAPTER 7] 1 **to lerne us this** This lesson about the need to contemplate the creator, described in 6.54–58. Parallels the opening of Chapter 6 • 2 **Sent** saint • 2 **highe wisdom and truth** An allusion to Mary's first appearance, in 4.24–35, on which this passage builds • 5 **reverend drede** reverent fear. This phrase, applied to the soul in 6.57, refers back to Mary's reverence in 4.27–29 and forward to a discussion of fear in Chapters 74–77. See also 8.20 • 6 **in regard of** by comparison with • 7 **by this grounde** on this foundation. Wisdom and truth lead to reverence of God and so to meekness, which in turn makes Mary worthy to receive grace. "Grounde" also alludes to the first revelation, which is the "strength and the grounde of alle" (6.55) • 8 **overpasseth alle creatours** transcends all created things. See 6.43, 47

to serve us at the simpilest office that to oure body longeth in kinde, for love of the
soule that he hath made° to his awne liknesse. For as the body is clad in the cloth,   35
and the flesh in the skinne, and the bones in the flesh, and the harte in the bowke,
so ar we, soule and body, cladde and enclosedde in the goodnes of God.

Yee, and more homely! For all these may waste and were away.° The goodnesse
of God is ever hole, and more nere to us without any likenes.° For truly oure lover
desireth that the soule cleve to him with all the mightes, and that we be evermore   40
cleving to his goodnes. For of alle thing that hart may thinke, it pleseth most God
and soneste spedeth. For oure soule is so presciously loved /fol. 13r/ of him that is
highest, that it overpasseth the knowing of alle creatures: that is to say, ther is no
creature that is made that may wit how mekille• and how swetely and how tenderly
oure maker° loveth us.   45

And therfore we may, with his grace and his helpe, stande in gostly beholding,
with everlasting marveling in this high, overpassing, unmesurable love that oure
lorde hath to us of his goodnes. And therfore we may aske of oure lover, with
reverence, all that we wille. For oure kindely wille is to have God, and the good
wille of God is to have us, and we may never blin° of willing ne of loving tille we   50
have him in fulhede of joy. And than we may no more wille. For he wille that we be
occupied in knowing and loving tille the time cometh that we shal be /fol. 13v/
fulfillede in heven.

And herefore was this lesson of love shewed, with alle that foloweth, as ye shall
see. For the strength and the grounde of alle was shewed in the furst sight. For of   55
alle thing, the beholding and the loving of the maker maketh the soule to seme lest
in his awne sight, and most filleth hit with reverent drede and trew meknesse, and
with plente of charite to his evencristen.

THE SEVENTH CHAPTER

And to lerne us this, as to my understanding, our good lorde shewed our lady,
Sent Mary, in the same time: that is to meane, the highe wisdom and truth
that she had in beholding of her maker. This wisdom and truth made her to beholde
her God so gret, so high, so mighty, and° so good. This gretnesse and this nobilnesse
/fol. 14r/ of her beholding of God fulfilled her of reverent drede. And with this she   5
sawe herselfe so litille and so lowe, so simple and so poor in regard of her God,
that this reverent drede fulfilled her of meknes. And thus by this grounde she was
fulfilled of grace, and of alle maner of vertues,° and overpasseth° alle creatours.

9–10 **gostely sight . . . bodely sight** After the elaborately articulated theology of Chapters 5–6, the physicality of the "bodely sight" is evoked by the startling homeliness of the imagery in this passage • 11 **pelottes** pellets or gobbets. A word used not only of rain but of stones, cannonballs, hunks of meat • 11–12 **seming . . . of the veines** Although the circulation of the blood was fully described only in the sixteenth century, it was known that "Blode is yette out [shed] when the cote [exterior] of the vesselles, that is, veines, is . . . opened or broken" (*The Cyrurgie of Guy de Chauliac*, 219) • 12 **browne rede** dark red. See 16.3, which has the phrase "browne blew." Blood coming out of the veins was called "brown" or "black" blood • 14 **browes** eyebrows. Julian is looking at the front of Christ's head. At this stage of the revelation, his face is not affected by the bleeding, but see Chapter 10 • 14–16 **And . . . livelyhede** At this stage of the revelation, Christ's blood is seen as inexhaustible • 14 **notwithstonding** although • 15 **fairhede** beauty • 16 **livelyhede** vitality • 17 **plentuoushede** abundance • 17–18 **of the evesing of an house** from the eaves of a house. The crown of thorns is like the eaves of a house, perhaps one roofed with thatch. The images here are alluded to nowhere else in *A Revelation* • 19 **bodely wit** natural intelligence • 19–20 **for the roundhede . . . of the forhede** in their roundness as they spread across the forehead, they resembled the scales of herring. Herring scales are round, shiny, closely linked, and very numerous. The fish itself was a basic, abundant source of food in medieval Norwich • 23–24 **quick . . . lovely** living and vivid, and hideous and frightening, and sweet and lovely • 25 **homely** intimate • 26 **liking and sekernesse** delight and confidence • 27 **he shewde . . . example** he revealed to me a lucid exemplum, or parable. One of several: see 14.19–21, 25.26–28, 51.1–51. As in 5.30–31, the phrase "to the understonding of this" introduces a meditative addition to the original revelation. All the exempla involving lords and servants point forward to the central chapter in the work, Chapter 51 • 29 **namely** especially • 29 **if he shew it himselfe . . . mening** if he makes it known personally (not just through his servants) with a deeply sincere intention • 30 **chere** expression • 30 **in previte and openly** in private and in public • 32 **marvelous homelyhede** wonderful intimacy. This oxymoron sums up the mixture of "reverent . . . dredfulle . . . homely and . . . curteyse" in the revelation (lines 25–26). Variations recur three times, at lines 35 ("grete homelyhede"), 42 ("marvelous curtesy and homelyhede"), and 45 • 33 **wer . . . strange in maner** behaved distantly. To be "strange" is to be formal or foreign, the opposite of "homely" • 33–35 **This bodely exsample . . . homelyhede** this story taken from everyday life was revealed in so sublime a way that this person's [the servant's] heart might well be overwhelmed and he come close to forgetting himself for joy of this great intimacy. The only use of "ravish" in *A Revelation* • 36 **Thus it fareth by . . . by us** thus it is between our Lord Jesus and us

And in alle that time that he shewd this that I have now saide in gostely sight, I
saw the bodely sight lasting of the plentuous° bleding of the hede. The gret droppes   10
of blode felle downe fro under the garlonde like pelottes, seming as it had comen
oute of the veines. And in the coming oute they were browne° rede, for the blode
was full thicke. And in the spreding abrode they were bright rede. And whan it
came at the browes, ther they vanished. And notwithstonding /fol. 14v/ the bleding
continued tille many thinges were sene and understonded, nevertheles the fairhede   15
and the livelyhede continued in the same bewty and livelines.

The plentuoushede is like to the droppes of water that falle of the evesing of an
house after a grete shower of raine, that falle so thicke that no man may nomber
them with no bodely wit. And for the roundhede,° they were like to the scale of
hering, in the spreding of the forhede. Thes thre thinges cam to my minde in the   20
time: pelettes, for the roundhede in the coming oute of the blode; the scale of
herring, for the roundhede in the spreding; the droppes of the evesing of a house, for
the plentuoushede unnumerable. This shewing was quick and lively, and hidous and
dredfulle, and swete and lovely. /fol. 15r/ And of all the sight that I saw, this was most
comfort to me: that oure good lorde, that is so reverent and dredfulle, is so homely   25
and so curteyse. And this most fulfilled me with liking and sekernesse in soule.

And to the understonding of this, he shewde this open example. It is the most
wurship that a solempne king or a gret lorde may do to a pore servante if he wille be
homely with him, and namely if he shew it himselfe of a fulle true mening and with
a glad chere, both in previte and openly. Than thinketh this pore creature thus: "Lo,   30
what might this noble lorde do more wurshippe and joy to me than to shew to me,
that am so litille, this marvelous homelyhede?• Sothly° it is more joy and liking to
me than if he gave me gret geftes,° and wer himselfe /fol. 15v/ strange in maner." This
bodely exsample was shewde so high that this mannes hart might be ravished and
almost forget himselfe for joy of this grete homelyhede.•   35

Thus it fareth by oure lorde Jhesu and by us. For sothly° it is the most joy that
may be, as to my sight, that he that is highest and mightiest, nobliest and wurthiest,

---

[VIS. 5.1–2] And in that time that oure lorde shewed this that I have nowe saide in gaste-
lye° sight, I saw° the bodilye sight lastande of the plentyouse bledinge of the hede.
/Rev. 7.10–24/

[VIS. 7.11–13] Of alle that I° sawe, this was the maste comforthe to me: that oure lorde ‡
es so hamlye and so curtayse. And this maste filled° me with likinge and syekernes in
saule. /Rev. 7.27–54/

38 **hamliest and curtysest** most intimate and most courteous • 39–40 **And this wille . . . make solace** and our good Lord wills this, that we believe and trust, rejoice and take pleasure, comfort and solace ourselves • 43 **in oure lorde . . . oure broder** Christ himself is a manifestation of God the Father's "homelyhede" • 45–54 **But . . . ende** The peroration of the first revelation. God's intimacy can only be known through revelation or inner grace, but it can be believed in and deserved by faith, hope, and charity, the cardinal virtues of 1 Cor. 13. Though the "shewing" reveals "prevy pointes" about God, it is ultimately the same as faith. This point is developed in Chapter 9, although see Chapter 45 for a more complex understanding of the relation between "shewing" and faith • 47 **mede** reward. Of God's "homelyhede" • 48 **in faith . . . oure life is grounded** Faith is the basis on which Christian living is built: the last of several uses of "ground" in the first revelation. See 1.6–7 • 48–49 **made to whom that God wille** Julian, writing in a period when visionaries were fairly numerous, does not think herself the sole recipient of a revelation of God's "homelyhede" • 49 **opened and declared** revealed and articulated • 50 **prevy pointes** secret details • 51 **in a time** at a particular point in time • 51 **passede and hidde** finished and hidden. That God's "homelyhede" can be hidden is a paradox of revelation, which is more temporary than "faith." The sentence acknowledges the passage of time between the revelation and this analysis of it, and how the divine "homelyhede" has not necessarily been present to Julian during that time • 52 **by the shewing** concerning the revelation • 53–54 **oure lordes mening . . . the last ende** See Chapter 86

[CHAPTER 8] 1 **plentuous bleding of the heed** plentiful bleeding from the head. See 4.1–5 • 2 **stinte of** stop saying • 2 **Benedicite dominus!** bless Lord. See 4.13 • 3 **six thinges** Befitting its status as the "ground" of the revelation as a whole, the first revelation is the only one to be followed by a summary of its contents. The summary, which differs from the earlier summary in 1.3–7, subdivides the revelation into its original elements, rather as Chapter 1 subdivides the revelation as a whole into sixteen smaller units. Apart from lines 9–13, the summary offers no new insights, though it does present the reader with the main evidence on the basis of which *A Revelation* has woven its exposition. The summary begins with the "bodily sight" of the blood, then moves to the "ghostly sights" by way of the vision of Mary, which is seen "ghostly in bodily likenes" (4.25). Beyond that, the principle of ordering is not clear, although the last four items move more or less backward through Chapter 5, reversing the direction of its argument • 4 **The furst** See 4.1–5, 7.9–26 • 4 **tokens** symbols. In medieval iconography, the crown of thorns, the cross, and the pillar to which Christ was bound were all regarded as synecdoches, or "tokens," of his Passion, detachable from the narrative of the Passion as objects of meditation in their own right, just as they are seen in *A Revelation* • 6 **The seconde** See 4.24–35, 7.1–8 • 6 **deerwurthy** precious • 7 **The thurde** See 5.14–27, understood as an actual revelation of the "blissful godhede"

is lowest and mekest, hamliest and curtysest. And truly and sothly° this marvelous
joy shalle he shew us all, when we shall see him. And this wille oure good lorde that
we beleve and trowe,° joy and like, comfort us and make solace, as we may with his   40
grace and with his helpe, into the time that we see it verely. For the most fulhede of
joy that we shalle have, as to my sight, is this marvelous curtesy and homelyhede• of
oure fader that is oure maker, in oure lorde Jhesu Crist that is oure broder and oure
/fol. 16r/ savior.

    But this marvelous homelyhede• may no man know in this life, but if he have it   45
by specialle shewing of oure lorde, or of gret plenty of grace inwardly given of the
holy gost. But faith and beleve with charite deserve the mede, and so it is had by
grace. For in faith, with hope and cherite, oure life is grounded. The shewing, made°
to whom that God wille, plainely techeth the same, opened and declared, with many
prevy pointes belonging to our faith and beleve which be wurshipful to be knowen.   50
And whan the shewing, which is given in a time,° is passede and hidde, than faith
kepeth it, by grace of the holy goste, into our lives ende. And thus, by the shewing:
it is none other than the faith, ne lesse ne more, as it may be seene by oure lordes
mening in the same matter, by than it come to the last ende. /fol. 16v/

THE EIGHTH CHAPTER

And as longe as I saw this sight of the plentuous bleding° of the heed, I might
never stinte of these wordes: "Benedicite dominus!" In which shewing I
understood six thinges.

    The furst is the tokens of the blisseful° passion and the plentuous sheding of his
precious blode.   5

    The seconde is the maiden that is his deerwurthy mother.

    The thurde is the blisseful• godhede that ever was and is and shalle be: alle
mighty, alle wisdom, and all love.

[*vis*. 5.3–9] And als longe as I sawe that sight ‡ *I saide often times:* "Benedicite dominus!"
    In this firste shewinge of oure lorde I sawe sex thinges in mine understandinge.
    The furste is the° takens of his blisfulle passion and the plenteous shedinge of his
precious blode.
    The seconde is the maidene, *that she is* his dereworthy modere.
    The thirde is the blisfulle godhede that ever was and es and ever shalle be: alle
mighty, alle wisdome, and alle love.

9 **The fourth** See 5.7–11 • 9–10 **wele I wot . . . good** I know well that heaven and earth and all that is created is vast and beautiful and broad and good. A reaction against 5.7–27 and its account of creation as "nought" • 11 **for I saw it** that I saw it • 14 **The fifth** See 5.12–13 • 16 **The sixth** See 5.5–6, much developed in Chapter 6 • 19 **beholde** contemplate • 19 **stinted** ceased • 19 **dwelled** remained • 20 **abode** waited • 20 **with reverent dred** Like Mary at the Annunciation, "fulfilled . . . of reverend drede" by her "beholding of God" in 7.4–7 • 20 **joyeng in that I saw** rejoicing in what I saw • 21 **durste** dared • 21 **to see more** Julian's earlier sense that her experience is a prelude to her death, in 4.17–20, is here represented as beginning to shift • 21 **lengar** longer • 22 **mekille sterede . . . to mine evenchristen** very much moved in charity toward my fellow Christians. The need to disseminate the revelation among "evenchristen" is implied by its deathbed setting, with Julian's friends gathered around • 24 **in generalle** As a message for everyone, rather than merely the personal act of divine comfort Julian at first supposed the revelation to be • 24–25 **them that were with me** Her companions are here treated as representatives of her "evenchristen" • 25 **It is todaye domesday with me** today is judgment day for me. This remark, though it follows the expectations of the deathbed scene in progress, seems at odds with the revelation just described, which notably makes no allusion to the judgment • 25 **wened** expected • 26–27 **that day . . . understanding** on the day that a man or a woman dies he is judged as he shall be without end, as I understand it. Recalls the teaching, commonly but not universally held in Julian's day, that the individual is judged by God at death, rather than at Judgment Day, and that this judgment remains fixed for eternity

The fourth is all thinge that he hath made. For wele I wot that heven and erth and alle that is made is mekille and° large and fair and good. But the cause why it sheweth so litille to my sight was for I saw it in the presence of him that is the maker. For to a soul° that seth the maker of all thing, all that is made semeth fulle /fol. 17r/ litille. 10

The fifth is that he has made° alle thing that is made for love. And by the same love it is kepte and shall be withoute ende, as it is° before saide. 15

The sixth is that God is alle thing that is good, as to my sight. And the goodnesse that alle thing hath, it is he.

And alle this our lorde shewde in the furst sight, and gave me space and time to beholde it. And° the bodely sight stinted, and the gostely sighte dwelled° in my understonding. And I abode with reverent dred, joyeng in that I saw, and desiring 20 as I durste to see more, if it were his wille, or lengar time the same.°

In alle this I was mekille• sterede in cherite to mine evenchristen, that they might alle see and know the same that I sawe, for I wolde that it were comfort to them. For alle this sight was shewde /fol. 17v/ in generalle. Than saide I to them that were with me: "It is todaye° domesday with me." And this I saide for I wened to have 25 died. For that day that man or woman dieth is he demede° as he shal be withoute

---

[VIS. 5.10–21] The ferthe is alle thinge that he has made. For wele I woote that heven and erth and alle that is made° is mekille and faire and large and goode. Botte the cause why it shewed so litille to my sight was for I sawe itte in the presence of him that es makere. For to a saule that sees the makere of alle thinge, alle that es made semes° fulle litille.

The fifte es that he has made alle thinge that is made for love. And thorowe the same love it is kepede and ever shalle be withouten ende, as it is before saide.

The sexte es that God is alle thinge that is goode ‡. And the goodenes that alle thinge has is he.

And alle this° oure lorde shewed **me** in the first sight, and gafe me space and time to behalde it. And the bodily sight stinted, and the gastely sight dwelled in mine understandinge. And I abode with reverente drede, joyande in that I sawe, and desirande as I durste for to see mare, if it ware his wille, or the same langer time.

[VIS. 7.8–11] And in alle this I was mekille stirrede in charite to mine evencristene, that thaye might alle see and knawe the same that I sawe, for I walde that it ware comforthe to thame /fol. 101v/ **alle, as it es to me.** For this sight was shewed in generalle **and nathinge in specialle.**

[VIS. 7.14–16] Than saide I to *the folke* that were with me: "It es todaye domesdaye with me." And this I saide for I wenede to hafe died. For that daye that man or woman dies is he demed as he shalle be withouten

28 **have minde** recollect • 28 **as they might se in exsample** Unable to convey her revelation, Julian offers to her fellows her death as an example of life's brevity • 29–30 **marveyle to me . . . perty** extraordinary to me and somewhat desperate. "Marveyle" and "sweme" (which means "grief," "despair," but also "swoon") are nouns, easiest to translate here as adjectives • 30 **avision** vision. A vaguer and less certain word than "shewinge" or "revelation" (see 1.1–2), and so appropriate to Julian's excited but appropriately uncertain state of mind at this time • 31 **of me** about myself • 31 **I mene . . . my evencristen** I mean to be interpreted as referring to all my fellow Christians. Exegetes often referred to passages of the Bible as voiced "in the person" of a certain group. References to Julian in *A Revelation* are to be interpreted according to the same principle • 32 **lerned in . . . he meneth so** taught by our Lord's spiritual revelation that he means so • 33 **counceyle** advise. "Counceyle" is what equals or friends offer each other • 34 **leve the beholding . . . shewde to** stop dwelling on the wretch to whom it was shown. Even though she has just offered herself "in exsample" (line 28), the passage makes a fierce plea for the anonymity of Julian's voice • 35–36 **wold shew it generally** wished to reveal it publicly • 37 **as Jhesu had . . . you** as if Jesus had shown it to you. See 7.45–54 for this idea that the revelation is to be experienced, not simply read about, by any person

[CHAPTER 9] 1 **For the shewing . . . better** I am not good merely because of the revelation unless I love God the better for it. This antielitism marks a return to the careful modesty of 3.40–44. *The Chastising,* adapting Alphonse, states that a true visionary can be known by "whether he hath any presumption of his visions, or maketh any bost of hem with veinglorye, or holdith himsilf the more of reputatioun, or hath any other men in dispite or indignation" (174). Elsewhere it notes "that visions . . . proven nat a man or woman holy or parfite" (182) • 2 **it is more** it is of more significance • 3 **wit** know • 3 **you that be simple** Julian is herself referred to as a "simple creature" in 2.1. Identifying with the simple, she addresses them as "you," whereas the "wise" in line 2 are "them" • 3–4 **For we be alle one in love** for we are all united by love, or are all part of the order of love • 4 **sothly** truly • 5–7 **For I am seker . . . than I** Compare 7.45–54, which does regard revelation as a "mede" for the practice of faith, hope, and charity • 5 **seker** certain

ende, as to my understanding. This I saide for I wolde they loved° God the better, for
to make them to have minde that this life is short, as they might se in exsample. For
in alle this time I wened to have died. And that was marveyle to me and sweme° in
perty, for methought this avision was shewde for them that shuld live.   30

   Alle that I say° of me, I mene in the person° of alle my evencristen, for I am
lerned in the gostely shewing of our lord God that he meneth so. And therfore I pray
you alle for Gods sake, and counceyle you for youre awne profite, that /fol. 18r/ ye
leve the beholding of a wrech that it was shewde to, and mightely, wisely, and mekely
behold God,° that of his curteyse love and endlesse goodnesse wold shew it   35
generally in comfort of us alle. For it is Goddes wille that ye take it with as grete joy
and liking as Jhesu had shewde it to you.°

THE NINTH CHAPTER

For the shewing I am not good but if I love God the better, and in as much as ye
love God the better, it is more to you than to me. I say not this to them that be
wise, for they wit it wele. But I sey it to you that be simple, for ease and comfort. For
we be alle one in love. For sothly° it was not shewde to me that God loveth me better
than the lest soule that is in grace. For I am seker• ther be meny /fol. 18v/ that never   5

[VIS. 7.16–19] ende ‡. This I saide for I walde thaye loved God mare **and sette the lesse prise
be the vanite of the worlde**, for to make thame to hafe minde that this life es shorte, as
thaye might se in ensampille **be me**. For in alle this time I wenede to hafe died. /Rev. 8.29–30/

[VIS. 6.1–18] Alle that I saye° of myselfe, I meene in the persone of alle° mine evencristene, for I am lernede in the gastelye shewinge of oure lorde that he meenes so. And
therfore I praye yowe alle for Goddes sake, and counsayles yowe for youre awne profit,
that ye leve the behaldinge of *the wrechid, /fol. 100v/ sinfulle creature*° that it° was shewed
unto, and that ye mightlye, wiselye, **lovandlye**, and mekelye behalde God, that of his curtays love and of his endles goodnes walde shewe *generalye this vision* in comforthe of us
alle. **And ye that heres and sees this vision and this techinge that is of Jhesu Criste to
edification of youre saule**, it is Goddes wille **and my desire**° that ye take it with als grete
joye and likinge as Jhesu hadde shewed it yowe **as he did to me**.
   For the shewinge I am not goode but if I love God the better, /Rev. 9.1–3/ **and so may
and so shulde ilke man do that sees it and heres it with goode wille and trewe meninge.
And so is my desire that it shulde be to everilke manne the same profitte that I desirede
to myselfe, and therto was stirred of God in the firste time when I sawe itte**, for it is
comon° and generale, *as we ar alle ane.* **And I am sekere I sawe it for the profitte of
many oder.** For sothly it was nought shewed unto me for that God loves me bettere
thane the leste saule that is in grace. For I am sekere thare is *fulle* many that nevere

7 **if I looke . . . myselfe** if I regard myself only as a single individual. See 35.3–4 and 37.3–4 for Julian's mistaken attempt to take the revelation "singulery"; 61.47–55 for further reflections on the communality of the church. "Singularity" is usually a negative term in Middle English, suggesting an inappropriate and prideful self-separation from others, a vice any visionary would be warned against. Rolle's *Form* lists "singulere wit" and "vaine glory" as two of the special temptations the devil sends "when he sees a man or a woman . . . turne haly [wholly] to God" (chap. 1, *YW* 1:5) • 7 **in general** in relation to everyone else • 8 **onehede of cherite** the unity of charity. This language of this passage is close to that of 1 John 4:7–8: "Beloved, let us love one another; for love is of God, and he who loves is born of God and knows God. He who does not love does not know God; for God is love" • 8 **evencristen** fellow Christians • 8–9 **For in this onehede . . . saved** The sentence is a little personification allegory, in which a character called Life takes a stand inside Unity of Charity. Compare the way all Christendom awaits the apocalypse inside the barn Unity at the end of Langland's *Piers Plowman* (B 20) • 9–14 **For God . . . loveth alle** A proof of the previous sentence and a defense of the "general." Salvation depends on the "onehede of cherite" with the saved because the saved, standing for the whole creation and with God within them, constitute the unity of all. The "onehede" of those in charity is the exact opposite of the claim to be "singuler" that visionaries might be tempted, inappropriately, to make • 12 **comprehended** included • 12–13 **alle that is made . . . alle** Unlike the creation as hazelnut (at 5.7–13), which is created by God but does not "comprehend" him, humanity ever since the Incarnation incorporates God • 13 **For in man . . . alle** A reference to a key theme in Julian's writings, the "mutual indwelling" in which God and humankind are each seen as "enclosed" in the other. Richly developed in Chapters 51–63 • 15 **beholdeth it thus** thinks about it in this way. Alludes back to the plea to "leve the beholding of a wrech" in 8.34 • 16 **truly taught** The revelation will not yield even its doctrinal truth to someone who insists on adulating Julian, rather than reading in the way just described • 16 **if him nedeth comfort** if he should need comfort. Presumably for having no "shewing ne sight but of the comen teching of holy church" (line 6) • 16–21 **I speke of them . . . contrary therto** According to this passage, *A Revelation* is not a general statement about humankind's relationship with God, but instead concerns only members of that unknowable body, the saved, and says nothing about anyone else: the double negative "no nother," nobody else, reinforcing this point. The phrase "that shalle be saved" is used some twenty-five times in *A Revelation* to qualify its teaching by making it more specific. Here, as often, it pulls against the universalizing logic of the surrounding passage, with its insistence on the "generalle" meaning of the revelation and heavy use of the word "alle." The tension between particular and universal readings of the "revelation of love" is the main topic of the thirteenth revelation (Chapters 27–40), with its explicit confrontation with ideas of universal salvation

had° shewing ne sight but of the comen teching of holy church that love God better than I. For if I looke singulery to myselfe, I am right nought. But in general I am, I hope, in onehede of cherite with alle my evencristen. For in this onehede° stondeth the life of alle mankind that shalle be saved. For God is alle that is goode, as to my sight, and God hath made alle that is made, and God loveth alle that he hath made. And he that generally loveth all his evencristen for God, he loveth alle that is. For in mankind that shall be saved is comprehended alle: that is to sey, alle that is made and the maker of alle. For in man is God, and in God is alle. And he that loveth thus, he loveth alle.

And I hope by the grace of God, he that beholdeth° it thus shalle /fol. 19r/ be truly taught and mightly comforted, if him nedeth comfort. I speke of them that

10

15

[*VIS.* 6.18–45] hadde shewinge ne sight botte of the comon techinge of haly kyrke that loves God better than I. For if I loke singulerlye to myselfe, I am right nought. Botte in generalle, I am ‡ in anehede of charite with alle mine evencristende. For in this anehede of charite standes the life of alle mankinde that shalle be safe. For God is alle that is goode, ‡ and God has made alle that is made, and God loves alle that he has made. **And if anye man or woman departe his love fra any of his evencristen he loves right nought, for he loves nought alle. And so that time he is nought safe, for he es nought in pees.** And he that generaly loves ‡ his evencristen ‡, he loves alle that es. For in mankinde that shalle be safe is comprehende *alle that is:* ‡ alle that is made and the makere of alle. For in manne is God, *and so in man is alle.* And he that *thus generalye loves alle his evencristene,* he loves alle. **And he that loves thus, he is safe.**

And thus wille I love, and thus I love, and thus I am safe. For I mene in the person of mine evencristene. And the more I love of this lovinge whiles I am here, the mare I am like to the blisse that I /fol. 101r/ **shalle°** have in hevene withouten ende: that is God, **that of his endeles love wolde become oure brothere and suffer for us.** *And I am sekere that* he that behaldes it thus he shalle be trewly taught and mightelye comforthtede, if° him nede comforthe.

Botte God forbede that ye shulde saye or take it so that I am a techere. For I meene nought so, no I mente nevere so. For I am a woman, lewed, febille, and freylle. Botte I wate wele, this that I saye I hafe it of the shewinge of him that es° soverayne techare. Botte sothelye charite stirres me to telle yowe it. For I wolde God ware knawen and min evencristene spede, as I wolde be myselfe, to the mare hatinge of sinne and lovinge of God. Botte for I am a woman shulde I therfore leve that I shulde nought telle yowe the goodenes of God, sine that I sawe in that same time that it is his wille° that it be **knawen? And that shalle ye welle see in the same matere that folowes after, if° itte be welle and trewlye taken.**

Thane shalle ye sone forgette me that am a wreche, and dose so that I lette yowe nought, and behalde Jhesu that is techare of alle. I speke of thame that

17–18 **in all thing . . . precheth and techeth** According to *The Chastising,* a vision can be judged by whether it is "enclined to ony errour of holy chirche, of the feith, or ony wondir or newe thing" (176) • 18 **the faith of holy church** the Christian faith as the church understands it • 19 **willefully kept** consciously observed • 19–20 **in use and in custome** according to practice and tradition • 20–21 **willing and meaning . . . contrary therto** desiring and intending never to accept anything that might be inconsistent with it. An allegory in which "faith" stands guard "in my sighte" (either within her line of vision or in her eye), filtering out any thought or perception inconsistent with itself • 23 **it them.** The revelation and the "faith of holy church." See 7.52–54 • 24 **by thre partes** in three modes. These distinctions between corporeal and spiritual vision and between vision and "locution" are traditional, deriving ultimately from Augustine • See 5.1–2 and side note to 5.2 • 24–25 **worde . . . understonding** See 13.1–5 • 25–26 **But the gostely . . . as I would** but I do not know how, nor have I the power, to declare the spiritual visions as explicitly or as completely as I would wish. The auxiliaries "can," "may," and "would" each relate to one of the faculties of the mind: memory, reason, and will. These parallel the "powers" associated with the persons of the Trinity. See sidenote to 1.10. For the ineffability of spiritual vision, see 73.1–6, a structural echo of this passage • 27 **shall** Here retains some of its earlier sense of "must." See 27.10

[CHAPTER 10] 1 **I saw . . . the crucifixe** As with the revelation of Christ's blood, this "bodely sight" effects a single transformation of the cross that has been placed before Julian's gazing eyes. Scenes of humiliation from Christ's trial appear "in" the image of Christ's head, which is "the face of the crucifixe," confusingly coexisting in Julian's gaze both with each other and with the sight of his slow death • 2–3 **dispite . . . buffeting** contempt, spitting, soiling, and buffeting. The torments Jesus is said to have suffered after trial by the Sanhedrin: "They lede him into theire chapetere-hous and examende him straitly [closely] . . . they . . . despisede him and spitte in his faire face, they hillide his eyen and bobbed him [shrouded his eyes and hit him]" (*The Privity,* prologue, *YW* 1:201, based largely on Matt. 26:67; see 4.3). In *The Privity* and the Gospels, these torments take place before the crowning of thorns evoked in the first revelation • 3 **languring paines** long agonizing pains • 3 **mo** more • 4 **often changing of colour** frequent changes of color. The torments are seen as changes of color on Jesus' face • 4 **And one time I saw** This revelation is fragmentary, consisting of discrete moments introduced by the phrases "one time," "sometime," "diverse times" (4, 16, 27–28). The relationship of these fragments is confused: it is not even clear whether different things are being seen, whether the same confused image is being interpreted in different ways, or whether the phrase "one time" refers to the accretion of images and explanations in the years since the original revelation • 5 **overyede . . . face** spread over with dry blood until it enclosed the middle of the face. A sight of Christ's blood very different from that in the first revelation, where the blood is fresh and does not occlude Christ's face. See 7.10–14

shalle be saved, for in this time God shewde me no nother. But in all thing I beleve as holy church precheth and techeth. For the faith of holy church, which I had beforehand understonde°—and, as I hope, by the grace of God willefully kept° in use and in custome—stode continually in my sighte, willing and meaning never to receive onything that might be contrary therto. And with this intent and with this meaning I beheld the shewing with all my diligence. For in all this blessed shewing I behelde it as one in Gods mening.°

All this was shewde by thre partes: that is to sey, by bodily sight, and by worde formede in my understonding, and by gostely sight. /fol. 19v/ But the gostely sight I can not ne may not° shew it as openly ne as fully as I would. But I trust in our lord God almighty that he shall, of his goodnes and for your love, make you to take it more ghostely and more sweetly then I can or may tell it.

20

25

ooooooooooooooooooooooooooooo

The Secunde Revelation
THE TENTH CHAPTER

And after this, I saw with bodely sight in the face of the crucifixe that hung before me, in the which I beheld continually a parte of his passion: dispite, spitting, solewing, and buffeting, and many languring paines, mo than I can tell, and often changing of colour. And one time I saw how halfe the face, beginning at the ere, overyede with drye bloud till it beclosed° into the mid face. And after that the

5

[vis. 6.45–49] shalle be safe, for in this time God shewed me no nothere. Bot in alle thing I lyeve as haly kyrke techis. /Rev. 9.18–22/ For in alle this° blissede shewinge **of oure lorde** I behelde it as ane in God *sight*. **And I understode never nathinge therein that stones me ne lettes me of the trewe techinge of halye kyrke.**

[vis. 7.1–7] *Alle this blissede techinge of oure lorde God* was shewed **to me** in thre parties: that is, be bodilye sight, and be worde formede in mine understandinge, and be gastelye sight. Botte the gastelye sight I maye nought ne can nought shewe it **unto yowe** als oponlye and als fullye as I wolde. Botte I truste in oure lorde God allemighty that he shalle, of his goodnes and for youre love, make yowe to take it mare gastelye and mare swetly than I can or maye telle it **yowe. And so motte it be, for we are alle one in love.**

[vis. 8.1–5] And after this, I sawe with bodely sight ‡ the face of the crucifixe that hange before me, in whilke I behelde continuely a party of his passion: despite, spittings, *sowlinge° of his bodye,* and *buffetinge in his blisfulle face,* and *manye langoures and paines,* ma than I can telle, and ofte changing of coloure, *and alle his blissede face a time closede in dry blode.* /Rev. 10.6–7/

6 **other halfe beclosed** the other half of the face was enclosed • 6 **therewhiles . . . this party** meanwhile the dried blood on the first side disappeared. As though the revelation were moving slowly forward and backward in time around the moment of the buffeting • 8 **bodely, swemly, and darkely** physically, sorrowfully, and obscurely. The revelation shows the bloody effects of blows but nobody delivering them, as though the blindfold over Christ's eyes during this scene in Luke 22:64, where Christ is taunted with "Who is it that struck you?" obscured Julian's vision also. In late medieval church roof bosses, the scene is also disturbingly fragmentary, the tormenters sometimes depicted merely as a spitting mouth or a slapping hand with no bodies attached • 10 **I saw him and sought him** The dimness of Julian's sight of Christ is what makes her want more • 12 **ought** anything • 12 **graciously** by grace • 14 **thus I saw him . . . wanted him** so I saw him and sought him, and I had him and lacked him. The dimness and discoloration of Christ's face suddenly takes on an erotic charge • 15 **this is . . . comen working** this is and ought to be our usual way of being. Reasserts the message of Chapter 9, which reassures readers who know God only through the "comen teching of holy church" (line 6) that lack of visionary experience is unimportant • 16–22 **One time my understanding . . . can tell** This passage may partly be based on Ps. 139:9–10 (Vulgate 138)—"If I take the wings of the morning and dwell in the uttermost parts of the sea, even there thy hand shall lead me"—or on the story of Jonah, as told in the contemporary Middle English poem *Patience*. Julian is like Jonah, safe at the bottom of the sea. The passage is given further resonance by the earlier, North Sea reference to herring scales in 7.19–22 • 17 **mosse begrowen** grown over with moss • 17 **wrake** debris • 19–20 **so as God . . . continually** in the sense in which God is always with a person • 21 **overpassing** more than that • 22 **thow** though • 23 **it be but litle** our sight of him is not much • 24 **abiden** waited for • 25–27 **This secounde shewing . . . or none** The anxiety expressed here confirms Julian's solidarity with her "evenchristen" who do not experience revelations expressed in Chapter 9 • 27 **For . . . in a feer** for I was sometimes worried • 27 **whether it was . . . or none** about whether it was a revelation. See 8.20–21 for Julian's desire "to see more," which the indistinctness of this revelation seems to frustrate. According to *The Chastising*, one "tokene" of a true vision is lucidity: a visionary's experience is true "whanne al the undirstonding [the entire meaning] of the matier that he seeth is verily shewid him [truly manifested to him] in soule and

clierly is opene [lucidly translated] to him" (179). This revelation does not easily meet this criterion • 27–28 **diverse times** on different occasions • 29 **foule, black, dede hame** foul, black, dead skin. "Hame" means skin or membrane. Often used of skin that is sloughed, it points forward to the "holy vernacle" in the next sentence. Jesus' bloodied face is an image of the ugliness inflicted on human selfhood by sin • 30–31 **holy vernacle of Rome** Alludes to the legend of Saint Veronica, who, in compassion for Christ's sufferings on the way to his death, wiped his face with a kerchief. The cloth retained the impression of his face and was preserved in St. Peter's basilica in Rome. In the Middle Ages, the cloth became an object of popular pilgrimage and a subject of meditation. Like any pilgrim to Rome, Chaucer's Pardoner wears "a vernicle . . . sowed upon his cappe" to show that he is "streight . . . comen fro the court of Rome" (*Canterbury Tales* I(A).685, 671) • 31 **portrude** imprinted • 32 **often changing of coloure** its frequent changes of color. Like Jesus' face in lines 4–7, although now Jesus is apparently on the way to Gethsemane, carrying his own cross. According to lines 54–56, the vernacle changes color as it is viewed at different times • 32–37 **Of the brownhead . . . fairhead?** *The Privity* calls Christ "speciouse [lovely] in beaute passande [transcending] all erthely mene [men]," until his scourging (see Chapter 12), after which the prophecy of Isa. 53:1–5 applies to him: "We behelde him all outcaste and vileste of all mene, and ther was in him neither fairenes nor beaute" ("Ad primam," *YW* 1:203) • 33 **rewlyhead and leenhead** piteousness and thinness • 34 **standing that** seeing that • 37 **I desire . . . as I have understonde** A rare digression from the material of the revelation to discuss an important devotional object (lines 38–56). Perhaps the vernacle, a woman's cloth imprinted by Christ, is to be taken as a figure for the revelation • 38–45 **We knowe in our faith . . . oure gainmaking** A passage of exposition similar in tone and teaching to Hilton's *Scale* 2.1, another quick exposition of the fundamentals of salvation history: "Oure lord God shop [shaped] in soule man to the image and the liknesse of him. . . . But thorugh sinne of the first man Adam it was disfigured. . . . [T]o that hevenely heritage it might never have come agen, but yif it hadde be reformed to the first shap and to the first liknesse. But that reforminge might not ben had [could not be achieved] by non erthely man. . . . Therfore it nedide bi don [had to be done] by him that is more thanne a man, and that is only God"

other halfe beclosed on the same wise, and therewhiles° it° vanished in this party, even /fol. 20r/ as it cam.

This saw I bodely, swemly, and darkely, and I desired mor bodely light to have seen more clerly. And I was answerede in my reason: "If God will shew thee more, he shal be thy light. Thee nedeth° none but him." For I saw him and sought him. For we be now so blinde and so unwise that we can never seke God till what time that he of his goodnes sheweth him to us. And whan we see ought of him graciously, then are we stered by the same grace to seke with great desire to see him more blissefully.• And thus I saw him and sought him, and I had him and wanted him. And this is and should be our comen working in this life, as to my sight.

One time my understanding was led downe° into the sea grounde, and ther saw I hilles and dales grene, /fol. 20v/ seming as it were mosse begrowen,° with wrake and gravel. Then I understode thus: that if a man or woman wher there, under the brode water, and he might have sight of God—so as God is with a man continually—he shoulde° be safe in soule and body, and take no harme. And overpassing, he should have mor solace and comforte then all this worlde may or can tell. For he will that we believe that we see him continually, thow that us thinke that it be but litle, and in this beleve° he maketh us evermore to get grace. For he will be seen, and he will be sought, and he will be abiden, and he will be trusted.

This secounde shewing was so lowe and so little and so simple that my spirites were in great traveyle in the beholding: morning, dredful, and longing. /fol. 21r/ For I was sometime in a feer whether it was a shewing or none. And then diverse times our lord gave me more sight, wherby that I understode° truly that it was a shewing. It was a figur and a liknes of our foule, black, dede hame° which° our faire, bright, blessed lord bare for our sinne. It made me to thinke of the holy vernacle of Rome, which he portrude with his owne° blessed face when he was in his hard passion, wilfully going to his death, and often changing of coloure. Of the brownhead and the blackhead, rewlyhead and leenhead of this image, many marveyled how that might be, standing that he portrude it with his blessed face, which is the fairhede° of heaven, flower of earth, and the frute of the maidens wombe. Then how might this image be so discolourede /fol. 21v/ and so farre from fairhead? I desire to say° as I have understonde by the grace of God.

We knowe in our faith and in our beleve, by the teaching and the preching of holy church, that the blissed• trinity made mankind to his image and to his likenes.

[vis. 8.5–8] This I sawe bodilye *and hevelye* and derkelye, and I desired mare bodelye light to hafe sene more clerelye. And I was answerde in my resone *that if God walde shewe me mare he shulde, botte me neded na light botte him. /Rev. 10.10–82/*

43 **overpassing** transcending it • 45 **gainmaking** remaking • 46 **thes two** "Oure furst making" and "oure gainmaking" • 47 **foulhede** foulness • 48 **before said** See line 29 • 50 **hid his godhede** The idea that Christ's divinity was hidden by his human body to trick the devil into unjustly killing him belongs to the "devil's rights" theory of redemption, challenged by Anselm in the early twelfth century but still popular in the fourteenth. In *Piers Plowman,* Christ jousts against the devil clad in Piers's armor (the human body), "that Crist be noght biknowe here for *consummatus Deus* [so that Christ is not recognized here as fully and truly God]," so that "gile is begiled and in his gile fallen [trickery is tricked and fallen as a result of his trickery]" (B 18.24, 361). Here, however, it is the discoloration of death, not the body itself, that hides • 50–51 **we ought to trowe** we ought to believe. The tradition of Christ's surpassing beauty was based on Ps. 45:2 (Vulgate 44.3): "You are the fairest of the sons of men; grace is poured upon your lips; therefore God has blessed you for ever" • 54 **ther it seyeth** See lines 30–32, an obscure sentence that this one attempts to clarify • 54–55 **it meneth . . . chere** it refers to the frequent change of coloring and expression in the vernacle. See "often changing of colour," lines 4, 31 • 56 **rewful and deadly** pitiful and deathlike • 56 **as it may be seen** Not, in this case, in the revelation, but in the real world, by pilgrims to St. Peter's • 57–70 **And this vision . . . my sight** After the long passage on Christ's sufferings and the vernacle, from line 25, this returns abruptly to the theme of "seeing and seeking," outlined in lines 7–24, the theme that now dominates until the end of the chapter, anticipating the theme of longing in the thirteenth revelation, especially Chapters 39–40 • 57–58 **continual seking of the soule** the soul's constant seeking • 58 **full mekille** very greatly • 60 **clernesse of finding** clarity that comes from finding God • 63 **for the time . . . traveyle** during the time that God wishes to allow the soul to be in labor • 65 **shall have him** shall behave itself • 66 **he shall teach himselfe** God himself will teach. Sudden changes of pronoun referent are common in Middle English • 68 **For a soule . . . God** for a soul that attaches itself only to God. See 6.1–2 • 68 **very true** • 69 **it is the most worshippe . . . do** cleaving to God is the greatest reverence the soul can pay • 72 **comen** available to all. See line 15 • 73 **and oweth . . . holy church** and ought to have by the discretion and teaching of holy church • 74–76 **The furst . . . vaine sorow** Anticipates the opening of the fifteenth revelation, 64.1–7 • 75 **as it may be** as much as we can • 76 **unskilfulle hevinesse** unreasonable sluggishness • 77 **gruching** grumbling

In the same maner wise, we know that when man fell so depe and so wretchedly by   40
sinne, ther was no nother helpe to restore man but thorow him that made man. And
he that made man for love, by the same love he woulde restore man to the same
blisse, and overpassing. And right as we were made like to the trinite in oure furst
making, our maker would that we should be like to Jhesu Crist, oure saviour in
heven without ende, by the vertu of oure gainmaking.°   45

Then betwene thes /fol. 22r/ two he would, for love and for worshipe of man,
make himselfe as like to man in this deadly life, in our foulhede and in our
wretchednes, as man might be without gilt. Wherof it meneth, as is before said: "It
was the image and the liknes of our foule, blacke, dede hame,"° wherein oure fair,
bright, blessed lorde hid his godhede. But full sekerly° I dare say, and we ought to   50
trowe,° that so fair a man was never none but he, tille what time that his fair coloure
was changed with traveyle and sorow, passion and dying. (Of this it speketh in the
eighth° revelation in the sixteenth chapter,° wher it speketh more of the same
liknesse. And ther it seyeth "of the vernacle of Rome," it meneth° by diverse
changing of colour and chere,° somtime more comfortable and lively, and sometime   55
more /fol. 22v/ rewful and deadly, as it may be seen.)°

And this vision was a lerning to my understanding that the continual° seking
of the soule pleseth God full mekille.° For it may do no more than seke, suffer,
and trust. And this is wrought in every soule that hath it by the holy gost. And the
clernesse of finding, it is of his special grace when it is his will. The seking with faith,   60
hope, and charity pleseth oure lord, and the finding pleseth the soule, and fulfilleth
it with joy. And thus was I lerned to my understanding that seking is as good as
beholding, for the time that he wille suffer the soule to be in traveyle. It is Gods
will that we seke into the beholding of him, for by that shall he shew us himself of
his special grace when he will. /fol. 23r/ And how a soule shall have him° in his   65
beholding he shall teach himselfe. And that is most worshippe to him, and most
profite to the soule, and most receiveth° of mekenesse and vertuse, with the grace
and leding of the holy gost. For a soule that only festeneth° him onto° God with very
truste, either in seking or in beholding,° it is the most worshippe that he may do, as
to my sight.   70

Theyse be two workinges that may be seen in this vision. That one is seking,
the other is beholding. The seking is comen: that, ech soule may have with his grace,
and oweth to have, by discretion° and teching of holy church. It is Gods will that we
have three thinges in our seking of his gifte. The furst is that we seke wilfully and
besily withoute slouth, as it may be /fol. 23v/ with his grace, gladly and merely   75
without unskilfulle° hevinesse and vaine sorow. The seconde is° that we abide him
stedfastely for his love, withoute gruching° and striving against him, into our lives

78–79 **of fulle seker faith** with truly confident faith ·
79 **he shall aper sodenly** At the end of time or at death ·
80–81 **For his working is prevy . . . sodeyn** for his activity is secret, and he wants to be recognized, and his appearing will be very sudden · 81 **trowed** believed ·
81–82 **hende, homely, and curteise** gracious, intimate, and courteous. See 7.38 and elsewhere

[CHAPTER 11] 1 **God in a pointe** A point in space, not time, as line 16 makes clear. Besides having an evocative, but inarticulate, relationship with the vision of the hazelnut in 5.7–13, the "pointe" anticipates the Christian Neoplatonism of Chapters 52–63: see, e.g., 62.10–17, with its account of the creation as "flowing out" from God at the center of being, before returning to him. A "point" is also a subdivision in an argument or a full stop in a sentence, meanings that give parts of the chapter a scholastic and dialogic cast · 1–2 **by which sight I saw** The use of "saw" here makes the perception "that he is in al thing" as much part of the revelation as the sight of "God in a pointe" that precipitates it · 2 **with avisement** with close attention · 4 **with a softe drede** with a gentle awe · 4 **"What is sinne?"** The second revelation's vision of the dry blood has already begun to expose the incongruous fact of sin. This question haunts the whole of *A Revelation*, especially from Chapter 27 on · 5–6 **by happe . . . aventure** by chance or by accident · 6–13 **If it be hap or aventure . . . aventure** An exploration of the human experience of chance. Both "hap" and "aventure" belong to the secular register, "hap" referring to any temporal chance or happiness, "aventure," more broadly, to a sequence of events or a large-scale reversal of fortunes. "Aventure" also recalls the literary genre of romance, in which protagonists experience their lives as a series of accidents, even as the audience is invited to view them as providential narratives. Having reached the end of his "unsely [unhappy] aventure" and seeing now "with ful avisement" the movement of the wandering stars as they help determine events on earth, Troilus laughs as he looks down from the heavens at the "blinde lust" of those left behind him, his perspective now united with eternity (Chaucer, *Troilus and Criseyde*, 1.35, 5.1811, 1824). For a philosophical exploration of this theme, see Chaucer's translation of Boethius's *Consolation of Philosophy*. Several passages in this chapter, as well as its allusions to dialogue, recall this work, still in the fourteenth century the classic exploration of divine providence and human will. The material for this passage is said to be "this shewing of love" (line 12), not this specific revelation but the whole (see 6.54) · 7 **unforsight** lack of foresight · 7 **tho** those · 8 **bene . . . beginning** exist from eternity · 9–10 **as it cometh . . . sodeynly** as God's purpose is fulfilled, happening to us unpredictably · 10 **unweting** unknowing · 12 **wot** know · 14 **me behoved nedes to grant** I am obliged to concede. The language of logic or dialectic, used to announce a conclusion that, given the fact of sin, might seem unexpected · 15 **the working of creatures** the behavior of created beings. Their exercise of free will · 16–17 **all he doth** he does all · 17–18 **sinne is no dede** sin is not a deed. In formal theology, sin is often described as a "privation of good," a nullity, in order to avoid the dualist notion of creative evil. See 27.22–23

ende, for it shall last but a while. The third is that we truste in him mightely, of
fulle seker° faith. For it is his wille that we know that he shall aper sodenly and
blissefully• to all his lovers. For his working is prevy, and he wille be perceived, and   80
his apering shalle be swithe° sodeyn. And he wille be trowed,° for he is fulle hende,
homely, and curteise.° Blessed mot he be!

The Third Revelation
THE ELEVENTH CHAPTER

And after this, I saw God in a pointe—that is to say, in my understanding—by
which sight I saw that he is in al thing. I beheld with avisement, seeing and
/fol. 23ar/ knowing in that sight that he doth alle that is done. I merveyled in that
sight with a softe drede, and thought: "What is sinne?" For I saw truly that God doth
alle thing, be it never so litile. And I saw truly° that nothing is done by happe ne by   5
aventure, but alle by the foreseing° wisdom of God. If it be hap or aventure in the
sight of man, our blindhede and our unforsight° is the cause. For tho things that
be in the foreseing° wisdom of God bene fro without beginning, which rightfully
and worshipfully and° continually he ledeth to the best ende as it cometh aboute,
falling to us sodeynly, ourselfe° unweting. And thus, by our blindhede• and our   10
unforsighte, we say these thinges be by happes and aventure. Thus I understonde in
this shewing of love, for wel I wot in the sight of /fol. 23av/ our lord God is no happe
ne aventure.

Wherfore me behoved nedes to grant that alle thinges that is done is welle done,
for our lord God doth all. For in this time the working of creatures was not shewde,   15
but of our lord God in the creature.° For he is in the mid point of all thinges, and all
he doth, and I was seker• that he doth no sinne. And here I saw sothly° that sinne is
no dede, for in alle this, sinne was not shewde.

[VIS. 8.9–17] And after this, I sawe God in a pointe—that es, in mine understandinge—
by whilke sight I sawe that he es in alle thinge. I behelde with visemente, *wittande* and
knawande in that sight that he dose alle that es done. I merveylede in this sight with a
softe drede, and thought: "Whate es sinne?" For I sawe trulye that God dothe alle thinge,
be it nevere so litille. *Nor nathinge es done* be happe ne be eventure, *botte be the endeles°
forluke of the wisdome of God.* /Rev. 11.6–13/ Wharefore me behovede nedes graunte that
alle thinge that es done es wele done, for our lord God doth all.° /Rev. 11.15–17/ And I was
seker that God dose na sinne. *Therfore it semed to me that sinne is nought,* for in alle this,
sinne° was nought shewed **me.**

20 **as it mighte be for the time** to the extent that it could be at that time. The passage that follows elaborates on perceptions that could only be glimpsed during the time of the revelation • 20 **rightfullehede** perfection, justice, or righteousness. The theme of the passage that follows • 22–25 **And so be . . . grace** Mercy and grace are not attributes of God's doings—these, like the creation that is their result, are perfect—but only of his response to the imperfections of his agents • 23 **faileth right nought** nothing at all fails • 24 **as I shall say after** See Chapter 27 for the "beholding of sinne," Chapter 35 for discussion of "mercy and grace" in the context of "rightfullehede" • 27 **generally of all his workes** of all he had made and done generally • 27–29 **alle his domes . . . God** See Chapter 45, a surprising elaboration of this distinction between human and divine perception • 27–28 **alle his domes . . . swete** all his judgments are easy and sweet. God is like a merciful judge • 29 **deming** judgment or perception • 30–31 **For man beholdeth . . . not so** From the perspective of the divine plan, nothing is ever less than perfect. See *The Consolation:* "For whiche it es that alle thingis semen to ben confus and trouble to us men, for we ne mowen nat considere thilke ordenaunce [for we cannot reflect on this principle of providential ordering]. Natheles [Nevertheless] the propre maner of everything, dressinge hem to gode [directing themselves toward the good], disponith hem alle [orders all of them], for ther nis nothing doon for cause of yvel [as a result of evil], ne thilk thing that is

doon by wikkid folk nis nat doon for yvel" (4.6.169–70) • 31 **alle that hath being in kinde** everything that has natural existence • 32 **in properte of Gods doing** an aspect of God's activity • 33–35 **And so wele . . . withoute beginning** See Ecclus. 39:33–34: "The works of the Lord are all good, and he will supply every need in its hour. And no one can say, 'This is worse than that,' for all things will prove good in their season" • 34 **properte** manner • 35 **hath it ordained . . . beginning** has endlessly ordained for it • 37–38 **rightfulle ordenance** perfect ordering of creation • 38 **or** before • 39–40 **no manner thing . . . that point** nothing at all will fall short of that objective. "Point" immediately refers back to "set in order" but contains all the resonances given it by lines 1–2 • 40 **in fulhed of goodnes** in the perfection of goodness • 42 **meaning thus** The speech that follows is a crystallization of the revelation and the chapter that describes it, "seeing" translated into "meaning." This mode of exposition by attributed speech is derived from medieval biblical exegesis and is common in *A Revelation,* often tending to diminish the distance between revelation and exposition • 43 **never lefte . . . workes** never took my hands away from what I made • 46–47 **Thus mightly . . . behoved nedes to assent** As though Julian has been questioning God about the righteousness of the creation in the fashion of a Boethius being questioned by Philosophy in *The Consolation.* Compare line 14

And I would no longer marveyle in this, but behelde our lorde, what he would shew. And thus, as it mighte be for the time, the rightfullehede• of Gods working was shewed to the soule. Rightfullehede• hath two fair properties: it is right and it is fulle. And so be all the workes of our lorde, and therto nedeth neither working of mercy ne grace, for they be alle rightfulle, wherin /fol. 24r/ faileth right nought. And in another time he shewde for beholding of sinne nakedly, as I shall say after, when he useth working of mercy and of grace. This vision was shewed to my understanding for our lord wille have the soule turned truly into the beholding of him, and generally of all his workes. For they be fulle good, and alle his domes be esy and swete, and to gret ees bringe° the soule that is turned fro the beholding of the blind deming of man into the fair, swete deming of our lorde God.

For man beholdeth some dedes wele done and some dedes eville, and our lorde beholdeth them not so. For as alle that hath being in kinde is of Gods making, so is alle thing that is done in properte of Gods doing. For it is esy to understand that the /fol. 24v/ beste dede is wele done. And so wele as the best dede is done° and the highest, so wele is the leest dede done, and all in the properte and in the order that our lord hath it ordained to fro° withoute beginning. For ther is no doer but he. I saw fulle sekerly• that he changeth° never his purpose in no manner of thing, ne never shalle without end. For ther was nothing unknowen to him in his rightfulle ordenance fro without beginning. And therfore all thinge was° set in order, or anything was made, as it should stand without ende, and no manner thing shalle faile of that point. For he hath made alle thing in fulhed of goodnes, and therfore the blessed trinite is ever fulle plesed in alle his workes.

And all this shewed he full blissefully,° meaning /fol. 25r/ thus: "See, I am God. See, I am in all thing.° See, I do all thing. See, I never lefte my handes of my workes, ne never shalle without ende. See, I lede all thing to the end that I ordaine it to, fro° without beginning, by the same might, wisdom, and love that I made it with. How shoulde any thing be amisse?" Thus mightly, wisely, and lovingly was the soule examined in this vision. Than saw I sothly° that me behoved° nedes to assent with great reverence, enjoying in God.°

[VIS. 8.17–19] And I walde no lenger mervelle of this, botte behalde oure lorde, whate he wolde shewe **me**. /Rev. 11.20–23/ And in another time God shewed **me** *whate sine es nakedlye be the selfe*, as I shalle telle afterwarde.° /Rev. 11.24–48/

[CHAPTER 12] 1–2 **in seming of the scorging** in a representation of the scourging. Unless "seming" is from "seam," a groove or wound, in which case the phrase means "through the wounds caused by the scourging." Christ is tied to a pillar and scourged with "sharpe knotty shourges," sometimes said to be tipped with lead (*The Privity*, "Ad primam," *YW* 1:203), before his crowning with thorns. See Matt. 27:26 • 2 **full depe** very deep • 3–4 **The hote blode . . . all blode** Again, see *The Privity*: "On every side stremes downe the kinges blode of hevene fro every parte of his blessed body" ("Ad primam," *YW* 1:203) • 5 **ther it vanished** The blood vanishes as it reaches the visual limit of the field of revelation. See 3.24–26 • 5 **Notwithstanding** nevertheless • 6 **avisement** attention • 7–8 **if it had . . . time** if it had actually been that plentiful at that time • 8 **it shulde . . . on bloude** it would have covered the bed completely in blood • 9–14 **God hath made waters . . . owne kinde** Despite the cruelty and sorrow of Christ's scourging, this brief meditation on the divine plenitude is detached from the narrative moment that gave birth to it. Rolle's *Meditations* similarly compares Christ's tormented body to a set of beautiful things: a net, a dovecot, a book, a meadow "ful of swete flouris and holsum herbis" (*YW* 1:96–97) • 9 **waters plentuous in erth** See Ps. 65:9–10 (Vulgate 64.10–11): "Thou visitest the earth and waterest it, thou greatly enrichest it; the river of God is full of water. . . . Thou waterest its furrows abundantly." In *The Pryckinge of Love*, it is said that Jesus shed his blood like water for the human soul, as he would never have done for the material creation: "Goddis sone . . . wolde not for savinge of alle the worlde have spillid oon drope of his blode. But for man he helde hit oute [poured it out] as watir" (39) • 11 **holsomly** healingly • 12 **licour** liquid. Perhaps in the sense "medicine," with an allusion to Communion wine •12 **liketh him . . . geve us** pleases him as much to give to us •

13 **plentuous . . . precious** The rest of the chapter is a meditation on these two words • 14 **it is our owne kinde** it shares our human nature • 15 **dereworthy bloude** precious blood • 16 **as verely** as truly • 17–18 **It descended downe into helle** Paintings of the Passion show the blood dripping down from the cross and into hell. Praying for sinners in passus 5 of *Piers Plowman* B, Repentance reminds Christ how, "aboute midday whan most light is and meel-time of seintes," Christ "feddest tho with thy freshe blood oure forefadres [ancestors] in derknesse" (492–93) • 18 **brak her bondes** broke their bonds. Unless "her" is not the southern version of "their," but rather the feminine singular "her." "Their" (those who "belong to the courte of heven" [line 19]) seems more logical, but the possessive plural pronoun occurs nowhere else in *A Revelation*. If "her" is taken as feminine, hell is being personified as a female monster. The gates of hell were often depicted as a pair of monstrous gaping jaws • 18–19 **deliverd them . . . courte of heven** The imagery derives from the narrative of Christ's harrowing of hell in the apocryphal *Gospel of Nicodemus*, in which, after his death, Christ binds Satan (see 13.14), releasing the souls of the just from limbo and taking them to heaven. The scene is the centerpiece of the climactic passus 18 of *Piers Plowman* B • 21–23 **The precious plenty . . . as long as us nedeth** Heb. 12:24 describes Christ's "sprinkled blood" as "speak[ing] more graciously than the blood of Abel." Christ's bleeding body remains in heaven until the Judgment, at which his wounds are manifested to all. See *The Pricke of Conscience*: "Crist sal shew than his woundes wide, / In heved, and fote, and in his side, / That freshe sal sem and alle bledand [still bleeding]" (5305–7). *The Pryckinge* brings out the underlying allusion to the Eucharist: "Cristes blood is yitt als hote and as fresh as hit was wene he died on Good Friday, and shal be so in holy chirche unto the day of doom" (35)

oooooooooooooooooooooooooooooo

The Fourth Revelation

THE TWELFTH CHAPTER

And after this I saw, beholding, the body plentuously° bleding in seming of the scorging, as thus: the fair skinne was broken full depe into the tender flesh, with sharpe smitinges all about the sweete /fol. 25v/ body. The hote blode ranne out so plentuously that ther was neither seen skinne ne wounde, but as it were all blode. And when it cam wher it shuld have falle downe, ther it vanished. Notwithstanding, the bleding continued a while till it might be seen with avisement. And this was so plentuous to my sight that methought, if it had ben so in kinde and in substance for that time, it shulde have made the bedde all on bloude, and have passede over all about.

Than cam to my minde that God hath made waters plentuous in erth to our servys, and to our bodely eese, for tender love that he hath to us. But yet liketh him better that we take full holsomly his blessed /fol. 26r/ blode to wash us of sinne, for ther is no licour that is made that liketh him so wele to geve us. For it is most plentuous, as it is most precious, and that by the vertu of the blessed godhead. And it is our owne kinde, and all° blissefully• overfloweth us by the vertu of his precious love. The dereworthy bloude of our lorde Jhesu Crist, also verely as it is most precious, as verely it is most plentuous.

Beholde and see the vertu of this precious plenty of his dereworthy blode! It descended downe into helle and brak her bondes and deliverd them, all that were there which belong to the courte of heven. The precious plenty of his dereworthy blode overfloweth all erth, and is redy to wash /fol. 26v/ all creatures of sinne which be of good will, have ben, and shall be. The precious plenty of his dereworthy blode ascendeth up into heven in the blessed body of our lorde Jesu Crist, and ther is in him, bleding, preying for us to the father, and is and shal be as long as us nedeth.

5

10

15

20

[*VIS.* 8.20–28] And after this I sawe, behaldande, the bodye plenteouslye bledande, **hate and freshlye and lifelye, right as I sawe before in the hede. And this was shewed°** /fol. 102r/ **me** in the semes of scourginge. /*Rev.* 12.2–6/ And this *ranne* so plenteouslye to my sight that methought, if it hadde bene so in kinde ‡ for that time, it shulde hafe made the bedde alle on blode, and hafe passede on aboute. ‡ God has made waterse plenteouse in erthe to oure service, and to oure bodilye ese, for tender love that he has to us. Botte it likes him better that we take *fullye* his blessede blode to washe us with of sinne, for thare is no likoure that es made that him likes so welle to giffe us. For it is so plenteouse ‡ and of oure kinde. /*Rev.* 12.14–25/

25 **fulfilling the number that faileth** making up the number who fail. Alludes to the belief that humanity was created to replace the fallen angels, so that the eventual number of the saved would be the same as that of the demons

[CHAPTER 13] 1 **or** before • 1 **sufferde** allowed • 2 **conveniable** suitable • 2 **understanding** meaning • 3–4 **he, without . . . lippes** The mode of revelation called "worde formede in my understonding" (9.24–25). These words are evidently not heard physically but in some sense also differ from the general words Julian hears in her understanding at 5.9–10. *The Chastising* quotes Gregory as saying: "whanne [God] spekith to us by himsilf, thanne is the hert enformed and taught of his worde, withoute any worde or sillable . . . also the speche of God inward to us is rather made or do [made or performed] thanne herd" (172). Christ's words in *A Revelation* are similar, but do assume precise verbal form. See 68.43–44 • 4–5 **Herewith is the feende overcome** by this (the blood seen in the fourth revelation) is the devil overcome. See 68.43–53 for the structural significance of these words • 5 **mening** referring to • 6 **fully his unmight** the whole of his impotence • 7 **the passion of him** the Passion of our Lord • 9 **also sore he traveyleth** he works just as hard • 9–10 **as continually . . . worshipfully** he sees just

as unfailingly that all chosen souls honorably escape him • 11 **full evil is he attemed** he is most terribly diminished. By comparison with the power he wielded before the Incarnation. "Full evil" is scornfully colloquial, since the diminishment of Satan's power is a good from every point of view except his own. "Attemed" is from "temen," to empty, pour out • 12 **mekille** much • 12–13 **geveth him leve to werke** allows him to act • 14 **his might . . . hande** his power is completely locked in God's hand. Repeated in 65.18–20. According to the *Gospel of Nicodemus,* Christ chained Satan during the harrowing of hell. See also Rev. 20:1–3: "Then I saw an angel coming down from heaven, holding in his hand the key of the bottomless pit and a great chain. And he seized the dragon, that ancient serpent, who is the devil and Satan, and bound him for a thousand years, and threw him into the pit" • 14–15 **But in God may be no wrath** Anticipates an important later theme developed, e.g., in 46.24–41 • 16–17 **with might . . . the reproved** stands with power and justice against the damned. As distinct from "wrath." The "reproved" would normally be souls destined for damnation, but in the context of this passage may rather be the demons • 17 **shrewdnes** wickedness • 17 **besye them** busy themselves • 18 **contrary** contradict

And evermore° it floweth in all heaven, enjoying the salvation of all mankind that be ther and shall be, fulfilling the number that faileth.

25

∞∞∞∞∞∞∞∞∞∞∞∞∞∞∞∞∞∞∞∞

The Fifth Revelation
THE THIRTEENTH CHAPTER

And after, or God° shewed any wordes, he sufferde me to beholde him a conveniable time, and all that I had seen, and all the understanding that was therin, as the simpilnes of the soule might take it. */fol. 27r/* Then he, without voys and opening of lippes, formed in my soule these wordes: "Herewith is the feende overcome." This worde saide our lorde mening his blessed passion, as he shewed before. In this, our lord shewed a parte of the feendes malice, and fully his unmight, for he shewed that the passion of him is the overcoming of the feende. God shewed that the feend hath nowe the same malice that he had before the incarnation, and also sore he traveyleth, and as continually he seeth that all soules of salvation eskape him worshipfully, by the vertue of his precious passion. And that is his sorow, and full evil is he attemed,° for all that God suffereth him to do turneth us to joy and him to shame and paine. And he */fol. 27v/* hath as mekille• sorow when God geveth him leve to werke as when he worketh not. And that is for he may never do as ille as he wolde, for his might is alle lokked in Gods hande. But in God may be no wrath, as to my sight. For our good lorde—endelessly having regard to his awne worshippe and to the profite of all them that shal be saved—with might and right he withstondeth the reproved, the which of malice and of shrewdnes besye them to contrary and do against Goddes will.

5

10

15

[*VIS. 8.29–41*] And after this, or° God shewed **me** any wordes,° he sufferde me to behalde *langere,* and alle that I hadde seene, and *alle that was therein* ‡. And than *was,* withouten voice and withoute openinge of lippes, formede in my saule this worde: "Herewith is the feende overcomen." This worde saide oure lorde menande° his ‡ passion, as he shewed **me** before. In this, oure lorde **brought unto my minde and** shewed **me** a perte of the fendes malice, and fully his unmight. *And, for that,* he shewed **me** that the passion of him is overcominge of the fende. God shewed **me** that he hase nowe the same malice that he had before the incarnation, and als sare he travailes, and als continuelye he sees that *alle chosene saules* eschapes him worshipfullye ‡. And that es alle his sorowe ‡. For alle that God suffers him to° do turnes us° to joye and him to paine and to shame. And he has als mekille sorowe when God giffes him leve to wyrke as when he werkes nought. And that es for he maye nevere do als ille as he wolde, for his might es alle lokene in Goddes hande. */Rev. 13.14–18/*

19 **scorne his . . . unmight** scorn the devil's malice and deride his impotence • 20–21 **that were aboute me** who were standing around me • 21 **was a liking to me** gave me pleasure • 21–22 **I thought that I wolde that I** thought how I wished that • 23 **But I saw not Crist laugh** Medieval lives of Christ note that the Gospels never describe the "man of sorrows" as laughing • 23 **wot** knew • 24–25 **in comforting of oureselfe** to comfort ourselves • 25–26 **ther I sawe . . . lorde** See line 19. Christ's scorn of the devil is an inner attitude. Julian sees this attitude intuitively, by "leding of my understanding," a phrase also used of a moment of intuitive insight in 51.36 • 26–27 **an inwarde . . . changing of chere** [Christ's scorn is] an interior manifestation of truthfulness, not involving any change of expression • 27–28 **it is a . . . durable** scorn of the devil is an honorable property of God, which is permanent. Thus it is not expressed as laughter, which is temporary • 29 **sadhede** state of seriousness • 29 **and saide** Julian again tries to communicate her revelation to her "evenchristen," this time offering an interpretation of the words she has just heard. See 8.22–30 • 29–30 **game, scorne, and ernest** play, scorn, and seriousness • 33 **sad traveyle** hard labor • 34–41 **ther I saide . . . helle** Words spoken by Julian are here interpreted as part of her revelation • 34 **ther** where • 34 **he is scorned** See "God scorneth him," line 31. God anticipates the devil's damnation • 35–36 **that the feende is dampned** Most medieval works other than *A Revelation* would assume this • 36–37 **he shalle be scornede at domesday** he will be scorned on Judgment Day • 37 **generally of all . . . saved** in common by all the saved • 40–41 **shalle endelsly go . . . helle** See Rev. 20:13–15, where, after the Judgment, death and hell are cast into the pit of fire: "And the sea gave up the dead in it, Death and Hades gave up the dead in them, and all were judged by what they had done. Then Death and Hades were thrown into the lake of fire. This is the second death, the lake of fire; and if any one's name was not found written in the book of life, he was thrown into the lake of fire"

Also I saw oure lorde scorne his malis and nought° his unmight, and he wille
that we do so. For this sight, I laught mightely, and that made them to laugh that   20
were aboute me, and ther laughing was a liking to me. I thought /fol. 28r/ that I
wolde that alle my evencristen had seen as I saw. Then shoulde all they have
laughed° with me. But I saw not Crist laugh.° But wele I wot that sight that he
shewed me made me to laugh, for I understode that we may laugh in comforting of
oureselfe and joyeng in God for the feend is overcome. And ther I sawe him scorne   25
his malis, it was be leding of° my understanding into oure lorde: that is to say, an
inwarde shewing of sothfastnesse without changing of chere. For as to my sight, it
is a wurshipful properte that is in God, which is durable.

And after this, I felle into a sadhede,• and saide: "I see thre thinges: game,
scorne, and ernest. I see game, that the feend is overcome. /fol. 28v/ And I se   30
scorne, that God scorneth him,° and he shalle be scorned. And I se ernest, that he
is overcome by the blisseful• passion and deth of oure lorde Jhesu Crist, that was
done in fulle ernest° and with sad traveyle."

And ther I saide "he is scorned," I ment that God scorneth him: that is to sey, for
he seeth him now as he shall do without ende. For in this, God shewde that the   35
feende is dampned. And this ment I ther I saide, "he shalle° be scorned." For I saw he
shalle be scornede at domesday generally of all that shal be saved, to whos salvation
he hath had gret envye. For then he shall see that all the wo and tribulation that he
hath done them shalle be turned into encrese of ther joy without ende. And all the
paine /fol. 29r/ and the sorow that he wolde have brought them to shalle endlesly°   40
go with him to helle.

[VIS. 8.42–52] Also I sawe oure lorde scorne his malice and nought *him,* and he wille
that we do *the same.* For this sight, I laugh mightelye, and that made tham to laugh that
were aboute me, and thare laughinge was likinge to me. I thought I wolde mine evencristene hadde sene as I sawe. Than shulde thaye alle hafe laughen with me. Botte I sawe
nought Criste laugh. ‡ *Nevertheless him likes that we laugh* in comforting of us and
enjoyande° in God for the feende is overcomen. /Rev. 13.25–28/

And after this, I felle into a saddehete, and saide: "I see° thre thinges: game, scorne,
and arneste. I see game, that the feende is overcomen. And I see scorne, /fol. 102v/ that
God scornes him, and he shalle be scornede. And I see arneste, that he es overcomen be
the ‡ passion of oure lorde Jhesu Criste, and be his dede that was done ful erneste and
with sadde travaile." /Rev. 13.34–41/

[CHAPTER 14] 1 **travelle** labor • 2 **namely of thy youth** especially in your youth. A commendation either of Julian's life of devotion before the revelation or, perhaps, of the three youthful requests to God described in Chapter 2 • 2–3 **lifted uppe into heven** Julian understands Christ's words to her as a premonition of the thanks he gives the saved: as though, undergoing her "domesday" (8.25), she has indeed died and been taken up into heaven • 4 **derewurthy** precious • 4 **solempne fest** solemn feast • 4–5 **taking no place** taking no seat • 5 **awne** own • 5–6 **I saw him ryally reigne . . . frendes** I saw him reign royally in his house, and he fills it quite full of joy and happiness, in order endlessly to gladden and comfort his precious friends. Instead of sitting at the center of the banquet, the Lord makes his friends its focus. Heaven was often depicted as a banquet in medieval religious writings, on the model of texts like Matt. 22:1–14, the parable of the wedding feast. See, e.g., the very different banquet, modeled on this parable, at the opening of the Middle English poem *Cleanness* • 10 **thre degrees of blisse** Middle English writings such as *The Pricke* often follow Anselm's categorization of the joys of heaven into seven spiritual and seven physical "dowries," which overlap with, and likely underlie, the list of "blisses" here • 11 **wilfully** consciously • 11 **in any degree** in any state of life. Probably alludes to the "three spiritual estates" of virgins, widows, and spouses, who are often taken to receive amounts of "blisse" that correspond to the yield of the fruitful seed in the parable of the sower (Matt. 13:3–8). Working out from this parable,

Holy Maidenhood states that "marriage brings forth her fruit thirtyfold in heaven, widowhood sixtyfold," while "virginity, with a hundredfold, outdoes both" (233). Here, each "degree" receives in different measure all the "thre degrees of blisse" described in lines 12–30 • 12 **wurshipfulle thanke** See Matt. 25:21: "Well done, good and faithful servant . . . enter into the joy of your master." According to *The Pricke*, "Thare [in heaven] es mare worshepe and honoure / Than ever had king here or emparoure" (7827–28) • 13 **when he is . . . paine** At death or after passing through purgatory • 13–14 **him thinketh it filleth him** it seems to the soul it (this first degree of bliss) fills him up. *The Pricke* likens heavenly joy to a bowl so full of water it "na mare [no more] water within may hald" (8049) • 14–16 **For methought . . . served God** for it seemed to me that all the pain and labor that could be suffered by everyone who has ever lived could not have merited the thanks that even one person shall receive who has willingly served God. Heaven is often described through tropes of inexpressibility. Compare the attempt to describe the extent of Christ's pain in 12.1–8 • 17–18 **alle the blessed . . . thanking** *The Pricke*, following Anselm, notes that the saved will see one another's joys and rejoice: "Thare salle ilk ane many thousandes se / In sere joyes, als himself salle be [there each one of them will see many thousand people in various joys, as he himself will be]" (8623–24) • 18 **he maketh his servys knowen** God makes the soul's service known • 19 **exsample** exemplum. See 7.27–35

The Sixth Revelation
THE FOURTEENTH CHAPTER

After this, our lorde saide: "I thanke the of thy servys and of thy travelle and namely of° thy youth." And in this, my understonding was lifted uppe into heven, wher I saw our lorde God as a lorde in his owne house, which lorde hath called alle his derewurthy frendes to a solempne fest. Than I saw the lorde taking no place in his awne house, but I saw him ryally reigne in his house, and all fulfilleth   5
it with joy and mirth, himselfe endlesly to glad and solace his derewurthy frendes, fulle homely and fulle curtesly, with mervelous melody of endelesse love,° in his /fol. 29v/ awne fair blissed• chere. Which glorious chere of the godhede fulfilleth alle heven of joy and blisse.

God shewde thre degrees of blisse that ech soule shalle have in heven that   10
wilfully° hath served God in any degree in erth.

The furst is the wurshipfulle° thanke of our lorde God that he shall receive when he is deliverde of paine. This thanke is so high and so wurshipfulle that him thinketh° it filleth him, though ther were no more. For methought that° alle the paine and traveyle that might be suffrede of all living men might not have deservede   15
the wurshipful thank that one man shalle have that wilfully hath served God.

For the secunde: that alle the blessed creatures that be in heven /fol. 30r/ shalle se that° wurshipfulle thanking. And he maketh his servys knowen to alle that be in heven. And in this time, this exsample was shewd: a king, if he thanke his subjettes, it is a gret wurshippe to them. And if he make it knowen to all the realme, then ther   20
wurship is mekille• incresed.

[vis. 8.53–54] After this, oure lorde saide: "I thanke the of thy service and of thy travaile and namly in thy youth." /Rev. 14.2–9/

[vis. 9.1–10] God shewed **me** thre degrees of blisse that ilke saule shalle hafe in hevene that wilfullye hase served God in any degree here in erthe.

The firste is the wyrshipfulle thankinge of oure lorde God that he shalle resayfe when he es deliverede fro paine. This thanke is so highe and so wyrshipfulle that him thinke it filles him, though thare ware no mare **blis**. For methought that alle the paine and tra-vaile that might be sufferde of alle liffande men might nought hafe° deservede the ‡ thanke that a man shalle hafe that wilfullye has servede God.

For the seconde: that alle the blissede creatures that er in hevene shalle see that wor-shipfulle thankinge **of oure lorde God**. And he makes his service to alle that er in heven knawen. /Rev. 14.19–21/

22 **as new and as liking** as freshly and as pleasingly •
22 **undertaken** received • 23 **so shalle it laste without
ende** *The Pricke* lists the sixth spiritual dowry as security: "For thay salle be thare siker and certaine / To have
endeles joy, and nevermare paine" (8559–60) • 23 **I saw
that . . . shewd** I saw that this was shown intimately and
sweetly. By Christ's words to Julian in lines 1–2 •
24–25 **be rewarded . . . for his time** Compare 3.7–10 •
25–26 **namly . . . wonderly thanked** This elevation of
youthful devotion evokes the account of the young virgins who sing before the throne of God and "follow the
Lamb wherever he goes" in Rev. 14:1–4, a passage central
to the medieval virginity tradition, as well as to the Middle English poem *Pearl.* Despite this, the ending of the
chapter is carefully inclusive of those whose "youth" is
not given to God • 25 **namly** especially • 26 **passinly**
surpassingly • 27 **turned** converted • 29 **lever** happier

[CHAPTER 15] 1 **he shewde . . . in my soule** he manifested a sensation of supreme spiritual delight in my
soul. This is consonant with the prevailing mood of
Chapters 13–14 • 2 **sekernesse** certainty • 2 **mightely
fastned** made powerfully secure. See 5.17 • 3 **peese**
peace • 4 **shulde have greved me** could have injured
me • 5 **turned and left to myselfe** The mood darkens,
partly in preparation for the Passion sequence in Chapters 16–18. The alternation of ease and difficulty, a common feature of accounts of the "servys and . . . travelle"
of religious living (14.1–2), is what *The Chastising*, following *Ancrene Wisse,* calls "the pley of love": "The pley
of love is joye and sorwe, the whiche two comen sundry
times oon aftir another, by the presence and absence of
him that is oure love" (99). The alternation reappears
later in *A Revelation* as the double experience of the
soul's "sensualite" and as the "mervelous medelur both
of wele and of wo" that is human living. See 44 and
52.6–7, and *The Scale* 2.41 • 6 **irkenes of myselfe** disgust
at myself • 6–7 **unneth . . . to live** I had scarcely enough
patience to stay alive. Compare the state described in
64.1–7 • 7 **faith, hope, and cherite** The three theological
virtues that form the basis of Christian living. See 1
Cor. 13:13: "So faith, hope, love abide, these three; but the
greatest of these is love" • 8 **in truth . . . in feling** The
dichotomy between truth or faith and feeling was traditional. At times of spiritual difficulty, faith must be
trusted, not feeling

And for the thurde: that as new and as liking as it is undertaken that time, right so shalle it laste without ende. And I saw that homely and swetly was this shewd: that the age of every man shal be knowen in heven and be rewarded for his wilfulle servys and for his time. And namly the age of them that wilfully and frely offer ther youth to God, passinly is rewarded and wonderly° thanked. /fol. 30v/ For I saw that, when or what time that a man or woman be truly turned to God, for one day servys and for his endelesse wille he shall have alle these thre degrees of blesse. And the more that the loving soule seeth this curtesy of God, the lever he is to serve him all the dayes of his life.°

25

30

∞∞∞∞∞∞∞∞∞∞∞∞∞∞∞∞∞∞∞∞∞∞

The Seventh Revelation
AND THE FIFTEENTH CHAPTER

And after this, he shewde a sovereyne, gostely likinge in my soule. In this liking, I was fulfillede of the everlasting sekernesse,• mightely fastned without any painefulle drede. This feling was so glad and so gostely that I was all in peese, in eese, and in reste, that ther was nothing in erth that shulde have greved me.

This lasted but a while, and I was turned and left to myselfe in hevines and werines of my life and irkenes of myselfe, that /fol. 31r/ unneth I could have patience to live. Ther was no comfort ne none eese to my feling, but faith, hope, and cherite, and these I had in truth, but fulle litille in feling.

5

[*VIS. 9.11–24*] And for the thirde: that als new ande als likande as it es *resayvede* that time, right so shalle it laste withouten ende. I sawe that *goodelye* and swetlye was this *saide and shewed* **to me**: that the age of everilk man° shalle be knawen in heven and rewarded for his wilfulle service and for his time. And namelye the age of thame that wilfullye and frelye offers thare youth unto God, es passande rewardede and wonderlye thanked. /Rev. 14.26–30/

And after this, oure lorde shewed **me** a soverayne, gastelye likinge in my saule. In this likinge, I was fulfilled of everlastande sekernesse, mightlye festnede withouten any ‡ drede. This felinge was so gladde **to me** and so *goodly* that I was° in pees, in ese, and in reste, so that there was nothinge in erthe that shulde hafe greved me.

This lasted botte a while, and I was turnede and lefte to myselfe in hevines and werinesse of myselfe and irkesumnesse of my life, that unnethes I couthe hafe patience to lyeve. Thare was none ese ne na comforthe to my felinge, botte hope, faithe, and charite, and this I hadde in trowthe, botte fulle litille in felinge.

9 **anon** soon • 11 **dissesede me** made me uneasy •
14 **with Saint Paule** See Rom. 8:38–39: "I am sure that
neither death, nor life, nor angels . . . nor anything else
in all creation will be able to separate us from the love of
God in Christ Jesus our Lord" • 14 **departe me fro** separate me from • 15 **with Saint Peter** A conflation of two
appeals to Christ on the Sea of Galilee, only one spoken
by Peter: Matt. 8:25 and 14:30 • 17–28 **This vision was
shewde me . . . liking that is God** A passage of spiritual
"counceyle" (8.33), the advice and reflection on experience Christians might give each other, and anchoresses
in particular should give their fellow Christians, when
in a state of difficulty. Hilton's *Scale* (1.83) suggests to its
anchoritic reader, "whoso cometh to thee, aske him
mekely what he wole; and yif he come to telle his disese
[difficulty] and to be comfortid of [by] thy speche,
heere him gladly, and suffre him to seye what he wole
for ese of his owen herte. And whanne he hath doon,
comfort him goodly and charitably." This is one of a
number of passages in *A Revelation* written in the mode
of the spiritual "remedy," in the tradition of Flete's *Remedy* • 17 **to lerne me at** to teach me in • 17–18 **spedfulle
to** profitable for • 19–20 **he kepeth us . . . wele** he keeps
us always equally secure, in woe and in well-being •
21 **sinne is not ever the cause** sin is not always the reason. This is the specific force of this moment of revelation, as the next sentence makes clear. Contrast *The
Chastising,* which is closer to Middle English religious
writing in general in advocating the opposite attitude
toward the "hevinesse" of Christ's absence: "I counceile
every man to rette it to his owne defaute [to consider it
his own fault] that grace is withdrawe" (111) • 21–22 **werefor I shulde . . . myselfe** in such a way that I ought to be
left to myself • 22 **sodeyne** quick • 23 **suffereth us in
wo** allows us to be in misery • 26 **to them** for those •
27 **folow** pay attention to • 28 **sodaynly** quickly •
28 **passe over** get over it

And anon after this, oure blessed lorde gave me again the comfort and the rest in soule: liking and sekernesse• so blisseful• and so mighty° that no drede, ne sorow, ne no paine bodely ne gostely that might be sufferde shulde have dissesede me. And than the paine shewed° again to my feling, and than the joy and the liking, and now that one, and now that other, diverse times, I suppose about twenty times. And in the time of joy, I might have saide with Saint Paule: "Nothing shalle departe me fro the charite of Crist." And in the paine, I might have said with Saint Peter: /fol. 31v/ "Lord, save me,° I perish."

This vision was shewde me to lerne me at my understanding° that it is spedfulle to some soules to feele on this wise: sometime to be in comfort, and sometime to faile° and to be lefte to themselfe. God wille that we know that he kepeth us ever in like seker,• in wo and in wele. And for profite of mans soule a man is somtime left to himselfe, althogh sinne° is not ever the cause. For in this time, I sinned not werefor I shulde be left to myselfe, for it was so sodeyne. Also I deserved not to have this blisseful• feling, but frely our lorde giveth it whan he wille, and suffereth us in wo sometime, and both is one love. For it is Goddes wille that we holde us in comfort with alle oure might. For blisse is lasting without ende, and paine is passing, and shall /fol. 32r/ be brought to nought to them that shall be saved. Therfore it is not Goddes wille that we folow the feling of paine° in sorow and mourning for them, but sodaynly passe over and holde us in the endlesse liking that is God.

10

15

20

25

[*VIS. 9.25–45*] And anone after, God gafe me againe the comforth and /fol. 103r/ the reste in saule: likinge and syekernesse so blisfulle and so mighty that no drede, no sorowe, no paine bodilye no gastelye that might be sufferde shulde have dissesede me. And than the paine shewed againe to my felinge, and than the joye and than the likinge, and than the tane and nowe the tothere, diverse times, I suppose aboute twentye sithes. And in the time of joye, I might hafe saide with Paule: "Nathinge shalle departe me fro the charite of Criste." And in paine, I might hafe saide with Sainte Peter: "Lorde, save me, I perishe."

This vision was shewed me to lere me atte my understandinge that it es *nedefulle* to *ilke man* to feele on this wise: sumtime to be in comforthe, and sumtime to faile and be lefte to himself. God wille that we knowe that he kepes us evere like seker, in wele and in wo, **and als mekille loves us in wo as in wele.** And sumtime, for the profitte of his saule, a man es lefte to himselfe. And *towhethere*, sinne es nought the cause. For in this time, I sinnede nought wherefore I shulde be lefte to myselfe, ‡ ne also I deservede nought to hafe this blisfulle felinge. Botte frelye God giffes *wele* when him likes, and suffers us° in wa sumtime, and bothe es of love. For it is Godes wille that we halde us in comforthe with alle oure might. For blis es lastande withouten ende, and pain es passande, and shalle be brought to nought ‡. Therefore it es nought Goddes wille that we folowe the felinges of paine in sorowinge and in mourninge for thaim°, botte sodaynlye passe over and halde us in endelesse likinge that es God **allemighty, oure lovere and kepare.**

[CHAPTER 16] 1 **nere his dying** near the time of his death. Again, the focus on a single detail, here the drying of Christ's body, is fierce. If the sight of the blood flowing from Christ in the first and fourth revelations is surprisingly joyful, the sight of dryness in *A Revelation* is always associated with absence and pain. This revelation intensifies the sense of horror expressed in the second and part of the seventh revelations, as Julian's youthful request to have "seen bodily the passion that our lord suffered for me" (2.8–9) reaches its climax • 1 **swete** sweet • 2 **pale dying** the pallor of death • 2 **sithen** afterward • 2 **deade** deathly • 3 **languring** languishing • 3 **than turned . . . browne blew** then turned more deathly blue, and afterward a duller blue • 4 **turned more depe dede** became more deeply dead • 4 **properly** explicitly • 5 **namely in his lippes** especially in his lips. The wounds in Christ's hands, feet, and side, and the crown of thorns on his head, were often separate objects of contemplation in Passion meditation, with prayers directed toward each of them. Not only are Christ's lips an addition to these standard "tokens" of the Passion; visionary contemplation here focuses, not on the lips themselves, but on the process they undergo as Christ dies. The object of contemplation is generally static. Here, the lips are seen in time • 5 **there I saw** where I saw • 5 **tho** those lips • 6 **fresh . . . liking** fresh and ruddy, lively and delicious. In Bridget's *Liber celestis*, Mary describes Christ's lips, when he was a young man, as "thike anogh and redyse [very thick and ruddy]" (4.70) • 6 **swemfulle** terrible • 7 **the nose clongen togeder** the nose withered into itself • 8 **waxid** grew • 10 **rode** cross • 10 **a dry, harre wind** a dry, bitter wind. Not a standard detail in accounts of the Passion, although *The Privity* notes that "the wedire was colde" ("Ad primam," *YW* 1:203). A cold east wind from the North Sea might have been a feature of many Good Fridays in fourteenth-century Norwich • 11–12 **the precious blode . . . therfro** all the precious blood was bled from the sweet body as could flow from it • 13 **Blodlessehed** bloodlessness • 15 **twain** two • 17 **lively spirites** sources or sparks of life. Medieval biology defined any living thing as a combination of body and spirit • 20 **paining** suffering • 20 **had be sennight deade** had been dead seven nights. The number of nights Julian has lain sick. See 3.2–4 • 20–21 **at the point of outpassing** at the point of the soul's departure from the body • 21 **ther I say** where I say. A sentence structured as a gloss on the previous sentence, perhaps to stress that the perception of Jesus as "sennight deade" should be taken as part of the revelation. The gloss is necessary to justify what looks like a historical inaccuracy: in the Gospels, Jesus' death takes place before nightfall • 22 **it specifieth** it indicates • 23 **dedly** deathly • 23 **pituous** piteous

oooooooooooooooooooooooooooooo

The Eighth Revelation
AND THE SIXTEENTH CHAPTER

After this, Crist shewde a parte of his passion nere his dying. I saw the swete face as it were drye and blodeles with pale dying; and sithen more° deade pale, languring; and than turned more deade into blew; and sithen more browne blew,° as the flesh turned more depe dede. For his passion shewde to me most properly in his blessed face, and namely in his lippes, there I saw° these four colours—tho that were   5 before fresh and rody, lively and liking to my sight. This was a swemfulle change,° to se this depe /fol. 32v/ dying. And also the nose clongen togeder and dried,° to my sight, and the swete body waxid browne and blacke, alle changed and turned oute of the fair, fresh, and lively coloure of himselfe into drye dying. For that same time that oure blessed saviour died upon the rode, it was a dry, harre wind, wonder colde° as to my   10 sight. And what time that the precious blode was bled out of the swete body that might passe therfro, yet ther dwellid° a moister in the swete flesh of Crist, as it was shewde.

Blodlessehed and paine dried within, and blowing of the winde and colde coming from without, met togeder in the swete body of Christ. And these four, twain withouten and twain within,° dried the flesh of Crist by process of time. And   15 thowe this paine was bitter and sharp, yet it was fulle longe lasting, as to my sight. /fol. 33r/ And the paine driede uppe alle the lively spirites of Cristes flesh.

Thus I saw the swete flesh dry in my sight, parte after parte, drying with mervelous paine. And as long as any sprite had life in Cristes flesh, so longe sufferde he paine.° This long paining° semede to me as if he had be sennight deade, dying, at the point of   20 outpassing, alwey suffering the gret paine. And ther I say, "it semed to me° as he had bene sennight dead," it specifieth that the swet body was so discoloured, so drye, so clongen, so dedly, and so pituous as he had bene sennight dead, continually dying. And methought the drying of Cristes flesh was the most paine, and the last, of his passion.

[VIS. 10.1–11] After this, Criste shewed **me** a partye of his passione nere his dyinge. I sawe that swete face as it ware drye and bludyelesse with pale dyinge; sithen mare dede° pale, langourande; and than turnede more dede to the blewe; and sithene mare *blewe,* as the fleshe turnede mare deepe dede. *For alle the paines that Criste sufferde in his bodye shewed to me in the blissede face, als farfurthe as I sawe it,* and namelye in the lippes, thare I sawe this foure colourse—thaye that *I sawe beforehande* freshlye and ruddy,° liflye and likande to my sight. This /fol. 103v/ was a *hevy* change, to see this deepe dyinge. And also the nese claungede° and dried to my sight. /Rev. 16.8–19/

This lange pininge semede to me as he hadde bene a sevennight dede, ‡ allewaye suf-ferande ‡ paine. /Rev. 16.21–23/ And methought the dryinge of Cristes fleshe was the maste paine of his passion and the laste.

[CHAPTER 17] 1 "**I thurst**" See John 19:28. Thus begins *A Revelation*'s great set piece on Christ's death by drying. Bridget of Sweden had seen many new details of Christ's suffering and his mother's intense feelings in viewing his death, recorded in the *Liber celestis*: see, e.g., the detailed narrative accounts of his bleeding and his different postures (*Liber celestis* 1.10 and 4.70). Julian here makes her own carefully focused contribution to the tradition, its theme the undoing of creation by sin • 2 **doubille thurst** A standard interpretation of Christ's words. See *The Privity:* "For thof [although] it were so that him thristede for the hele of manes soule, nevertheles in sothefastnes him thirsted bodily; and that was no wonder, for thurghe sheddinge of his preciouse blode so habundandly . . . he was all inwardly drye and thristy" ("Meditatione of None," *YW* 1:207) • 3–4 **as I shalle sey after** See 31.10–16 • 4 **failing of moister** lack of moisture. Compare 16.11–12 • 5–7 **The blessed body . . . body** the blessed body dried all alone for a long time, with the wrenching of the nails and the weight of the body • 7 **for tendernes** because of the tenderness. According to Bridget, Christ's skin "was so tendir that, were he nevir so softly scourged, anone the blode wente furth" (*Liber celestis* 1.10) • 8 **grevoushede** terribleness • 8 **waxid** grew • 9 **satilde for weight** sank because of its weight • 9 **persing and rasing** piercing and scraping • 10 **crowne** crown of thorns • 10 **baken** baked • 11 **swet here** sweet hair • 12–22 **in the beginning . . . fall** Now the moisture in Jesus' body ceases to be life-giving, as it has been in Chapter 16, and becomes part of what tears his body, as it adds to the weight of his flesh and skin. See the textual notes for the Sloane manuscript's version of this passage • 12–13 **continualle sitting of the thornes** Bridget has Mary recall that the thorns "prikked so sharply the reverent hede of my son that his eene [eyes] were filled of the blode that flowed oute, his eres were stopped, and all his berde was besene [drenched] tharewith" (*Liber celestis* 1.10) • 14–15 **was alle rased . . . thornes** was all scraped and loosened on top by the thorns • 15 **pecis** pieces • 15–16 **as they wolde** as if they would • 16 **while it . . . moister** while it still contained its natural moisture • 17–18 **boistrous . . . the garlonde** rough, terrible pushing-on of the garland of thorns. A reminiscence of the opening of the first revelation, where the "sitting on" of the crown of thorns has just occurred. See 4.1–3 • 18 **that alle tho brake** that at that time quite broke. "Tho" is here an adverb (at that time, then). The wounds Julian now sees are the result of his earlier crowning with thorns (compare 4.2–3) • 19 **losed** loosed. Read "and loosed" • 19 **Wherthorow** for which reason • 20 **as a cloth** A sad evocation of "He is oure clothing" (5.3) • 24 **stint** diminish • 25 **environed** surrounded • 26 **as it were garland upon garland** The torn, bleeding skin makes a ring of flesh around and above the crown of thorns. "Garland" is already associated more readily with flowers than with blood and thorns in Middle English, so the phrasing here is bitterly ironic • 26 **deyde** dyed • 27 **clotered blode** clotted blood • 28 **semed of the . . . body** seemed to be part of the face and the body. "Semed" suggests it is no longer possible to be sure where the torn skin and flesh belonged on Jesus' body

THE SEVENTEENTH CHAPTER   */fol. 33v/*

And in this drying was brought to my minde this worde that Crist said: "I thurst." For I sawe in Crist a doubille thurst: on bodely, and another gostly. This worde was shewed for the bodily thurste, and for the gostely thurst was shewed as I shalle sey after. And I understode by the bodily thurste that the body had failing of moister, for the blessede flesh and bones was lefte alle alone without blode and moister. The blessed body dried alle alon long time, with wringing of the nailes and weight of the body. For I understode that for tendernes of the swete handes and the swete feet, by the gretenes, hardhede, and grevoushede° of the nailes, the woundes waxid wide. And the body satilde for weight by long time hanging, and persing and rasing° of the heed, and binding of the crowne, alle */fol. 34r/* baken with drye blode, with the swet here clinging the drye flesh to the thornes and the thornes to the flesh, drying.

And in the beginning, while the flesh was fresh and bleding, the continualle sitting of the thornes made the woundes wide. And ferthermore I saw that the swet skinne and the tender° flesh, with the here and with the blode, was alle rased and losede above with the thornes, and broken in many pecis, and were hanging as they wolde hastely have fallen downe while it had kinde moister. How it was done I saw not, but I understode that it was with the sharpe thornes and the boistrous, grevous sitting on of the garlonde, not sparing and without pitte, that alle tho brake the swet skinne, with the flesh and the here, losed it from the bone. Wherthorow it was broken on peces as a */fol. 34v/* cloth and sagging downwarde, seming as it wolde hastely have fallen for hevines and for loosenes. And that was grete sorow and drede to me, for methought that I wolde not for my life have seene it fall.

This continued a while, and after it began to change, and I behelde and marveyled how it might be. And than I saw it was for it beganne to dry and stint a parte of the weight that was round about the garland, and so it was environed all about, as it were garland upon garland. The garlonde of thornes was deyde with the blode. And that other garlond and the hede, all was one coloure, as clotered blode when it was dried. The skinne and the fleshe that semed of the face and of the body

5

10

15

20

25

[*VIS.* 10.12–18] And in this dryhede was brought to my minde this worde that Criste saide: "I thriste." For I sawe in Criste a doubille thirste: ane bodilye, ane othere gastelye. This worde was shewed **to° me** for the bodilye thirste, and for the gastelye thirste was shewed **to me** als I shalle saye efterwarde. And I understode of bodelye thirste that the bodye hadde failinge° of moistere, for the blessede fleshe and banes ware lefte allane withouten blode and moistere. The blissed bodye driede allane° lange time, with wringinge of the nailes **and paysinge of the hede°** and weight of the bodye, */Rev. 17.7–37/*

29 **smalle rumpelde** slightly wrinkled • 29 **drye bord whan it is aged** Jesus' flesh and the wood of the cross, or the crucifix in which the scene is set, begin to look alike • 31 **blodlesse** blood loss • 32 **eyer** air • 33 **the bodely kinde asked licoure** his bodily nature required moisture • 35–36 **thus clinging** withering in this way. See 16.7, 23 • 36–37 **wrought to the drying** created by the drying • 37–39 **that other . . . paines** and the other, slow pain created by the withering and the drying, by the blowing of the wind from without, which dried him more and tormented him more with cold than my heart can think—and there were other pains. The sentence, which lingers over the details mentioned in 16.13–15, breaks down under its own intensity • 39–40 **For which paines . . . may not be tolde** concerning which pains I saw that everything that I say is too little, for it cannot be told. Despite the brutal focus here on physical, rather than spiritual, suffering, the description must still end by asserting the scene's inexpressibility • 41 **The shewing . . . fulle of paines** An equivalence between Christ's Passion and the devout Christian's compassion, a common aim of meditation and the basis of Julian's first desire, is achieved. In *The Pryckinge,* the meditator's focus on Christ's pain guarantees "that thou shalt be wounded with his woundes and over-helte [overcome] with peynes of his passioun" (15) • 41–42 **I wiste welle . . . but onys** I knew well he suffered only once. See Heb. 10:10: "And by [God's] will we have been sanctified through the offering of the body of Jesus Christ once for all" • 42–43 **but as he wolde . . . desirede** except insofar as he wished to show me it, and fill me with recollection, as I had asked for before. See 2.5–16. Julian acknowledges she is seeing a representation of the Passion, not the Passion itself • 43 **presens** presence • 44 **I knew fulle litille what . . . I asked** See Matt. 20:22, Jesus' answer to the mother of James and John: "You do not know what you are asking. Are you able to drink the cup that I am to drink?" • 45 **as a wrech I repented me** like a wretch I took back my wish. See 66.23, where Julian again calls herself "wrech" • 45 **wiste** known • 47 **Is ony paine in helle lik this?** Is any pain in hell like this? See Lam. 1:12: "Look and see if there is any sorrow like my sorrow". A version of a commonly asked question, whether Christ's pain was worse than hell: "Thenne may sum mon [person] seyen that the sorwe that he suffrede for us on the crois was grettere then the peine of helle is," as Edmund of Abingdon's *Mirror of Holy Church* has it ("Contemplation biforen Midday," *YW* 1:256). Unlike *The Mirror,* which accepts the question, *A Revelation* stresses the difference in kind between these pains • 48 **dispair** The worst pain because by definition eternal. According to *The Pricke,* the damned "ay [always] dwelle" in despair "withouten hope of mercy," since they realize the truth of Job's words: "For in hell . . . es na redemptioune" (7234–51) • 50 **sothfastly** truthfully

was smalle rumpelde, with a tawny coloure, like a drye bord whan it is aged, and the
face more browne than the body.   30

I saw /*fol. 35r*/ four maner of drying. The furst was blodlesse. The secunde, paine
folowing after. The thurde is that he was hanging uppe in the eyer, as men hang a
cloth for to drye. The fourth, that the bodely kinde asked licoure, and ther was no
maner of comfort ministred to him. A, hard and grevous was that paine, but moch
more harder and grevous it was when the moistur failed, and all began to drye, thus   35
clinging. These were two paines that shewde in the blissed hed: the furst wrought to
the drying while it was moist; and that other, slow, with clinging and drying, with
blowing of winde fro without that dried him more and pained with colde than my
hart can thinke—and other paines.° For which paines, I saw that alle is to litille that
I can sey, for it /*fol. 35v*/ may not be tolde.   40

The shewing of Cristes paines filled me fulle of paines. For I wiste welle he
sufferede but onys, but as he wolde shewe it me and fille me with minde, as I had
before desirede. And in alle this time of Cristes presens, I felte no paine but for
Cristes paines. Than thought me, I knew fulle litille what paine it was that I asked.
And as a wrech I repented me, thinking if I had wiste what it had be, loth me had   45
been to have preyde it. For methought my paines passed ony bodely deth. I thought:
"Is ony paine in helle lik this?" And I was answered in my reson: "Helle is another
paine, for ther is dispair. But of alle paines° that leed to salvation, this is the most: to
se thy love suffer.° How might ony paine be more then to /*fol. 36r*/ see him that is
alle my life, alle my blisse, and alle my joy suffer?" Here felt I sothfastly° that I loved   50

[*VIS. 10.19–36*] with blawinge of winde fra withouten that dried mare, and pined him
with calde mare, than min herte can thinke, and **alle** othere paines.

Swilke paines I sawe that alle es to litelle that I can *telle or saye,* for it maye nought
be tolde. **Botte ilke saule, after the sayinge of Sainte Paule, shulde "feele in him that in
Criste Jhesu."** This shewinge of Criste paines filled me fulle of paines. For I wate wele he
suffrede nought botte anes, botte as he walde shewe it me and fille me with minde, as I
hadde desirede before.

**My modere, that stode emanges othere and behelde me, lifted uppe hir hande
before me face to lokke min eyen. For she wened I had bene dede or els I hadde diede.
And this encresed mekille my sorowe. For noughtwithstandinge alle my paines, I wolde
nought hafe been letted for love that I hadde in him. And towhethere,** in alle this time
of Cristes presence, I feled no paine botte for Cristes paines. Than thought me, I knewe
ful litille° whate paine it was that I asked, /*Rev. 17.45–46*/ for methought that my paines
passede any bodilye dede. I thought: "Es any paine in helle like this paine?" And I was
answerde in my resone that "*dispaire is mare, for that es gastelye paine. Bot bodilye paine
es nane mare than this.* Howe might *my* paine be more° than to see him that es alle my
life, alle my blis, and alle mye /*fol. 104r*/ joye suffer?" Here° feled I sothfastlye that I lovede

51–52 **ther was no paine . . . to see him in paine** The pain of compassion is so severe as to blot out, for a time, Julian's sense even of the pain that is its object

[CHAPTER 18] 1 **the compassion of . . . Mary** Mary's presence at the foot of the cross made her the first, as well as the best-informed, person to experience the Passion , and as such an object of identification and veneration. As in 4.33–35, she is again seen here as the highest thing in creation below Jesus • 2 **oned** united • 2 **mekillehede** magnitude • 3–4 **a substance . . . to him** an essential basis of the natural love, continued by grace, that his creatures have for him. The extent of Mary's suffering with Jesus reveals the intimacy of the relationship between Christ and his creation that is a result of his Incarnation and death. "Kinde love" is often the love felt between close relatives or lovers. See 60.41: "To the properte of moderhede longeth kind love" • 4–5 **was most . . . overpassing** was most abundantly and transcendently revealed in his sweet mother • 5 **For so mekille** for as much • 8 **alle his tru lovers** See 2.7–10: both Mary Magdalene and the company of Christ's lovers she represents, those who through meditation or vision are at the scene of the Passion "that time" • 8–9 **ther awne bodely dying** their own physical death • 9 **seker** sure • 11 **oning** cause of union ("one-ing") • 13–14 **alle creatures . . . dying** the whole creation that God has made to serve us, the heavens and the earth, failed in their own way for sadness at the time of Christ's death. Refers to the eclipse and the earthquake that, in Luke 23:44–45 and Matt. 27:45, 51, follow the death of Jesus. In Bridget's *Liber celestis,* Mary describes how, "in the deing [death] of my son, all thinges were turbled [troubled]. . . . All the elementes were disesed. The son and the mone withdrawen [withdrew] ther light in tokening of [as a sign of] compassion, the erth tremlid, the stones braste [burst open]" (6.11). Langland's *Piers Plowman* B evokes the scene in a single line: "The day for drede withdrough and derk bicam the sonne" (18.60) • 15 **it longeth . . . properte** it belongs naturally to their order • 16–17 **then behoved . . . with him** then because of their nature they necessarily failed with him • 18 **generally alle** in a general way everyone • 19–20 **save . . . keping of God** except the comfort provided by God's powerful secret sustaining. Compare the hazelnut in 5.11–13

Crist so much above myselfe that ther was no paine that might be suffered like to that sorow that I had to see him in paine.

THE EIGHTEENTH CHAPTER

Here I saw in parte the compassion of our lady,° Saint Mary. For Crist and she was so oned in love that the gretnes of her love was cause of the mekillehede° of her paine. For in this I saw a substance of kinde love, continued by grace, that his creatures have to him, which kinde love was most fulsomly shewde in his swete mother, and overpassing. For so mekille• as she loved him more then alle other, her paine passed alle other. For ever the higher, the mightier, the swetter that the love is, the more sorow /fol. 36v/ it is to the lover to se that body in paine that he loved. And so alle his disciples and alle his tru lovers suffered paines more° than ther awne bodely dying. For I am seker,• by my awne feling, that the lest of them loved him so farre aboven themselfe that it passeth alle that I can sey.

Here saw I a gret oning betwene Crist and us, to my understonding. For when he was in paine, we ware in paine, and alle creatures that might suffer paine suffered with him: that is to say, alle creatures that God hath made to oure servys, the firmamente and erth, failed for sorow in ther kind in the time of Cristes dying. For it longeth kindly to ther properte to know him for ther lorde, in whom alle ther vertuse stondeth. And whan he failed, /fol. 37r/ then behoved nedes to them for kindnes to faile with him, in as moch as they might, for sorow of his paines.

And thus tho that were his frendes suffered paine for love, and generally alle: that is to sey, they that knew him not sufferde for failinge of all maner comfort, save

5

10

15

[vis. 10.36–49] Criste so mekille aboven myselfe that **methought it hadde beene a grete ese to me to hafe diede bodilye ‡**.

Herein I sawe in partye the compassion of oure ladye, Sainte Marye. For Criste and sho ware so anede in love that the gretnesse of hir love was the cause of the mekillehede of hir paine. /Rev. 18.3–5/ For so mekille as sho loved him mare than alle othere, her paine passed alle othere. /Rev .6–7/ And so alle his disciples and alle his trewe lovers sufferde paines mare than thare awne bodelye dying. For I am seker, be min awne felinge, that the leste of thame luffed him° *mare than thaye did thamselfe.*

Here I sawe a° grete aninge betwyx Criste and us ‡. For when he was in paine, we ware in paine, and alle creatures that might suffer paine sufferde with him. **And thaye that knewe him nought, this was thare paine: that alle creatures, sone and the mone, withdrewe thare service and so ware thaye alle lefte in sorowe for the time.** /Rev. 18.13–19/

And thus thaye *that loved him* sufferde paine for luffe ‡, *and thay that luffed him nought sufferde paine for failinge of comforthe of alle° creatures.* /Rev. 18.19–30/

20 **two maner of people** two kinds of people. People who did not, and people who did, convert • 21 **Pilate** Pontius Pilate, who condemned Jesus to be crucified. According to the *Gospel of Nicodemus* 11:2, Pilate, troubled by his unjust condemnation of Christ, took note of the eclipse and "sent for the Jews and said unto them: 'Did ye see that which came to pass?' But they said: 'There was an eclipse of the sun after the accustomed sort'" • 22 **Saint Dionisy of France** Saint Dionysius the Areopagite, Paul's only named convert from Athens in the Book of Acts (17:34). Legend identified him as the Denis who was patron saint of France. This account stays close to the wording of James of Voragine's life of Dionysius in his great collection *The Golden Legend*, which has a detailed description of the natural disturbances caused by the Passion. Dionysius opines: "Either the God of nature has suffered death or else the ordinance of nature in this world is dissolved"; then he proceeds to erect "the altar of the unknown God" • 22 **paynim** pagan • 23 **merveyles** marvels • 24 **elles** else • 24 **maker of kindes** maker of natural things, the Creator • 25 **This is . . . unknowen God** this is an altar to the unknown God. The altar Paul claims to have seen in Athens with this epithet inscribed upon it, Acts 17:23 • 25 **awter** altar • 26–27 **that maketh . . . cursede** who makes the planets and the elements [earth, air, fire, water] to work after their natures on behalf of the blessed man and the cursed • 27 **in that time . . . fro both** in that time, the working of the creation was withdrawn from blessed and cursed • 29 **noughted** humiliated • **as I shalle sey after** See 27.14–17

[CHAPTER 19] 1 **wolde have . . . crosse** wanted to look away from the cross. Julian has been looking at the cross since 3.22 • 1 **durst** dared • 1 **wist** knew • 3 **perelle** peril • 3–4 **no sekernesse . . . fends** no safety because of the horror of fiends. See 3.26–27. The demons cluster around both Julian's deathbed and the dying figure of Christ • 4 **profer** proposition • 4 **as it had ben frendely** as though it were friendly. The status of the "profer" is never clarified, though the phrasing here suggests a sinister source for the words that follow • 5 **Loke uppe** look up. As Julian is looking up in 3.18–21, before lowering her eyes to the cross • 6–7 **might have dissesede me** could have given me trouble • 7 **either me behoved . . . answere** I must either look up or else answer • 7 **answered inwardly** Julian's earlier statements, at 8.24–25 and 13.29–33, are made aloud • 8 **Nay, I may not!** Julian's change of mind is not explained, although it seems connected not only with her desire to suffer with Christ but with her desire to live beyond her experience of dying—with both the first two "desires" described in Chapter 2. Fidelity to the sufferings of the human Jesus is often prized in medieval women's writings: see *The Book of Margery Kempe,* chaps. 35–37, on Margery's devotion to Christ's humanity and reluctance to undergo mystical marriage to the godhead. When Julian denies her revelation in Chapter 66, her devastation leads to an episode of demonic temptation to despair • 8 **For thou art my heven** Hilton's *Scale* 2.33 begins an account of the contemplative's sight of heaven with "What is hevene to a resonable soule? Sothly, not ellis but Jhesu God" • 9 **For I had lever . . . tille domesday** for I would rather have been in that pain until Judgment Day. A formulation that links Julian's pain with the pains of purgatory, which cease on the Day of Judgment • 10–11 **he that bounde me so sore** he who bound me so tight. The image is erotic. In Chaucer's *Troilus and Criseyde* 3.1358, Troilus asks Criseyde: "How koude ye withouten bond me binde?" Here, however, the bonds are mutual. As part 7 of *Ancrene Wisse* makes clear, when it comes to love, Christ is as bound to humanity as humanity is to him: "Love binds our Lord, so that he cannot do anything except with love's leave" (198)

the mighty prive keping of God. I mene of two maner of people that knew him not, 20
as it may be understand by two persons. That one was Pilate, that other person was
Saint Dionisy of France, which was that time a paynim. For whan he saw wonders
and merveyles, sorowse and dredes, that befelle in that time, he saide: "Either the
worlde is now at an ende, or elles he that is maker of kindes suffereth." Wherfore he
did write on an awter: "This /fol. 37v/ is an awter of the° unknowen God." 25

God of his goodnes, that maketh planettes and the elementes to worke in ther
kinde to the blessed man and to the cursede, in that time it was withdraw fro both.
Wherfor it was that they that knew him not were in sorow that time. Thus was oure
lord Jhesu noughted° for us, and we stonde alle in this maner noughted° with him,
and shalle do tille that we come to his blisse, as I shalle sey after. 30

THE NINETEENTH CHAPTER

In this time I wolde have lokede fro the crosse, and I durst not, for I wist wele
while that I behelde the crosse I was seker• and safe. Therfore I wolde not assent
to put my soule in perelle, for beside the crosse was no sekernesse• for ugging of
fends.° Than had I a /fol. 38r/ profer in my reason,° as it had ben frendely, saide to
me: "Loke uppe to heven to his father." And than sawe I wele, with the faith that I 5
felt, that ther was nothing betwene the crosse and heven that might have dissesede
me, and either° me behoved to loke uppe or elles to answere. I answered inwardly
with alle the might of my soule, and said: "Nay, I may not! For thou art my heven."
This I saide for I wolde not. For I had lever have bene° in that paine tille domesday,
than have come to heven otherwise than by him. For I wist wele that he that bounde 10
me so sore, he shuld unbind me whan he wolde.

[VIS. 10.50–60] In this time I walde hafe loked beside the crosse, botte I durste nought,
for I wiste wele whiles I *luked upon* the crosse I was seker and safe. Therfore I walde
nought assente to putte my saule in perille, for beside the crosse was na syekernesse,°
botte uglinesse of feendes. Than hadde I a profer in my resone, as if it hadde beene frendelye, isaide to me: "Luke uppe to heven to his fadere." Than sawe I wele, with the faithe
that I feled, that thare ware nathinge betwyx the crosse and heven that might hafe
desesed me, and othere me behoved loke uppe or els answere. I answerde ‡ and saide:
"Naye, I may nought! For thowe erte mine heven." This I saide for I walde nought. For I
hadde lever hafe bene in that paine to domesdaye, than hafe comen to hevene otherewise
than be him. For I wiste wele, he that bonde me so sare° shulde unbinde me when he
walde.

12 **chese** choose • 12 **whom I saw only in paine** The conflation of pain and heaven here is profoundly contradictory. According to *The Pricke,* life in heaven is defined by "hele and liking" (health and pleasure) and the absence of "ivel" and "paine" (8011–12). "Paine," on the other hand, is a synonym for "hell" • 13 **no nother** no other • 17–18 **though I . . . prayde it** See 17.45–46 • 19 **gruging and daunger of the flesh** reluctance and resistance on the part of the flesh • 19 **assent of the soule** In later medieval theology, a thought or deed is sinful only if made with the assent of the soul. The passage exonerates Julian for what might appear to be her sin in behaving as a "wrech" (line 17) • 21–22 **Repenting . . . at that time** regret (at having asked to experience Christ's suffering) and conscious choice (the choice just made to continue to do so) are two opposite responses, which I felt both together at that time • 22 **And tho be two partes** and I did so with two different parts of the self. This passage anticipates the distinction drawn in Chapter 45 between the soul's "sensual" and "substantial" natures, and is discussed in some detail with respect to the soul of Christ in 55.40–49 • 22 **that on** the one • 23 **dedely flesh** mortal body • 24 **whereof I felte moch** of which pain and woe I felt much • 24–25 **And that party . . . repented** and it was that part of the self that regretted • 26 **prively** intimately • 28–29 **nought charging . . . willes of that** not reckoning or taking notice of the desires of the outer self • 29 **alle the intent and the wille** all the inner part's intent and desire • 29 **to be oned to** to be united with • 30 **That the outward . . . shewde to me** Sin can be defined as the submission of the inner self to the outer, spirit to flesh, servant to "sovereyne." The sentence acknowledges that such submission is possible but, as ever in this revelation, "sinne was not shewde" (11.18)

[CHAPTER 20] 1 **languring** languishing • 1–3 **oning . . . might** unification with the divinity of Christ gave strength to his humanity to suffer more than anyone could, or than everyone put together could. The next sentence resolves the ambiguity • 3–5 **I meene . . . the last day** Edmund, in *The Mirror,* writes: "Theigh alle the seknesses and alle the serwes [sorrows] of this world were in o [one] monnes body . . . hit were not but litel, or as nought, to regard of [it would not be more than a little, or nothing, by comparison with] the serwe that he suffrede for us in on houre of the day" ("Contemplation biforen Midday," *YW* 1:256). *A Revelation* is more precise: as members of the body of Christ, all the saved participate in his suffering (see 21.12–13), but even added together their pains can represent only a small portion of his • 4 **all men of salvation** all the saved. As 17.46–50 argues, the pains of the damned are in a different category

Thus was I lerned to chese Jhesu for my heven, whom I saw only in paine at that
time. Me liked no nother heven than Jhesu, which /fol. 38v/ shalle be my blisse when
I come ther. And this hath ever be a comfort to me, that I chose Jhesu to be my
heven, by his grace, in alle this time of passion and sorow. And that hath ben a
lerning to me, that I shulde evermore do so, to chese Jhesu only to my heven in wele
and in woe. And though I as a wrech hath repented me—as I saide before, "If I had
wist what paine it had be, I had be loth to have prayde it"—heer I saw sothly° that it
was gruging and daunger° of the flesh without assent of the soule, in which God
assigneth no blame.

Repenting and wilfulle choyse be two contrarites, which I felt both in one°
at that time. And tho be two partes: that on outward, that other inwarde. The
outwarde party is our dedely flesh, which is now in paine and now /fol. 39r/ in wo,
and shalle be in this life, whereof I felte moch in this time. And that party was that
repented.° The inward party is a high and a blisseful• life, which is alle in peece and
in love, and this is more prively felte. And this party is in which mightly, wisely, and
wilfully, I chose Jhesu to my heven. And in this, I saw sothly° that the inward party is
master and sovereyne to the outward, nought charging nor taking hede of the willes
of that. But alle the intent and the wille is set endlesly to be oned to our lorde Jhesu.
That the outward party sholde drawe the inward to assent was not shewde to me.
But that the inwarde party draweth the outward party, by grace, and both shalle be
oned in blisse without ende by the vertu of Christ, this was shewde. /fol. 39v/

15

20

25

30

THE TWENTIETH CHAPTER

And thus saw I oure lorde Jhesu languring long time. For the oning of the
godhed gave strength to the manhed for love to suffer more than alle men°
might. I meene not only more paine than alle men° might suffer, but also that he
sufferd more paine than all men° of salvation that ever was, from the furst

---

[VIS. 11.1–9] *Thus chese I Jhesu* for my heven, wham I saw° onlye in paine at that time.
Me likede no nothere hevene /fol. 104v/ than Jhesu, whilke shalle be my blisse when I am
thare. And this has ever beene a comforthe to me, that I chesed Jhesu to my hevene ‡ in
alle time of passion and of sorowe. And that has beene a lerninge to me, that I shulde
evermare do so, and chese anly him to my heven in wele and in wa. /Rev. 19.17–32/

And thus sawe I *my* lorde Jhesu langoure lange time. For the aninge of the godhede
for love gafe strenght to the manhede to suffer mare than alle men might. I mene nought
anly mare paine anly than alle men might suffer, bot also° that he sufferde mare paine
than alle men ‡ that ever was, fra the firste

6 **having regard to** taking account of • 7 **dispiteous** pitiless • 8 **fulliest noughted . . . dispised** most fully humiliated and most utterly despised. See Phil. 2:6–8, a statement of Christ's self-humiliation through Incarnation and Passion: "Though he was in the form of God, [he] . . . emptied himself, taking the form of a servant. . . . And being found in human form he humbled himself and became obedient unto death, even death on a cross" • 8–9 **hyest point** most sublime consideration • 9–10 **what he is that suffered** what he who suffered is • 10 **seeing after** reflecting on it after • 10 **which be lower** which are less sublime. Like the structure of the eighth revelation, meditation is here seen as moving from the lower to the higher • 12 **in this** in this reflection • 14 **which be together oned** the two of which (godhead and body) are fused together • 14–15 **the lothhede . . . paine** our natural reluctance to suffer pain • 15–16 **For as much as . . . mighty to suffer** Compare Bridget, *Liber celestis* 1.10: "For [because] he was of the beste kinde [having taken from Mary "the clenneste body and beste complexiond"], therefore was thare a strong fight in his body bitwene life and dede" • 18–20 **For in as mekille . . . in kinde** for to the extent that our lady sorrowed for his pains, to that extent he suffered sorrow for her sorrows, and more besides, to the extent that his sweet humanity was worthier in nature. The idea that Christ's and Mary's awareness of one another's sorrow makes their own worse is found, e.g., in Rolle's *Meditations on the Passion:* "Heo [she] fel in dede swoune [a dead faint] ofter than ones [more than once] for sorewe of the peines that to hire herte smiten. The sorewe that heo made and the mykel dool [great grief] agregged manifold [multiplied many times] alle thin othere peines. So whan heo [she] wiste that it so was, than was hire wel wers, and thou also for hire wepist. So was youre sorewe, either for other, waxenge manifold with hepinge sorewes" (*YW* 1.86) • 20 **passible** capable of suffering. A technical word for a characteristic of the human nature of Christ not shared by his divinity • 21 **uppe resin** resurrected • 22 **as I shalle sey after** See 21.20–23 • 23–24 **the love . . . oure soule** the love that he has for our souls was so strong • 24 **wilfully he chose it** he deliberately chose suffering • 27 **which paines . . . joy** those pains that shall be turned into eternal joy. The pains of hell are again excluded. See 17.46–52

[CHAPTER 21] 1–2 **It is Gods wille . . . passion** Begins a complex summing-up of Julian's revelation concerning the Passion that stretches over three chapters and incorporates both the ending of the eighth and the whole of the ninth revelations • 2 **The furst** For the second and third, see 22.37–38, 23.5–6, both part of the ninth revelation • 2–3 **contrition and compassion** Two of the three wounds desired by Julian in 2.34–36 • 3 **in this time** at the time of the revelation. This first "maner of beholding" is the chief subject of the eighth revelation • 5 **loked after** anticipated • 5 **with alle my mightes** with all the powers of my soul • 5 **wende** expected • 6 **alle dead** completely dead • 6–7 **by seming** to all appearances

beginning into the last day. No tongue may telle, or herte fully thinke, the paines 5
that oure saviour suffered for us,° having regard to the worthines of the highest,
worshipful king and the shamfulle, dispiteous, and painful° deth. For he that is
highest and worthiest was fulliest noughted° and utterliest° dispised. For the hyest
point that may be seen in his passion is to thinke and to know what he is that
suffered,° seeing after these other two pointes, which be lower: that one is what 10
he suffered; and that other, for /fol. 40r/ whom that he suffered.

And in this, he brought to mind in parte the hight° and the nobilite of the
glorious godhede, and therwith the precioushede and the tendernesse of the
blisseful• body, which be together oned, and also the lothhede• that in our kinde
is to suffer paine. For as much as he was most tender and clene, right so he was 15
most strong and mighty to suffer. And for every mannes sinne that shal be saved he
suffered. And every mannes sorow, desolation, and anguish he sawe and sorowd for
kindnes and love. For in as mekille• as our lady sorowde for his paines, as mekille•
sufferde he sorow for her sorowse, and more over, in as mekille• as the swete
manhed of him was wurthier in kinde. For as long as he was passible, he sufferde 20
for us and sorowde for us. And now he is uppe resin and no more passibille, yet he
suffereth with us, as I /fol. 40v/ shalle sey after.

And I, beholding alle this by his grace, saw that the love in him was so strong
which he hath to oure soule that wilfully° he chose it with gret desyer, and mildely
he suffered it with gret joy. For the soule that beholdeth thus whan it is touched by 25
grace, he shalle verely see that tho paines of Cristes passion passe all paines:° that is
to sey, which paines shal be turned into everlasting joy by the vertu of Cristes
passion.

THE TWENTY-FIRST CHAPTER°

It is Gods wille, as to my understanding, that we have thre maner of beholding of
his blessed passion. The furst is the harde paine that he suffered, with contrition°
and compassion. And that shewde oure lorde in this time, and gave me might and
grace to see it.

And I loked after the departing with alle my mightes and wende to have seen the 5
body alle dead. But I saw him not so. And right in the same time that methought by

---

[vis. 11.9–13] beginninge to the laste daye. No tonge maye telle, ne herte fully thinke, the
paines that oure savioure sufferde for us, haffande rewarde to the worthines of the hyest,
worshipfulle kinge and to the shamefulle, dispittous, and painfulle dede. For he that was
hieste and worthiest was fulliest noghthede and witterliest dispiside. /Rev. 20.8–21.8/

7 **lenger** longer • 8 **behoved nedes to be nye** had to be close • 8 **sodenly** Again, this word announces visionary transformation. See 3.30, 4.1 • 8 **beholding in . . . crosse** as I looked into the same cross. Even the following joyful scene is played out "in the face of the crucifixe" (10.1) • 8–9 **he changed in blissful chere** his face transformed into an expression of joy. A change that completes the story of the Passion by alluding to the Resurrection, but that also proves to reveal new facts about the Passion itself as an act of joy. See 23.5–22 • 10–11 **Wher is . . . agrefe?** where is any part of your pain or of your sorrow now? • 12 **in our lordes mening** according to our Lord's intention • 12 **in his crosse with him** The choice of "in," not "on," here and throughout this passage conveys an understanding of the cross as a mode of being, not just a thing. *Ancrene Wisse,* part 6, describes its anchoritic readers as "night and day . . . up on God's cross," and quotes Gal. 6:14 as referring especially to them—"Christ forbid that I should have any joy in this world except in the cross of Jesus Christ my Lord, through whom the world is nothing to me"—concluding that for anchoresses "all . . . joy is to be hung, painfully and shamefully, with Jesus on his cross" (176–78). This passage extends such language to everyone • 12–13 **in our paines . . . dying** All the earthly suffering of the saved participates in the Passion of Christ • 13–15 **And we, wilfully abiding . . . in heven** See 1 Cor. 15:51–52: "Lo! I tell you a mystery. We shall not all sleep, but we shall all be changed, in a moment, in the twinkling of an eye, at the last trumpet." This theme is developed in the fifteenth revelation, Chapter 64 • 13 **wilfully abiding** willingly awaiting • 15 **Betwene . . . that other** between the pain on the cross and being with him in heaven • 15 **shalle alle be one time** no time at all shall pass • 19 **ne in no nother place** nor in any other place. Christ's "blissful chere" could light up purgatory or hell. Compare 15.1–4 • 19 **that shuld agreve us** that should grieve us • 20–21 **But for he sheweth . . . asketh** but because he shows us an expression of suffering, just as he bore his cross in this life, for this reason we are in discomfort and labor with him, as our nature requires. Life on earth is life lived in response to Christ's "chere of passion" • 22 **eyers** heirs • 23–24 **for this litille paine . . . knowing** This theme is extensively developed in Chapter 51 • 25 **worshippe** reward

[CHAPTER 22] 1 **Arte thou well apaid** are you fully satisfied • 2 **gramercy** "grant merci," great thanks • 2 **blessed mot thow be** may you be blessed

seming /fol. 41r/ that the life might no lenger last, and the shewing of the ende
behoved nedes to be nye—sodenly, I beholding in the same crosse, he changed in
blisseful• chere. The changing of his blisseful° chere changed mine, and I was as glad
and mery as it was possible. Then brought oure lorde merily to my mind: "Wher is   10
now any point of thy paine or of thy agrefe?"° And I was fulle mery.

    I understode that we be now,° in our lordes mening, in his crosse with him in our
paines and in our passion, dying. And we, wilfully abiding in the same crosse, with his
helpe and his grace, into the last point, sodeynly he shalle change his chere to us, and
we shal be with him in heven. Betwene that one and that other shalle alle be one time,   15
and than shall alle be brought into joy. And so ment he in this shewing: "Wher is now
any /fol. 41v/ point of thy paine or of thy agrefe?" And we shalle be full blissed.°

    And here saw I sothfastly° that if he shewde now to us his blisseful• chere, there
is no paine in erth ne in no nother place that shuld agreve° us, but alle thing shulde
be to us joy and blisse. But for he sheweth us chere of passion, as he bare in this life   20
his crosse, therfor we be in disees and traveyle with him, as our kind asketh. And
the cause why that he suffereth is for he wille of his goodnes make us the eyers with
him in his blisse. And for this litille paine that we suffer heer, we shalle have an high,
endlesse knowing in God, which we might never have without that. And the harder
oure paines have ben with him in his crosse, the more shalle our worshippe be with   25
him in his kingdom.

○○○○○○○○○○○○○○○○○○○○○○○○○○○○○○○○○

The Ninth Revelation

AND THE TWENTY-SECOND CHAPTER

/fol. 42r/

Then saide oure good° lorde, asking: "Arte thou well apaid that I suffered for
thee?" I saide: "Ye, good lorde, gramercy. Ye, good lorde, blessed mot thow be."
Then saide Jhesu, our good lord: "If thou arte apaide, I am apaide. It is a joy, a blisse,

---

[vis. 11.17–20] And sodaynlye, me behaldande in the same crosse, he chanchede into
blisfulle chere. The chaunginge of his chere changed mine, and I was alle gladde and
mery as it was possibille. Than brought oure lorde merelye to my minde: "*Whate es* any
pointe of thy paine or of thy grefe?" And I was fulle merye. /Rev. 21.12–26/

[vis. 12.1–3] Than saide oure lorde, askande: "Arte thou wele paide that I sufferde for
the?" "Ya, goode lorde," quod I, "Gramercy goode lorde, blissed mut thowe be!" "If thowe
be payede," quod oure lorde, "I am payede. It es a joye and a blisse

4–5 **if I might . . . wolde suffer more** The liturgy for Good Friday contains the words: "What more should I do for you and have not done?" See Isa. 5:4; also the lyric "Woefully Arrayed," where Christ on the cross laments, "What might I suffer more / Then I have sufferde, man, for thee?" • 6 **lefted uppe** lifted up • 7 **thre hevens** Compare Paul's vision of the third heaven in 2 Cor. 12:2–4: "I know a man in Christ who fourteen years ago was caught up into the third heaven—whether in the body or out of the body I do not know, God knows. . . . and he heard things that cannot be told." As 23.1–4 makes clear, the "thre hevens" emerge from the three words "joy," "blisse," and "liking" spoken by Jesus in lines 3–4, though they are anticipated by 19.8 ("thou art my heven") and 21.13–15 • 7 **I was gretly merveyled** I was greatly astonished • 8 **alle of the blissed manhed** "Of," always a difficult word in Middle English, seems to mean both "for" and "consisting of" • 9 **the furst heven** For the second and third heavens, see 23.1–4 • 10 **in no bodely liknesse** *A Revelation* is self-conscious about any thought that it is representing the persons of the Trinity visually. See also 51.273–76 • 10 **properte** character • 10 **wurking** activity • 10–11 **that is to sey . . . the father is** The first person of the Trinity is here deduced from Christ and his joy: a clear example of the hermeneutic principle announced at the beginning of the revelation, 4.11–12 • 11–12 **that he geveth mede . . . Crist** that he gives reward to his Son, Jesus Christ. See Phil. 2.9–10: "God has highly exalted him and bestowed on him the name which is above every name, that at the name of Jesus every knee should bow, in heaven and on earth and under the earth" • 13 **his father might have . . . better** his Father could have given him no reward that could have pleased him more. Initially, it seems as if the reward is the Father's gift and the gift is the Son's joy at the reward, but by line 17 the gift has become more specific: "we be his mede" • 14 **plesing of the father** the

Father's delight. See 23.2–4 • 16 **about our salvation** concerning our salvation • 16 **not only his by his buying** not only his through his buying. Economic language was and is basic to discussion of the "redemption." Christ has "bought" the human race back from sin and owns them • 17 **curteyse gifte of his father** The underlying image switches to the courtly register, and the language of gift and reward, not purchase. Having been bought by Christ, humankind is given him again by his Father as a reward ("mede") for his service. Humans owe Christ a double allegiance. From Philippians, the underlying biblical source shifts to Hebrews 1–2, where Christ, "when he had made purification for sins, . . . sat down at the right hand of the Majesty on high," all things "in subjection under his feet" (1:3, 2:8) • 17–18 **We be his blisse . . . crowne** Humankind here replaces the crown of thorns that, in the first and eighth revelations, causes the shedding of Jesus' blood. This sentence is quoted in 31.27–28 as though it is here spoken by God, and the parenthetical remark "And this was a singular marveyle" (lines 18–19) implies the same. Revelation and exposition are indistinguishable. See Heb. 2:7: "Thou hast crowned him with glory and honour" • 19–20 **setteth at naught** considers as nothing • 21–23 **And in these wordes . . . done it** An attempt to define the infinitude of Christ's love by the infinitude of his willingness to undergo suffering. In *Liber celestis* the devil speaks to Christ about Bridget: "If it were possibil, thou wald moste gladly suffir in ilke of thy membres [in each one of your limbs] swilke one pain spiritually [a spiritual version of each pain] as thu suffird ones in all the membris [in all your limbs] upon the cross, or thou wald forgo her [before you would give her up]" (1.34). *A Revelation* similarly imagines Christ suffering again, but for each one of the saved, rather than for a specially precious individual • 21–22 **I saw sothly . . . wolde** I saw truly that as often as he could die, so often he would die

an endlesse liking to me that ever I sufferd passion for the. And if I might suffer
more, I wolde suffer more."°   5

In this feling, my understanding was lefted uppe into heven, and ther I saw
thre hevens. Of which sight I was gretly merveyled, and thought: "I see thre hevens,
and alle of the blissed• manhed of Criste. And none is more, none is lesse, none is
higher, none is lower, but even like in blisse." For the furst heven, Crist shewed me
his father, in no bodely liknesse but in his properte and in his wurking: that is to sey,   10
I saw in Crist that the father is. The werking of the father is this: that he geveth mede
to /fol. 42v/ his sonne Jhesu Crist. This gift and this mede is so blisseful• to Jhesu
that his father might have geven him no mede that might have liked him better.°

For the furst heven, that is the plesing of the father, shewed to me as an heven,
and it was fulle blisseful.• For he is fulle° plesede with alle the dedes that Jhesu hath   15
done about our salvation, wherefor we be not only his by his buying, but also by the
curteyse gifte of his father. We be his blisse, we be his mede, we be his wurshipe, we
be his crowne. (And this was a singular marveyle and a full delectable beholding,
that we be his crowne!) This that I sey is so grete blisse to Jhesu that he setteth at
naught all° his traveyle and his harde° passion, and his cruelle and shamfulle deth.   20
And in these wordes—"If I might suffer more, I /fol. 43r/ wolde suffer more"—I saw
sothly° that as often as he might die, as often he wolde, and love shulde never let
him have rest tille he had° done it.

[VIS. 12.3–22] and ane endlesse likinge to me that ever I sufferde passion for the. For if I
might suffer mare, I walde suffer."

In this felinge, mine understandinge was lifted uppe into heven, and thare I sawe
thre hevens. Of the whilke sight I was gretlye merveyelede, and /fol. 105r/ thought: "I sawe
thre hevens, and alle of the blessed manhede of Criste. And nane is mare, nane is lesse,
nane is hiare, nane is lawere, botte evene like in blisse." For the firste heven, shewed
Criste me his fadere, bot in na bodelye liknesse botte in his properte and in his
wyrkinge.‡° The wyrkinge of the fadere it is this: that he giffes mede tille his sone
Jhesu Criste. This gifte and this mede is so blisfulle to Jhesu that his fadere° might haffe
giffene na mede that might hafe likede him bettere.

For the firste heven, that is *blissinge* of the fadere, shewed to me as a heven, and it
was fulle blisfulle. For he is fulle *blissede* with alle the dedes that *he* has done aboute oure
salvation, wharefore we ere nought anely his thurgh byinge, botte also be the curtayse
gifte of his fadere. We ere his blisse, we er his mede, we er his wyrshippe, we er his
crowne. /Rev. 22.18–19/ This that I saye is so grete blisse to Jhesu that he settes atte
nought his travaile and his harde passion, and cruelle and shamefulle dede. And in this
wordes—"if I might suffer mare, I walde suffer mare"—I sawe sothly that *if he might die
als ofte als fore everilke man anes that shalle be safe as he died*° anes for alle, love shulde
never late him hafe reste to he hadde done it. /Rev. 22.24–26/

24 **I behelde . . . might** I contemplated with great energy to find out how often he would wish to die if he were able. Compare the earlier account of Christ's blood like raindrops "that falle so thicke that no man may nomber them with no bodely wit" (7.17–18) • 25 **ferre** far • 26 **cold not** could not • 27 **or shuld** or was about to die • 27 **alle thinketh him but litille** for it all seems to him only little. Recalls the hazelnut image of 5.7–13. "Alle" and "litille" could be taken as abstract nouns: "for infinity seems to him like littleness" • 28 **in regard of** by comparison with • 28–29 **For though . . . seese of profer** A striking way of defining two infinities: that of the love of the human Jesus, fully demonstrated by his dying once; and that of the divine Christ, which even an impossible number of deaths cannot exhaust. See 23.23–28 • 28 **onse** once • 29 **seese of profer** stop offering himself • 30 **make . . . new erthes** See Isa. 65:17: "For behold, I create new heavens and a new earth; and the former things shall not be remembered or come into mind" • 30–31 **it ware . . . regarde** it would be only a little, by comparison • 34 **Than meneth he thus** See 11.42–46 for another example of this mode of exposition by direct speech • 35 **greveth** grieves • 35 **sethen** since • 36 **having no regard to** taking no notice of • 37 **seconde**

beholding See 21.1–3 for the first beholding. The impossibility of counting the times Jesus would die if he could has built toward this new insight • 39 **wurshipfulle** honorable • 39 **done in a time** done at a single time • 42 **He saide not** Like the exposition by direct speech in lines 34–36, this technique of exposition by contrast, quoting what was not said instead of what was, derives from medieval biblical exegesis • 42 **nedfulle** necessary. According to medieval theological opinion, the Passion itself was formally unnecessary. In *La lumere as lais,* the lay voice asks, "Could Christ have delivered humanity any other way than through death and pain?" to receive a resounding "Veire!" "For sure!" in response (5099–107) • 43 **and he might . . . wolde** and if he could suffer more, he would • 44 **ordained** ordered • 45–47 **I saw a fulle blisse . . . was done** Only perfect suffering could have given Christ perfect bliss. The thought recalls Christ's last words on the cross in John 19:30, as retold by *The Privity:* "The sexte worde was whene he saide: 'It es all done,' as who say: 'Fader, the obedience that thou bad me do, I have fulfillede it; and yit, if thare be any more that ye will that I do, I am redy to fulfill it'" ("Meditatione of None," *YW* 1:207)

And I behelde with grete diligence for to wet how often he wolde die if he might. And sothly° the nomber passed my understanding and my wittes so ferre that my reson might not, nor cold not, comprehende it ne take it. And whan he had thus ofte died, or shuld,° yet he wolde set it at nought for love, for alle thinketh him but litille in regard of his love. For though the swete manhode of Crist might suffer but onse, the goodnes of him may never seese of profer: every day he is redy to the same, if it might be. For if he saide he wolde for my love make new hevens and new erthes, it ware but litille in regarde. For this /fol. 43v/ might he do ech day, if that he wolde, without any traveyle. But for to die for my love so often that the nomber passeth creatures reason—this is the highest profer that oure lorde God might make to mannes soule, as to my sight. Than meneth he thus: "How shulde it than be that I shulde not for thy love do all that I might? Which deed greveth me nought, sethen that I wolde for thy love die so often, having no regard to my harde paines."

And heer saw I for the seconde beholding in his blissed• passion: the love that made him to suffer it passith as far alle his paines as heven is above erth. For the paine was a noble, precious, and wurshipfulle dede done in a time by the working of love. And love was without beginning, is, and shall be without ende. For which love he saide /fol. 44r/ fulle swetely this worde: "If I might suffer more, I wolde suffer more." He saide not, "if it were nedfulle to suffer more" but, "if I might suffer more." For though it were not nedfulle, and he might suffer more he wolde.

This dede and this werke about oure salvation was ordained as wele as God might ordaine it, it was don as wurshipfully as Crist might do it. And heerin, I saw a fulle blisse in Crist, for his blisse shuld not have ben fulle if it might ony better have ben done than it was done.

25

30

35

40

45

[VIS. 12.22–24] And *when he hadde done it,* he walde sette it atte nought for luff, for alle thinke° him botte litille in regarde of his love. /Rev. 22.28–37/

[VIS. 11.13–16] *Botte* the love that made him to suffere **alle this**, it passes als fare alle his pains as heven es aboven erthe. For the paines was a ‡ dede done in a time be the wyrkinge of love. *Botte* luffe was withouten beginninge, and es, and evere shalle be with-outen any ende.

[VIS. 12.24–31] *And that shewed he me wele sobarly, sayande this worde:* "If I might suffere mare ‡." He saide nought, "if it ware nedfulle to suffer mare," botte, "if I might suffer mare." For though it be nought nedefulle and he might suffer mare, mare he walde.

This dede and this werke aboute oure salvation was ‡ als wele as he might ordayne it, it was done als wyrshipfullye as Criste might do it. And in this, I sawe a fulle blisse in Criste, botte this blisse shulde nought hafe bene done fulle if it might any bettere hafe bene done than it was done.

[CHAPTER 23] 1 **And in these thre wordes** See 22.3–4. The whole of this chapter is a meditation on these earlier words of Christ • 2–3 **plesance of the father** delight of the Father. See 22.14, which introduces the first of the three heavens, then leaves the topic hanging • 3 **wurshipe of the sonne** honoring of the Son. See 22.17, "we be his wurshipe" • 5 **heer saw . . . thirde beholding** here I saw material concerning the third beholding. See 21.2–4 for the first beholding • 6 **the joy . . . to like it** the joy and the bliss that causes Christ to take pleasure in the Passion. These words paraphrase Christ's words quoted in line 1, where "liking" has been attributed to the Holy Spirit, and lead into an analysis of the joyfulness of the Passion organized around the words "joy," "bliss," and "liking" • 7 **bleding of the hede** See Chapters 4 and 8 • 8 **discolouring of his blessed face** See Chapter 10 • 9 **in seming of scorging** as a representation of the scourging. See Chapter 12 • 9 **depe drying** See Chapters 16–17 • 12 **strengthed** strengthened • 13–14 **For we be his blisse** See 22.17 • 14 **in us he liketh** he is pleased with us • 15–16 **was never cost ne charge to him** never caused him expenditure or difficulty. In Christian thought, God cannot experience these things, only the human Jesus. This is why the "thre hevens" of lines 1–4 are "alle of the blissed manhed of Criste" (22.8). The imagery is financial, as befits discussion of "redemption" (line 18) • 16 **that he did in our manhede** what he did in our humanity • 17 **Ester morow** Easter morning • 17 **dured** lasted • 19 **as it is befor said** See 22.3–4 • 19–20 **Jhesu wille . . . of our salvation** Jesus wants us to pay heed to the joy that is in the blessed Trinity over our salvation • 21 **as it is before said** See lines 12–14 • 21–22 **be like to the joy** be as much like the joy • 22 **here** in this life • 23 **habondance** abundance • 24 **maidens sonne** maiden's son. The human Jesus, not the divine Christ • 24 **werof** in which • 26 **By that other worde** it was also showed by the other word. The syntax is informal

THE TWENTY-THIRD CHAPTER

And in these thre wordes—"It is a joy, a blisse, an° endlesse liking to me"— were shewed thre hevens, as thus: for the joy, I understode the plesance of the father; and for the blisse, the wurshipe of the sonne; and for the endlesse /fol. 44v/ liking, the holy gost. The father is plesed, the sonne is wurshiped, the holy gost liketh.

And heer saw I for the thirde beholding in his blisseful• passion: that is to sey, the joy and the blisse that maketh him to like it. For oure curteyse lorde shewed his passion to me in five manneres: of which the furst is the bleding of the hede, the seconde is° discolouring of his blessed face, the thirde is the plentous bleding of the body in seming of scorging, the fourth is the depe drying—theyse four as it is before saide for the paines of the passion—and the fifte is this that was shewed° for the joy and the blisse of the passion. For it is Goddes wille that we have true liking with him in oure salvation, and therin he wille that we be mightly comforted and strengthed, and thus wille /fol. 45r/ he merily with his grace that oure soule be occupied. For we be his blisse, for in us he liketh without end, and so shall we in him° with his grace. Alle that he hath done for us, and doeth,° and ever shalle, was never cost ne charge to him ne might be, but only that he did° in our manhede, beginning at the swete incarnation, and lasting to the blessed uprising on Ester morow. So long dured the cost and the charge about our redemption in deed, of which dede he enjoyeth° endlesly, as it is befor said. Jhesu wille we take hede° to this blisse that is in the blisseful• trinity of our salvation, and that we desire to have as much gostly liking, with his grace, as it is before said: that is to say, that the liking of our salvation be like to the joy that Crist hath of oure salvation as it may be while we /fol. 45v/ be here.

Alle the trinite wrought in the passion of Crist, ministring habondance of vertuse and plente of grace to us by him. But only the maidens sonne suffered, werof alle the blessed trinite endelessly° enjoyeth. And this was shewed in this worde: "Arte thou welle apaide?" By that other worde that° Crist seid—"If thou arte apaid, I am

5

10

15

20

25

[VIS. 12.31–38] And in this thre wordes—"It is a joye, a blisse, and ane endeles likinge to me"—ware shewed **to me** thre hevens, as thus: for the joye, I understode the plesance of the fadere; for the blisse, the wirshippe of the sone; for the endeles likinge, the haly gaste. The fadere is plesed, the sone is worshipped, the haly gaste likes. /Rev. 23.5–19/ Jhesu wille that we take heede to this blisse that is in the blissedfulle trinite of oure salva-tion, and that we *like als mekille, /fol. 105v/* with his grace, /Rev. 23.21–22/ whiles we er here. /Rev. 23.23–25/ And this was shewed **me** in this worde: "Erte thow wele payed?" Be the tothere worde that Criste saide—"if thowe be payed, I am

27–28 **I aske . . . apaye the** I ask nothing else for my labor except that I might satisfy you • 29 **properte** quality • 29 **gladde gever** glad giver. See 2 Cor. 9:7: "God loves a cheerful giver" • 29–34 **A glade gever . . . loveth** A type of exemplum known as a "similitude," in which a truth is explored by way of a close analogue, described in highly abstract form, concerning how someone "would" behave in a given situation. The resulting insight into the subject, here "the properte of a gladde gever," is then applied back to God • 30 **taketh but litille hede at** takes small notice of • 32 **setteth at nought** considers as nothing • 35 **Think . . . "Ever"** also think intelligently about the magnitude of this word: "Ever." See 22.4: "that ever I sufferd passion for the," the only clause in Christ's speech not to have been expounded to this point, though the focus in the following passage is on the single word "ever" itself. The injunction to "think" briefly makes readers colleagues in the exposition of the revelation • 35–36 **in that was shewed . . . salvation** in that word was revealed an elevated knowledge of the love that he has in our salvation. This "high knowing" is Christ's. When understood as an intensifier, "ever" reveals Christ's awareness of the extent of his love for humankind • 37 **in dede** in fact. Here "ever" means "at a particular time." Christ has already suffered and will do so no more • 38–40 **That other . . . endlesse blisse** Here "ever" means "endlessly" or "with effects that are endless"

[CHAPTER 24] 1 **loked** looked • 1 **into his side** The wound in Christ's side made by a spear in John 19:34. According to the fifteenth-century *Treatise of Ghostly Battle,* building on this verse, "his side was openede and his herte clovene a-two [sliced in two] with a sharpe spere and . . . he shadde [shed] oute both bloode and water . . . yef he had hade [if he had had] more bloode, more he wolde have yevene for mannes soule to the fadere of hevene" (*YW* 2:426) • 2–3 **with his swete loking . . .**

within with his sweet look he directed the understanding of his creature through the same wound within, into his side. Julian's bodily sights all involve transformations of Christ's head. Here, too, only his eyes move, and the vision of the wound in the side takes place in Julian's "understanding," not as a "bodily sight" • 3–4 **ther he shewed . . . saved** there [within his body] he showed a beautiful, pleasing place, wide enough for all humankind that is to be saved. An important focus of Passion meditation, this place inside Christ is often imagined as a refuge for the meditator and associated with the hiding place in the rocks of Song of Sol. 2:14. According to *The Pryckinge,* "al . . . swetnesse is plentiously hid in Jhesu," in the wound opened in his side: "Lo, now the gate of paradise is opened and thorou vertu of his blod is put awey the brennande pliaunt swerd [the burning supple sword, held by the angel who guards the gates to Eden]. . . . Lo, for mikelnesse of love he opened his holy side for to yeve the his herte" (11–12). In *A Revelation,* the place is big enough, not just for one person, but for everyone. In the sixteenth revelation the image is reversed, and Christ sits in the kingdom of the soul. See Chapter 67 • 4 **inow** enough • 5–6 **blode and . . . water** See John 19:34 • 7 **hart** heart • 7 **even cloven on two** split right in two. The image of the Sacred Heart, from which the healing liquids of blood and water flow • 8 **blessed godhede** The godhead is also found inside Christ's Sacred Heart in *The Pryckinge,* as the goal of the meditative journey: "Love thou that fleshe not only for itself [itself] but for that [what] is hid therinne. Wat is that? A precious soule. And wat is in the soule? The fulnesse of the godhede" (6) • 8 **as farforth as he wolde** to the extent that he wished to • 9 **strengthing . . . saide** strengthening the poor soul to understand what can be put into words. Christ's divinity is ineffable, and only its effect ("the endlesse love"), not its nature, can be stated

apaide"°—as if he had saide: "It is joy and liking enough to me, and I aske not elles of the for° my travayle but that I might apaye the."

And in this, he brought to my mind the properte of a gladde gever. A glade gever° taketh but litille hede at the thing that he giveth, but alle his desir and alle his intent is to plese him and solace him to whome he giveth it. And if the receiver take the gift gladly and thankefully, than the curtesse gever setteth at nought alle his cost and alle his traveyle, for joy and delight that he hath for he hath plesed and solaced /fol. 46r/ him that he loveth. Plentuously and fully was this shewed.

Think also° wisely of the gretnesse of this worde: "Ever." For in that was shewed° an high knowing of love that he hath in our salvation, with manifolde joyes that folowen of the passion of Crist. One is that he joyeth that he hath done it in dede, and he shalle no more suffer. That other is that he hath therwith bought us from endlesse paines of helle. Another is that he brought us up into heven and made us for to be his crowne and his endlesse blisse.

30

35

40

oooooooooooooooooooooooooooooooo

The Tenth Revelation

AND THE TWENTY-FOURTH CHAPTER

With a glad chere° oure good lorde loked into his side and behelde, enjoyenge.° And with his swete loking he led forth the understanding of his creature by the same wound into his sid, within. And ther he shewed a fair, delectable° place, and large inow for alle mankinde that shalle be saved to rest° in pees and in love. And therwith he /fol. 46v/ brought to minde his dereworthy blode and his precious water which he let poure all out° for love. And with the swete beholding he shewed his blissful• hart even° cloven on two. And with this swete enjoyeng° he shewed to my understanding, in part, the blessed° godhede, as farforth as he wolde that time, strengthing the pour soule for to understande as it may be saide: that is to mene, the endlesse love that was without beginning, and is, and shal be ever.

5

10

[VIS. 12.38–43] paid"—**he shewed me the understandinge,** as if he had saide: "It is joye and likinge enough to me, and I aske nought els ‡ for my travaile botte that I might paye the." /Rev. 23.29–34/ Plentyouslye and fully was this shewed **to me.** Thinke also wiselye of the gretnesse of this worde: *"That ever I suffred passion for the."* For in *that worde was* a hye knawinge of luffe **and of likinge** that he hadde in oure salvation. /Rev. 23.36–40/

[VIS. 13.1] *Fulle merelye and gladlye* oure lorde loked into his side and behelde, /Rev. 24.1–10/

11 **loved the** loved you • 11–12 **as if he had saide** For this technique of commentary by analytic paraphrase, see 11.42 • 17 **or that** before • 17 **that I wolde die for the** that I wanted to die for you • 18 **sufferd wilfully that I may** willingly suffered what I can. See 22.4–5 • 19–21 **How shulde . . . grante it the?** This sudden introduction of the topic of prayer anticipates the fourteenth revelation, 41.8–10 • 21 **my liking is thine holinesse** what I want is your holiness • 23 **mery** merry. See 23.13

[CHAPTER 25] 1 **loked downe** As in Chapter 24, this eye movement is the only moment of "bodily sight" in the revelation • 1–2 **the right side . . . our lady stode** In late medieval painting and sculpture Mary is usually depicted on the right side of the cross, from Christ's perspective, while the apostle John stands on the left. The portable crucifix in which Julian is seeing the revelation would not include either figure • 3 **Wilt thou see her?** do you want to see her? • 3–4 **as if he had said** it was as if he had said. The first of four interpretations of Jesus' words in the chapter • 4 **wot** know • 4 **se** see • 5–6 **And most she is desired . . . creatures** and all my blessed creatures desire to see her most of all. See 4.34–35: "For above her is nothing that is made but the blessed manhood of Christ" • 7 **maiden . . . mother . . . layde** According to medieval Christianity, Mary's three roles in the scheme of salvation • 8–9 **as by the mening . . . saide** according to this interpretation of his sweet word, as if he said. The paraphrase of "Wilt thou see her?" that follows, which emphasizes the mutual love between Jesus and Mary, shows how the saying can be made to reveal the "enjoyeng" of Mary • 11–14 **this swete word . . . that it do the** Now Mary becomes the representative of all humankind, and Christ's love of her reveals his love of all

And with this, oure good lorde saide full blissefully,° "Lo, how I loved° the," as if he had saide: "My darling, behold and see thy lorde, thy God, that is thy maker and thy endlesse joy. See thin owne brother, thy saviour. My childe, behold and see what liking and blisse I have in thy salvation, and for my love enjoye with me."

And also, to more understanding: this blessed worde was saide, /fol. 47r/ "Lo how I loved° thee," as if he had saide: "Behold and see that I loved thee so much, or that I died for thee, that I wolde die for the. And now I have died for the, and sufferd wilfully° that I may. And now is all my bitter paine and alle my harde traveyle turned to endlesse° joy and blisse to me and to the. How shulde it now be that thou shuldest anything pray me that liketh° me, but if I shulde fulle gladly grante it the? For my liking is thine holinesse and thy endlesse joy and blisse with me."

This is the understanding, simply as I can sey, of this blessed worde: "Lo how I loved the." This shewed oure good lorde to make us glade and mery.

15

20

∞∞∞∞∞∞∞∞∞∞∞∞∞∞∞∞∞∞∞∞

The Eleventh Revelation
THE TWENTY-FIFTH CHAPTER

And with this same chere° of mirth and joy, our good lord loked downe on the /fol. 47v/ right side, and brought to my minde where our lady stode in the time of his passion, and said: "Wilt thou see her?" And in this swete word, as if he had said: "I wot welle that thou wilt se my blessed mother, for after myselfe she is the highest joy that I might shewe the, and most liking and worshipe to me. And most she is desired to be seen of alle my blessed creatures." And for the marvelous, high, and singular love that he hath to this swete maiden, his blessed mother, our layde Saint Mary, he shewed° her highly enjoyeng,° as by the mening of this swete word, as if he saide: "Wilte thou se how that I love her, that thou might joy with me in the love that I have in her and she in me?"

And also, to more understanding: this swete word oure good lorde speketh in love to all mankind that shall be saved, as it were alle to one person, /fol. 48r/ as if he

5

10

[VIS. 13.1–9] and saide *this worde*—"Lo, how I loved the"—as if he° hadde saide: **"My childe, if thow kan nought loke in my godhede, see here howe I lette open my side, and my herte be clovene in twa, and lette oute blude and watere alle that was tharein. And this likes me, and so wille I that it do the."** /Rev. 24.12–23/ This shewed oure lorde **me** to make us gladde and mery.

And with the same *chere and mirthe* he loked downe on the right side, and brought to my minde whare oure ladye stode in the time of his passion, and saide: "Wille thowe see hir?" /Rev. 25.3–19/

15–16 lerned . . . bodely presens taught to desire to see her physical presence. The revelations of two of Julian's most famous predecessors, Bridget of Sweden and Elizabeth of Hungary, feature many visions of and conversations with Mary. Julian's more frugal revelation does not teach her to aspire to such experiences • **16–17 truth . . . wisdom . . . reverently drede** Terminology already used in Mary's earlier appearances in 4.26–29 and 7.1–8 • **19 gramercy** "grant merci," great thanks • **20 wend** expected • **21 Jhesu in that worde . . . her** in the statement "Do you want to see her?" Jesus showed me a spiritual sight of her. The words themselves generate the sight. Apart from the demonic temptations of Chapters 67 and 69, there are no further "bodily sights" in the revelation • **22 seen her before** See 4.24–26 • **22–23 high . . .**

above all creatures Cycles of paintings and sculptures of the life of Mary end with her Assumption and coronation, the scenes evoked here • **24 tho that like . . . in her** those who delight in him must delight in her. "Like" is a more intimate word in this context than "love," and alludes punningly back to "likenes" (line 20) • **27 wille make** wants to make • **29–30 in this worde . . . of her** in this word that Jesus said—"Do you want to see her?"— it seemed to me there lay the most delightful remark he could have given me about her • **31 in specialle** individually. The phrase also occurs in 35.9, 37.6, 42.43, 73.10 • **32 thre times** See Chapters 4, 18, 25. These appearances correspond to the three epithets "maiden," "mother," and "layde" used of her in line 7

saide: "Wilt thou se in her how thou art loved? For thy love I have made her so high, so noble, so wurthy. And this liketh me, and so wille I that it do the." For after himselfe she is the most blissful• sight. But hereof am I not lerned to long to see her bodely presens while I am here, but the vertuse of her blissed• soule—her truth, her wisdom, her cherite—wherby I may leern° to know myself, and reverently drede my God.

And whan oure good lorde had shewed this, and saide this worde—"Wilte thou see her?"—I answered and saide: "Ye good lorde, gramercy.° Ye good lorde, if it be thy wille." Oftentimes I preyde this, and I wend to have seen her in bodely likenes.° But I saw her not so. And Jhesu in that worde shewed me a gostly sight of her. Right as I had seen her before litille and /fol. 48v/ simple, right so he shewed her than high and noble and glorious and plesing to him above all creatures. And so he wille that it be knowen that all tho that like in him shuld like in her, and in the liking that he hath in hir and she in him.°

And to mor understanding, he shewed this exsample: as if a man love a creature singularly above alle creatures, he wille make alle other creatures to love and to like that creature that he loveth so mekille.•

And in this worde that Jesu saide—"Wilte thou see her?"—methought it was the most liken worde that he might have geve me of her,° with the gostely shewing that he gave me of her. For oure lorde shewed me nothing in specialle but oure lady Sent Mary. And her he shewed thre times: the furst was as she conceived; the secunde was° as she was in her sorowes under the crosse; and the thurde was as she is now, /fol. 49r/ in likinge, worshipe, and joy.

15

20

25

30

[VIS. 13.9–21] And I answerde and saide: "Ya goode lorde, gramercy, ‡ if it be thy wille." Ofte times I prayed it, and wened to haffe sene here in bodely likenes. Botte I sawe hir nought so. And Jhesu in that worde shewed me a gastelye sight of hire. Right as I hadde before sene hire litille and simpille, right so he shewed here than hye and nobille and gloriouse and plesante to him aboven alle creatures. And so he wille that it be knawen that alle tha that likes in him shulde like in hire, and in the likinge that he hase in hire and sho in him. /Rev. 25.26–28/

And in that worde that Jhesu saide—"Wille thowe see hire?"—methought I hadde the maste likinge that he might hafe giffen me, with the gastelye shewinge that he gafe me of hire. For oure lorde shewed me nothinge in specialle botte oure lady Sainte Marye. And here he shewed **me in** thre times: the firste was as she consayved; the seconde was as sho were in hire sorowes undere the crosse; and the thrid as sho is nowe, in likinge, wirshippe, /fol. 106r/ and joye.

[CHAPTER 26] 1 **more glorified** The glorification of Mary in Chapter 25 now gives way to that of Jesus, as the contemplation of Mary is seen as no more than a stage on the way to the higher contemplation of God. The Christ who announces himself in the lines that follow is once again the Christ of Phil. 2:9–11, the passage from which the devotion to the Holy Name of Jesus derives. See 22.11–12 • 2–3 **oure soule . . . joye** See 5.24–26 • 3–4 **homely . . . life** intimate and courtly and full of bliss and true life • 4 **I it am** I am the one. Despite Chapter 25's attention to Mary "in specialle" (line 31), Jesus' words of wooing leave little room for devotion to anyone other than himself. The aggressively masculine Jesus of *Ancrene Wisse,* part 7, is likely a model: "Am I not the fairest one? Am I not the richest king? Am I not the highest born?" (194). However, "I it am" (not "I am he") goes out of its way not to emphasize this Jesus' maleness • 6 **that thou meneste** to whom your intention is directed • 7 **precheth the** preaches to you • 8 **that shewde me ere** who showed myself before • 8 **number . . . wittes** the number of the repetitions overwhelmed my wits. Compare 22.25. Twelve repetitions of "I it am" are quoted • 9 **they were in the highest** they were the most exalted utterances • 10 **I can not telle what** I do not know how to tell what. The words become ineffable to Julian as their invocations of Christ's exaltation multiply, each phrase pointing inexorably back to him • 11 **hart** heart • 12 **be not declared here** are not expounded here. They are, however, given partial explication later, in Chapters 31 and 59 • 12 **geveth** gives • 13 **in our lordes mening** according to our Lord's intention

[CHAPTER 27] 1–2 **longing . . . to him before** the longing I had for him before the time of the revelation. "Wilfil longing" is the third of the "thre woundes" for which Julian asks in 2.34–37. The thirteenth revelation opens by returning Julian to her somber starting point • 2 **nothing letted me but sinne** nothing prevented me except sin. Perhaps to be taken as a digest of the meaning of the first twelve revelations • 2–3 **so I behelde . . . alle** this I saw to be generally true of us all • 3–4 **have be clene . . . as he made us** have been as pure and as like our Lord as he made us

The Twelfth Revelation
AND THE TWENTY-SIXTH CHAPTER

And after this, oure lorde shewed° him more glorified as to my sight than I saw him before. Wherin I was lerned that oure soule shalle never have reste tille it come into him, knowing that he is fullhede° of joye: homely and curteys and blisseful• and very life. Often times oure lorde Jhesu° saide: "I it am, I it am. I it am that is highest. I it am that thou lovest. I it am that thou likest. I it am that thou servest. I it am that thou longest. I it am that thou desirest. I it am that thou meneste. I it am that is alle. I it am that holy church precheth the and techeth thee. I it am that shewde me ere° to the." The number of the words passeth my wittes and my understanding and alle my mightes, for they were in the highest, as to my sight. For therin /fol. 49v/ is comprehended I can not telle what. But the joy that I saw in the shewing of them passeth alle that hart can think or soule may desire. And therfore these wordes be not declared here. But every man, after the grace that God geveth him in understanding and loving, receive them in our lordes mening.

The Thirteenth Revelation
THE TWENTY-SEVENTH CHAPTER

And after this, oure lorde brought to my minde the longing that I had to him before. And I saw that nothing° letted me° but sinne. And so I behelde generally in us alle, and methought: "If sinne had not be, we shulde alle have be

---

[*vis.* 13.22–34] And efter this, oure lorde shewed him **to me** mare glorified as to my sight than I sawe him before. And in this was I lerede that **ilke saule contemplatife to whilke es giffen to luke and seke God shalle se hire and passe unto God by contemplation ‡.**

And efter this techinge, hamelye, curtayse, and blisfulle and verray life, ofte times oure lorde Jhesu saide **to me:** "‡ I it am that is hiaste. I it am that thowe luffes. I it am that thowe likes. I it am that thowe serves. I it am that thowe langes. I it am that thowe desires. I it am that thowe menes. I it am that is alle. I it am that haly kyrke preches the and teches the. I it am that shewed me are to the." /Rev. 26.8–12/ *Thies wordes I declare nought,* botte for ilke man, efter the grace that God giffes him in understandinge and lovinge, resayfe tham in oure lordes meninge.

And efter, oure lorde brought unto my minde the langinge that I hadde to him before. And I sawe that nathinge letted me bot sin. And so I behelde generallye in us alle, and methought: "If sin hadde nought bene, we shulde alle hafe bene

5–6 why . . . letted why, by the great, foreseeing wisdom of God, the beginning of sin was not prevented. In Pierre D'Abernon's translation of Honorius's *Elucidarium, La lumere as lais,* the lay voice also asks: "Why would God create humankind when he knew it would sin?" and "Why did God allow humankind to be tempted?" (*pur quei suffri Deu tempter humme?* [70]). Langland's *Piers Plowman* B has "heighe men" asking the latter question with "crabbede wordes: / 'Why wolde oure saveour suffre swich a worm in his blisse, / That biwiled the woman and the wye [man] after?'" (10.106–8) • **6 alle shulde have be wele** all would have been well or must have been well. The phrase is picked up by Christ in line 10 and again by Julian in 29.2–3 • **7–8 This stering . . . discretion** this thought was much to be repudiated, and nevertheless I mourned and sorrowed over it without reason or moderation • **9 enformed . . . me neded** gave me information about everything necessary to me. Regardless of how fully this question was "to be forsaken" • **10 behovely** necessary or fitting, also good or opportune. The sole adjectival use in *A Revelation,* though as an impersonal verb, in the forms "behoveth" and "behoved," the word is common. See 11.14–15, where the word means "was necessary," although the word "nedes" is brought in to make this clear; elsewhere the word can mark a stage in an argument, announce a custom, express satisfaction at a good fit with something. The statement "Sinne is behovely" may echo words from the Easter liturgy, where the Fall is invoked in words of paradoxical joy: "O happy fault, O necessary sin of Adam!" (*O felix culpa, O necessarium peccatum Ade*). If so, "behovely" might be considered a translation of both *felix* and *necessarium* • **10 alle shalle be wele** everything is going to be well, or everything must be well. "Shall" implies necessity at least as strongly as futurity, as Christ's distinction between "shalle" and "wille" in 31.1–9 shows. "Alle," used more than six hundred times in *A Revelation,* already has resonances derived from the visions of the hazelnut ("all that is made") and God in a point ("God doth alle thing") in 5.10, 11.4–5, the second of which asks, "What is sinne?" "Alle shalle be wele" dominates the many arguments and insights of the thirteenth revelation and recurs at two structurally key moments later: at the end of the long digression after the fourteenth revelation and the end of the revelations as a whole. See 63.39–40, 68.60; also 85.10–13 • **11 naked worde "sinne"** simple word "sin" • **12 shamful despite and the utter noughting** shameful contempt and the absolute humiliation. Refers not only to Christ's sufferings during his lifetime but to the "noughting" of the Incarnation. See 5.19–27 for the various meanings of "nought" • **13–14 alle the paines . . . bodely** all the physical and spiritual pains and sufferings of all his creatures. "Sinne" in this formulation includes all creaturely suffering • **14 in party noughted** partly negated • **14 shal be** ought to be • **16 of oure dedly flesh** of our mortal flesh • **16 inwarde affections** inner impulses • **17 very good** truly good • **19–20 and with . . . overpassing** and for all this pain, I understood Christ's Passion to be the greatest and transcendent pain. See 20.3–5 • **20 touch** moment • **20 redely** easily • **21 aferde** afraid • **22–23 I believe . . . cause of** I believe it has no kind of actuality, nor any share of existence, nor could it be apprehended were it not for the pain it causes. This theme has already been introduced in 11.3–13. Although it sounds daring, this is a theological commonplace: far from being an active principle, sin is merely "a lackinge of love and of light . . . a wantinge of God [some manuscripts read 'good']," as Hilton puts it in *The Scale* 1.53

clene and like to oure lorde as he made us." And thus in my foly before this time,
often I wondred why, by the grete forseeing° wisdom of God, the beginning of sinne   5
was not letted. For then thought me that alle /fol. 50r/ shulde have be wele.

   This stering was mekille˙ to be forsaken, and neverthelesse morning and
sorow I made therfore withoute reson and discretion. But Jhesu, that in this vision
enformed me of alle that me neded, answered by this worde and saide: "Sinne is
behovely, but alle shalle be wele, and alle shalle be wele, and alle maner of thinge   10
shalle be wel." In this naked worde "sinne," oure lorde broughte to my minde
generally alle that is not good, and the shamful despite and the utter noughting°
that he bare for us in this life, and his dying, and alle the paines and passions of alle
his creatures,° gostly and bodely. For we be alle in party noughted,° and we shal be
noughted,° folowing our master Jhesu, tille we be fulle purged: that is to sey, till we   15
be fully noughted° of oure dedely flesh, and of alle oure inwarde affections which
/fol. 50v/ be not very good.

   And the beholding of this, with alle the paines that ever were or ever shalle
be—and with alle this,° I understode the passion of Criste for the most paine and
overpassing—and alle this was shewde in a touch, and redely passed over into   20
comfort. For oure good lorde wolde not that the soule were aferde of this ugly
sighte. But I saw not sinne. For I beleve it hath° no maner of substance, ne no part of

---

[VIS. 13.34–55] clene and like to oure lorde as he made us." And thus in my folye before
this time, ofte I wondrede why, be the grete forseande wisdome of God, ‡ sin was nought
letted. For than thought me that alle shulde hafe bene wele.

   This stirringe was mekille to forsayke, and ‡ mourninge and sorowe I made therfore
withouten resone and discretion **of fulle grete pride.** *Neverthelesse Jhesu in this vision*
enfourmede me of alle that me neded. **I saye nought that me nedes na mare techinge.
For oure lorde, with the shewinge of this, hase lefte me to haly kyrke; and I am hungery
and thirstye and nedy and sinfulle and freele, and wilfully submittes me to the techinge
of haly kyrke, with alle mine evencristen, into the ende of my life.**

   He answerde be this worde and saide: "Sinne is behovelye." /Rev. 27.10–11/ In this ‡
worde "sinne," our lorde brought to my minde generallye alle that is nought goode: the
shamefulle dispite and the utter noghtinge that he bare for us in this life and in his
dyinge, and alle the paines and passions of alle his creatures, gastelye and bodelye. For
we ere alle in party noghted, and we shulde be noghted, folowande oure maister Jhesu,
to we be fulle purgede: that is to say, to we be fully /fol. 106v/ noghted of oure awne
dedely fleshe, and of alle oure inwarde affections° whilke ere nought goode.

   And the behaldinge of this, with alle the paines that ever ware or ever shalle be,
/Rev. 27.19–20/ alle° this was shewed **me** in a toch and redely passed overe into comforth.
For oure goode lorde God walde noght that the saule ware afferde of this uglye sight.
Botte I sawe noght sinne. Fore I lefe it has na manere of substance, na partye of

24 **For it purgeth** Sin is defined only in relation to its positive effects • 26 **alle this** all the effects of sin • 26 **and so is his blessed wille** and this (that his Passion comfort us) is his blessed will • 27 **to alle that shalle be saved** See 9.16–17 for the first use of this phrase, repeatedly used later in *A Revelation* to qualify what would otherwise be its explicit universalism • 28 **soth** true • 30 **ne to none** nor to anyone • 31 **sithen** since • 33 **an high, mervelous previte** a lofty and wonderful secret. The first of several "prevites" discussed in the thirteenth revelation. See Chapters 30, 32, 34 • 34 **openly . . . to us in heven** According to *The Pricke,* the first spiritual dowry of the blessed "Es [is] wisdom: for thay salle knaw and se / Alle that was, and es, and yit salle be [will be in the future] / . . . Thay salle knaw alle thing and wit, / That God has done and salle do yit / . . . Thare salle be shewed than tille tham, apertly [openly], / Sere privetese [many secrets] of God allemighty . . . Thay salle than se thare, openly, / Of alle thinges the skille and the cause why [the reason and the cause why]" (8189–244). However, knowledge of God's "prevites" does not in this poem explicitly extend to knowledge of the reason why God allowed sin • 35 **se** see

[CHAPTER 28] 1 **compassion on us . . . sinne** compassion for us by reason of sin. A reason that is still hidden at this stage in *A Revelation* and to some extent remains so. See 27.34–35 • 1–2 **right as . . . like** just as . . . in the same way • 2 **before** See Chapters 16–19 • 3 **in party** in part • 3 **fulfilled** filled • 3 **compassion . . . evencristen** A main theme in this and the next chapter • 4–6 **Holy church . . . winde** A prophecy that may refer to the church's usual state of struggle but could also predict a coming ordeal: perhaps the ordeal precipitated by the coming of the Antichrist that is imagined at the end of *Piers Plowman* and that was ever more widely expected in the late fourteenth century, as the papal schism continued. The image of the shaken cloth alludes to 17.32–33, where it refers to Christ's body on the cross • 8 **herof** out of this • 8–9 **Ye, so far-forth I saw** yes, I saw even as much as this. Announces a claim that is evidently to be taken as unusual

being, ne it might not be knowen but by the paine that it is cause of.° And this
paine, it is somthing,° as to my sighte, for a time. For it purgeth and maketh us to
know oureselfe and aske mercy. For the passion of oure lorde is comfort to us agenst 25
alle this, and so is his blessed wille. And for the tender love that oure good lorde
/fol. 51r/ hath to alle that shalle be saved, he comforteth redely and swetly, mening
thus: "It is soth° that sinne is cause of alle this paine, but alle shalle be wele, and alle
maner of thing shalle be wele." Theyse wordes were shewde fulle tenderly, shewing
no maner of blame to me, ne to none that shalle be safe. Than were it a gret° 30
unkindnesse of me to blame or wonder on God for my sinne,° sithen he blameth
not me for sinne.

And in theyse same wordes, I saw an high, mervelous previte hid in God, which
privite he shalle openly make knowen° to us in heven. In which knowing we shalle
verely se the cause why he sufferde sinne to come, in which sight we shalle endlessely 35
have joye.

THE TWENTY-EIGHTH CHAPTER

/fol. 51v/

Thus I saw how Crist hath compassion on us for the cause of sinne. And right as
I was before in the passion of Crist fulfilled with paine and compassion, like in
this I was in party fulfilled with compassion of alle my evencristen. For fulle wele he
loveth pepille that shalle be saved: that is to seye, Goddes servantes. Holy church
shalle be shaked in sorow and anguish and tribulation in this worlde as men shaketh 5
a cloth in the winde.

And as to this oure lorde answered, shewing on this maner: "A, a gret thing
shalle I make herof in heven of endlesse wurshippe and of everlasting joye." Ye, so

---

[VIS. 13.55–67] beinge, na it might nought be knawen bot be the paines that it is cause
of. And this paine, it is sumthinge, as to my sight, for a time. For it purges us and makes
us to knawe oureselfe and aske mercy. For the passion of oure lorde is comforth to us
againes alle this, and so is his blissed wille. And for the tender love that our goode lorde
hath° to alle that shalle be safe, he comfortes redely and swetlye **be his wordes**, *and says:*
"‡ Botte alle shalle be wele, and alle maner of thinge shalle be wele." Thies wordes ware
shewed wele tenderlye, shewande na manere° of blame to me, na to nane that shalle be
safe. Than were it a grete unkindenesse of me to blame or wonder of God for my sinnes,
sen he blames not me for sinne. /Rev. 27.33–36/

Thus I sawe howe Criste has compassion of us for the cause of sinne. And right as I
was before with the passion of Criste fulfilled with paine and compassion, like in this I
was in party filled with compassion° of alle min evencristene. /Rev. 28.3–17/

9 **oure lord . . . sarvantes** our Lord rejoices in the tribulations of his servants. This is indeed a step beyond that usually taken in Middle English writing on tribulation and temptation, such as *The Chastising* and *The Remedy*, both of which focus on the utility of tribulation for the soul, not its effect on God • 10–15 **to ech person . . . everlasting** Common teaching about suffering and persecution, this is the central theme of *The Chastising of God's Children,* explaining that work's title. The language used here, with its emphasis on the persecution of the righteous, is unusually forceful by the standards of the fourteenth century outside the writings of Lollards and other reformists, as though in reaction against the language of enjoyment and comfort in the surrounding passages • 10 **to his blisse for to bring** in order to bring them to his joy • 11 **lacked** abused or scorned • 12 **raped** abused. Literally "snatched," the word can already refer to sexual assault in Middle English • 12–13 **for to let . . . take** in order to prevent the damage they would otherwise receive • 14 **heynen them** raise them up • 15 **For he seyth** Perhaps meant as a restatement of lines 4–6 and 7–8 • 15 **tobreke you from** tear you away from • 16 **vaine affections** useless desires • 16 **gader** gather • 17 **by oning to me** through union with me • 18 **ech kinde compassion . . . evencristen** every natural feeling of compassion that someone has for his fellow Christians • 19 **That ech maner noughting** that same kind of negation. See 20.7–8 • 19–20 **it was shewde . . . compassion** it was shown again here in this revelation of compassion. Here, "compassion" refers back to Christ's words in 27.9–11, which line 1 of this chapter defines as "how Christ hath compassion." The "noughting" of Christ and his people is implied by the word "sinne" •

20 **wherin . . . understondinges** in which revelation of compassion were contained two lessons • 21 **the blisse . . . brought to** Alluded to in the phrase "alle shalle be wele" (27.10) • 22 **he wille that we wit** he wants us to know • 23 **turned us to wurship** turned for us into honor • 24 **right nought** not at all • 25 **grounde** foundation • 25–26 **And that we see his paines . . . full thought** See 27.19–20 • 27 **gruging** complaining • 27 **feling** feeling • 28–30 **of his gret curtesy . . . unlothfulle** Christ's ability to perceive humankind as blameless is a result of "curtesy," an aristocratic virtue (Latin *curialitas*) that combines politeness and generosity and does not insist on differences of rank. The word is first important in 7.36–44. God's special way of seeing humankind is central to Chapters 45 and 51 • 28–29 **doth away alle oure blame** See 27.30–32 • 29 **ruth and pitte** compassion and pity • 29–30 **innocens and unlothfulle** innocent and not loathsome

[CHAPTER 29] 1 **But in this I stode** but at this point I stood still or dug my feet in • 1 **beholding . . . mourningly** contemplating widely, anxiously, and mournfully • 2 **in my mening** in my intention. Julian does not speak aloud • 3 **the gret harme . . . creatures** the great damage that has come to your creation because of sin. *La lumere* devotes several questions and answers to this damage, under headings like "Whether humankind can know how things would have been if it had never sinned" (79–84) • 4 **desyered** desired • 4 **as I durste** so far as I dared • 4 **more open declaring** more explicit exposition • 4–5 **wherwith . . . this** through which I could feel easier about this farforth I saw: oure lord enjoyeth of the tribulations of his sarvantes, with pite and compassion. And to ech person that he loveth, to his blisse for to bring, he leyth /fol. 52r/ on them° som thing that is no lacke in his sight, wherby they be lacked° and dispised in this worlde, scorned and raped° and cast out. And this he doth for to let the harm that they shulde take of the pompe and of the pride and the vaineglorye of this wreched life, and make ther wey redy to come to heven, and heynen them° in blisse without ende everlasting. For he seyth: "I shal alle tobreke you from youre vaine affections and youre viscious pride. And after that I shalle togeder gader° you, and make you meke and milde, clene and holy, by oning to me." And than saw I that ech kinde compassion that man hath on his evencristen with charite, it is Crist in him.

10

15

That ech maner noughting that he shewde in his passion, it was shewde agene here in this compassion, /fol. 52v/ wherin were two maner of understondinges in oure lordes mening. That one was the blisse that we be brought to, wherin he wille that we enjoye. That other is for comfort in oure paine. For he wille that we wit that it alle shalle be turned us to wurship° and to profite by the vertu of his passion. And that we witte that we suffer° right nought alone, but with him, and see him oure grounde. And that we see his paines and his noughting° passe so ferre alle that we may suffer that it may not be full thought. And the well beholding of this wille save us° from gruging and despair in the feling of our paines. And if we see sothly° that oure sinne deserve it, yet his love° excuseth us. And of his gret curtesy he doth away alle /fol. 53r/ oure blame, and beholdeth us with ruth and pitte as children, innocens and unlothfulle.

20

25

30

THE TWENTY-NINTH CHAPTER

But in this I stode, beholding generally, swemly, and mourningly, seying thus to oure lorde in my mening with fulle gret drede: "A, good lorde, how might alle be wele for the gret harme that is come by sinne to thy creatures?" And here I desyered as I durste° to have some more open declaring wherwith° I might be esed

[VIS. 13.67–69] And than sawe I that ilke kinde compassione that man hase of his evencristene with charite, that it is Criste in him. /Rev. 28.19–30/

[VIS. 14.1–5] Bot in this I stode,° behaldande generallye, *drerelye,* and mournande, sayande thus to oure lorde in my meninge with fulle grete drede: "A, goode lorde, howe might alle be wele for the grete harme that is comon by sinne to thy creatures?" And I desired as I durste to hafe sum mare open declaringe wharewith I might be hesed

6 **Adams sinne was the most harme** Christ puts a face to Julian's word "harme" in line 3. Adam is a central character in Chapter 51, where, as here, he takes full responsibility for the first sin, incorporating Eve. *La lumere* describes the gravity of eating the apple and the process by which "the sin of Adam [*le pecché Adam*] passes to all those engendered from him" (75–76, 85–87) • 7–8 **this is openly knowen . . . in erth** this is known publicly by the whole of holy church on earth. An endorsement of standard teaching on sin. Underneath Julian's question in lines 2–3 lies doubt about whether that teaching can be correct • 9 **lerned** taught • 9 **I shulde beholde the glorious asseeth** I should see the glorious Atonement. The "asseeth" is Christ's Passion: in *A Treatise of Ghostly Battle,* Christ makes "aseeth to the fader in hevene for the gilt of mankinde" (*YW* 2:421). Julian is promised that she will see the efficacy of this "asseeth" in heaven: perhaps in the form described in *The Pricke* (5271–302), in which all the "tokens" of the Passion, including the cross, are displayed in the sky at the Day of Judgment to encourage the blessed and reprove the sinful • 10 **asseeth-making** act of reparation • 13 **take hede to this** pay attention to this message • 13 **sithen** since • 13 **the most harm** The harm caused by Adam's sin • 14 **therby** from this fact

[CHAPTER 30] 1 **He gave me understonding** This formulation leaves it unclear how this teaching is conveyed • 1 **two parties** two categories, or kinds, of truth. These continue Christ's answer to Julian's anxious question in 29.2–3: "How might alle be wele?" • 1–2 **That one party . . . oure salvation** one category is our savior and our salvation. Knowledge of Christ and of the moral, ritual, societal, and theological truths pertinent to human living and dying • 2–3 **open . . . plentuouse** explicit and lucid and lovely and easy and plentiful. "Plentuouse" is earlier used of Christ's blood. See especially Chapter 12 • 4 **comprehended** included • 4–6 **Hereto . . . the same grace** to this category of truth we are bound and led by God and counseled and taught by the Holy Spirit within and, through the same grace, by holy church without • 6 **joyeng** rejoicing • 6 **for** because • 7 **take of this** partake of this category of truth

in this. And to this oure blessed lorde answered fulle mekely and with fulle lovely   5
chere, and shewd that Adams sinne was the most harme that ever was done or ever
shalle to° the worldes end. And also he shewde that this is openly knowen in alle
holy church in erth.

Ferthermore he lerned that I shulde beholde /fol. 53v/ the glorious asseeth. For
this asseeth-making is more plesing to the blessed godhed and more wurshipfulle   10
for mannes salvation withoute comparison than ever was the sinne of Adam
harmfulle. Then meneth oure blessed lorde thus in this teching,° that we shulde
take hede to this: "For sithen° I have made welle the most harm, than it is my wille
that thou know° therby that I shalle make wele alle that is lesse."

THE THIRTIETH CHAPTER

He gave me° understonding of two parties. That one party is oure saviour
and oure salvation. This blessed parte is open and clere and fair° and light
and plentuouse. For alle mankinde that is of good wille and that shalle be is
comprehended in this part. Hereto we be bounde of God and drawen and conceyled
and lerned inwardly by the /fol. 54r/ holy gost and outward by holy church in the   5
same grace. In this wille oure lorde that we be occupied, joyeng° in him for he
enjoyth in us. And the more plentuously that we take of this, with reverence and

---

[VIS. 14.5–21] in this. And to this oure blissede lorde answerde fulle mekelye and with
fulle lovelye chere, and shewed **me** that Adames sinne was the maste harme that ever
was done or ever shalle to the warldes ende. And also he shewed **me** that this is openly
knawen° in alle haly kyrke in erthe.

Forthermare he lered **me** that I shulde behalde the gloriouse asethe. For this aseth-
makinge is mare plesande to the blissede godhede and mare wyrshipfulle to mannes
salvation withoutene comparison than ever was the sinne of Adam harmfulle. Thane
/fol. 107r/ menes oure blissede lorde° thus in this techinge, that we shulde take hede to
this: "For sen I hafe made wele the maste harme, it is my wille that thowe knawe therby
that I shalle make wele alle that is the lesse."

He gaffe me understandinge of twa parties. The ta party is oure saviour and oure salvation. This blissed party is open and clere and faire and light and plentiouse. For alle
mankinde that is of goode wille *or* that shalle be es comprehended in this partye. Hereto
ere we *bidden* of God and drawen and consayled and lered inwardlye be the haly gaste
and outwarde by haly kyrke by the same grace. In this wille oure lorde that we be occupied, enjoyande in him for he enjoyes in us. And the mare plentyouslye that we take of
this, with reverence and

8 **spede** benefit • 9 **Oure parte is oure lorde** Perhaps from Ps. 119:57 (Vulgate 118): "The Lord is my portion" • 10 **sparred fro** locked away from. The word is also used in 6.30 • 10 **beside oure salvation** irrelevant to our salvation • 11 **prevy concelle** secret counsel. The term is political, rather than religious, referring to the king's inner circle of advisers or to confidential matters of state. In Chaucer's *Man of Law's Tale,* the sultan sends for his "privee conseil" to consult them about his marriage (II [B] 204). The expected word here would be "privetes," which often means "heavenly secrets," as when the apostle John, in Hilton's *Scale,* is "raveshid by love into contemplation of Goddis privetees" (1.17) • 11–13 **it longeth . . . conceyles** it is proper to God's royal lordship to hold his secret counsels peacefully, and it is proper to his servants, out of obedience and reverence, not to desire to know his counsels. The image of God as king is anticipated by the exempla in 7.27–35, 14.19–21 • 14 **for that some creatures . . . therin** because some people make themselves so anxious about them [God's "privy conceyles"] • 14 **seker** certain • 15 **wist how mekille** knew how greatly • 15 **to leve it** to leave it alone • 16 **wille nothing wit** desire to know nothing • 16 **but that** except what • 17 **ther charite . . . lorde** their

love and desire is ruled according to the will of our Lord. The blessed have nothing to do with speculation. According to *The Pricke,* although wisdom is the first spiritual dowry or joy of the blessed, who "salle knaw and se / Alle that was, and es, and yit salle be," this wisdom is still limited to "that God vouches safe / That any creature knawing may have" (what God allows any creature to have knowledge of) (8187–206) • 18 **nothing wille ne desyer** neither will nor desire anything • 19 **For we be . . . mening** for from God's perspective we are all the same • 20 **we shalle . . . Jhesu** we should only rejoice in our blessed savior, Jesus. This sounds conclusive, but, characteristically, the next chapter pushes back

[CHAPTER 31] 2 **comfortabely** comforting • 2–3 **may . . . can . . . wille . . . shalle** The auxiliary verbs refer, respectively, to God's power to make well ("may"), his wisdom ("can"), his will ("wille"), and his intention ("shalle"). Compare Flete's *Remedy:* "Nothinge to him is impossible. . . . Thinke ferthermore that his might and power may do all, that his wisdome can, and his goodnes wil. And therfore truste fully that by his goodnes he will save you" (chap. 4, *YW* 2:112)

mekenesse, the more thanke we deserve of him and the more spede to oureselfe.
And thus may we sey, enjoyeng:° "Oure parte is oure lorde."

That other is hid and sparred fro us: that is to sey, alle that is beside oure salvation.   10
For that is oure lordes prevy concelle, and it longeth to the ryalle lordshippe of God
to have his privy conceyles in pees, and it longeth to his sarvantes for obedience and
reverence not wille to witte° his conceyles. Oure lorde hath pitte and compassion on
us, for that some creatures make them so besy therin. And I am seker• if we /fol. 54v/
wist how mekille° we shuld plese him and ese oureselfe to leve it, we wolde. The   15
saintes in heven, they wille nothing wit but that oure lorde wille shew them, and
also ther charite and ther desyer is ruled after the wille of oure lorde. And thus oght
we to wille to be like to them.° Than shalle we nothing wille ne desyer but the wille
of oure lorde, like as they do. For we be alle one in Goddes mening. And here was I
lerned that we shalle° onely enjoye in oure blessed savioure Jhesu, and trust in him   20
for alle thing.

THE THIRTY-FIRST CHAPTER

And thus oure good lorde answered to alle the questions and doutes that I
might make, sayeng full comfortabely: "I may make alle thing wele, and I can
make alle thing welle, and I wille make alle thing /fol. 55r/ wele, and I shalle° make
alle thing welle. And thou shalt se thyselfe that alle maner of thing shall be welle."

[*vis.* 14.22–35] mekenesse, the mare we deserve thanke of him and the mare spede to
oureselfe. And thus maye we saye, enjoyande: "Oure parte is oure lorde."

The tother parte is spared fra us and hidde: that is to saye, alle that is beside oure salvation. For this is oure lordes prive consayles, and it langes to the ryalle lordeship of God
for to have his prive consayles° in pees, and it langes to his servantes for obedience and
reverence nought to wille witte his councelle. Oure lorde has pite and compassion of
us, for that sum creatures makes tham so besy therin. And I am seker if we wiste howe
mekille we shulde plese him and ese oureselfe for to lefe it, we walde. The saintes in
heven wille nathinge witte bot that oure lorde wille shewe thame, and also there charite
and ther desire is rewled efter the wille of oure lorde. And thus awe we to willene to be
like to thame.° And than shalle we nathinge wille ne desire botte the wille of oure lorde,
as thaye do.° For we er alle ane in Goddes meninge. And here was I lered that we shalle
anely enjoye in oure blissid saviour Jhesu, and trist in him for alle thinge.

[*vis.* 15.1–4] And thus oure goode lorde answerde to alle the questions and doutes that
I might make, sayande fulle comfortabelye **on this wise**: "I may make alle thinge wele, I
can make alle thinge wele, I wille make alle thinge wele, and I shalle make alle thinge
wele.° And thowe shalle se it° thyselfe that alle thinge shalle be wele."

5–9 There he seyth . . . trinite The auxiliary verbs correspond to the properties associated with the persons of the Trinity: power (the Father), wisdom (the Son), love (the Holy Spirit). The unity of the Trinity is then deduced from "shalle" (intention), and humanity's participation in God from "thou shalt se thyselfe" • **8 thre persons and on truth** three persons and one truth. All three persons of the Trinity agree on the truth of "alle shalle be wele." Alludes to the creedal formulation "three persons in one God" • **9 oning** uniting • **10 in theyse five wordes . . . pees** in fulfilling these five promises God will be immersed in rest and in peace. The "wordes" are fulfilled at the end of time, after the Last Judgment. God's "enclosing" by the soul is the theme of the sixteenth revelation, Chapter 68. See also 54.13–21 • **11 gostly thirst of Crist** the spiritual thirst of Christ. See 17.3–4. In *Piers Plowman* B 18.368–70, Christ also anticipates that his thirst for souls can be slaked only at the Judgment: "I faught so, me thursteth yet, for mannes soule sake; / May no drinke me moiste, ne my thurst slake, / Til the vendage [harvest] falle in the vale of Josaphat," that is, as the dead rise up on the Last Day • **12 love-longing** Christ cannot suffer lack, but he does suffer "love-longing," the emotion of the lover not yet united with the beloved in Song 2:5 and 5:8: "For I languish for love" (our translation; RSV: "am sick with love"). The paradoxical view of divine need implied by the word runs throughout the work, resurfacing, still partly unresolved, as late as 79.30–80.35 • **12 till we se . . . domesday** until we see that sight (see line 4) at the Judgment • **13–14 some ben . . . into that day** some are still here, and some are to come, and so will some continue to be until the Last Day. See Matt. 16:28: "Some standing here . . . will not taste death before they see the Son of man coming in his kingdom" • **16 For we be not . . . than** for we are not now so completely brought together in him as we will be then. Standard teaching, alluded to as such in 12.21–25 • **17–33 For we know . . . blisse** Carefully makes the orthodox distinction between Christ's divinity, which is impassible (incapable of suffering), and his humanity, which is passible. See 20.20–22 • **17 in oure faith** as part of standard Christian belief • **17 it was shewde in alle** The first time in *A Revelation* that the entire revelation is brought in to produce evidence for a theological point. This becomes a common practice from Chapter 44 on. The passage that follows backs up the claim here by citing different revelations that bear on Christ's two natures • **18 aneynst** concerning • **18 fro** from • **19 very true** • **19–20 never be highed . . . selfe** never be made more elevated or lowered so far as Christ's own selfhood is concerned • **20 plentuously sene . . . shewing** plentifully seen in all of the revelations • **21 namely in the twelfth** especially in the twelfth revelation. See 26.4–8 • **22 and also shewde** and was also part of the revelation • **22 vertu** power • **24 the workes . . . manhed** the deeds performed by Christ in his human nature • **25 in the ninth** in the ninth revelation. See 22.3–4 • **27 ther he seyth** where he says • **27–28 We be his blisse . . . crowne** See 22.17–18 • **28–29 aneynst . . . oure hede** insofar as Christ (in his divinity) is our head. See Eph. 4:15 • **29 unpassible** impassible • **29–30 as anenst his body . . . knit** concerning his body, in which all his members are joined. Refers both to Christ's physical body and the body of his church, of which all Christians are members (see 1 Cor. 12:14–30) and which must still suffer until the Judgment

There he seyth "I may," I understonde for the father; and there he seyth "I can," I 5
understond for the sonne; and there he seyth "I wille," I understonde for the holy
gost; and there he seyth "I shalle," I understonde for the unite of the blessed trinite,
thre persons and on truth. And there he seyth "thou shalt se thyselfe," I understond
the oning° of alle mankinde that shalle be saved into the blisseful• trinite.

And in theyse five wordes God will be enclosed° in rest and in pees. And thus 10
shalle the gostly thirst of Crist have an end. For this is the gostly thirst of Crist: the
love-longing that lasteth and ever shall till we se that sight at domesday. For we that
shalle be safe, and shalle be /fol. 55v/ Cristes joy and his blisse, some° ben yet here,
and some be to come, and so shalle some be into that day. Therfore this is his
thurste: a love-longing to have us all togeder, hole in him to his endlesse blisse,° 15
as to my sight. For we be not now fully as hole in him as we shalle be than.

For we know in oure faith, and also it was shewde in alle, that Crist Jhesu is both
God and man. And aneynst the godhed: he is himselfe highest blisse, and was fro
without beginning and shalle be without end, which very endlesse blesse may never
be highed nor lowede in the selfe. And this was plentuously sene in every shewing, 20
and namely in the twelfth, wher he seyth: "I it am that is° highest." And as aneynst
Cristes manhode: it is knowen in our faith and also shewde, that he, with the vertu
of the godhede, /fol. 56r/ for love to bring us to his blisse, suffered paines and
passion and died. And theyse be the workes of Cristes manhed, wherin he enjoyeth.
And that shewde he in the ninth, where he saith: "It is a joy, a blisse, an endlesse 25
liking to me that ever I sufferd passion for the." And this is the blisse of Cristes
werkes, and thus he meneth ther he seyth in the same shewing: "We be his blisse, we
be his meed, we be his worship, we be his crowne." For as aneynst that Crist is oure
hede, he is glorified and unpassible. And° as anenst his body, in which alle his

---

[VIS. 15.4–16] There he says he "maye," I understande for the fadere; and there he says he
"can," I understande for the sone; and ther he says /fol. 107v/ "I wille," I understande for
the haly gaste; and there he says "I shalle," I undirstande for the unite of the blissede trinite, thre persones in a trewthe. And there he says "thowe shalle se thyselfe," I understande the aninge of alle mankinde that shalle be sayfe into the blisfulle trinite.

And in this five wordes God wille be closed in reste and in pees. And thus has the
gastely thirst of Criste ane ende. For this is the gastely thirste: the luff-langinge that lastes°
and ever shalle to we see that sight atte domesdaye. For we that shalle be safe, and shalle
be Cristes joye and his blisse, *ere yit here* ‡ *and shalle be* unto the daye. Therefore this is
the thirste: *the falinge of his blisse, that he has us nought in him als haelye as he shalle*
thane haffe. /Rev. 31.17–41/

31 **the rode tre** the cross • 31–32 **which desire . . . without beginning** Christ's "I thirst" is interpreted as part of the godhead from creation to the end of time. It is as though "longing and thirst" are synonymous with the Christ of the opening of John's Gospel: "In the beginning was the Word, and the Word was with God, and the Word was God" (1:1) • 34 **as verely . . . ruth and pite** as truly as there is in God a quality of compassion and pity. An allusion to 28.29 • 35 **thurst and longing** Despite the impassibility of Christ's divinity as described in the previous passage • 35–36 **of the vertu . . . to him** by the power of Christ's longing we are obliged to long for him in return • 37 **endlesse goodnes** See 8.35 • 39 **sondry propertees** different properties • 39–40 **in this standeth . . . thirst** in this the source of Christ's spiritual thirst is situated. "This" probably refers to "the endlesse goodnes of God" (line 37), making the sentence "And though . . . as to my sight" parenthetical • 42 **shewing of compassion** Apparently another name for the thirteenth revelation, the first to twelfth revelations being "the shewing of passion." See especially 28.19–20: "That ech maner noughting that he shewde in his passion, it was shewde agene here in this compassion" • 42–43 **that shalle ceasen at domyesday** compassion will cease at the Day of Judgment. Along with Christ's thirst and all his promises, as they come to fulfillment • 44 **suffer not the ende . . . best time** do not allow the end of the world to happen until the best time. According to Hilton, *The Scale* 2.4, this delay in completing the work of salvation "unto the laste day" is "for this skile [reason]: oure lord Jhesu of his mercy hath ordained a certain nombre of soulis to salvation" and waits for that number to be fulfilled. *A Revelation* alludes to this exclusivist theology of salvation in 12.25. Chapter 32 manifests some of this theology's latent tensions

[CHAPTER 32] 1–2 **One time . . . another time** See 27.10–11 and 31.4 • 1 **a** of • 3 **toke sundry maner** received different kinds • 3 **On** one • 4 **he wille we witte** he wants us to know • 5 **and to one and to other** both to the one (the great) and to the other (the little) • 6 **in that he seyeth** in what he says • 7 **lest thing . . . forgeten** the smallest thing will not be forgotten. An optimistic variation on the common Judgment scene in which all souls must give a complete account of how they have lived: "For men sal than straite acount yelde [must give a strict account] / Of alle thair time of youthe and elde / . . . And specialy of ilka moment, / Of alle the time that God tham lent" (*The Pricke* 5644–50) • 7 **Another understanding** Relating to the second promise, "Thou shalt se thyselfe" • 8 **so gret harmes take** such great injuries suffered • 9 **unpossible** impossible • 9–10 **And upon . . . therfore** and we look upon this evil, with sorrow and mourning over it • 10–11 **so that we can not rest . . . shuld do** Faced with the fact of evil, we cannot imitate the patience of the saints in heaven described in 30.15–19 • 11–12 **the use of oure reson . . . simple** Hilton and others argue that human reason, having been "mad cleer and bright withouten errour or derkenesse" (*The Scale* 1.43), is "blinde" because of the Fall • 13–14 **And thus meneth he** and so this is what he means

membris be knit, he is not yet fulle glorified ne all unpassible. For the same thurst 30
and longing that he had uppe on the rode tre—which desire, longing and thirste, as
to my sight, was in him from /fol. 56v/ without beginning—the same hath he yet, and
shalle into the time that the last soule that shalle be saved is come uppe to his blisse.

For as verely° as ther is a properte in God of ruth and pite, as verely ther is a
properte in God of thurst and longing. And of the vertu of this longing in Crist 35
we have to long agene to him, without which no soule cometh to heven. And this
properte of longing and thirst cometh of the endlesse goodnes of God, right as the
properte of pitte cometh of his endlesse goodnesse. And though he have longing
and pitte, they ben sondry propertees, as to my sight. And in this standeth the
pointe of gostly thirst, which is lasting in him as long as we be in need, us drawing 40
uppe to his blisse.

And alle this was seen in shewing /fol. 57r/ of compassion, for that shalle ceasen
at domyesday. Thus he hath ruthe and compassion on us, and he hath longing to
have us, but his wisdom and his love suffer not the ende to come till the best time.

THE THIRTY-SECOND CHAPTER

One time oure good lorde saide, "Alle maner a thing shalle be wele," and
another time he saide, "Thou shalt se thyselfe that alle maner of thing shalle
be wele." And in theyse two the soule toke sundry maner of understonding. On was
this: that he wille we witte that not only he taketh heed to nobille thinges and to
gret, but also to litille and to small, to lowe and to simple, and to one and to other. 5
And so meneth he in that he seyeth: "Alle maner thing shall be welle." For /fol. 57v/
he wille that we wit that the lest thing shall not be forgeten. Another understanding
is this: that ther be many dedes evil done in oure sight and so gret harmes take that
it semeth to us that it were unpossible that ever it shuld come to a good end. And
upon this we loke, sorowing and morning° therfore, so that we can not rest us in 10
the blisseful• beholding of God as we shuld do. And the cause is this: that the use of
oure reson is now so blinde, so lowe, and so simple, that we can not know the high,
marvelous wisdom, the might, and the goodnes of the blisseful• trinite. And thus

---

[vis. 15.16–19] Alle this was *shewed me* in the shewinge of compassion, for that shalle
sese atte domesdaye. Thus he hath reuthe and compassion of us, and he has langinge
to hafe us, botte his wisdome and his love suffers nought the ende to come to the beste
tym. /Rev. 32.1–16/

15–16 **"Take now hede . . . fulhede of joye"** "pay attention now faithfully and trustingly, and at the end of time you will truly see in fullness of joy." The object of "hede" and "se" is not stated, but in both cases is implicitly the promise "Alle maner thing shall be welle" • 16 **wordes** clauses. The clauses of Christ's speech in 31.2–4 • 17 **"I may make all thing wele"** Understand "etcetera" after "wele" 17 **a mighty comfort** The prophecy that follows, evidently generated by the "five wordes" just referred to • 17–18 **of alle the workes** concerning all the deeds • 19–30 **There is a deed . . . not welle** This prophecy sets out to resolve two conundrums: a rational conundrum concerning sin, punishment, and the assertion that "alle shalle be wele"; and an emotional conundrum concerning the soul's need to understand and its need to rest in trust. The first will be resolved, it asserts, outside the present order, on the "last day"; even the angels know no more than that. The second should be resolved on reading the prophecy, though the issues it attempts to settle continue to dominate much of the rest of the work. The only further hints as to the nature of the "deed" are in 75.13–39 • 20–21 **unknowen of . . . beneth Crist** unknown to all created beings beneath Christ. Christ's humanity is the sole created being to know the timing and nature of this plan. Compare Mark 13.32, on the day of Judgment: "But of that day or that hour no one knows, not even the angels in heaven, nor the Son, but only the Father" • 23 **heyle** conceal • 24–25 **the cause . . . oure soule** the reason why he wants us to know it in this sense is that he wants us to be made to feel easier in our souls • 25 **peesed** made peaceful • 25–26 **leving the beholding . . . him** turning away from the contemplation of all the agitations that might hinder us from truly rejoicing in him • 32 **longeth to oure faith** it is part of our faith • 33 **Goddes worde shalle be saved** God's word will be preserved. See Matt. 24:35: "Heaven and earth will pass away, but my words will not pass away" • 33–38 **And one point . . . to beleve** The traditional categories into which the damned are divided: fallen angels, anyone not a Christian, and wicked Christians. See, e.g., *The Scale* 2.3, a formal statement of a conservative salvation theology: "Two maner of men aren not reformed by vertu of his passioun. Oon is of hem that troweth it not [one is those who do not believe it]; anothir is of hem that loven it not. Jewes and paynemes [pagans] han not the benefetes [benefits] of this passioun. . . . Thanne thinketh me that thise men gretly . . . erren that seyn that Jewis and Saracenes and paynemes . . . mown be mad saaf. . . . False Cristen men, the whiche are out of charite and leven [live] and dien in dedly sinne . . . gon to peines of helle endlesly, as Jewes and Sarcenes doon." Following this argument only to cast doubt on it, *A Revelation* here makes quite explicit the tension between what "holy church techeth" and what Julian interprets her vision to imply • 34 **as angelis . . . for pride** such as angels who fell out of heaven because of their pride. See Isa. 14:12–15, traditionally understood as an account of the fall of Satan: "How are you fallen from heaven, O Day Star, son of Dawn! . . . You said in your heart, 'I will ascend to heaven; above the stars of God I will set my throne on high . . . I will make myself like the Most High.' But you are brought down to Sheol, to the depths of the Pit" • 35 **out of the faith** outside the faith • 36 **tho** those • 36 **man that hath received cristondom** someone who has received Christianity. Any baptized person • 37 **oute of cherite** outside the state of charity. For the phrase, see 9.8–9 • 38 **stonding alle this** this being so • 41–42 **That that is unpossible . . . to me** that which is impossible for you is not impossible for me. With a similar resistance to orthodox salvation theology, Langland at the climax of *Piers Plowman* has Christ say: "I may do mercy thorugh rightwisnesse, and alle my wordes trewe," even though "Holy Writ wole that I be wroke of hem [avenged on those] that diden ille [evil]" (B 18.390–91). Both Langland and Julian allude to Luke 18:26–27: "Those who heard it said, 'Then who can be saved?' But he said, 'What is impossible with men is possible with God'" • 42 **save my worde** preserve my word • 44–45 **and therwith that** and in addition to that • 45 **stonde** stand firm • 45 **sadly** steadily

meneth he where he seyth, "Thou shalt se thyselfe that alle manner thing shall be
wele," as if he saide: "Take now hede° faithfully and trustely, and at the last end thou   15
shalt /fol. 58r/ se verely in fulhede of joye." And thus in the same five wordes before
saide—"I may make all thing wele"—I understonde a mighty comfort of alle the
workes° of oure lorde God that are for to come.

There is a deed the which the blissefulˑ trinite shalle do in the last day, as to my
sight. And what the deed shall be and how it shall be done, it is unknowen of alle   20
creatures which are beneth Crist, and shall be tille whan it shalle be done. The
goodnesse and the love of our lorde God wille that we witte that it shall be. And the
might and the wisdom of him, by the same love, wille heyle it and hide it fro us,
what it shalle be and how it shalle be done. And the cause why he wille we witte it
thus is for he wille we be the more esed in oure soule and peesed° in love, leving the   25
beholding of alle /fol. 58v/ tempestes that might let us of true enjoyeng in him. This
is the gret deed ordained of oure lorde God fro without beginning, tresured and hid
in his blessed brest, only knowen to himselfe, by which deed he shalle make all thing
wele. For right as the blessed trinite made alle thing of nought, right so the same
blessed trinite shalle make wele alle that is not welle.   30

And in this sight I marveyled gretly, and beheld oure faith, mening thus: oure
faith is grounded in Goddes worde, and it longeth to oure faith that we beleve that
Goddes worde shalle be saved in alle thing. And one point of oure faith is that many
creatures shall be dampned: as angelis that felle out of heven for pride, which be
now fendes, and man° in erth that /fol. 59r/ dyeth out of the faith of holy church—   35
that is to sey, tho that be hethen—and also man° that hath received cristondom and
liveth uncristen life, and so dyeth oute of cherite. All theyse shalle be dampned to
helle without ende,° as holy church techeth me to beleve. And stonding alle this,
methought it was unpossible that alle maner of thing shuld be wele, as oure lorde
shewde in this time.   40

And as to this, I had no other answere in shewing of oure lorde but this: "That
that is unpossible° to the is not unpossible to me. I shalle save my worde in alle
thing, and I shalle make althing wele." And in this I was taught by the grace of God
that I shuld stedfastly holde me in the faith as I had before understond, and therwith
that I shulde stonde and sadly beleve /fol. 59v/ that alle maner thing shall be welle, as   45

[*VIS.* 15.20–23] And in thies same five wordes before saide—"I may make alle thinge
wele"—I understande a mighty comforthe of alle the werkes of oure lorde that ere for to
come. /*Rev. 32.19–29*/ For right as the blissed trinite made alle thinge of nought, right so
the same blissed trinite shalle make wele alle that es nought wele. /*Rev. 32.31–33.22*/

46–48 **this is the grete dede . . . not welle** The deed at the end of time is thus defined as the reconciliation of orthodox teaching on damnation with God's message of love to Julian • 49 **wot it, ne shalle wit it** knows it, nor will know it

[CHAPTER 33] 1 **yit in this** yet in thinking about this "deed" • 1 **as I durste** so far as I dared • 1–2 **hel and of purgatory** Hell and purgatory are common destinations for visionaries from the apocryphal *Apocalypse of Paul* (fourth century) on, and it is no more surprising that Julian should have expected to see them in the course of her revelation than that she expected a "bodily sight" of Mary (see Chapter 25). Hell and purgatory are clearly relevant to meditation on a deed that promises to reconcile the doctrine of eternal damnation with "alle shalle be wele." See 32.46–48 • 2 **not my . . . onything** not my intention to put anything to the test • 2–3 **that longeth to** that has to do with • 4 **techeth for** teaches about • 4–5 **for lerning . . . faith** to gain information about everything to do with my faith. Julian has formed the idea that her revelation is to be a comprehensive guide to the faith • 6 **culde** could • 7 **in the fifte shewing** See 13.34–36 • 8–11 **In which sight . . . nought** *The Apocalypse of Paul* similarly states that God and the saints do not remember the damned: "The angel turned and said to me, 'If any are thrown into the well of the abyss, and it is sealed over them, there will never be any recollection made of them in the presence of the Father and the Son and the Holy Ghost or of the holy angels'" (43). It is perhaps in the same spirit that visionary journeyers to the other world are often barred from the deep pit where the finally damned dwell. Paraphrasing Ps. 58.10 (Vulgate 57.11)—"The righteous will rejoice when he sees the vengeance; he will bathe his feet in the blood of the wicked"—*The Pricke* articulates the more common

position, that the elect actively rejoice to see the damned suffer: "Ilka rigthwise [righteous] man / Fulle glad and blyth [cheerful] salle be than, / When thay Godes vengeance se / On the sinfulle, that than dampned salle be" (8443–46) • 9 **and therin ende** and end their lives in this condition. The possibility of salvation remains right to the point of death • 10 **alle his holen** all his holy • 15 **in the furst** See Chapters 4–9 • 15 **in the secunde** See Chapter 10 • 15 **in the fourth** See Chapter 12 • 15 **in the eighth** See 18.1–10 • 15–16 **as it is before saide** See 23.6–11 • 16 **wherin** in all of which • 17 **properly specified** specifically indicated • 17–18 **the Jewes . . . to deth** the Jews who put him to death • 18 **in my faith** as a matter of orthodox belief • 18–19 **acursed . . . without ende** In *La lumere*, the lay voice asks why it is that the Jews who "mistrent nostre seignur a la mort [put our savior to death]" should not be rewarded, rather than condemned, "kar grant biens par iceo nus firent [since they did us a great deal of good through this deed]" (5167–74). Their envy and malice is quickly asserted • 19 **saving tho . . . by grace** except for those who were converted by grace. The work avoids directly suggesting that anyone other than the devil is damned • 21 **therin in the faith** • 23 **have grete regarde** pay close attention • 24 **he wille . . . shalle do** by it ["alle the dedes that he hath done"] he wants us to know, trust, and believe everything he is going to do. The Day of Judgment is often presented as a time of justice and fear, when Christ returns in wrath to condemn the wicked. According to *The Pricke*: "Alle sal haf gret drede that day, / Bath gude and ille [both the good and the evil], als we here clerks say. / Thar sal be nouther aungel na man / That thay ne sal tremble for drede than [then]" (5368–71). Christ's manifestation of love for humankind in the past, as seen in the first through twelfth revelations, refocuses this picture

oure lorde shewde in that same time. For this is the grete dede that oure lorde God shalle do, in which dede he shalle save his worde in alle thing and he shalle make wele all that is not welle. But what the dede shal be, and how it shall be done, there is no° creature beneth Crist that wot it, ne shalle wit it, till it is done, as to the understanding that I toke of oure lordes mening in this time. 50

THE THIRTY-THIRD CHAPTER

And yit in this I desyered as I durste that I might have had full° sight of hel and of purgatory. But it was not my mening to take prefe of onything that longeth to oure faith. For I beleved sothfastly that hel and purgatory is for the same ende that holy church techeth for. But my mening was that I might have seen for lerning /fol. 6or/ in alle thing that longeth to my faith, wherby I might live the more to 5 Goddes wurshippe and to my profite. And for ought that I culde desyer, I ne culde se of this right nought but as it is before saide in the fifte shewing, wher that I saw the deville is reproved of God and endlessly dampned. In which sight I understond that alle the creatures that be of the devilles condition in this life, and therin ende,° ther is no more mention made of them before God and alle his holen then of the deville, 10 notwithstonding that they be of mankinde, wheder they have be cristend or nought.

For though the revelation was shewde of goodnes, in which was made litille mention of eville, yet I was not drawen therby from ony point of the faith that holy church techeth me to beleve. For I had sight of the passion of Crist in diverse shewing: in the furst, in the secunde, in the /fol. 6ov/ fourth, and° in the eighth, as 15 it is before saide, wherin I had in part feling of the sorow of oure lady and of his tru frendes that saw his paines. But I saw not so properly specified the Jewes that did him to deth. But notwithstonding, I knew in my faith that they ware acursed and dampned without ende, saving tho that were converted by grace. And I was strenghed and lerned generally to kepe me in the faith in every point and in all, as I 20 had before understonde, hoping that I was therin with mercy and the grace of God, desiring and preyeng in my mening that I might contenue therin unto my lives ende.

It is Goddes wille that we have grete regarde to alle the dedes that he hath done. For he wille therby we know, trust, and beleve alle that he shalle do. But evermore us

---

[*vis.* 15.23–26] It is Goddes wille that we hafe grete rewarde to alle the dedes that he has done. For he wille that we knawe thereby ‡ alle that he shalle do. **And that shewed he me in this worde that he saide: "And thowe shalle see thyselfe that alle manere of thinge shalle be wele."**

25 **leve the beholding . . . shalle be** stop imagining what the deed will be. See 32.48–50 • 25–26 **like to oure . . . heven** like our brothers who are the saints in heaven • 26 **wille right nought** do not desire anything at all. An allusion to 30.15–18 • 27–28 **be welle apaide . . . shewing** be well satisfied both with what God hides and what he reveals. See the alternation of presence and absence in Chapter 15, and, for the phrase "welle apaide," 22.1–5

[CHAPTER 34] 1 **two maner of prevites** two kinds of secrets. This distinction opens this chapter's attempt to sort out the complex relation between revelation and "previte" that has emerged since Chapter 27. If the revelation is a "shewing" of divine truth, how then does it not belong to the category of "previte"? • 1 **One is this gret previte** Announced in Chapter 32 • 2 **theyse** these • 2 **we know thus hid** we know them as hidden in the way described. This formulation aligns the "gret privite" of Chapter 32 with the "privy conceyles" of Chapter 30. Both are answers to Julian's cry in 29.2–3: "A, good lorde, how might alle be wele?" • 3 **into** until • 3 **That other are** the others are • 4 **himselfe** he himself • 4 **tho** those • 5 **he wille . . . them** he wants us to know that it is his will we know them • 6–7 **not only . . . prevites to us** not only because he wants them to be secrets to us • 7 **oure blindhed and oure unknowing** These are also qualities of the soul during its earthly journey in 10.10–11 and 11.6–7 • 8 **reuth** pity • 8 **make them open to us himselfe** make them manifest to us himself • 8 **wherby** so that through them • 9 **cleve** cling • 9–11 **For alle . . . holy church** for our good Lord

most courteously desires to reveal to us the truth about all that it is useful to us to know and to understand, besides all the preaching and teaching of holy church. "With" could mean "through," but makes better sense here as "besides," "as a supplement to," since the passage as a whole is about the dynamics of divine revelation, and the passage immediately following reacts sharply against it • 12 **plesance** pleasure • 13 **take** accept • 13 **the preching . . . holy church** A corrective account of the need to accept the church's teaching and of the adequacy of that teaching despite the importance of the "privities" contained in the revelation. Hilton similarly writes of how most souls do no more than "liven mekely in the trouthe of holy chirche" and are nonetheless saved by the church's prayers (*The Scale* 2.10) • 13–14 **For he it is, holy church** A definition of the church as the body of Christ that ultimately derives from 1 Cor. 12:12, 27: "For just as the body is one and has many members, and all the members of the body, though many, are one body, so it is with Christ. . . . Now you are the body of Christ and individually members of it." In sacramental theology, the church affirms its identity with Christ every time its members consume his body at the Mass. Here, this affirmation has the effect of diminishing the dichotomy between revelation and church teaching in the first part of the chapter • 14 **grounde** foundation • 15 **the mede . . . traveleth** the reward for which every true soul labors • 16–17 **And I hope . . . God** and I have true hope that all those who seek in this way (through "preching and teching of holy church") will prosper, for they seek God

nedeth leve the beholding what the dede shalle be, and desyer we to be like to oure   25
bretherne */fol. 61r/* which be the saintes in heven, that wille right nought but Goddes
wille. Than shalle we only enjoye in God and be welle apaide both with hiding and
shewing. For I saw sothly° in our lordes mening, the more we besy us to know his
prevites in that or in any other thing, the ferthermore shalle we be from the knowing.

THE THIRTY-FOURTH CHAPTER

Oure lord shewed two maner of prevites. One is this gret previte with all the
prevy pointes therto belonging: and theyse prevites he wille we know thus hid
into the time that he wille clerly shew them to us. That other are the prevites which
himselfe shewed openly in this revelation: for tho are prevites which he wille make
open and knowen to us. For he wille that we wit that it is his wille we knowe them.   5
They are prevites to us, but not only for that he wille they */fol. 61v/* be prevites to
us, but they are prevites to us for oure blindhed and oure unknowing. And therfore
hath he gret reuth. And therfore he wille make them open to us himselfe, wherby we
may knowe him and love him and cleve to him. For alle that is spedfulle to us to wit
and for to knowe, fulle curtesly oure good lorde wille shew us what it is, with alle   10
the preching and teching of holy church.

God shewde fulle gret plesance that he hath in alle men and women that mightly
and mekely and wisely° take the preching and the teching of holy church. For he it is,
holy church. He is the grounde, he is the substance, he is the teching, he is the techer,
he is the ende, and he is the mede wherfore every kinde soule traveleth. And this is   15
knowen and shall be knowen° to ech soule to which the holy gost declareth it. And I
hope sothly° that alle tho that seke thus they shalle spede, */fol. 62r/* for they seke God.

[*VIS.* 15.27–31] **This I understande in twa manerse: ane, I am wele payed that I wate it
noght; anothere, I am gladde and mery for I shalle witte it. It is Goddes wille that we
witte that alle shalle be wele in generalle. Botte it is nought Goddes wille that we shulde
witte it nowe, botte as it langes to us for the time. And that is the techinge of haly kyrke.**
/Rev. 33.24–34.11/

[*VIS.* 16.1–7] God shewed **me** fulle grete plesance that he has in alle men and women
that mightelye and mekelye and *wyrshipfullye* takes the prechinge and the techinge of
haly kyrke. For he is haly kyrke. For he is the grounde, he is the substance, */fol. 108r/* he is
the techinge, he is the techare, he is the ende, he is the mede° wharefore ilke *trewe* saule
travailles. And this is knawen° and shalle be knawen to ilke saule to whame the haly gaste
declares it. And I *am seker* that alle tho that sekes thus shalle spede, for thay seke God.

18–21 **Alle this that I have . . . shalle be wele** The passage alludes back to the third revelation, of "God in a pointe" (11.14–18), with its perception that God "doth alle that is done," and forward, less explicitly, to various passages, especially the exemplum of the lord and the servant in Chapter 51 • 19 **in the thirde shewing** See 11.14–18 • 20 **whan God shewede me for sinne** See Chapter 27

[CHAPTER 35] 2–3 **I desired . . . good leving** I wanted to know whether a certain person whom I loved would continue in a virtuous life. Prophetic information about the living or the dead was often part of visionary experience, as Julian's expectations here suggest. Margery Kempe is shown "hy revelations . . . of many soules, sum for to ben saved and sum for to ben dampned," even though she attempts to refuse them (*Book* 1.59) • 4 **singular desyer** desire to know something about a particular person • 4 **I letted myselfe** I stood in my own way. Compare 33.1–11 • 5 **frendfulle mene** friendly intermediary. Perhaps an angelic or saintly voice • 5–6 **Take it generally** understand the revelation to be about general truths. An injunction *A Revelation* obeys even as it tells of Julian's "singular desyer," by referring to the person in question with the anonymous and genderless term it usually reserves for Julian herself: "creature" • 6 **as he sheweth to the** in the form in which he shows it to you.

Rather than try to pull the revelation in her own direction • 7 **specialle** particular • 8 **therwith** with that • 9 **like in** take pleasure in • 9–10 **onything in specialle** anything in particular. Special or particular truths thus prove to fall into the category of the "prevites he wille we know . . . hid" (34.2) • 9–10 **do wisely . . . teching** behave wisely in accordance with this teaching • 10 **not be glad . . . in specialle** not be glad on account of anything specific. Julian has sought the gladness of "specialle" knowledge of the destiny of her friend or relative, the "creature" • 10 **dissesed** made anxious • 12 **For the ful- hed . . . alle** for the fullness of joy is to contemplate God in everything • 13 **the same end** That is, "to beholde God in alle" • 13 **ledeth it** leads everything • 15 **in the furst** in the first revelation. See 5.5: "He is all thing that is good" • 15 **the thirde . . . God in a point** See Chapter 11 • 17–18 **Alle that oure lorde . . . wurshipfulle** all that our Lord makes happen is just or perfect, and all that he lets happen is worthy of reverence. "Suffereth" can mean "allows" or "endures." The next chapter builds on the account of seeing God "in alle" in lines 12–16, returning to the theme of "rightfullehede" from Chapter 11 before complicating this theme with an account of what God in his mercy "suffereth." Anticipates the account of the two "domes" pertaining to the substance and the sensuality in Chapter 45 • 18 **in theyse two** in doing and suffering

Alle this that I have now saide, and more that° I shalle sey after, is comforting against sinne. For in the thirde shewing, whan I saw that God doeth all that is done, I saw not sin. And than saw I that alle is welle. But whan God shewede me for sinne, than said he: "Alle shalle be wele."

THE THIRTY-FIFTH CHAPTER

And when God almighty had shewed so plentuosly and so fully of his goodnesse, I desired to wit of a serteyn creature that I loved if it shulde continue in good leving, which I hoped by the grace of God was begonne. And in this singular desyer it semed that I letted myselfe, for I was not taught° in this time. And then was I answered in my reson, as it were by a frendfulle mene: "Take it generally, and beholde the curtesy of thy lorde God as he sheweth° to the. For it is more wor- /fol. 62v/ shipe to God to beholde him in alle than in any specialle thing." I assented, and therwith I lerned that it is more wurshippe to God to know althing in generalle than to like in onything in specialle. And if I shuld do wisely after this teching, I shuld not be glad° for nothing in specialle, ne gretly dissesed for no manner of thing,° for alle shalle be wele.

For the fulhed of joy is to beholde God in alle. For by the same blissed might, wisdom, and love that he made alle thing, to the same end oure good lorde ledeth it continually, and therto himselfe shalle bring it. And when it is time we shalle see it. And the ground of this was shewed in the furst, and more openly in the thirde, wher it seyth: "I saw God in a point."

Alle that oure lorde doeth is rightfulle,° and alle that he suffereth is wurshipfulle. And in theyse two is comprehended good and eville. /fol. 63r/ For alle that is good

---

[VIS. 16.8–21] Alle this that I hafe nowe saide, and mare that I shalle saye efter, es comforthinge againe sinne. For *first,* when I sawe that God does alle that es done, I sawe nought sinne. And than sawe I that alle is wele. Bot when God *shewed me sinne,* than saide he: "Alle shalle be wele."

And when God allemightye hadde shewed **me** plentyouslye and fully of his goodnesse, I *desired of* a certaine person that I loved *howe it shulde be with hire* ‡. *And in this desire I letted myselfe,* for I was noght taught in this time. And than was I answerde in my reson, als it ware be a frendfulle meen:° "Take it generally, and behalde the curtaysy of thy lorde God as he shewes it to the. For it is mare worshippe to God to behalde him in alle than in any specialle thinge." I assented, and therwith I lered that it is mare wyrshippe to God to knawe alle thinge in generalle than to like in anything in specialle. And if I shulde do wisely efter this techinge, I shulde nought be glad for nathing in specialle, na desesed for na manere of thinge, for alle shalle be wele. /Rev. 35.12–36.61/

21 **mildhed** mercifulness • 21–22 **by this werking . . . grace** by God's activity of mercy and grace • 23 **Rightfulhed** perfection, justice, or righteousness. The term combines "fulhed" (line 12) and "rightfulle" (line 17) • 24–25 **as they be ordained . . . beginning** as they have been endlessly ordained. See 11.34–35: all is done "in the order that our lord hath it ordained to fro withoute beginning" • 27 **the same ende** "the best" • 28 **this blisseful acord** this happy accord. The harmony between what God ordains and how he brings it into being • 32 **marcy is a werking . . . God** mercy is an activity that proceeds from the goodness of God. "Mercy" is the manifestation of goodness (line 20), whereas "rightfullehede" is goodness itself. Mercy is a secondary quality, tied to time • 34 **leve to pursew** Compare the lament of Haukyn "the Actif Man" in Langland's *Piers Plowman* B 14.322–23: "'So hard it is,' quod Haukyn, 'to live and to do sinne, / Sinne seweth [pursues] us ever,' quod he, 'and sory gan wexe'" • 35 **brought into** reconciled with • 35 **stonde** remain • 35 **By his sufferance** with his permission • 37 **mercy and grace** For the relation between these two qualities of God, often mentioned in tandem in *A Revelation*, see 48.21–32 • 37 **manifolde more joyes** many times more joyes. That is, than we would have had if we had not fallen • 39 **paide with both** satisfied with the fact of "rightfullehede" and "mercy." Able not to worry about "onything in specialle" (line 9). Parallels "welle apaide" in 33.27

[CHAPTER 36] 1–5 **Oure lorde God . . . working** A second prophecy about a deed. Compare 32.19–30. This new deed is the means by which God brings "alle . . . into rightfullehede" (35.35), but in a more limited sense than is the case with the first deed. If the first deed encompasses both "hethen" and those who "liveth uncristen life" (32.36–37), the implications of the second deed at first seem restricted to "alle his lovers in erth" (line 9), though it is later extended to "alle that shalle be safe" (line 29) • 2 **plentuous** plentiful • 2 **by me** for my sake or in relation to me • 4 **I shalle do right nought but sinne** I will do nothing at all except sin • 5 **sinne shall not let . . . working** sin will not hinder the working of his goodness. Anticipates the argument of Chapter 38, that "sinne shalle be no shame, but wurshipe to man" • 5–7 **the beholding . . . Goddes wille** contemplation of this transformation of sin into good is a heavenly joy in a fearful soul who always desires God's will, naturally and by grace. For reasons the chapter explores, contemplation of sin as joy makes the soul fearful • 8 **This dede . . . begon here** Unlike the first deed, which takes place only at the end of time and in the next world • 9–10 **And ever . . . joy** Unlike the first deed, this deed will be known at death • 10 **And it shalle . . . last day** and it will in this way continue in its activity until the Judgment. Aligns this deed, aimed at transforming the sins of "alle his lovers in erth" into "goodnes," with the "werking" of mercy in 35.32–34

oure lorde doeth, and that is evil oure lord suffereth. I say not that eville is wurshipfulle, but I sey the sufferance of oure lorde God is wurshipfulle, wherby his goodnes shalle be know without ende, and his mervelous mekenesse and mildhed, by this werking of mercy and grace.

Rightfulhed is that thing that is so good that may not be better than it is. For God himselfe is very rightfulhed, and all his werkes be done rightfully, as they be ordained fro without beginning by his high might, his high wisdom, his high goodnesse. And right as he hath ordained° it to the best, right so he werketh continually, and ledeth it to the same ende. And he is ever fulle plesed with himselfe and with alle his workes. And the beholding of this blisseful° acord is full swete to the soule that seeth it by grace. Alle the soules that shalle be saved in heven /fol. 63v/ without ende be made rightfulle in the sight of God and by his awne goodnesse, in which rightfullehede• we be endlessly kepte and marvelously, above all creatures.

And marcy is a werking that cometh of the goodnes of God, and it shalle last in wurkinge° as long as sinne is suffered to pursew rightfulle soules. And whan sinne hath no lenger leve to pursew, than shalle the werking of mercy cees. And than shalle alle be brought into rightfullehede• and therin stonde withoute ende. By his sufferance we falle, and in his blessed love, with his might and his wisdom, we are kept. And by mercy and grace we be raised to manifolde more joyes.° And thus in rightfullehede• and in mercy he will be know and loved, now and without ende. And the soule that wisely beholdeth in grace is wele paide with both, and endlessely enjoyeth.

THE THIRTY-SIXTH CHAPTER

/fol. 64r/

Oure lorde God shewde that a deed shalle be done, and himselfe shalle do it, and it shall be wurshipfulle and mervelous and plentuous. And by me° it shall be done, and himselfe shalle do it (and this is the highest joy that the soule understode, that God himselfe shall do it!), and I shalle do right nought but sinne. And my sinne shall not let his goodnes working. And I saw that the beholding of this is a hevenly joy in a dredfulle soule which evermore kindly by grace desyereth Goddes wille.

This dede shalle be begon here, and it shalle be wurshipfulle to God and plentuously profetable to alle his lovers in erth. And ever as we come to heven we shalle se it in marvelous joy. And it shalle last thus in werking to the last day. And the worshippe and the blisse of that shalle last in heven before God and alle his holy° without ende. /fol. 64v/

20

25

30

35

5

10

13 **Thus was this dede . . . meyning** The end of this moment of revelation and the beginning of its exegesis • 14–17 **When I saw . . . before saide** The implication of the awkward phrasing is that, until the revelation moved on, Julian expected to learn "what the dede shuld be" (line 18). But this episode turns out to be a "close showing" (see lines 23–24), not an open one • 15–16 **it was shewede . . . for to come** it was a revelation about a great deed that at that time was still to come. "Than for to come" could mean no more than "destined to be completed at the Last Day" (as line 10 has already said), but combined with all the "shalls" in this chapter, it seems rather to suggest that the deed has not yet begun but is about to do so. If so, the pattern of thinking here is apocalyptic, aligning *A Revelation* with texts such as *Piers Plowman* that see the world as entering the "last times" before the final Judgment • 18 **privy to me** secret from me • 19 **in this** in the revelation about the "deed" • 19 **he wille not . . . shewth** he does not want us to fear to know the things he shows. The other side of the teaching against curiosity in Chapter 30. Here, knowledge of the role of sin in the "deed" causes fear • 21 **like in him** take pleasure in him • 23 **now have prevy** keep secret for now • 23–24 **yet . . . sheweth them close** even these in his great goodness he reveals in a hidden fashion • 27 **ees** ease • 27 **endlesse . . . therfore** we shall have endless thanks from him for it • 28–29 **this is the understonding . . . safe** this is the meaning of the phrase "that it will be done for my sake": that is, for people in general, that is to say, for all who will be saved. The two "that is" phrases offer glosses of "me" • 33–36 **Than meneth . . . most plese me** A sustained exercise in the method of exegesis by analytic paraphrase used several times earlier, e.g., 22.34–36, 24.12–14, 25.9–10, 29.12–14. The speech expounds the previous sentence, "That God himselfe shalle do it," etc. • 35 **noughting thiselfe**

humbling yourself • 36 **for of alle thing . . . plese me** for in this way (by "enjoying in me"), out of all the ways, you could please me most • 38 **beholding of the reproved** thinking about the damned. The "reproved," if any, are excluded from "the generalle man" (line 29) for whom God's "deed" is done. Although participants in the "sinne" that generates the "deed," they would be outsiders to the transformations that make sin meaningful. The only other use of the term in *A Revelation* occurs at 13.17 • 39 **Let me alone** do not interfere with me • 39 **derwurdy** precious • 39 **intende** attend • 39–40 **I am inogh to the** I am enough for you. See 2 Cor. 12:9: "My grace is sufficient for you, for my power is made perfect in weakness" • 40–41 **this is oure lordes werking in us** To decide not to meditate on the damned is to do God's will. Such an idea echoes standard teaching on refusing to succumb to doubt in one's own salvation, such as *The Remedy*'s counsel against paying heed to any "imagination or temptation . . . by the whiche ye doubte of salvation" (chap. 4, *YW* 2:112), but extends it to include everyone. Contrast *The Book of Margery Kempe* 1.59–60, which teaches the necessity of taking note of damnation • 41 **perced** pierced. By the realization of the folly of "the beholding of the reproved" • 43 **excludeth not the specialle** does not exclude anyone in particular. Alludes to the opening of this extended reflection, 35.1–3 • 43 **poure** poor • 45 **that other before saide** See 32.19–30 • 45 **it is not both one** they are not the same. As 32.31–50 makes clear, the first "deed" differs because, among other things, it does not exclude the damned • 45 **sondry** different • 47 **in party** in part • 49–50 **special understanding . . . of miracles** Miracles are among the aspects of the "deed" that can be "knowen here in party" (line 47). How this "special understanding" is conveyed is unclear: the phrase is used nowhere else in *A Revelation*

Thus was this dede seen and understonde° in oure lordes meyning. And the cause
why he shewede it is to make us to enjoy in him and in alle his werkes. When I saw
the shewing continued, I understode it was shewede for a gret thing that was than   15
for to come, which thing God shewde that himselfe shuld do it, which dede hath the
propertes before saide. And this shewde he full blissefully,• mening that I shuld take
it wisely, faithfully, and trustely. But what the dede shuld be, it was kepte privy to me.

And in this I saw that he wille not we drede to know tho thinges that he shewth.
He sheweth them for he wille we know them, by which knowing he wille we love   20
him and like in him and endlesly enjoy in him. And for the gret love that he hath
to us, he sheweth us alle that is wurshipfulle and profitable for the time. And tho
thinges that he wille /fol. 65r/ now have prevy, yet of his gret goodnesse he sheweth
them close. In which shewing, he wille we beleve and understande that we shall° se it
verely in his endlesse blisse. Than oughte we to enjoy in him for alle that he sheweth   25
and for all that he hideth. And if we wilfully and mekely do thus, we shalle finde
therin gret ees, and endlesse thanking we shalle have of him therfore.

And this° is the understonding of this worde, "that it shalle be done by me": that
is, the generalle man, that is to sey, alle that shalle be safe. "It shalle be wurshipfull,
mervelous, and plentuous, and by me it shalle be done, and God himselfe shalle do   30
it." And this shalle be the highest joy that may be beholden of the dede: "That God
himselfe shalle do it, and man shall do right nought but sinne."

Than meneth oure good lorde thus, as if he saide: "Beholde and se. Here hast
thou matter of mekenesse, /fol. 65v/ here hast thou matter of love, here hast thou
matter of noughting thiselfe,° here hast thou matter of enjoying in me. And for my   35
love enjoy in me, for of alle thing therwith might thou most plese me."

And as long as we be in this life, what time that we by oure foly turne us to the
beholding of the reproved, tenderly oure lorde toucheth us and blissefully• calleth
us, seyeng in oure soule: "Let me alone, my derwurdy childe, intende to me, I am
inogh to the. And enjoy in thy saviour and in thy salvation." And that this is oure   40
lordes werking in us I am seker.• The soule that is perced therwith by grace shalle
se it and fele it. And though it be so that this dede be truly take for the general man,
yet it excludeth not the specialle. For what oure good lorde wille do by his poure
creatures, it is now unknowen to me.

But this dede and that other before saide, it is not both one, but two sondry. But   45
this dede shalle /fol. 66r/ be knowen soner, and that shalle be as we come to heven.
And to whom oure lorde geveth it, it may be knowen here in party. But the gret dede
aforesaide shalle neither be knowen in heven nor in erth tille that it be done.

And farthermore he gave special understanding and teching of working and
shewing of miracles, as thus: "It is knowen that I have done miracles here before,   50

51 **fele** many • 52 **shall do in coming of time** will continue to do so in the time to come. Another hint of the apocalypticism of lines 15–16 • 54 **to meke us** to make us meek • 57 **so as it may be** to the extent it may be • 57 **strenghing** strengthening • 58 **encrese oure hope** increase of our hope • 59–61 **he wille that . . . before miracles coming** The role "sorows and tempestes" have in presaging miracles parallels the role of sin in somehow enabling the "deed" through which God's goodness is to be manifested. Miracles are, as it were, the "deed" in miniature • 59–60 **borne overlowe** made too depressed

[CHAPTER 37] 1 **I shuld sinne** I must or would sin. This perception is similar to the one that begins Chapter 36, though it is developed in a different direction • 1 **for liking** because of the pleasure • 2 **entended not redely** did not pay immediate attention • 3 **abode** waited • 3–4 **toke singularly to myselfe** applied to myself individually. That this is not right has already been argued in 36.28–29 • 4 **as ye shalle see** See especially Chapters 78–79, which meditate further on the material presented here • 6–7 **by me alone . . . alle** the revelation that I individually must sin must be interpreted to apply to everyone • 8 **softe drede** quiet fear • 8–9 **I kepe the fulle sekerly** I protect you in complete security. Ostensibly the topic of discussion from here to the end of Chapter 40 • 11 **right so . . . shewede** just so was the comfort revealed. Just as God's words about Julian's sin apply to all, so do his words of comfort

many and fele,° high and mervelous, wurshipfulle and gret. And so as I have done
I do now continually, and shall do° in coming of time." It is knowen that before
miracles come sorows and anguish and trobil. And that is that we shuld know oure
owne febilnesse and mischef that we be fallen in by sinne, to meke us and make us
to drede God, crying for helpe° and grace. And gret miracles come after, and that of   55
the high might and wisdom and goodnesse of God, shewing his vertu /fol. 66v/ and
the joyes of heven, so as it may be in this passing life, and that for the strenghing of
our faith, and encrese oure hope in charite. Wherfor it pleseth him to be knowen
and worshipped in miracles. Then meneth he thus: he wille that we be not borne
overlowe for sorows and tempestes that falle to us, for it hath ever so been before   60
miracles coming.

THE THIRTY-SEVENTH CHAPTER

God brought to my° minde that I shuld sinne. And for liking that I had in
beholding of him, I entended not redely to that shewing. And oure lorde
fulle marcifully abode, and gave me grace for to entende. And this shewing I toke
singularly to myselfe. But by alle the gracious comfort that foloweth, as ye shalle see,
I was lerned to take it to alle /fol. 67r/ min evencristen, alle in generalle and nothing   5
in specialle. Though oure lorde shewed me that I shuld sinne, by me alone is
understonde alle.

  And in this, I conceived a softe drede. And to this oure lorde answered: "I kepe
the fulle sekerly."• This worde was saide with more love and sekernesse• of gostly
keping than I can or may telle. For as it was afore shewde to me that I shuld sinne,   10
right so was the comfort shewede: sekernesse of keping° for alle min evencristen.

[VIS. 16.22–26] God brought to my minde that I shulde sinne. And for likinge that I
hadde in behaldinge of him, I entendid nought redely to that shewinge. And oure lorde
fulle *curtayslye abayde to I walde entende.* /Rev. 37.3–5/ *And than oure lorde brought to*
minde with my sinnes the sinne of alle mine evencristen, alle in generalle and nathinge in
specialle.

[VIS. 17.1–6] *If alle oure* lorde shewed me that I shulde sinne, be me allayn I understode
alle. In this, I consayved a softe drede. And to this oure lorde answerde **me thus**: "I kepe
the fulle sekerly." This worde was saide **to me** with mare love and sekernes of gastely
kepinge than I can or maye telle. For as it was be- /fol. 108v/ fore shewed to me that I
shulde sinne, right so was the comforth shewed **to me**: sekernesse of kepinge for alle
mine evencristen.

13 **alle one soule** all a single soul. God's dealings with Julian's soul imply his dealings with all • 14–17 **For in every soule . . . ever good** This claim for the absolute goodness of part of the soul, perhaps implicit in Christ's "I kepe the fulle sekerly," previews the detailed discussion of the soul's "substance" and "sensuality" in the fourteenth revelation and later (Chapters 45–53) and functions in *A Revelation* as a first sketch of that discussion. The near repetition of these lines in 53.9–12 suggests their structural importance. *The Remedy* has a similar passage on resistance to sin, aimed at stiffening the resolve of those so severely beset by temptation that they believe they may already have succumbed to sin: "Every man and woman hath two willes, a good will and an evil. The evil will cometh of sensualite, the whiche is ever inclininge downwarde to sinne. And the good will cometh of grace, which alweye stireth the soule upwarde to all goodnes. . . . Though ye . . . be enclined to sensualite, yet ye do it not, ne consent therto, but it is the sensualite that doth it in you. And your good will abideth in you still unbroken" (chap. 5, *YW* 2:114) • 15–17 **Right as . . . good** just as there is a bestial will in the lower part of the soul that can will nothing good, even so there is a godly will in the higher part, a will so good that it can never will evil, but always good. "Bestely" here may be merely a synonym for "impure," but the human soul was thought to include an "animal soul," whose mode was instinctive rather than rational or ethical; "godly" could just be a spelling of "goodly" (the spelling in the parallel passage of *A Vision*), for in the sense "divine" the word was rare before the sixteenth century; the two words often appear interchangeably in Middle English. However, throughout *A Revelation* the word is generally spelled "godly" in both main manuscripts • 17 **therfore** in relation to the goodness of the godly will • 18–19 **in the holhed of love** by means of the wholeness of the love. If there were no godly will in the soul in this life, God's love for us now would not be the same as his love for the saved • 21 **for failing . . . traveyle** all our anguish in this life is due to a failure of love on our part. An axiom in Chapter 45

[CHAPTER 38] 1 **sinne shalle be . . . man** sin will not be a cause of humiliation but will do a person honor. A paradox derived from "I kepe the fulle sekerly" (37.8–9)

almost as startling as the doctrine of the "godly wille" (37.14–21). *The Pricke* 8297–364, following Anselm, argues that the saved in heaven remember their sins without shame: "Na mare than Petre now has shame / Of that, that he forsoke our Lord by name; / Or Mary Maudelayne now has of hir sin / That sho [she] som time delited in" (8333–36). This chapter's introduction of the idea of sin as "wurshipe" takes the argument a significant step further • 1–3 **For right as . . . blisse by love** for just as truth creates for every sin a corresponding pain, so love gives the same soul a specific joy for every sin. "Answering" is a past participle. "Truth" means both "divine justice" and "causality." "A" in Middle English often means "a single" • 3 **ponished** punished • 4 **after . . . grevous** depending on how serious they are • 8 **but which sinne . . . rewarded** without this sin's being rewarded • 8–9 **it is made knowen without end** the sin is made known forever. Compare Chapter 14 • 9 **overpassing** transcendent • 11 **merely** merrily • 11 **David** King David. The first in a list of holy sinners, included here because of his adultery with Bathsheba. See 2 Sam. 11–12 • 11 **other in the olde lawe** other people who lived under God's covenant with the Jews, as represented in the Old Testament • 12 **new lawe** the law of Christ initiated by his life and teaching • 12 **Magdaleyne** Mary Magdalene, mentioned in 2.7 and traditionally associated with the sinful woman of Luke 7:36–50 • 12 **Peter** Peter, who denied Christ. See Matt. 26:69–75 • 13 **Paule** Paul, who (under the name Saul) persecuted the early church until his conversion. See Acts 8–9 • 13 **Thomas of Inde** the apostle Thomas, who doubted Christ's resurrection and is said to have founded the Nestorian church in India. See John 20:19–29 • 13–29 **Sent John . . . continually** Saint John of Beverley, in Yorkshire (died 721). His cult was vigorous in the late fourteenth century, his feast day being May 7, either the day after Julian fell sick or the day before the revelation (see 2.1–2 and 3.1–5). The only version of his life that makes him into a serious sinner is late, lurid, and not English: a sixteenth-century Dutch narrative describes him as a repentant murderer who became a hermit with such a reputation for dealing with serious sinners that the pope mistakenly referred him to himself when he went to Rome to seek forgiveness. Perhaps Julian and her readers knew a now lost English version of a similar narrative

What may make me more to love min evencristen than to see in God that he loveth alle that shalle be saved, as it were alle one soule?

For in° every soule that shalle be saved is a godly wille that never assented° to sinne, nor never shalle. Right as there is a bestely wille in the lower /fol. 67v/ party that may wille no good, right so there is a godly will° in the higher party, which wille is so good that it may never wille eville, but ever good. And therfore we be that he loveth, and endlesly we do that he liketh. And this shewede oure good lorde in the holhed of love that we stande in, in his sight: yea, that he loveth us now as welle while that we be here as he shalle do when we be there before his blessed face. But for failing of love in oure party, therfore is alle oure traveyle.

THE THIRTY-EIGHTH CHAPTER

Also° God shewed that sinne shalle be no shame, but wurshipe to man. For right° as to every sinne is answering a paine by truth, right so for every sinne to the same soule is geven a blisse by love. Right as diverse sinnes be ponished with divers paines /fol. 68r/ after that they be grevous, right so shalle they be rewarded with divers joyes in heven after as the sinne have ben painfulle and sorowfulle to the soule in erth. For the soule that shalle come to heven is so precious to God, and the place so wurshipfulle, that the goodnes of God suffereth never that soule to sinne that shalle come ther but which sinne shal be rewarded. And it is made knowen without end and blissefully restored by overpassing worshipes.°

For in this sight my understanding was lifted up into heven, and then God brought merely° to my minde David and other in the olde lawe with him, without number. And in the new lawe he brought to my minde furst Magdaleyne, Peter and Paule, Thomas of Inde,° Sent John of Beverly, and other, also without number: how

15

20

5

10

[*vis.* 17.6–17] What may make me mare to luff mine evencristen° than to see in God that he loves alle that shalle be safe, as it ware alle a saule?

And in ilke saule that shalle be sayfe is a goodely wille that never assented to sinne, na never shalle. For as ther is a bestely wille in the *nethere* party that maye wille na goode, so is thare a *goodely* wille in the *over* partye ‡ that maye wille nane eville, botte ever goode, **na mare than the persones of the blissed trinite** /Rev. 37.17–18/. And this shewed oure lorde **me** in the holehed of luffe that we stande in, in his sight:° ya, that he luffes us nowe als wele whiles we ere here as he shalle do when we ere thare before his blissed face. /Rev. 37.20–21/

Also God shewed **me** that sin *is* na shame, bot wirshippe to man. /Rev. 38.1–9/ For in this sight min understandinge was lifted up into heven, and than *com verrayly* to my minde David, /Rev. 38.11–12/ Peter and Paule, Thomas of Inde and the Maudelayn ‡: howe

15–17 **And therfore . . . worshippe** and for this reason our courteous Lord causes them (in their sin and its honoring) to be known in this life in part as they are known in the next life in fullness. For in the next life the badge of sin is transformed into honor • 19 **for homely-hed** to be intimate • 19–20 **a hende neighbur . . . knowing** a lovely neighbor and a local. The town of Beverley, where John's shrine was located, is in East Yorkshire, north of Norwich. Although John had been dead for nearly seven hundred years when *A Revelation* was written, his cult (like any saint's cult) worked on the assumption that he was still vividly and effectively present in the place with which he was associated and where his body lay. In this sense, he was Julian's "neighbour" • 20 **plainly** simply • 23 **dereworthy sarvant** precious servant • 23 **full mekille God . . . dreding** very greatly loving and fearing God • 25 **ne lost no time** and lost no time. For the importance of time to *A Revelation*'s theology of reward, see 14.22–30 • 25 **manifolde** many times • 26 **contrition** sorrow for sin • 27 **overpassing** transcendent • 28–29 **God sheweth . . . continually** God shows on earth by continually performing plentiful miracles around John of Beverly's body. A saint's ability

to generate miracles was taken as a sure sign of holiness • 30 **mery** merry. See line 11

[CHAPTER 39] 1 **Sinne is the sharpest scorge** In this fourth of five chapters on sin, Chapter 38's account of the sins and rewards of the saints are applied to the ordinary soul. In the process, the notion that sin does the sinner honor in heaven is qualified by discussion of the damage sin does, as penitential language takes the place of the language of remedy and comfort. The earlier account of tribulation in Chapter 15 is relevant to much of the discussion that follows • 2 **forbeteth** beats down. "For" is an intensifier • 2 **forbreketh him** breaks him to pieces • 2 **noyeth** disgusts • 3–4 **so ferforth . . . into helle** so much that sometimes he thinks himself only worthy to sink, as it were, into hell • 5 **touching** inspiration • 5 **bitternesse** bitterness of sin • 6 **quicken** revive • 6 **turned** converted • 7–8 **wilfully . . . shame** The characteristics of true confession in part 5 of *Ancrene Wisse* include all these items: "Confession must be accusing, bitter with sorrow . . . naked . . . full of shame . . . true and willing" (159–60)

they be /*fol. 68v*/ knowen in the church on erth with ther sinnes, and it is to them
no shame, but alle is turned them to worshippe. And therfore oure curtesse lorde 15
sheweth for them here in party like as it is ther in fulhed. For there, the token of
sinne is turned to worshippe.

And Saint John of Beverley, oure lorde shewed him full highly in comfort of us,
for homelyhed,° and brought to my minde how he is a hende° neighbur, and of
oure knowing. And God called him Saint John of Beverley, plainly as we do, and 20
that with a fulle glade and swet chere, shewing that he is a full high saint in his sight
and a blisseful.° And with this he made mention that in his youth and in his tender
age he° was a dereworthy sarvant to God, full mekille° God loving and dreding. And
neverthelesse God suffered him to falle, him mercifully /*fol. 69r*/ keping, that he
perished not ne lost no time. And afterward God raised him to manifolde more 25
grace. And by the contrition and the mekenesse that he had in his living, God hath
geven him in heven manifolde joyes, overpassing that he shuld have had if he had
not sinned or fallen. And that this is soth,° God sheweth in erth with plentuous
meracles doing abought his body continually. And alle was this to make us glad
and mery in love. 30

THE THIRTY-NINTH CHAPTER

Sinne is the sharpest scorge that ony chosen soule may be smitten with. Which
scorge alle forbeteth° man and° woman, and alle forbreketh° him, and noyeth°
him in his owne sight—so ferforth that otherwhile he thinketh himselfe he is not
wurthy but as it were to sinke into helle—/*fol. 69v*/ tille when contrition taketh him
by touching of the holy gost, and turneth the bitternesse into hope of Goddes mercy. 5
And than begin his woundes to heele and the soule to quicken, turned into the life of
holy church. The holy gost ledeth him to confession, wilfully to shew his sinnes,

---

[vis. 17.17–28] thaye er knawen in the kyrke of erth with thare sinnes **to thayre wirshippe.**
And it is to tham no shame that thay hafe sinned, /*Rev. 38.15–16*/ **no mare it is in the blisse
of heven.** For thare, the takeninge of sinne is turned into wirshippe. **Right so oure lorde
God shewed me tham in ensampille of alle othere that shalle cum theder.** /*Rev. 38.18–30*/

Sin is the sharpeste scourge that any chosen saule maye be *bette* with, whilke scourge
it alle forbettes man and woman, and alle forbrekes tham, and *noghtes* thamselfe° in
thare awne sight, sa fareforth *that him thinke that* he is noght worthy bot as it ware to
sinke into helle. *Botte* when contrition takes him be the touchinge of the haly gaste, *than*
turnes the bitternesse° into hope of Goddes mercye. And than beginnes his woundes to
hile and the saule to quiken, turned in to the life of haly kyrke. The haly gaste leddes him
to confession, wilfully to shewe his sinnes,

8 **nakedly** plainly • 8–9 **defouled . . . God** defiled the lovely image of God in his soul. A common understanding of sin. *The Scale* 1.52 claims that an image of sin replaces the image of God (see Gen. 1:27) in the fallen soul • 9–10 **Than undertaketh . . . holy church** then, as enjoined by his confessor, he performs the penance that is grounded in holy church for every sin. Confessors consulted lists of penances to be imposed for sins • 11 **mekille** much • 11–12 **and also . . . sending** and bodily sickness sent by God, when it is humbly received, also pleases God. According to *Ancrene Wisse,* part 4: "Sickness that God sends" washes past sins, protects against future ones, "tries patience, keeps one humble, increases one's reward, makes the patient person equal to a martyr" (115) • 12–14 **also . . . gostly and bodely** so does public grief and shame accompanied by the world's repudiation and contempt, as well as every kind of misfortune, and the spiritual and physical temptations that we are thrown into. A list of what treatises on meekness. After its discussion of sickness, *Ancrene Wisse,* part 4, likewise goes on to commend the usefulness of "temptation that comes from human evil" and offers various remedies (116–17). Then it describes "inner temptation . . . of two kinds, bodily and spiritual: bodily as in lechery, gluttony, and sloth; spiritual, as in pride, envy and anger, and also covetousness" (119) • 15 **neer** nearly • 18 **also whom . . . specialle grace** of his special grace our Lord also visits whom he wishes • 18–19 **so gret contrition . . . God** Like the earlier reference to bodily sickness (lines 11–12), this echoes the "three desires" described in Chapter 2, in this case the third wish, in lines 34–36 • 19–20 **they be**

sodeynly . . . saintes This seems to be an account, not of spiritual ecstasy in this life, but of physical death in a state of love-longing for Christ. Desire for such death is a frequent theme in the writings of Rolle, who in his *Ego Dormio* describes how, "Fro [from the time that] thou or I or another be broght into this joy of love, we mow nat [cannot] live longe after as other men doth. Bot as we live in love, also we shal dey in joy, and passe to him that we have loved" (249–52). Compare Christ's ecstatic account of death in 64.9–12 • 20 **of sinne and of paine** from sin and from pain • 20 **even with** equal to • 22 **thre menes** three ways. The three sources of "mekenesse" described in the chapter: through sin (lines 1–10), tribulation (lines 11–17), love-death (lines 18–23) • 24 **For by theyse medicins . . . heled** for every sinful soul must be healed by these medicines. Pastoral texts such as *Ancrene Wisse* often describe remedies for sin as medicines • 25 **Though that he be heled** if he ("every sinfulle soule") is healed • 25–26 **not as woundes but as wurshippes** See 38.10–17 • 26 **on the contrary wise** in the opposite way • 26 **as we be ponished here** to the same extent we are punished in this life • 28 **that wille . . . no degre** who desires that nobody who comes there should lose his labor to the slightest extent. See 38.23–26 • 28–30 **For he beholdeth . . . love** for he regards sin as sorrow and suffering in his lovers, to whom, because of love, he attributes no guilt. Alludes back to Chapters 27–28 and forward to the exemplum of the lord and servant in Chapter 51 • 31 **mede** reward • 31 **undertake** receive • 33–34 **For oure curtesse lorde . . . grevous falling** See 51.1–51

nakedly and truly, with gret sorow and with gret shame that he hath so defouled the fair image of God. Than undertaketh he penance for every sinne, enjoined by his domesman, that is grounded in holy church by the teching of the holy gost. 10

And this is one mekenesse that mekille° pleseth God; and also, meekely taken,° bodely sicknesse of Goddes sending; also sorow and shame outwardly with reprefe and despite of the worlde, with alle maner of grevance, and temptations that we be cast in, gostly and bodely. Fulle preciously oure good /fol. 7or/ lorde kepeth us, whan it semeth to us that we be neer forsaken and cast away for oure sinne, and for we se 15 that we have deserved it. And because of the meekenes that we get hereby, we be raised fulle high in Goddes sight by his grace.

And also whom oure lord wille he visiteth of his specialle grace with so gret contrition, and also with compassion and tru longing to God, that they be sodeynly deliverde of sinne and of paine, and taken up to blisse and made even with saintes. By 20 contrition we be made clene, by compassion we be made redy, and by tru longing to God we be made wurthy. Theyse be thre menes, as I understode, wherby that alle soules com to heven—that is to sey, that have ben sinners in erth and shalle be saved.

For by theyse medicins behoveth that every sinfulle /fol. 7ov/ soule be heled. Though that he be heled, his woundes be sene before God not as woundes but as 25 wurshippes. And so on the contrary wise, as we be ponished here with sorow and with penance, we shall be rewarded in heven by the curtesse love of oure lord° God almighty, that wille that none that come ther leese his traveyle in no degre.° For he beholdeth sinne as sorow and paines to his lovers, in whom he assigneth no blame for love. 30

The mede that we shal undertake shall not be litille, but it shalle be high, glorious, and wurshipfulle. And so shalle alle shame turne to worshippe and to more° joy. For oure curtesse lorde wille not that his servantes despair for ofte falling

---

[VIS. 17.28–39] nakedlye and trewly, with grete sorowe and grete shame that he hase swa defouled the faire image of God. Than he takes penance for ilke a sine, enjeuned be his domesman, that is grounded in haly kyrke be the techinge of the haly gaste. /Rev. 39.11–23/

Be *this medicin* behoves everilke sinfulle saule be heled, **and namlye of sinnes that ere dedely in the selfe.** /fol. 109r/ Though he be heled, his woundes er sene before God nought as woundes bot as wyrshippes. And so on contrarye wise, as *it es* punished here with sorowe and with penance, *it* shalle be rewarded in heven be the curtayse love of oure lorde God alle mightye, that wille that nane that comes thare lese his travaile ‡. /Rev. 39.28–30/ That mede that we salle *resayfe thare* salle nought be litelle, bot it shalle be hy, gloriouse, and wirshipfulle. And so shalle alle shame turne into wyrshippe and into mare joye. /Rev. 39.33–40.4/

34 **letteth not him to love us** does not hinder him from loving us • 38 **enmes** enemies • 38 **felle** dangerous • 38 **fers** fierce • 38–39 **And so much . . . by oure falling** and our reward is all the greater by the extent to which we give him the opportunity (to reward us) by our falling

[CHAPTER 40] 1 **sovereyne frenship** supreme act of friendship • 1–2 **that he kepeth . . . sinne** The theme of Chapters 38–39, beginning with the account of Saint John of Beverly in 38.18–30 • 2 **toucheth** moves • 3 **prevely** intimately • 4–5 **then we wene . . . sinne** then we believe that God is angry at us on account of our sin. Rather than at the sin, as is really the case. According to *Pore Caitif,* "God hatith . . . nothing but sinne and wickidnesse: nethir soule ne body, ne non othir thing that man hath" (87). Chapter 45 explains how the perception that God is angry with the self, even though not true, is nonetheless useful • 5–6 **Than be we stered . . . God** then we are moved by the Holy Spirit through sorrow

for sin into prayer and the desire for amendment of ourselves with all the powers of our soul, in order to appease the anger of God • 7 **unto the time . . . consciens** until the time comes that we find a certain peace in our souls and an easiness of conscience. Treatises on tribulation such as *The Remedy* and *The Chastising* assume that the sensation of ease or peace is a true sign of divine favor, even as they offer strategies for dealing with what happens when "the felinge of swetnes is withdrawn from a man . . . for the best to the helth of his soule" (*The Remedy,* chap. 5, *YW* 2:115) • 8 **soth** true • 9 **merely** merrily • 9 **of fulle glad chere** with a very joyful expression • 11–12 **now seest thou my loving** now you recognize my love • 12 **oned** united • 14 **as oftetimes as it cometh** as often as the soul returns to God • 15 **vertu** power • 16 **made redy to us** made ready for us • 17 **so ferforth that** with the result that • 18 **for we mey . . . fulhed** because we cannot have peace and charity in their fullness • 19 **it befalleth . . . live** we should always live • 20–21 **as it is before saide** See 31.10–16

ne for grevous falling. For oure falling letteth not him to love us. Pees and love
is ever in us, being and working, but we be not ever in pees /fol. 71r/ and in love. 35
But he wille we take hede thus: that he is ground of alle oure hole life in love, and
ferthermore that he is oure everlasting keper, and mightely defendeth us agenst alle
oure enmes that be full felle and full fers upon us. And so much oure mede° is the
more for we geve him° occasion by oure falling.

THE FORTIETH CHAPTER

And this is a sovereyne frenship of oure curtesse lorde, that he kepeth us so
tenderly while we be in oure sinne. And ferthermore he toucheth us fulle
prevely, and sheweth us oure sinne by the swet light of mercy and grace. But
when we se oureselfe so foule, then we wene that God were wroth with us for oure
sinne. Than be we stered of the holy gost by contrition into prayer and desyer to 5
amending° of oureselfe with alle oure mightes,° to slake /fol. 71v/ the wrath of God,
unto the time we finde a rest in soule and softnes in consciens. And than hope we
that God hath forgeven us oure sinne, and it is soth.° And than sheweth oure
curtesse lorde himselfe to the soule merely and of fulle glad chere, with frendfulle
wellcoming,° as if it had ben in paine and in preson, seyeng thus: "My dere darling, 10
I am glad thou arte come to me. In alle thy woe I have ever ben with the, and now
seest thou my loving,° and we be oned in blisse." Thus are sinnes forgeven by grace
and mercy, and oure soule worshipfully received in joy, like as it shalle be whan it
cometh into heven, as oftetimes as it cometh by the gracious werking of the holy
gost and the vertu of Cristes passion. 15

Here understond° I sothly° that alle maner of thing is made redy to us by the
gret /fol. 72r/ goodnes of God, so ferforth that, what time we be oureselfe in pees
and in charite, we be verely safe. But for we mey not have this in fulhed while we
be here, therefore it befalleth us ever to live in swete prayeng and in lovely longing
with oure lorde Jhesu. For he longeth ever for to bring us to the fulhed of joy, as it is 20
before saide, wher he sheweth the gostly thriste.

[*VIS.* 19.59–66] And than wenes *he* that God ware wrathe with *him* for *his* sinne. *And
than is he stirred to contrition and be confession and othere goode dedes* to slake the wrathe
of God, unto the time *he* finde a reste in saule and softnesse in conscience. *And than him
thinke* that God hase forgiffen *his* sinnes, and it es soth. *And than is God, in the sight of
saule, turnede into the behaldinge of the saule,* as if it had bene in paine or in preson,
sayande thus: " ‡ *I am gladde that thowe erte comen to reste, for I hafe ever loved the and
nowe loves the, and thowe me.*" /Rev. 40.12–21/

22–25 **if any man . . . of the enemy** See Rom. 6.1–2: "Are we to continue in sin that grace may abound? By no means!" In *The Remedy,* after describing the power of the divine mercy, Flete adds a similar warning: "God forbede . . . that ony creature be the more . . . bolde to sinne wilfully [on purpose]. For in so moche [because] the mercy of God is so large [generous] we ought to be the more besy and diligent to love and praise him" (chap. 4, *YW* 2:113) • 23 **stered by foly** moved by foolishness • 23 **If this be soth** if this should be true • 24 **more mede** greater reward • 24 **or elles . . . sinne** or else to ascribe less weight to sin • 26 **alle this comfort** All the comfort contained in the words "I kepe the fulle sekerly." See lines 44–45 and 37.8–13 • 27 **hate sin only for love** hate sin alone for the sake of love. "Only" could qualify "for love" and mean "purely," but see lines 41–44. Probably an allusion to Ps. 97:10 (Vulgate 96): "The Lord loves those who hate evil." Paralleling the "comfort" of the revelation with a citation from Scripture, the sentence implies that the teachings of the revelation have quasi-biblical authority. As if in answer, the thirteenth revelation ends with perhaps the greatest concentration of biblical quotations and allusions in the work • 27 **awne** own • 28 **seeth this** realizes the truth of this • 28–29 **the lother is him to sinne** the more unwilling he is to sin • 30–31 **For if . . . sinne** for if (on the one hand) all the pain in hell and purgatory and on earth—including death and other pains—were laid before me and (on the other hand) sin. A hyperbolic statement designed to

shock the reader out of any complacency induced by the "comfort" of the last few chapters • 31 **chese** choose • 32 **so mekille for to hate** so much to be hated • 32–33 **may be liconned . . . sinne** cannot be compared to any pain that is not sin. Sin is categorically different from everything else in the universe and can be "likened" only to itself • 33–34 **to me was shewed . . . sinne** to me was shown no hell more severe than sin. See Julian's thwarted desire to see hell in Chapter 33 • 33–34 **a kind soule . . . sinne** a good soul hates no hell except sin. Hell, it seems, is not to be hated. See 63.1–22 and 76.1–11 • 35 **whan we geve . . . meknesse** when we focus on love and humility. Rather than on the temptation to exploit the divine mercy by sinning • 37 **mighty . . . wise . . . willing** The properties of the Trinity: power, wisdom, love. The whole Trinity joins in the salvation of humankind • 38 **ground of alle . . . men** the foundation of all the laws of Christian people. Christ is the basis of the "new lawe" that, in Christian belief, supersedes the"olde lawe" God gave the Jews. See 38.11, 12 • 38–39 **he taught us . . . eville** See Matt. 5:38–48, a passage that explicitly contrasts the old law and the new. See also Luke 6:27: "Love your enemies, do good to those who hate you" • 39 **he is himselfe this charite** See 1 John 4:8 and 16: "God is love." Chapter 4 of 1 John seems to lie behind much of this passage • 39–40 **doeth to us . . . to do** does to us as he teaches us to do to others. Paraphrases Matt. 7:12: "So whatever you wish that men would do to you, do so to them; for this is the law and the prophets"

But now because of alle this gostly comfort that is before saide, if any man or woman be stered by foly to sey or to thinke, "If this be soth,° than were it good for to sinne to have the more mede," or elles to charge the lesse to sinne, beware of this stering. For sothly,° if it come, it is untrue and of the enemy. For the same tru love that techeth us alle this comfort,° the same blessed love techeth us that we shalle hate° sin only for love. And I am seker• by /fol. 72v/ my awne feling, the more that ech kinde soule seeth this in the curtesse love of our lorde God, the lother is him to sinne, and the more he is ashamed.

For if it were leyde before us, alle the paine that is in hell and in purgatory and in erth—deed and other—and° sinne, we shulde rather chese alle that paine than sinne. For sin is so vile and so mekille for to hate that it may be liconned to no paine which paine is not sinne. And to me was shewed none harder helle than sinne. For a kind soule hateth no helle° but sinne, for alle is good but sin, and nought is evel but sinne. And whan we geve oure intent to love and meknesse by the werking of mercy and grace, we be made alle fair and clene.

And as mighty and as wise as God is to save man, as willing he is. For Crist himselfe is ground of alle the lawes /fol. 73r/ of cristen men, and he taught us to do good agenst eville. Here we may se that he is himselfe this charite, and doeth to us as

25

30

35

[VIS. 18.1–4] Bot ‡ *if thowe be stirred* to saye or to thinke, "*Sen this is* sothe, than ware it goode for to sinne for to hafe the mare mede," ‡ beware of this stirringe **and dispice it,** for ‡ it is of the enmy. **For whate saule that wilfully takes this stirringe, he maye never be safe to he be amended as of dedely sinne.** /Rev. 40.25–27/

[VIS. 17.39–41] And I am sekere be min awne felinge, the mare that ilke kinde saule sees this in the *kinde and curtayse* love of God, the lathere es him for to sinne ‡.

[VIS. 18.4–14] For if it ware laide before *me,* alle the paine that is in helle and in purgato-rye and in erth—dede and othere—and sinne, *I had* lever chese alle that paine than sinne. For sinne is so vile and so mekille for to hate that it maye be likened to na paine whilke paine es nought sin. /Rev. 40.33–34/ For alle thinge is goode botte sinne, and nathinge is *wikked* botte sinne. /Rev. 40.35–36/ **Sinne es nowthere deed no liking. Botte when a saule cheses wilfully sinne—that is, paine—as fore his God, atte the ende he hase right nought. That paine thinke me the herdeste helle, for he hase nought his God: in alle paines a saule may hafe God botte in sinne.**

And als mighty and als witty as God is for to safe man, als willy he is. For Criste him-selfe is grounde of alle the lawe of cristen men, and he has taught us to do goode againes eville. Here may we see that he es himselfe this charite, and does to us as

40 **holhed** wholeness • 41–42 **No more . . . evencristen** no more than Christ's love for us is broken because of our sin, no more does he desire that our love for ourselves or for our fellow Christians be broken. Knowledge of sin is not to lead to despair or hatred of others • 43 **but nakedly hate sinne . . . loveth it** but we should openly hate sin and endlessly love the soul just as God loves it. *The Scale* 1.65 stresses the difficulty of keeping this distinction clear: "It is a greet maistrye [feat] for a man to kunne love [know how to love] his evencristene in charite and wisely hate the sinne of him and love the man" • 44 **hate sinne like as God hateth it** hate sin in the way God hates it. See lines 26–27 and 52.44–45, 63.1–2 • 45 **I kepe the fulle sekerly** See 37.8–9. A formal ending to a four-chapter exposition of this divine promise

[CHAPTER 41] 1 **shewed for prayer** gave a revelation concerning prayer. The new topic follows from the thirteenth revelation's analysis of humanity's role in God's activities • 1–2 **I saw two . . . mening** I saw two characteristics of prayer in our Lord's intention • 2 **rightfulle prayer** just prayer. Prayer offered in the proper way in both a spiritual and a formal sense—just, ordered, and properly understood—the topic of lines 24–55 • 2 **seker trust** certain trust. Glances back to "I kepe the fulle sekerly," 40.45, suggesting that the word "seker" is a bridge between the revelations. The topic of 42.11–56 • 3 **oftime . . . not fulle** often our trust is not complete. *Pore Caitif* describes "ful trist and stidfast hope in him that me preyeth to" as the seventh "needful thing" in prayer, quoting James 1:5–8: "He that doutith is liik the flood of the see" (95) • 3–4 **as we thinke for oure unwurthinesse** on account of our unworthiness, as we think • 4 **fele right nought** feel nothing at all • 4–5 **as bareyne and as drye** as barren and as dry. Compare Julian's own state in 66.9–10 on awakening from the revelation: "as baren and as drye as I had never had comfort but litille" • 5–6 **And thus . . . wekenesse** and so, as we imagine, our foolishness is the reason for our weakness. Subjectively, it seems that the weakness of prayer is caused by "foly," here synonymous with "unwurthinesse" (line 4) • 6 **have I felt in myselfe** Like the thirteenth revelation, the fourteenth revelation begins with a meditation on Julian's experience

he techeth us to do. For he wille that we be° like him in holhed of endlesse love to
oureselfe and to oure evencristene. No more than his love is broken to us for oure
sinne, no more wille he that oure love be broken to oureselfe nor to our evencristen,
but nakedly hate sinne, and endlesly love the soule as God loveth it. Than shulde we
hate sinne like as God hateth it, and love the soule as God loveth it. For this word°
that God said is an endlesse comfort: "I kepe the fulle sekerly." •

40

45

oooooooooooooooooooooooooooooo

The Fourteenth Revelation
THE FORTY-FIRST CHAPTER

After this, oure lorde shewed for prayer, in which shewing I saw two conditions
in our lordes mening. One is rightfulle prayer; /fol. 73v/ another is seker trust.
But yet oftime oure trust is not fulle. For we be not seker• that God hereth us, as we
think for oure unwurthinesse, and for we fele right nought. For we be as bareyne
and as drye oftetimes after oure prayers as we were before. And thus, in oure feling,
oure foly is cause of oure wekenesse. For thus have I felt in° myselfe.

5

[*VIS.* 18.14–19] he teches us to do. For he wille that we be like to him in *anehede* of endeles luffe to oureselfe and to oure evencristen. Na mare than his love es broken to us for
oure sinne, na mare wille he that oure love be broken to oureselfe ne to oure evencristen,
botte nakedlye hate sinne, and endeleslye love the saule as God loves it. /*Rev. 40.43–44*/
For this worde that God saide es ane endelesse comforth: *that "he kepes us* fulle sekerlye." °

[*VIS.* 19.1–16] After this, oure lorde shewed **me** for° prayers. *I sawe two conditions in tham
that prayes, after that I hafe feled in myselfe.* Ane /fol. 109v/ es ‡, **thaye wille nought praye
for nathinge that may be, botte that thinge that es Goddes wille and his wirshippe.
Anothere is that thay sette tham mightelye and continuely to beseke that thinge that es
his wille and his wirshippe. And that es as I hafe understandide be the techinge of haly
kyrke. For in this oure lorde lered me the same: to hafe of Goddes gifte faith, hope, and
charite, and kepe us therein to oure lives ende. And in this we say Pater noster, Ave, and
Crede with devotion, as God wille giffe it. And thus we praye fore alle oure evencristen
and for alle manere of men, that Godes° wille es. For we walde that alle maner of men
and women ware in the same vertu and grace that we awe to desire to oureselfe.**

Botte yit **in alle this** oftimes oure triste is nought fulle. For we ere nought sekare
that God almighty heres us, as us thinke for oure unworthinesse, and fore we fele right
nought. Fore we ere als barayne and als drye oftimes efter oure prayers as we ware
before. And thus, in oure felinge, oure foly es cause of oure waykenesse. For thus hafe I
felede in myselfe.

8 **I am . . . beseking** I am the foundation of your prayer • 9 **sithen** next • 9–10 **and thou besekest it!** and you ask for it! • 11 **in the furst reson** in the first clause of Christ's promise. Analysis of the passage divides it into six "resons" • 12 **in the same wordes** in the words themselves. Because they make clear that prayer has its source in the one who can answer it, God • 13 **there he seyeth** where he says • 14 **mede** reward • 15 **for an unpossible** as an impossible thing • 17–18 **For of alle thing . . . beginning** for our good Lord himself has prescribed for us from eternity all he causes us to ask for • 19–20 **oure beseching . . . goodnesse** God's own goodness, not our asking, is the reason for the goodness and grace he does us. See Hilton, *The Scale* 1.24: "For though it be so that prayer is not the cause for whiche our lord geveth grace, nevertheles it is a weye by the whiche grace frely given cometh to a soule." In other contexts, this formal truth is often ignored in favor of a more immediate and intimate way of conceptualizing prayer. *Pore Caitif* notes comfortably that God "wol heere hise frendis and graunte hem al resonable thing that they asken of him" (92) • 20 **sothfastly** truly • 21 **alle theyse swete wordes** All six "resons" • 21–22 **our good lorde . . . in erth** our good Lord desires that this be known by his earthly lovers. This, it seems, is the most urgent message God wishes to communicate through the fourteenth revelation. For other such declarations of intent, see 40.22–29,

53.7–17. 70.1–9 • 23 **wisely take** wisely understood • 24–25 **Beseching . . . holy gost** intercessory prayer is a true, grace-inspired, enduring act of will on the part of the soul, united and fastened to the will of our Lord by the sweet, secret activity of the Holy Spirit. Both "conditions" of lines 1–2 are involved in this definition, but the emphasis for the rest of the chapter is the examination and categorization of "rightfulle prayer." See *The Chastising*, which divides prayer into four categories, the first two of which involve "beseching," or intercession: first, prayer for the self "for mercy and for grace," as well as whatever special prayers "cometh to youre minde by the gift of God for that time"; second, prayer for friends, enemies, and all others (224) • 26 **he is the furst receivoure** he is the first recipient. Prayers are not dealt with by an angelic bureaucracy. A startling remark, given the wealth of medieval prayers directly addressed to Mary, the orders of angels, and the saints, unless we read "first" as meaning "most important." Compare Chapter 6 and its attack on the use of "meanes" by those praying. In the next passage, prayer is a reification of the good deed that it constitutes on the part of the one praying • 27 **in tresure** in a treasury • 28 **wher it shall never perish** See Matt. 6:20: "Lay up for yourselves treasure in heaven, where neither moth nor rust consumes and where thieves do not break in and steal" • 28 **It is ther . . . holy** it is there before God with all his saints

And all this broughte our lorde sodenly to my minde, and shewed theyse wordes and saide: "I am grounde of thy beseking. Furst it is my wille that thou have it, and sithen I make the to wille it, and sithen I make the to beseke it—and thou besekest it!° How shoulde it than be that thou shuldest not have thy beseking?"° And thus in the furst reson, with the thre that folowe, oure good lorde sheweth a mighty comfort, as it may be sene in the same wordes. And in the fifth° reson /fol. 74r/ — there he seyeth, "and thou besekest° it!"—ther he sheweth full gret plesance and endlesse mede that he wille geve us for oure beseking. And in the sixth reson—there he seyth, "How shuld it than be?"—this was saide for an unpossible.° For it is the most unpossible that may be that we shulde seke mercy and grace and not have it. For of alle thing that oure good lord maketh us to beseke, himselfe hath° ordained it to us from without beginning.

Here may we than see that oure beseching is not cause of the goodnesse and grace that he doeth to us, but his proper goodnesse. And that shewed he sothfastly° in alle theyse swete wordes, ther he seyeth: "I am ground." And our good lorde wille that this be knowen of his lovers in erth. And the more that we know, the more shalle we besech, if it be wisely take. And so is our lordes /fol. 74v/ mening.

Beseching is a trew, gracious,° lesting wille of the soule, oned and fastened into the wille of oure lorde by the swet, prevy werking of the holy gost. Oure lorde himselfe, he is the furst receivoure of our prayer, as to my sight, and he taketh it full thankefully. And, highly enjoyeng, he sendeth it uppe above, and setteth it in tresure wher it shall never perish. It is ther before God with all his holy,° continually

10

15

20

25

[*VIS.* 19.17–33] And alle this brought oure lorde sodaynlye to my minde, **and mightely and lifely, and comfortande me againes this maner of waykenesse in prayers,** ‡ and saide: "I am grounde of thy besekinge. First it is my wille that thowe hafe it, and sene I make the to will it, and sene I make the to beseke it—and thowe beseke it!° Howe shulde it than be that thowe shulde nought hafe thy besekinge?" And thus in the firste reson, with the thre that folows eftere, oure lorde shewed a mighty comfort ‡. And the fifth°— thare he says, "And thowe beseke it!"°—thare he shewes fulle grete plesance and endelese mede that he wille giffe us for oure besekinge. And in the sixth° reson—thare he sais, "Howe shulde it than be **that thowe shulde noght hafe thy besekinge?"—thare he shewes a sobere undertakinge. For we tryste nought als mightelye als we shulde do. Thus wille oure lorde that we bath praye and triste. For the cause of the resones befor-saide is to make us mighty againes waiknesse in oure prayers.**

For it is Goddis wille that we pray, and therto he stirres us in thies wordes befor-saide. For he wille that we be sekere to hafe oure prayere. For prayer pleses God. Prayer pleses man with himselfe, and makes him sobure and meke that beforehand /fol. 110r/ **was in strife and travaile.** /*Rev.* 41.15–42.56/

29 **speding** furthering • 29 **undertake** receive • 30 **a degre of joy** a specific measure of joy. Each prayer adds a specific amount to the soul's reward. Compare the "thre degrees of blisse" described in 14.10–30 • 31 **he loketh therafter** he expects it • 32–33 **like to himselfe . . . in kinde** like him in condition as we are in nature. By nature, humans are the image of God, but the image is partly effaced by the Fall. Prayer restores it. The language here anticipates the opening of Chapter 43 and alludes back to the account of the "godly wille" in 37.14–21 • 33–38 **Pray interly . . . in my sight** Formally, this passage is an analytic paraphrase of Christ's earlier words, written as though spoken by him in the revelation, with only the present tense of "For he seyth thus" to indicate its status. (Compare 36.33–36.) In practice, it reads exactly like part of the revelation. On the need to keep praying, see *The Chastising*: "Though preyer savourith nat at that time [a time "of hevinesse"], it is accepted ful high to God, and turneth paraventure [perhaps] to more mede than though he [the one praying] were visited with likinge and swetnesse" (111) • 33–34 **Pray interly . . . savour the not** Pray wholeheartedly, though it seem to you that it does not give you any sensation of spiritual benefit. "Not" and "nought" both have the sense "nothing" in this passage • 34 **inough** enough • 35–36 **though thou fele . . . might not** even if you feel nothing, even if you see nothing, yes, even if you think you can do nothing. See lines 4–6 • 40 **traveyl** labor • 42 **resonable with discretion** reasonably, with moderation. The need to avoid praying to excess is a topic in Edmund's *Mirror*, which instructs the reader to "make no fors [do not struggle] to multeplien mony *Pater Noster* [to say multiples of the Lord's Prayer]" ("Sevene Preyeres of the Pater Noster," *YW* 1:253), while *The Scale*

similarly counsels against reciting prayers "gredily ne reklesly [carelessly]" (1.27) • 42 **keping oure mightes to him** keeping the powers of our soul directed toward him • 43–44 **in the fifteenth revelation** See 64.11 • 45 **Also to prayer longeth thanking** thankfulness is also part of prayer. The fourth category of prayer according to *The Chastising* (see lines 24–25 and sidenote): "worshippes, heryenges [praises], and thankinges" (225) • 45–47 **Thanking is . . . inwardly** The definition parallels that of "beseching" in lines 24–25 • 46 **drede** awe • 46–47 **turning oureselfe . . . stereth us to** turning us and all the powers of our souls toward the task our Lord stirs us to • 48 **plenteoushede** plentifulness • 51–52 **rehersing . . . goodnes** rehearsing his blessed Passion and his great goodness. A standard remedy for temptation, practiced by Julian herself when under diabolic attack in 69.12–19 • 52 **so the vertu . . . soule** thus the power of our Lord's word (as "rehersed") converts the soul • 53 **entreth by his grace into tru werking** initiates a true work of the soul by God's grace

[CHAPTER 42] 1 **namely** especially • 1–2 **thre thinges . . . oure prayer** These prove to be the basis of the "seker trust" needed for prayer (41.2), the topic of this chapter • 2–3 **by whom . . . springeth** from whom and how our prayer arises • 3 **I am grounde** See 41.8 • 4 **Furst it is my wille** See 41.8 • 5 **use oure prayers** make our prayers useful • 5–6 **oure wille be turned . . . enjoyeng** An allusion to "thy will be done," the most fundamental of all the petitions in the Lord's Prayer, to which all prayer can be reduced • 6–7 **I make the to wille it** See 41.9. The subordination of the listener to the "I" who makes this statement itself implies the purpose of prayer • 8 **oned** united • 8 **althing** everything

received, ever speding oure nedes. And whan we shalle undertake oure blisse, it shall
be geven us for a degre of joy, with endlesse, wurshipfulle thanking of him. 30

Ful glad and mery is oure lord of oure prayer, and he loketh therafter, and he
will have it. For with his grace it maketh us like to himselfe in condetion as we be in
kinde, and so is his blisseful° wille. For he seyth thus: "Pray interly:° thoughe the
thinke it savour the not, /fol. 75r/ yet it is profitable inough, though thou fele it
nought. Pray interly:° though thou fele nought, though thou se nought, yea, though 35
thou think thou might not. For in dryehede• and barrenhede,• in sicknesse and in
febilhede,• than is thy prayer fulle plesant to me, though thou think it saver the not
but litille. And so is all thy living prayer in my sight." For the mede and the endelesse
thanke that he wille geve us therfor, he is covetous to have us prayeng continually in
his sight. God accepteth the good wille and the traveyl of his servantes, howsoever 40
we fele.° Wherfore it pleseth him that we werke in prayer and in good living by his
helpe and his grace, resonable with discretion, keping oure mightes to him till whan
we have him that we seke in fulhede of joy: that is, Jhesu. And that shewed he in the
fifteenth revelation, /fol. 75v/ wher he seyth: "Thou shalt have me to thy mede."

Also to prayer longeth thanking. Thanking is a true, inward knowing, with 45
gret reverence and lovely drede, turning oureselfe with alle oure mightes into the
werking that oure lorde stereth° us to, enjoyeng and thanking inwardly. And
sometime, for plenteoushede,• it breketh out with voice and seyth:° "Good lorde,
grant mercy, blessed mot thou be." And sometime, whan the harte is dry and feleth
nought, or elles by temptation of oure enemy, than it is dreven by reson and by 50
grace to cry upon oure lorde with voice, rehersing his blessed passion and his
gret goodnes. And so the vertu of oure lordes worde turneth into the soule, and
quickeneth the hart, and entreth by his° grace into tru werking, and maketh it to
pray fulle blissefully,• and truly to /fol. 76r/ enjoy in oure lorde. It is a fulle lovely
thanking in his sight. 55

THE FORTY-SECOND CHAPTER

Oure lorde wille that we have tru understanding, and namely in thre thinges
that longeth to oure prayer. The furst is by whom and howe that oure prayer
springeth. By whom, he sheweth whan he seyth, "I am grounde"; and how, by his
goodnesse, for he seyth, "Furst it is my wille." For the seconde: in what maner and
how that we shulde use oure prayers. And that is that oure wille be turned into the 5
wille of oure lorde, enjoyeng. And so meneth he whan he seyth: "I make the to wille
it." For the thurde: that we know the fruit and the ende of oure prayer: that is, to be
oned and like to oure lorde in althing. And to this mening and for this ende was

9 **alle this lovely lesson** The entire revelation. For a similar phrase, see 6.54 • 10 **as he seyth himselfe** In the clause "I make the to wille it" • 11 **For this is oure lordes wille** Begins a discussion (through line 41) of God as "ground" • 11 **that oure prayer . . . alike large** that our prayer and our trust be similarly ample. "Large" can also mean "broad," "generous," or "ambitious." According to *The Mirror*, the phrase "Our Father," as used to open the Lord's Prayer, implies "Certeyn hope to haven [obtain] that we asken; and studefast [steadfast] beleeve in whom that we hopen [in the one we trust]" ("Sevene Preyeres of the Pater Noster," *YW* 1:252). The passage of *A Revelation* that follows explains why "trust" should be "large" • 13 **tary** delay • 13 **paine** trouble • 14 **oure lorde is grounde** See line 3 • 15 **that it is . . . by grace** that prayer is given us by grace. Prayer begins with God, not with the one who prays • 16 **of oure lordes gefte** by the gift of our lord • 17 **tru mening** honest intention • 18 **geven** given • 20 **have not oure asking** have not received what we asked for • 21 **hevy** depressed. See 10.76 • 21 **abide** await • 21–22 **a better time . . . or a beter gifte** In a long account of how to pray and what prevents answer to prayer, *The Holy Boke Gratia Dei* points out that "It es noghte ay beste in prayere to be hert to oure propir will [it is not always the best thing for our prayer to be heard according to our own desire]. . . . God grauntes us noghte ay that we for pray [what we pray for], for he will gife us better then we after yerne [than we yearn for]" (52) • 22–23 **we have . . . being** we have real knowledge in him that he is being • 24–25 **in this grounde . . . oure wonning** upon this ground (of our knowledge of his being) he wants us to make our dwelling place and our home • 27 **making** creation • 28 **derwurthy** precious • 28 **againe-buying** buying back, or redemption • 28–29 **the thirde . . . kepeth it** the third, everything he has made beneath us to serve us and that he protects for our love. The world • 30–31 **I have done . . . prayest me** I have done all this even before you make your prayer. And now you exist, and are praying to me. God's past behavior and achievements are proof of his engagement in and desire to respond to prayer. On the study of God's present and future character by means of his past deeds, see also 33.23–24 • 31 **it longeth to us to wit** it is right for us to know • 31–32 **the grettest dedes . . . techeth** the greatest deeds have already been done, just as holy church teaches • 33 **ow** ought • 33 **the dede . . . doing** the deed that is now being done. The deed through which God's lovers are saved, possibly the deed described in Chapter 36 • 34–35 **therefore he hath done alle** so he has done everything. God is doing as well as being. Recalls the third revelation, the sight of "God in a pointe," in Chapter 11 • 36 **that we se . . . therfore** that we both recognize that God does the deed (see line 33) and pray for it. Begins a passage aimed at reconciling the need to recognize that "oure beseching is not cause of the goodnesse . . . that he doeth to us" (41.19–20) with the need to pray, arguing for their close interrelationship • 36–37 **For that one is not inow** for just one of these is not enough • 38 **doughtfulle** doubtful • 38 **not his wurshippe** not to his honor • 39 **we do not oure det** we do not render our debt. On the nature of the "det" to pray, see *The Holy Boke*: "It es noghte by [it is not the same with] hevenly werke as by other werkes . . . whareto [in which] mane es ofte constreynede [forced] to wyrke againe his will. . . . Bot this werke . . . wil be done with a fredome of spirit. . . . Forthy [therefore] he that will pay God prayer, als to him falles [as it is proper for him to do], offer his prayer to God with a free will and lufand hert" (45–46) • 39–40 **and so may . . . beholding** and in this situation it (what "we se that he doth") cannot be (take place): that is to say, in this situation it is not present in his contemplation. A difficult passage that argues in philosophical terms for the absolute necessity of prayer. Everything seen by God's "foreseing wisdom" (11.6) happens, but this includes our prayers "fore the dede that is now in doing" (line 33), which is integral to the deed itself. As a result, if people want to see what God has foreseen and that he has foreseen it, they must pray for it • 40 **withalle** all the same • 41 **sped** benefited • 42–43 **Althing . . . generalle** Prayer joins with divine foresight and providence in the work of human salvation • 45–47 **prayer is . . . trust** prayer is a just understanding of the fullness of joy that is to come, accompanied by true longing and certain trust. Rewrites the earlier definition of "beseching" in 41.24–25. One of the new elements is "longing," a benign version of the lack that makes those who do not trust "hevy" (line 21)

alle this lovely lesson shewed. And he wille helpe us, and he shalle make /fol. 76v/ it
so, as he seyth himselfe. Blessed mot he be!   10

For this is oure lordes wille: that oure prayer and oure trust be both alike large.
For if we trust not as mekil as we praye, we do not fulle worshippe to oure lorde in
oure prayer, and also we tary and paine oureselfe. And the cause is, as I beleve, for
. we know not truly that oure lorde is grounde in whom that oure prayer springeth.
And also that we know not that it is geven us by grace of his love. For if we knew   15
this, it wolde make us to truste to have, of oure lordes gefte, alle that we desyer. For
I am seker• that no man asketh mercy and grace with tru mening but mercy° and
grace be furst geven to him.

But somtime it cometh to oure minde that we have prayde long time, and yet it
thinketh us that we have not oure asking. But herefore shulde /fol. 77r/ we not be   20
hevy, for I am seker• by oure lordes mening that either we abide a better time, or
more grace, or a beter gifte. He wille that we have true knowing in himselfe that he
is being. And in this knowing, he wille that oure understanding be grounded with
alle oure mightes, and alle oure intent, and alle our mening. And in this grounde, he
wille that we take oure stede and oure wonning.°   25

And by the gracious light of himselfe he wille that we have understanding of
thre thinges that folow. The furst is our noble and excelent making; the seconde,
oure precious and derwurthy againe-buying; the thirde, althing that he hath made
beneth us to serve us and, for oure love, kepeth it. Than meneth he thus, as if he
saide: "Beholde and se that I have done alle this before thy prayer. And now /fol. 77v/   30
thou arte, and prayest me." And thus he meneth that it longeth to us to wit that the
grettest dedes be done, as holy church techeth. And in the beholding of this, with
thanking, we ow to pray fore the dede that is now in doing: and that is that he ruwle
us and gyde us to his wurshippe in this life, and bring us to his blisse. And therefore
he hath done alle.   35

Than meneth he thus: that we se that he doth it, and we pray therfore. For
that one is not inow: for if we pray and se not that he do it, it maketh us hevy and
doughtfulle, and that is not his wurshippe. And if we se that he doth it and we pray
not, we do not oure det,° and so° may it not be: that is to sey, so is it not in his
beholding. But to se that he doeth it and to pray forth withalle, so is he worshipped   40
and we sped.

Althing that oure lorde hath ordained to do, it is his wille that /fol. 78r/ we pray
therfore either in specialle or in generalle. And the joy and the blisse that is to him,
and the thanke and the wurshippe that we shalle have therfore, it passeth the
understanding of all creatures in this life, as to my sight. For prayer is a rightwis   45
understanding of that fulhed of joy that is for to come, with tru longing and seker•

47 **Failing of oure blisse . . . longe** the imperfection (in this life) of the joy for which we are ordained naturally makes us long (for "fulhed of joy") • 47–48 **Trew understonding** See lines 22–24 • 48 **mind in** memory of • 48 **graciously** by the working of grace • 50 **these two werkinges** these two activities of longing and trust • 50–52 **For it is our det . . . diligence thereto** for longing and trust are our duty, and his goodness cannot make us responsible for less than what is proper for us to do, to do work diligently at it. According to *The Holy Boke,* commenting on the statement "[it] behoves mane ever pray and never faile [a person must continually pray and never stop]," prayer is a spiritual equivalent of respiration: "Righte es it by prayere als by draweyng of . . . ayere [prayer is just the same as breathing]" (44) • 53 **do we as we may** let us do what we can • 54–55 **I am grounde** See 41.8 • 55 **with the shewing** with what was revealed about the words • 56 **overcoming against** overcoming of • 56 **doutful dredes** doubting fears. Fears that tell against the "seker trust" (41.2) the chapter enjoins on believers. "Doubtful drede" becomes a major theme in Chapter 74 and its successors

[CHAPTER 43] 1 **oneth** unites • 1–2 **be ever like . . . in kinde and in substance** is always in the likeness of God in its essential nature and substance. The optimistic view of the state of the fallen soul given here forms a bridge between the doctrine of the "godly wille" in 37.14–21 and the full exposition of the doctrine of the soul's substance, which begins in Chapter 45 • 2 **unlike in condetion** unlike God in its actual state • 2–3 **by sinne of mannes perty** because of sin on humanity's side. "Ceesing of sinne and leving to do yvel" is the first "needful thing" in prayer in *Pore Caitif:* "For medicin helith not while the arwhed [arrowhead] is in the fleish" (93) • 3 **Than is prayer . . . will** then prayer is a witness that the soul still wills what God wills. "Thy will be done" (see 42.5–6 and sidenote) is thus the soul's union with God • 4 **ableth man to grace** prepares a person for grace • 5 **beholdeth us in love** perceives us through his love for us • 6 **perteyner** partner. An accomplice in an action or a member of an association • 7 **therfore . . . him to do** for this reason (to make us partners with him) he moves us to pray for what he wants to do • 8 **that we have of his gifte** which we have because he gives them to us • 9 **And thou besekest it!** See 41.9–10 • 10 **so . . . so** such . . . such • 10 **plesance** See 41.13 • 10–11 **as he were mekille beholden to us** as if he were much indebted to us • 11–12 **And for that . . . as if he said** and because we vehemently ask him to do the thing he wants to do, it is as if he were saying. "Mightly" may modify "do" rather than (or as well as) "besech"

trust. Failing of oure blisse° that we be ordained to kindely maketh us to longe. Trew understanding and love, with swete mind° in oure savioure, graciously maketh us to trust. And thus have we of kinde to long and of grace to trust.

And in these two werkinges oure lord beholdeth us continually. For it is our 50 det,° and his goodnes may no lesse assine in us that longeth to us, to do oure diligence thereto. And when we do it, yet shall us thinke that it is nought. And soth° it is, but do we as we may, /fol. 78v/ and mekly aske mercy and grace, and alle that us faileth we shalle it finde in him. And thus meneth he there he seyth: "I am grounde° of thy beseching." And thus in theyse blisseful• wordes, with the shewing, I saw a 55 fulle overcoming against alle oure wekenesse° and alle oure doutful dredes.

THE FORTY-THIRD CHAPTER

Prayer oneth the soule to God. For though the soule be ever like to God in kinde and in substance, restored by grace, it is ofte unlike in condetion, by sinne of mannes perty. Than is prayer a witnesse that the soule wille as God will, and comforteth the conscience, and ableth man to grace. And thus he techeth us to pray and mightily to trust that we shalle have it. For he beholdeth us in love, and 5 wille make us perteyner of his good wille and dede.

And therfore /fol. 79r/ he stereth us to pray that that liketh him to do, for which prayer and good wille, that we have of his gifte, he wille rewarde us and geve us endlesse mede. And this was shewed in this worde: "And thou besekest it!" In this worde, God shewed so gret plesance and so gret liking as he were mekille• 10 beholden° to us for ech good dede that we do. And yet it is he that doth it. And for

---

Prayer anes the saule to God. For though the saule be ever like God in kinde and in substance, ‡ it is oft unlike in condition, thurgh sin of mannes party. *Than makes prayer the saule like unto God when the saule wille as God wille,* **and than es it like to God in condition as it es in kinde.** ‡ And thus he teches us to pray and mightely tryste that we shalle hafe *that we praye fore.* **For alle thinge that es done shulde be done though we never prayed it.** *Botte the luff of God es so mekille that he haldes us partners of his goode deede.*

And therfore he stirres us to praye that him likes to do, for whate prayere or goode wille, that we hafe of his gifte, he wille rewarde us and gife us endelese mede. And this was shewed **me** in this worde: "And thou beseke it!" In this worde, God shewed **me** so grete plesance and so grete likinge as if he ware mekille behaldene to us for ilke goode dede that we do, *alle if it es he that does it.* And for

14 **doen** do • 14 **acorded** reconciled • 16 **we have that we desyer** we have what we desire. The longing that generates prayer in 42.45–47 has now gone. This account of silent contemplative prayer runs to the end of the chapter. Compare *The Scale* 1.32: "The thridde maner of prayer is only in herte withoute speche, by grete reste of the body and of soule." Those who pray in this way "comen into reste of spirit, so that here [their] affectioun is turned into gostly savoure, that they moun neer continuely praye in here herte, and love and praise God" • 16 **what we shulde more pray** anything more we should pray about • 17 **entent** attention • 17 **mightes** powers of the soul • 17 **hole** wholly • 18 **an high, unperceivable prayer** a sublime, imperceptible prayer. A wordless prayer such as that described in detail in *The Cloud*. In that work, only the soul's faculty of love contemplates, the rest falling behind. Here, true to the Trinitarian thinking of *A Revelation*, this form of prayer involves "alle oure mightes," the powers of memory and reason as well as love • 18–19 **alle the cause . . . to whom we pray** the whole reason for which we pray (longing and trust, see 42.45–49) is integrated into the sight and contemplation of him to whom we pray. Even though nothing is asked for in this mode of praying, the fact that it still has a "cause" allows it to be part of the loop between intercessory prayer and divine action described in Chapter 42 • 20 **reverent drede** The emotion felt by Mary at the Annunciation, according to 7.1–8 • 20 **so such** • 21 **but as he stereth . . . time** except insofar as he moves us at the time • 21 **welle I wot** I well know • 21–22 **the more the soule seeth . . . by grace** The fulfillment of desire in this "high, unperceivable prayer" also has the effect of increasing it. One of the doctrines associated with the so-called free-spirit heresy was Marguerite Porete's claim that the free soul "has no will at all," having given up its desire. Condemnation of this doctrine at the Council of Vienne in 1311 obliged writers to make special note of the persistence and growth of desire at all stages of the spiritual life. *The Chastising* devotes an entire chapter to "freedom of spirit," condemning those who "seye [say] that they bien poore in

spirite, bicause they bien withoute wil or desire" (140). In lines 33–34, once again, even though the soul "can do no more but beholde him," contemplation is again firmly said to generate "desyer to be alle oned into him" • 23–24 **for failing . . . to Jhesu** because of our weakness and to prepare ourselves for Jesus. According to *The Chastising*, in its treatment of the "play" of Christ's presence and absence, "in his absence we bien al cold and drye . . . the wreched saule sodanly is chaunged and made ful hevy and ful of sorwe and care" (98) • 24 **tempted, trobled** Feelings associated with "false drede," according to Chapter 74 • 24–25 **lefte to itselfe** See 15.5 • 25 **unrest** distress • 25 **himselfe** itself • 25 **suppul** compliant • 25 **buxom** obedient • 26 **But he . . . suppel to him** but by no kind of prayer does the soul make God compliant to him • 27–28 **I saw that . . . foloweth us** I saw that at whatever time we see a need for which we pray, then our Lord God follows us • 29 **seyeng** seeing • 30 **fulsom** abundant • 31 **fulfilleth all oure mightes** satisfies all the powers of our soul • 32 **overpasseth** transcends • 33 **wene or thinke** imagine or think • 34 **alle oned into him** wholly united with him • 35 **entende to his wonning** give due attention to his dwelling place. That is, to the soul, where the "oning" of God and the self takes place. See 68, 81.9–12 • 36–47 **And thus shalle we . . . the tym** Anticipates death as the final fulfilment of what prayer, in its alternations, can only foreshadow. Since the goal of prayer is contemplative union, the end of this discussion of prayer properly evokes that union. The language of this passage is unusually sensual for *A Revelation*, describing union of God, not with the "mightes" or Trinitarian powers of the soul, but rather with the spiritual senses (see lines 40–43) • 37 **come into him** move into him. The phrase is repeated in line 40 • 37–38 **by many prevy touchinges . . . bere it** by way of many secret inspirations of sweet, spiritual sights and feelings, dealt out to us as our simple natures can bear them. The sensation of God's presence is intermittently part of prayer thoughout life. See Chapter 15 for the revelation's presentation of the intermittency of the divine presence

that we besech him mightly to do that thing that him liketh, as if he said: "What might thou plese me more then to besech mightly, wisely, and wilfully to do that thing that I wille doen?"° And thus the soule by prayer is acorded with God.

But whan oure curtesse lorde of his special grace sheweth himselfe to oure soule, we have that we desyer. And then we se not for the time what we shulde more pray, but all oure /fol. 79v/ entent with alle oure mightes is set hole into the beholding of him. And this is an high, unperceivable prayer, as to my sighte. For alle the cause wherfore we pray is oned° into the sight and the beholding of him to whom we pray, mervelously enjoyeng with reverent drede and so gret swetnesse and delighte in him that we can pray right nought but as he stereth us for the time. And welle I wot, the more the soule seeth of God, the more it° desyereth him by grace.

But whan we se him not so, than fele we nede and cause to praye, for failing and for abling° of oureselfe to Jhesu. For whan a soule is tempted, troblede, and lefte to itselfe° by unrest,° then is it time to praye to make himselfe° suppul and buxom to God. But he° by no manner of prayer maketh God suppel to him. For he is ever alike° in love. And thus I saw that what time we se nede wherfore /fol. 8or/ we praye, then our lord God foloweth us, helping our desire. And whan we of his special grace plainly beholde him, seyeng none other nedes, then we folowe him, and he draweth us into° him by love. For I saw and felt that his mervelous and his fulsom goodnesse fulfilleth all oure mightes. And therwith I saw that his continual werking in alle maner thinges is done so godly, so wisely, and so mightely that it overpasseth alle oure imagining and alle that we can wene or thinke.° And than we can do no more but beholde him, enjoying,° with an high, mighty desyer to be alle oned into him, and entende to his wonning,° and enjoy in his loving, and delighte in his goodnesse.

And thus shalle we, with his swete grace, in our owne meke, continual prayer come into him now in this life by many prevy touchinges of swete, gostly sightes and

15

20

25

30

35

[VIS. 19.44–55] that we beseke *besily* to do that thinge that him likes, as if he saide: "Whate might thowe plese me mare than to bisike *besily,* wisely, and wilfullye to do that thinge that I wille do?"

And thus makes prayere accorde betwix God and mannes saule. **For whate time that mannes saule es hamelye with God, him nedes nought to praye, botte behalde reverent-lye whate he says. For in alle this time that this was shewed me I was noght stirred to praye, botte to hafe allewaye this welle in my minde for comforth:** *that when we see God we hafe that we desire, and than nedes us nought to praye.* /Rev. 43.17–22/ *Botte when we se nought God, than nedes us to pray* for failinge and for habelinge of oureselfe to Jhesu. For when a saule es tempted, trubled, and lefte to itselfe be unreste, than es it time to pray and to make himselfe souple° and boxsom to God. Bot he be na maner of prayer° makes God souple to him. For he is ever ylike in love. /Rev. 43.27–47.12/

39 **so long . . . longing for love** until at long last we die in longing for love. The theme of spiritual love-death, closely associated with Rolle in late medieval England, has already been introduced in 39.19–20 • 40–41 **God fulsomly having** abundantly having God. "Having" is opposite of "longing." The word here clearly has a sexual sense • 41 **had in God** gathered into God • 41–42 **him verely seyeng . . . feling** truly seeing and abundantly feeling him • 43 **swetly swelwing** sweetly swallowing. The image of eating God is Eucharistic • 43 **homely** intimately • 45 **may no man se God and live after** See Exod. 33:20: "Man shall not see me and live" • 46 **aboven the selfe** above the self's own power • 47 **mesureth the shewing** moderates the force of the revelation • 47 **the tym** This should probably be considered the end of the fourteenth revelation, although the manuscripts give no indication of this. Most of what follows between here and the fifteenth revelation, in Chapter 64, is in another, nonnarrative mode and is far from the topics listed under the fourteenth revelation in 1.40–43. The few references to the time of the revelation, such as at 45.12–14 and 50.5–9, are structural, announcing new stages in the argument in the manner of a dialogue. In response to what is taught, Julian raises new difficulties, which then become the topic of succeeding chapters. This is similar to the dialogue format of a work such as *La lumere*

[CHAPTER 44] 1 **God shewed in all the revelations** Marks a shift from analysis of each revelation on its own to synthesis of insights based on different revelations, or all of them together. See 51.63–72 for an account of this mode of analysis. Prayer is no longer the topic, but interest continues to focus on humanity's role in the divine plan. The topic of this chapter is the soul • 1–2 **man werketh . . . stinting** humanity perpetually performs God's will and his honor, lastingly and without ceasing. A claim whose implications are worked out over many chapters • 3 **in the furst** in the first revelation. See 4.26–27: "Also God shewed me in part the wisdom and the truth of her soule." *A Revelation* now returns to this passage and finds new insights there • 3 **grounde** place • 4–5 **by truth and wisedom** in relation to Mary's truth and wisdom • 5 **how** how this "werking" was showed • 6–17 **Truth seeth . . . endlesly kepeth him** With this important exposition of humanity's creation in the image of God (see Gen. 1:27) compare *The Scale* 1.43, here telling of Adam's soul before the fall: "The soule of a man is a liyf, made of thre mightes, minde, resoun, and wille, to the image and the likenes of the blissid holy trinite: holy, perfight, and rightwise. . . . So that a mannes soule, whiche may be callid a mad [created] trinite, was fulfillid in minde, sight, and love, of the unmad [uncreated] blissid trinite, whiche is oure

lord" • 6 **Truth seeth . . . wisdom beholdeth** The distinction here is between "truth" as awareness and assent and "wisdom" as spiritual contemplation • 6–7 **of theyse two . . . thurde** the third quality (love) comes from these two • 7–8 **Where truth . . . there is love** where there is truth and wisdom, truly there is love. Love is not mentioned in Chapter 4's account of Mary's soul, but is said to be implicit there • 8 **coming of them both** As the Holy Spirit proceeds from the Father and the Son in Western Trinitarian theology, Mary's soul as seen in the first revelation thus affirms the Trinitarian affinity between humankind and God • 9 **endlesse sovereyne truth** eternal absolute truth • 10 **unmade** uncreated • 10 **a creature in God** a created being dwelling in God • 10–11 **which hath . . . made** which has in created form the same trinity of characteristics as God • 11 **evermore . . . made for** The chapter's central claim, explored and justified in many succeeding chapters. Having been introduced as a revelation of the Trinitarian structure of the soul, the perfect truth, wisdom, and love displayed by Mary at the Annunciation here evolves into a revelation of the soul's continuing perfection. The rest of the chapter is full of echoes of the first revelation, in which language originally applied to Mary is reapplied to the "creature," that is, to "mans soule" • 12 **Wherfore** for which reason. Because of the reciprocity between God and humankind • 13–14 **in which merveling . . . of him** Further echoes of 4.28 and 7.3–6 • 14–15 **that unnethes . . . to the selfe** that the creature scarcely seems of any value to itself • 15 **clernesse** clarity • 15 **clennesse** purity • 16 **beknowen** recognize • 16 **he is made for love** he is made because of love. See 6.33–35, 8.14–15

[CHAPTER 45] 1 **demeth us upon** judges us according to. "Deme" is a legal word, applied to the judgment of the soul at death in 8.26. "Dome," from which derives "domesday," Judgment day, is the noun. The distinction made here between the "domes" of God and those of humankind, on the basis of Chapter 44's account of the soul of Mary, is fundamental to the argument of Chapters 45–63 • 1 **kindely substance** created substance or essential part of the soul: the trinitarian structure described in Chapter 44. The term begins to be closely defined only in Chapter 53, then dominates *A Revelation* through Chapter 63 • 1 **which is ever kepte one in him** which is always kept united in him. An unusual claim for the integrity of part of the soul. See the account of the "godly wille" in 37.14–21 • 2 **this dome is of his rightfulhede** this judgment proceeds from his justice. God has no need to treat the sinless substance of the soul with mercy • 2–3 **man demeth** humankind judges itself

felinges, mesured to us as oure simpilhed may /fol. 80v/ bere it. And this is wrought
and shall be by the grace of the holy gost, so long till we shall die in longing for love.
And than shall we alle come into oure lorde, oureselfe clerely knowing and God   40
fulsomly having; and we endlesly be alle had° in God, him° verely seyeng and
fulsomly feling, and him gostely hering, and him delectably smelling, and him
swetly swelwing. And than° shall we se God face to face, homely and fulsomly. The
creature that is made shall see and endlesly beholde God which is the maker. For
thus may no man se God and live after, that is to sey, in this dedely life. But whan he   45
of his special grace will shewe him here, he strengtheth the creature aboven the selfe,
and he mesureth the shewing after his awne wille, as° it is profitable for the tym.

THE FORTY-FOURTH CHAPTER

God shewed in all the revelations oftetimes that man werketh evermore his
wille and his wurshippe, /fol. 81r/ lastingly° without stinting. And what this
werking is was shewed in the furst—and that in a mervelous grounde, for it was
shewed in the werking of the blisseful• soule of our lady Sent Mary, by truth and
wisedom. And how, I hope, by the grace of the holy gost, I shall sey as I saw.   5
   Truth seeth God, and wisdom beholdeth God. And of theyse two cometh the
thurde, and that is a mervelous, holy delight° in God, which is love. Where truth
and wisedom is, verely there is love, verely coming of them both, and alle of Goddes
making. For God is endlesse sovereyne truth, endelesse sovereyne wisdom, endelesse
sovereyne love unmade. And mans° soule is a creature in God, which hath the same   10
propertes made, and evermore it doeth that it was made for: it seeth God, and it
beholdeth God, and it loveth God. Wherfore God enjoyeth in the creature and the
creature in God, endelesly merveling, in /fol. 81v/ which merveling he seeth his God,
his lorde, his maker, so hye, so gret, and so good in regard of him that is made, that
unnethes the creature semeth ought to the selfe. But the clernesse and clennesse° of   15
truth and wisedome maketh him to see and to beknowen° that he is made for love,
in which love God endlesly kepeth him.

THE FORTY-FIFTH CHAPTER

God demeth us upon oure kindely substance, which is ever kepte one in him,
hole and safe without ende, and this dome is of his rightfulhede. And man

3 **changeable sensualite** inconstant sensual nature. Humanity's fallen nature, the self experienced in daily living, compounded of body and soul. See Chapters 55–63, where the term comes into its own, and compare the "bestely wille" of 37.15. Hilton describes the fallen soul as an inversion of its unfallen self: as a result of Adam's fall "thou also lostest it [Adam's "worshipe and dignite"] in him and fell from that blissid trinite into a foule merk [murky] wrecchid trinite: that is, into forgetinge of God and unknowinge of him, and into beestly [bestial] likinge of thisilf" (*The Scale* 1.43). Chapters 45–63 of *A Revelation* are a determined attempt to reconcile this picture with the revelation's insistence on the continuing existence and deeper reality of the soul in its unfallen state, as described in Chapter 44 • 3 **which semeth now one and now another** which seems at one time one way and then another way. "One" also means "united," as in line 1 • 4 **after that it taketh . . . outward** depending on which of its parts it draws from and shows outwardly. Sometimes the soul seems to itself "godly," sometimes "bestely." In Flete's *Remedy,* the "bestely" part of the soul is identified with the "sensualite, the whiche is ever inclininge downwarde to sinne" (chap. 5, *YW* 2:114; see *Rev.* 37.14–17). Here, the "sensualite" is a more ambiguous, and more positive, aspect of the soul • 4–5 **And this dome is medeled . . . grevous** and this human self-judgment is mixed, for sometimes it is good and comforting, and sometimes it is harsh and terrible • 5–6 **in as mekille** inasmuch • 6 **it longeth to the rightfulhede** it participates in divine justice • 8 **thorow** through • 9 **acorded** harmonized • 9 **yet it shall be knowen, both** yet both of them will be known. See 38.1–9, where human sin "is made knowen without end" in heaven "by overpassing worshipes" • 11–12 **that is of his . . . love** that proceeds from his own sublime, endless love • 13 **in which I saw . . . blame** See 39.29–30: God "beholdeth sinne as sorow and paines to his lovers, in whom he assigneth no blame for love." See also 27.28–30, where the phrase "no maner of blame" picks up the rhythm and vocabulary of "alle maner of thing" • 13–14 **though this . . . not be fulle esed** As in 29.1–3 ("A, good lorde, how might alle be wele?"), Julian's perplexi-

ties push the argument on • 14 **only in the beholding of this** in the contemplation of this alone • 15 **for the dome of holy church** because of the judgment of holy church. A "dome" that follows and reinforces the "medeled" judgment of the "changeable sensualite" described in lines 2–10 • 16 **continually in my sight** As stated earlier, in 9.18–21 • 16 **by this dome** according to this judgment • 16–17 **methought that me . . . to know** it seemed to me that I must recognize • 18–19 **sinners . . . see in God** Anticipates the argument of 46.24–31 • 18 **be sometime wurthy blame** sometimes deserve blame • 20–21 **higher dome . . . lower dome** A formulation in which the church's teaching on sin is clearly subordinated to that of the revelation • 22 **by no weye leve** by no means abandon • 23–24 **that I might se . . . sight** that I be able to see in God the sense in which what holy church teaches about sin and guilt is true in God's sight • 25 **ware** would be • 26 **I ne had no nother** I never had any other. In Middle English, extra negatives mean extra force. Here are three. Much hangs on the "mervelous example of a lorde and of a servant" • 27 **as I shall sey after** See Chapter 51 • 27 **mistely** obscurely • 28 **yet I stond in desyer** still I remain in desire. All of life becomes a process of discerning how God's judgment and that of the church apply to the self • 29 **know theyse . . . to me** understand what is relevant to me about these two ways of judging • 34 **therto** for that • 35 **sithen** since

[CHAPTER 46] 1–12 **But oure passing . . . joy** From Chapter 45's account of the "domes" follows this first account of the separation between substance and sensuality, which is a vital part of *A Revelation*'s model of the soul. The theme of self-knowledge, an important feature of many contemplative programs, is given more extended treatment in Chapter 56 • 1 **oure passing living** our mortal selfhood • 1 **in oure sensualite** in the sensual part of our soul. The only part of the soul to which everyday consciousness has access • 1–2 **what oureselfe is** what we are in ourselves • 2 **but in our faith** except through our faith. Only faith can glimpse the purity that belongs to the soul's substance

demeth upon oure changeable sensualite, which semeth now one and now another, after that it taketh of the parties and sheweth° outward. And this dome is medeled, for somtime it is good and esy, and somtime it is hard and grevous. And in as mekille° as it is good and esy, it longeth to the rightfulhede.° And in as /fol. 82r/ mekille° as it is hard and grevous, oure good lorde Jhesu reformeth it by mercy and grace thorow vertu of his blessed passion, and so bringeth into the rightfulhede.° And though these two be thus acorded and oned, yet it shall be knowen, both, in heven without ende.

The furst dome, which is of Goddes rightfulhede,° and that is of his owne high, endlesse love—and that is that fair, swete dome that was shewed in alle the fair revelation, in which I saw him assigne° to us no maner of blame. And though this was° swete and delectable, yet only in the beholding of this I culde not be fulle esed. And that was for the dome of holy church, which I had before understonde° and was continually in my sight. And therfore, by this dome, methought that me behoveth nedes to know myselfe a sinner. And by the same dome I understode /fol. 82v/ that sinners be sometime wurthy blame and wrath, and theyse two culde I not see in God. And therfore my advice and desyer was more than I can or may telle. For the higher dome God shewed himselfe in the same time, and therfore me° behoved nedes to take it. And the lower dome was lerned me before time in holy churche, and therfore I might not by no weye leve the lower dome. Then was this my desyer: that I might se in God in what manner that the dome of holy church herein techeth° is tru in his sight, and howe it longeth to me sothly° to know it, whereby they might both be saved, so as it ware wurshipfulle to God and right wey° to me. And to alle this I ne had no nother answere but a mervelous example of a lorde and of a servant, as I shall sey after, and that full mistely shewed.

And yet I stond° in desyer, and wille into my /fol. 83r/ lives ende, that I might by grace know theyse two domes as it longeth to me. For alle hevenly thinges and alle erthely thinges that long to heven be comprehended in theyse two domes. And the more knowing and understonding by the gracious leding of the holy gost that we have of these two domes, the more we shalle see and know oure failinges.° And ever the more that we see them, the more kindly by grace we shall long to be fulfilled of endlesse joy and blisse, for we be made therto. And oure kindely substance is now blisseful° in God, and hath bene sithen it was made, and shalle be withoute ende.

THE FORTY-SIXTH CHAPTER

But oure passing living that we have here in oure sensualite knoweth not what oureselfe is but in our faith. And when we know and see, verely and clerely, what /fol. 83v/ oureselfe is, than shalle we verely and clerly see and know oure lorde

4 it behoveth nedes to be it has to be • **5 the more we shall long** See 42.45–49 • **6 knowing of oureselfe** *Nosce teipsum*, know thyself, means entirely different things in medieval contemplative writing. *Rev.* 45.15–17 records Julian's obligation, according to the "dome of holy church," to "know myselfe a sinner." Here, however, the emphasis falls on knowing the soul in its ideal, unfallen, or "substantial" state, as a means of finally attaining God. Compare Edmund's *Mirror:* "Forthy [that] he is threo persones and o God [three persons and one God], the selve may every mon sen in himself [everyone may recognize the same truth within himself]," by contemplating the trinitarian powers of the soul. "Such manere of knowing is foundement [the basis] of contemplation," on which is eventually built knowledge of "God . . . in his oune kinde" ("Contemplation of God and of His Deite," *YW* 1:259) • **6–7 oure high kind** our sublime nature. The substance, already called the "kindely substance," 45.1 • **7 encrese and wax** increase and grow • **7 forthering and speding** assistance and helping • **8 we may never . . . last point** we may never fully know ourselves until the last moment. For the "last point" as the moment of death, see 21.14 • **10 it longeth properly to us** it is proper for us • **13 fro the beginning to the ende** from the beginning of the revelation to the end • **15 For of this was all the shewing** for the entire revelation partook of this • **17 wilfully having in use** consciously living by. See 9.18–20: "the faith of holy church . . . willefully kept in use and in custome" • **17–18 cam not from me** did not leave me • **18 therfro** from it • **19 wherby** by doing which • **20 hyer** higher • **20–21 in alle this beholding** in all this contemplation. Of holy church's teaching • **21 methought it behoved nedes** it seemed necessary to me • **24–25 And notwithstonding . . . shall** and despite all this, I saw truly that our Lord was never angry and never will be. This important claim is developed over several chapters, to the end of Chapter 49. In one sense, the claim is a theological commonplace. As Chapter 31 explains, God does not experience desires or passions. However, divine anger is an omnipresent image in medieval depictions of the Last Judgment and

other areas of pastoral theology. *The Pricke* devotes many lines to "the wrethe of the lamb" at the Judgment (5060–108), basing its account on the irreproachable authority of the Books of Revelation and Job. In his Epistle to the Romans Paul, too, writes that "the wrath of God is revealed from heaven against all ungodliness and wickedness of men" (1:18), associating that wrath with the inexorable demands of divine law • **26 might . . . wisdom . . . charite . . . unite** The qualities that define God as Father, Son, Holy Spirit, and godhead • **27 against the properte of his might** inconsistent with the quality of his power • **29 not but goodnes** nothing except goodness. Seen as a fundamental quality of God from the first revelation on. See Chapter 6 • **31 fulsomly** abundantly • **32 right nought** nothing at all • **32–41 And to this understanding . . . oweth** A passage of justification for continuing to explore a "hye marveyle" (lines 40–41) • **34 That it is thus** that this is so. That God is not angry and that the soul and God are "fulsomly oned" • **35 he wille we desyer to wit** he wants us to desire to know it • **35–36 as it longeth . . . to witte it** so far as it is proper to a created being to know it. Chapter 45 has insisted that the creature needs also to know the "lower dome" of the church, in which the fiction of divine anger plays an important part. It is thus structural to "the faith" that the "higher dome" described here be known only in part • **36 simple soule** Julian herself (see 2.1), who had understood the revelation of the "two domes" only in part and still "stond[s] in desyer," to "know theyse two domes as it longeth to me" (45.28–29) • **37–38 For those thinges . . . love** for he himself, out of love, powerfully and wisely conceals those things he wants to keep secret. See 33.27–29, which enjoins readers to be "welle apaide both with hiding and shewing" • **38–39 moch privete is hid** many secrets are hid. Both kept out of the showing and concealed within it. See 51.61–62: "every shewing is full of privites" • **40 apaide** satisfied • **40 abiding** waiting for • **41 my moder holy church** my mother, holy church. A common image of the church, later linked to the image of Jesus as mother (Chapers 58–62) • **41 oweth** ought to do

God in fulhed of joye. And therfore it behoveth nedes to be that the nerer we be
oure blisse, the more we shall long, and that both by kinde and by grace. We may   5
have knowing of oureselfe in this life by continuant helpe and vertu of oure high
kind, in which knowing we may encrese and wax by forthering and speding of
mercy and grace. But we may never fulle know oureselfe into the last point, in which
pointe this passing life and alle manner of wo and paine shalle have ane ende. And
therfore it longeth properly to us, both by kinde and by grace, to long and desyer   10
with alle oure mightes to know oureselfe, in which full knowing we shall verely and
clerely know oure God in fulhede of endlesse joy.

  And yet in alle this time, fro the beginning /fol. 84r/ to the ende, I had two
manner of beholdinges. That one was endlesse continuant love with sekernesse•
of keping and blissful salvation. For of this was all the shewing. That other was the   15
comen teching of holy church, of which I was befor enformed and grounded and
wilfully having in use and in understonding. And the beholding of this cam not from
me. For by the shewing I was not stered nor led therfro in no manner point, but I had
therin teching to love it and like it, wherby I might, with the helpe of oure lorde and
his grace, encrese and rise to more hevenly knowing and hyer loving. And thus, in   20
alle this beholding, methought it behoved nedes to se and to know that we be sinners
and do many evilles that we oughte to leve, and leve many good dedes undone that
we oughte to do, wherfore we deserve paine, blame, and /fol. 84v/ wrath.

  And notwithstonding alle this, I saw sothfastly° that oure lorde was never wroth
nor never shall. For he is God, he is good, he is truth, he is love, he is pees. And° his   25
might, his wisdom, his charite, and his unite suffereth him not to be wroth. For I
saw truly that it is against the properte of his might to be wroth, and against the
properte of his wisdom, and against the properte of his goodnes. God is that
goodnesse that may not be wroth, for God is not but goodnes. Oure soule is oned to
him, unchangeable goodnesse. And betwen God and oure soule is neither wrath nor   30
forgevenesse in his sight. For oure soule is so fulsomly oned to God of his owne
goodnesse that betwene God and oure soule may be right nought. And to this
understonding was the soule led by love and drawen by might in every shewing.
That it is thus, oure /fol. 85r/ good lorde shewed. And how it is thus: sothly,° of his
gret goodnesse. And that he wille we desyer to wit: that is to sey, as it longeth to his   35
creature to witte it. For all thing that the simple soule understode, God will that it be
shewed and knowen. For those thinges that he wille have prevy, mightely and wisely
himselfe hideth them for love. For I saw in the same shewing that moch privete is
hid which may never be knowen into the time that God of his goodnes hath made
us wurthy to se it. And therwith I am well apaide, abiding oure lords wille in this hye   40
marveyle. And now I yelde me to my moder holy church, as a simpil childe oweth.

[CHAPTER 47] 1 **Two pointes longe . . . by det** two things are proper for our soul to do as a matter of obligation. See the account of prayer as "det" in 42.38–41, 50–52 • 1–2 **One is . . . meekly suffer** one is that we marvel with reverence. The other is that we endure with humility. The proper attitude toward divine "privete," demonstrated at the end of Chapter 46, in Julian's "abiding" of "oure lords wille in this hye marveyle," the marvel of his lack of anger. Yet again, the language recalls Mary at the Annunciation in 4.28–29 and 32–33, in her "marvayling with great reverence" and her saying "full meekely to Gabriel: 'Lo me here, Gods handmaiden'" • 4–5 **notwithstonding . . . God** Announces a new topic arising out of the claim that God is never angry. If God is not "wroth," how can he forgive? This topic, in combination with what at first seems the unrelated topic of Julian's responses to this moment of revelation, persists through Chapter 49 • 6 **should be . . . his wrath** was going to be the forgiveness of his anger. The popular poem *Pety Job* (the little book of Job) succinctly exemplifies this belief. The speaker asks, "Who to me may yeve [give] or graunte / For love or any affectione / Fro thy wrathe that is duraunte / I may have protectione? [that I may have protection from your lasting anger]," and answers, "But woldes thou, lorde, me unbinde, / Thorough the vertu [powers] of thy pite, / Thanne were I gladde and light as linde [linden leaf] / To have *parce michi domine* [to have attained this answer to "spare me, Lord"]" ("Quis michi hoc tribuat?" *YW* 2:385) • 7 **mening** intention • 8 **I toke that** I supposed that. Before receiving the revelation • 9 **principal pointes** main aspects • 10 **for noughte . . . this point** I could not see this aspect of forgiveness for anything that I could contemplate or long

for • 11 **the working of mercy** See 35.32–34 • 11 **I shall sey somdele** I shall somewhat describe. Analysis of mercy takes until the end of Chapter 49, although the language with which it opens also anticipates the exemplum of the lord and the servant in Chapter 51 • 13 **changeabil** The main characteristic of the "sensualite" according to 45.3 • 14 **uncunning** ignorance • 14 **unmighty and unwise** powerless and foolish • 14–15 **his will is overlaide** his will is occluded. All the trinity of the soul's "mightes" are corrupted by sin • 15 **in tempest** in turmoil • 17 **serveth to sinne** inclines one to sin • 18–30 **Thus saw I . . . not gretly painful** The most extensive account of Julian's immediate responses to her experience in *A Revelation*. The passage describes how, during the revelation itself, her understanding of the truth about divine anger and mercy was so "lowe and smalle" (line 20) as to evoke an ambigous reaction, albeit a reaction kept from complete confusion by "seker hope of his merciful keping" (line 29). Even in her most exalted state, Julian, bound to her "sensualite," needs the assurance of divine mercy. *What* mercy is thus matters less than *that* mercy is • 18–19 **the sight and the feling** Of God in the revelation • 19 **in regarde that** in comparison to how • 21 **I felt in me . . . werkinges** in the revelation I felt in myself five kinds of response • 22 **seker hope** certain hope • 24 **failing** failure. Personal weakness or the intermittent quality of the revelation • 26–27 **that that sight shulde faile** that the revelation would end • 27 **I to be lefte to myselfe** The certainty of this happening is made clear in the seventh revelation, where periods of "gostely likinge" alternate with times when "I was turned and left to myselfe" • 28 **the blisse** heaven • 29 **joying** rejoicing

THE FORTY-SEVENTH CHAPTER

Two pointes longe° to our soule by det. One is that we reverently marveyle. That other is that we meekly suffer, ever enjoyeng /*fol. 85v*/ in God. For he will that we witte° that we shalle in short time se clerely in himselfe all that we desyer.

And notwithstonding all this, I behelde and merveyled gretly what is the mercy and forgevenesse of God. For by the teching that I had before, I understode that the mercy of God should° be forgevenesse of his wrath after the time that we have sinned. For methought that, to a soule whose mening and desyer is to love, that the wrath of God were harder than ony other paine. And therfore I toke that the forgevenesse of his wrath shulde be one of the principal pointes of his mercy. But for noughte° that I might beholde and desyer, I culde not see this point in all the shewing. But how I saw and understode of the working of mercy I shall sey somdele, as God will give me grace.

I understode thus: Man is changeabil in this life, and by frailte /*fol. 86r*/ and uncunning° falleth into sinne. He is unmighty and unwise of himselfe, and also his will is overlaide in this time. He is in tempest and in sorow and woe. And the cause is blindhede,• for he seeth not God. For if he saw God continually, he shulde have no mischevous feling, ne no maner stering no sorowing that serveth to sinne.

Thus saw I and felt in the same time. And methought that the sight and the feling was hye and plentuous and gracious, in regarde that oure commun feling is in this life. But yet methought it was but lowe and smalle, in regard of the gret desyer that the soule hath to se God. For I felt in me five maner of werkinges, which be theyse: enjoyeng, morning, desyer, drede, and seker• hope. Enjoyeng: for God gave me knowing and understonding that it was himselfe that I sawe. Morning: /*fol. 86v*/ and that was for failing.° Desyer: that was that I might se him ever more and more, understonding and knowing that we shalle never have fulle rest tille we se him, clerly and verely, in heven. Drede was for it semed to me, in alle that time, that that° sight shulde faile, and I to be lefte to myselfe. Seker• hope was in the endlesse love that I saw: that I shulde be kepte, by his mercy, and brought to the blisse. And the joying in his sight, with this seker• hope of his merciful keping, made me to have feling and comfort, so that morning and drede were not gretly painful.

5

10

15

20

25

30

[VIS. 19.56–59] *Botte in the time that man is in sinne, he is so unmightye, so unwise, and so unluffande that he can nought love God ne himselfe. ‡ The maste mischefe that he hase es blindnesse, for he sees nought alle this.* /*Rev. 47.16–30*/ **Than the hale luffe of God allemighty, that ever is ane, giffes him sight** /*fol. 110v*/ **to himselfe.**

[VIS. 19.67–68] **And thus with prayers as I hafe before saide, and with othere goode werkes that ere °custumabille° be the techinge of haly kyrke, is the saule aned to God.** /*Rev. 48–63*/

34 **anon we falle into oureselfe** after a bit we fall back into ourselves. See 66.1–11, where this comes to pass • 35 **contrariousnes** opposition or perversity. Anticipates the word's emergence into prominence in Chapter 48 • 35 **that of the olde rote ... sinne** that perversity emerging out of the ancient root of our original sin. Original sin is often imaged either as the root of a great tree or as the source of a great river. Elsewhere in *A Revelation*, as in 49.3–4, it is always love that is the "rote" • 36 **all that foloweth ... continuance** all the sin that follows from it of our own continuing activity • 36–37 **we be traveyled and tempested** we are belabored and agitated. Anticipates the last moment of revelation proper, in 68.55–57, where Christ does not say, "Thou shalt not be tempestid, thou shalt not be traveyled," but says instead, "Thou shalt not be overcom." "Traveyle" and "tempest" are permanent features of life

[CHAPTER 48] 1 **which is endlesse life ... soule** who is eternal life dwelling in our soul • 2 **therin** in the soul • 3 **buxom** obedient • 3 **accordeth it to God** reconciles it with God. As does prayer in 43.14 • 3 **this is the mercy** this is the activity of mercy. Mercy, then, is not the "forgevenesse of his wrath" (47.9) but the Holy Spirit's care of the "sensualite" • 5 **I saw no wrath ... perty** I saw no anger except on humanity's part. A statement that begins the chapter's restatement of the doctrine of divine forgiveness • 6–7 **a frowerdnes ... to love** a rebelliousness and an opposition to peace and to love • 8 **in oure party** on our own part • 9 **continuant contrariousnes** enduring opposition. "Contrariousnes" is a more serious condition than the "changeable" nature of

the sensuality (45.3), operating as a principle of perversity whose origin is the "olde rote of oure furst sinne" (47.35) • 10 **that shewed he ... pitte** This "chere" (expression) is described in 28.28–30, 71.8–10 • 10 **ruth** compassion • 11 **keping** protection • 12 **of the properte of mercy** with respect to the property of mercy • 13 **all one in love** wholly unified in love. Mercy is an aspect, not of the "forgevenesse of his wrath" (47.6), but of love. Forgiveness thus becomes a somewhat problematic category • 14–15 **medled with plentuous pitte** mixed with plentiful pity • 16 **by mesure** up to a limit • 17 **in as moch ... in so mekille** to the extent ... to the same extent • 19 **shamful** shameful • 21 **departeth never from us** never separates itself from us • 22 **ceseth** ceases • 23 **the properte of grace** the quality of grace. With "forgiveness" at this point a term in search of a satisfactory definition, "grace" enters the discussion as a better synonym for "mercy," one better able to account for its activities • 23 **which have ... one love** which have two varieties of activity as parts of the same love. Alludes to the doctrine of the "hypostatic union" of divine and human in Christ, implying an analogy with the relation between grace and mercy • 24 **pitteful** compassionate • 24 **longeth to moderhode** pertains to motherhood • 25 **longeth to ryal lordshippe** pertains to royal lordship • 26 **keping ... heling** protecting, tolerating, enlivening, healing. The acts of a mother, according to Chapters 58–62, which this passage anticipates. Also the acts of Christ during his years on earth • 27 **raising** resurrecting • 27–28 **endlessly overpassing ... deserveth** eternally transcending what our loving and our labor deserves

And yet in all this I behelde in the shewing of God that this maner sight of him may not be continuant in this life, and that for his owne wurshippe and for encrese of oure endlesse joy. And therfore we faile oftimes of the sight of him, /fol. 87r/ and anon we falle into oureselfe, and than finde we no° feling of right nought but the contrariousnes° that is in oureselfe, and that of the olde rote of oure furst sinne with all that foloweth of oure owne continuance. And in this we be traveyled and tempested° with feling of sinne and of paine in many diverse maner, gostely and bodely, as it is knowen to us in this life.

THE FORTY-EIGHTH CHAPTER

But oure good lorde the holy gost, which is endlesse life wonning° in oure soule, full sekerly• kepeth us, and werketh therin a pees, and bringeth it to ees by grace, and maketh it buxom, and accordeth it to God. And this is the mercy and the wey that oure good lord continually ledeth us in, as longe as we be in this life which is changeable. For I saw no wrath but on mannes perty, /fol. 87v/ and that forgeveth he in us. For wrath is not elles but a frowerdnes and a contrariousnes to pees and to love. And either it cometh of failing of might, or of° failing of wisdom, or of failing of goodnesse, which failing is not in God, but it is in oure party. For we by sinne and wrechednesse have in us a wrath and a continuant contrariousnes to pees and to love, and that shewed he full ofte in his lovely chere of ruth and pitte. For the ground of mercy is in love, and the werking of mercy is oure keping in love. And this was shewed in such a manner that I culde not perceive of the properte of mercy otherwise but as it were all one in love.°

That is to sey, as to my sight: mercy is a swete, gracious werking in love, medled /fol. 88r/ with plentuous pitte. For mercy werketh, us keping, and mercy werketh, turning to us all thing to good. Mercy for love suffereth us to faile by mesure. And in as moch as we faile, in so mekille• we falle, and in as mekille• as we falle, in so mekille• we die. For us behoveth nedes to die in as moch as we faile sighte and feling of God that is oure life. Oure failing is dredfulle, oure falling is shamful, and oure dying is sorowful.

But yet in all this the swet eye of pitte and of love deperteth never from us, ne the werking of mercy ceseth not. For I behelde the properte of mercy, and I behelde the properte of grace, which have two maner of working in one love. Mercy is a pitteful properte, which longeth to moderhode in tender love. And grace is a wurshipful properte, /fol. 88v/ which longeth to ryal lordshippe in the same love. Mercy werketh—keping, suffering, quicking, and heling—and alle is of tendernesse of love. And grace werketh with mercy: raising, rewarding (endlesly overpassing that

28–29 **spreding abrode . . . lordshippe** disseminating and revealing the sublime, plentiful generosity of God's royal lordship. The works of mercy, the mother, focus on the soul. Although those of grace, the lord, are about the Lord's own worship, they too work with mercy in order to save the soul • 30 **habundance** abundance • 30 **grace werketh . . . failing** grace transforms our fearful failure. See lines 19–20 • 33–35 **For I saw . . . overpassing** Compare the "deed" in which "I shalle do right nought but sinne," 36.4 • 35 **blisse overpassing** transcendent joy • 35 **so ferforth that** to such an extent that • 39–40 **me behoved nedes to grant** it was necessary for me to grant. The phrase is used in a similar context, summing up a controversial piece of argumentation, in 11.14–15: "Wherfore me behoved nedes to grant that alle thinges that is done is welle done, for our lord God doth all" • 40–41 **mercy . . . is to slake and waste oure wrath** mercy . . . exists in order to assuage and lay waste our anger. Rather than God's, as the sinful soul is said to believe in 40.1–7, turning to "amending of oureselfe with alle oure mightes, to slake the wrath of God." The temporary paradox on which the chapter ends is thus that the only thing God has to forgive is humanity's inability to forgive itself

[CHAPTER 49] 1–2 **continuantly shewed in alle** revealed constantly in all the revelations • 2 **with gret diligence beholden** contemplated with great diligence • 2–3 **God . . . may not forgeve** God, with respect to himself, cannot forgive. Drives home the point of the paradox that ends Chapter 48. The careful separation of the concept of mercy from the concept of divine anger during the course of Chapters 47–48 can now be seen to have rendered the idea of divine forgiveness obselete • 3 **for he may not be wroth** since he cannot be angry. See 46.24–31 • 5–7 **to the soule . . . wrath** for the soul who

by God's special grace sees deeply enough into the high, wonderful goodness of God, and sees that we are eternally kept one with him in love, it is the greatest impossibility that can be that God could be angry. A more forceful restatement of the earlier statements on anger, from Chapter 46 on, which leads in turn to an analysis of the concept of "wrath" • 8 **frenshippe** friendship. See 14.2–9 • 8 **two contraries** 72.3 quotes a scientific adage to the effect that "two contrares [shalle] not be togeder in one stede [two opposites cannot coincide in a single place]" • 9–10 **it behoveth nedes to be that** it must be the case that • 10 **contrariouse to** in opposition to • 11 **where oure lorde apereth** where our Lord appears. In the world, the revelation, and this account of it • 11 **pees is taken** peace is established or understood. An allusion to Jesus' resurrection appearances in John 20:19, 26, where he says "Peace be with you": words that are also spoken by the priest at Mass, after he has pronounced the absolution of sins. In the rest of the chapter, peace, rather than forgiveness, becomes the proper antonym for wrath, and the term that most properly describes God • 11 **wrath hath no stede** anger has no home • 13 **if God might be wroth a touch** if God could be angry even for a bit • 14–15 **For as verely . . . also verely** for as truly . . . so truly • 15 **we have oure keping** As is made alarmingly clear in the Middle English poem *Cleanness*, creation's existence is dependent on the stability of God's character. This passage alludes to the "hazelnut" revelation in Chapter 5: "It lasteth and ever shall, for God loveth it. And so hath all thing being by the love of God" (5.12–13) • 17 **wrath, debate, and strife** The reverse of "might . . . wisdom . . . love" • 17 **beclosed** enclosed • 18 **mildehed . . . mekehed . . . beningnite . . . buxomhede** gentleness . . . meekness . . . benevolence . . . obedience • 19 **stede** home

oure loving and our traveyle deserveth), spreding abrode, and shewing the hye, plentuouse° largesse of Goddes ryal lordshippe in his mervelouse curtesy. And this is of the habundance of love. For grace werketh oure dredful failing into plentuouse and endlesse solace, and grace werketh oure shameful falling into hye, wurshippeful° rising, and grace werketh oure sorowful dying into holy, blisseful° life.

For I saw full sekerly° that ever as oure contrariousnes werketh to us here in erth paine, shame, and sorow, right so, on /fol. 89r/ the contrary wise,° grace werketh to us in heven solace, wurship, and blisse overpassing°—so forforth that, when we come uppe and receive that swete reward which grace hath wrought to us, there we shall thanke and blisse oure lorde, endlessly enjoyeng that ever we suffered wo. And that shalle be for a properte of blessed love that we shalle know in God, which we might never have knowen withoute wo going before. And whan I saw all this, me behoved nedes to grant that the mercy of God and the forgivenesse is to slake and waste oure wrath.°

THE FORTY-NINTH CHAPTER

For this° was an hye marveyle to the soule, which was continuantly shewed in alle and with gret diligence beholden:° that oure lorde God, as /fol. 89v/ aneynst himselfe, may not forgeve, for he may not be wroth. It were unpossible. For this was shewed: that oure life is alle grounded° and roted in love, and without love we may not live. And therfor, to the soule that of his special grace seeth so forforth of the hye, marvelous goodnesse of God, and° that we be endlesly oned to him in love, it is the most unpossible that may be that God shulde be wrath.

For wrath and frenshippe be two contraries.° For he that wasteth and destroyeth oure wrath and maketh us meke and milde, it behoveth nedes to be° that he be ever in one love, meke and milde, which is contrariouse° to wrath. For I saw full sekerly• that where oure lorde apereth, pees is taken and wrath hath no stede. For I saw no manner of wrath in /fol. 90r/ God, neither for shorte time nor for long. For sothly,° as to my sight, if God might be wroth a touch,° we shuld neither have life, ne stede, ne being. For as verely as we have oure being of the endlesse might of God, and of the endlesse wisdom, and of the endlesse goodnesse, also verely we have oure keping in the endles might of God, in the endlesse wisdom, and in the endlesse goodnesse. For thowe we fele in us wrath, debate, and strife, yet we be all mercifully beclosed in the mildehed of God and in his mekehed, in his beningnite and in his buxomhede.•

For I saw full sekerly° that alle oure endlesse frenship, oure stede, our life, and oure being is in God. For that same endlesse goodnesse that kepeth us when we /fol. 90v/ sinne, that we perish not, that same endlesse goodnesse continually

22 **treteth in us** nurtures in us • 22–23 **maketh us to see . . . forgivenesse** makes us realize, with true fear, our need vehemently to seek God in order to have his forgiveness. Although God does not forgive (lines 2–3), his goodness impels penitent souls to seek forgiveness • 25 **be wrath** by wrath • 26 **deseses** distress • 27 **sekerly safe** securely safe. Not in danger of damnation • 28 **blissefully safe** joyfully safe. As though already in heaven • 29–31 **full plesed with God . . . as love liketh** A state that, despite the soul's "contrariousnes," can apparently be attained in this life. *Ancrene Wisse*, part 4, compares the spiritual life to the Israelites' long years in the desert but likewise insists that devout souls can enjoy "rest, and all prosperity and joy, all their heart's desire and body's ease and happiness . . . here . . . in this world, before they come to heaven" (128–29) • 30 **domes** judgments • 30 **pesible** peaceful • 33 **God is our very peas** God is our true peace. See John 14:27, part of Christ's final words at the Last Supper: "Peace I leave with you; my peace I give to you; not as the world gives do I give to you. Let not your hearts be troubled, neither let them be afraid" • 33–34 **be . . . at unpeas** lack peace • 35 **by the werking . . . grace** See 48.14–32 • 36 **Sodenly . . . truly peesed in the selfe** the soul is immediately united to God when it is made truly peaceful in itself. As with mercy and forgiveness, the key to divine peace is peace with oneself • 38 **we finde no contrariousnes . . . letting** we do not find opposition in any kind of obstacle. Difficulties will not make the soul at peace resistant to God • 38–44 **And that contrariousnes . . . endlesse wurshipe** The opposition to God caused by sin is redeemed by God's goodness and made the occasion of eternal reward. The "contrariousnes which is now in us" thus joins human

sin, suffering, and prayer as these wait for the soul in heaven, ready to be transformed into eternal reward. See 38, 41.25–30 • 45 **unchaungeable** Once "contrariousnes" has been turned to reward in heaven, at death, the "changeable" sensuality at last takes on the "unchangeable" stability of the substance

[CHAPTER 50] 1 **dedly** mortal • 1 **mercy and forgevenesse** The return to these two terms signals the end of the discussion begun in 47.4–5, in preparation for a new topic, about to be launched as the result of a new question from Julian • 3 **deed** dead • 3 **as to mannes dome** according to human judgment • 3–4 **the soule . . . ne never shall** The phrasing here evokes the "godly wille" in 37.14–15 "that never assented to sinne, nor never shalle" • 5–6 **But yet here . . . mening thus** Announces the new topics to be discussed: how it can be that God does not blame humankind for sin; and, behind that, how the revelation as a whole can teach such a doctrine, given what Julian has held as the church's teaching. These topics, which persist until 53.7–17, are in a sense no more than intensifications of matters raised in Chapters 44–49. However, Chapter 51 brings important new revelatory evidence to the discussion • 6 **mening thus** to this effect • 7 **we sin grevously all day** Probably an allusion to Prov. 24:16: "For a righteous man falls seven times [some medieval Bibles added "a day"], and rises again; but the wicked are overthrown by calamity" • 7–9 **And I may neither . . . blame** and I can neither abandon my knowledge of this truth (of human sin), nor can I see you (despite your being "very truth") attributing to us any kind of guilt • 10–11 **fro the furst man** from the time of Adam

treteth in us a pees against oure wrath and our contrariouse falling, and maketh us
to see oure nede, with a true drede, mightely to seke unto God to have forgivenesse
with a gracious desyer of oure salvation. For we may not be blesfully saved till we be
verely in pees and in love, for that is oure salvation. And though we, be wrath and 25
the contrariousnes that is in us, be nowe in tribulation, deseses,° and wo, as falleth
to oure blindnesse and oure frailte,° yet be we sekerly° safe by the merciful keping
of God, that we perish not. But we be not blissefully safe in having of oure endlesse
joye till we be all in pees and in love: that is to sey, full plesed with /fol. 91r/ God and
with alle his werkes and with alle his domes, and loving and pesible° with oureselfe 30
and with oure evencristen and with alle that God loveth, as love liketh. And this
doth Goddes goodnes in us.

   Thus saw I that God is our very peas, and he is oure seker• keper when we be
oureselfe at unpeas, and he continually werketh to bring us into endlesse peas. And
thus when, by the werking of mercy and grace, we be made meke and milde, than 35
we be full safe. Sodenly is the soule oned to God when it is truly peesed in the selfe,°
for in him is founde no wrath. And thus I saw, whan we be alle in peas and in love,
we finde no contrariousnes in no manner of letting. And that contrariousnes which
is now in us, oure lorde God of his goodnes maketh it to us fulle profitable. For
contrariousnes is cause of alle oure tribulation and alle oure /fol. 91v/ wo. And oure 40
lorde Jhesu taketh them and sendeth them uppe to heven, and then they ar made
more swete° and delectable than hart may thinke or tonge can tell. And when we
come theder we shalle finde them redy, alle turned into very fairnesse and endlesse
wurshipe. Thus is God oure stedfast ground, and shall be oure full blisse, and make
us unchaungeable as he is when we be ther. 45

THE FIFTIETH CHAPTER

A nd in this dedely life, mercy and forgevenesse is oure way that evermore ledeth
us to grace. And by the tempest and the sorow that we fall in on oure perty, we
be ofte deed, as to mannes dome in erth. But in the sight of God, the soule that shall
be safe was never deed, ne never shall.

   But yet here I wondrede and merveyled with alle the diligence of my soule, 5
mening thus: "Goode lorde, I see the that thou /fol. 92r/ arte very truth, and I
know sothly° that we sin grevously all day and be mekille• blamewurthy. And I may
neither leve the knowing of this sooth, nor I se not the shewing to us no manner of
blame. How may this be?" For I knew be the comen teching of holy church and by
my owne feling that the blame of oure sinnes continually hangeth upon us, fro the 10
furst man into the time that we come uppe into heven. Then was this my merveyle,

14 **traveyled** exercised • 14–15 **by my blindhede** because of my blindness. Anticipates the account of the servant in 51.22, who is "blinded in his reson" • 15 **for drede** for fear. This fear of not being "enformed . . . of alle that me neded" (27.9) has already been mentioned (in 47.26–27) as haunting this part of the revelation • 15 **culde have no rest** So far, God's revelation of himself as peace, not wrath, has done nothing except deprive Julian of her own peace. Far from being comforting, the teaching of the last chapters is in danger of working like the "divers temptations in doubtes of the faith and dredes of salvation" Flete calls characteristic of his and Julian's times (*The Remedy,* chap. 1, *YW* 2:107). Much is thus at stake in relieving Julian of her "drede" here • 16 **to be lefte . . . sinne** to be left in ignorance of how he perceives us in our sin • 17–19 **either me behoved . . . blame** either I needed to see in God that sin was completely done away with, or else I needed to see in God how he thinks of it, through which I could truly know how I ought to think of sin and the manner of our guilt • 21 **nor no blamewurthy** nor in any way guilty • 22 **it semeth as** it seems as if • 22 **erre** err, or fall into heresy • 22 **knowing of this soth** knowing the truth of sin. See line 8 • 24 **sothnes** truth • 25 **make me hardy to aske it** make me brave enough to ask it. The present tense of "make" could be taken to suggest that lines 25–30 continue Julian's soliloquy from lines 21–24 • 25 **so lowe a thing** so modest a matter. See 47.20, where Julian's ability to understand how God cannot be angry is described as "but lowe and smalle." Revelation of God's relation to the world is "lowe" compared to the vision of God itself. Her question here is thus not a prying into God's "prevy concelle" (30.10–21), although it is hard to read the theological adventure embarked on in these lines as "lowe" • 26 **adred** afraid • 27 **special and prevy** See Chapter 35 on the need not to ask "special" questions • 27–28 **it nedeth me to wit** I need to know it. If so, God desires to show it, according to 36.19–25. The account of Julian's anxiety in lines 14–24 makes this the most powerful of the three reasons given here • 29 **deperte them asonder** separate them in two • 31–33 **I cryde inwardly . . . se it in the?** The drama of this pause in the narrative is similar to that just before the

revelation begins, in Chapter 4 • 32 **esede** made easy • 32–33 **that me nedeth to wit** what I need to know

[CHAPTER 51] 1 **answered in shewing** responded in a revelation • 1 **fulle mistely** most secretly. "Mistely" is related both to "mist" and "mystic," and is often used to refer to difficult, especially allegorical texts, such as the Book of Revelation (see, e.g., *The Pricke* 4364) • 2 **example** exemplum. A standard part of a late medieval sermon. The word has already been used to describe an "open example" about a lord and a servant in 7.27. Like another such short narrative, in 23.29–34, this exemplum is formally a "similitude," a genre of narrative associated with Anselm and especially common in *Ancrene Wisse,* in which divine truths are described in closely analogous human terms. Significance is generated not by the gap between vehicle and tenor, story and meaning—as is the case in some of Jesus' parables, whose improbability is their point—but by their contiguity. Here, the result is as close to algebra as a narrative mode can be. Indeed, numbers play an important part in the exemplum's interpretation, from the fact that it is "shewed double" (line 3) to the fact it has to be read methodically in relation to the "thre propertes" it implies (line 63) • 3 **shewed double** manifested on two different levels. That is, the characters and details in the exemplum signify allegorically in two ways • 4 **one perty** one level. One aspect of the lord's and the servant's double natures • 4 **gostly in bodely liknesse** in spiritual vision but in bodily form. This phrase introduces a new refinement to the modes of vision described in 9.24–28 • 5 **more gostly** in more elevated spiritual vision • 7 **therwith** with that sight • 8 **sitteth . . . stondeth** As in a modern joke ("A man goes into a bar"), the present tenses bring us into the realm of vivid but generalized fiction • 9 **lovely** lovingly • 10–14 **The servant . . . weye** the servant doesn't just go, he suddenly leaps up and rushes off as fast as he can because he so much loves doing his lord's will. But as soon as he does, he falls into a hollow and gets badly hurt. And then he groans and moans and wallows and writhes. But there's no way he can get up or look after himself • 12 **slade** valley, hollow, ditch, or any declivity in the ground

that I saw oure lorde God shewing to us no more blame then if we were as clene and as holy as angelis be in heven.

And betwene theyse two contraries, my reson was gretly traveyled by my blindhede• and culde have no rest, for drede that his blessed presens shulde passe fro my sight, and I to be lefte in unknowing how he beholde us in oure sinne. For either me behoved to se in God that sinne were alle done awey, or els me behoved /fol. 92v/ to see in God how he seeth it, wherby I might truly know how it longeth to me to see sinne and the manner of oure blame. My longing endured, him continuantly beholding. And yet I culde have no patience for gret feer and perplexite, thinking: "If I take it thus, that we be no sinners nor no blamewurthy, it semeth as I shulde erre and faile of knowing of this soth. And if it be tru that we be sinners and blamewurthy, good lorde, how may it than be that I can not see this sothnes° in the, which arte my God, my maker, in whom I desyer to se alle truth?"

For thre pointes make me hardy to aske it. The furst is for it is so lowe a thing: for if it were an hye, I shulde be adred. The secunde is that it is so comon: for if it were special and prevy, also I shulde be adred. The therde is that it nedeth me to wit—as me /fol. 93r/ thinketh—if I shall live here, for knowing of good and evil, wherby I may by reson and by grace the more deperte them asonder, and love goodnesse and hate evil as holy church techeth.

I cryde inwardly with all my might, seking into God for helpe, mening thus: "A, lorde Jhesu, king of blisse, how shall I be esede? Who shall tell me and tech me that me nedeth to wit, if I may not at this time se it in the?"

THE FIFTY-FIRST CHAPTER

And then oure curteyse lorde answered in shewing, full mistely, by a wonderful example of a lorde that hath a servant, and gave me sight to my understanding of both. Which sight was shewed double in the lorde, and the sight was shewed double in the servant. That one perty was shewed gostly in bodely liknesse. That other perty was shewed more gostly withoute bodely liknes.

For /fol. 93v/ the furst, thus: I sawe two persons in bodely liknesse, that is to sey, a lorde and a servant, and therwith God gave me gostly understanding. The lorde sitteth solempnely in rest and in pees. The servant stondeth before his lorde reverently, redy to do his lordes wille. The lorde loketh upon his servant full lovely and swetly, and mekely he sendeth him into a certaine place to do his will. The servant not onely he goeth, but sodenly he sterteth and runneth in gret hast for love to do his lordes wille. And anon he falleth in a slade, and taketh ful gret sore.° And

15 **most mischefe** worst damage • 15 **failing of comfort** From the start the servant's sufferings matter only because he is cut off from the lord • 16 **he culde not turne** Now that the action of the anecdote is over, the analytic past tense reasserts itself, though the present periodically breaks through • 16–17 **which was to him full nere** who was very close to him. The servant has not run far • 17–18 **But as a man . . . in wo** but like someone who was completely weak and stupid for the moment, he focused on how badly he felt and how long it went on • 19 **sevene gret paines** These physical pains acquire connotations as the exemplum is interpreted but at this stage simply categorize the servant's suffering. There is no association, here or later, with the common trope of the "seven deadly sins," used, e.g., in *The Scale* 1.53–55 to describe the effects of the fall on the soul • 20 **sore brosing** painful bruising • 21 **hevinesse** weight or dullness • 21 **febilnesse** weakness • 23 **stoned** stunned • 23 **so ferforth that** to such an extent that • 25–26 **I loked alle about . . . no helpe** See Lam. 1:12, often taken to depict the voice of Christ on the cross: "Is it nothing to you, all you who pass by? Look and see if there is any sorrow like my sorrow which was brought upon me" • 26–27 **a lang, harde, and grevous** a deep, difficult, and terrible one. The language here is suggestive of the quest, as though the hero of a romance has fallen at the first test he has faced • 29 **I behelde with avisement** A phrase used earlier, in 11.2, to describe Julian's response to the unlikely sight of "God in a pointe" • 30 **assigne in him . . . blame** attribute to him any kind of guilt. This phrase parallels 50.7–9 and represents the earliest gesture in the chapter toward interpretation of the exemplum • 32 **unlothful** unhateful • 34 **doubil chere** double expression. Alludes to the double nature of the revelation in lines 3–5 • 34–35 **rewth and pitte** compassion and pity. See 28.19–30 for these qualities as "properties" of God • 35 **this was of the furst** this belonged to the first level of insight • 36–37 **I saw him hyely enjoy** Recalls 28.8–10: "Ye, so farforth I saw: oure lord enjoyeth

of the tribulations of his sarvantes, with pite and compassion" • 37 **for** on account of • 37 **wurshipful restoring and noble** reverential and noble restoring • 37 **shall** must • 38 **this was of that other shewing** this belonged to the other mode of revelation (see line 3) • 40 **Lo, my beloved servant** In retrospect, though not on first reading, this alludes to Isa. 42:1, the first mention of the figure of the "suffering servant," who is traditionally identified with Christ in biblical exegesis: "Behold my servant, whom I uphold, my chosen, in whom my soul delights." The most clearly relevant of the suffering-servant passages is Isa. 53:1–12: "Who has believed what we have heard? And to whom has the arm of the Lord been revealed? For he grew up before him like a young plant, and like a root out of dry ground; he had no form or comeliness that we should look at him, and no beauty that we should desire him. He was despised and rejected by men; a man of sorrows, and acquainted with grief" (1–3). Yet although this resonates with many features of the servant and his story, at this point in the text the servant is unidentified; and his first identity is not as Christ but as Adam—as saved, not as savior • 41 **disses** trouble • 41–42 **yea, and for his good wille!** yes, and out of his good will! • 42 **skille** reasonable • 42 **reward him** reward him for • 42 **his frey and his drede** his fright and his fear. "Dred of afray" (fear caused by panic) is the first of the four kinds of fear in Chapter 74 • 43 **maime** injury • 43–44 **falleth it not . . . bene?** am I not obliged to give him a gift that is better for him and more honorable than his own health would have been? See 38.1: "Sinne shalle be no shame, but wurshipe to man" • 45 **els** if I did otherwise • 45 **me thinketh** it seems to me • 45 **I did him no grace** I would not be behaving rightly by him. "Grace" here is used in a courtly, more than a theological, sense • 46–47 **in which I saw . . . owne wurshippe** in which I saw it must necessarily be, in light of his great goodness and his own honor • 49 **that he shulde have be** what he would have been • 49 **so forforth** to such an extent

than he groneth and moneth and walloweth and writheth.° But he may not rise nor helpe himselfe by no manner of weye.

And of all this, the most mischefe that I saw him in was failing of comfort. For he culde not turne his face to loke uppe on his loving lorde, which was to him full nere, /fol. 94r/ in whom is full comfort. But as a man that was full febil and unwise for the time, he entended to his feling and enduring in wo. In which wo he suffered sevene gret paines.

The furst was the sore brosing that he toke in his falling, which was to him felable° paine. The seconde was the hevinesse of his body. The thirde was febilnesse that foloweth of theyse two. The fourth was that he was blinded in his reson and stoned in his minde so forforth that almost he had forgeten his owne love. The fifth was that he might not rise. The sixth was paine most mervelous to me, and that was that he leye alone. I loked alle about and behelde, and ferre ne nere, ne hye ne lowe, I saw to him no helpe. The seventh was that the place which he ley in was a lang, harde, and grevous.

I merveyled how /fol. 94v/ this servant might thus mekely suffer all this wo. And I behelde with avisement, to wit if I culde perceive in him ony defaute, or if the lorde shuld assigne in him ony maner of blame. And sothly° there was none seen. For only his good will and his gret desyer was cause of his falling. And he was as unlothful and as good inwardly as he was when he stode before his lorde, redy to do his wille. And right thus continuantly his loveing lorde full tenderly beholdeth him, and now with a doubil chere. One outwarde, full mekly and mildely, with gret rewth and pitte: and this was of the furst. Another inwarde, more gostly: and this was shewed with a leding of my understanding into the lorde, in which I saw him hyely enjoy for the wurshipful restoring and noble that he will and shall bring his servant to by his plentuous grace.° And this was of that other shewing. /fol. 95r/ And now was my understanding ledde againe into the furst, both keping in mind.

Than saide this curteyse lorde in his mening: "Lo, my beloved servant, what harme and disses he hath had and taken in my servis for my love—yea, and for his good wille! Is it not skille° that I reward him his frey and his drede, his hurt and his maime, and alle his wo? And not only this, but falleth it not to me to geve him a gifte that be better to him and more wurshipful than his owne hele shuld have bene? And els me thinketh I did him no grace." And in this, an inwarde gostely shewing of the lordes mening descended into my soule, in which I saw that it behoveth nedes to be, standing his gret goodnes and his owne wurshippe, that his deerworthy servant, which he loved so moch, shulde be hyely and blissefully• rewarded withoute end, above that he shulde have /fol. 95v/ be if he had not fallen. Yea, and so forforth that

51 **overpassing** transcendent • 52–56 **at this point . . . ees in that time** At the time, the exemplum is only partially successful in easing the anxiety expressed in Chapter 50 • 54 **forthleding** ushering on • 54 **marveyling of the example** state of wonder about the exemplum • 55 **my desyer** Alludes not only to Julian's anxious questioning in Chapter 50 but to her closely related reflections on the "two domes" of God in Chapter 45 (see especially lines 22–27) • 56–57 **that was shewed for Adam** who was shown as a representation of Adam • 57 **as I shall sey** See line 86 • 58 **by no manner . . . Adam** in no way be attributed to Adam on his own • 58–59 **stode mekille in unknowinge** remained in a great deal of ignorance • 59 **mervelouse example** An exemplum is meant to clarify: it is a popularizing form, not the all but insoluble riddle that makes this exemplum "mervelouse" • 60 **misty** secret. Already used of the exemplum in line 1 • 60–61 **be yet mekille hid** are still very much hidden • 61–62 **every shewing is full of privites** See 46.38–40 • 63 **telle thre propertes** describe three properties of, or ways of learning from, the revelation. The influence of these "propertes" as interpretive devices has been implicit from the beginning of *A Revelation*. Now they become explicit. The rest of the chapter, from line 85, analyzes the revelation in relation to each of these properties in turn • 63–64 **somdele esed** As Julian has cried out to be in 50.31–33 • 64 **The furst is the beginning . . . time** the first way of learning is through the beginning of God's teaching, which I understood while the revelation was happening. Julian's memory of the revelation, which in *A Revelation* as a whole is associated with phrases such as "I saw" and "in that time" • 65 **the inwarde lerning . . . sithen** the inner teaching I have understood in it since then. Julian's reflection on the meaning of the revelation, which in *A Revelation* as a whole is often associated with passages beginning with the word "understand." See, e.g., the hermeneutic rule laid down at the outset: "Wher Jhesu appireth" in the revelation, "the blessed trinity is understand [is to be understood], as to my sight," 4.11–12 • 65–66 **The third . . . revelation** the third way of learning is in light of the whole of the revelation. Often associated with the passages based on "all the revelations" (44.1) or with references to individual revelations • 67–68 **theyse thre . . . deperte them** these three ways of learning are so unified, as I understand them, that I have neither skill nor power to separate them • 68–69 **by theyse thre as one** by these three ways of learning all

together. The phraseology echoes language about the Trinity as "three and one," as the three "propertes" are revealed to correspond both to the persons of the Trinity and to the "mightes" of the mind: memory, reason, and will • 69 **ow** ought • 71–72 **he shall declare it . . . will** See 36.19–27 • 73 **twenty yere . . . thre monthes** February 1393, according to the date of the revelation given in 2.2 • 74–75 **the propertes and the condetions** the features and the qualities. Attention is needed to minor facts and their implications. The rest of the chapter treats the exemplum as a mystery or puzzle, with clues and a final solution • 76 **indefferent** meaningless • 77 **avisement** close attention • 77 **pointes** details • 79–84 **at the manner . . . his unlothfulhede** The close observation of the exemplum that begins here, after the command to "take hede to . . . propertes and . . . condetions," involves Julian in asking of the exemplum a series of questions that have some relation to the very common lists of "topics," for structuring and elaborating a discourse, found in rhetorical manuals: general topics such as "Who, Where, What," or specific ones such as (under "Who") "Name, Nature, Manner of Life," one of which might in turn generate the yet more detailed "Expression, Clothing, Gesture, Action" (see, e.g., Cicero's *De inventione* 1.24). During the rest of the chapter, this structure of disclosure by systematic exegesis is in counterpoint with analysis of the exemplum in relation to the "propertes" described in lines 63–72. Much of the skill of the exposition lies in keeping back essential detail until the proper moment: see especially line 157: "Ther was a tresoure in the erth" • 80 **manner of shape** how his clothing was styled • 81 **nobley** nobility • 81–82 **manner of . . . servant** how the servant stood • 84 **unlothfulhede** innocence • 85–102 **The lorde . . . to his blisse** This brief passage represents the "beginning of teching" (line 98), in which the lord and servant receive their preliminary identies as God and Adam, and the lesson already learned in the thirteenth revelation, as well as in the sequence of chapters on all the revelations (45–50), is reiterated in abbreviated form • 87–88 **one man . . . alle manne and his falling** *The Scale* 1.43 states that "whanne Adam sinnede . . . he loste al this worshipe . . . and thou also lostest it in him." As with *The Scale*, the shift in *A Revelation* from a historical account of the Fall to its ethical and spiritual consequences is immediate. No interest is shown in the actuality of Eden, and there is no place in the analysis for Eve or serpent

his falling and alle his wo that he hath taken thereby shalle be turned into hye,° 50
overpassing wurshippe and endlesse blesse.

And at this point the shewing of the example vanished, and oure good lorde
ledde forth my understanding in sight and in shewing of the revelation to the ende.
But notwithstanding all this forthleding, the marveyling of the example went never
fro me, for methoght it was geven me for answere to my desyer. And yet culde I 55
not take therein full understanding to my ees in that time. For in the servant that
was shewed for Adam, as I shall sey, I sawe many diverse properteys that might
by no manner be derecte to singel Adam. And thus in that time I stode mekille in
unknowinge.° For the full understanding of this mervelouse example was not geven
me in that time, in which misty /fol. 96r/ example the privites of the revelation be 60
yet mekille• hid. And notwithstanding this, I sawe and understode that every
shewing is full of privites.

And therefore me behoveth now to telle thre propertes in which I am somdele
esed. The furst is the beginning of teching that I understode therin in the same time.
The secunde is the inwarde lerning that I have understonde therein sithen. The third 65
is alle the hole revelation, fro the beginning to the ende, which oure lorde God of his
goodnes bringeth oftimes frely to the sight of my understonding. And theyse thre
be so oned, as to my understonding, that I can not nor may deperte them. And by
theyse thre as one, I have teching wherby I ow to beleve and truste in oure lorde
God, that of the same goodnesse that he shewed it and for the same end, right so 70
of the same goodnes and for the same end he shall declare it to us when it /fol. 96v/
is his will.

For twenty yere after the time of the shewing, save thre monthes, I had teching
inwardly, as I shall sey: "It longeth to the to take hede to alle the propertes and the
condetions that were shewed in the example, though the thinke that it be misty and 75
indefferent to thy sight." I assented wilfully with gret desyer, seeing inwardly, with
avisement, all the pointes and the propertes that were shewed in the same time, as
ferforth as my wit and my understanding wolde° serve: beginning my beholding
at the lorde and at the servant; at the manner of sitting of the lorde and the place
he sat on, and the coloure of his clothing and the manner of shape, and his chere 80
withoute and his nobley and his goodnes within; at° the manner of stonding of the
servant, and the place, where and how; at° his manner of clothing, the coloure and
the shape; at his outwarde behaving;° and at his inwarde /fol. 97r/ goodnes and his
unlothfulhede.•

The lorde that sat solemply in rest and in peas, I understonde that he is God. 85
The servant that stode before him, I understode that he was shewed for Adam:
that is to sey, one man was shewed that time, and his falling, to make thereby to be

89–91 **This man was hurte . . . lorde** Returns for the first of many times to the details, given earlier, in lines 15–27 • 90 **stoned** stunned • 91 **his wille . . . Gods sight** See 45.1–2, where the "kindely substance . . . is ever kepte one in him [God], hole and safe without ende" • 92 **himselfe** his selfhood • 92–93 **letted . . . will** frustrated and blinded from knowing his own will. Flete's discussion of the "good will" in *The Remedy,* which has some relation to the thirteenth revelation's concept of the "godly wille" (see 37.14–17), argues that, in the state of tribulation, "your good will . . . standeth alwaye unbroken in you by the grace of almighty God, though ye fele it not thrugh travaillous thoughtes [as a result of laborsome thoughts] whiche taketh away the sighte of your knowlege" (chap. 5, *YW* 2:114) • 93 **grevous disses** terrible anguish • 96 **theyse two** "his loving lord" and "what himselfe is" in the Lord's sight • 98 **this was . . . of teching** Concludes discussion of the first "property" (see lines 63–68) • 99 **what manner . . . oure sinne** In 50.16, Julian was in deep anxiety to know "how he beholde us in oure sinne" • 101 **socurreth** helps • 101 **ever . . . in glad chere** See 21.18–26, where Julian explains why Christ for now shows us not his "blissful chere" but rather "chere of passion" • 103–4 **The place . . . wildernesse** the place the Lord sat on, alone in a wilderness, was simply barren and empty ground. The beginning of the second "property" of the exemplum, "the inwarde lerning that I have understonde therein sithen" (line 65), beginning with the Lord and introducing for the first time the topic of "place." The "wildernesse" is not a sign of the Fall, since the Lord is already sitting there before this occurs, but an image of latency. Wilderness precedes civilization in the spiritual realm as in the civic (see lines 123–25). The exemplum ends not in the wilderness but in the city of the human soul (lines 278–80) • 104 **side** ample • 106 **fair brown** a beautiful brown • 108 **an hey ward . . . hevens** a high refuge, long and wide, quite full of endless heavens. See 54.13–21, on humanity's enclosure in God. As in an erotic narrative, heaven is seen in the beloved's eyes • 109 **loking that he loked** expression with which he looked • 111 **shewed of** was revealed as • 111 **semely medelur** fitting mixture • 112 **rewth and pitte** See the account of God's attitude toward fallen humanity in 28.28–30: "Of his gret curtesy he doth away alle oure blame, and beholdeth us with ruth and pitte as children, innocens and unlothfulle" • 112–13 **passeth as ferre . . . erth** surpasses the compassion and the pity as far as heaven is above earth • 114–16 **The rewth and the pity . . . fader** In order to explain the Lord's "joy and blisse," these sentences anticipate the final phase of the analysis of the servant, in 179–227 • 116 **which is even with the fader** who is equal with the Father. A tenet of Trinitarian theology • 116–18 **The merciful beholding . . . deth** God's regard of Adam followed him to hell and protected him there. Adam's release from hell is described in 12.17–19, where Christ's blood is seen as having "descended downe into helle" in order to "brak [the] bondes" of "all that were there which belong to the courte of heven" • 120–23 **But man is blinded . . . is not man** The Lord is God the Father, shown as though he were a man because human blindness makes this necessary. "Blinded in this life" brings sharply to mind the fact that writer and readers alike are all represented by the servant • 122 **homely, as man** familiarly, as a man • 123–24 **is thus to mene** means this. A passage of detailed allegorical reading follows • 124 **to be his owne citte** The image is filled out in Chapter 68, where the human soul is described as though it were the New Jerusalem

understonde how God beholdeth alle manne and his falling. For in the sighte of
God alle man is one man, and one man is alle man. This man was hurte in his
mighte and made fulle febil, and he was stoned in his understanding, for he was 90
turned fro the beholding of his lorde. But his wille was kepte hole° in Gods sight.
For his wille I saw oure lorde commende and aprove, but himselfe was letted and
blinded of the knowing of this will. And this is to him gret sorow and grevous disses,
for neither he seeth clerly his loving lorde, which is to /fol. 97v/ him full meke and
milde, nor he seeth truly what himselfe is in the sight of his loving lord. And welle I 95
wot, when theyse two be wisely and truly seen, we shall get rest and peas: here in
party, and the fulhede• in the blisse in heven, by his plentuous grace.

And this was a beginning of teching which I saw in the same time, wherby I
might come to knowing in what manner he beholdeth us in oure sinne. And then I
saw that only paine blameth and ponisheth, and oure curteyse lorde comforteth and 100
socurreth. And ever he is to the soule in glad chere, loving and longing to bring us
to his blisse.

The place that the lorde sat on was simply on the erth, bareyn and deserte,
alone in wildernesse. His clothing was wide and side and full semely, as falleth to
a lorde. The colour of the clothing was blew as asure, most sad and fair. His chere 105
was merciful. The colour of /fol. 98r/ his face was fair brown,° with full semely
countenance. His eyen were blake, most fair and semely, shewing full of lovely pitte,
and within him an hey ward, long and brode, all full of endlesse hevens.° And the
lovely loking that he loked on his servant continually—and namely in his falling—
methought it might melt oure hartes for love and brest them on two for joy. 110

This fair loking shewed of a semely medelur, which was marvelous to beholde.
That one was rewth and pitte, that other joy and blisse. The joy and blisse passeth
as ferre the rewth and the pitte as heven is above erth. The pity was erthly and the
blisse hevenly. The rewth and the pity of the fader was of the falling of Adam, which
is his most loved creature. The joy and the blisse was of the falling of his deerwurthy 115
son, which is even with the fader. The merciful beholding /fol. 98v/ of his lovely
chere fulfilled all erth and descended downe with Adam into helle, with which
continuant pitte Adam was kepte fro endlesse deth. And this mercy and pitte
dwelleth with mankinde into the time that we come uppe into heven.

But man is blinded in this life, and therefore we may not se oure fader, God, as 120
he is. And what time that he of his goodnesse will shew him to man, he sheweth him
homely, as man. Notwithstonding that, I saw sothly° we ought to know and beleve
that the fader is not man. But his sitting on the erth, bareyn and desert, is thus to
mene: he made mannes soule to be his owne citte and his dwelling place, which is
most pleasing to him of all his workes. And what time man was fallen into sorow 125

126 **not all semely** not entirely fitting. A courteous understatement • 126 **of that noble office** in that noble role • 127 **adight him** prepare himself • 128 **medled with erth** made partly of earth. See Gen. 2:7: "The Lord God formed man of dust from the ground, and breathed into his nostrils the breath of life; and man became a living being" • 128–29 **till what time . . . traveyle** The Son's task is to restore his Father's kingdom. The allegory again takes on attributes of medieval romance—somewhat against its own grain, since in the exemplum the kingdom has, strictly speaking, never been lost. The identity of the servant with Christ has still not been formally announced • 129 **the nobil fairhede** the state of noble beauty • 130 **blewhed . . . stedfastnesse** blueness of the clothes signifies his loyalty. A traditional understanding of the color blue • 130–32 **brownhed . . . sobernesse** darkness of his lovely face, with the fitting blackness of his eyes, was most appropriate to display his holy sobriety • 132 **flamming about** billowing about • 133 **he hath beclosed in him** See line 108 • 134 **a touch** a brief moment • 134–35 **wher I sey . . . grace** See lines 36–38 • 137 **yet I marveyled** Now the topic shifts to the servant. Recalls the phrase that introduces the analytic part of the chapter, "mervelouse example" (line 59) • 139 **doubil understanding, one without, another within** two interpretations, one external, the other internal • 140 **a laborer . . . traveyle** a laborer ready to work. At this stage, we know for certain only that this figure is Adam. That many of the following details do not quite fit Adam is meant to puzzle • 141 **not even foranenst** not exactly in front of • 141 **in perty aside** slightly to one side • 142 **whit kirtel** white tunic • 142 **singel** in a single layer. See lines 207–9 • 142 **defauted** deficient. Compare "defaute," line 29 • 142–43 **dyed with swete of his body** stained with the sweat of his body • 143 **straite fitting** close-fitting • 143 **an handful beneth the knee** reaching a hand's breadth below the knee. The garment of a peasant • 144 **worne uppe** worn out • 144 **ragged** ripped up for rags • 145 **This is now an unsemely clothing** The worn-out clothing is strange because the servant as Adam is wearing what look like tokens of punishment before his fall. For "unsemely," see line 126 • 147–48 **even like to** the same as. See line 116: "even with the fader" • 149 **The wisdom of the servant** Wisdom is identified with Christ, the second person of the Trinity, as early as 1.10, where God is "al mighty, all wisdom, and all love" • 149 **sawe inwardly** the lord does not command the servant. The servant realizes that he can serve the lord • 150 **wurshippe to the lord** honor to the lord. "Wurshippe" is the only thing that, in his absolute self-sufficiency, the lord lacks • 151 **might fall of him** might happen to him • 151 **deed sterte** did jump up. See lines 10–12 • 152–56 **For it semed . . . before** The paradox is later resolved, with the "continuant laborer" as Adam, after his fall, and the "newed" as Christ • 154 **traveler laborer** • 154 **of long time** of long standing • 155 **newed** new hire • 157 **Ther was a tresoure in the erth** A crucial new item of information enters the exemplum: after the topics of "person" and "place," discussion moves to the "thing" (see lines 79–84) . See Matt. 13:44: "The kingdom of heaven is like treasure hidden in a field" • 158 **mete** food • 159 **lovesom and plesing** appealing and appetizing. The lord has no actual need of the "mete" but would still like some • 161 **no servant . . . sent out** Any householder of modest means would have more servants than this lord • 163–64 **the hardest traveyle . . . gardener** After the Fall, God tells Adam: "Cursed is the ground because of you; in toil you shall eat of it all the days of your life. . . . In the sweat of your face you shall eat bread" (Gen. 3.17–19). Christ is associated with gardening in John 20:15, where, after his resurrection, Mary Magdalene mistakes him for a gardener. In the exemplum the hard work of gardening is accepted by the servant even before the fall—indeed, gardening and fall prove to be the same thing

and paine, he was not all semely to serve of that noble office. And therfore oure
/fol. 99r/ kinde fader wolde adight° him non other place but to sit upon the erth,
abiding mankinde which is medled with erth, till what time by his grace his deerwurthy
sonne had brought againe his citte into the nobil fairhede° with his harde traveyle.
The blewhed of the clothing betokeneth his stedfastnesse. The brownhed of his fair   130
face, with the semely blackhede of the eyen, was most according to shew his holy
sobernesse. The larghede° of his clothing, which was fair, flamming about, betokeneth
that he hath beclosed in him all hevens and all endlesse joy and blisse. And this was
shewed in a touch, wher I sey° that "my understanding was led into the lorde, in
which I saw him heyly enjoye for the worshipful restoring that he will and shall   135
bring his servant to by his plentuous grace."

   And yet I marveyled, /fol. 99v/ beholding the lorde and the servant before saide.
I saw the lorde sit solemply, and the servant standing reverently before his lorde—in
which servant is doubil understanding, one without, another within. Outward: he
was clad simply, as a laborer which was disposed to traveyle. And he stod full nere   140
the lorde, not even foranenst him but in perty aside, and that on the lefte side. His
clothing was a whit kirtel, singel, olde, and alle defauted, dyed with swete of his
body, straite fitting° to him and shorte, as it were an handful beneth the knee, bare,
seming as it shuld sone be worne uppe, redy to be ragged and rent. And in this I
marveled gretly, thinking: "This is now an unsemely clothing for the servant that   145
is so heyly loved to stond in before so wurshipful a lord!" And inward: in him was
shewed a ground of love, which love he had /fol. 100r/ to the lorde that was even like
to the love that the lord had to him.

   The wisdom of the servant sawe inwardly that ther was one thing to do which
shuld be wurshippe to the lord. And the servant for love, having no regarde to   150
himselfe nor to nothing that might fall of him, hastely deed sterte and runne at the
sending of his lorde to do that thing which was his wille and his wurshippe. For it
semed by his outwarde clothing as he had ben a continuant laborer and an hard
traveler of long time. And by the inward sight that I had both in the lorde and in the
servant, it semed that he was a newed: that is to sey, new beginning for to traveyle,   155
which servant was never sent out before.

   Ther was a tresoure in the erth which the lorde loved. I merveyled and thought
what it might be. And I was answered in my understanding: "It /fol. 100v/ is a mete
which is lovesom and plesing to the lorde." For I saw the lorde sit as a man, and I
saw neither meet nor drinke wherwith to serve him. This was one merveyle. Another   160
merveyle was that this solempne lorde had no servant but one, and him he sent out.
I beheld, thinking what manner labour it may be that the servant shulde do. And
then I understode that he shuld do the grettest labour and the hardest traveyle that

164 **delve and . . . swete** dig and make ditches and work and sweat • 165 **seke the depnesse** search the depths of the earth • 166–67 **nobille and plentuous fruite** rich and abundant fruit • 168 **never turne againe** never return (to the lord) • 168–69 **dighte this met alle redy** got this food all ready • 169 **as he knew . . . the lorde** as he knew the lord liked it • 172 **And yet I merveyled** As at line 137, the phrase announces another new phase of analysis • 172 **whens the servant came** whence the servant came. The lord's existence is taken to be self-evident, but that of the servant is a puzzle. After explaining why this is so, the answer follows in lines 179–91 • 174 **that was grounded** even that had its ultimate source. As God, the lord cannot suffer lack and is the source of all • 174 **mervelous depnesse** The treasure that the servant finds when he "seke[s] the depnesse" (line 165) is united with the lord's own "depnesse" • 175 **it was not . . . wurship** the treasure did not fully do him honor. In a sense, the "tresure" actually is "wurship," the purpose for which the "citte" of the human soul was created and redeemed. See lines 123–29 • 176 **in himselfe present** into his own presence • 176 **without** around • 177 **I understode . . . ment** I did not entirely understand what this exemplum signified • 179 **In the servant . . . trinite** the second person of the Trinity is included in the meaning of the servant. The servant, like the "tresure," ultimately comes from the lord. Here exegesis by description gives way to a more intensively interpretive analysis • 180–81 **whan I sey "the sonne"** The servant acquires a new name, Son. See line 114 • 181 **is even with the fader** is equal to the Father. See line 116 • 182–84 **By the nerehed . . . Adam** See lines 140–41 • 182 **nerehed** closeness • 185 **even love** equal love. See lines 146–48 • 185–86 **When Adam felle, Godes sonne fell** Plays a variation on 1 Cor. 15:21–22: "For as by a man came death, by a man has come also the resurrection of the dead. For as in Adam all die, so also in Christ shall all be made alive" • 186 **For the rightful oning** because of the perfect

union. See John 1:3–4 for the doctrine of God the Son's role as life and light of humankind: "All things were made through him, and without him was not anything made that was made. In him was life, and the life was the light of men" • 187 **seperath** separated • 187–88 **Adam fell fro life to deth . . . hell** In *The Scale* 2.1, it is the "image of God" that fell, "thorugh sinne of the first man Adam . . . from that gostly light and that hevenely foode into that peynful mirkenesse and beestly lust of this wrecchid liyf, exiled and flemed out [cast out] fro the heritage of hevene" • 188 **slade** hollow • 188 **into hell** See lines 116–18 • 188–89 **Goddes son fell with Adam** See Phil. 2:6–8, the source of the Christian doctrine of kenosis. See 20.7–8 • 191 **mightely . . . out of hell** For an earlier allusion to the harrowing of hell, see 12.17–19 • 192–95 **By the wisdom . . . but one man** Alludes back to lines 149, 139–44. As both Adam and Christ, the servant by this point in the exemplum resembles Piers in one of his final manifestations in *Piers Plowman*, as a figure for the humanity of Christ. At the Passion, Jesus jousts "in Piers armes, / In his helm and in his haubergeon [mail coat], *humana natura* [human nature]" (B 18.22–23), although we already know that Piers is in reality no knight but a laborer, clad in "clothes, yclouted and hole [both patched and whole]" (B 6.59). Even so, the Son, several times in this chapter associated with the protagonist of a romance, takes on the likeness of a laborer to restore his Father's kingdom (see lines 128–29, 211–12, 276–78) by rescuing Adam "out of hell" (line 191). Romances involving disguise, sometimes called Fair Unknown romances, are common: several episodes in Sir Thomas Malory's *Morte d'Arthure* follow this pattern • 195 **but one man** as only one person. The union of divine and human natures in Christ • 200–202 **Thus was he . . . heven** Begins a discussion (to line 227) of the servant's standing as an expression of Christ's eternal intention to redeem

is: he shuld be a gardener: delve and dike and swinke and swete and turne° the erth
up and down, and seke the depnesse, and water the plantes in time. And in this he   165
shulde continue his traveyle, and make swete flodes to runne, and nobille and
plentuous fruite° to spring which he shulde bring before the lorde and serve him
therwith to his liking. And he shulde never turne againe till he had dighte this met
/fol. 101r/ alle redy, as he knew that it liked to the lorde, and than he shulde take this
met with the drinke, and bere it full wurshiply before the lorde. And all this time the   170
lorde shulde sit right on the same place, abiding the servant whom he sent oute.

   And yet I merveyled fro whens the servant came. For I saw in the lord that he
hath within himselfe endlesse life and all manner of goodnes, save the tresure that
was in the erth, and that was grounded within the lord in mervelous depnesse of
endlesse love. But it was not alle to his wurship till his servant hath thus nobly   175
dighte it and brought it before him in himselfe present. And without the lorde was
right noght but wildernesse. And I understode not alle what this exampil ment, and
therfore I marveyled from wens the servant came.

   In the servant is /fol. 101v/ comprehended the seconde person of the trinite, and
in the servant is comprehended Adam: that is to sey, all men. And therfore whan   180
I sey "the sonne," it meneth the godhed, which is even with the fader; and whan I
sey "the servant," it meneth Cristes manhode, which is rightful Adam. By the nerehed
of the servant is understand the sonne, and by the stonding on° the left side is
understond Adam. The lorde is God the father; the servant is the sonne Jesu Crist;
the holy gost is the even love which is in them both. When Adam felle, Godes sonne   185
fell. For the rightful° oning which was made in heven, Goddes sonne might not be
seperath from Adam, for by Adam I understond alle man. Adam fell fro life to deth:
into the slade of this wreched worlde, and after that into hell. Goddes /fol. 102r/ son
fell with Adam into the slade of the maidens wombe, which was the fairest doughter
of Adam—and that for to excuse Adam from blame in heven and in erth—and   190
mightely he feched him out of hell.

   By the wisdom and the goodnesse that was in the servant is understond Goddes
son. By the pore clothing as a laborer, stonding nere the left side, is understonde the
manhode and Adam,° with alle the mischefe and febilnesse that foloweth. For in alle
this, oure good lorde shewed his owne son and Adam but one man. The vertu and   195
the goodnesse that we have is of Jesu Crist, the febilnesse and blindnesse that we
have is of Adam: which two were shewed in the servant. And thus hath oure good
lorde Jhesu taken upon him all oure blame, and therfore oure fader may nor will no
more blame assigne /fol. 102v/ to us than to his owne derwurthy son, Jhesu Crist.

   Thus was he the servant, before his coming into erth, stonding redy before the   200
father in purpos, till what time he wolde sende him to do the wurshipful deede by

202–5 **notwithstonding . . . oure charge** although he is God, equal with the Father with respect to his divinity, even so in relation to his foreseen plan—that he would become a human to save humanity in carrying out the will of his Father—in that sense he stood before his Father as a servant, consciously taking all our burden upon himself • 206 **sterte full redely** jumped up very readily. See lines 150–52 • 207–10 **The whit kirtel . . . laborar** See lines 141–44. *Ancrene Wisse,* part 6: "Our old dress is the flesh which we have from Adam our first father" (181) • 208 **singlehede** singleness. Of the tunic • 209 **straighthede** tightness • 209–10 **The elde . . . Adams traveyle** If the servant is like the virtuous laborer Piers in *Piers Plowman* (see lines 195–99), he is also like Piers's antonym, the figure of Haukyn, whose "cote . . . / Hath manye moles and spottes . . . / . . . bihinde and bifore," signs of wear that symbolize Haukyn's sinfulness (B 13.314–16) • 209 **elde is of Adams wering** the kirtle has aged from Adam's wear • 209 **defauting** deficiency • 210 **servant laborar** the servant's status as a laborer • 211 **seing** saying • 211–12 **Lo . . . Adams kirtel** Parallels the lord's speech in lines 40–45. In Robert Grosseteste's great theological poem *Le chateau d'amour,* dramatizing Phil. 2:7 ("taking the form of a servant"), Christ similarly stands before the Father and says: "Del serf prendrai la vesture, / En verité e en dreiture [I shall take the clothing of a thrall, as it is true and right to do]" (101) • 212 **wolde be** want to be • 213 **to don** to do • 214 **Full sothfastly wist the son** the Son knew very well. God the Son knew when the Incarnation would take place. In *Le chateau d'amour,* the Son, as divine wisdom, proposes the Incarnation as a solution to sin • 215 **as anemptes** as regards • 216 **this mening** Christ's speech in lines 211–14 • 218–19 **he is the heed . . . membris** See 1 Cor. 12:12, alluded to in 31.28–30: "For just as the body is one and has many members, and all the members of the body, though many, are one body, so it is with Christ" • 219–20 **to which membris . . . fulfilled** See Mark 13:32,

perhaps already in play in lines 211–14: "But of that day or that hour no one knows, not even the angels in heaven, nor the Son, but only the Father." Now what is unknown is not the Incarnation but the Judgment • 221 **Which day . . . desireth** 1 Pet. 1:12 describes the gospel "preached . . . through the Holy Spirit sent from heaven" as containing "things into which angels long to look" • 222 **theder** there • 223–24 **which desyering . . . kirtel** See 31.10–16, Christ's "gostly thirst," generalized in this passage to include all saved humanity • 224 **or elles** or otherwise • 225 **apered** appeared • 226–27 **and all of the charite . . . to us** and all by God's love, along with our obedience, humility, and patience, and the other virtues appropriate to us • 228 **Also in the merveylous example** Ends analysis of the second "properte," begun on line 103, and begins exposition of the third, working from the exemplum's relationship to the "hole revelation" (see lines 63–68). This mode of exposition persists until Chapter 63. Analysis by way of the third "properte" focuses on the mystery of the union of human and divine in Christ, offering a narrative account of salvation history that is simpler than the material in the previous section • 229 **beginning of an A. B. C.** beginning of an education • 229–30 **oure lordes mening** our Lord's general intention. For this phrase, see 86.11–17 • 230 **privites of the revelation** secrets of the revelation • 230 **therin** in the example • 232 **The sitting of the fader** The details of the exemplum in this passage are all taken from its second telling, lines 103–48. God is often seen seated in the Bible: Isaiah sees "the Lord sitting upon a throne, high and lifted up" (Isa. 6:1) • 232–33 **that is to sey . . . traveyle** that is to say, indicates rest and peace, since there can be no work in the godhead • 234 **standen** standing • 235 **on side and on the lefte** that the servant stands to one side and on the left • 236 **even right before** right in front of • 238 **falling into . . . kinde** falling into the assumption of our nature • 239 **as swithe** at once

which mankinde was brought again into heven. That is to sey, notwithstonding that he is God, even with the fader as anenst the godhede, but in his forseeing purpos— that he woulde be man to save man in fulfilling of the will of his fader—so he stode before his fader as a servant, wilfully taking upon him alle oure charge. And than he 205 sterte full redely at the faders will, and anon he fell full lowe in the maidens wombe, having no regarde to himselfe ne to his harde paines. The whit kirtel is his fleshe. The singlehede is that ther was right noght betwen /fol. 103r/ the godhede and the manhede. The straighthede° is poverte. The elde is of Adams wering. The defauting is the swete of Adams traveyle. The shorthede• sheweth the servant laborar. 210

And thus I saw the sonne stonde, seing in his mening: "Lo, my dere fader, I stonde before the in Adams kirtel, alle redy to sterte and to runne. I wolde be in the erth to don° thy worshippe,° whan it is thy will to send me. How long shall I desyer it?" Full sothfastly° wist the son whan it was the faders will, and how long he sholde desyer: that is to sey, as anemptes the Godhed, for he is the wisdom of the fader. 215 Wherfore this mening was shewed in understonding of the manhod of Crist. For all mankinde that shall be saved by the swete incarnation and the blisseful passion° of Crist, alle is the manhode of Crist. For he is the heed, and we be his /fol. 103v/ membris, to which membris the day and the time is unknowen whan every passing wo and sorow shall have an ende and the everlasting joy and blisse shall be fulfilled. 220 Which day and time for to see, all the company of heven longeth or desireth. And all that be under heven which shall come theder, ther way is by longing and desyering; which desyering and longing was shewed in the servant stonding before the lorde— or elles thus, in the son stonding afore the fader in Adam kirtel. For the longing and desyer of all mankind that shall be safe apered in Jhesu. For Jhesu is all that shall 225 be saved, and all that shall be saved is Jhesu°—and all of the charite of God, with obedience, mekenesse, and patiens, and vertues° that longeth to us.

Also in this merveylous example I have /fol. 104r/ teching within me, as it were the beginning of an A. B. C., wherby I may have some understonding of oure lordes mening. For the privites of the revelation be hid therin, notwithstonding that alle 230 the shewing be full of prevites.

The sitting of the fader betokeneth the godhede: that is to sey, for shewing of rest and pees, for in the godhede may be no traveyle. And that he sheweth himselfe as lorde betokeneth to oure manhod. The standen of the servant betokeneth traveyle, and on side and on the lefte° betokeneth that he was not alle wurthy to 235 stonde even right before the lorde. His sterting was the godhed, and the renning was the manhed. For the godhed sterte fro the fader into the maidens wombe, falling into the taking of oure /fol. 104v/ kinde. And in this falling he toke grete sore. The sore that he toke was oure flesh, in which as swithe° he had feling of dedely paines.

241 **honest** decent • 243 **wonne his peece** won his peace • 244 **by the lefte . . . son** by the servant's standing on the "left" side is meant that the Father "left" his own Son. The left side is the less favored side, but the interpretation here relies on a pun • 245 **without sparing of him** See Rom. 8:32: "He . . . did not spare his own Son but gave him up for us all." See also 17.18: the crown of thorns is pressed on Christ's head "not sparing and without pitte." Initiates a series of allusions back to the Passion sequence in Chapters 1–26 • 247 **sweppes** blows • 247 **scorges** whippings • 247 **drawing** pulling • 248 **his tender flesh renting** tearing his delicate flesh. See 12.2, on the scourging of Christ: "the fair skinne was broken full depe into the tender flesh" • 248 **As I saw in some party** as I saw to some extent. See Chapter 17 for all these details • 249 **headpanne** skull • 249 **unto the time . . . failed** until the bleeding stopped • 250 **cleving** clinging • 250 **walowing** tossing about • 251 **all mightly** with full power • 252–53 **he yelding the soule** See Luke 23:46: "Jesus, crying with a loud voice, said, 'Father, into thy hands I commit my spirit!' And having said this he breathed his last" • 254 **furst to show his might** See line 251, "he might never rise all mightly" • 255 **the gret root** the mighty company ("rout"). Those kept in hell from their death until hell's harrowing by Christ. See 12.17–19 • 255–56 **depe depnesse** The same "depnesse" that the servant has sought in his gardening, in line 165 • 259–64 **And oure foule dedely flesh . . . wurshippe** See Rev. 1:13, where "in the midst of the lampstands" John sees "one like a son of man, clothed with a long robe and with a golden girdle round his breast" • 260 **straite, bare, and shorte** narrow, threadbare, and short • 261 **side** ample • 263 **semely medolour** fitting mixture. See line 111 • 263 **I can it not discrive** I cannot describe it • 264 **all of very wurshippe** entirely made of true praise • 266 **seet ... in heven** See Ps. 103:19 (Vulgate 102): "The Lord has established his throne in the heavens, and his kingdom rules over all" • 267 **dredfully** fearfully • 267 **unornely** wretchedly • 268 **stondeth before . . . even righte** stands right in front of the Father • 268–69 **clothed . . . largenesse** clothed with joyous amplitude • 269–70 **it was shewede** See 22.17–18 • 273 **he sitteth on the faders right hande** Compare the Apostles' Creed, where Christ "sitteth at the right hand of God in the glory of God the Father." See Col. 3:1 • 273–76 **But it is not ment . . . joy** Compare lines 122–25, on the topic of allegorical reading

By that that he stode dredfully before the lorde, and not even righte, betokeneth 240
that his clothing was not honest to stonde even right before the lorde. Nor that
might not, nor shulde not, be his office while he was a laborer. Nor also he might
not sit with the lord in rest and pees till he had wonne his peece rightfully with his
hard traveyle. And by the lefte side: that the fader lefte his owne son wilfully in the
manhed to suffer all mans° paine without sparing of him. 245

By that his kertel was at the point to be ragged and rent is understond the
sweppes and the scorges,° the thornes and the nailes, the drawing and the dragging,
his tender flesh /fol. 105r/ renting.° As I saw in some party, the flesh was rent fro the
headpanne, falling on peces unto the time the bleding failed. And than it beganne
to dry againe, cleving to the bone. And by the walowing and writhing, groning and 250
moning,° is understonde that he might never rise all mightly fro that time that he
was fallen into the maidens wombe, till his body was slaine and dede, he yelding the
soule into the faders hand, with alle mankinde for whome he was sent.

And at this point, he beganne furst to show his might, for then he went into
helle. And whan he was ther, than he raised uppe the gret root oute of the depe 255
depnesse, which rightfully was knit to him in hey heven. The body ley in the grave
till Easter morow, and fro that time he ley /fol. 105v/ never more. For ther was
rightfully ended the walowing and the writhing, the groning and the moning.°
And oure foule dedely flesh, that Goddes son toke upon him—which was Adams
olde kirtel, straite, bare, and shorte—then by oure savioure was made fair, new, whit, 260
and bright, and of endlesse clennesse, wide and side, fair and richar than was the
clothing which I saw on the fader. For that clothing was blew, and Cristes clothing
is now of fair, semely medolour which is so mervelous that I can it not discrive, for
it is all of very wurshippe.

Now sitteth not the lorde on erth in wildernesse, but he sitteth on his riche and 265
nobil seet which he made in heven most to his liking. Now stondeth not the son
before the fader as a servant before the lorde, dredfully, unornely° clothed, in perty
/fol. 106r/ naked, but he stondeth before the fader even righte richely clothed in
blissefull largenesse, with a crowne upon his hed of precious richenes. For it
was shewede that "we be his crowne"; which crowne is the faders joy, the sonnes 270
wurshippe, the holy gostes liking, and° endlesse, mervelous blisse to alle that be
in heven. Now stondeth not the sonne before the fader on the lefte side as a laborer,
but he sitteth on the faders right hande in endlesse rest and pees. (But it is not ment
that the sonne sitteth on the right hand beside as one man sitteth by another in this
life—for ther is no such sitting, as to my sight, in the trinite. But he sitteth on his 275
faders right honde: that is to sey, right in the hyest nobilite of the faders joy.) Now

277–78 **his loved wife . . . maiden of endlesse joy** The soul or church, or the personification "Endless Joy" itself. The very common medieval image of Christ as the spouse of the church or soul derives from a tradition of allegorical interpretation of the bride and bridegroom in the Song of Songs. Rarely evoked in *A Revelation* (although see 52.2, 58.12–13), here it gives a traditional conclusion to the exemplum considered as a romance narrative • 278–79 **in his citte . . . in pees** The development from wilderness to city is complete, and government of the city has been granted to the Son • 279 **dighte to him** prepared for him. See Rev. 21:2: "I saw the holy city, new Jerusalem, coming down out of heaven from God, prepared as a bride adorned for her husband." See also Chapter 68

[CHAPTER 52] 1 **enjoyeth that** has joy because • 1–2 **that he is our moder** Mentioned here and in 54.16–17, the theme of God as mother dominates Chapters 58–63. Its relation to the exemplum is not, at this stage, obvious • 2 **very spouse** true spouse • 6–7 **Alle that shall be saved . . . of wo** during our present lifetimes, all those of us who shall be saved have in ourselves a strange mixture both of happiness and of misery. "Medelur" recalls the servant in 51.128, whose being is "medled with erth"; also the "semely medelur" with which the lord looks upon the servant, mingling "rewth and pitte" with "joy and blisse" (51.111–12). The sentence begins a chapter-long summing-up of the exemplum in Chapter 51 as an account of the individual soul's experience of being alive • 7–8 **We have . . . Adams falling** See 1 Cor. 15:22: "For as in Adam all die, so also in Christ shall all be made alive," already alluded to in 51.185–86 • 7–8 **up resin** resurrected • 8–9 **Dying by Crist** dying with Christ. See 1 Cor. 15:36, 42: "What you

sow does not come to life unless it dies. . . . So is it with the resurrection of the dead. What is sown is perishable, what is raised is imperishable" • 9 **lastingly** eternally • 9 **by . . . touching** through his gracious inspiration • 9–10 **seker trust of salvation** See 2.14–15 • 11 **we be . . . so blinde** The servant's blindness is described in 51.92–93. The theme is fully developed in 72.25–33, which describes the blindness of "oure gostly eye" and the "weight of oure deadely flesh and darkhede of sinne" • 12 **unnethes** scarcely • 12 **in oure mening . . . God** Similar language is used in 10.76–79 • 14 **ey of oure understanding** A phrase used in 5.9, 60.8. Here, the open eye enables humankind to perceive reality from Christ's joyful point of view, rather than Adam's sorrowful one • 15 **sometime more and somtime lesse** See 83.13: "This light is mesured discretly" • 15 **after that God . . . take** according to the ability God gives to receive it • 15–16 **And now . . . into that other** Compare the alternating pattern of divine presence and absence described in Chapter 15 • 17–19 **And thus . . . fele him** and so this mixture in us is so strange that we hardly know of ourselves or of our fellow Christians what state we are in, such is the strangeness of this inconsistent sensation—except at each moment of holy affirmation in which we affirm God when we sense him • 23 **ayeen** again • 25 **we assent never therto** See 19.17–20, 37.14–15. "Assent" is the will's agreement with an improper thought, word, or action • 25–26 **groge ther agenst** complain against it • 29 **very man . . . updrawing** a true human being in his own self, drawing us up after him. *Rev.* 31.40–41 describes how Christ is continually "us drawing uppe to his blisse" • 29–30 **and that . . . gostely thirst** See 31.14–16 • 30–31 **that . . . in the thirde** See 11.44: "See, I lede all thing to the end that I ordaine it to"

is the /fol. 106v/ spouse, Goddes son, in pees with his loved wife, which is the fair
maiden of endlesse joy. Now sitteth the son, very God and very man, in his citte in
rest and in pees, which his fader hath dighte to him of endlesse purpose, and the
fader in the son, and the holy gost in the fader and in the son.   280

THE FIFTY-SECOND CHAPTER

And thus I saw that God enjoyeth that he is our fader, and God enjoyeth that he
is our moder, and God enjoyeth that he is our very spouse, and our soule his
loved wife. And Crist enjoyeth that he is our broder, and Jhesu enjoyeth that he is
our saviour. Theyse be five hye joyes, as I understonde, in which he wille that we
enjoye: him praising, him° thanking, him loving, him endlessly blessing.   5

Alle that shall be saved, for the time of this life we have in us a mervelous
/fol. 107r/ medelur both of wele and of wo. We have in us oure lorde Jhesu Crist up
resin, and we have in us the wrechednesse and the mischef of Adams falling. Dying
by Crist, we be lastingly kept, and by his gracious touching we be raised into seker•
trust of salvation. And by Adams falling we be so broken in oure feling on diverse   10
manner by sinne and by sondry paines, in which we be made derke and so blinde
that unnethes we can take any comforte. But in oure mening we abide God, and
faithfully trust to have mercy and grace. And this is his owne werking in us, and
of his goodnesse openeth the ey of oure understanding—by which we have sight,
sometime more and somtime lesse, after that God geveth abilte to take. And now we   15
are° raisede in- /fol. 107v/ to that one, and now we are suffered to fall into that other.

And thus is that medle so mervelous in us that unnethis we knowe of oureselfe
or of oure evencristen in what wey we stonde, for the mervelousshede• of this
sondrye feling—but that ech holy assent that we assent to God when we fele him,
truly willing to be with him with all oure herte, with all oure soule, and with all   20
oure mighte. And than we hate and dispise oure evil stering and all that mighte be
occasion of sinne, gostely and bodely. And yet neverthelesse, whan this swetnesse
is hid, we fall ayeen into blindnesse and so into wo and tribulation on diverse
manners. But than is this oure comfort: that we knowe in oure faith that by the
vertu of Crist, which is oure keper, we assent never therto. But /fol. 108r/ we groge   25
ther agenst and endure in paine and in wo, prayeng into that time that he sheweth°
him ayeen to us. And thus we stonde in this medelur all the dayes of oure life.

But he will we trust that he is lastingly with us, and that in thre manner. He is
with us in heven, very man in his owne person, us updrawing; and that was shewd
in the gostely thirst. And he is with us in erth, us leding; and that was shewde in the   30

31 **wonning** home • 32 **rewling and yeming** ruling and governing • 32 **that . . . in the sixteenth** See 68.6–8, where Christ "ruleth and yemeth heven and erth" from his dwelling in the soul • 33–35 **And thus . . . Goddes son** See 51.192–99 for this double sight of the servant • 35 **the rewth and the pitte** See 51.34–35 • 36–37 **in the lorde . . . mankinde is come to** in the lord was manifested the great nobility and the endless honor to which humanity has come. By becoming the Lord's "owne citte and his dwelling place" (51.124) • 38 **mightely . . . his falling** the lord rejoices mightily in the servant's falling • 39 **overpassing . . . have had** transcending what we would have had. See 51.43–51, where the phrase "overpassing wurshippe" is used • 40–41 **And thus to se . . . falle** and in order to see this surpassing nobility, my understanding was led into God at the same time I saw the servant fall. This happens in 51.35–38 • 41–42 **we have . . . morning** at the moment we have cause to mourn • 45 **hateth nought but sinne** In 40.26–27 "the same blessed love techeth us that we shalle hate sin only for love." The self is not to be hated, even in a state of sin • 46 **unmesurable contrarys** extreme opposites • 47–48 **alle holy** quite completely • 49 **sinnes . . . endlesse paine** Deadly sins, severe enough to damn anyone who dies without repenting them • 49 **as holy church techeth us** Every parish priest had to expound the deadly sins to his flock several times a year • 50 **eschewe** eschew, shun • 50 **venial** venial sins. Sins that do not damn the soul • 50 **resonably uppe oure might** to a reasonable extent, so far as is within our power. Orthodox medieval theology assumes the persistence of venial sin in even the holiest souls • 51 **ony** any • 51 **that we redely rise** that we should quickly rise up. The phrase is governed by "I sawe and understode" (lines 46–47) and parallels "that we may not" and "that we may wele" as part of a long sentence (broken into four here for clarity) that persists to line 57 • 52 **upon . . . holy church** according to the teaching of holy church • 52–53 **after that the**

sinne is grevous depending on how serious the sin is • 53–55 **And neither . . . oure febilhede** and that we neither on the one side fall too low, inclining to despair, nor on the other side be too reckless, as if we did not care, but openly acknowledge our frailty • 55 **witting** knowing • 56 **twingling** twinkling • 56 **cleve** cling • 58 **For otherwise . . . beholding of man** for God looks at things in one way and humankind looks at them in another. Returns discussion to the two "domes," that of God and that of holy church and humankind, introduced in Chapter 45, associating these with the "doubil chere" of the lord as he looks at the fallen servant (see lines 60–62). Although the emphasis falls differently, no obvious intellectual gain has been made between the earlier passage and this one. What has mainly changed is the tone, as the exemplum reduces the extreme anxiety of Chapters 45 and 50. The new theological ideas it makes possible are yet to come • 59–60 **For it longeth . . . excuse man** for it is appropriate for humankind humbly to accuse himself, and it is appropriate to our Lord God's own goodness courteously to excuse humankind. The first use of "accuse" in *A Revelation*, a word associated with the confessional and the lawcourt. In *Ancrene Wisse*, part 5, the first "branch" of confession is that it "must be accusing": the one confessing must lay the charges against him- or herself, even if they should turn out to be exaggerated. In 77.27–28, limits are placed on human self-accusation, as Christ commands: "Accuse not thyselfe overdon mekille [much too much]" • 61 **doubil chere** See 51.33–39 • 65 **cum therof** come from it • 65 **witting** knowing • 65 **that we may never restoren it** An important axiom of the Christian theology of sin. Hilton, working with a passage from Anselm, writes that the reformation of the image of God in the soul "might not ben had [could not be achieved] by non [any] erthely man, for . . . non might suffice to helpe himsilf. . . . Therfore it nedide bi don [it had to be done] by him that is more thanne a man" (*The Scale* 2.1) • 66 **sen** see

thirde, wher I saw God in a point. And he is with us in oure soule, endlesly wonning, rewling and yeming° us; and that was shewde in the sixteenth, as I shalle sey.

And thus in the servant was shewde the blindhede• and the mischefe of Adams falling; and in the servant was shewde the wisdom and the goodnesse of Goddes son. And in the lorde was shewde /fol. 108v/ the rewth and the pitte of Adams wo; and in the lorde was shewde the hye noblite and the endlesse wurshippe that mankinde is come to, by the vertu of the passion and the deth of his deerwurthy son. And therfore mightely he enjoyeth in his falling, for the hye raising and fulhed of blisse that mankinde is come to, overpassing that we shuld have had if he had not fallen. And thus° to se this overpassing noblete was my understonding led into God in the same time that I saw the servant falle. And thus we have now° mater of morning, for oure sinne is cause of Cristes paines. And we have lastingly mater of joy, for endlesse love made him to suffer.

And therfore the creature that seeth and feleth the working of love by grace hateth nought but sinne. For of alle thing, as /fol. 109r/ to my sight, love and hate be hardest and most unmesurable contrarys. And notwithstonding all this, I sawe and understode in oure lordes mening that we may not in this life kepe us fro sinne alle holy, in full clenesse, as we shall be in heven. But we may wele by grace kepe us fro the sinnes which wolde lede us to endlesse paine, as holy church techeth us, and eschewe venial resonably uppe oure might. And if we, by oure blindhede• and oure wrechednesse, ony time falle, that we redely rise, knowing the swete touching of grace, and wilfully amend us upon teching of holy church, after that the sinne is grevous, and go forth with God in love. And neither on that one side fall over lowe, enclining to dispairs, ne on that other side be over rechelesse, /fol. 109v/ as if we geve no forse, but nakidly° know oure febilhede,• witting that we may not stonde a twingling of an ey but with keping of grace, and reverently cleve to God, in him only trusting.

For otherwise is the beholding of God, and otherwise is the beholding of man. For it longeth to man mekely to accuse himselfe, and it longeth to the proper goodnesse of oure lorde God curtesly to excuse man. And theyse be two parties that were shewde in the doubil chere in which the lorde behelde the falling of his loved servant. That one was shewde outward, full mekely and mildely, with gret rewth and pitte, and that other of inwarde endlesse love. And right thus wille oure good lorde that we accuse oureselfe, wilfully and sothly seing and knowing our falling and all the harmes that cum therof, seing and witting that we may never restoren it; and therwith, that we wilfully° and truly sen and know his everlasting love /fol. 110r/ that he hath to us, and his plentuous mercy. And thus graciously to se and know both

68–69 **And . . . there it is** and it is he who is at work where this combination is found • 70 **the lower party of mannes life** What Chapters 45–46 first call the "sensualite." See 55.42 • 70–71 **and it was . . . chere** Here Julian unexpectedly begins to use the lord in the exemplum to deduce truths, not about God, but about the self. The lord and his servant become figures for the two parts of the soul, what the next chapters will call the substance and the sensuality, the terms first introduced in Chapter 45 • 72 **asseth** atonement. Seen in the lord's "pitte" (line 63). For the "asseth," see 29.9–12 • 73 **more hyly and all one** in a more elevated way and all the same. The higher "party" of the human soul, the substance, is simple, not double • 73–75 **For the life . . . by grace** for the life and power that we have in the lower part of the soul derives from the higher part, and it comes down to us out of natural self-love through grace. The soul's "hyer" part, or substance, joins with divine grace in infusing life and virtue into the soul. The language here is reminiscent of 6.25–26, where the "goodnes of God . . . cometh downe to us, to the lowest party of our need" • 75 **that one and that other** "kinde love" and "grace" • 76–77 **doubil werking** See "doubil chere," line 61 • 80 **holy restorid** wholly restored. See 38.1–9 for the restoration of sin and its transformation into "overpassing worshipes"

[CHAPTER 53] 1 **wit** know • 1 **he taketh no herder** he takes no worse • 2 **tok** took • 2 **which** whom • 5 **gentil** honorable • 5 **defaute** fault • 5–6 **in whome he shall be ever blessed** to someone in whom God is going to be blessed forever • 7 **was my desyer . . . answered.** See 45.22–27, 51.54–55. Marks the end of the exposition of the exemplum of the lord and servant, who are not explicitly mentioned again until 82.8–9, even though the traces of the structure of ideas they represent are omnipresent over the next ten chapters. Discussion now turns to the topic of the soul in its dual natures as substance and sensuality, building on the argument of the last part of Chapter 52 • 7–8 **my grete fere** See 50.20 • 8–12 **In which shewing . . . God** A nearly exact repetition of 37.14–17, much developed and presented now, "full sekerly," as revelation • 12–14 **Therefore . . . Jhesu Crist** so our Lord wants us to know this teaching about the godly will as a matter of faith and belief, and specifically that we have all this blessed will entire and safe in our Lord Jesus Christ. An important claim. To "know" something "in the faith" is to accept it as an authentic and necessary part of Christian doctrine. In Chapter 9 and elsewhere (e.g., 7.52–54), *A Revelation* implicitly differentiates between the revelation and "the faith of holy church" (9.18). Here Julian proposes that this distinction be erased, not by subordinating the revelation to existing teaching but by adding a new doctrine to what is considered "the faith of holy church." Making this formal theological claim about the godly will, based on the arguments of Chapters 37–52, this sentence also announces the topic of Chapters 53–57: the nature of the soul and its unfallen, "substantial" will • 14 **ech kinde** every variety of being. Angelic as well as human • 14–15 **behoveth . . . rightfulhede** must necessarily of God's perfection • 15 **knit and oned** joined and united. "Knit" has earlier been used to describe the relation between Christ and his "membris" (31.29–30) and between Christ and those raised to heaven at the harrowing of hell (51.256) • 15–16 **were kepte a substance** Reintroduces the term "substance" from Chapters 45–46, which now begins to receive a careful composite definition • 17 **thorow . . . purpose** as a result of his own good will in his eternal providential purpose • 19 **againe-buying** redemption • 19 **nedful and spedful** necessary and profitable togeder is the meke accusing that oure good lorde asketh of us. And himselfe wurketh there it is.

And this is the lower party of mannes life, and it was shewde in the outwarde chere, in which shewing I saw two partes. The one is the ruful falling of man; that other is° the wurshipful asseth that oure lorde hath made for man. That other chere was shewde inwarde, and that was more hyly and all one. For the life and the vertu that we have in the lower perty is of the hyer, and it cometh downe to us of the kinde love of the selfe by grace. Betwene that one and that other is right nought— for it is all one love, which one blessed love hath now in us doubil /fol. 110v/ werking. For in the lower perty be pains and passions, ruthis and pittes, mercis and forgevenesse and such other, which be profitable. But in the hyer perty be none of theyse, but all one hye love and mervelous joy, in which marvelous joy all paines be holy restorid.°

And in this, not only oure good lorde shewde our excusing, but also the wurshipfulle noblite that he shall breng us to, torning all oure blame into endlesse wurshippe.

THE FIFTY-THIRD CHAPTER

And thus I saw that he will that we wit° he taketh no herder the falling of any creatur that shalle be saved than he tok the falling of Adam, which we know was endlessly loved and sekerly• kepte in the time of all his nede, and now is blissefully• restored in hye, overpassing joyes. /fol. 111r/ For oure lorde God is so good, so gentil, and so curtesse that he may never assigne defaute° in whome he shall be ever blessed and praised.

And in this that I have now saide was my desyer in perty answered, and my grete fere somdele esed, by the lovely, gracious shewing of oure lorde God. In which shewing I saw and understode full sekerly• that in ech a soule that shall be safe is a godly wille that never assented to sinne, ne never shall. Which will is so good that it may never wille evil, but evermore continually° it willeth good and werketh good in the sight of God. Therefore oure lorde wille we know it in the faith and the beleve, and namly and truly that we have all this blessed will hole and safe in oure lorde /fol. 111v/ Jhesu Crist. For that ech kinde that heven shall be fulfilled with behoveth° nedes of Goddes rightfulhede• so to be knit and oned in him, that therein were kepte a substance which might never nor shulde be parted from him, and that thorow his awne good will in his endlesse forseeing° purpose.

And notwithstonding this rightful knitting and this endlesse oning, yet the redemption and the againe-buying of mannekinde is nedful and spedful in

21 **began never to love mankinde** never started loving humankind. The substance is associated with the eternity of divine love • 21–22 **righte . . . blesse** in exactly the same way as humankind will be in eternal joy • 22–23 **fulfilling . . . (as anemptis his werkes)** completing God's joy (with regard to what God has done) • 23–24 **righte so . . . loved** just so has the same humanity been known and loved in the providence of God • 25–26 **mid person** second person of the Trinity • 26 **this fair kinde . . . come** this beautiful principle of being from which we have all come. "Mankind," here considered as a collective entity or idea in God. See Col. 1:15–17: "He is the image of the invisible God, the first-born of all creation; for in him all things were created, in heaven and on earth. . . . He is before all things, and in him all things hold together" • 27 **wenden** go • 27–28 **in him . . . heven** See 19.8 "Nay, I may not! For thou art my heven" • 30 **or that . . . loved us** he loved us even before he created us. The statement makes sense within the framework of Christian Neoplatonism, becoming increasingly important in this chapter, in which humankind exists as an eternal idea in the mind of God. The rest of the chapter concerns the nature of the soul in its creation, which at once separates it from God and "knits" it to God • 31 **kindly . . . goodnesse** natural and essential goodness • 33 **made of God** created by/from God. The ambiguity is explored here and in Chapter 54 • 34 **made of nought** created from nothing • 35 **shulde** was about to • 36 **toke the slime of the erth** See Gen. 2:7 • 38 **wolde take . . . made it** wished to take nothing at all, but simply made the soul. The first phrase could be translated "wished to take only nothingness." The soul is created *ex nihilo* • 38–39 **thus is the kinde . . . God** so is created being justly united to the maker, who is essential uncreated being, that is, God. The difficulty of the phrase "substantial kinde unmade" is characteristic both of this group of chapters and of

the words "substance" and "kinde." The phrase makes sense in this specific context, where the soul has just been described as "kinde made." Compare another phrase for divine being, "substantial kindhede," 56.34, and see Gen. 1:27: "So God created man in his own image" • 40 **ther may . . . soule** See 5.16–18 • 40–41 **in this endlesse love . . . hole** The safety of the godly will derives from the moment and the mode of humanity's creation • 44 **oure soule is a life** An axiom of medieval theories of selfhood: being created by God "of nought" (line 34), the soul can exist separate from the body, but not the other way around • 46–47 **tresured in God and hid** Like the "deed" in 32.27–28, "tresured and hid in his blessed brest, only knowen to himselfe." Whatever else it is, the deed is thus an essential part of the idea of humankind eternally kept in the mind of God • 48–49 **fulleste substance . . . soule of Crist** the soul of Christ is the most complete being and sublimest power. The created thing nearest the uncreated from which it has being. This is consistent with 4.34–35, which says of Mary that "above her is nothing that is made but the blessed manhood of Christ" • 49–54 **And ferthermore . . . holy in this holyhede** Christ's soul is united with God in the very process of its creation, and the souls of all saved humankind are united to God through this primal act of union. This is how 52.28–29 can argue "that he is lastingly with us . . . in heven, very man in his owne person, us updrawing" • 50–51 **Which knot . . . mighty** which knot is so intricate and strong. A "suttel knot" is both a love knot, symbol of union between lover and beloved, and a mystery or paradox: the word is used in intellectual contexts to describe an apparent contradiction. In *A Revelation,* the word "knot" is used only here and in line 53 • 53 **knit in this knot** included in this knot. God's union with the most sublime thing he made incorporates the entirety of saved humankind • 54 **holyhede** holiness

everything, as it is done for the same entent and the same ende that holy church in   20
oure faith us techeth. For I saw that God began never to love mankinde. For righte
the same that mankind shall be in endlesse blesse, fulfilling the joy of God (as
anemptis his werkes), /fol. 112r/ righte so the same mankind hath be, in the
forsighte of God, knowen and loved fro without beginning in his rightful entent.
And by the endlesse entent and assent and the full acorde of all the trinite, the mid   25
person wolde be grounde and hed of this fair kinde out of whom we be all come, in
whom we be alle enclosed, into whom we shall all wenden,° in him finding oure full
heven in everlasting joy, by the forseeing purpose of alle the blessed trinite fro
without beginning.

For or that he made us he loved us, and when we were made we loved him. And   30
this is a love° made of the kindly, substantial goodnesse of the holy gost, mighty in
reson of the mighte of the fader, and wise in minde of the wisdom of the son. And
/fol. 112v/ thus is mannes soule made of God, and in the same pointe knite to God.

And thus I understode that mannes soule is made of nought. That is to sey, it is
made, but of nought that is made, as thus: whan God shulde make mannes body,   35
he toke the slime of the erth, which is a mater medeled and gadered of alle bodely
thinges, and therof he made mannes body. But to the making of mannes soule he
wolde take right nought, but made it. And thus is the kinde made rightfully oned to
the maker, which is substantial kinde unmade, that is God. And therfore it is that
ther may ne shall be right noughte betwene God and mannis soule. And in this   40
endlesse love, mannis soule is kepte hole, as all the mater of the revelation meneth
and sheweth, in which endlesse love we be ledde and /fol. 113r/ kepte of God, and
never shalle be lost.

For he will that we wit° that oure soule is a life; which life, of his goodnesse and
his grace, shall last in heven without ende, him loving, him thanking, him praising.   45
And right the same that we shulde be without end, the same we ware tresured in
God and hid, knowen and loved fro without beginning. Wherfore he will we wit
that the nobelest thing that ever he made is mankinde, and the fulleste substance
and the hyest vertu is the blessed soule of Crist. And ferthermore, he will we wit that
this deerwurthy soule was preciously knit to him in the making. Which knot is so   50
suttel and so mighty that it is oned into God, in which oning it is made endlesly
holy. Farthermore, he will we wit that all the soules that /fol. 113v/ shalle be saved in
heven without ende be knit in this knot, and oned in this oning, and made holy in
this holyhede.•

[CHAPTER 54] 2 **deperting in love** distinction as to how he loves • 3 **trowe** believe • 3 **wonning** home, perhaps with a pun on "oning" • 6 **Hyely owe** greatly ought • 6 **wonneth** lives • 7 **mekille hyly** very greatly • 8–9 **Our soule is made . . . unmade** The "knot" of 53.53, the mutual indwelling of God and Christ's soul, in which all souls are "knit," derives from the mode of creation described in 53.34–43. Mutual indwelling, first described in Chapter 9, remains a major theme until Chapter 57. For Christ "wonning" in the soul, see Chapter 68 • 10–12 **a higher understanding . . . substance** it is a higher and greater understanding to see within and to know that our soul, which is made, has its home in God in its substance • 12 **of which substance . . . that we be** from which substance, through God, we are what we are. As lines 22–29 go on to make clear, although the self is split into sensual and substantial halves, and although the sensuality has no direct access to the substance, it is nonetheless the substance that determines the character and destiny of the self • 13 **I sawe no difference . . . all God** I saw no distinction between God and the soul's substance, but it was as if all of it was God. This perception seems to follow from the claim that "or that he made us he loved us," for if there is divine love for a soul not yet made, it can be argued that what God loves in the soul is unmade, that is, part of God. If this perception were made into a theological claim, it would thus lay *A Revelation* open to the charge of autotheism, the heresy for which Eckhart and Marguerite Porete were found guilty. For Eckhart, God and the soul are ultimately united "without distinction," so that the claim that part of the soul (what he calls its *scintilla*, or spark) is uncreated being, or God, is correct. Here, though, Julian's perception remains only that, and *A Revelation*'s argument as a whole, in which the soul is able to render God worship and a place of "wonning," has no place for understanding the soul as anything other than a created entity • 15 **a creature in God** a created being living within God • 17 **beclosed** enclosed. The repetition of this word over the next few lines speaks out strongly against

the notion of "union without distinction" • 22–23 **oure faith . . . holy gost** our faith is a power that comes out of our own substance into our sensual soul by way of the Holy Spirit. Reintroduces the "sensual soul," not mentioned since 46.1, to begin exploration of its role in relation to God and the substance. The sensual soul is the psychic and physical self as it knows itself, cut off from knowledge of its substance. This is an unusual definition, for although "sensuality" is often used of the part of the soul that interacts with body and senses, consciousness itself is usually associated with the substance. According to Reginald Pecock's mid-fifteenth-century theological treatise, *The Reule of Crysten Religioun*, e.g., "Oure soule in his ful substaunce is departable from oure body by deth . . . withoute eny hurting of the soulis substaunce and withoute eny apeirement [impairment] of his resoning and his willing, though al the use of the sensual outward and inward wittis [outer and inner senses] whiche were exercisid by instrumentis of the body before, at thilke time of his departing from the body shal be voide from worching [will cease to work at the time the soul departs from the body]" (109–10). The role of "faith" in uniting sensuality and substance is explored in Chapter 55. The phrase "by the holy gost" declares God's essential role in the mechanism by which the substance and sensuality are joined • 25 **seker truste of oure being** Sensuality is united with God and the substance through trust. See Heb. 11:1: "Faith is the assurance of things hoped for, the conviction of things not seen" • 27–28 **we graciously according to him** we are by grace reconciling with him

[CHAPTER 55] 1–2 **Crist in his body . . . heven** All the saved are the body of Christ • 2 **bereth** carries • 2–3 **us alle having . . . by him** having in him all of us who shall be saved by him • 3 **wurshipfully presenteth . . . with us** Souls are offered to God the Father like the defeated or freed knights and maidens a romance hero sends back to the royal court as proofs of his prowess

THE FIFTY-FOURTH CHAPTER

Ande for the grete endlesse love that God hath to alle mankinde, he maketh no deperting in love betwen the blessed soule of Crist and the lest soule that shall be saved. For it is full esy to beleve and trowe° that the wonning° of the blessed soule of Crist is full high in the glorious godhede. And sothly,° as I understode in oure lordes mening, where the blessed soule of Crist is, there is the substance of alle the soules that shall be saved by Crist. Hyely owe we to enjoye that God wonneth° in oure soule, and mekille• hyly we owe to enjoye that oure soule wonneth° in God. Our soule is made to be Goddes wonning;° and the wonning° of oure soule is God, which is unmade. /fol. 114r/ A hye understanding it is inwardly to se and to know that God, which is oure maker, wonneth° in oure soule; and a higher understanding it is and more, inwardly to se and to know oure soule, that is made, wonneth° in God in substance—of which substance, by God, we be that we be.

And I sawe no difference betwen God and oure substance, but as it were all God. And yet my understanding toke that oure substance is in God: that is to sey, that God is God and oure substance is a creature in God. For the almighty truth of the trinite is oure fader, for he made us and kepeth us in him. And the depe wisdome of the trinite is our moder, in whom we are all beclosed.° And the hye goodnesse of the trinite is our lord, and in him we are beclosed° and he in us. /fol. 114v/ We are beclosed° in the fader, and we are beclosed° in the son, and we are beclosed° in the holy gost. And the fader is beclosed in us, the son is beclosed in us, and the holy gost is beclosed in us: all mighty, alle wisdom, and alle goodnesse; one God, one lorde.

And oure faith is a vertu that cometh of oure kinde substance into oure sensual soule by the holy gost, in which vertu alle oure vertues comen to us. For without that no man may receive vertues. For it is nought eles but a right understanding with trew beleve and seker• truste of oure being, that we be in God and he in us, which we se not. And this vertu, with all other that God hath ordained to us coming therin, werketh in us grete thinges. For Crist marcifully is werking in us, and we graciously according to him /fol. 115r/ thorow the yefte and the vertu of the holy gost. This werking maketh that we be Cristes children and cristen in living.

THE FIFTY-FIFTH CHAPTER

And thus Crist is oure wey, us sekerly• leding in his lawes, and Crist in his body mightely bereth us up into heven. For I saw that Crist, us alle having in him that shall be saved by him, wurshipfully presenteth his fader in heven with us. Which present fulle thankfully his fader receiveth, and curtesly geveth it unto his

6 **that to us longeth** which concern us • 8 **in the nineth shewing** "Joy," "blisse," and "liking" in lines 5–6 are the "thre hevens" of 22.3–4, 7–9 • 10 **wo or wele** misery or happiness. See 52.6–7 • 10–11 **God will . . . erth** From here to Chapter 57, the perspective shifts to that of the sensual soul • 11–17 **Oure faith . . . holy gost** The first of the three theological virtues, faith, is made of love of self (the substance's love for the sensuality: see 52.73–75, 54.22–23), reason, and primal knowledge of God: all three faculties of the soul (see lines 33–35). Faith is born, in fact, at the moment of the soul's creation in the Trinitarian image of its creator. Once the soul is in the body, divine mercy and grace, in order to preserve the sensuality, create the second theological virtue, hope, out of faith • 12 **clere lighte of oure reson** See 56.33–51 • 13–14 **enspired in oure body** breathed into our bodies • 14 **in which we be made sensual** in which we are created as sensual beings • 14 **as swithe** at once • 15 **having of us cure and keping** taking care of and sustaining us • 18–19 **sensualite . . . grace** the sensuality is founded in being, in mercy, and in grace. Attributes of all three persons of the Trinity, which enable the sensuality to reach back up to God and the substance • 19 **ableth** enables • 19–21 **For I saw full sekerly . . . God is** for I saw very surely that our substance is kept in God. And I also saw that God is present in our sensuality. A succinct way of formulating the difference between *A Revelation*'s doctrine of the mutual indwelling of God and the soul and the Eckhartian notion of the soul as divine, mentioned in 54.13 • 21–22 **in the same . . . citte of God** See 51.129 and 278–80, 56.19–21. The work's fundamental justification for the existence and sufferings of the sensual soul. God's dwelling place in the soul is at the point of union between the substance, which dwells in him, and the sensuality, which is separate, fallen, and redeemed. The place is analogous to the union between divine and human in Christ and the Lord's seat on the ground in 51.123–36 • 22 **ordained to him** predestined to be his • 23 **never shall remeve it** will never leave • 24 **in the sixteenth**

shewing See 68.12 • 28 **waxen** grown • 29–30 **broughte up into stature** grown to maturity. After the "soule is enspired in oure body" (lines 13–14), Jesus looks after God's gifts to the soul until the age of responsibility. Jesus, that is, the humanity of Christ in heaven, provides the "cure and keping" of mercy and grace in line 15: an idea that clearly points forward to the account of God as mother from Chapter 58 on • 30 **as kinde werketh** according to nature • 32–49 **And thus . . . in the god-hede** The final passage in the chapter steps back from the difficult analysis of the soul in its relation to the godhead carried out in the previous two chapters to give an account of salvation history from the perspective this analysis has made available • 32–33 **to se in him . . . to know** Four verbs of knowing to correspond to the persons of the Trinity and the Trinity itself • 33–34 **a made trinite . . . blessed trinite** a created trinity similar to the uncreated blessed Trinity. See Hilton, *The Scale* 1.43, writing of humankind before the fall: at that time "a mannes soule, which may be callid a mad [created] trinite, was fulfilled in minde, sight, and love, of the unmad blissed trinite" • 35 **as it is before saide** See 53.30–33 • 38 **fro doubil deth** death of body and soul • 40 **to whome . . . furst making** to whom the highest was united in the first creation. "Whom" refers to the "lower party," or sensuality; "hyest," to the substance, united to both. Restoration of body and soul could not take place before the Incarnation • 40–41 **theyse two . . . one soule** Christ's own soul was compounded of substance and sensuality • 41–43 **The hyer perty . . . salvation of mankind** This notion that only the sensual part of the soul of Christ, not the substance, suffered at his Passion clearly follows from the account of the substance that has been developed. It also suggests the influence of the doctrine of the "hypostatic union," Christ's union of divine and human natures, on *A Revelation*'s account of the soul. The substance of Christ's soul is here seen to share in what has been called the "unpassible" (impassible) nature of his divinity (see 31.30)

sonne Jhesu Crist. Which gifte and werking is joy to the fader and blisse to the 5
son and liking to the holy gost. And of alle thing that to us longeth, it is most liking
to oure lorde that we enjoye in this joy, /fol. 115v/ which is in the blessed trinite of
oure salvation. And this was sene in the nineth shewing, where it speketh more of
this matere.

And notwithstonding all oure feling, wo or wele, God will we understond and 10
beleve that we be more verely in heven than in erth. Oure faith cometh of the kinde
love of oure soule, and of the clere lighte of oure reson, and of the stedfaste minde
which we have of God in oure furst making. And what time oure soule is enspired
in oure body, in which we be made sensual, as swithe° mercy and grace beginne to
werke, having of us cure and keping with pitte and love. In which werking the holy 15
gost formeth in oure faith hope that we shall come againe up aboven to our substance,
/fol. 116r/ into the vertu of Crist, encresed and fulfilled throw the holy gost.

Thus I understode that the sensualite is grounded in kinde, in mercy, and in
grace, which ground ableth us to receive giftes that leed us to endlesse life. For I saw
full sekerly• that oure substance is in God. And also I saw that in oure sensualite 20
God is. For in the same point that oure soule is made sensual, in the same point is
the citte of God, ordained to him fro without beginning; in which citte he cometh,
and never shall remeve it. For God is never out of the soule, in which he shalle
wonne° blissefully° without end. And this was said in the sixteenth shewing, where it
seyth: "The place that Jhesu taketh in oure soule he shall never remeve it." 25

And all the giftes that God may geve to the creature he /fol. 116v/ hath geven
to his son Jhesu for us. Which giftes he, wonning in us, hath beclosed in him into
the time that we be waxen and growen, oure soule with oure body and oure body
with oure soule, either of them taking° helpe of other tille we be broughte up into
stature, as kinde werketh. And than, in the ground of kind, with werking of mercy 30
the holy gost graciously enspirith into us giftes leding to endlesse life.

And thus was my understanding led of God to se in him, and to wit, to
understonde, and to know, that oure soule is a made trinite like to the unmade
blessed trinite, knowen and loved fro without beginning, and in the making oned to
the maker, as it is before saide. This sight was /fol. 117r/ fulle swete and mervelous to 35
beholde, pesible and restful, seker• and delectabil. And for the worshipful oning that
was thus made of God between the soule and the body, it behoved nedes to be that
mankind shuld be restored fro doubil deth. Which restoring might never be into
the time that the seconde person in the trinite had taken the lower party of mankind,
to whome that hyest was oned in the furst making. And theyse two perties were in 40
Crist, the heyer and the lower, which is but one soule. The hyer perty was ever in

44 **in the eighth shewing** See Chapters 17–20 • 44–45 **fulfilled . . . dying** See 17.41–44 • 46–47 **that was shewed . . . heven** See 19.1–11, 21–32. The second of these passages is an account of the division between Julian's outer and inner "partes," the second of which is described as a "high and a blisseful life, which is alle in peece and in love, and this . . . more prively felte" (lines 25–26). At this stage of *A Revelation,* the earlier passage can be clearly seen as an allusion to the now developed doctrine of the two natures of the soul • 47 **for the mene profer** despite the suggestion by an intermediary. See 19.4–5 • 47 **ech** same • 48 **the inwarde life** Christ's hidden source of life, his substantial soul

[CHAPTER 56] 1–2 **And thus I saw . . . soule** In contemplative theology, self-knowledge is a stage on the way to God. According to Edmund's *Mirror,* "such manere of knowing is foundement [the basis] of contemplation" ("Contemplation of God and of His Deite," *YW* 1:259; see sidenote to 46.5–6). Here, however, the model is daringly reversed, as the quest for self-knowledge becomes a quest for the integration of sensuality and substance in which God is for a few lines seen, not as the end of contemplation, but as the means by which the self comes to know the self • 3–4 **we may not come . . . God** we may not have knowledge of the soul until we first have knowledge of God • 5 **kindly of fulhed** out of an instinct for our completion • 7–8 **we shall know them both in one** we shall know God and the soul both in one act of knowing • 8–9 **it is both good and trew** both are good and true • 9 **more nerer** closer • 9 **he is grounde** See 53.25–29 • 10–11 **mene that kepeth . . . togeder** the intermediary who keeps the substance and the sensuality together. As has

already been made clear, God keeps the soul together as a "mene" through the instrumentality of "oure faith" (54.22) • 11 **it shall never departe** substance and sensuality shall never be separated • 12 **seker** confident • 14–15 **comening and dalyance** conversation and dalliance, or love talk • 15 **it behoveth** it is necessary • 16 **in the sixteenth shewing** See Chapter 68 • 17–19 **as anemptis . . . God** concerning our substance: it can properly be called our soul. And concerning our sensuality: it can properly be called our soul, and that is because of the union that it has in God. Union, that is, with the substance, with God as the "mene" (line 10). Knowledge of the soul implies knowledge of both the substance and the sensuality, since both can be called "soul" • 19–21 **That wurshipful citte . . . godhed** The sensuality is "oned" in God because the human Jesus is enclosed in it, while the substance is enclosed in the human Jesus, along with Christ's soul, all in turn enclosed within God. Theological Russian dolls declare the intricacy of the "knot" that ties God and human. For this "knot" and the importance to it of "the blessed soule of Crist," see 53.47–54 • 23 **so depe into God** The language of depth again belongs to Christian Neoplatonism, with its model of a God who can be known more fully as the soul penetrates (or, here, is "led") into the divine being. This is the model that governs the structure, and the title, of Bonaventure's *Itinerarium mentis in Deum,* the soul's journey into God. See also "hye depnesse [exalted depth]" in lines 24–25, a phrase of deliberately oxymoronic force that perhaps echoes Eccles. 7:24 (on the topic of wisdom): "That which is, is far off, and deep, very deep [Vulgate *alta profunditas,* "a great or high depth"]; who can find it out?"

pees with God, in full joy and blisse. The lower perty, which is sensualite, suffered
for the salvation of mankind. And theyse two perties were seene and felte /fol. 117v/
in the eighth shewing, in which my body was fulfilled of feling and mind of Cristes
passion and his dying; and, ferthermore, with this, was a suttel feling and a prevy
inwarde sighte of the hye party.° And that was shewed in the same time, wher I
mighte not, for the mene profer, loke up into heven. And that was for that ech
mighty beholding of the inwarde life. Which inwarde life is that hye substance,
that precious soule, which is endlessly enjoyeng in the godhede.

THE FIFTY-SIXTH CHAPTER

And thus I saw full sekerly• that it is redier to us and more esy to come° to the
knowing of God then to know oure owne soule. For oure soule is so depe
grounded in God, and /fol. 118r/ so endlesly tresored, that we may not come to the
knowing therof tille we have furst knowing of God, which is the maker to whome it
is oned. But notwithstonding, I saw that we have kindly of fulhed to desyer wisely
and truly to know oure owne soule, wherby we be lerned to seke it ther it is, and that
is into God. And thus, by the gracious leding of the holy gost, we shall know them°
both in one. Whether we be stered to know God or oure soule, it is both good and
trew. God is more nerer to us than oure owne soule. For he is grounde in whome
oure soule standeth, and he is mene that kepeth the substance and the sensualite
togeder, so that it shall never departe. For oure soule sitteth in God in very rest, and
oure /fol. 118v/ soule stondeth in God in seker° strenght, and oure soule is kindely
roted in God in endlesse love.

And therfore, if we wille have knowing of oure soule, and comening and
dalyance therwith, it behoveth to seke into oure lord God in whom it is enclosed.
And of this enclosing I saw and understode more in the sixteenth shewing, as I shall
sey. And as° anemptis oure substance: it may rightly be called oure soule. And
anemptis oure sensualite: it may rightly be called oure soule, and that is by the
oning that it hath in God. That wurshipful citte that oure lorde Jhesu sitteth in, it is
oure sensualite, in which he is enclosed. And oure kindly substance is beclosed in
Jhesu, with the blessed soule of Crist sitting in rest in the godhed.

And I saw full sekerly• that it behoveth nedes to be that /fol. 119r/ we shulde be
in longing and in penance, into the time that we be led so depe into God that we
verely and trewly know oure owne soule. And sothly° I saw that into this hye
depnesse our good lorde himselfe ledeth us, in the same love that he made us
and in the same love that° he boughte us, by mercy and grace, thorow vertu of his
blessed passion.

45

5

10

15

20

25

28–29 And notwithstanding . . . oure owne soule A characteristic reversal of viewpoint, resembling the apparent *volte-face* on "meanes" and the divine goodness in Chapter 6 • **29–30 For into the time . . . full holy** for until the soul attains its full powers, we cannot be fully holy. The substance is not complete without the sensuality • **30 that is that** that is when • **31–32 with . . . oure tribulation** The virtues and rewards gained by the sensuality in this life • **33 I had in perty . . . kind** I had a glimpse of spiritual intuition, and it (the soul or the soul's doubleness) is grounded in being or nature. Unless the phrase "and it is grounded in kind" describes the source of this moment of "touching" or simply alludes back to 55.18, it appears to be the "touching" itself: a moment of new revelation that takes place as Julian writes. For "touchings," moments of insight outside the original revelation, see 65.29–31. The rest of the chapter, beginning with the elucidating phrase "that is," expands this "touching," which explores further the double nature of the soul in relation to the concept of "kind": a word that here means "being," "nature," and "creation," all used as synonyms for "substance." The basic argument is that, although the soul participates in God's perfect being so far as its substance is concerned, it paradoxically cannot be complete until it has first been "doubled," split off into substance and sensuality, so that aspects of divinity other than "kind," namely mercy and grace, can be brought to bear on it. Although this is not made explicit, the argument is shaped around the exemplum of the lord and the servant, with the substance standing in for the lord, the sensuality for the servant • **34 reson** A partial synonym for the substance • **34 which is substantial kindhede** who is the ultimate source of being • **35 mercy and grace . . . spredeth into us** See 55.13–15, where "mercy and grace" begin to work as soon as the self comes into being. "Reson" can have existence as the soul's substance in and of itself. "Mercy and grace," which are needed for the self to be complete, are from God and can only function in relation to the sensuality. This is why sensuality has to be part of the self, in addition to substance • **38 encres and . . . fulfilling**

growth and completion. These only come about through mercy and grace in their dealings with the sensuality • **38–39 thre propertes in one goodnes** "Kinde," mercy, and grace are one, like the members of the Trinity • **39–40 which be now longing to us** which are now appropriate for us • **40–44 God wille we understande . . . his love** To know the self in full is thus to know "kinde," mercy, and grace, since these are the qualities that make up the life of the soul, according to lines 37–38: its "life," which pertains especially to the substance; and its "encres and fulfilling," which pertain to the sensuality • **41 of them** of "kinde," mercy, and grace • **45–46 evenly . . . love** memory and love equally with reason. The created trinity of the human faculties described in 55.32–35 • **46–47 Ne onely . . . saved** nor may we be saved solely through our essential ground that we have in God. The substance cannot save us on its own • **50 onely in oure spirite** in our spirit on its own • **51 doubil** double. Substantial and sensual, and so able to receive God's mercy and grace as well as being. By the end of the chapter, the soul's self-division and consequent lack of ability to know itself in this life is understood and accepted

[CHAPTER 57] **1 anemptes our substance** as regards our substance. This final chapter on the doctrine of the substance, declared in 53.12–14, synthesizes the teachings of the previous chapters, describing the course of the life of the soul from the creation of the sensuality on • **3–4 For sothly . . . stinting** Compare 44.1–2: "God shewed . . . that man werketh evermore his wille . . . lastingly without stinting" • **4 ony stinting** any ceasing • **4–5 grete richesse and . . . high noble** Of the soul's substance • **5 vertues by mesure** a proportion of virtues. Reprises 54.22–24 and 55.11–15 • **6 we be made sensual** we are made sensual beings • **7–8 which failing . . . goodhede** God will restore and complete this failing by the activity of mercy and grace, flowing into us plentifully from his own natural goodness. Reprises the account of mercy and grace in 56.33–51

And notwithstanding all this, we may never come to the full knowing of God tille we knowe furst clerely oure owne soule. For into the time that it is in the full mightis, we may not be alle full° holy—and that is that oure sensualite, by the vertu of Cristes passion, be brought up into the substance, with all the profites of oure tribulation that oure lorde shall make us to get by mercy and grace.

I had in perty /fol. 119v/ touching, and it is grounded in kind: that is to say, oure reson is grounded in God, which is substantial kindhede.° Of this substantial kindhede,° mercy and grace springeth and spredeth into us, werking all thinges in fulfilling of oure joy. Theyse be oure groundes, in which we have oure being, oure encrese, and oure fulfilling. For in kinde we have oure life and oure being, and in mercy and grace we have oure encres and oure fulfilling. It be thre propertes in one goodnes. And where that one werketh, alle werken in the thinges which be now longing to us. God wille we understande, desyering with all oure hart and alle oure strength to have knowing of them, ever more and more, into the time that we be fulfilled. For fully to know them and /fol. 120r/ clerely to se them is not elles but endles joy and blisse that we shall have in heven; which God will we beginne here in knowing of his love.

For only by oure reson we may not profite, but if we have evenly therwith minde and love. Ne onely in oure kindly grounde that we have in God we may not be saved, but if we have, coming° of the same grounde, mercy and grace. For of these thre werkinges alle togeder we receive alle oure goodes: of which the furst be goodes of kinde. For in oure furst making, God gave us as moch good and as grete good as we might receive onely in oure spirite. But his forseeing perpos in his endlesse wisdom wolde that we were doubil.

THE FIFTY-SEVENTH CHAPTER

And anemptes oure substance, /fol. 120v/ he made us so nobil and so rich that evermore we werke his wille and his worshippe. Ther I sey "we," it meneth man that shall be saved. For sothly° I saw that we be that he loveth, and do that him liketh lastingly withoute ony stinting. And of this grete richesse and of this high noble, vertues by mesure come to oure soule, what time that it is knit to oure body, in which knitting we be made sensual. And thus in oure substance we be full and in oure sensualite we faile; which failing God wille restore and fulfil by werking of mercy and grace, plentuously flowing into us of his owne° kinde goodhede.• And thus this kinde goodhede• maketh that mercy and grace werketh in us, and the kinde goodhede• that we /fol. 121r/ have of him ableth us to receive the werking of mercy and grace.

12 **oure kinde** the soul's substance • 12 **diversites** different things. Another reference to the theory of emanation central to Christian Neoplatonism, in which the divine one flows outward into the many. Here, however, the "hole" is the quality of "kinde [being]," which has also been referred to as "reson" (56.34), which is the soul's substance. "Diversites" include the various qualities of the sensuality, sustained by mercy and grace (lines 4–11) and by "oure faith" (line 22) • 14 **of theyse** of these different things • 14 **perished** lost • 15 **in the making** through its creation • 15–16 **oure kinde . . . the lower party** The sensuality also participates in "kinde," as the lower half of the soul's two natures. Again, Christ's union of divine and human appears to be the source of the idea • 16 **in oure flesh taking** through the Incarnation • 16 **in Crist . . . oned** in Christ our two natures are united. See 56.10–11. The soul is incoherent in its doubleness without Christ. "Kinde" means sensuality as well as substance • 18 **the secund parson** Christ • 18–19 **which kind furst to him was adight** which nature was prepared for him from the first. In Col. 1:16–17, Paul writes that "all things were created through [Christ] and for him. . . . and in him all things hold together." See 58.1–3 • 22 **The nexte good** the next "diversite" • 22 **is oure faith** After the sensuality comes into being before birth (lines 5–6), faith is administered through baptism • 22 **profeting** profiting. The process by which the sensuality earns reward for its earthly existence • 23 **it cometh . . . oure sensual soule** The claim that "faith," also called a "seker truste of oure being," is the contribution made by the substance to the sensual soul has been elaborated in 54.22–29 • 24–25 **the werking of mercy and grace** As described in 56.33–51, where mercy and grace are essential to the existence of the sensuality and come, not from the substance, but from God • 25 **therof** From the "faith" as "grounded" by mercy and grace • 26–32 **the commaundementes . . . all manner**

vertuse Faith is a conduit for the understanding of Christian living, instilling knowledge of the Ten Commandments and the seven sacraments, as well as of the virtues. All these, in other words, come into the sensual soul from the substance, which knows them intuitively as a result of its hidden enclosure in the godhead • 27 **we owe** we ought • 32–34 **the same vertuse . . . renewed** the same virtues that we have received from our substance, given to us through nature by the goodness of God [see line 5], these same gifts are given us through grace by the activity of mercy, renewed by the Holy Spirit. God "cooperates" with the substance in instilling faith and the virtues in the soul • 35–39 **in that same time . . . man** A remarkable claim developed from the earlier discussion of the soul of Christ in 53.44–54.12 and with roots in the exemplum of the lord and servant. The redemption of humankind is understood as the uniting of the sensuality and the substance in Christ as perfect and collective human being. Human selfhood thus emerges as incoherent except in Christ. See, again, the first chapter of Colossians, where Christ is called "the first-born of all creation" and "the head of the body, the church" • 40 **oure lady is oure moder** The claim just made also makes Mary into the mother of humankind in a new way—although the sense in which Christ is himself the mother now comes to the fore • 42 **oure saviour . . . moder** A central theme in Chapters 58–63 • 44 **in the furst** See 6.29 • 45 **in the sixteenth shewing** See 68.6–7 • 46–50 **For it is his liking . . . trusting in him** The dizzying abstraction of the chapter's teaching on the two natures of the human soul, the sensuality's dependence on divine mercy and grace, and the role of Jesus as the power that makes the soul one with itself all resolves into a narrative picture of Christ enthroned in the soul like a king at the center of his kingdom • 47 **wonne** dwell

I saw that oure kinde is in God hole, in which he maketh diversites, flowing oute of him, to werke his wille, whom° kinde kepeth, and mercy and grace restoreth and fulfilleth. And of theyse, none shalle be perished. For oure kinde, which is the hyer party, is knitte to God in the making; and God is knit to oure kinde, which is the lower party, in oure flesh taking. And thus in Crist oure two kindes be oned. For the trinite is comprehended in Crist, in whom oure hyer party is grounded and roted. And oure lower party, the secund parson hath taken, which kind furst to him was adight. For I saw full sekerly° that alle the werkes that /fol. 121v/ God hath done, or ever shall, were full knowen to him and before seen fro without beginning. And for love he made mankind, and for the same love himselfe wolde become man.

The nexte good that we receive is oure faith, in which oure profeting beginneth. And it cometh of the hye richesse of oure kinde substance into oure sensual soule; and it is grounded in us, and we in that, throw the kinde goodnes of God by the werking of mercy and grace. And therof come alle other goodes° by which we be led and saved. For the commaundementes of God come therein, in which we owe to have two manner of understanding. That one is that we owe to understand and know which be his biddinges, to love them and to kepe them. That other is that /fol. 122r/ we owe to knowe his forbiddinges, to hate them and refuse them. For in theyse two is all oure werking comprehended. Also in oure faith come the seven sacramentes, eche following other in order as God hath ordained° them to us, and all manner vertuse. For the same vertuse that we have received of oure substance, geven to us in kind of the goodnes of God, the same vertuse by the werking of mercy be geven to us in grace, throw the holy gost renewed; which vertuse and giftes are tresoured to us in Jhesu Criste. For in that same time that God knit him to oure body in the maidens wombe, he toke oure sensual soule. In which taking— he us all having beclosed in him—he oned it to oure substance, in which oning he was perfit man. For Crist, having /fol. 122v/ knit in him all man that shall be saved, is perfete man.

Thus oure lady is oure moder, in whome we be all beclosed and of her borne in Crist. For she that is moder of oure savioure is mother of all that ben saved in our savioure. And oure savioure is oure very moder, in whome we be endlesly borne and never shall come out of him. Plentuously, fully, and swetely was this shewde; and it is spoken of in the furst, wher it saide: "We be all in him beclosed." And he is beclosed in us; and that is spoken of in the sixteenth shewing, where he seyth: "He sitteth in oure soule." For it is his liking to reigne in oure understanding blissefully,° and sitte° in oure soule restfully, and to wonne° in oure soule endlesly, us all werking into him. In which werking he /fol. 123r/ wille we be his helpers, geving to him alle

15

20

25

30

35

40

45

49 **keping his lore** retaining his teaching • 50 **For sothly . . . God** Brings to a close the discussion of this doctrine

[CHAPTER 58] 1–3 **God . . . to make mankinde** A stately generalized opening to the chapter, which signals arrival at a new stage in the discussion and a new topic, God as mother. To this point, every chapter since Chapter 49 has begun with "and" • 2 **purpose endlesse** endless purpose • 3 **which fair kind** Human nature • 3 **dight to** assigned to • 3 **the second person** Christ. The focus of the next group of chapters concerns the special part Christ plays in the life of the soul • 4 **when he woulde** when Christ desired it. "He" could also be God in trinity, but in context it seems to be Christ in particular who is intended here • 4 **alle at ones** all in an instant • 5 **he knit us** See 53.49–52, where the soul of Christ is "knit to [God] in the making"; also 57.35–39 • 6 **that ech precious** that same precious • 9 **the godly wille before saide** See 53.9–10, drawing on a discussion in Chapter 37. The godly will, or substance, by virtue of its createdness, must "love oure maker and like him" • 12–13 **we his loved wife . . . maiden** Returns to language used only in the last lines of Chapter 51 and the first lines of Chapter 52, where the soul is described in the spousal language of the Song of Songs. Compare 51.277–78: "his loved wife, which is the fair maiden of endless joy." The allusion serves a structural purpose, locating the discussion that follows in the aftermath of the historical events described in Chapter 51: that is, in the present when, after his life and death, Christ's redemptive work has reached its final phase • 13 **For he seyeth** The following declaration, in which Christ speaks to humankind as the bridegroom to the bride, is important enough to be repeated twice near the end of the work, in 79.13–15 and 82.15–16, by which point it has attained the status of part of the revelation • 14 **oure love . . . in two** See *The Scale* 1.8, after quoting 1 Cor. 6:17: "Whoso by raveshinge of love is fastned to God, thanne God and a soule aren not

two but bothe oon. . . . And sothely in this oninge is the mariage mad bitwixe God and the soule which shal nevere be broken." However, Hilton here writes of contemplative union between the pure soul and Christ. *A Revelation* concerns a state of unity already attained by the very fact of the soul's creation as substance and sensuality and the "knitting" together of these two in Christ • 15–24 **I beheld . . . plentuous grace** This passage describes the workings of the Trinity in brief, in terms already evolved in Chapters 53–57. These relatively basic observations are thus intended to sum up what has been established about God in his dealings with humankind to this point • 18 **as anemptes** as regards • 21–22 **moder, broder, and saviour** Correspond to "keping," "restoring," "saving." See the earlier use of these terms for Christ in 52.1–3 • 22 **yelding** payment • 25–27 **all oure life . . . grace** Discussion now focuses more specifically on the teaching of 56.33–44 on "kinde," mercy, and grace, "being . . . encresing . . . fulfilling." This then becomes the germ of *A Revelation*'s next major exposition • 27–30 **For the furst . . . substantial making** Lines 15–24, which assign each part of life a person of the Trinity, lead one to expect that "kinde" will continue to be associated with the Father. But in *A Revelation* the Trinity is always process more than state, and all three persons turn out to be implicated in the soul's "being," its "kinde" or substance, with the Son taking a special role of his own • 27 **For the furst** as to the first • 30 **oure substantial making** creation of the substantial part of our souls • 30–32 **the seconde person . . . moder sensual** the second person, who is mother to the substance, this same precious person has now become mother to our sensuality. Through the Incarnation. The emphasis of Chapters 58–62 is increasingly on God's motherhood and the sensuality, as in lines 19–21. This and the next chapter, however, both start from the argument that Christ is mother to the substance before he is mother to the sensuality • 32 **we be doubel** See 56.50–51

oure entent, lerning his lawes, keping his lore, desyering that alle be done that he
doth, truly trusting in him. For sothly° I saw that oure substance is in God.　　　　50

God, the blisseful• trinite, which is everlasting being, right as he is endlesse
fro without beginning, righte so it was in his purpose endlesse to make
mankinde; which fair kind furst was dight to his owne son, the second person. And
when he woulde, by full accorde of alle the trinite, he made us alle at ones. And in
oure making he knit us and oned us to himselfe, by which oning we be kept as clene　　5
and as noble as we were made. By the vertu of that ech precious oning we /fol. 123v/
love oure maker and like him, praise him and thanke him and endlesly enjoye in
him. And this is the werking which is wrought continually in ech soule that shalle be
saved, which is the godly wille before saide. And thus in oure making God almighty
is oure kindly fader, and God alle wisdom is oure kindly mother, with the love and　　10
the goodnes of the holy gost, which is alle one God, one lorde. And in the knitting
and in the oning he is oure very tru spouse, and we his loved wife and his fair
maiden, with which wife he was never displesed. For he seyeth: "I love the and
thou lovest me, and oure love shall never be departed° in two."

　　I beheld the werking of alle the blessed trinite, in which beholding I saw and　　15
/fol. 124r/ understode these thre propertes: the properte of the faderhed, and the
properte of the motherhed, and the properte of the lordhede° in one God. In oure
fader almighty we have oure keping and oure blesse, as° anemptes oure kindely
substance, which is to us by oure making fro without beginning. And in the seconde
person, in wit and wisdom, we have oure keping, as° anemptes oure sensualite, oure　　20
restoring, and oure saving. For he is oure moder, broder, and savioure. And in oure
good lorde the holy gost we have oure rewarding and oure yelding for oure living
and oure traveyle, and endlessly overpassing alle that we desyer in his mervelous
curtesy of his hye, plentuous grace.

　　For alle oure life is in thre: in the /fol. 124v/ furst we have° oure being, and in° the　　25
seconde we have oure encresing, and in the thirde we have oure fulfilling. The furst
is kinde, the seconde is mercy, the thirde is grace. For the furst: I saw and understode
that the high might of the trinite is oure fader, and the depe wisdom of the trinite
is oure moder, and the grete love of the trinite is oure lorde. And alle these have we
in kinde and in oure substantial making. And fertheremore I saw that the seconde　　30
person, which is oure moder substantially, the same derewurthy person is now
become oure moder sensual. For we be doubel of Gods making: that is to sey,
substantial and sensual. Oure substance is the hyer perty, which we have in oure

34–35 **the seconde person . . . grounded and roted** See lines 2–3, where the Son is given the task of creation • 36 **in oure sensualite taking** by taking our sensuality. See 57.35–36 • 37–38 **in whom oure pertes . . . undeperted** in whom our parts are kept undivided. Christ as mother first produced and now preserves the integrity of sensuality and substance. A process described in Chapter 57 • 40 **oneth** unites • 41 **buxom and obedient** compliant and obedient. As good children are in Middle English. The first hint that the motherhood of God is to be associated with discipline as well as love • 42 **namely** especially • 42 **as it was shewde** Perhaps a reference to 48.21–32, which anticipates the present discussion of mercy and grace, though without making specific reference to the Holy Spirit • 43 **he werketh . . . geving** the Holy Spirit works, rewarding and giving. These "two propertes" are then defined • 44 **Rewarding is . . . traveyled** reward is a generous gift according to pledge that the Lord makes to those who have labored. The gift of salvation • 45–46 **geving is . . . creatures** giving is a courteous act that God performs freely of his grace, completing and transcending all that is deserved by created beings. Although the "reward" of salvation itself involves "geving" as well as human desert, "geving" here pertains to the rewards other than salvation the saved are to receive. The distinction between reward and gift is anticipated in 51.40–45, where the lord asks with regard to the servant, "Is it not skille that I reward him . . . ?" then adds, "falleth it not to me to geve him a gifte . . . ?" • 48–49 **in whom . . . perfite man** In 57.35–39, Christ is described as perfect man • 49–50 **by yelding . . . fulfillede** we are completed by the grace of the Holy Spirit through his paying and giving • 53–57 **oure sensualite . . . the holy gost** Although the chapter continues to reaffirm the indivisibility of the Trinity, by its end it has established the second person, Christ, as fundamental to the life of the sensuality, just as he is to the life of the substance. The way is now clear for a discussion of Jesus' maternal relation to the sensual soul • 53 **oure sensualite . . . seconde person** Only Christ took flesh •

54–55 **we be mightly taken out of hell** An allusion to the harrowing of hell described in 51.188–91. Note that the word "we" here identifies writer and readers with their sensual souls • 56 **blissefully oned . . . substance** joyfully united with our substance. See 56.22–27 • 56 **nobly** nobility

[CHAPTER 59] 2–3 **but if that properte . . . blisse** if that property of goodness that is God, through which we have this joy, had not been opposed. The Fall is crucial to human selfhood, a point made throughout the chapter, whose main concern is with the role of evil in soul making and its relation to the theme of divine motherhood. Use of "contraried" here suggests a relationship between this chapter and Chapter 48, which makes an early attempt at issues analyzed in this chapter, describing the "contrariousnes" that anger sustains in the soul because of "sinne and wrechednesse" (lines 6–9) • 3–4 **hath been suffered to rise contrary** has been allowed to rise in opposition • 4 **goodnesse of . . . grace** A specialized aspect of God's goodness, designed to combat wickedness by mercy and grace • 4–5 **contraried against** strove against • 6 **it is that properte** goodness of mercy and grace is that property • 7 **very true** • 7–8 **we have oure being . . . beginneth** The soul's substance takes its being from the place in Christ where the various manifestations of his property of motherhood are grounded. See lines 37–41 • 10 **As verely as . . . moder** as truly as God is our Father, as truly he is our Mother. A significant claim, since "father" is the name used for one of the persons of the Trinity, and so one of the most deeply institutionalized of all Christian metaphors. In Chapter 60, the argument is made that "mother" is more than a mere metaphor for Christ • 10–11 **that shewde he in all** he revealed that in all the revelations • 11 **there he seyth** where he says • 11 **I it am** See Chapter 26 • 11 **That is to sey** A set of elaborations of "I it am" different from those elucidated in 26.4–8

fader God almighty. And the /fol. 125r/ seconde person of the trinite is oure moder
in kind in oure substantial making, in whom we be grounded and roted, and he is   35
oure moder of mercy in oure sensualite taking.

  And thus oure moder is to us diverse manner werking, in whom oure pertes
be kepte undeperted. For in oure moder Crist we profit and encrese, and in mercy
he reformeth us and restoreth, and by the vertu of his passion, his deth, and his
uprising oneth° us to oure substance. Thus worketh oure moder in mercy to all his   40
beloved children which be to him buxom and obedient. And grace werketh with
mercy, and namely in two propertes, as it was shewde, which werking longeth
to the thurde person, the holy gost: he werketh, rewarding and geving. /fol. 125v/
Rewarding is large geving of trewth° that the lorde doth to them that hath traveyled,
and geving is a curtesse werking which he doth frely of grace, fulfilling and   45
overpassing alle that is deserved of creatures.

  Thus in oure fader God almighty we have oure being. And in oure moder of
mercy we have oure reforming and oure restoring, in whom oure partes be oned
and all made perfite man. And by yelding and geving in grace of the holy gost we be
fulfillede. And our substance is in oure fader, God almighty, and oure substance is in   50
oure moder, God all wisdom, and oure substance is in oure lorde God the holy gost,
all goodnes. For oure substance is hole in ech person of the trinite, which is one
God. And oure sensualite is only in the seconde person, /fol. 126r/ Crist Jhesu, in
whom is the fader and the holy gost. And in him and by him we be mightly taken
out of hell and oute of the wrechednesse in erth, and wurshipfully brought up into   55
heven, and blissefully• oned to oure substance, encresed in richesse and nobly by all
the vertu of Crist, and by the grace and werking of the holy gost.

THE FIFTY-NINTH CHAPTER

And all° this blisse we have by mercy and grace, which manner blisse we might
never have had and knowen, but if that properte of goodnesse which is God°
had ben contraried, wherby we have this blisse. For wickednesse hath been suffered
to rise contrary to that goodnesse, and the goodnesse of mercy and grace contraried
against that wickednesse, and turned all to goodnesse /fol. 126v/ and wurshippe to all   5
that shall be saved. For it is that properte in God which doth good against evil. Thus
Jhesu Crist, that doth good against evil, is oure very moder: we have oure being of
him, where the ground of moderhed beginneth, with alle the swete keping of love
that endlesly foloweth.

  As verely as God is oure fader, as verely is God oure moder. And that shewde he   10
in all, and namely in theyse swete wordes there he seyth: "I it am." That is to sey: "I it

16–17 **For ther . . . ther** for where . . . there. The highest place in the soul, its substance, is also the lowest, humbled before the totality of Christ's "I it am" • 17–18 **of this substantial grounde** from this ground of the substance • 18–19 **we have . . . profite** Retraces ground covered in 54.22–24, 55.11–15 • 19 **speding** assisting • 20–21 **almighty God . . . before ony time** See 53.30: "For or that he made us he loved us" • 22 **forseeing endlesse councel** providential eternal design. "Councel" could also allude to the Council in Heaven most famously described in Grosseteste's *Chateau d'amour,* in which God the Son is duly appointed savior of mankind after consideration by all the Trinity, aided by various allegorical personages • 23 **oure moder . . . savioure** See 52.1–4 • 24–25 **Oure fader willeth . . . confirmeth** The structure is still that of the trinity of "kinde, mercy, and grace," as lines 29–31 make clear • 27 **of oure making** for our creation • 28 **mercy and pitte** See the lord's "fair loking" at his fallen servant in 51.111–19 • 29 **in these three . . . life** Similar to 58.25 • 29 **werof** from which • 30 **hating of sinne** See 52.44–45 • 30–31 **longeth properly** is appropriate • 31 **vertuse** virtues • 32–33 **thus is Jhesu . . . kinde made** The shift toward Christ as mother to the sensuality, rather than the substance, now becomes more pronounced • 33 **by taking . . . made** by taking our created nature • 33–34 **the swete . . . motherhed** the sweet, natural functions associated with precious motherhood. These are a major topic of Chapters 60–63 • 34 **is inpropred to** is assigned to • 35 **this godly wille** See 53.8–14. The final reference to the godly will in the work •

37 **thre manner . . . in God** three modes of insights concerning motherhood in God • 40 **forthspreding** spreading forth. The image of the pouring-forth of goodness from the one into the many belongs to Christian Neoplatonism. See 48.28, 56.34–36, 57.12–13, and also the image of the "spreding abrode" of Christ's blood on his forehead in 7.9–26 • 40–41 **of length and brede . . . ende** of a length and a breadth, of a height and a depth, without end. See Eph. 3:17–19: "That you, being rooted and grounded in love, may have power to comprehend with all the saints what is the breadth and length and height and depth, and to know the love of Christ which surpasses knowledge"

[CHAPTER 60] 1 **now me behoveth . . . more of** now I need to say a little more about. After the theological intricacy of much of the last nine chapters, the opening of this chapter suggests an informal excitement and enthusiasm. What follows further extends the idea of Christ as mother, giving him a literal, physically maternal role in ordinary human processes • 1 **forthspreding** spreading forth. See 59.40, and compare "forthbringing" in lines 42–43 • 2–4 **how that we . . . leeveth us** how we are brought back by the motherhood of mercy and grace into our natural home, where we were created by the motherhood of essential love, which never leaves us. The return of the soul to God—a process reciprocal to the divine "forthspreding" whose goal is to bring this return about—is a major motif in this and the next three chapters

am, the might and the goodnes of faderhode. I it am, the wisdom and the kindnes°
of moderhode. I it am, the light and the grace that is all blessed love. I it am, the
trinite. I it am, the unite. I it am, the hye sovereyn goodnesse of all manner thing. I
it am that maketh the to love.° I it am that makith the to long. I it am, the endlesse   15
fulfilling of all true desyers." /fol. 127r/ For ther the soule is hyest, nobliest, and
wurshipfullest, ther it is lowest,° mekest, and mildest. And of this substantial
grounde, we have all oure vertuse in oure sensualite by gift of kind, and by helping
and speding of mercy and grace, withoute which we may not profite.

Oure hye fader, almighty God, which is being, he knew° us and loved us fro   20
before ony time. Of which knowing, in his full mervelous depe charite, by the
forseeing endlesse councel of all the blessed trinite, he woulde that the seconde
person shulde become oure moder, oure brother, and oure savioure. Whereof it
foloweth that as verely as God is oure fader, as verely God is oure mother. Oure
fader willeth, oure mother werketh, oure good lorde the holy gost confirmeth.   25
/fol. 127v/ And therfore it longeth to us to love oure God in whome we have oure
being, him reverently thanking and praising of oure making, mightly prayeng to
oure moder of mercy and pitte, and to oure lorde the holy gost of helpe and grace.
For in these three is alle oure life: kind, mercy, and grace, werof we have mekehede,°
mildehed, patience, and pitte, and hating of sinne and wickednesse—for it longeth   30
properly to vertuse to hat sinne and wickednesse.

And thus is Jhesu oure very moder in kind of oure furst making, and he is oure
very moder° in grace by taking of oure kinde made. Alle the fair werking and all the
swete kindly officis of dereworthy motherhed is inpropred to the seconde person.
For in him we have this godly wille,° hole and safe without ende, both in kinde and   35
in grace, of his owne /fol. 128r/ proper goodnesse.

I understode thre manner of beholdinges of motherhed in God. The furst is
grounde of oure kinde making. The seconde is taking of oure kinde, and ther
beginneth the moderhed of grace. The thurde is moderhed in werking, and therin
is a forthspreding by the same grace, of length and brede, of high and of depnesse   40
without ende. And alle is one love.

THE SIXTIETH CHAPTER

But now me behoveth to seye a litil more of this forthspreding, as I
understonde° in the mening of oure lord: how that we be brought againe,
by the motherhed of mercy and grace, into oure kindly stede where that we ware
made° by the moderhed of kind love, which kinde love never leeveth us.

5–6 for he wolde . . . thing because he wanted to become altogether our mother in all things • **7 in the furst** see 4.24–26: "He brought our lady Saint Mary to my understanding . . . in the stature as she was when she conceivede" • **9–11 our hye God . . . thing** God was born of a mother in order to become a mother • **10 he arayed . . . him** he arrayed and prepared himself • **12 sekerest** surest • **13–14 This office . . . he alone** none but he alone might or could fully perform this office • **15 We wit . . . to dying** we know that all our mothers deliver us into pain and death. Opens an extended discussion of Christ first as better than earthly mothers, then, from line 39, as more genuinely motherly than earthly mothers • **16–17 bereth us to joye . . . leving** delivers us into joy and eternal life • **18 traveyled into the full time** was in labor until the fullness of time. "The full time" means that he carried humanity to term, but also alludes to Eph. 1:10, where Christ is the manifestation of the divine purpose as God's "plan for the fulness of time, to unite all things in him, things in heaven and things on earth." See also Gal. 4:4–5 • **18–19 sharpest throwes . . . shalle be** the sharpest birth pangs and the most severe pains that were ever felt or will ever be felt. Humanity's birth is accomplished at Christ's death • **20 make aseeth to** give satisfaction to. The word is elsewhere used of the Passion, as in 52.72 • **21 in theyse . . . wordes** See 22.4–5 • **22 might no more die** might not die any more • **23 stinte of werking** stop working. Having given birth to humankind, his work is only just begun, and in this sense his earlier pledge to suffer more if he could is fulfilled • **23 him behoveth to fede us** he has to feed us • **24 dettour to us**

debtor to us. In the same sense that a mother owes a child the debt of her responsibility for the child's existence • **25 The moder . . . milke** the mother may give her child her milk to suck • **27 fode of very life** food of true life. Christ feeds his people with his flesh in the Mass, where the congregation affirms its membership in the body of Christ by eating it in the form of bread • **29 theyse blessed wordes** See 26.7 • **31–32 that is ordained . . . the** that is ordained for you by holy church • **34 homely lede** intimately lead • **34 into his blessed brest . . . open side** Late medieval devotion often saw an association between the wound in Christ's side and a breast from which blood, not milk, is sucked. See *The Pryckinge:* "For this shal thou love that holy flesh and souke out of hit at his woundes that aren so wide the swetnesse of grace that is hid withinne. . . . And yif thou wolt have grace, or vertu, or help, or swetnesse, or comfort, souke hit out and drawe hit out of the swete flesh of Jhesu Crist and of his precious manhede" (6) • **36 in the tenth** See 24.1–10, where "with his swete loking he led forth the understanding of his creature by the same wound into his sid, within" and "shewed . . . in part the blessed godhede" • **39–41 may not verely . . . alle** may not truly be said of anyone, nor to anyone, but of him and to him who is true mother of life and of all. With this turn, "mother" is claimed to be more than a metaphor for Christ, and earthly mothering emerges as only a shadow of, or at best a passive participant in, heavenly mothering. The rest of the chapter explores this claim • **42 forthbringing** delivery

Oure kinde moder, oure gracious moder, for he /fol. 128v/ wolde alle holy° 5
become oure moder in alle thing, he toke the grounde of his werke full lowe and full
mildely in the maidens wombe. And that shewde he in the furst, wher he broughte
that meke maiden before the eye of my understonding, in the simpil stature as she
was whan she conceived: that is to sey, oure hye God, the sovereyn wisdom of all, in
this lowe place he arayed him and dight him all redy in oure poure flesh, himselfe to 10
do the service and the office° of moderhode in alle thing.

The moders service is nerest, rediest, and sekerest:• nerest, for it is most of kind;
rediest, for it is most of love; and sekerest, for it is most of trewth. This office ne
might nor coulde never none done to the full but he alone.

We wit that alle oure moders bere us to paine and to dying. A, /fol. 129r/ what 15
is that? But oure very° moder Jhesu, he alone bereth us to joye and to endlesse
leving—blessed mot he be! Thus he sustaineth us within him° in love, and
traveyled° into the full time that he wolde suffer the sharpest throwes and the
grevousest paines° that ever were or ever shalle be, and died at the last. And whan
he had done, and so borne us to blisse, yet might not all this make aseeth to his 20
mervelous love. And that shewd he in theyse hye, overpassing wordes of love: "If I
might suffer more, I wold suffer more." He might no more die, but he wolde not
stinte of° werking. Wherfore him behoveth to fede° us, for the deerworthy love of
moderhed hath made him dettour to us.

The moder may geve her childe sucke° her milke. But oure precious moder 25
Jhesu, he may fede us /fol. 129v/ with himselfe, and doth full curtesly and full
tenderly with the blessed sacrament that is precious fode of very life. And with all
the swete sacramentes he sustaineth us full mercifully and graciously. And so ment
he in theyse blessed wordes where he saide: "I it am that holy church precheth the
and techeth the." That is to sey: "All the helth and the life of sacramentes, alle the 30
vertu and the grace of my worde, alle the goodnesse that is ordained in holy church
to the, I it am."

The moder may ley her childe tenderly to her brest. But oure tender mother
Jhesu, he may homely lede us into his blessed brest by his swet, open side, and shewe
us therein perty of the godhed and the joyes of heven, with gostely sekernesse• of 35
endlesse blisse. And that shewde he in the tenth,° geving the same understanding in
this swet worde where he seyth: /fol. 130r/ "Lo, how I loved° thee," beholding° into
his blissed side, enjoyeng.

This fair, lovely worde, "moder," it is so swete and so kinde in itselfe that it may
not verely be saide of none, ne to none, but of him and to him that is very mother 40
of life and of alle. To the properte of moderhede longeth kind love, wisdom, and
knowing; and it is God. For though it be so that oure bodely forthbringing be but

43–44 yet it is he . . . done yet it is he who does this (brings us forth) in those created beings by way of whom it is done. Christ's agency in biological processes has already been claimed for excretion in 6.25–37. Now it is claimed for childbirth • **45–50 The kinde, loving moder . . . done** Similar to *The Chastising*, amplifying a passage from part 4 of *Ancrene Wisse:* "A goode lovinge modir suffrith hir childe souke and tendrely be norisshed, til it have more strength to suffre more hardnesse. Than she withdraweth a litel and a litel the milke and other delicacies, and makith him asaye of [makes him try] sharper and harder metis. She withdraweth hir glad chiere and sumtime spekith sharply . . . and the stenger he wexith [grows], the sharper rodde she taketh, and sharply leith on" (113). In *A Revelation*, however, the "kinde, loving moder" is also an earthly mother, in whom Christ is working. Again, the metaphoric nature of divine motherhood is denied • **45 kinde, loving moder** a natural, loving mother • **45 woot** knows • **46–47 as it waxeth . . . stature** Similar to 55.26–31 • **47 she changeth her werking** she alters her strategies • **48 wexid** grown • **50 oure lord . . . done** our Lord performs this work (of good parenting) in those by means of whom it is done • **51 Thus he is . . . lower perty** so he is our mother in a natural sense through the working of grace in the lower part of the self. Christ is in actual mothers and causes the good they do • **53–54 alle oure det . . . moderhod** Alludes to the Fourth Commandment: "Honor your father and your mother," Exod. 20:12. Christ as mother has been called "dettour to us" in line 24. Now this debt becomes reciprocal. See also 42.39, where humans have a "det" to pray to God • **56 wher he seyth** See 26.5

[CHAPTER 61] **1 gostly forthbringing** spiritual delivery. The topic of this chapter, as distinct from the "bodely forthbringing" discussed in the last. See 60.42–43. The language of the opening silently alludes a number of times to earlier moments in the revelation, which become a kind of model for the process of "gostly forthbringing" • **2 likenes** comparison • **2 by as moch as** to the same extent as • **3–5 He kindeleth . . . blissful godhede** As

"gostly" mother, Christ is concerned with the spiritual education of his charges. These are partly the activities of a good priest or of "mother" church, who comes increasingly to the fore as Christ's representative as the chapter moves gradually toward a penitential approach to the spiritual life, invoking the language of contrition, confession, and satisfaction • **4–5 geveth us in party . . . godhede** Compare "he shewed . . . , in part, the blessed godhede," 24.7–8 • **5–6 gracious minde in his . . . passion** Compare Julian's first desire for "mind of the passion," 2.3 • **6–7 merveling in his . . . goodnesse** Compare "marveling in this high, overpassing, unmesurable love that oure lorde hath to us of his goodnes," 6.47–48 • **7–8 be well apaide** be well satisfied. Compare "Arte thou well apaid that I suffered for thee?" 22.1–2 • **8–9 whan we falle . . . touching** Compare "And if we . . . falle, that we redely rise, knowing the swete touching of grace," 52.50–52 • **9 becleping** embracing • **11 lestingly** everlastingly • **12–13 he suffereth . . . before** As though the lord were to allow the servant to fall more than once. "Falle," "hard," "grevously" recall 51.20–27 • **13–14 And than wene . . . begonne** Compare "then we wene that God were wroth with us for oure sinne," 40.4–5 • **13–14 wene we . . . wise** then we, who are not completely wise, suppose • **14 that all were . . . begonne** that what we have begun to be has been brought all to nothing • **15 it nedeth us . . . see it** we need to fall, and we need to recognize it. As is most difficult for the servant, "blinded in his reson" in 51.22. The next two paragraphs treat these two points in order • **16–17 how wreched . . . of oureselfe** how miserable we are in our own right. See 66.26: "Here may you se what I am of myselfe." In *The Chastising*, the "second cause" of God's "withdrawinge" from the soul is "that we shuld [ought to] knowe oure owne infirmite, and that is ful profitable" (101) • **17 fulsomly** completely • **20 the lesse of price** of less value • **20–21 by the assey of this falling** through the experience of this lapse. Heroes of medieval romances must overcome "assays," or tests • **21 we shalle have . . . knowing of love** Compare "And for this litille paine that we suffer heer, we shalle have an high, endless knowing in God," 21.23–24

litle, lowe, and simple in regard of oure gostely forthbringing, yet it is he that doth it
in the creatures by whom that it is done.

The kinde, loving moder that woot and knoweth the neede of her childe, she   45
kepeth it full tenderly, as the kinde and condition of moderhed will. And ever as
it waxeth in age and in stature, she changeth her werking,° but not her love. And
when it is wexid of more age, she suffereth /fol. 130v/ it that it be chastised in breking
downe of vicis, to make the childe to receive° vertues and grace. This werking, with
all that be fair and good, oure lord doth it in hem by whome it is done.   50

Thus he is our moder in kinde by the werking of grace in the lower perty, for
love of the hyer. And he wille that we knowe it, for he wille have alle oure love
fastened to him. And in this I sawe that alle oure° det that we owe by Gods bidding
to faderhod and moderhod is fulfilled in trew loving of God, which blessed love
Crist werketh in us. And this was shewde in alle, and namly in the hye plentuous   55
wordes wher he seyth: "I it am that thou lovest."

THE SIXTY-FIRST CHAPTER

Ande in oure gostly forthbringing he useth more tendernesse in keping,
without ony likenes,° by as moch as oure soule is of more /fol. 131r/ price in
his sight. He kindeleth oure understonding, he prepareth oure weyes, he eseth oure
consciens, he conforteth oure soule, he lighteth oure harte and geveth us in party
knowing and loving in his blisseful• godhede—with gracious minde in his swete   5
manhode and his blessed passion, with curtesse merveling in his hye, overpassing
goodnesse—and maketh us° to love all that he loveth for his love, and to be well
apaide with him and with alle his werkes. And whan we falle, hastely he raiseth us by
his lovely becleping and his gracious touching. And when we be strengthed by his
swete werking, than we wilfully chose him, by his swete grace,° to be his servantes   10
and his lovers, lestingly without ende.

And yet, after this, he suffereth some of us to falle more hard and more
grevously then ever we did before, as us thinketh. /fol. 131v/ And than wene we,
that be not alle wise, that all were noughte that we have begonne. But it is not so.
For it nedeth us to falle, and it nedeth us to see it.   15

For if we felle not, we shulde not knowe how febil and how wreched we be of
oureselfe, nor also we shulde not so fulsomly know the mervelous love of oure
maker. For we shalle verely see in heven without ende that we have grevously sinned
in this life. And notwithstonding this, we shalle verely see that we were never hurt in
his love, nor we were never the lesse of price in his sight. And by the assey of this   20
falling we shalle have an high and a mervelous knowing of love in God without

23 for trespas because of sin • **23 this is one . . . profite** this is one profitable realization • **24 lownesse . . . we shall get** In *The Chastising*, the "firste cause" of God's "withdrawinge" is "that the lover shulde nat falle by pride" (101) • **24 by the sight of** through the recognition of • **27 if we se it not . . . profite us** if we do not recognize it, then it may not be profitable to us, even if we should feel it • **28 furst we falle . . . se it** we fall first and recognize it only later • **29–32 The moder may suffer . . . perish** See Isa. 49:15: "Can a woman forget her sucking child, that she should have no compassion on the son of her womb? Even these may forget, yet I will not forget you." Compare Christ's promise to intervene on behalf of all his "kin" in speaking at the harrowing of hell in *Piers Plowman*: "For blood may suffre blood bothe hungry and acale [for one may put up with one's kinsmen going both hungry and cold], / Ac blood may noght se blood blede, but him rewe [but not with seeing one's kin bleed, without feeling pity]" (B 18.395–96). Like an earthly mother who always intervenes to prevent her child from dying, so Jesus steps in to prevent the souls of his children perishing in spiritual death or damnation • **30 for the own profite** for its own profit • **30 ony any** • **31 though oure erthly moder . . . perish** even if our earthly mother did allow her child to die • **33 Blessed mote he be!** may he be blessed! • **34–35 sore adred** sorely afraid • **35–36 unnethis we wit . . . holde us** we scarcely know where to put ourselves. Contrition for sin, the first stage of the penitential process. Compare "Sinne is the sharpest scorge . . . [w]hich scorge alle forbeteth man and woman . . . so forforth that otherwhile he thinketh himselfe he is not wurthy but as it were to sinke into helle," 39.1–4 • **36–46 But then . . . in wele and in wo** In *The Chastising*, the "fourthe cause" of

Christ's "withdrawinge" is "that we shuld the more besily seeke him, wepe and crye aftir him, as the child aftir the modir" (101) • **36–37 But then wille not . . . nothing lother** but then our courteous mother does not want us to flee away, for nothing would be less pleasing to him • **37 use the condition** take on the qualities of • **38 dissesed and adred** distressed and afraid • **39 cryeth on** cries to • **39 alle the mightes** all its strength, or all the powers of its soul. The phrase is also used in 6.39–41 • **40–42 My kind moder . . . grace** Confession, the second stage of the penitential process • **42–43 if we feele . . . wise moder** if we are not then at once made easy, let us be confident that he is taking on the qualities of a wise mother • **44 ruth** compassion • **47–49 he wille that we take us . . . comon** The private confession to Jesus in lines 40–42 is formalized as the sacrament of confession, as mother Jesus becomes mother church • **48–49 all the blessed comon** the whole blessed community • **49 singular** individual • **51–52 to wille mekly . . . holy church** to desire humbly and vehemently to be joined and united to our mother holy church • **53 deerworthy blode . . . water** See 24.5–6. Priestly absolution of the sinner after confession was often described as washing the soul of its sin • **53 is plentuous** is plentiful enough. See Chapter 12 for an elaboration of this motif • **56 useth . . . kinde nurse** takes on the same employment as an actual nurse • **56–57 that hath not . . . her childe** who has nothing else to do except to attend to the salvation of her child. A yet humbler image for Christ's care of the soul, since a nurse might be a paid professional • **59–60 in these gracious wordes** See 37.8–9. The previous chapter has also ended by quoting one of Christ's declarations from earlier in the revelation: "I it am that thou lovest," 60.56

ende. For hard and mervelous is that love which may not, nor will not, be broken
for trespas. And this is° one understanding of profite.

Another° is the lownesse and mekenesse that we shall get by the sight of
/fol. 132r/ oure falling. For therby we shall hyely be raised in heven, to which rising   25
we mighte never have comen without that meknesse. And therfor it nedeth us to see
it, and if we se it not, though we felle, it shuld not profite us.

And comonly, furst we falle and sethen we se it, and both is of the mercy of God.
The moder may suffer the childe to fall sometime and be dissesed on diverse manner
for the own° profite, but she may never suffer that ony manner of perel come to her   30
childe, for love. And though oure erthly moder may suffer her childe to perish, oure
hevenly moder Jhesu may never suffer us that be his children to perish. For he is
almighty, all wisdom, and all love, and so is none but he. Blessed mote he be!

But oftimes when oure falling and oure wrechednes is shewde us, we be so sore
adred and so gretly ashamed of oureselfe that unnethis we wit wher /fol. 132v/ that we   35
may holde us. But then wille not oure curtesse moder that we flee away, for him were
nothing lother, but he will than that we use the condition of a childe. For when it is
dissesed and adred,° it runneth hastely to the moder. And if it may do no more, it
cryeth on the mother for helpe with alle the mightes. So will he that we done as the
meke childe, seyeng thus: "My kind moder, my gracious moder, my deerworthy   40
moder, have mercy on me. I have made myselfe foule and unlike to thee, and I may
not nor canne amende it but with thine helpe and grace." And if we feele us not than
esed as swithe,° be we seker• that he useth the condition of a wise moder. For if he see
that it be more° profite to us to morne and to wepe, he suffereth it° with ruth and pitte
into the best time, for love. And he wille then that we use the properte of a childe, that   45
ever- /fol. 133r/ more kindly trusteth to the love of the moder in wele and in wo.

And he wille that we take us mightly to the faith of holy church, and find
there oure deerworthy mother in solas and trew understanding with all the blessed
comon. For one singular person may oftentimes be broken, as it semeth to the selfe,
but the hole body of holy church was never broken, nor never shall be without ende.   50
And therfore a seker• thing it is, a good and a gracious, to wille mekly and mightly
be fastened and oned to oure moder holy church, that is Crist Jhesu. For the flode of
mercy that is his deerworthy blode and precious water is plentuous to make us fair
and clene. The blessed woundes of oure saviour be open and enjoye to hele us. The
swet, gracious handes of oure moder be redy and diligent about us.   55

For he, in alle this /fol. 133v/ werking, useth the very office of a kinde nurse, that
hath not elles to done but to entende° about the salvation of her childe. It is his
office to save us, it is his worshippe to do it, and it is his wille we know it. For he will
we love him swetely and trust in him mekely and mightly. And this shewde he in
these gracious wordes: "I kepe the fulle sekerly."•   60

[CHAPTER 62] 1 **in that time** in the time of the revelation • 1 **brekinges** breakdowns. For "breking" as an effect of sin, see 52.10–11: "by Adams falling we be so broken in oure feling on diverse manner by sinne and by sondry paines." See also 78.13–26 • 2 **noughtinges** humiliations. See 27.14: "For we be alle in party noughted" • 2 **dispites and . . . outcastings** times of being despised and cast out. See 28.1–12, an account of how "oure lord enjoyeth of the tribulations of his sarvantes" and has the soul "dispised in this worlde, scorned and raped and cast out" • 2–3 **as farreforth . . . in this life** to the degree, it seemed to me, that these things could happen in this life • 4–6 **that he kepeth us . . . solace and comfort** See 15.17–28 • 8 **never to lese time** See 38.24–25, where Saint John of Beverley, despite his sin, "lost no time" • 9 **kinde goodnes** natural goodness • 10–17 **God is kind . . . wurshippe** This passage returns to the abstract theological language of Chapters 53–57 in order to initiate the summing-up of the "motherhood" argument of Chapters 58–63. The passage moves between several of the many senses of "kind" in play in Chapters 51–63: "creation," "natural," "good," "attribute." Chapter 61 describes the merciful engagement of Christ the "kind" mother in the soul's life of penitence. Now the perspective shifts from mercy back to "kind" • 10 **that goodnesse . . . is God** any goodness that is essentially good, it is God. The force of the clause is its claim that "kind" and "good" are synonyms • 10–11 **He is the . . . substance** Compare 34.14 • 11 **kindhede** being • 12–14 **alle kindes . . . werking of grace** See 57.12–14 for this language of "outflowing." Here the outflowing of God includes many "kindes," all the attributes of the species that make up creation and whose purpose is fulfilled in the salvation of humanity, as creation flows back into God • 14–15 **For of all kindes . . . the hole** for of all the attributes that God has parceled out to different beings, the entirety of them is in humankind. This is close to *The Mirror*'s account of how "creatures" collectively display the powers of the Trinity: "Thorw his miht [through his power] ben alle thinges formed, thorw his wisdam ben wonderliche ordeinet [set in order], thorw his goodnesse ben every day multipliede." Different attributes of creatures separately reflect attributes of godhead: "His wisdam . . . hath yiven to every creature beoing [being]; to summe, beoing withoute more [without anything else], as to stones; to summe, beoing and living, as to treon [trees]; to summe, beoing, living, and feling, as to beestes." Only

"men hath beoinge with stones, livinge with herbes, felinge with beestes, resoun with angeles. Thus thou maiht seon [can see] the dignite of monkinde" ("Whuche Manere [In what manner] Mon Shal Knowe God in Every Creature," *YW* 1:244–45) • 18–19 **bounde to God . . . for grace** tied to God because of nature and tied to God because of grace. "Kind" and grace have been crucially different qualities earlier in the argument, where "kind" has pertained to the soul's substance, grace and mercy to the sensuality: see, e.g., Chapter 55. Here, the stage is being set for their ultimate assimilation to one another, achieved in Chapter 63 • 19–20 **us nedeth . . . sondry kindes** we do not very much need to search far away in order to get to know a variety of natures. Despite its traditional place as part of the ladder of contemplation, study of the book of nature is of limited relevance • 20–21 **to holy church . . . owne soule** Reverses the movement of 61.34–55, in which the sinner seeks Christ first within, then through the church • 21 **wonneth** dwells. See 68.1–13 • 21 **ther shall we finde alle** Since the soul is in the image of God and encloses him, it also contains all that is scattered through the "kindes" of the world • 23–24 **no man . . . it is general** See 8.31–37 and 37.3–6. The warning is directed against an autotheistic reading of line 21: "Ther shall we finde alle." Compare 54.13–14 • 24–25 **For it is . . . making** for it is our precious mother Christ (who is "alle," not we ourselves), and for him was this lovely human nature prepared, on account of the reverence and nobility of humanity's creating

[CHAPTER 63] 1 **Here may we see** In the fact of God's "kindhede." See 62.10–12 • 1 **we have verely . . . to hate sinne** we truly must by nature hate sin. Despite the positive effects of sin described in Chapter 61, under the jurisdiction of "mercy." A theme first introduced in 40.26–27—"we shalle hate sin only for love"—and given sustained treatment in that chapter • 2–5 **For kind is all good . . . of grace** After "kind" flows out from God, grace is sent out after it to bring it back home. "Grace was sent" suggests the servant of Chapter 51 in the role of Christ going out to save the same servant in the role of Adam • 4 **the blessed point** See Chapter 11, the revelation of "God in a pointe" • 6 **kind hath ben . . . tribulation** creation has been tested in the fire of tribulation. A standard image in discussion of individual tribulation, though here it is the whole creation that is tested

THE SIXTY-SECOND CHAPTER

For in that time he shewde oure frailte and oure falling, oure brekinges and oure noughtinges, oure dispites and oure outcastings,° and alle oure wo, as farreforth as methought that it might falle in this life. And therwith he shewde his blissed might, his blessed wisdome, his blessed love: that he kepeth us in this time as tenderly and as swetely to his wurshippe, and as sekerly° to oure salvation, as /fol. 134r/ he doth when we be in most solace and comfort; and therto raiseth us gostly and hyely in heven, and turneth alle to his wurship and to oure joye without ende. For his precious love, he suffereth us never to lese time. And all this is of the kinde goodnes of God, by the werking of grace.

God is kind in his being: that is to sey, that goodnesse that is kind, it is God. He is the grounde, he is the substance, he is the same thing that is kindhede,° and he is very fader and very moder of kindes. And alle kindes that he hath made to flowe out of him to werke his wille, it shall° be restored and brought againe into him by salvation of man throw the werking of grace. For of all kindes that he hath set in diverse creatures by party, in man is alle the hole /fol. 134v/ in fullhed and in vertu, in fairhed and in goodhed, in ryalte and in noblye, in alle manner of solempnite of precioushede° and wurshippe.

Here may we see that we be all bounde to God for kind, and we be bounde to God for grace. Her may we see that us nedeth not gretly to seke ferre out to know sondry kindes, but to holy church, into oure moders brest: that is to sey, into oure owne soule wher oure lord wonneth.° And ther shall° we finde alle: now, in faith and in understanding, and after, verely in himselfe, clerely, in blisse.

But no man ne woman take this singularly to himselfe, for it is not so: it is general. For it is oure precious moder Crist, and to him was this fair kinde dight, for the wurshippe and the nobly of mans making, and for the joye and the blisse of mannes salvation, right as he saw, wist, and knew fro without beginning. /fol. 135r/

THE SIXTY-THIRD CHAPTER

Here may we see that we have verely of kind to hate sinne, and we have verely of grace to hate sinne. For kind is all good and fair in itselfe, and grace was sent oute to save kinde, and kepe kinde, and destroy sinne, and bring againe fair kinde into the blessed point from thens it cam—that is, God—with more noblines and wurshippe, by the vertuse wurking of grace. For it shall be seen before God of all his holy, in joy without end, that kind hath ben assayde in the fyer of tribulation,

9 **ne none be deperted** nor can either be separated from the other • 10 **by the mercy of God** The topic of mercy is introduced for the last time in this part of the work, in a final synthesis of *A Revelation*'s teaching on the place of sin in the divine plan • 11 **sinne is wurse . . . than hell** See 40.30–32: "For if it were leyde before us, alle the paine that is in hell . . . and sinne, we shulde rather chese alle that paine than sinne" • 12 **liknesse** comparison • 12 **contrarious** antithetical. For a related use of the word, see 47.31–38 • 13 **sinne is unkinde** sin is perverse. The one use of "unkinde" in *A Revelation*, a word on which the Middle English poem *Cleanness* provides a brilliant and lugubriously severe meditation. Julian's language here seems almost as harsh, but her usage needs to be read in light of her idiomatic use of the noun "unkindnesse," in 27.30–31 ("were it a gret unkindnesse of me to blame or wonder on God for my sinne") and 66.23 ("This was a gret sinne and a gret unkindnesse"), where the word is little more than a synonym for "sinne" • 15 **but inasmoch as dred may spede** except insofar as fear may be useful. See the discussion of the utility of "dred" in Chapter 74 • 15–16 **make we oure mone . . . mother** The final return of the motherhood theme, with Christ's birthing the soul, as he is described doing in Chapter 60 • 16–17 **And he shall . . . fulle milde** See Rolle's *Meditations*: "Whe! [Ah!], lord, a drope of thi blood to droppe on my soule in minde of thy passion may hele al my sore, souple and softe in thy grace it that is so harde [make it that is so hard (my soul) soft and supple through your grace]" (*YW* 1.90) • 16 **besprinkil** sprinkle • 19 **of this swete . . . nor stinte** he shall never cease or end this sweet, beautiful activity. Sprinkling souls with his blood. Alludes to 60.22–23, where Christ's

death is described as a birthing of humankind, which he desires to follow by feeding his children with his blood: "He might no more die, but he wolde not stinte of werking" • 19–20 **tille all his deerwurthy children . . . forth** If humankind as a whole was born at the Passion, all the time between Passion and Judgment is needed for Christ to birth his children in an individual sense • 21 **the gostely thurst** See 31.10–16 • 25 **in the taking of oure kind** in assuming our nature • 25 **he quicked us** he conceived us • 27 **fedeth us and fordreth us** feeds us and fosters us. Like a nursing mother • 27–28 **hye, sovereyne kindnesse** high, absolute kindness • 31–32 **that long to children in kinde** that children naturally have • 33–34 **eche one of them other** each one of them loves the other • 36–37 **I understode none . . . witte** I understood that we attain no higher status in this life than childhood, in our frailty and failures of strength and intelligence • 39 **wher he seyth** See 32.1–3 • 39 **Alle shalle be welle** The first allusion to Christ's promise since the end of the thirteenth revelation, brought in here as the peroration of this long passage of theological rumination. Compare the other return of the promise in 85.10–13, almost at the end of *A Revelation* • 40–41 **than shalle the blisse . . . fader God** then shall the happiness of our motherhood in Christ be set to begin anew in the joys of God our Father • 42 **which new beginning . . . beginning** which new beginning will last without end, always beginning anew. The return of all to God is not the end of the purpose of creation but its beginning. As grand a finale to this part of the work as the peroration of the whole in Chapter 86 • 43–44 **Thus I understode . . . grace** A one-sentence summary of the argument of Chapters 58–63

and therin founde no lack nor no defaute. Thus is kind and grace of one accorde: for grace is God, as unmade kinde is God. He is two in manner werking, and one in love, and neither of them werketh without /fol. 135v/ other, ne none be deperted.

And whan we, by the mercy of God and with his helpe, accorde us to kinde and to grace, we shall se verely that sinne is wurse, viler, and painfuller than hell without ony liknesse, for it is contrarious to our fair kinde. For as sothly° as sinne is unclene, as sothly° sinne is unkinde, and thus° an horrible thing to see to the loving soule that wolde be alle fair and shining in the sight of God, as kind and grace techeth. But be we not adred of this (but inasmoch as dred may spede), but mekely make we oure mone to oure derewurthy mother. And he shall all besprinkil us in his precious blode, and make oure soule full softe and fulle milde, and heele us fulle fair by processe of time, right as it is most wurshipe to him and joye to us without ende. And of this swete, fair werking /fol. 136r/ he shalle never ceese nor stinte, tille all his deerwurthy children be borne and brought forth. And that shewde he where he gave the understanding of the gostely thurst: that is, the love-longing that shalle last tille domesday.

Thus in oure very moder Jhesu oure life is grounded in the forseeing wisdom of himselfe fro without beginning, with the hye might of the fader and the sovereyne goodnesse of the holy gost. And in the taking of oure kind he quicked us, and in his blessed dying upon the crosse he bare us to endlesse life. And fro that time, and now, and ever shall into domesday, he fedeth us and fordreth us, right as the hye, sovereyne kindnesse of moderhed wille, and as the kindly nede of childhed asketh. Fair and swete is our hevenly moder in the sight of oure soule. Precious and lovely be the gracious children in the sight of oure hevenly moder, /fol. 136v/ with mildhede˙ and mekenesse and alle the fair vertuse that long to children in kinde. For kindly the childe dispaireth not of the moders love, kindly the childe presumeth not of itselfe, kindly the childe loveth the moder, and eche one of them other. Theyse be as fair vertues, with alle other that be like, wherwith oure hevenly moder is served and plesed.

And I understode none higher stature in this life than childehode, in febilnesse and failing of might and of witte, into the time that oure gracious° moder hath brought us up to oure faders blisse. And ther shall it verely be made knowen to us, his mening in the swete wordes wher he seyth: "Alle shalle be welle, and thou shalt see it thyselfe that alle manner thing shall be welle."° And than shalle the blisse of oure moderhed in Crist be new to beginne in /fol. 137r/ the joyes of oure fader God; which new beginning shall last without end, new beginning.

Thus I understode that all his blessed children which be come out of him by kind shall° be brougt againe into him by grace.

[CHAPTER 64] 1–7 **Afore this time . . . felle to do** Compare the openings of the thirteenth and fourteenth revelations, Chapters 27 and 41, which similarly narrate Julian's desires and questions before the revelation. The longing for death described here is a common feature of meditative writing from Paul on. See Phil. 1:23: "My desire is to depart and be with Christ, for that is far better" • 1–2 **I had grete longing . . . this worlde** I had a great longing and desire to be delivered from this world by God's gift. See 2.27: "For I desired to be soone with my God and maker" • 2 **here** on earth • 3 **wele** happiness • 3 **blessed being** blessed existence • 3 **if** even if • 3 **ben** been • 5 **to morne . . . longe** to mourn and anxiously desire. A state of love-longing described in 42.47–49 and 43.38–39 • 5–6 **of my owne wretchednesse** because of my own misery • 6 **that me liked not** so that it pleased me not • 6 **traveyle** labor • 6–7 **as me felle to do** as it was my duty to do • 8 **for comfort and patiens** to give comfort and instill patience • 10 **disese** discomfort • 11 **to thy mede** as your reward • 12–13 **thou shalte never more . . . withoute end** you shall never more have any kind of pain, any kind of sickness, any kind of displeasure, any frustration of your desire, but always joy and eternal bliss. The many double negatives here ("never . . . no . . . no . . . no . . . no . . .") increase the forcefulness of the promise. *The Pricke* writes similarly of the "dowries," or joys, of the saved: "The fift blis, als clerkes wate [know] wele, / Es hele [health] that the saved bodyse salle fele, / Withouten seknes or grevaunce, / Or angre, or paine, or penaunce"; "And what-swa [whatever] thay wille think in thought, / Alle salle be at thair wille thare wroght [everything shall be done as they want it]"; "The sevend blis es joy parfite. . . . For thare salle be mare sere joyes [there will be more different joys] than / Than ever couth noumbre erthly man [than anyone on earth could count" (8007–10; 8493–94; 8601, 8615–16) 14 **What shulde . . . awhile** why then should it grieve you to be patient for a while • 14 **sithen** since • 14–15 **my wurshippe** for my honor • 16 **worde** clause • 16–17 **God rewardeth . . . time** God rewards people for the patience that they exercise in waiting on God's desire and for their proper time to die. This is similar to the argument of 14.22–30 • 18–19 **man length . . . passing** people stretch their patience out over the whole time they are alive, because of their ignorance about the time of their death. This and the next sentences are full of commonplaces. In Rolle's *Form*, the second of four things the contemplative must keep in mind is "uncertente of oure ending. For we wate [know] never when we sal die, ne whare we sal die, ne how we sal die, ne whider we sal ga [where we will go] when we er dede. And . . . God wil that this be uncertain til us: for he will that we be ay redy to die" (chap. 4, *YW* 1:19)

The Fifteenth Revelation
AND THE SIXTY-FOURTH CHAPTER°

Afore this time I had grete longing and desyer of Goddes gifte to be deliverde of this worlde and of this life. For oftimes I behelde the wo that is here and the wele and the blessed being that is there. And if there had ben no paine° in this life but the absens of oure lorde, methought sometime that it was more than I might bere. And this made me to morne and besely to longe, and also of my owne wretchednesse, sloth, and werinesse, that me liked not to live and to traveyle as me felle to do.

And to all this oure curteyse lorde answered for comfort and patiens, and saide these wordes: "Sodeynly thou shalte be taken from /fol. 137v/ all thy paine, from alle thy sicknesse, from alle thy disese,° and fro alle thy wo. And thou shalte come up above,° and thou shalt have me to thy mede, and thou shalte be fulfilled of joye and blisse. And thou shalte never more have no manner of paine, no manner of sicknes, no manner of misliking,° no wanting of wille, but ever joy and blisse withoute end. What shulde it than agreven thee to suffer awhile, sithen it is my wille and my wurshippe?"

And in this worde, "Sodeynly thou shalte be taken," I saw that God rewardeth° man of the patience that he hath in abiding Goddes wille and of his time, and that man length his patience over the time of his living, for unknowing of his time of

---

[VIS. 20.1–16] Before this time I hadde **ofte** grete langinge, and *desired* of Goddes gifte to be delivered of this warlde and of this life, **for I shulde be with my God in blisse whare I hope sikerlye thurgh his mercye to be withouten ende.** For oftetimes I behelde the wa that is here and the wele and the blissede beinge thare. And if thare hadde bene na pain *in erthe* bot the absence of oure lorde God, methought sumtime it ware mare than I might bere. And this made me to mourne and beselye lange /Rev. 64.5–7/.

Than God saide to me for patience and for sufferance thus: "Sudanly thowe shalle be takene fra alle thy paine, fra alle thy sickenesse,° fra alle thy dissese, and fra alle thy wa. And thowe shalle comen up aboven, and thowe shalle hafe me to thy mede, and thowe shalle be fulfillede of joye and blisse. And thowe shalle never hafe na maner of paine, na maner of sekenes, na maner of mislikinge, na wantinge of wille, botte ever joye and blisse withouten ende. Whate shulde it than greve the to suffer awhile, sen it is my wille and my wirshippe?"

Also in this *reson,* "Sudanly thou shalle be taken," I sawe how God rewardes man of the patience that he has in abidinge of Goddes wille *in his time,* and that man lengthes his patience overe the time of his liffinge, for unknawinge of his time of

20 **over** during • 20–21 **God wille . . . taken** Rolle writes: "God . . . wol that we be ever redy to dey" • 21 **at the pointe to be taken** at the point of being taken from this world • 21–22 **For alle this life . . . but a point** for all this life and this suffering that we have here is no more than an instant. In *The Form*, the first of the four things the contemplative must keep in mind is: "The mesur of thy lif here, that sa short es that unnethis es it oght [that it is scarcely anything]. For we live bot in a point, that es the leste thing that may be. And sothely [truly] oure life es les [is less] than a point, if we liken it to the life that lastes ay [eternally]" (chap. 4, *YW* 1:19) Contrast 11.1, where the "pointe" means "point in space" • 24–28 **I sawe a body . . . into heven** Julian's memory of her desire "to be deliverde of this worlde" (lines 1–2) leads to a general vision of death. Lying recumbent on the ground, the body might be that of the servant from the exemplum in 51.1–39, fallen into his "slade" and still unable to rise • 24–25 **which body shewde . . . feerfulle** which body appeared gross and fearful • 25 **withoute shape and forme** Like the account of the chaos that precedes creation in Gen. 1:2: "The earth was without form and void" • 25 **as it were a swilge stinking mire** as if it were a bog of stinking mud. The body as it seems at the moment when it is left behind • 25–28 **And sodeynly . . . into heven** A traditional late medieval image of dying, in which the soul springs out of the mouth of the dying person • 26 **a litille child** The image glances back at 63.36–38, where all human life is in a state of "childehode" • 26–28 **full shapen . . . heven** perfectly shaped and formed, quick and alive and whiter than the lily, which glided swiftly up into heaven • 28 **swilge** bog • 28 **betokeneth** signifies • 29 **puernesse** purity • 30–31 **With this body . . . of the body** no beauty of the child remains in the body, nor does any foulness of the body dwell in the child • 31–32 **It is fulle blesfulle . . . man** it is very blessed that a person be taken from pain, more so than that pain be taken from a person • 34 **in this behest** in this promise. See line 16, "Sodeynly thou shalte be taken" • 35 **curtesse behiting** courteous promising • 35–36 **clene deliverance** pure or absolute liberation • 37 **the overpassing joy** transcendent joy • 39–40 **the point of oure thought** the focus of our contemplation. "Point" alludes to earlier uses of the word, lines 21–22 • 42 **ladde of** led by • 43 **whan we falle againe to oureselfe** See 47.33–35: "And anon we falle into oureselfe, and than finde we no feling of right nought but the contrariousnes that is in oureselfe, and that of the olde rote of oure furst sinne" • 43 **hevines and gostely blindhede** Two pains experienced by the servant in 51.20–23 • 45 **forget** forgotten

passing. This is a greate profite. For if a man° knew his time, he shulde not have patience over that time. And also God wille that while the /fol. 138r/ soule is in the body, it seeme to itselfe that it is ever at the pointe to be taken. For alle this life and this langor° that we have here is but a point, and when we be taken sodeynly out of paine into blesse, than pain shall be nought.

And in this time I sawe a body lyeng on the erth, which body shewde hevy and feerfulle and withoute shape and forme, as it were a swilge stinking mire. And sodeynly oute of this body sprong a fulle fair creature, a litille child, full shapen and formed, swift and lifly and whiter then the lilye, which sharpely glided uppe into heven. The swilge of the body betokeneth grette wretchednesse of oure dedely flesh, and the littilhede• of the childe betokeneth the clennes and the puernesse of oure soule. And I thought: "With this body bliveth no fairhede• of this childe, ne of this childe dwelleth no foulhede• of the body. /fol. 138v/ It is fulle blesfulle,• man to be taken fro paine, more than paine be taken fro man. For if paine be taken from us, it may come againe. Therfore this is a sovereyne comfort and a blesful beholding in a longing soule, that we shall be taken fro paine." For in this behest I saw a marvelous° compassion that oure lorde hath in us for oure wo, and a curtesse behiting of clene deliverance.

For he wille that we be comforted in the overpassing joy. And that he shewde in theyse wordes: "And thou shalte come uppe above, and thou shalte have me to thy mede, and thou shalt be fulfilled of joy and blisse." It is Goddes wille that we set the point of oure thought in this blesfulle beholding as oftime as we may and as long time kepe us therin with his grace. For this is a blesfulle contemplation to the soule that is ladde of God, and fulle mekille• to his wurshippe for the time that it lasteth. /fol. 139r/ And whan we falle againe to oureselfe, by hevines and gostely blindhede,• and felinge of paines gostely and bodely by oure frailte,° it is Goddes wille that we know that he hath not forget us. And so meneth he in theys wordes and seyth for comforte: "And thou shalt never more have paine in no manner, nor no manner of sicknes, no manner of misliking, no wanting of will, but ever joy and blisse without ende. What shuld it than agreve° the to suffer a while, sithen it is my wille and my

---

[VIS. 20.17–23] passinge. This is a grete profitte. For if a man knewe his time, he shulde noght hafe patience overe that time. Also God wille that whiles the saule es in the bodye, that it semen to itselfe that it es ever atte the pointe to be taken. For alle this /fol. 111r/ life *in this langoure* that we hafe here is bot a pointe, and when we ere takene sodaynly oute of paine into blisse *it* shalle be nought. /Rev. 64.24–45/

And therfore saide oure lorde: /Rev. 64.46–48/ "Whate shulde it than greve the to suffere a while, sen it is my wille and my

49 **take** understand • 50 **largely** comprehensively •
50–51 **oure abidinges and oure disseses** the lingerings
and distresses of our lives • 51 **lightely** cheerfully •
52 **lesse price . . . love** the less we set store by them, out
of love

[CHAPTER 65] 1–3 **And thus I understode . . . grace**
After all the references to "alle mankind that shalle be
saved" (e.g., 9.9), many of them possible to read as arguing a strongly predestinarian position, it is stated here
that the chosen soul is anyone who chooses God •
2 **with endlesse love** by means of an eternal love • 3 **that
werketh . . . grace** Love chooses those who will love •
3 **that grace** The grace of choosing God • 3 **kepe** recollect • 3 **trustly** trustfully • 3–4 **as seker in hope . . .
heven** as secure in the hope of the bliss of heaven. Reinforces 2.14–15: "For I beloved to be saved by the marcy of
God" • 4–5 **in sekernesse . . . there** in certainty when
we are there. "Sekernesse" is another "dowry" of the
blessed, according to *The Pricke:* "For thay salle be thare
siker and certaine / To have endeles joy, and nevermare
paine" (8559–60) • 6 **the better liketh him** the better it

pleases him • 7–8 **this reverence . . . knit** "Reverence,"
"drede," and "meekenes" are often linked in the work,
beginning with the first revelation's account of the soul
in contemplation of the maker, as Mary contemplated
God: "the beholding and the loving of the maker
maketh the soule to seme lest in his awne sight, and
most filleth hit with reverent drede and trew meknesse"
(6.56–57) • 8–9 **and that is that . . . mervelous litle** and
the cause of that (fear and humility) is that a creature
can see the Lord as wonderfully great and the self as
wonderfully small • 9–11 **these vertues . . . whan it is**
these virtues are possessed in eternity by those beloved
of God, and can now be seen and experienced in part
through the gracious presence of our Lord, when it
comes • 12–13 **mervelous sekernesse . . . drede** wonderful confidence of true faith and certain hope, through
the greatness of fearful love. The presence of God evokes
all three of the "theological virtues" of faith, hope, and
charity in the soul, tempered by "drede," the quality of
awe evoked by "sekernesse" • 13–14 **as mekille bound** as
greatly bound

wurshippe?" It is Goddes wille that we take his behestes and his comforting as
largely and as mightly as we may take them. And also he wille that we take oure   50
abidinges and oure dissesses as lightely as we may take them, and set them at nought.
For the lightlier that we take them, and the lesse price that we set at them for love,
the lesse° paine shalle we have in the /fol. 139v/ feeling of them, and the more thanke
and mede shalle we have for them.

THE SIXTY-FIFTH CHAPTER

And thus I understode that what man or woman wilfully choseth God in this
life for love, he may be seker• that he is loved without end, with endlesse love
that werketh in him that grace. For he wille we kepe this trustly, that we be as seker
in hope of the blisse of heven while we are here as we shalle be in sekernesse° when
we ar there. And ever the more liking and joye that we take in this sekernesse, with   5
reverence and meekenes, the better liketh him.

For, as it was shewed, this reverence that I meane is a holy, curtious drede of our
lorde, to which meekenes is knit: and that is that a creatur see the lord mervelous
great and the selfe° mervelous litle. For these vertues ar had endlesly to the loved of
God, and it may now be seen and felt in /fol. 140r/ mesure by the gracious presence   10
of oure lord, whan it is. Which presence in all thing is most desirid, for it worketh
that mervelous sekernesse in true faith and seker hope by greatnes of charitye in
drede that is sweet and delectable. It is Gods will that I see myselfe as mekille•

[VIS. 20.23–34] wyrshippe?" It is Goddes wille that we take his behestes and his confortinges als largelye and als mightelye as we maye take thame. And also he wille that we
take oure abidinge and oure desese als lightelye as we may take tham, and sette tham atte
nought. For the lightlyere we take tham, the lesse price we sette be tham for luff, the lesse
paine salle we hafe in the felinge of tham, and the mare thanke ‡ we shalle hafe for tham.
In this blissed revelation I was trewly taught that whate man or woman wilfully cheses
God in this° life ‡, he may be sekere that *he is chosene* ‡. *Kepe this treulye, for sothly it is
Godes wille* that we be als sekere *in tryste* of the blis in heven whiles we ere here as we
shulle° be in sekernesse when we ere thare. And ever the mare likinge and the joye that we
take in this sekernesse, with reverence and mekenes, the bettere likes him. /Rev. 65.7–14/

14 as if . . . all that he hath done as if he had done every-thing that he has done specifically for me. The obverse of the work's frequent injunctions not to understand the revelation or its teaching as for a specific individual. See Chapter 9, where the principle is established • **15 in regard of his lover** in relation to its lover • **19 witte** know • **19–20 loked in our frendes hande** locked in our friend's hand. A near repetition of 13.14: "For his might is alle lokked in Gods hande." See the account of the binding of the devil in Rev. 20:1–2. Satan is "loked," God's lovers are "bound" (line 14). The weakness of the devil is one of the remedies against despair in *The Chastising*: "The fiende is so fieble of himself that he hath no power to overcome a mans soule, but a man wil himself [unless a person himself wants it so]" (153) • **20 wote sekerly this** knows this for sure • **20–21 not dred but . . . loveth** A formulation of the relation between fear and love much expanded in Chapter 74 • **21–22 Alle other dredes . . . imaginations** all other kinds of fear, he attributes them to the passions and bodily disease and fantasies. Anticipates the diabolical visions that flank the final revelation, as described in Chapters 67 and 69. *The Chastising* describes the many fears to which contemplatives are subject, including the fear that Christ's Passion will not be efficacious in one's own case. Those "travelid in imaginatiouns [attacked by fantasies] and thoughtis of predestinatioun and of the prescience of God [divine foreknowledge of the soul's damnation]"

are most inclined to despair (156) • **22–23 though we ben in so much paine . . . nought** Anticipates, and for-gives in advance, Julian's confused behavior in Chapter 66 • **23–24 us thinkith . . . we feele** it seems to us that we can think about absolutely nothing except what state we are in or what we are feeling • **24 passe we lightly over** we move cheerfully on • **25 God will be knowen** God wants to be known. Alludes to 5.24–26, part of the exposition of "God in a pointe": "God will be knowen, and him liketh that we rest us in him. For all that is beneth him suffiseth not to us. And this is the cause why that no soule is rested till it is noughted of all things that is made" • **26 we shall have patience** One of the objects of this revelation, according to 64.8 • **27 in these wordes** See 64.14–15 • **29–30 as God whitsafe . . . minde** as God has vouchsafed to present them to my memory • **30 lighteninges and touchinges** illuminations and inspi-rations. See 56.33 • **30 I hope of the same spirite** com-ing, I trust, from the same spirit • **31–32 erly in the morninge** See 3.14–15 • **32 oure** hour • **32–33 shewing by processe . . . other** revealing themselves in sequence, very beautifully and seriously, each following the last. "Processe" could mean "procession," in which case the allusion would be to a festivity such as Corpus Christi, when, in Norwich and elsewhere, the mystery plays were performed. Revelation after revelation has rolled by on divine pageant wagons before Julian's eyes • **33 none** noon • **33 or paste** or later

bound to him in love as if he had done for me all that he hath done. And thus shuld everye soule thinke in regard of his lover. That is to say, the charite of God maketh in us such a unitye that when it is truly seen, no man can parte themselfe from other. And thus ought ech soule to thinke that God hath done for him all that he hath done.

And this shewith he to make us to love him, and liken him, and nothing dred but him. For it is his will we witte° that all the° might of our enemy is loked° in our frendes hande.° And therfore the soule that wote sekerly this, he° /fol. 140v/ shall not dred but him that he° loveth. Alle other dredes, he setteth° them among passions and bodely sicknesse and imaginations. And therfore, though we ben in so much paine, wo, and disese that us thinkith we can thinke right nought but that we are in or that we feele, as soone as we may, passe we lightly over, and set we it at nought. And whi? For God will be knowen. For if we know him and love him and reverently drede him, we shall have patience and be in great rest, and it shuld bin great liking to us, all that he doth. And this shewid our lord in these wordes: "What shuld it than agrieve thee to suffre a while, seeing it is my will and my worshipe?"

Now have I tolde you of fifteen shewinges, as God whitsafe to minister them to my minde, renewde by lighteninges and touchinges, I hope of the same spirite that shewed° them alle. Of which fifteen shewinges the /fol. 141r/ furst beganne erly in the morninge, aboute the oure of four, and it lasted—shewing by processe,° fulle fair and soberly, eche folowing other—tille it was none of the day or paste.

15

20

25

30

[*VIS. 20.34–49*] **For I am seker if thare hadde nane ben bot I that shulde be safe,** *God wolde hafe done alle that he hase done for me.* And so shulde ilke saule thinke in *knawinge* of his lovere, **forgettande, if he might, alle creatures,** /Rev. 65.15–17/ *and thinkande* that God hase done for him alle that he hase done.

And this thinke me shulde stirre a saule for to luff and like him, and nought drede bot him. For it is his wille that we witte that alle the might of oure enmye is loken in oure frendes hande. And therfore a saule that wate sekerly this shalle nought drede botte him that he loves, and alle othere dredes sette tham emange passions and bodelye sekenesse and imaginations. And therfore, if *a man* be in so mekille paine, in so mekille wa, and in so mekille deseses, that *him* thinke that *he* can thinke right nought bot that that *he* es in or that *he* feles, als sone as *he* maye, passe lightlye overe and sette it atte nought. And why? For God wille be knawen. For if we knewe him and luffed him ‡, we shulde hafe /fol. 111v/ patience and be in grete reste, and it shulde be likinge to us, alle that he does. And this shewed oure lorde **me** in thies wordes that he saide: "Whate shulde it than greve the to suffer a while, sen it is my wille and my wirshippe?" /Rev. 65.29–66.6/

[CHAPTER 66] 2 **as I shalle sey after** See Chapter 68 • 2–3 **conclusion and confirmation** Rhetorical terms for the peroration of an argument. Compare the opening description of the first revelation, "in which all the shewinges that foloweth be groundide and oned" (1.6–7) • 3 **me behoveth to telle you** I need to tell you. Since the sixteenth revelation refers to the scene described in this chapter. See 68.4–6 • 3–4 **as anenst my febilnes** about my weakness • 4 **febilnes . . . blindnes** These epithets now have particular resonances from their association with the fallen servant in the exemplum. See 51.196–97: "The febilnesse and blindnesse that we have is of Adam." The narrative of Chapters 66–68—in which Julian, left alone in her "baren" state (line 9), sins through blindness, suffers God's absence, and is answered by a vision of Christ unchanged in his love and seated in her soul— is an individual manifestation of the exemplum's universal story • 4–6 **I have saide . . . in shewing** I said at the beginning, where it says, "And in this all my pain was suddenly taken from me"—I had no grief or discomfort from this pain as long as the fifteen revelations continued to be revealed. The syntax of the sentence is informal • 4 **wher it seyth** See 3.30 • 7 **close** finished • 7 **anone** soon • 8 **cam agene** came back • 8–9 **furst in my hed . . . before** The progress of Julian's sickness, on its return to her body, runs opposite to the course it had followed when she earlier felt herself dying. See 3.14–35 • 8 **dinne** noise • 9 **fulfilled** filled • 9–10 **as baren and as drye** The terms are elsewhere used in the context of prayer. See 41.4–5: "For we be as bareyne and as drye oftentimes after oure prayers as we were before" • 10–11 **as a wrech . . . paines** like a wretch complained and

tossed about because of the physical pain I was feeling. "A wrech" is also used in 8.34 and 17.45 • 11 **failing of comforte** lack of comfort • 12–16 **Then cam . . . rechelesnesse** Julian's denial of Christ here is treated as a serious sin in the rest of *A Revelation,* and certainly this scene has little in common with the decorum of *The Chastising,* where the visionary submits experiences "lowely to the doom of his gostly fadir [humbly to the judgment of his spiritual father], or of other discreet and sad gostly livers [careful and serious spiritual persons], for drede of illusion" (174). As described, however, Julian's revelation passes even the severe tests suggested by *The Scale.* Although doubtful "whether ther be ony" true visionary "livande in erthe [living on earth]," *The Scale* admits the possibility of an experience that "though it be so that it stonyeth [amazes] thee in the first biginninge, nevertheles aftirward it turneth and quikeneth thin herte to more desire of vertues and encreseth thy love more bothe to God and to thin evenecristen; also, it maketh thee more meke in thyn owen sight" (1.11) • 12 **religious person** a member of a religious order. Probably a friar or canon • 13 **loght** laughed • 13 **enterly** sincerely • 13–14 **The crosse . . . fast** See 4.1–5, 7.9–10 • 14 **methought it bled fast** I thought it bled heavily • 15 **waxed all sad and merveyled** grew all serious and marveled • 15 **anone** straightaway • 15 **astoned** stunned. A sad echo of the beginning of the revelation, 4.13–16 • 16 **sadly** seriously • 16 **lest** least • 17 **that sawe no more therof** who knows no more of it than that • 19 **wolde have bene shriven** would have liked to take confession

The Sixteenth Revelation
AND THE SIXTY-SIXTH CHAPTER

Ande after this the goode lorde shewde the sixteenth revelation on the night folowing, as I shalle sey after; which sixteenth was conclusion and confirmation to all the fifteen. But furst me behoveth to telle you as anenst my febilnes, wretchednes, and blindnes. I have saide at the beginning, wher it seyth, "And in this sodeynly all my paine was taken fro me," of which paine I had no grefe ne no disesse° as long as the fifteen shewinges lasted in shewing. And at the ende alle was close, and I saw no more, and soone I felt that I should life longer.° And anone my sicknes cam agene: furst in my hed, with a sounde and a dinne;° and sodeynly all my body /fol. 141v/ was fulfilled with sicknes like as it was before, and I was as baren and as drye as I had never had comfort but litille, and as a wrech morned and heved° for feeling of my bodely paines and for failing° of comforte, gostly and bodely.

Then cam a religious person to me and asked me how I fared, and I saide I had raved to day. And he loght loude and enterly.° And I saide: "The crosse that stode before my face, methought it bled fast." And with this worde, the person that I spake to waxed all sad and merveyled, and anone I was sore ashamed and astoned for my rechelesnesse. And I thought: "This man taketh sadly the lest worde that I might sey, that sawe no more therof."

And when I saw that he toke it so sadly and with so grete reverence, I waxed full gretly ashamed, and wolde /fol. 142r/ have° bene shriven. But I coulde telle it to no

5

10

15

[VIS. 20.50] *And here was ane ende of alle that oure lorde shewed me that daye.*

[VIS. 21.1–13] **And efter this sone I felle to myselfe and into my bodelye seknes,** *understandande that I shulde life, and as a wrech hevyed° and mourned° for the bodely paines that I feled,* **and thought grete irksumnes that I shulde langere liffe.** ‡ And I was als barane and drye as if I hadde never had comforth before bot litille, *for fallinge to my paines and failinge of gastelye felinge.*

Than com a religiouse person to me and asked me howe I farde, and I saide that I hadde° raved that daye. And he laughed loude and enterlye. And I saide: "The crosse that stode *atte my bedde feete,* ‡ it bled faste." And with this worde, the person that I spake to wex alle sadde and mervelande, and onane I was sare ashamed ‡ for my reklessenes. And I thought thus: "This man takes it sadlye the leste worde that I might saye, that *says* na mare *therto.*"

And when I sawe that he toke it so sadelye and with so grete reverence, I wex right gretly ashamed, and walde haffe bene shrifen. Bot I couth telle it na

20 **How shulde a preste believe me?** Even though a "religious person" just has. The confusion and difficulty of bringing the revelation back into the world begins immediately • 21 **This I beleft . . . saw him** I truly believed the revelation during the time in which I saw him • 22 **fole** fool • 23 **unkindnesse** unnaturalness • 23–24 **for foly of . . . paine** out of folly caused by feeling a little bodily suffering. "Foly" is similar in nuance to "rechelesnesse," line 16. See 41.5–6 • 26 **of myselfe** by myself • 26–27 **herein . . . leeve me** our courteous Lord would not leave me in this state

[CHAPTER 67] 1 **fende** devil • 1 **set him in my throte** took me by the throat. The physicality of the demonic assault in this passage is in accord with late medieval understandings of the devil's power to afflict the body through disease and illusion. According to *The Chastising,* holy men since antiquity have been "chastised sodeynlie with bodily infirmitees, and sumtime grevously travelid with illusions of wikked spirites" (164) • 2 **putting forth . . . yonge man** pushing right into my face a visage like a young man's • 3 **wonder leen** amazingly skinny • 3 **I saw never none such** I never saw anything like it. The note struck in the description is that of the scorn and laughter directed at the devil in 13.19–21 • 3–5 **The coloure was red . . . thonwonges** In its color,

shape, and ability to evoke images of familiar household objects, the devil's face seems to parody the face of Christ Julian sees in the first and eighth revelations, Chapters 4–7 and 16–17 • 3–4 **red** Compare Christ's blood in 4.1–2 • 3–4 **the tilestone whan it is new brent** the hearth tile just after a fire, or newly fired. Compare "evesing of a house," 7.22 • 4 **blacke spottes . . . freknes** with black spots in it like freckles. Soot, grease, or heat marks on the tile, as though a cooking fire has recently burned over the "tilestone" • 4 **here** hair • 5 **not scored afore** not shorn in front • 5 **with side lockes . . . thonwonges** with dreadlocks hanging from his temples. Compare Christ's hair and blood hanging like a garland in 17.12–30 • 6 **shrewde** cunning • 6 **whit teth** white teeth • 7 **Body ne handes . . . shaply** his body and his hands were ill-formed • 8 **woulde have** wanted to • 9 **This ugly shewing . . . none other** this disgusting revelation happened while I was asleep, unlike any of the others. Dreams were usually thought less authoritative than waking visions, partly because they were more easily infiltrated by demons • 10 **trusted to be saved . . . God** The purpose of the devil's visit is to induce despair. The correct counterattack is thus trust in divine mercy • 11 **unnethes had I my life** I was scarcely alive • 11 **persons** people

prest. For I thought: "How shulde a preste believe me? I beloved not oure lorde God."° 20
This I beleft sothfastly° for the time that I saw him, and so was than my wille and
my mening ever for to do without end. But as a fole I let it passe from° my minde.
A, lo I, wrech!° This was a gret sinne and a gret unkindnesse, that I, for foly of feling
of a litille bodely paine, so unwisely left for the time the comfort of alle this blessed
shewing of oure lorde God. 25

Here may you se what I am of myselfe. But herein woulde oure curtesse lorde
not leeve me. And I ley stille tille night, trusting in his mercy, and than I began to
slepe. /fol. 142v/

THE SIXTY-SEVENTH CHAPTER

Ande in my slepe, at the beginning, methought the fende set him in my throte,
putting forth a visage fulle nere my face like a yonge man, and it was longe and
wonder leen. I saw never none such. The coloure was red, like the tilestone whan it is
new brent, with blacke spottes therein like freknes,° fouler than the tilestone. His here
was rede as rust, not scored afore, with side lockes hanging on the thonwonges. He 5
grinned upon me with a shrewde loke; shewde me whit teth and so mekille, methought
it the more ugly. Body ne handes had he none shaply, but with his pawes he helde me
in the throte, and woulde have strangled me,° but he might not.

This ugly shewing was made sleping, and so was none other. And in all this time
/fol. 143r/ I trusted to be saved and kepte by the mercy of God. And oure curtesse 10
lorde gave me grace to wake, and unnethes had I my° life. The persons that were
with me beheld me and wet my temples, and my harte beganne to comfort. And

[*VIS.* 21.13–26] preste. For I thoght: "Howe shulde a preste leve me? I leved nought oure
lorde God." This I leved sothfastlye for the time that I sawe him, and so was than my
wille and my meninge ever for to do withouten ende. Bot as a fule I lette it passe fro
my minde. Lo, I, wrich! This was a grete sinne and a grete unkindnes, that I, for folye of
felinge of a litille bodelye paine, so unwiselye lefte for the time the comforth of alle this
blissede shewinge of oure lorde God.

Here maye ye see whate I am of myselfe. Botte herein walde nought oure curtayse
lorde leve me. And I laye stille tille night, tristande in his mercye, and than I begane to
slepe. And in my slepe, atte the beginninge, methought the fende sette him in my throte
/*Rev. 67.2–8*/ and walde hafe strangelede me, botte he might nought. /*Rev. 67.9–11*/ *Than
I woke oute of my slepe,* and unnethes hadde I my life.

The persones that ware with me beheld me and wette my temples, and my herte
began to comforth. And

13 **dorre** door • 13 **foule stinch** foul stench. Smoke, smells, and heat traditionally accompany demons. *The Pricke* lists "filthe and stink" as the third pain of hell, caused by fire, brimstone, and pitch (6683–94) • 14 **Benedicite dominus!** bless Lord! See 4.13 for this ungrammatical cry • 14 **I wened** I supposed • 14 **it had bene** it was • 15 **shuld have burned** was going to burn • 16 **felt ony stinch** noticed any stench • 17 **wist I wele** knew I well • 17 **tempest me** torment me • 18 **I toke me to . . . shewed me** I recollected what our Lord had showed me

[CHAPTER 68] 2–4 **I saw the soule . . . citte** The city in the soul is where the Son is seated at the end of the exemplum of the lord and servant. See 51.278–80. The city in the soul resembles the New Jerusalem of Rev. 21:1–27, as represented in art and poems such as *Pearl* or *The Pricke,* where the vision of God "es mast joy" of the city of heaven, a city so "large and wide" it has space for all the saved, all of whom can nonetheless clearly see "the face of God allemighty" (9207–31). In the chapter as a whole, the city is taken to be a figure for both the individual soul and the collective souls of "alle that shalle be saved" • 2 **so large as it were** as expansive as if it were • 2 **an endlesse warde** an eternal citadel. Compare 51.107–8 • 3 **by the conditions . . . therein** judging by the fittings I saw in it • 4 **wurshipfulle citte** honorable city • 4–5 **sitteth oure lorde Jhesu** In *The Book of Margery Kempe* 1.86, the Trinity and the whole court of heaven come to sit in Margery's soul. In *Piers Plowman* B 5.605–7, Piers tells the pilgrims that, if they search diligently for truth, they will eventually find him in their own hearts: "Thou shalt see in thiselve Truthe sitte in thin herte, / In a cheyne of charite, as thou a child were [as if you were a child], / To suffren him and segge nought ayein thy sires wille [to submit to him and to say nothing against your lord's will]" • 5 **very God and very man** true God and true human. The God who is "enclosed in rest and in pees" in the human soul at the end of time (see 31.10) is the incarnate Christ • 5 **a fair person and of large stature** See Mary's account of Christ's beauty and size in Bridget's *Liber celestis,* where he is "so fare in visage [so beautiful of face] that ilka man [everyone] that saw it had likinge tharein," and "large of persone, noght fleshely bot bony" (4.70) • 6–7 **clothed solemply in wurshippes** solemnly clad in honors. Christ wears the badges not only of his triumphant suffering and the "mede" given him by his Father in Chapter 22 but of his triple office as bishop, king, and lord • 7 **sitteth . . . even righte** sits squarely in the middle of the soul. "Even righte" also has an ethical connotation, "impartially" or "justly" • 8 **yemeth** governs • 9–10 **instrument or besinesse** assistance or work. Like the lord in the exemplum in Chapter 51, Christ as God does not need to make any effort to rule. Now, however, as at the end of the exemplum, the humanity of Christ, as well as his divinity, is at rest, ruling creation directly, not through intermediaries

anon a littil smoke cam in at the dorre with a grete heet and a foule stinch. And than
I said: "Benedicite dominus! Is it alle on fyer that is here?" And I wened it had bene a
bodely fyer that shuld have burned° us all to deth. I asked them that were with me if   15
they felt ony stinch. They saide "nay," they felt none. I saide: "Blessed be God!" For
than wist I wele it was the fende that was come to tempest me.°

And anon I toke me to that oure lorde had shewed me on the same daye, with
alle the faith of holy church—for I behelde it as both one°—and fled therto as to my
/fol. 143v/ comfort. And anon alle vanished awey, and I was brought to grete reste   20
and peas, without sicknesse of body or drede of conscience.

THE SIXTY-EIGHTH CHAPTER

And then oure good lorde opened my gostely eye and shewde me my soule in
the middes of my harte. I saw the soule so large as it were an endlesse warde,
and also as it were a blissefull° kingdom, and by the conditions that I saw therein
I understode that it is a wurshipfulle citte. In middes of that citte sitteth° oure
lorde Jhesu, very God and very man: a fair person and of large stature, highest   5
bishoppe, solempnest° kinge, wurshipfullest lorde. And I saw him clothed solemply
in wurshippes. He sitteth in the soule even righte in peas and rest, and he ruleth and
yemeth° heven and erth and all that is. The manhode /fol. 144r/ with the godhed
sitteth in rest; the godhede ruleth and yemeth° withouten ony instrument or

---

[*vis.* 21.26–35] onane a litelle smoke come in atte the dore with a grete hete /fol. 112r/
and a foule stinke. I saide: "Benedicite dominus! Is alle on fire that is here?" And I wened
it hadde bene a bodely fire that shulde hafe brenned us to dede. I asked tham that ware
with me if thaye feled any stinke. Thay saide "naye," thay feled nane. I saide: "Blissede be
God!" For than wiste I wele it was the fende was comen to tempest me.

And onane I tuke *tha* that oure lorde hadde shewed me on the same daye, with alle
the faith of haly kyrke—for I *holde* it as bathe ane—and fled therto as to my comforth.
And al sone alle vanished awaye, and I was brought to gret reste and pees, withoutene
seknes of bodye or drede of conscience.

[*vis.* 22.1–9] **Bot than lefte I stille wakande,** and than oure lorde openede my gastely
eyen and shewed me my saule in middes of my herte. I sawe *my* saule swa large as it ware
‡ a kingdome, and be the conditions that I sawe therin, *methought* it was a wirshipfulle
cite. In middes of this cite sittes oure lorde Jhesu, verraye God and verray man: a faire
persone and of large stature, ‡ *wyrshipfulle, hiest* lorde. And I sawe him cledde solemplye
in wyrshippes. He sittes in the saule even right in pees and reste, and he rewles and
yemes heven and erth and alle that is. The manhede with the godhede sittis in reste;
and the godhede rewles and yemes withouten any instrumente or

10 **the soule . . . godhed** the soul is wholly possessed by the blessed godhead • 12 **remove** leave • 13 **homeliest** most intimate • 13 **wonning** dwelling • 13–14 **And in this he shewde** Apparently in the phrase "his homeliest home and his endlesse wonning" • 14 **liking** pleasure • 14–16 **as wele as . . . so it was done** The auxiliary verbs "might, "couth," and "wolde" represent the power, wisdom, and love of the persons of the Trinity as they create humankind. There is a resemblance, here and in lines 30–35, to a passage on the perfection of the Passion of Christ in 22.44–47: "This dede and this werke about oure salvation was ordained as wele as God might ordaine it. . . . And heerin, I saw a fulle blisse in Crist, for his blisse shuld not have ben fulle if it might ony better have ben done than it was done" • 15 **couth** knew how to • 18 **he sawe . . . ende** he always foresaw what was always to please him. See 53.30: "Or that he made us he loved us" • 19 **sheweth** declares • 20–21 **a creature . . . lorde** a person who is taken to see the great nobility and the kingdoms that belong to a lord. The last exemplum in the work • 24 **oure soule . . . have rest** See 5.16–27, which alludes to a famous adage at the outset of Augustine's *Confessions* or to one of its many vernacular adaptations, such as Hilton's *Scale* 1.43 • 25–26 **whan it cometh . . . God** when it arrives at itself, above all created beings, even then it cannot rest in the contemplation of itself, but all its contemplation is joyfully fixed on God. The creature's contemplative progress here follows that of *The Mirror,* whose discussion of contemplation of God through creation also resembles parts of Chapter 62. After contemplating God through the trinity of its own faculties, "then thou shalt heven up thin herte in heigh contemplation of thy creatour. The soule wolde fayn sen [would like to see] God thorw contemplation in his owne nature, but hit may not. And thenne hit turneth to his oune degres [its own stairs; read: "then it returns to itself and makes itself stairs"] by whuche hit may mounten to the contemplation of God" ("Contemplation of God and of His Deite," *YW* 1:259) • 27 **very wonning** true home • 27–29 **the highest light . . . God** Alludes to Rev. 21:23: "And the city has no need of sun or moon to shine upon it, for the glory of God is its light, and its lamp is the Lamb" • 29–30 **what may . . . enjoyeth in us** Similar to 30.6–7 • 32 **full plesed** See 11.40–41 • 33–34 **But for . . . a creature** but because he made the human soul as beautiful, as good, as precious as he could make it, as a created thing • 36 **depnesse of the erth** Compare "depe depnesse," 51.255–56, a term for hell • 38 **while we are here** while we are in this life • 38 **sped** profit

besinesse; and the soule is alle occupied with the blessed godhed: that is, sovereyne 10
mighte, sovereyne wisdom, and sovereyn goodnesse.

The place that Jhesu taketh in oure soule he shall never remove it° withouten
ende, as to my sight, for in us is his homeliest home and his endlesse wonning.° And
in this he shewde the liking that he hath of the making of mannes soule. For as wele
as the fader might make a creature, and as wele as the son couth° make a creature, 15
so wele wolde the holy gost that mannes soule were made. And so it was done. And
therfore the blessed° trinite enjoyeth without ende in the making of mannes soule,
for he sawe without beginning what shulde like him without ende.

Al thing that he /fol. 144v/ hath made sheweth his lordshippe—as understanding
was geven in the same time by example of a creature that is led to se grete noblinesse 20
and kingdoms longing to a lorde. And when it had sene alle the nobilnes beneth,
than, merveling, it was stered to seke uppe above to that high place where the lorde
wonneth,° knowing by reson that his dwelling is in the wurthiest place. And thus I
understonde sothly° that oure soule may never have rest in thing that is beneth
itselfe. And whan it cometh above alle creatures into itselfe, yet may it not abide in 25
the beholding of itselfe, but alle the beholding is blissefully• set in God, that is the
maker, wonning° therin. For in mannes soule is his very wonning.° And the highest
light and the brightest shining of the citte° is the /fol. 145r/ glorious love of oure
lorde God, as to my sight. And what may make us more enjoye in God than to see in
him that he enjoyeth in us, highest of all his werkes? For I saw in the same shewing 30
that if the blisseful° trinite might have° made mannes soule ony better, ony fairer,
ony nobeler than it was made, he shulde not have° been full plesed with making
of mannes soule. But for he made mannes soule as fair, as good, as precious as he
might make it, a creature, therfore the blessed trinite is fulle plesed withoute ende in
the making of mannes soule. And he wille that oure hartes be mightly raised above 35
the depnesse of the erth and alle vaine sorowes, and enjoye in him.

This was a delectable sighte and a restfulle shewing that is without ende. And the
beholding of this while we are here, it is fulle plesant to God, and fulle grete sped to us.

[VIS. 22.9–15] besines. And *my* saule is° *blisfullye occupied with the godhede: that is,* sufferayn might, sufferayne wisdome, sufferayne goodnesse.

The place that Jhesu takes in oure saule he shalle never remove it withouten ende, ‡
for in us is his haymelieste hame and **maste likinge to him to dwelle in.** /Rev. 68.13–36/

This was a delectabille sight and a *restefulle, for it is so in trowth withouten ende.*
And the behaldinge of this whiles we ere here es fulle plesande to God, and fulle grete
spede to us.

39 **And the soule . . . beholde** contemplation transforms the soul who contemplates in this way into the image of that which is contemplated. See 2 Cor. 3:18: "And we all, with unveiled face, beholding the glory of the Lord, are being changed into his likeness from one degree of glory to another" • 40 **oneth** unites • 41 **that I saw him sitte** Rather than assume any other posture • 41 **the sekernesse . . . dwelling** the stability of his sitting meant he would stay there forever • 42 **he gave me knowing . . . alle before** he gave me the knowledge that it was truly he who showed me everything before. This knowledge precedes Christ's words in lines 45–47, which in a sense do no more than make public what, it is said here, Julian had already understood. Christ's occupancy of the soul, and the fact that "I saw him sitte" (line 41), in themselves not only act as "confirmation" of the truth of all the revelations (see 66.3), by gathering up so many of its strands, but refute her reckless claim to have been "raving" (66.13). Christ has, from the beginning, been in full command not only of the revelation but, from his seat in Julian's soul, of her apprehension of it • 43 **behold this with avisement** contemplated this with deliberation. A deliberation exemplified by the length of this chapter's buildup to Christ's words that follow •

44–45 **right as he had done afore** See 13.3–4, where Christ speaks in the same voiceless and lipless way • 45 **Wit it now wele** now know it well • 45 **it was no raving** it was no madness. See 66.12–13 • 47–51 **Theyse last wordes . . . overcome** Christ's last words confirm the revelation not only by what they say but by the formal beauty of their allusion to his first words. The repetition of "overcome" brings the revelation full circle. The intricate circular structure of *Pearl* has an analogous function • 48 **for lerning . . . sekernesse** to teach absolute certainty • 49 **the furst worde** Spoken by Christ in 13.4–5 • 51 **mening us alle** referring to all of us. Despite the fact that "thou" in "Thou shalt not be overcome" is singular • 52 **generalle to** generally applicable to • 52–53 **as it is afore saide** See 8.31–32: "Alle that I say of me, I mene in the person of alle my evencristen, for I am lerned in the gostely shewing of our lord God that he meneth so" • 53 **and so is Gods wille** and such is God's will • 54 **sharply** fiercely • 55–56 **He saide not** For this mode of exposition by means of what was not said, see 22.42 • 56 **Thou shalt not . . . traveyled** See 47.36–37: "And in this [this "contrariousnes"] we be traveyled and tempested" • 56 **tempestid** tormented • 56 **traveyled** wearied

/fol. 145v/ And the soule that thus beholdeth, it maketh it like to him that is beholde, and oneth° it in rest and in pease by his grace. And this was a singuler joye and blisse to me that I saw him sitte,° for the sekernesse of sitting shewde endlesse dwelling.° And he gave° me knowing sothfastly° that it was he that shewde me alle before.

And whan I had behold this with avisement, then shewed oure good lorde° wordes fulle mekely, without voice and without opening of lippes, right as he had done afore, and saide full swetely: "Wit it now wele, it was no raving that thou saw today. But take it and beleve it, and kepe thee therin, and comfort thee therwith, and trust thee therto,° and thou shalt not be overcome." Theyse last wordes were saide for lerning of full tru sekernesse, that it is oure lorde Jhesu° */fol. 146r/* that shewed me alle. And right as in the furst worde that oure good lorde shewde, mening his blessed passion—"Herewith is the fende overcome"—right so he saide in the last worde with full tru sekernesse,° mening us alle: "Thou shalt not be overcome." And alle this lerning and this tru comfort, it is generalle to alle mine evencristen, as it is afore saide, and so is Gods wille.

And this worde, "Thou shalt not be overcom," was saide fulle sharply and full mightly for sekernesse and comfort against all tribulations that may come. He saide not, "Thou shalt not be tempestid,° thou shalt not be traveyled, thou shalle not be

40

45

50

55

[VIS. 22.15–33] And the saule that thus behaldes, it makes it like to him that is behaldene, and anes in reste and in pees ‡. And this was a singulere joye and a blis to me that I sawe him sitte, *for the behaldinge of this sittinge shewed to me sikernes of his endelesse dwellinge. And I knewe sothfastly* that it was he that shewed me */fol. 112v/* alle before.

And when I hadde behalden this with **fulle** avisement, than shewed oure lorde **me** wordes fulle mekelye, withouten voice and withouten openinge of lippes, as he hadde done before, and saide fulle *soberlye:* "Witte it ‡ welle, it was na ravinge that thowe sawe today. Botte take it, and leve it, and kepe the° therto, ‡ and thowe shalle nought be overcomen." This laste wordes ware saide **to me** for lerninge of fulle trewe sikernes, that it is our lorde Jhesu that shewed me alle. For right as in the firste worde that oure lorde shewed **me**, menande his blissed passion—"Herewith is the fende overcomen"—right so he saide in the laste worde, with fulle trewe sikernesse ‡ : "Thow shalle nought be overcomen." And this lerninge and this trewe comforthe, it es generalle to alle mine evencristen, *as I haffe* before saide, and so is Goddes wille.

And this worde, "Thowe shalle nought be overcomen," was saide fulle sharpely and fulle mightely for sekernes and comforth againe alle tribulations that maye com. He saide nought, "Thowe salle not° be tempested, thowe shalle not be travailed, thowe shalle not be

57 **dissesed** distressed. The mood that makes a child run to its mother in 61.29–30, 37–38 • 57 **take hede at** pay attention to • 60 **all was close** everything was finished. The end of the revelation

[CHAPTER 69] 1 **feende** devil • 1 **with his heet . . . stinch** See 67.13 • 1–2 **made me fulle besy** kept me very busy. As described in lines 12–19. "Besy" and "besines" are used often in this chapter. The word "besy" sometimes has negative connotations in Middle English religious writing and through most of this work, but Julian's "besines" is justified by that of her tempters • 2–3 **the bodely heet also . . . traveylous** the physical heat equally frightening and exhausting. "Bodely heet" might seem like a reference to fever, but "body" is used several times in this passage to convey the disgusting physicality of the demons, and the phrase probably refers to the same diabolical heat Julian mentioned in line 1 • 3 **harde** heard • 3 **bodely jangeling** audible squabbling • 3 **as it had been of two bodies** as if it had been between two bodies. "Bodies," not "persons" or "creatures," terms that would dignify the demonic presence • 4–5 **as if they had holde . . . besines** as if they were conducting a parliament with much energy. The devil's "besines" parodies Julian's (line 2). A "perlement" is a meeting to decide something: here, perhaps, Julian's eternal destiny • 6–8 **as they scorned bidding of bedes . . . prayer** as if they were parodying the recitation of prayers when they are said crudely with the mouth, lacking that devout attention and wise care we owe God in our prayer. The "boistosly" mumbled words in the first

instance parody the prayers said around Julian's bed all through her illness, but also reflect her "rechelesnesse" in 66.16, where she has not exercised "wise diligence" in relation to her revelation • 9–10 **to comfort my soule . . . traveyled** comforted my soul by speaking aloud, as I would have done for any other who had been in similar in difficulty. Talking to herself to drown out the mutterings of the demons, Julian follows a course of action suggested in *The Remedy,* which recommends that the tempted person "strength himselfe and be mery [cheerful], though it be ayenst his herte [not in accordance with how he feels], and drede nothinge the fendes malice" (chap. 6, *YW* 2:116) • 11 **Methought that besines . . . bisines** A curious remark, since the entire account has consisted of "likening" the temptation to "bodely bisines." It evokes the inverted ineffability of the scene, as far below words and metaphors as the divine is above them • 12–13 **afore that time** See 3.18–23 • 13 **my tong . . . holy church** my tongue to talk of Christ's Passion and rehearsal of the faith of holy church. Standard remedies in temptation, meant to awaken faith, hope, charity. *The Remedy* notes that if "the fende cometh and tempteth a soule fiersly like a dragon," the tempted "creature" should "strength himselfe saddely in the passion of almighty God and arme him with that holy passion" (chap. 4, *YW* 2:112) • 14 **my harte to fasten on God** Julian is attempting to recapture the experience she describes in 15.2–3, when she was "fulfillede of the everlasting sekernesse, mightely fastned without any painefulle drede" • 15 **mening** thinking this • 15 **Thou hast nowe great besenes** now you have to make a big effort

dissesed," but he saide, "Thou shalt not be overcom." God wille that we take hede at this worde, and that we be ever mighty in seker° trust, in wele and wo. For /fol. 146v/ he loveth us and liketh us, and so wille he that we love him and like him and mightely trust in him, and all shall be welle. And sone after all was close,° and I saw no more.°   60

THE SIXTY-NINTH CHAPTER

After this,° the feende came againe with his heet and with his stinch, and made me fulle besy. The stinch was so vile and so painfulle, and the bodely heet° also dredful and traveylous. Also I harde a bodely jangeling,° as it had been of two bodies, and both to my thinking jangled° at one time, as if° they had holde a perlement with greate besines. And all was softe muttering,° and I understode not what they said.   5
And alle this was to stere me to dispere, as methought, seming to me as they scorned bidding of bedes which are saide boistosly with mouth,° failing /fol. 147r/ devout intending and wise diligence, the which we owe to God in oure prayer. And oure good lorde God gave me grace mightly to trust in him, and to comfort my soule with bodely spech, as I shulde have done° to another person that had been traveyled.   10
Methought that besines might not be likened to no bodely bisines.°

My bodely eye° I set in the same crosse there I had seen in comforte afore that time, my tong with spech of Cristes passion and rehersing the faith of holy church, and my harte to fasten on God with alle the truste and the mighte that was in me. And I thought° to myselfe, mening: "Thou hast nowe great besenes to kepe the in   15

[VIS. 22.33–37] desesed," bot he saide, "Thowe shalle nought be overcomen." God wille that we take hede *of his worde,* and that we be ever mighty in *sekernesse,* in wele and in wa. For he luffes us and likes us, and so wille he that we luff him and like him and mightely triste in him, and alle shalle be wele. And sone efter alle was close, and I sawe na mare.

[VIS. 23.1–15] After this, the fende com againe with his heete and with his stinke, and made me fulle besye. The stinke was so vile and so painfulle, and the bodely heete also dredfulle and travailous. And also I harde a bodely jangelinge **and a speche,** as it hadde bene of two bodies, and bathe to my thinkinge jangled at anes, as if thay had haldene a parliamente with grete besines. And alle was softe mutteringe, and I understode nought whate thay saide. Botte alle this was to stirre me to dispaire, as methought. /Rev. 69.6–8/ *And I triste besely in God and comforthede* my saule with bodely speche, as I shulde hafe done to anothere person **than myselfe** that hadde so bene travailede. Methought this besines might nought be /fol. 113r/ likned to na bodely besenes.

My bodelye eyen I sette on the same crosse *that I hadde sene comfort in* before that time, my tunge **I occupied** with speche of Cristes passion and rehersinge of the faith of haly kyrke, and my herte *I festende* on God with alle the triste and alle the might that was in me. And I thought to myselfe, menande: "Thowe hase nowe grete besines. /Rev. 69.15–16/

16 **for that thou shuldest not be taken of** so that you are not captured by • 18–19 **Were I safe . . . soule** if I were safe from sin, I would be completely safe from all the devils of hell and enemies of my soul. *The Remedy* argues that "somtime . . . the fende tempteth and travailleth a rightwise soule so sharpely that it is . . . driven to dispaire. And yet all that time, though the soule perceive it not, it dwelleth still in the drede and love of God. . . . for our lorde . . . arrecteth [attributes] not to the soule that sinne which himselfe suffreth the fende to werke in the soule without the consente . . . of the said selfe soule" (chap. 1, *YW* 2:107) • 20 **he occupied me** The two devils reduce again to one • 21 **prime day** early morning • 24 **saide afore** See 13.4–5

[CHAPTER 70] 1–2 **In alle this blessede . . . passe** throughout this blessed revelation our Lord made it understood that the vision would end. This might seem obvious, but Julian's Continental contemporaries, Bridget of Sweden and Catherine of Siena, had many years of visionary experience, and the career of her closest English equivalent, Margery Kempe, was equally full of visionary episodes. The end of this revelation is anticipated from the second revelation on, where it is said that Julian "was sometime in a feer whether it was a shewing or none" (10.27) • 2 **which blessed shewing . . . wille** which blessed revelation faith preserves with God's own good will. See 2 Cor. 5:7: "For we walk by faith, not by sight." "Faith" here is Julian's personal faith, but in the rest of the chapter the word aspires to a more general meaning • 3 **For he lefte . . . might know it** Perhaps a reference to the symbols of the divine presence associated with other visionaries, such as Katherine of Alexandria's ring or Francis of Assisi's stigmata. "Signes" and "tokens" are also legal proofs, which, had they been available to Julian, would have helped this chapter to make its case for the authority of the revelation • 6 **that it**

is in the faith that he shewde that what he showed is part of orthodox faith. A claim made earlier for the doctrine of the "godly wille" (see 53.12–14) now extends to the whole revelation. However, where Chapter 53 declares flatly, "Therefore oure lorde wille we know it in the faith and the beleve," here the phrase "that it is in the faith" is dependent on a personal "I beleve." (See also line 7: "I am bounde.") The absence of any "signe" or "token" signifies the absolute necessity of personal faith in apprehending not only the revelation but *A Revelation*. Hence, in line 9, "the faith" has again become "my faith" • 7 **therto I am bounde . . . mening** I am bound to believe by the full force of his own intention. "Bounde" has erotic and feudal connotations, as in 19.10–11, but also religious ones, referring to the tie created by a monastic or other formal vow. The revelation binds Julian as much as do her anchoritic vows of poverty, chastity, and stability of abode • 8 **with the nexte wordes that folowen** as stated in the following words. First quoted in 68.46–47. The language is deliberately formal • 9–11 **For on the same day . . . raved** See 66.12–17. Julian's failure to believe until the revelation had been confirmed becomes a further reason she is bound to belief • 12 **wolde not let it perish** "Perish" suggests that Julian's failure to believe put the entire revelation in peril. "Perish" often means "perish in hell" in Middle English, as in 61.31–32: "Oure hevenly moder Jhesu may never suffer us that be his children to perish" • 12–13 **he shewde hit all agene** Presumably through the words from 68.45–46 quoted in the next lines • 15–16 **For the sighte . . . the** because the vision had left you • 17–18 **This was saide . . . folowing** this was said not only to apply to that specific time, but also to build the foundation of my faith on it, where he says immediately afterward. Belief is based on obedience and trust, not sight, but these are still a "grounde"

the faith, for that thou shuldest not be taken of thine enemes. Woldest thou now fro this time evermore be so besy to kepe the fro sinne, this /*fol. 147v*/ were a good and a sovereyne occupation." For I thought sothly:° "Were I safe fro sinne, I were fulle safe fro alle the feendes in helle and enemes of my soule."

And thus he occupied me alle that night and on the morne° tille it was about   20
prime day. And anon they were alle gone and passed, and there lefte nothing but stinke, and that lasted still a while. And I scornede him, and thus was I delivred of him by the vertu of Cristes passion. For "therwith is the feend overcome," as oure lorde Jhesu Crist saide afore.

THE SEVENTIETH CHAPTER

In alle this blessede shewing oure good lorde gave understanding that the sight shulde passe, which blessed shewing the faith kepeth with his owne good wille and his grace. For he lefte with me neither signe ne token whereby I might know it. But he lefte with me his owne blessed worde in tru understanding, /*fol. 148r*/ bidding me fulle mightly that I shulde believe it, and so I do. Blessed mot he be! I believe that   5
he is oure savioure that shewed it, and that it is in the faith that he shewde. And therfore I beleve° it, ever joyeng. And therto I am bounde by alle his owne mening, with the nexte wordes that folowen: "Kepe thee therein, and comforte thee therwith, and truste therto." Thus I am bounde° to kepe it in my faith. For on the same day that it was shewde, what time the sight was passed, as a wrech I forsoke it, and   10
openly I saide that I had raved.

Than oure lorde Jhesu of his mercy wolde not let it perish, but he shewde hit all agene within my soule, with more fullehed, with the blessed light of his precious love, seyeng theyse wordes full mightely and fulle mekely: "Wit it now welle, it was no raving that thou saw this day"—as if he had /*fol. 148v*/ saide: "For the sighte was   15
passed fro the, thou lost it and couth or might not kepe it. But wit it now: that is to seye, now thou seest it." This was saide not onely for the same time, but also to set

---

[*VIS. 23.15–22*] Walde thowe nowe fra this time evermare be so besy to kepe the fro sinne, this ware a soferayne and a goode occupation. For I *trowe* sothlye, ware I safe fra sinne, I ware fulle saife fra alle the fendes of helle and enmyse of my saule."

And thus *thay* occupied me alle the night and on the morn tille it was aboute prime dayes. And than onane thay ware alle gane and passed, and there lefte nathinge bot stinke, and that lasted stille a while. And I scorned *thame,* and thus was I delivered of *tham* be the vertu of Cristes passion. For "tharewith is the fende overcomen," as Criste saide before **to me.** /*Rev. 70.1–72.49*/

18–20 **take it . . . overcom** See 68.46–47 • 21–22 **In theyse six wordes . . . hert** Now the "I" who must have "faith" in the revelation becomes "we" readers, according to the logic of Julian's exemplarity outlined in Chapters 8–9 • 22–23 **he wille it dwelle . . . joye** Christ desires the revelation to remain with readers in faith until the end of our lives and afterward in fullness of joy • 23 **we have . . . trust** we always have certain trust. See 41.2 • 24 **contraried** opposed • 29–31 **For above the faith . . . we kepe us** Expounds the "therein" of "kepe thee therin," line 19. "Above the faith" is the knowledge God chooses to keep hidden, as much of the thirteenth revelation has explained. "Beneth the faith" is doubt as to the veracity of the revelation. "Faith" and the revelation have merged • 33 **asayde** tested

[CHAPTER 71] 1–2 **Glad . . . soules** This chapter continues Chapter 70's exploration of faith and sight. Christ's "glad chere" is felt in this life as a matter of faith more than sight (lines 16–22) • 1 **chere** expression • 2–3 **For he beholdeth . . . to him** Despite his awareness of human longing for him, Christ desires to be shown a "glad chere." A typically anti-ascetic stance. Again, see

The Remedy: "A man . . . ought to the honour of God . . . to strength himselfe and be mery, though it be ayenst his herte" (chap. 6, *YW* 2:116) • 2 **love-longing** The one time this word is applied to humanity, not Christ. Compare 63.21 • 3 **to yelde him his mede** See 22.17–18 • 3–4 **thus I hope . . . inner** so I hope that by his grace he has drawn the outward expression closer to the inner, and will do so all the more. Alludes to 51.33–38, the lord's "doubil chere" toward the fallen servant, although here both Christ's "chere" toward us and ours toward him are at issue at once • 6–7 **chere of passion** See 21.20: "He sheweth us chere of passion." As shown in Chapters 3–21 • 9 **pitte . . . compassion** See 31.42, summing up Chapters 27–31: "Alle this was seen in shewing of compassion" • 11 **blissful chere** See 21.8–9, introducing Chapters 21–26: "He changed in blissful chere" • 11–12 **oftenest shewed** From the exemplum of the lord and servant on, Chapters 51–68 • 14 **beer** bear • 17 **therwith meddeling the thirde** mixing the third expression in with them. Whereas in the revelation Christ's third, "blissful chere . . . was oftenest shewed" (lines 11–12), this is not the case in ordinary life

thereupon the grounde of my faith, where° he seyeth anone folowing: "But take it, and beleve it,° and kepe thee therin, and comfort the therwith, and trust therto, and thou shalt not be overcom."° 20

In theyse six wordes that foloweth wher he seyth, "Take it," his mening is to fasten it faithfully in oure hert. For he wille it dwelle with us in faith into oure lifes ende, and after in fullehed of joye, willing° that we have ever seker° trust of his blisseful• behestes,° knowing his goodnesse. For oure faith is contraried in diverse maner by oure owne blindhede• and /fol. 149r/ oure gostely enemes, within and 25 withoute. And therefore oure precious lover helpeth us with gostely lighte and tru teching on diverse manner within and withoute, whereby that we may know him. And therfore in what manner that he techeth us, he wille that we perceve him wisely, receive° him swetly, and kepe us in him faithfully. For above the faith is no goodnesse kept in this life, as to my sight, and beneth the faith is no helth of soule. 30 But in the faith, there will oure lorde we kepe us. For we have by his goodnesse and his owne werking to kepe us in the faith, and by his suffrance throw gostely enmite we are asayde in the faith and made mighty. For if oure faith had not enmite it shulde deserve no mede, as by the understanding that I have in oure lordes /fol. 149v/ meyning. 35

THE SEVENTY-FIRST CHAPTER

Glad and mery and swete is the blisseful,• lovely chere of oure lorde to oure soules. For he beholdeth° us ever living in love-longing, and he wille oure soule be in glad chere to him, to yelde him his mede. And thus I hope with his grace he hath—and more shall—drawe the utter chere to the inner, and make us all at one with him, and ech of us with other in tru, lasting joye that is Jhesu. 5

I have mening of thre° manner of cheres of oure lorde. The furst is chere of passion, as he shewde while he was with us in this life, dying. And though this beholding be morning and swemfulle, yet it is glad and mery, for he is God. The seconde manner of chere, it is pitte and ruth and compassion, and this sheweth he to all his lovers with sekernesse of keping that hath nede to his mercy. The thirde is 10 the blisseful• /fol. 150r/ chere as it shalle be withouten ende, and this was oftenest shewed and longeste continued.

And thus in the time of oure paine and oure wo, he sheweth to us chere of his passion and his crosse, helping us to beer it by his owne blessed vertu. And in time of oure sinning he sheweth to us chere of reuth and pitte, mightely keping us and 15 defending against all oure enmes. And theyse two be the comen cheres which he sheweth to us in this life, therwith meddeling the thirde, and that is his blisseful°

18 **like in perty . . . heven** partly like how his expression will be in heaven • 18–19 **gracious touching . . . life** the touch of grace in the form of a sweet illumination of our spiritual life. The same language of "touching" and "lightening" describes both the periods of spiritual well-being experienced in the seventh revelation and the means by which God renews the revelation to Julian after it is passed. See 1.18–19: "gracious touching and lightning, with true sekernes of endlesse joy"; 65.30: "renewde by lighteninges and touchinges"

[CHAPTER 72] 1–2 **me behoveth to telle . . . for sinne** I need to describe in what way I saw mortal sin in those people who will not be damned for their sin. (Compare the opening of Chapter 60.) This chapter's subject arises from the work's claim that Christ "sheweth . . . chere of reuth" even "in time of oure sinning" (71.14–15), a claim that seems to imply that those who will be saved are incapable of "deadly," or mortal, sin. In late medieval theology venial sin does not damn the soul but subjects it to punishment in purgatory, unless it is confessed and penance is performed. An unconfessed mortal sin, however, may send the soul to hell, a place normally considered beyond the reach of Christ's "chere of reuth." How can he then pity, or save, mortal sinners? Although not a mortal sin by most definitions, Julian's own sin of disbelief in Chapter 66 may also be in question. This is the first of a number of addenda dealing with specific topics arising from the revelation, though the formal opening of the revelation's coda takes place in Chapter 73 • 3 **two contrares . . . stede** opposites cannot coexist in the same place. An adage from medieval physics • 4–6 **The highest blesse . . . fullhede of joye** the highest happiness that there is, is to possess God in the clarity of the endless light, truly seeing him, sweetly feeling him, all peacefully possessing him in fullness of joy. Evokes the account of the soul's assimilation into God after death, at 43.36–47, where "we" are "alle had in God, him verely seyeng and fulsomly feling" • 6–7 **thus was the blisseful chere . . . in perty** As just explained in 71.16–18 • 7–8 **most contrary** most opposed. To the "blisseful chere" of God • 8 **meddled** mixed. Alluding to the use of this word in 71.17 • 9 **horiblier** more horrible • 9 **depper** further • 11 **parelle of deth** peril of death • 11 **in a party of helle** in a region of hell. See 63.10–12: "Whan we . . . accorde us to kinde . . . we shall se verely that sinne is wurse, viler, and painfuller than hell without

ony liknesse" • 12 **thus we are dead** in this sense we are dead. "Deedly" sin is not misnamed, although the word now implies a subjective experience of death in a situation of mere "parelle of deth." "Deedly" does not, for the saved, mean "damnable" • 12 **very sight** true sight • 13 **we be not dead . . . God** The argument is similar to that made in Chapter 45 about the two "domes" of God and holy church, where God's knowledge of the final salvation of the elect—of their substantial souls—allows him to see them as always already perfect • 13–14 **ne he passeth never from us** nor does he ever leave us • 16 **geten therto** brought there • 16 **sinne is deadly . . . time** The resolution of the contradiction articulated in lines 1–2. In a sense it is obvious that "the blessed creatures of endlesse life" cannot finally experience sin as "deadly." But the issue at stake is not so much intellectual as personal: since "deadly" sin remains always a possibility in this life, how can Julian and the reader be sure that the revelation's picture of Christ's "reuth" for them as sinners, and his final promise "thou shalt not be overcome" (68.47), apply to them? "Sekernesse," spiritual confidence, is one of the attitudes most frequently insisted on in *A Revelation*: e.g., in 71.8–10, where Christ's "chere" of "ruth and compassion" signifies "sekernesse of keping." The concept of "deadly" sin need not threaten that "sekernesse" • 19–21 **oure lorde God . . . may never leve us** See 5.3–5: "He is oure clothing, that for love wrappeth us and windeth us, halseth us and all becloseth us, hangeth about us for tender love, that he may never leeve us" • 19 **wonneth** dwells • 20 **halseth** embraces • 22 **stinte of morning ne of weping** In his capacity as "wise moder," Jesus allows his children "to morne and to wepe" for a time and to their profit in 61.44, the only earlier reference to weeping in *A Revelation*. Here, however, "morning" and "weping" become conditions of earthly existence, precipitated in part by the inevitability of sin • 24 **ther may no wo . . . faile** no sorrow can linger nor joy fail • 25 **mater of merth . . . morning** reason for mirth and reason for mourning. Compare 52.6–7: "a mervelous medelur both of wele and of wo" • 26–27 **sekernesse . . . goodnes** certainty of our protection by his great goodness • 28 **boren downe** weighed down • 28 **deadly flesh** mortal flesh • 28 **darkhede** darkness • 28–29 **that we may not see . . . clerly** The situation of the servant in 51.15–19 • 30 **unnethes** scarcely • 30 **trowe** trust • 31 **that I sey** See line 22

chere, like in perty as it shalle be in heven. And that is by gracious touching of swete
lightening of gostly life, wherby that we ar kept in seker° faith, hope, and charite,
with contrition and devotion and also with contemplation and alle manner of tru   20
solace° and swete comfortes. The blisseful• chere of oure lorde God werketh
/fol. 150v/ it in us by grace.

THE SEVENTY-SECOND CHAPTER°

But now me behoveth to telle in what manner that I saw sinne deadly in the
creatures which shall° not die for sinne, but live in the joye of God withoute ende.
I saw that two contrares shulde not be togeder in one stede. The most contrarious that
are is the highest blesse and the deppest paine. The highest blesse that is, is to have God
in cleerte of endlesse light, him verely seing, him swetly feling, him all peasable having   5
in fullhede of joye. And thus was the blisseful• chere of oure lorde God shewde in perty.
In which shewing I saw that sinne° was the most contrary, so ferforth that as long as we
be meddled with any part of sinne we shall never see clerly the blisseful° chere of God.
And the horiblier and the grevouser that oure /fol. 151r/ sinnes be, the depper are we for
that time fro this blisseful° sighte. And therfore it semeth to us oftentimes as we were in   10
parelle of deth and in a party of helle, for the sorow and the paine that sinne is to us.
And thus we are dead for the time fro the very sight of oure blisseful• life.

But in all this I saw sothfastly° that we be not dead in the sight of God, ne he
passeth never from us. But he shall never have his fulle blesse in us tille we have oure
full blesse in him, verely seing his fair, blisseful° chere. For we are ordained therto in   15
kinde and geten therto by grace. Thus I saw how sinne is deadly for a short time to
the blessed creatures of endlesse life. And ever the more clerly that the soule seeth
the blisseful chere by grace of loving, the mor it longeth to se it in /fol. 151v/ fulhed,
that is to sey in his owne liknes. For notwithstonding that oure lorde God wonneth°
now in us, and is here with us, and halseth° us and becloseth us for tender love that   20
he may never leve us, and is more nere to us than tonge may telle or harte may
thinke, yet maye we never stinte of morning ne of weping, nor of seking nor of
longing, till whan we se him clere in his blisseful• chere. For in that precious sight
ther may no wo abide nor wele faile.

And in this I saw mater of merth and mater of morning. Mater of merth: that oure   25
lorde, oure maker, is so nere to us and in us, and we in him by sekernesse° of keping of
his great goodnes. Mater of morning: for oure gostly eye is so blinde, and we be° so
boren downe with weight of oure deadly flesh and darkhede• of sinne, that we may
not see oure /fol. 152r/ lorde God clerly in his fair,° blisseful• chere. No, and because of
this darkhede,° unnethes° we can beleve or trowe his grete love and oure sekernesse°   30
of keping. And therfore it is that I sey, we may never stinte° of morning ne of weping.

32–33 **This weping . . . understanding** This weeping not only signifies the pouring of tears from our physical eye, but also includes a more spiritual interpretation. Although Margery Kempe, Julian's younger contemporary, lived a spiritual life full of physical tears, and *A Revelation* here leaves them as a legitimate devout response, this is the work's only reference to "teeres." Even in the Passion sequences, the pain of Christ's dying is evident not as tears but, to the contrary, as dryness. In his *Incendium amoris,* Rolle argues influentially that "tears and weeping are for new converts and beginners" (chap. 41), and *A Revelation* appears to hold the same. Chapters 73–74 are both written against a penitential attitude of fear and sorrow that would overemphasize the sense of sinfulness • 34 **unmesurable** immeasurable • 34 **if it were yeve . . . nobley** if all the noble things were given us for our solace and our comfort • 37 **painful longing** See 51.221–22: "All that be under heven which shall come theder, ther way is by longing and desyering." Weeping is here assimilated to this form of spiritual longing • 38 **that hart may . . . telle** A formula used in lines 21–22, as also in 20.5 and 49.42 • 41 **shule us not greve** should not grieve us • 40 **ende** the end • 41 **hye, mervelous wordes** See 26.4–8 • 43–47 **It longeth to us . . . to my understanding** *A Revelation* here defines its purpose as providing knowledge of God, knowledge of self as seen by God, and knowledge of the self as felt by the self. For the first two, see especially Chapter 56 • 44–45 **what we ar . . . grace** what we are through him in nature and in grace • 45 **what oureselfe is** See 66.26: "Here may you se what I am of myselfe" • 45 **anemptes** with regard to

This weping meneth not all in poring out of teeres by oure bodely eye, but also to more gostely understanding. For the kindly desyer of oure soule is so gret and so unmesurable that if it were yeve us to oure solace° and oure comfort alle the nobley that ever God made in heven and in erth, and we saw not the fair, blissful° chere of himselfe, yet shuld we never stinte of° morning ne of gostely weping—that is to sey of painful longing—till whan we se verely the fair, blissful° chere of oure maker. And if we were in all the paine that hart may think /fol. 152v/ or tong may telle, and we might in that time se his fair,° blissful° chere, alle this paine shule us not greve. Thus is that blissful° sight ende of alle manner of paine to loving soules, and fulfilling of all manner joy and blisse. And that shewde he in the hye, mervelous wordes where he seyth: "I it am that is highest, I it am that thou lovest, I it am that is alle."

It longeth to us to have thre manner of knowing. The furst is that we know oure lorde God. The seconde is that we know oureselfe, what we ar by him in kinde and in grace. The thirde is that we know mekely what oureselfe is, anemptes oure sinne° and anemptes oure febilnes.° And for these thre was alle this shewing made, as to my understanding.

[*VIS.* 23.23–48] A, wriched sinne! Whate ert thowe? Thowe er nought. For I sawe that God is alle thinge: I sawe nought the. And when I sawe that God hase made alle thinge, I sawe the nought. And when I sawe that God is in alle thinge, I sawe the nought. And when I sawe that God does alle thinge that is done, lesse and mare, I sawe the nought. And when I sawe oure lorde Jhesu sit in oure saule so wyrshipfully, and luff and like and rewle and yeme alle that he has made, I sawe nought the. And thus I am seker that thowe erte nought. And alle tha that luffes the and likes the and folowes the and wilfully endes in the, I am seker thay shalle be brought to nought with the, and endleslye confounded. God shelde us alle fra the. Amen par charite.

And whate wrechednesse is I wille saye, as I am lernede be the shewinge of God. Wrechednesse es alle thinge that is nought goode: the gastelye blindehede that we falle into in the firste sinne, and alle that folowes of that wrechednesse, passions and paines, gastelye or bodely; and alle that es in erth or in othere place whilke es nought goode. And than may be asked of this: "Whate er we?" /fol. 113v/ And I answere to this: if alle ware departed fra us that is nought goode, we shulde be goode. When wrechidnesse is departed fra us, God and the saule is alle ane, and God and man alle ane. "Whate is alle in erthe that twinnes us?" I answere and saye: in that that it serves us, it is goode; and in that that it shalle perish, it is° wrichednes; and in that that a man settes his herte theropon otherewise than thus, it is sinne. And for that time that man or woman loves sinne, if any be swilke, he is in paine that passes alle paines. And when he loves nought sinne, botte hates it and luffes God, alle is wele. And he that trewlye does thus, though he sin sumtime by frelty or unkunninge in his wille, he falles nought, for he wille mightely rise againe and behalde God wham he loves in alle his wille. God has made him° to be loved of him or hire that has bene a sinnere. Bot ever he loves, and ever he langes to hafe oure luffe. And when we mightelye and wisely luffe Jhesu, we er in pees.

[CHAPTER 73] 1–3 **Alle . . . sighte** See 9.24–25 for these modes of revelation. The repetition signals a structural parallel between the introductory first revelation and the coda that begins here • 1 **by thre partes** in three modes • 3–4 **For the bodely sighte . . . them me** Julian claims to have represented both the first two kinds of vision with fullness and precision. "Truly" is often used to describe paintings or images that are faithful depictions of what they represent. "I have saide them right" insists that Julian has reproduced the specific words spoken by Christ in the revelation • 5 **somedele** some part • 6 **stered** stirred • 7–8 **unpatiens or slouth** impatience or sloth. Impatience is conventionally linked to the rigors of the religious life. Patience is the subject of a short tract in *Pore Caitif* (taken from Rolle's *Emendatio vitae*), which follows immediately after the tract on the "perfect" life of the contemplative. It is also the implied subject of parts 3 and 4 of *Ancrene Wisse*, as of any treatment of temptation, sin, and tribulation. Sloth, the monastic sin of *accidia*, is often understood to be the sin closest to despair. Though often manifested as torpor, it could also take the frenzied form of "unpatiens" • 8 **traveyle** labor • 8–9 **dispair or doughtfulle drede** despair or doubting fear. Despair is a preoccupation of Flete's *Remedy* and of *The Chastising*, associated with diabolic temptation to intellectual doubt and self-recrimination • 9 **as I shalle sey after** See 74.11–14, though the topic resonates for several chapters • 10 **in special . . . theyse two** For "unpatiens," see 15.6–7: God's absence is so severe that "unneth I could have patience to live"; 64.5–6: the same absence "made me to morne and besely to longe, and also of my owne wretchednesse, sloth, and werinesse." For despair, see 69.6, where the second appearance of the devil, in the form here of "two bodies," "was to stere me to dispere, as methought" • 11 **traveyleth and tempesteth** tasks and torments • 11 **as by that oure lorde shewde me** according to what our Lord showed me. See 68.55–56: "He saide not: 'Thou shalt not be tempestid, thou shalt not be traveyled'" • 12–14 **I speke of . . . to theyse** Lovers of God are more inclined to impatience and despair than others, presumably because of their intense awareness of sin. Much of this coda appears to be addressed to this more particularized readership, almost as if it is picking up one by one the questions and suggestions of the devout circle who likely constituted the work's earliest readers. See pages 10–12 of the Introduction • 13 **dispose them** set themselves • 13–14 **by oure gostly . . . hevinesse** because of our spiritual blindness and bodily sluggishness. Sloth and despair put God's lovers in the state of the servant in the exemplum, who also suffers sluggishness and blindness. See 51.21–23 • 14 **enclining** susceptible

THE SEVENTY-THIRD CHAPTER

Alle this blessed teching of oure /fol. 153r/ lorde God was shewde by thre partes: that is to sey, by bodely sight, and by worde formed in mine understonding, and by gostely sighte. For the bodely sighte, I have saide as I sawe, as truly as I can. And for the words, I have saide them right as oure lorde shewde them me. And for the gostely sighte, I have saide somedele, but I may never fulle telle it. And therfore of this gostely sight I am stered to sey more, as God wille geve me grace.

God shewde two manner of sicknesse that we have. That one is unpatiens or slouth, for we bere oure traveyle and oure paine hevily. That other is dispair or doughtfulle drede, as I shalle sey after. Generally, he shewde sinne, wherin alle is comprehended. But in special, he shewde none but theyse two. And theyse two are it that /fol. 153v/ moste traveyleth and tempesteth° us, as by that oure lorde shewde me, of which he wille we be amended. I speke of such men and women that for Goddes love hate sinne and dispose them to do Goddes wille. Than, by oure gostly blindhed and bodely hevinesse, we are most enclining to theyse. And therfore it is Goddes wille that they be knowen, and than shall° we refuse them, as we do other sinnes.

5

10

15

[VIS. 23.49–55] Alle the blissede techinge of oure lorde God was shewed **to me** be thre parties **as I hafe saide before**: that es to saye, be bodely sight,° and be worde formed in min understandinge, and by gastelye sight. For the bodely sight, I haffe saide as I sawe, als trewlye as I can. And for the wordes **fourmed**, I hafe saide tham right as oure lorde shewed me thame. And for the gastely sight, I hafe saide somdele, bot I maye never fully telle it. And therfore of this gastely sight I am stirred to say more, as God wille gife me grace.

[VIS. 24.1–9] God shewed **me** twa maners of sekenes that we hafe, **of whilke he wille that we be amended.** The tone es inpatience ‡, for we bere our travaille and oure paine hevely. The tothere is dispaire or° doutefulle drede, as I shalle saye efterwarde. /Rev. 73.9–10/ And thiese twa er it that moste travailes us and tempestes us, as by that oure lorde shewed me, *and maste lefe to him that thiese be amendede.* I speke of swilke /fol. 114r/ men and women that for Goddes love hates sinne and disposes tham to do Goddes wille. **Than ere thiese twa prive sinnes, and maste besye aboute us.** /Rev. 73.13–14/ Therefore it is Goddes wille that thay be knawen, and than shalle we refuse tham, as we do othere sinnes.

16–18 **full mekely oure lorde shewd . . . for love** See Chapters 16–22 • 18 **in example** by way of example • 19–20 **cause why . . . them** the reason we are exercised about them (i.e., "oure paines") • 20 **unknowing of love** ignorance of love. A phrase also used in 6.3 • 21 **alle even in the selfe** completely equal in themselves • 22 **the soule toke most understanding in love** my soul learned most about the property of love • 24–25 **For some of us . . . there we stinte** See 31.5–9 for the auxiliary verbs used here • 25 **there we stinte** at that belief we baulk. This passage on love anticipates the conclusion of the work. See 86.13–16 • 26 **letteth** hinders • 26 **Goddes lovers** For this phrase, see 2.8, 18.8, 41.22, 71.10 • 27 **by the ordinance of holy church** according to the rules established by holy church. Through contrition, confession, and satisfaction • 28–29 **yet ther dwelleth . . . sinnes** there still remains a fear that holds us back through our contemplation of ourselves and of our earlier sins, and with some of us of our everyday sins. This is a serious problem, according to *The Remedy:* "Also the

fende is full besy to meve men and women to tender conscience . . . and somtime that is well done they thinke it sinne, and maketh a venial sinne as grevous as a dedly. And somtime also the fende encombreth them so gretely that, whatsoever they do or leve undone, they be so sore bitten in conscience that they can no while togider have ony reste in themselfe" (chap. 8, *YW* 2:118). This is what would come to be called the sin of "scrupulosity" • 30 **setteth us in** Through baptism and penance • 32 **unnethes** scarcely • 33–34 **this drede . . . wekenesse** we sometimes take this fear for humility, but it is an ugly blindness and a weakness. If *A Revelation* is read as a practical work of pastoral theology, this exposure of what is seen as false "drede" can be understood as its most pressing message • 34–35 **And we can not dispise it . . . enmite** Since this sin appears to Christ's lovers under the form of "mekenes," it is not easy to scorn it, despite its demonic origins. The unusually strong phrase "foule blindhede" offers a model for that scorn • 35 **enmite** demonic enmity • 35 **againe** against

And for helpe against this, full mekely oure lorde shewd the patiens that he had in his harde passion, and also the joy and the liking that he hath of that passion for love. And this he shewde in example that we shulde gladly and esely bere oure paines, for that is great plesing to him and endlesse profite to us. And the cause why we are traveyled with them is for unknowing of love.

20

Though the thre persons of the blessed trinite be alle /fol. 154r/ even in the selfe, the soule toke most understanding in love. Ye, and he wille in alle thing that we have oure beholding and oure enjoyeng in love. And of this knowing are we most blinde. For some of us beleve that God is almighty and may do alle, and that he is alle wisdom and can do alle. But that he is alle love and will do alle, there we stinte.°

25

And this unknowing it is that most letteth Goddes lovers, as to my sight. For whan we beginne to hate sinne, and amend us by the ordinance of holy church, yet ther dwelleth a drede that letteth us by the beholding of oureselfe and of oure sinne afore done, and some of us for oure everyday sinnes. For we holde not oure covenants° nor kepe not° oure clennes that oure lorde setteth us in, but fall oftimes into so moche wrechednes that shame it is to say it. And the beholding of this maketh /fol. 154v/ us so sory and so hevy that unnethes we can see ony comfort. And this drede we take sometime for a mekenes, but it is a foule blindhede• and a wekenesse.° And we can not dispise it as we do another sinne that we know, for it cometh of enmite° and it is againe truth.

30

35

[VIS. 24.10–26] *And thus* fulle mekelye oure lorde shewed **me** the pacience that he hadde in his harde passion, and also the joye and the likinge that he hafes of that passion for love. And this° he shewed **me** in ensampille that we shulde gladlye and esely bere oure paines, for that es grete plesinge to him and endelesse profitte to us. And cause why we ere travailed with tham is for unknawenge° of luffe.

Though the ‡ persones in the blissede trinite be alle even *in properte, luffe was moste shewed to me*, **that it is moste nere to us alle.** /Rev. 73.22–23/ And of° this knawinge er we moste blinde. For *many men and women* leves that God is allemighty and may do alle, and that he is alle wisdome and can do alle. Botte that he is alle love and wille do alle, thar *thay* stinte.

And this unknawinge it is that most lettis Goddes luffers ‡. For when *thay* begin to hate sinne, and to amende *tham* by the ordinance of holye kyrke, ȝit there dwelles a drede that *stirres tham to behaldinge* of *thamselfe* and of *ther* sinnes before done. /Rev. 73.29–32/ And this drede *thay take* for a mekenesse, bot this is a foulle blindehede and a waykenesse. And we can it nought dispise, **for if we knewe it we**° **shulde sodaynly dispice it**, as we do ane othere sinne that we knawe, for it comes *of the enmy* and it is againe the trewthe.

37 **sekernesse** confidence • 37–38 **love maketh might . . . meke to us** God's love makes his power and wisdom very humble before us. God's majesty is mediated through his homeliness • 39 **as anemptes** with regard to • 40 **unskil-fulle hevinesse** unreasonable anxiety

[CHAPTER 74] 1 **four manner of dredes** four kinds of fear. The four fears described here are similar to those in other Middle English texts, such as *Contemplations* (which lists three; see chap. C, "What Is Drede," *YW* 2:76–77), though the schema adopted here seems specific to this work • 1–2 **One is dred of afray, . . . freelte** one is the fear of attack (or alarm), which comes over one suddenly out of vulnerability. *Ancrene Wisse* offers the example of fear caused by someone's shouting "Fire! Fire!" (136) • 2–3 **to purge man** See 2.24–26 and 27.13–16 • 4 **taken** received • 5 **drede of paine** fear of suffering. This is similar to the "servile fear" or "drede of servage," fear of God's punishment, described in *Contemplations* (chap. C, "What Is Drede," *YW* 2:76): the

same fear a text like *The Pricke* sets out to arouse with its evocations of hell and judgment. Lines 7–8 emphasize how in this state it is punishment itself, more than God, that is feared • 5 **sterid** stirred • 5 **waked** wakened • 6 **harde of slepe of sinne** fast asleep in sin. Jonah's sleep during a storm at sea, as described in the Middle English poem *Patience*, provides the model for this traditional image • 7 **undertaken** undergone • 7–8 **drede of . . . enemes** fear of the pain of bodily death and of spiritual enemies • 9 **entre** gateway. See Prov. 1:7: "The fear of the Lord is the beginning of knowledge" • 9–10 **abileth . . . contrition** enables us to experience sorrow for sin • 10 **by the blisseful touching** by the blessed inspiration • 11 **doubtful drede** doubting fear. Doubt as to the reality of God's forgiveness • 11–12 **inasmoch as it draweth . . . love** insofar as it pulls us toward despair, God wants to have it converted into love in us by our true recognition of love. In 73.8–9, "doughtfulle drede" is actually synonymous with despair

For of° alle the propertees of the blisseful˙ trinite, it is Goddes will that we have most sekernesse° and liking in love. For love maketh might and wisdom fulle meke to us. For right as by the curtesy of God he forgeteth oure sinne after the time that we repent us, right° so wille he that we forget oure sinne, as anemptes° oure unskilfulle hevinesse and oure doughtfulle dredes.

40

THE SEVENTY-FOURTH CHAPTER

For I understonde four manner of dredes. One is dred of afray, that cometh to man sodeynly by freelte. /fol. 155r/ This dred doth good, for it helpeth to purge man, as doth bodely sicknesse or such other paine that is not sinne. For all such paines helpe man, if they be patiently taken.

The seconde is drede of paine, wherby man is sterid and waked fro slepe of sinne. For man that is harde of slepe of sinne, he is not able for the time to receive the softe comforte of the holy goste, tille he hath undertaken this drede of paine of bodely deth and of gostly enemes. And this drede stereth us to seke comfort and mercy of God. And thus this drede helpeth us as an entre, and abileth us to have contrition by the blisseful˙ touching of the holy gost.

The thurde is doubtful drede. Doubtfulle drede, inasmoch as it draweth to dispair, God wille have it turned in us into love by tru knowing of love: that is to sey,

5

10

[vɪs. 24.27–31] For of alle the propertees of the blissed trinite, it is Goddes wille that we hafe moste sekernesse *in likinge and luffe*. For luffe makes might and wisdome fulle meke to us. For right as be the curtasye of God he forgettes oure sinne *for time* we repente us, right so wille he that we foregette oure sinne, *and alle oure hevinesse, and alle oure doute-fulle dredes. /fol. 114v/*

[vɪs. 25.1–13] Fore I *saw* foure maner of dredes. One is drede of afray, that comes to a man sodanly be frelty. This drede *is* good, for it helpes to purge a man, as does bodely seknes or swilke odere paine that is nought sinne. For alle swilke paines helpes man, if thay be patiently taken.

The secunde is drede of paine, wharby a man is stirred and wakned fro slepe of sin. For man that is harde in slepe of sin, he is nought able for the time to resayfe the soft comfort of the haly gaste, to he hafe *geten* this drede of paine of bodely dede and *of the fire of purgatory*. And this drede stirres *him* to seke comfort and mercy of God. And thus this drede helpes *him* as ane antre, and ables *him* to hafe contrition be the blisfulle touchinge° of the haly gaste.

The thirde is a doutfulle drede. ‡ **For though it be litille in the selfe and it ware knawen, it is a spice of dispaire. For I am seker that alle doutefulle dredes God hates, and he wille that we hafe tham departed fro us** *with trewe knawinge of luffe.*° /Rev. 74.12–14/

15 **reverent drede** reverent fear. Respect or awe. Similar to the "frendely drede" described in *Contemplations:* "Whan a man dredeth the longe abidinge here for grete desire that he hath to be with God" (chap. C, "What Is Drede," *YW* 2:76). Exemplified earlier in Mary's reaction to the Annunciation and Julian's to the revelation. See 7.1–8 and 8.20–21 • 16 **full softe** very easy. See 11.4 and 37.8 for "softe drede" • 17 **Love and drede are bredren** love and fear are brothers. According to *Contemplations:* "Frendly drede . . . cometh of love and that pleaseth moche God" (chap. C, "What Is Drede," *YW* 2:76) • 18–20 **We have of kind to love . . . to drede** Compare 63.1–2. "Kind" and "grace" are progenitors of creation and salvation respectively in Chapters 53–63. Inseparable from both, "reverent drede," like love, is part of the essential character of the soul • 23–24 **And, though . . . wurking** and, nonetheless, this reverent fear and love are not both the same, but they are different in their nature and in how they are expressed • 26 **dredeth** fears • 27–28 **Alle dredes . . . not so tru** A surprising turn to the argument, since "dred of afray" and "drede of paine," just described as good things in themselves, are now categorized with "doubt-fulle drede" as "not so tru." *Contemplations,* on the other hand, argues that "drede of servage," its equivalent of "drede of paine," "may be . . . proufitable," and proceeds to show how (chap. C, "What Is Drede," *YW* 2:77). The next passage provides nuancing of the categories • 27 **profered** offered • 28 **under coloure of holinesse** disguised as holiness. A phrase often used in relation to

hypocrisy or diabolic temptation. Hilton writes: "Thou shalt not resieve non opinioun, ne fantasye, ne singuler conceit under colour of more holinesse, as summe don that aren not wise" (*The Scale* 1.21) • 28–29 **hereby . . . onsonder** they can be distinguished from one another in this way • 29–34 **That dred . . . good and true** A sustained evocation of the account of the sinful soul and Jesus as mother in 61.34–46. The subject of the sentence, "that dred," is repeated in line 33 • 29 **fle** flee • 30 **as the childe into the moders barme** like the child into its mother's bosom. As does the child in 61.37–38 when it recognizes its sinfulness: "For when it is dissesed and adred, it runneth hastely to the moder." Although the original passage is not explicit on this point, the child's response is here presented as an example of "reverent drede," rather than "drede of paine" • 31 **knowing** acknowledging • 32 **only seking . . . salvation** reaching out into him alone for salvation • 33 **cleving to** clinging to him. See 6:39–41: "For truly oure lover desireth that the soule cleve to him with all the mightes, and that we be evermore cleving to his goodnes" • 33 **that bringeth . . . wurking** which induces this behavior in us • 34 **contrarious** opposite • 35 **medelde** mixed • 36 **to knowe them both** to recognize good and bad kinds of fear • 36–37 **the kinde properte . . . life** the God-created kind of fear that we have in this life • 38 **gentille . . . delectabile** honorable, courteous, most delicious. Reverent fear is a courteous attitude to maintain before a lord. See lines 20–21 that the bitternesse of doubt /fol. 155v/ be turned into swetnes of kinde love by grace. For it may never plese oure lorde that his servantes doubt in his goodnesse.

The fourth is reverent drede. For ther is no drede that fully pleseth God in us but reverent drede, and that is full softe,° for the more it is had, the lesse it is felte, for swetnesse of love. Love and drede are bredren, and they are roted in us by the goodnesse of oure maker, and they shall never be taken from us without end. We have of kind to love, and we have of grace to love. And we have of kind to drede, and we have of grace to drede. It longeth to the lordeshippe and to the faderhed to be dred, as it longeth to the goodnes to be loved. And it longeth to us that are his servantes and his children to drede him for lordshippe and faderhed, as it longeth to us to love him for goodhed. And, though, this reverent drede and love be not /fol. 156r/ both in one, but they are two° in properte and in wurking, and neither of them may be had without other. And therfore, I am seker,• he that loveth, he dredeth, though he feele it but litille.

Alle dredes other than reverent drede that are profered to us, though they come under coloure of holinesse, they are not so tru. And hereby may they be knowen onsonder. That dred that maketh us hastely to fle fro alle that is not goode and falle into oure lordes brest, as the childe into the moders barme,° with alle oure entent and with alle oure minde—knowing oure febilnes and oure greate nede, knowing his everlasting goodnesse and his blisseful° love, only seking into him for salvation, cleving to with seker° trust—that° dred that bringeth us into this wurking, it is kinde and gracious and good and true. And alle that is contrarious to this, either it is wrong, or it is medelde with wrong. /fol. 156v/

Than is this the remedy, to knowe them both, and refuse the wrong. For the kinde properte of drede which we have in this life by the gracious werking of the holy gost, the same shall be in heven afore God: gentille, curteyse, fulle delectabile.°

15

20

25

30

35

[VIS. 25.14–26] The fourthe is reverente drede. For thare is na drede that ‡ pleses him in us bot reverente drede, and that is *fulle swete and softe* ‡ *for mekillehede of luffe. /Rev. 74.17–23/ And yit is* this reverente drede and luffe nought bathe ane, bot thay er twa in properte and in wyrkinge, and nowthere of tham may be hadde withouten othere. Therfore I am sekere, he that luffes, he dredes, though he fele bot litille.

Alle dredes othere than reverente dredes that er proferde to us, though thay come undere the coloure of halines, thay ere not so trewe. And hereby may thaye be *knawen and discerned whilke is whilke:* **for this reverente drede, the mare it is hadde, the mare it softes and comfortes and pleses and restes, and the false drede it travailes and tempestes and trubles.** /Rev. 74.29–35/

Than is this the remedye, to knawe tham bath and refuse the° fals, **righte as we walde do a wikked spiritte that shewed him in liknes of a goode angelle. For right as ane ille**

39 **homely and nere** intimate and near • 40 **both in one . . . even** both equally in the one manner. Heaven's courtiers will stand before their Lord in an attitude blended of fear and love • 43 **mightilier** more powerfully • 44 **that we trust in** in whom we trust • 44–46 **if us faile . . . for that time** if we fail in this reverent fear and this humble love, as God forbid we should, our trust will quickly be misruled during that time. "Misruled" seems to imply the overconfidence of a love that is not "meke" because not combined with "reverent drede." "Meke love," mentioned four times in this paragraph but nowhere else in *A Revelation*, revisits and revises the confident "love maketh might and wisdom fulle meke to us" in 73.37–38, by way of the statement "Love and drede are bredren" in line 17 • 46 **us nedeth mekille** we greatly need

[CHAPTER 75] 1–2 **us nedeth** (× 2) we need • 2 **love, longing, and pitte** Longing and pity are linked earlier, in 31.34–41. Pity has been discussed, as an aspect of mercy, in Chapters 48, 51, and others, but the sense in which God can be said to long for humanity has not yet been developed • 3 **thurst of God** See 31.14–15: "Therfore this is his thurste: a love-longing to have us all togeder, hole in him to his endlesse blisse" • 4 **the generalle man** humanity in general. *Rev.* 36.30 defines "the generalle man" as "alle that shalle be safe" • 4 **drawen** A pun: both "drawn toward himself" and "taken a draft of" • 5 **so getting his lively membris** in this way bringing in his living limbs. Chosen souls are "membris" of Christ's body • 5–6 **ever he draweth . . . longeth** he is always drawing and drinking, and still he thirsts and longs. The image is apocalyptic. See *Piers Plowman* B 18.366–73, Christ speaking at the harrowing of hell: "For I that am lord of lif, love is my drinke, / And for that drinke today, I deide upon erthe. / I faught so, me thursteth yet, for mannes soule sake; / May no drinke me moiste, ne my thurst slake, / Till the vendage falle [vintage take place] in the vale of Josaphat [where the dead congregate on the last day], / That I drinke right ripe must [wine from thoroughly ripened grapes], *resureccio mortuorum* [at the resurrection of the dead]. / And thanne shal I come as a king, crouned, with aungeles, / And have out of helle alle mennes soules." • 7–8 **of which . . . in us** Divine and human longing are the same • 8 **of the same vertue** from the same power • 9 **lerne** teach • 10 **spedefulle** profitable • 11 **to have us uppe into blisse** See Julian's desire to be taken up into heaven in 64.1–13. Here it is God, not the soul, that is in longing • 13 **The thurde . . . on the last day** See 31.10–16 • 13 **the last day** the Day of Judgment • 14 **ever to last** to last eternally • 14 **than** then

And thus we shalle in love be homely and nere to God, and we shalle° in drede be
gentille and curtesse to God, and both in one manner, like even.   40

Desyer we than of oure lorde God to drede him reverently and to love him°
mekly and to trust in him mightly. For when we drede him reverently and love him
mekly, oure trust is never in vaine. For the more that we trust and the mightilier, the
more we plese and wurshippe oure lorde that we trust in. And if us faile this
reverent drede and meke love, as God forbid we shuld, oure trust shalle sone be   45
misruled for that time. And therfore /fol. 157r/ us nedeth mekille• to praye oure
lorde of grace, that we may have this reverent drede and meke love of his gifte, in
hart and in worke, for without this no man may plese God.

THE SEVENTY-FIFTH CHAPTER

I saw that God may do alle that us nedeth. And theyse thre that I shall say us
nedeth: love, longing, and pitte. Pitte in love° kepeth us in the time of oure nede,
and longing in the same love draweth us into heven. For the thurst of God is to have
the generalle man into him, in which thurst he hath drawen his holy soules that be
now in blisse. And so getting his lively membris, ever he draweth and drinketh, and   5
yet him thursteth and longeth.

I saw thre manner of longing in God, and alle to one ende, of which we have the
same in us, and of the same vertue, and for the same end.°

The furst is for that he longeth to lerne us to know him and to love him ever
more /fol. 157v/ and more,° as it is convenient and spedefulle to us.   10

The seconde is that he longeth to have us uppe into blisse, as soules are whan
they be taken oute of paine into heven.

The thurde is to fulfille us of blisse, and that shall be on the last day fulfilled,
ever to last. For I saw, as it is knowen in oure faith, that than paine and sorow shall

---

[VIS. 25.26–35] spirit, though he com undere the coloure and the liknes of a goode
angelle—his daliance and his wirkinge though he shewe never so faire—first he travailes and tempestes° and trubles the person that he spekes with, and lettes him and
lefes /fol. 115r/ him alle in unreste. And the mare that he comones with him, the mare he
travailes him, and the farthere is he fra pees. Therfore it is Goddes wille and oure spede
that we knawe tham thus ysundure.

For God wille ever that we be sekere in luffe, and pesabile and ristefulle as he is to
us. And right so of the same condition as he is to us, so wille he that we be to oureselfe,
and to oure evencristen. Amen.

Explicit Juliane de Norwich. /Rev. 74.36–86.25/

15–17 **And not only . . . fulfille us** The new "blisse" traditionally associated with the Day of Judgment is the reunion of the soul and the resurrected body. However, this is an event never explicitly mentioned in *A Revelation,* and the allusion here seems rather to be to the "deed" prophecied in Chapter 32, perhaps associated with Rev. 21:1: "I saw a new heaven and a new earth" • 16 **a new** a new bliss • 17 **beflowe oute** flow out. A return to the Neoplatonic language of 62.12–13: "Alle kindes that he hath made to flowe out of him . . . shall be restored and brought againe into him" • 19–22 **Theyse goods . . . suffered** See 32.26–29: "This is the gret deed ordained of oure lorde God fro without beginning, tresured and hid in his blessed brest, only knowen to himselfe, by which deed he shalle make all thing wele" • 19 **into that time** until that time • 21 **overmore** furthermore • 24 **overpassing . . . before** transcending what has been seen and felt before • 24–25 **that the pillours . . . quake** that the pillars of heaven shall tremble and quake. Probably an allusion Job 9:1–13, in which Job asks, "How can a man be just before God?" and goes on to describe the divine anger: "He . . . removes mountains . . . when he overturns them in his anger; [he] shakes the earth out of its place, and its pillars tremble. . . . God will not turn back his anger." In the version of this prophetic passage given here, the "reverent drede" experienced by the creation takes the place of divine anger as what makes the "pillours . . . tremelle and quake." Compare the account of the Passion in 18.13–14, where "alle creatures that God hath made to oure servys, the firmamente and erth, failed for sorow in ther kind in the time of Cristes dying" • 27 **thus to be beholde of his creatures** to be looked at in this way by his creation • 28 **mekehede** meekness • 28–29 **merveyling . . . alle that is made** This combines 4.31–32, concerning Mary at the Annunciation, with 5.10, the vision of the hazelnut that immediately follows: "Knowing the greatnes of her maker and the littlehead of herselfe that is made"; "It is all that is made." The first revelation is tapped to present a picture of the Judgment as a new annunciation, rather than a day of terror • 29 **litilhede** insignificance • 30 **maketh creature mervelous meke and milde** makes a creature wonderfully humble and mild • 32 **to wille have knowing of this** to want to have knowledge of this • 33 **oneth** unites • 34 **as mekille** as much • 35 **drad** feared • 35–36 **this reverent dred . . . face** Alludes to 74.36–40, where "the kinde properte of drede" experienced on earth is also "in heven afore God: gentille, curteyse, fulle delectabile" • 36–38 **And as mekille . . . now** and by as much as he will be known and loved, transcending how he is now, by so much he will be feared, transcending how he is now • 38–39 **Wherfore . . . quake** See lines 24–25

[CHAPTER 76] 1–17 **I speke but litille . . . compassion** A reframing of topics covered in earlier discussions of hatred of sin, especially in Chapters 40 and 63. The chapter as a whole deals with different kinds of sin, especially accusation of others and self-accusation, and their remedies. It is the first of four chapters on sin • 1–2 **seen . . . afore saide** "Reverent dred" is mentioned fifteen times in *A Revelation,* reverence itself nearly forty times, but the claim here is more generally that reverence and fear are contained in the "matter" of the work itself • 2 **thoe** those • 4 **it hateth more sinne** it hates sin more • 4–5 **than it doeth . . . helle** See 63.11: "sinne is wurse, viler, and painfuller than hell" • 6 **hateth no helle but sinne** Alludes to 40.33–34: "For a kind soule hateth no helle but sinne." If "thoe that dred" God hated hell in itself, this would suggest their fear of him included "drede of paine" as well as "reverent dred" (74.5–26). But according to Chapters 74–75, the only truly good fear is "reverent" • 8 **reyse redely** quickly rise up

be ended to alle that shalle be saved. And not only we shalle receive the same blisse   15
that soules afore have had in heven,° but also we shall receive a new, which plentuously
shalle beflowe° oute of God into us and fulfille us. And tho be the goodes which he
hath ordained to geve us fro without beginning.

Theyse goods are tresoured and hid in himselfe. For into that time, creature is
not mighty ne worthy to receive them. In this we shalle° se verely the cause /fol. 158r/   20
of alle the dedes that God hath done. And, overmore, we shalle° see the cause of alle
thinges that he hath suffered. And the blisse and the fulfilling shalle be so depe and
so high that, for wonder and° merveyle, all creatures shalle° have to God so gret
reverent drede—overpassing that hath be sene and felte before—that the pillours
of heven shulle tremelle and quake.   25

But this manner of tremeling and drede shalle have no manner of paine. But it
longeth to the worthy majeste of God thus to be beholde of his creatures: dredfully
tremeling and quaking for mekehede° of joy, endlesly merveyling of the greatnesse
of God the maker, and of the litilhede° of alle that is made. For the beholding of this
maketh creature mervelous meke and milde.   30

Wherfore God wille, and also it longeth /fol. 158v/ to us both in kinde and in
grace, to wille have knowing of this, desyering the sighte and the wurking. For it
ledeth us in right wey, and kepeth us in tru life, and oneth us to God. And as good
as God is, as gret he is. And as mekille˙ as it longeth to his godhed to be loved, so
mekille˙ it longeth to his grethede° to be drad. For this reverent dred is the fair   35
curtesy that is in heven before Goddes face. And as mekille˙ as he shall be knowen
and loved, overpassing that he is now, in so mekille˙ he shall be drad, overpassing
that he° is now. Wherfore it behoveth nedes to be that alle heven, alle erth, shall
tremelle and quake whan the pillers shall tremelle and quake.

THE SEVENTY-SIXTH CHAPTER

I speke but litille of this reverent dred, for I hope it may be seen in this matter
afore saide. But wele I wot, oure lorde shewd me no soules but thoe that dred
him. For welle I wot, the soule that truly taketh the teching of the /fol. 159r/ holy
gost, it hateth more sinne, for the vilehede˙ and the horiblite, than it doeth alle the
paine that is in helle. For the soule that beholdeth the kindnesse of oure lorde Jhesu,   5
it hateth no helle but sinne,° as to my sight. And therfor it is Goddes wille that we
know sinne, and pray besily and traveyle wilfully and seke teching mekly, that we
falle not blindly therein; and if we falle, that we reyse redely. For it is the most paine
that the soule may have, to turne fro God ony time by sinne.

10–17 **The soule that wille . . . compassion** A passage deploring attention to the sins of others. Compare 36.37–44, against thinking about the damned. Compare *The Scale* 1.17, against reproving others for their faults: "But now seist thou . . . it is a dede of a charite for to undirneme [reprove] men of here defautis [their faults], and for to deme hem for here amendinge [judge them in order to amend them]. . . . As to this I answere . . . that to thee or to ony othir which hath the stat and the purpose of lif contemplatif it fallith not for to . . . underneme othir men." This was a controversial stance in late fourteenth-century England, in which many reformers considered it the responsibility of all Christians to reprove one another's faults as needed • 11 **againe that** against the temptation to reflect on the sins of others • 13 **fairhede** beauty • 14 **them** The sins of others • 14 **him** The sinner • 15 **noyeth and tempesteth** disgusts and torments. See 39.1–3: "Sinne . . . noyeth him in his owne sight" • 16 **letteth** hinders • 16–17 **shewing of the compassion** The phrase is used in 31.42 and there refers to all the thirteenth revelation. The reference here is probably to the discussion of sin in Chapter 39, and perhaps also to 35.1–7, Julian's desire to "wit of a serteyn creature that I loved if it shulde continue in good leving," and the warning she received to "take it generally," not to pay attention to one being • 18 **contrarious** opposites • 21 **his highest sovereyn frende** See John 15:15: "No longer do I call you servants . . . but I have called you friends." In much Middle English religious writing, as here, Jesus' "frendes" are those who follow his "councelles" as well as his commands • 24 **For wele . . . fle**

him for good or ill, he never wants us to run from him • 25 **for the changeablete** because of the state of changeableness. See "changeable sensualite," 45.3 • 26 **this** The evil advice that follows • 27 **they** The devil ("oure enemy"), the soul's "foly," and the soul's "blindhede" • 27–30 **Thou wottest wele . . . lesing of time** Repeats the accusations against the soul made, then criticized, in 73.26–35 • 27 **Thou wottest wele** you know well • 28 **covenant** agreement with God • 28 **behotest** promise • 29 **in the same** into the same sin • 30 **lesing of time** loss of time. See 62.8: "For his precious love, he suffereth us never to lese time" • 30 **that is the beginning of sinne** listening to such accusations is the beginning of sin • 33 **adred** fearful • 34–35 **his false drede . . . wrechednesse** the spurious fear he makes us feel of our misery • 35 **for paine that he threteth us by** by means of the pain he threatens us with. "Drede of paine" (74.5–10) again emerges as a false fear in those who are more than spiritual beginners

[CHAPTER 77] 1 **Oure good lord . . . fende** See 13.6–14, the exposition of Christ's words "Herewith is the feende overcome," in which is seen "a parte of the feendes malice." Widens the discussion of "false drede" in Chapter 76 to include the devil from whom it comes • 2 **contrarious to** contrary to • 4–5 **enmye ought winneth of us** enemy wins anything from us • 5 **for it is his liknes** because our fall is modeled after his. Falling into sin, the soul partly loses the likeness of God and takes on that of the devil • 5 **leseth manyfold more** loses many times more • 7 **brinneth** burns

The soule that wille be in rest, when other mennes sinnes come to minde he   10
shuld fle it as the paine of helle, seking into God for remedye° for helpe againe that.
For the beholding of other mennes sinne, it maketh as it were a thick mist afore the
eye of the soule, and we may not for the time se the fairhede of God, but if we may
beholde them with contrition with him, with compassion on him, and with holy
desyer to God for him. For without this it noyeth and tempesteth° and /fol. 159v/   15
letteth the soule that beholde them. For this I understande in the shewing of the
compassion.

In this blisseful• shewing of oure lorde I have understanding of two contrarious.
That one is the most wisdom that ony creature may do in this life, that other is the
most foly. The most wisdom is a creature to do after the will and the councelles   20
of his highest sovereyn frende. This blessede frend is Jesu, and it is his wille and
counceyle that we holde us with him, and fasten us homely to him evermore, in
what state so ever we been. For whether we be foule or clene, we are ever one in his
loving. For wele ne for wo, he wille never we fle him.

But for the changeablete that we are in, in oureselfe,° we falle often into   25
sinne. Than have we this by the stering of oure enemy, and by oure owne foly and
blindhede.• For they sey thus: "Thou wottest wele thou arte a wrech, a sinner, and
also /fol. 160r/ untrew, for thou kepest not thy covenant.° Thou behotest° oftentimes
oure lorde that thou shalt do better; and anon thou fallest againe in the same,
namely in slouth and in lesing of time." For that is the beginning of sinne, as to   30
my sighte, and namely to the creatures that have geven themselfe to serve oure
lorde with inwarde beholding of his blisseful• goodnesse. And this maketh us
adred to appere afore oure curteyse lorde.

Than is it oure enmye that wille put us aback with his false drede of oure
wrechednesse, for paine that he threteth us by. For it is his mening to make us so   35
hevy and so sory in this that we shuld let out of minde the fair blisseful• beholding
of oure everlasting frende.

THE SEVENTY-SEVENTH CHAPTER

Oure good lord shewde the enmite of the fende, wherby I understode that alle
that is contrarious to love and to peace, it is of the feende and of his /fol. 160v/
perty. And we have of oure febilnesse and oure foly to falle, and we have of mercy
and of grace of the holy gost to rise to more joye. And if our enmye ought winneth
of us by oure falling, for it is his liknes, he leseth manyfold° more in oure rising by   5
charite and mekenesse. And this glorious rising, it is to him so great sorow and
paine, for the hate that he hath to oure soule, that he brinneth continually in envy.

8 **it shall turne into himselfe** it will turn into his own sorrow • 8–10 **And for this . . . to laugh** The last direct reference to the devil in *A Revelation*. See 13.19–20: "I saw oure lorde scorne his malis and nought his unmight, and he wille that we do so. For this sight, I laught mightely" • 11 **Than is this the remedy** The phrase is also used at 74.36. The topic is still "false drede of oure wrechednesse" (*Rev.* 76.33–34) • 11 **we be aknowen of oure wrechednes** we acknowledge our wretchedness • 12 **more neder** needier • 12 **spedfulle** profitable • 13–15 **I knowe wele . . . tenderly** Answers the demonic speech in 76.27–30 by welcoming punishment for sin, not from the devil, but from God. *The Scale* 2.22 offers similar advice for when "enemies" say "that thou arte not worthy for to have the love of God." "Trowe [believe] hem not, but go forth, and seye thus: 'Not for I am worthy, but for I am unworthy, therfore wolde I love God. For yif I hadde it, that shulde make worthy me [that would make me worthy]'" • 15 **skillefully** appropriately • 16 **abide** remain • 18 **skorging** scourging • 19–20 **holde us paide with him** be satisfied with him • 21 **For that penance . . . himselfe** Ascetic mortifications such as fasting, vigils, wearing of hair shirts, and self-"skorging" • 23–24 **that penance . . . geveth us** The suffering and sin of everyday life. Chapter 39 is a reference point for this passage • 24 **with minde of his blessed passion** See 2.3, the first of Julian's desires before the revelation; also her resistance to the devil in 69.12–14 • 25–26 **then we suffer . . . saw it** then we suffer with him, just as his friends did who saw it. See 18.11–18, on the suffering of Christ's friends at his Passion • 26 **And this was shewd** The passage requires the sense "and this was also shown" • 27 **where it speketh of pitte** See 28.1–6, which itself alludes to Chapter 18 • 27 **For he seyeth** An interpretation of Chapter 28 as though in Christ's mouth. See especially 28.27–28: "we see sothly that oure sinne deserve it, yet his love excuseth us." The need to

combat the sin of self-accusation here effectively produces a new "word" from Christ, as the "highest sovereyn frende" to the soul (see 76.21) • 28 **overdon mekille** much too much • 28 **deming** judging • 28 **defaut** fault • 29 **undiscretly** without discretion • 29–30 **howsoever thou do** however you behave • 30–32 **therfore I wille . . . for thy penance** so I desire that you wisely recognize your penance (the "wo" just mentioned), which you continually suffer, and that you take it humbly as your penance. To see life as penance and to accept it as such are here two different moments • 32 **alle this living is penance** See the opening of *Ancrene Wisse*, part 6: "All you ever endure is penance, and hard penance, my dear sisters; all the good you ever do, all you suffer, is martyrdom for you in the most severe of orders, for night and day you are up on God's cross" (176) • 33 **This place is prison** A standard image, in ascetic texts, for human life in the world • 35–36 **he that shalle be . . . there** See 19.13–14: "Me liked no nother heven than Jhesu, which shalle be my blisse when I come ther" • 36–37 **oure keper . . . heven** For these epithets, see, respectively, 39.37, 55.1, 19.8: "He is oure everlasting keper"; "Crist is oure wey"; "For thou art my heven" • 38–39 **where he made . . . heven** See 19.1–17 • 40 **Flee we to oure lorde** See the account of the child fleeing to its mother in 61.34–46 • 40–41 **Touch we him . . . clene** See Matt. 9:20–22, where the sick woman says, "If I only touch his garment, I shall be made well," and is healed • 41 **Cleve** cling • 43–44 **But be we ware . . . leve curtesye** but we must be wary that we do not take this intimacy so carelessly that we forgo courtesy. "Homelyhed" and "curtesye" have been in play in *A Revelation* since Chapter 4. After language evocative of the intimacy of family relationships, the more formal gestures of respect implied by "curteyse" need to be emphasized. Human courtesy is here seen as modeled on divine • 45 **curtesse** courteous

And alle this sorow that he would make us to have, it shall turne into himselfe. And
for this it was that oure lorde skorned him, and shewde that he shalle be skorned,
and this made me mightely to laugh. 10

Than is this the remedy: that we be aknowen of oure wrechednes and fle to oure
lorde. For ever the more neder that we be, the more spedfulle it is to us to touch
him. And sey we thus in oure meaning: "I knowe wele I have deservede /fol. 161r/
paine, but oure lorde is almighty, and may ponish me mightly; and he is all wisdom,
and can ponish me skillefully;° and he is alle goodnesse, and loveth me tenderly." 15
And in this beholding it is spedfulle to us to abide. For it is a fulle lovely mekenes of
a sinfulle soule, wrought by mercy and grace of the holy gost, whan we will wilfully
and gladly take the skorging and the chastising that oure lorde himselfe wille geve
us. And it shalle be fulle tender and fulle esy, if we wille onely holde us paide° with
him and with alle his werkes. 20

For that penance that man taketh upon himselfe, it was not shewde me: that is
to sey, it was not shewde me specified. But this was shewde specially and highly and
with fulle lovely chere: that we shulde mekely and patiently bere and suffer that
penance that God himselfe geveth us, with minde /fol. 161v/ of his blessed passion.
For whan we have minde of his blessed passion, with pitte and love, then we suffer 25
with him, like as his frendes did that saw it. And this was shewd in the thirteenth,
nere at the beginning, where it speketh of pitte. For he seyeth: "Accuse not thyselfe
overdon mekille, deming° that thy tribulation and thy wo is alle thy defaut; for I
wille not that thou be hevy ne sorowfulle undiscretly. For I telle thee, howsoever
thou do, thou shalle have wo. And therfore I wille that thou wisely know thy 30
penance, which thou arte in continually, and that thou mekely take it for thy
penance. And than shalt thou truly se that alle this living is penance profitable."
This place is prison, this life is penance, and in the remedy he wille that we enjoy.
The remedy is that oure lorde is with us, keping us and leding into fulhed of joy.
For this is an endlesse /fol. 162r/ joy to us in oure lordes mening: that he that shalle 35
be oure blesse when we are there, he is oure keper while we are here, oure wey and
oure heven, in tru love and seker° trust. And of this he gave understanding in alle,
and namely in shewing of his passion, where he made me mightly to chose him
for my heven.

Flee we to oure lorde, and we shall be comforted. Touch we him, and we shalle 40
be made clene. Cleve we to him, and we shalle be seker• and safe from alle manner
of perilles. For oure curtese lorde wille that we be as homely with him as hart may
thinke or soule may desyer. But be we ware that we take not so rechelously this
homelyhed for to leve curtesye. For our lorde himselfe is sovereyn homelyhed,
and so homely as he is, as curtesse he is. For he is very curteyse. And the blessed 45

48 **wet not** know not • 49 **he shalle lerne us** he shall teach us. Divine courtesy with respect to sin is the topic of the next chapter

[CHAPTER 78] 1–2 **Oure lorde . . . himselfe** Christ shows sin in Chapter 27, though this chapter meditates widely on different passages • 2 **horrible** Also used of sin in 63.13, 72.9, 76.4 • 2–3 **he of his curtesy . . . mercy** Due to divine courtesy God does not show people their sins in their absolute form but already tempered by his mercy. First part of the lesson of courtesy promised in 77.48–50 • 4–5 **he is the grounde** foundation. Stated repeatedly, but see 41.8: "I am grounde" • 7 **are fulle felle upon us** beset us very fiercely. This sentence is similar to 39.38–39: "Oure enmes that be full felle and full fers upon us. And so much oure mede is the more for we geve him occasion by oure falling" • 8 **parell** peril • 8–9 **know not oure awne nede** do not know our own need. The passage supposes that the sin in question is hidden from the sinner, as is true of the sin of self-accusation described in Chapter 76 • 10 **curtesly** courteously • 11 **changeth no chere** does not change his expression. Evokes the lord's constant expression of "gret rewth and pitte" in 51.33–35: "And right thus continuantly his loveing lorde full tenderly beholdeth him" • 12 **oned** united • 13 **profitable without dispair** profitably without despair. Despair has been an implied topic since Chapter 73, as the peril into which the soul beset by the wrong kind of fear can fall. In this passage, the case is made that any direct confrontation with one's sin, not mediated by divine "mercy" (line 3), would induce despair • 14 **us nedeth** we need • 15 **broken downe . . . presumption** broken down with respect to our pride and our presumption. As Christ

promises threateningly in 28.15–16: "I shal alle tobreke you from youre vaine affections and youre viscious pride," words on which the next passage comments, circling especially around the word "tobreke": see "broken" (line 20), "breking" (line 23) • 16 **us behoveth verely to see** it is necessary that we truly see • 17–18 **by the sight . . . which we se not** by the sight of the smaller part of our sin that our Lord shows us, the greater part, which we do not see, is laid waste. The contemplation of the small portion of our sin that "oure lorde of his mercy" (line 1) allows us to recognize creates shame, breaking down "oure pride and oure presumption" (line 15) to such an extent that it also helps break down the much larger portion of our sin he courteously conceals from us because (as lines 18–19 go on to say) it would be unendurable to contemplate directly • 21–22 **than shalle . . . one us to him** See the second half of Christ's speech in 28.16–17: "And after that I shalle togeder gader you, and make you meke and milde, clene and holy, by oning to me" • 23 **This breking . . . general man** such breaking and healing our Lord intends for humanity in general. This passage against spiritual elitism draws on the account of the unity of the Christian people in Chapters 8–9 and replicates its self-conscious modesty • 24–25 **I that am the leste . . . saved** See 1 Cor. 15:9: "I am the least of the apostles, unfit to be called an apostle" • 26–29 **Whan he shewde . . . entende** See 37.1–3: "God brought to my minde that I shuld sinne. And for liking that I had in beholding of him, I entended not redely to that shewing. And oure lorde fulle marcifully abode, and gave me grace for to entende." This passage continues to resonate into Chapter 79

creatures that shalle be in heven with him without /fol. 162v/ ende, he wille have them like unto himselfe in alle thing. And to be like° to oure lorde perfetly, it is oure very salvation and oure fulle blisse. And if we wet not how we shall do alle this, desyer we of oure lorde, and he shalle lerne us, for it is his owne liking and his wurshippe. Blessed mot he be.

50

THE SEVENTY-EIGHTH CHAPTER

Oure lorde of his mercy sheweth us oure sinne and oure febilnesse by the swete gracious light of himselfe. For oure sinne is so foule and so horrible that he of his curtesy wille not shewe it us but by the light of his mercy.

Of four thinges it is his wille that we have knowing. The furst is that he is the grounde, of whom we have alle oure life and oure being.

The seconde is that he kepeth us mightly and mercifully, in the time that we are in oure sinne, among alle oure enmes that are fulle felle upon us. And so mekille˙ we are in the more parell, /fol. 163r/ for we geve them occasion therto, and know not oure awne nede.

The thirde is howe curtesly he kepeth us and maketh us to know that we go amisse.

The fourth is how stedfastly he abideth us, and changeth no chere, for he wille that we be turned and oned to him in love as he is to us.

And thus by gracious knowing we may se oure sinne, profitable without dispair. For sothly us nedeth to see it, and by the sighte we shulde be made ashamed of oureselfe and broken° downe, as anemptes° oure pride and oure presumption. For us behoveth verely to see that of oureselfe we are right nought but sinne and wrechednesse. And thus by the sight of the lesse that oure lorde sheweth us, the more is wasted, which we se not. For he of his curtesy mesureth the sight to us, for it is so foule and so horrible that we shulde not endure to se it as it is. And thus by this meke /fol. 163v/ knowing, thorow contrition and grace, we shall be broken from alle thing that is not oure lorde; and than shalle oure blessed saviour perfetely hele° us and one us to him.

This breking and this heling° oure lorde meneth by the general man. For he that is highest and nerest with God, he may se himselfe sinful and nedy with me. And I that am the leste and the lowest of tho that shalle be saved, I may be conforted with him that is highest. So hath oure lorde oned us in charite. Whan he shewde me that I shuld sinne, and for joy that I had in beholding him I entended not redely to that shewing, oure° curteyse lorde rested there, and wolde no ferther tech me tille whan that he gave me grace and wille to entende. And herof was I lerned, though that we

5

10

15

20

25

34 **nor of none . . . enmes** or from any of our spiritual enemies • 34–35 **they wille not us so mekille goode** they do not desire so much good for us

[CHAPTER 79] 1–2 **in this . . . singuler person** Continues the discussion of the opening of Chapter 37 from the end of Chapter 78. For this passage, see 37.3–6: "And this shewing I toke singularly to myselfe. But by alle the gracious comfort that foloweth, as ye shalle see, I was lerned to take it to alle min evencristen, alle in generalle and nothing in specialle" • 2 **nakedly** plainly • 2 **min owne singuler person** my own individual self • 2–3 **non otherwise stered** not moved to do differently • 3–4 **high gracious comfort . . . after** See 37.8–9: "And . . . oure lorde answered: 'I kepe the fulle sekerly'" • 4 **the generalle man** humanity in general. The rest of the sentence offers a more precise definition, without explicitly limiting it to the saved • 5–6 **of which man . . . I hope** of which group I am a member, as I trust • 6 **large** spacious. Although the sentence as a whole concerns "I kepe the fulle sekerly" from 37.8–9, "large" evokes the wound in Christ's side as described in 24.2–4: "And with his swete loking he led forth the understanding of his creature by the same wound into his sid, within. And ther he shewed a fair, delectable place, and large inow for alle mankinde that shalle be saved" • 7 **ther was I lerned** in the revelation I was taught. Begins a series of short lessons learned from Chapter 37, which then broaden to encompass the entire revelation • 7–8 **I shulde se . . . my**

evencristen As also discussed in 76.10–17 • 7 **awne** own • 8 **but if it may be** unless it be • 9 **ther I saw . . . ther was I lerned** where I saw . . . there I was taught • 9–10 **to be dradful . . . myselfe** to be fearful out of uncertainty about myself. See 37.8: "And in this, I conceived a softe drede" • 11 **wolde I have wist, dredful** fearful, I wanted to know. This wish has not been mentioned before, unless "I conceived a softe drede" implies it • 12–13 **Also oure curteyse lorde . . . love** See, again, "I kepe the fulle sekerly" • 14 **his grace inwardely keping** his grace protecting us within • 15 **deperted in two** separated. See 58.14: "Oure love shall never be departed in two" • 15–18 **in the dred . . . dispair** Paraphrases the speech imputed to Christ in 36.33–35: "Here hast thou matter of mekenesse, here hast thou matter of love, here hast thou matter of noughting thiselfe, here hast thou matter of enjoying in me" • 15–16 **in the dred** Described in line 9 • 19 **Alle this homely shewinge** Refers to the entire revelation. For the next passage, see especially Chapter 40 • 23–25 **if that we be stered . . . stering** if we are inclined to be more reckless in our living, or in guarding of our hearts, because we have knowledge of this plentiful love, then we need especially to beware of this inclination. Returns to the topic of spiritual complacency that ends the thirteenth revelation, 40.22–25: "If any man or woman be stered by foly to sey or to thinke, 'If this be soth, than were it good for to sinne to have the more mede' . . . beware of this stering. For sothly, if it come, it is untrue and of the enemy"

be hyely lifted into contemplation by the specialle gifte of oure lorde, yet us   30
behoveth nedes /fol. 164r/ therwith to have knowing and sight of oure sinne and
of oure febilnes. For without this knowing we may not have trew meknesse, and
withouten this we may not be safe. And also I saw we may not have this knowing
of oureselfe, nor of none of all oure gostly enmes, for they wille not us so mekille•
goode. For if it were by ther wille, we shoulde never se it tille oure ending day. Than   35
are we mekille• bounde to God, that he wille himselfe for love shewe it us in time of
mercy and of grace.

THE SEVENTY-NINTH CHAPTER

Also, I had in this more understanding: in that he shewde me that I shulde
sinne, I toke it nakedly to min owne singuler person, for I was non otherwise
stered in that time. But by the high gracious comfort of oure lorde that folowde
after, I saw that his mening was for the generalle man: that is to sey, alle man which
is sinfulle and shall be into the last day, /fol. 164v/ of which man I am a membre, as   5
I hope, by the mercy of God. For the blessed comfort that I sawe, it is large inough
for us alle. And ther was I lerned that I shulde se my awne sinne and not other
mennes, but if it may be for comfort or helpe of my evencristen. And also in the
same shewing ther I saw that I shuld sinne, ther was I lerned to be dradful for
unsekernesse of myselfe, for I wot not how I shalle falle, ne I know not the mesure   10
ne the gretnesse of my sinne. For that wolde I have wist, dredful,° and therto I had
no answere. Also oure curteyse lorde, in that same time, he shewde fulle sekerly° and
fulle mightely the endleshed and the unchangeabilte of his love. And also, be his
grete goodnesse and his grace° inwardely keping, that the love of him and of oure
soules shalle never be deperted in two° withouten ende. /fol. 165r/ And thus in the   15
dred, I have matter of mekenesse, that saveth me fro presumption. And in the
blessed shewing of love, I have mater of true comforte and of joy, that saveth
me fro dispair.

Alle this homely shewinge of oure curteyse lorde, it is a lovely lesson and a swete
gracious teching of himselfe in comforthing of oure soule. For he wille that we   20
know, by the swetnesse of the homely love of him, that alle that we see or fele,
within or withoute, which is contrarious to this, that it is of the enmy, and not of
God. As thus: if that we be stered to be the more rechelesser of oure leving, or of the
keping of oure harte, by cause that we have knowing of this plentuous love, than
nedeth us gretely to beware of this stering. If it come, it is untrew, and greatly we   25
owe to hate it, for it hath no liknes /fol. 165v/ of Goddes wille. And whan we be fallen

27 **freelte** frailty • 28 **mekely be it aknowen** meekly acknowledge it. See 77.11–12: "Than is this the remedy: that we be aknowen of oure wrechednes and fle to oure lorde" • 30 **to wrechedfulle on oureselfe** too self-recriminating • 31 **that we hastely entende to him** See 36.39, where Christ says: "Intende to me" • 31–32 **he stondeth . . . come** he is standing all alone, and he waits for us continuously, anxiously, and sorrowfully, until the time we come. Adapts the language used elsewhere of the sufferings of the human Jesus to describe Christ's poignant impatience to have the love of his chosen. The careful practicality of these last few chapters is suddenly interrupted by this rich evocation of divine longing, very different in tone from the earlier discussion of the "thurst of God" in 75.1–18. Many of the details are drawn from the description of the servant in Chapter 51; there may also be echoes of the parable of the Prodigal Son from Luke 15. Despite these echoes, the ending of this chapter and parts of the next one (especially 80.21–24) treat this sentence as a moment of new revelation, another "touching" from God (see 65.30), and comment on it accordingly • 33 **salve** remedy • 34–36 **There I sey . . . shewing** where I say "he stands all alone," I do not allude to the blessed company of heaven, but speak of his office and labor here on earth, as the mode of the revelation directs. See 80.18–21

[CHAPTER 80] 1 **By thre thinges man stondeth in this life** humanity is sustained in this life by three things • 2 **sped** profited • 2 **kindly reson** natural reason. See

56.33–34 for the grounding of the "reson," a partial synonym for the soul's substance, in God, who is "kindhede" • 3 **comen teching** usual teaching • 6 **to which he wille we . . . accorde us therto** which he wants us to regard highly and conform ourselves to • 8–10 **And these be gret thinges . . . fulhed in heven** Reason, church teaching, and the "werking" of the spirit can only reveal their secrets dimly in this life. See 51.228–30 for the "A. B. C." image. This reflection on the mystery of truth may be a reaction to the ending of Chapter 79, with its startling image of a yearning, lonely God • 11 **that God . . . kinde** that only God took our physical nature. The stress throughout the passage is on "alone," which alludes to "he stondeth alle alone" in 79.31 • 12–13 **longeth to oure salvation** have to do with our salvation. "Longeth" is singular, but is here used as a plural • 13 **in the last end** in these last times • 14–15 **he wonneth . . . blesse** See 68.7–8: "He sitteth in the soule even righte in peas and rest, and he ruleth and yemeth heven and erth and all that is" • 14 **wonneth** dwells • 14 **yemeth** governs • 16 **so farforth** to such an extent • 18 **ministration of holy angeles** Both in their relation to human needs and in their duties as members of Christ's entourage, who ensure that he is not in a real sense "alle alone" (line 17). Builds on 79.33–36, which provides the earliest reaction to "for he stondeth alle alone" • 18 **as clarkes telle** as clerics expound • 21–23 **And there I sey . . . moning** Returns directly to the vexed passage, 79.31–32, rephrasing it so that now it is the soul, not Christ, who mourns

by freelte or blindhede,• than oure curtesse lord, touching us, stereth us and kepeth us. And than wille he that we se oure wrechednesse and mekely be it aknowen.

But he wille not that we abide therwith, ne he wille not that we besy us gretly aboute oure accusing, ne he wille not that we be to wrechedfulle on oureselfe. But he wille that we hastely entende to him. For he stondeth alle alone, and abideth us continually, swemefully, and moningly,° tille whan we come. And he hath haste to have us to him, for we are his joy and his delight, and he is oure salve and° oure life. (There I sey "he stondeth alle alone," I leeve the speking of the blessed company in heven, and speke of his office and his werking here in erth, uppe the condition of the shewing.)

30

35

THE EIGHTIETH CHAPTER

/fol. 166r/

By thre thinges man stondeth in this life, by which three God is wurshipped and we be sped, kepte, and saved. The furst is use of mannes kindly reson. The seconde is the comen teching of holy church. The third is the inwarde gracious werking of the holy gost. And theyse thre be alle of one God. God is grounde of oure kindly reson, and God is the teching of holy church, and God is the holy gost. And alle be sondry giftes, to which he wille we have grete regarde, and accorde° us therto. For theyse wurke in us continually, alle togeder.

And these° be gret thinges, of which gretnesse he wille we have knowing here, as it were in an A. B. C. That is to sey, that we may have a litille knowing, whereof we shulde have fulhed in heven. And that is for to spede us.

We know in oure faith /fol. 166v/ that God alone toke oure kinde, and none but he; and ferthermore that Crist alone did alle the gret werkes that longeth to oure salvation, and none but he. And righte so he alone doth now in the last end. That is to sey, he wonneth° here in us, and rewleth us, and yemeth° us in this living, and bringeth us to his blesse. And thus shalle he do as long as any soule is in erth that shalle come to heven. And so farforth that if ther were none such soule in erth but one, he shulle be with that alle alone, tille he had brought it uppe to his blesse.

I believe and understonde the ministration of holy angeles, as clarkes telle, but it was not shewde me. For himselfe is nerest and mekest, highest and lowest, and doeth all. And not onely alle that us nedeth, but also he doeth alle that is wurshippefulle to oure joy in heven. And there I sey "he abideth /fol. 167r/ us, swemefully and moningly,"° it meneth alle the trew feling that we have in oureselfe, in contrition and in compassion, and alle sweming and moning° for we are not oned with oure lorde. And such as is spedful, it is Crist in us. And though some of

5

10

15

20

25 **selden** seldom • 27 **leve the minde of him** cease contemplation of him • 28 **bereth Crist** Christ bears • 30–31 **He is here . . . he is here** Meditates punningly on the word "alone," which as well as meaning "solitary" has the sense "exclusively, for one reason" • 31–32 **And what time . . . or sloth** and in that time that I am alienated from him on account of sin, despair or sloth. "Straunge" also has erotic overtones, "distant" or "aloof." For "dispair or sloth," see 73.7–9 • 32 **in as mekille as he is in me** to the extent that he is inside me • 34 **lastingly** eternally

[CHAPTER 81] 1–2 **Oure good lorde . . . soule** This chapter reemphasizes the significance of the final revelation of Christ's "wonning" in the soul as his present and permanent home (Chapter 68). The reminder provides further context for the "swemly and moning" Christ of Chapters 79–80 • 1 **his creature** Julian. See 2.1 • 2 **But I saw him . . . soule** See Chapter 68 • 2–3 **shewde him in erth . . . passion** Christ's physical presence on earth in history. See most of Chapters 5–25 • 3–4 **in other manner . . . where I saide** Christ's informing presence on earth at the root of creation. See 11.1 • 4–5 **And in other manner . . . us** Christ's eschatological presence on earth

as the body of Christ, or the church. See 52.30: "He is with us in erth, us leding"; also 55.1–2: "And thus Crist is oure wey, us sekerly leding in his lawes, and Crist in his body mightely bereth us up into heven." The phrase "as it were a pilgrimage," the only use of this image in *A Revelation,* imparts a visionary glow to the more abstract "leding" • 7 **as it is aforesaide** See, e.g., 14.5, where "I saw him ryally reigne in his house" • 7–8 **principally in mannes soule** See 68.1–11, which the rest of the paragraph draws on and develops • 9 **see** throne of a bishop • 9 **never rise ne remeve** never get up nor leave. See 68.12: "The place that Jhesu taketh in oure soule he shall never remove it" • 10 **wonneth** dwells • 15 **alle oure living . . . penance** See 77.32 • 15–16 **kinde longing . . . penance in us** the natural longing for him that is in us is a permanent source of penance to us • 17–18 **his wisdom . . . with his rightfulhed** See 35.24–26: "God himselfe is very rightfulhed, and all his werkes be done rightfully . . . by his high might, his high wisdom, his high goodnesse" • 20–21 **whan we shall have . . . mede** See 64.10–11: "And thou shalte come up above, and thou shalt have me to thy mede" • 21 **set oure hartes in the overpassing** fix our hearts upon the transcendent

us feele it selden, it passeth never fro Crist tille what time he hath brought us oute of   25
alle our wo. For love suffereth him never to be without pitte.

And what time that we falle into sinne and leve the minde of him and the keping
of oure owne soule, than bereth Crist alone alle the charge of us. And thus stondeth
he swemly and moning.° Than longeth it to us for reverence and kindnesse to turne
us hastely to oure lorde, and let him not alone. He is here alone with us alle. That is   30
to sey, only for us he is here. And what time I be straunge to him by sinne, /fol. 167v/
dispair or sloth, then I let my lorde stonde alone, in as mekille• as he is in me. And
thus it fareth with us all which be sinners. But though it be so that we do thus
oftentimes, his goodnesse suffereth us never to be alone, but lastingly he is with
us and tenderly he excuseth us, and ever kepeth us from blame in his sight.   35

THE EIGHTY-FIRST CHAPTER

Oure good lorde shewde him to his creature in diverse manner both in heven
and in erth. But I saw him take no place but in mannes soule. He shewde him
in erth in the swete incarnation and his blessed passion. And in other manner he
shewde him in erth, where I saide: "I saw God in a point." And in other manner he
shewde him in erth thus, as it were a pilgrimage: that is to sey, he is here with us   5
leding us, and shalle be tille when he hath /fol. 168r/ brought us alle to his blisse in
heven. He shewde him diverse times reigning, as it is aforesaide, but principally in
mannes soule. He hath take there his resting place and his wurshipfulle citte, oute of
which wurshipfulle see he shalle never rise ne remeve withoute ende. Mervelous and
solempne is the place where the lorde wonneth,° and therfore he wille that we redely   10
intend to his gracious touching, more enjoyeng in his hole love than sorowing in
oure often fallinges.

For it is the most wurshippe to him of ony thing that we may do that we live
gladly and merely for his love in oure penance. For he beholdeth us so tenderly
that he seth alle oure living here to be penance. For kinde longing in us to him is a   15
lasting penance in us, /fol. 168v/ which penance he werketh in us, and mercifully he
helpeth us to bere it. For his love maketh him to long, his wisdom and his truth with
his rightfulhed maketh him to suffer us here, and in this manner he wille se it in us.
For this is oure kindly penance, and the highest to my sight. For this° penance
cometh never fro us, tille what time that we be fulfilled, whan we shall° have him   20
to oure mede. And therfore he wille that we set oure hartes in the overpassing: that
is to sey, fro the paine that we feele into the blisse that we trust.

[CHAPTER 82] 1 **the moning . . . oure soule** Now the soul is in a state similar to that of Christ in Chapters 79–80, oppressed not by the penance of longing described in 81.13–22 but by the inevitability of sin's place in that penance • 2 **wot** know • 6 **disese** upset • 6 **And it is soth** and this is true. "It" is the previous two sentences, in which Christ paraphrases the soul's claim to desire to live without sin • 6 **to mekille agreved** too greatly troubled • 8–9 **here I understode . . . blame** See 51.29–30: "And I behelde with avisement, to wit if I culde perceive in him ony defaute, or if the lorde shuld assigne in him ony maner of blame. And sothly there was none seen." Also 51.99–101: "And then I saw that only paine blameth and ponisheth, and oure curteyse lorde comforteth and socurreth" • 9 **passing** transitory • 9 **asketh not to live . . . blame** does not require to be lived wholly without guilt • 10 **customeably** habitually • 11 **sorow and morne discretly** Unlike Julian in 27.7–8, where she makes "morning and sorow . . . withoute reson and discretion" as she reflects on the Fall • 12 **cleving . . . goodnesse** See 6.40–41: "that we be evermore cleving to his goodnes" • 12 **he is oure medicine** See 12.9–16 • 13 **we do nought but sinne** See 36.4: "And I shalle do right nought but sinne" • 15–16 **"I love . . . suffer"** The speaker is Christ. Apart from the last clause, a direct quotation from 58.13–14 • 17 **I kepe the full sekerly** See 37.8–9, a direct quotation • 19–20 **as alle this lesson of love sheweth** as the whole of this lesson of love shows. *A Revelation* is first called a "lesson of love" at 6.54. For Christ's desire "that we shalle live in . . . longing and enjoyeng," see, e.g., 40.19–20: "It befalleth us ever to live in swete prayeng and in lovely longing with oure lorde Jhesu"; 36.35–36: "For my love enjoy in me, for of alle thing therwith might thou most plese me" • 20–21 **alle that is contrarious . . . enmite** See 77.1–3: "Alle that is contrarious to love and to peace, it is of the feende and of his perty" • 22 **If any such liver be in erth** if any such person be living on earth • 24–25 **For in the beholding . . . stonde not** for in God's view of us we do not fall, and in our own view of ourselves we do not stand. The words create a web of allusions to the exemplum in Chapter 51 • 26 **sothnes** truth • 28 **high sothnes** That in God's sight "we falle not" • 29 **se** see • 29–30 **the higher beholding . . . the lower beholding** See 45.1–22

THE EIGHTY-SECOND CHAPTER

But here shewde oure curteyse lorde the moning and the morning of oure soule, mening thus: "I wot well thou wilt live for my love, merely and gladly suffering alle the /fol. 169r/ penance that may come to the. But for as moch as thou livest not without sinne, therfore thou arte hevy and sorowfulle. And if thou mightest live without sinne, thou woldest suffer for my love alle the wo, all the tribulation and disese° that might come to the. And it is soth. But be not to mekille˙ agreved with sinne that falleth to the against thy wille."

And here I understode that the lorde behelde the servant with pitte and not with blame, for this passing life asketh not to live alle without blame and sinne.° He loveth us endlessly, and we sinne customeably, and he sheweth it us fulle mildely. And than we sorow and morne discretly, turning us into the beholding of his mercy, cleving to his love and to his goodnesse, seeing that he is oure medicine, witting that we do nought° but sinne. And thus by the /fol. 169v/ mekenesse that we get in the sight of oure sinne—faithfully knowing his everlasting love, him thanking and praising—we plese him. "I love the and thou lovest me, and oure love shall never be deperted on two, and for thy profite I suffer": and all this was shewde in gostly understonding, seyeng this blessed worde: "I kepe the full sekerly."

And be the gret desyer that I saw in oure blessed lorde that we shalle live in this manner—that is to sey, in longing and enjoyeng, as alle this lesson of love sheweth—thereby I understonde that alle that is contrarious to this is not of him, but it is of enmite. And he wille that we know it by the swete gracious light of his kinde love. If any such liver be in erth which is continually kepte fro falling, I know it /fol. 170r/ not, for it was not shewde me. But this was shewde: that in falling and in rising we are ever preciously kepte in one° love. For in the beholding of God we falle not, and in the beholding of oureselfe we stonde not. And both theyse be soth, as to my sight, but the beholding of oure lord God is the higher sothnes.

Than are we mekille˙ bounde to him, that he wille in this living shew us this high sothnes. And I understode while we be in this life, it is full spedful to us that we se theyse both at ones. For the higher beholding kepeth us in gostly solace° and trew enjoying in God. That other, that is the lower beholding, kepeth us in drede, and maketh us ashamed of oure- /fol. 170v/ selfe. But oure good lorde wille ever that we holde us mekille˙ more in the beholding of the higher, and nought leve the knowing of the lower, into the time that we be broughte uppe above, where we shalle have oure lorde Jhesu to oure mede, and be fulfilled of joy and blisse withoute ende.

[CHAPTER 83] 1 **I had ... God** I had in part illumination, vision, and awareness of three characteristics of God • 3 **in the twelfe** in the twelfth revelation. See Chapter 26, revisited in 59.10–16 • 4 **life, love, and light** "Light" is the key term in this and the next chapter, the last topic to be discussed in *A Revelation* before the closing account of love. The argument is elusive, drawing on two difficult Chapters, 55–56, in an account of how the light of knowledge is mediated to the soul. The discussion doubles as a last attempt to describe the way in which the revelation can be considered as true—a topic discussed as recently as 80.1–10—and as a description of everyday Christian experience, as, at the end, these two blend into one another • 5 **endlesse kindhede** eternal being • 6–7 **into which goodnesse ... mightes** to which goodness my reason desires to be united and to cling with all its powers. Although the word "reson" primarily refers to the intellectual faculty with the help of which Julian has understood her revelation and which desires union with "goodnesse," it is also here a faculty of the higher part of the soul, or substance, as described in 55.11–13: "Oure faith cometh of the kinde love of oure soule, and of the clere lighte of oure reson, and of the stedfaste minde which we have of God in oure furst making" • 7 **I behelde** This phrase here suggests that the "touching, sight, and feeling" of "life, love, and light" are experienced as a new moment of revelation • 7–9 **I behelde ... God** I realized with reverent fear—and marveling highly in the sight and sensation of this sweet harmony—that our reason is in God • 10 **grounded in kind** grounded in the substance or in God. See 56.33–34, where "kind" is the substance and "substantial kindhede" is God: "I had in perty touching, and it is grounded in kind: that is to say, oure reson is grounded in God, which is substantial kindhede" • 13 **This light ... night** this light is measured with discretion, standing beside us as we need it in the night. "Stonding to," a phrase used nowhere else in the work, implies not only the helpfulness of the light, illuminating only what we need to see, but also the obliqueness of the truth it provides. Thus does *A Revelation* comment on the nature of its own illumination of the "night" • 16–17 **wilfully know ... mightely** know and believe in our light purposefully, living within it wisely and with determination • 17 **oure eye shalle be opened** See 72.28: "For oure gostly eye is so blinde"

[CHAPTER 84] 1 **This light is charite** Having been identified with faith and reason in Chapter 83, the light now reveals its source to be charity • 2–3 **For neither the light ... fro us** for neither is the light so great that we may clearly see our blissful day, nor is it all hidden from us. Meditates on "nedfully" in 83.13. "Sperred" evokes God's "prevy concelle" in 30.10–13, which is "hid and sparred fro us" • 4 **medfully** in a way worthy of reward • 5 **in the sixth shewing** See 14.1–2 • 10–12 **that is a gracious gifte ... for God** "given charity" is a spiritual activity given by grace in which we love God for his own sake, and ourselves in God, and everything that God loves, for his own sake. The height of charity is the disinterested love of God. This seems to allude to the account of the third and fourth degrees of love in Bernard of Clairvaux's *De diligendo Deo* (On loving God), in the lower of which "man loves God for God's sake," while in the higher, attainable only for short periods in this life, he "loves himself only for the sake of God" (118–19)

THE EIGHTY-THIRD CHAPTER

I had in perty touching, sight, and feeling in thre propertees of God, in which the strength and the effecte of alle the revelation stondeth. And it were seen in every shewing, and most properly in the twelfe, were it seyeth often times: "I it am." The propertees are theyse: life, love, and light. In life is mervelous homelyhed, in love is gentille curtesse, and in light is endlesse kindhede.• Theyse three propertees° were 5 seen in one goodnesse, into which /fol. 171r/ goodnesse my reson wolde be oned and cleve° to with alle the mightes. I behelde with reverent drede—and highly merveling in the sight and in feeling of the swete accorde—that oure reson is in God, understanding that it is the highest gifte that we have received, and it is grounded in kind. 10

Oure faith is a light, kindly coming of oure endlesse day that is oure fader, God; in which light oure moder, Crist, and oure good lorde, the holy gost, ledeth us in this passing life. This light is mesured discretly, nedfully stonding° to us in the night. The lighte is cause of oure life, the night is cause of oure paine and alle oure wo, in which woe we deserve endlesse mede and thanke of God. For we, with mercy 15 and grace, wilfully know and beleve oure lighte, going /fol. 171v/ therin wisly and mightely. And at the end of woe, sodeynly oure eye shalle be opened, and in clernes of sight oure light shalle be fulle, which light is God oure maker, fader and holy gost in Crist Jhesu oure saviour. Thus I sawe and understode that oure faith is oure light in oure night, which light is God, oure endlesse day. 20

THE EIGHTY-FOURTH CHAPTER

This light is charite, and the mesuring of this light is done to us profitably by the wisdom of God. For neither the light is so large that we may se clerly oure blisseful• day, ne it is all sperred fro us, but it is such a lighte in which we may live medfully with traveyle, deserving the wurshipful thanke of God. And this was sene in the sixth shewing, wher he seyth: "I thanke the of thy servise and of thy traveyle." 5 Thus charite kepeth us in faith and in hope, /fol. 172r/ and faith and hope ledeth us in charite. And at the ende alle shalle be charite.

I had three manner of understondinges in this light of charite.° The furst is charite unmade, the seconde is charite made, the thirde is charite geven. Charite unmade is God, charite made is oure soule in God, charite geven is vertu. And that 10 is a gracious gifte of wurking, in which we love God for himselfe, and oureselfe in God, and alle that God loveth, for God.

[CHAPTER 85] 1 **in this sight** Probably "life, love, and light," 83.4. Here these characteristics of God are seen, not as they operate in this life, but as evidence of the providential nature of his purposes for humankind • 2–3 **in this wurking enjoyeng** rejoicing in this activity. The activity of disinterested love, which God can already see the soul performing here, despite "oure simpille living." From the divine viewpoint, the soul is already rejoicing in the pure love of God in heaven • 3–4 **to beleve it** to believe in his rejoicing • 4 **shulle** shall • 6 **loved . . . fro without beginning** See 53.30: "For or that he made us he loved us" • 7 **in which . . . he made us** in which eternal love he created us. Love is therefore by definition a part of the soul, whatever its present sense of itself • 8–13 **And therfore . . . ony thing was made** Julian's account of her revelation ends with a string of allusions to the thirteenth revelation, Chapters 27, 30, 32 • 10 **hid to us** hidden from us • 10–11 **in ony thing** about any thing • 13 **thin** thy

[CHAPTER 86] 1–2 **This boke . . . to my sight** this book has been begun by the gift of God and with his grace, but it is not yet fully perfected, as I see it. "Perform," here used in both its rhetorical and its architectural senses, occurs nowhere else in *A Revelation*. In the passage that follows, the work's imperfection is linked to the conditions of worldly living, as responsibility shifts from writer to readers to continue to "perform" *A Revelation* until it is done. The chapter is full of the language of beginning and ending as it seeks to make thematic sense of its own need to attain closure under conditions when the "light" it has shed is still necessarily partial • 2–3 **For**

charite . . . enjoyeng This is how the book will be "performed." "With Goddes wurking" alludes back to the "gracious gifte of wurking" that is disinterested charity in 84.11, which here can be attained by prayer • 3 **thus wille . . . be prayde** this is how our good Lord wants to be prayed to • 4 **in the swete wordes** See 41.8 • 6–7 **he shewde . . . knowen more than it is** he revealed it because he wants it better known than it is. The subject of the sentence is presumably charity, here about to be revealed as the summation of the entire revelation • 7–10 **For he beholde . . . are in** Sums up the purpose of the revelation as Julian sees it: to "give us more light and solace in hevenly joye." The revelation is part of "the mesuring of this light" described in 84.1, increasing the amount of light that is available to readers to help them better to live "medfully with traveyle" (84.4) • 12 **mening** intention • 12 **fifteen yere after** Presumably late in 1388. Five years before the exemplum of the lord and the servant was at last clarified, according to 51.73–74 • 13 **woldest thou wit** would you know • 14 **Wit it wele** know it well • 14 **love was his mening** Provides *A Revelation* not only with its peroration but with a justification of its hermeneutic. Every aspect of the revelation has been interpreted in accordance with the "mening" (in Latin rhetorical language, the *intentio*) of the author, God • 14–15 **Who . . . What . . . Wherfore?** A final trinitarian pattern argues for the integrity of the revelation in the threefold unity of the divine Trinity • 15 **Holde the therin** hold yourself in love • 18 **or God made us he loved us** Again, 53.30 • 18 **sleked** satiated • 20–23 **In oure making . . . ende** Not just a final rhetorical flourish, an allusion to 85.4–7

THE EIGHTY-FIFTH CHAPTER

Ande in this sight I merveyled highly. For notwithstonding oure simpille living and oure blindhede˙ heer, yet endlessly oure curtesse lorde beholdeth us, in this wurking enjoyeng. And of alle thing we may plese him best, wisely and truly to beleve it, and to enjoy with him and in him. For as verily as we shulle /fol. 172v/ be in blisse of God without end, him praising and thanking, as verily we have been in the forsight of God loved and knowen in his endles purpose fro without beginning, in which unbegonne love he made us. In the same love he kepeth us, and never suffereth us to be hurt by which oure blisse might be lessed. And therfore whan the dome is geven, and we be alle brought uppe above, than shalle we clerely see in God the previtees which now be hid to us. And then shalle none of us be stered to sey in ony thing: "Lorde, if it had ben° thus, it had ben wele." But we shalle alle sey with one voice: "Lorde, blessed mot thou be, for it is thus, it is wele. And now we see verely that alle thing is done as it was thin ordinance, or ony thing was made."

THE EIGHTY-SIXTH CHAPTER

This boke is begonne by Goddes /fol. 173r/ gifte and his grace, but it is not yet performed, as to my sight. For charite pray we alle togeder, with Goddes wurking: thanking, trusting, enjoyeng. For thus° wille oure good lord be prayde, by the understanding that I toke in alle his owne mening, and in the swete wordes where he seyth fulle merely: "I am ground of thy beseching." For truly I saw and understode in oure lordes mening that he shewde it for he will have it knowen more than it is. In which knowing he wille geve us grace to love him and cleve to him. For he beholde his hevenly tresure with so grete love on erth that he will give us more light° and solace in hevenly joye, in drawing of oure hartes fro sorow and darknesse which we are in.

And fro the time that it was shewde, I desyerde oftentimes to witte° what was oure lords mening. And fifteen yere after and mor, I was answered in gostly /fol. 173v/ understonding, seyeng thus: "What, woldest thou wit thy lordes mening in this thing? Wit it wele, love was his mening. Who shewed° it the? Love. What shewid he the? Love.° Wherfore shewed° he it the? For love. Holde the therin, thou shalt wit more in the same. But thou shalt never wit therin other withouten ende." Thus was I lerned that love is oure lordes mening. And I sawe fulle sekerly˙ in this and in alle, that or God made us he loved us, which love was never sleked, ne never shalle. And in this love he hath done alle his werkes, and in this love he hath made alle thinges profitable to us. And in this love oure life is everlasting. In oure making we had

23 **Deo gracias** thanks be to God · 24–25 **Explicit . . .
Deus** here ends the book of the revelations of Julian,
anchorite of Norwich, in whose soul may God be
pleased

beginning, but the love wherin he made us was in him fro without beginning, in which love we have oure beginning. And alle this shalle we see in God with-/fol. 174r/ outen ende. Deo gracias.

Explicit liber revelationum Juliane anacorite Norwiche, cuius anime propicietur Deus.

25

TEXTUAL NOTES

In these notes "**A**" refers to London, British Library MS Additional 37790, the surviving manuscript of *A Vision;* "**P**" to Paris, Bibliothèque Nationale MS Fonds Anglais 40, our base manuscript in editing *A Revelation;* "**S**" to London, British Library MS Sloane 2499; "**W**" to London, Westminster Cathedral Treasury MS 4, the surviving manuscript of the Westminster Compilation. For conventions in use within the textual notes, see the Introduction, section 4.2a.

A Vision Showed to a Devout Woman

[RUBRIC] 1 **Here A** reads "There," the first of at least two places where the rubricator, writing the large red initial letters that begin each section of *A Vision*, seems to have made a mistake. See 1.1 • 2 **1413 A** reads "millesimo ccccxiii"

[SECTION 1] 1 **I** the rubricator wrote a large *S*, as though beginning the word "she," rather than "I" • 1 **Cristes A** reads "cryste es" • 15 **belevande his paines that time and sithene** See textual note to *Rev.* 2.12 • 27 **othere** from **P/S**: **A** reads "thayre," probably omitting the initial *o* by mistake • 27 **safe** added above the line by a corrector, likely, though not certainly, a person different from the original scribe. This corrector made a number of changes and additions, especially in the first few folios of *A Vision*. Many of these are straightforward corrections of simple slips on the part of the scribe, though a few are more difficult to interpret. This first addition, "safe," is suggestive, because it is not a response to any obvious omission in the text: "alle manere of thayre paynes of the owte passynge of the sawlle" makes good sense as it stands. The implication is that, here, at least, the corrector was working from another copy of *A Vision*, probably, though not necessarily, the same one as was used by the scribe. **P/S** read "save" • 28 **hoped** final *d* added above the line by the corrector. **P/S** also read "hoped" • 34 **youth** from **P/S**: **A** reads "thought." One of the two words is clearly a mistake for the other: easily

done, given spellings such as "þowth" and "yowth." "In my thought," however, seems a redundant phrase, unlikely to be correct • 35 **in threttye** "in" added above the line by the corrector • 40 **wounde** from **P/S**: **A** reads "woundys" • 41 **and** added above the line by the corrector. **P/S** also read "and" • 42 **so** added above the line by the corrector. **P/S** also read "so"

[SECTION 2] 9 **langere** from **P/S**: **A** reads "lange" • 9 **that I might** from **P/S**: **A** reads "that myght" • 11 **had lyevede A** initially read "wolde lyeve." The corrector substituted "hadd" for "wolde" above the line, but neglected to correct the tense of "lyeve." **P/S** read "had leved" • 13 **I was answerde** "I" added above the line by the corrector. This is the second time the original scribe omitted the important but perhaps troubling first-person pronoun in this section (see line 9) • 17 **to be sette** "be" added above the line by the corrector. **P/S** read "to be set" • 39 **prive A** initially read "journe," but this has been stroked out in red ink, and "pryve" added above the line by the corrector. "Journe" could be a version of "derne" (secret, hidden). **P/S** read "previe." (Hereafter, corrections in **A**, when adopted in our text, correspond to the readings of **P/S** unless otherwise stated)

[SECTION 3] 3 **minde and felinge** from **P/S**: **A** reads "mynde of felynge" • 16–17 **he wolde be so homlye A** has "homblye"; **P/S** read "he that is so reverent and so dreadfull will be so homely." The added phrase could be the result of revision, but it is possible the phrase was already present in *A Vision* but was omitted in error in **A**, as a line of the exemplar was missed by the scribe and its absence not noticed by the corrector • 17 **fleshe** from **P/S**: **A** reads "fleschly" • 22 **sawe** from **P/S**: **A** reads "saye," which gives much less good sense

[SECTION 4] 2 **hamly A** initially read "anly," but the corrector added an initial *h* and an extra minim to the *n* above the line. "Anly" would mean "solitary" or "unique" • 3 **clethinge, that** from **P/S**: **A** reads "clethynge" only, making "love" the subject of the rest of the sentence • 4 **becloses us** from P/S: A reads "beteches us us" • 8 **that it was as rounde** P/S omit "that," a word that complicates the syntax in A and may be a mistake • 14 **it** added above the line by the corrector • 17 **full reste** from P/S: A reads "love, reste," but this both upsets the parallelism with "verray blisse" and seems out of tune with Julian's theology as a whole • 24 **the** from P/S: not in A • 25 **hire** the scribe initially wrote "oure," but "hyre" has been substituted over the line by the corrector • 27 **that was made** from P: A reads "that was a sympille creature of his makynge," repeating the line the scribe had just copied, an instance of dittography. See Introduction, p. 34, n. 86 • 28 **wisdome and trowthe, knawande** from P/S: A reads "wysdome of trowthe, and knawande," "and" being added above the line by the corrector. Perhaps the corrector meant to change "of" to "and," but placed the correction incorrectly • 29 **for to** added at the end of line, in the right margin, by the corrector • 41 **all in ese** from P/S: A reads "here of his," the final *re* of "here" being written over an erasure, the first two letters of which were *he*. A's reading suggests that the worldly are already not God's (even "here," in this life, not "of his," of God's people), a sentiment common in medieval religious writing but inconsistent with the passage that follows and with Julian's thought

[SECTION 5] 1 **saide in gastelye** from P/S: A reads "saydene in gastelye," with the "in" added above the line by the corrector. It is likely that the *ne* of "saydene" is a mistaken transcription of the missing "in" from the exemplar, which the corrector failed to cancel • 2 **saw** A initially read "saye," but "saw" has been substituted above the line by the corrector • 5 **the** added above the line by the corrector • 10–11 **For wele I woote that heven and erth and alle that is made** from P/S: not in A, probably omitted because of eyeskip between the two occurrences of "made" • 12 **shewed** added in the margin by the corrector • 13 **semes** from P/S: A reads "semyd" • 16 **goodenes that** A initially read "goodenes of," but "that" has been substituted above the line by the corrector • 18 **And alle this** A initially read "and alle thynge," but "this" has been substituted above line by the corrector

[SECTION 6] 1 **saye** from P/S: A reads "sawe" • 1 **alle** added above the line by the corrector • 4 **wrechid, sinfulle creature** A reads "wrechid worlde synfulle creature," with "worlde" as the last word on fol. 100r. The phrase does not make good sense, even if one reads "worlde" as a possessive or an adjective. Perhaps the folio break encouraged the scribe to write the formulaic phrase "wrechid worlde" • 4 **it** added above the line by the corrector • 9 **desire** A reads "desyrere" • 15 **is comon** from P/S: A reads "comon" • 31 **that I shalle** A reads "that I that I schalle," repeating the "that I" across the folio break between fol. 100v and fol. 101r • 34 **if** written over an erasure by the corrector • 37 **that es** A

reads "thas es" • 42 **that it is his wille** from P/S: A reads "that is his wille" • 43 **if** added above the line by the corrector • 47 **alle this** A reads "alle thynge this," apparently repeating the word from the previous line in error

[SECTION 7] 11 **I** added above the line by the corrector • 12 **filled** this word is broken between lines, as "fil-lyd," with *fil* written over an erasure by the corrector

[SECTION 8] 1 **the face of the crucifixe** P/S plausibly precede this phrase with "in" • 3 **spitting, sowlinge** from P/S: A reads "spittynge in sowlynge" • 13–14 **be the endeles** from P/S: A reads "the endeles" • 15 **for our lord God doth all** from P/S: not in A. The clause seems necessary for the logic of the argument here. In the process of her revisions, Julian adds this gloss on the idea: "For in this time the working of creatures was not shewde, but of our lord God in the creature. For he is in the mid point of all thinges, and all he doth" (*Rev.* 11.15–17). The gloss circles back to its beginning point—"our lord God doth all"—providing further evidence for this sentence's place in the first version. *A Revelation* often comments on statements in *A Vision* in this way • 16–17 **Therfore it semed to me that sinne is nought, for in alle this, sinne** added by the corrector at the foot of the page; noted in margin with a ⚏ • 19 **afterwarde** the second *a* is corrected above an *o* in the text • 21 **shewed** A reads "schewyd schewyd" over a folio break • 26 **fullye** compare P/S, "full holsomly," a plausible possibility here • 29 **or** from P/S: A reads "houre" • 29 **wordes** from P/S: A reads "wondes" • 29–30 **behalde langere, and alle that I hadde seene** it is tempting to read "behalde him langere," taking "him" from P/S's "beholde hym a conveniable tyme," to make sense of the conjunction "and" • 32 **menande** from P/S: A reads "mevande" • 38 **to** added above the line by the corrector • 39 **us** written over an erasure by the corrector • 47 **enjoyande** A reads "er joyande" • 48 **I see** strangely, the corrector adds a second "I see" above these words, turning the phrase into "I see I see"

[SECTION 9] 6 **hafe** added in the margin by the corrector • 11 **resayvede** compare P/S, "undertaken"/"underfongyn," and see textual note to *Rev.* 2.19 • 13 **man** added above the line by the corrector. The word is not strictly necessary to the sense: "the age of everilk schalle be knawen" is comprehensible on its own • 19 **I was** added above the line by the corrector • 40 **us** from P/S: not in A • 44 **thaim** the *i*, with an abbreviation for *m*, is written over an erasure by the corrector

[SECTION 10] 2 **dede** the final *de* is written over an erasure by the corrector • 7 **ruddy** the final *dy* is written over an erasure by the corrector • 8 **claungede** from S: A reads "changede," P "cloeggeran." A's reading is presumably influenced by "chaunge" earlier in the line • 14 **to** written in the margin at the end of the line by the corrector • 16 **hadde failinge** from **P/S**: **A** reads "hadde of faylynge" • 17 **allane A** reads "alle ane" • 18 **hede** *ede* written over an erasure by the corrector • 31 **ful litille A** reads "fully tylle" • 35 **be more** written in the margin at the end of the line by the corrector • 36 **suffer?"** Here from **P/S**: **A** reads "suffyrde hir," perhaps losing the thread of the sentence over the folio break • 43 **him** added above the line by the corrector • 44 **a** added above the line by the corrector • 49 **of alle** written by the corrector over an erasure • 53 **syekernesse** the *r* is added above the line by the corrector • 59–60 **bonde me so sare** from **P/S**: **A** reads "bought me so sare," a formulaic phrase in many Middle English texts but less relevant to the context than the **P/S** reading

[SECTION 11] 1 **saw** written over an erasure by the corrector • 8 **bot also** from **P/S**: **A** reads "bot anly" • 19 **Whate P/S** both read "wher," repeating this word in their subsequent analysis of Christ's statement (building on *A Vision*), and "whare," not "whate," might be the correct reading here. **P/S** also include a "now" not in *A Vision*: "Wher is now." Generally, Christ's words remain stable between *A Vision* and *A Revelation*

[SECTION 12] 11 **wyrkinge** from **P/S**: **A** reads "lykynge," but see the opening of the next sentence • 12 **his fadere** from **P/S**: **A** reads "fadere" • 21 **died** the *e* is added over the line by the corrector • 23 **thinke** from **P/S**: **A** reads "thynge" • 36–37 **that we like als mekille, with his grace, whiles we er here P/S** read "that we desyre to have as much gostly lykyng, with his grace, as it is before seyde: that is to say, that the lykyng of our salvacion be lyke to the joy that Crist hath of oure salvation as it may be whylle we be here." It is tempting to incorporate the phrase "as it is before seyde" into *A Vision*, since **A**'s reading does not complete the implied "as . . . as" structure, but the missing phrase could also be "as it may be," from the end of the passage quoted

[SECTION 13] 2 **he A** reads "he he" • 25 **And efter this techinge, hamelye, curtayse, and blisfulle and verray life A**'s reading seems a little confused here. The equivalent sentence in **P/S** reads "Wher in I was lerned that oure soule shalle nevyr have reste tylle it come into hym, knowyng that he is full [**S** "fullhede"] of joye, homely and curteys and blessydfulle and very lyfe." Although *A Revelation* is revising *A Vision* here, something may have gone missing in **A** • 51 **affections** from **P/S**: **A** reads "affeccion" • 53 **alle** from **P/S**: **A** reads "and" • 59 **And for the tender love that our goode lorde hath** from **P/S**: not in **A**. **A**'s reading just makes sense: "and so is his blyssyd wille to alle that schalle be saffe." But it leaves the first verb in **A**'s next sentence (beginning "He comfortes") without an object • 62 **manere** from **P/S**: **A** reads "mare" • 66–67 **like in this I was in party filled with compassion** added at the foot of the page by the corrector, with insertion marks in the margin

[SECTION 14] 1 **Bot in this I stode** from **P/S**: **A** reads "Bot in this ye schalle studye." Although it is tempting, drawing the reader into the process of understanding, **A**'s reading is incoherent in context. It is also too similar to **P/S** for both to be correct. Somehow the pronoun "Y" has become "ye," the verb "stode" "studye," and then the auxiliary "schalle" has been imported to make sense of the result • 1 **drerelye** likely a dialect translation of **P/S**'s word "swemly" • 8 **knawen A** reads "knawynge" • 12 **blissede lorde** from **P/S**: **A** reads "lorde blyssede" • 18 **bidden P/S** plausibly read "bounde," a word that could easily be confused with "bidden" (in the form "bounden"). However, there is no clear case for preferring either word • 25–26 **and it langes to the ryalle lordeship of God for to have his prive consayles** added at the foot of the page by the corrector, with insertion marks in the margin • 32 **thame** from **P/S**: **A** reads "him." This ("like to Christ") is just plausible here, but the repetition of the singular pronoun in the next sentence (see next note) is nonsensical, since the "saintes" have only been referred to in the plural. The **A** scribe must have misread a form of the plural pronoun like that used in **S**, "hem," as the singular "him" • 33 **as thaye do** from **P/S**: **A** reads "as he does." This "he" cannot be Christ, and the sentence makes no clear sense as it stands. Again, "he" could have been a misreading of a form of the plural pronoun "hi," or it could have arisen as a rationalization, following the scribe's copying of "him" in the previous sentence

[SECTION 15] 2–4 **I may make alle thinge wele, I can make alle thinge wele, I wille make alle thinge wele, and I shalle make alle thinge wele A** reads "I wille make alle thynge wele, I schalle make alle thynge wele, I maye make alle thynge wele, and I can make alle thynge wele," but the order of "may . . . can . . . wille . . . schalle" is presumably meant to be the order in which the passage is glossed later in the paragraph • 4 **it** added above the line by the corrector: not in **P/S** • 12–13 **the luff-langinge that lastes A** reads "the luff langynge, and that lastes," but "and" confuses the syntax

[SECTION 16] 2 **wyrshipfullye** see textual note to *Rev.* 34.13 • 5 **mede** from **P/S**: **A** reads "myddes," which gives less good sense and is likely a scribal misreading of "mede" • 5 **this is knawen** from **P/S**: **A** reads "he is knawen," but see "it" at the end of the sentence • 15 **meen** from **P/S**: **A** reads "man"

[SECTION 17] 6 **What may make me mare to luff mine evencristen** added at the head of the page by the corrector, with correction marks in the margin. The initial omission of this line was probably the result of eyeskip • 12 **in, in his sight** from **P/S**: **A** reads "in his sight" • 22 **bette** compare **P/S**, "smitten." Either could be right, but it seems unlikely one was changed to the other • 23 **noghtes** compare **P/S**, "purgyth"/"noyeth" •

24 **thamselfe** A reads "hymselfe," perhaps misreading a form of the plural pronoun such as "hemself." P/S also read "himselfe," but have been using singular pronouns throughout the sentence. A also switches to singular pronouns as the sentence goes on • 26 **the bitternesse** from P/S: A reads "he bitternesse," which is only just possible • 37 **resayfe** compare P, "undertake," and see textual note to *Rev.* 2.19

[SECTION 18] 19 **that "he kepes us fulle sekerlye"** A reads "that kepes us fulle sekerlye": P/S read "I kepe the fulle truly/sekerly." Julian is clearly alluding to Christ's words at 17.2–3 in *A Vision* as in *A Revelation*, only in indirect speech

[SECTION 19] 1 **for** from P/S: A reads "foure" • 9 **Godes** A reads "god es" • 20 **and thowe beseke it!** From P/S: A reads "And if thowe beseke it." See the repetition of the clause in lines 23, 42, where the "if" has gone. See also textual note to *Rev.* 41.9–10. "If" could have been added by a scribe understanding "and thowe beseke it" as a conditional statement and wanting to make that more explicit • 23 **fifth** A reads "fyrst." See textual note to *Rev.* 41.12 • 23 **And thowe beseke it!** from P/S: A reads "and thowe beseke" • 24 **sixth** from P/S: A reads "fourte," written by the corrector over an erasure, apparently "sext" • 54 **souple** from P/S: A reads "simple," but "souple" in the following sentence • 55 **Bot he be na maner of prayer** from P/S/W (with P reading "she" for "he"): A reads "Bot he be boxom na maner of prayer." This makes good sense in context ("Bot he be boxom, na maner of prayer makes God souple to hym," with "bot" here in the sense of "unless"), but the agreement of the other manuscripts, the cruder theology of A's reading, and what we know of Julian's habits of revision combine to make the reading unlikely • 68 **custumabille** from P/S: A reads "custumabelye"

[SECTION 20] 1 **desired** compare P/S, "desire," the noun rather than the verb. This could be a deliberate change, since "desired" suggests a formal request for death on the model of the three requests described in Section 1; it is difficult to see such an implication surviving into *A Revelation*. But it is also possible that the past tense of "desired" here is scribal • 8 **fra alle thy sickenesse** from P/S: not in A. The clause seems required by 10–11, which parallels absence of "paine," "sekenes," "mislikinge," and "wantinge of wille" with the clauses in 8 • 30 **this** from P/S: A reads "his" • 32 **shulle** from P/S: A reads "schulde"

[SECTION 21] 2 **as a wrech hevyed** adapted from P/S: A reads "as a wrech that heved," which renders the sentence ungrammatical • 2 **mourned** "mned" with "r" added above the line • 7 **haddе** from P/S: A reads "hafe" • 11 **that says na mare therto** compare P/S, "saw no more thereof." This might represent a revision to *A Vision,* but the two phrases are sufficiently similar that one may be a scribal substitution for the other • 33 **holde** compare P/S, "behelde"

[SECTION 22] 9 **is** from P/S: not in A • 23 **the** added above line by the corrector • 32 **Thowe salle not** written in the margin by the corrector

[SECTION 23] 40 **is** not in A • 46 **God has made him** the whole sentence in A reads: "God has made tham to be loved of hym or hire that has bene a synnere," a remark that makes less sense the more one thinks about it, since the apparent antecedent of "tham" is the same as that of "hym or hire," i.e. the "man or woman" of 42. Two solutions present themselves, neither quite satisfactory. One would be to assume that "of" was added in error by a scribe attempting to make sense of a difficult sentence, so that "tham" and "hym or hire" do indeed have the same antecedent: "God has made tham to be loved: hym or hire that has bene a synnere." But the resulting sentence is weak and fits the context poorly. The other is to assume that a scribe has misread the original reading, "him," as "hem," the southern form of "tham," and to emend accordingly. This solution does create one new problem, since "God has made him" could be understood, not as "God has caused himself," but as "God has created himself," a theological solecism. In other respects, however, this solution is clearly the better of the two. Perhaps several words, even lines, have gone missing here • 50 **be bodely sight** A reads "be the bodely syght," perhaps because "the bodely" occurs in the next line

[SECTION 24] 3 **or** A reads "of" • 12 **this** *i* written in over an erasure by the corrector • 14 **unknawenge** *g* written in over an erasure by the corrector • 16 **of** added above the line by the corrector • 24 **knewe it we** A originally read "knewe it that we," but the "that" has omission marks below it

[SECTION 25] 10 **touching** from P/S: A reads "techynge" • 13 **luffe** from P/S: A reads "lyfe" • 24 **the** A reads "ye" • 28 **tempestes** A reads "tempes"

A Revelation of Love

[CHAPTER 1] The text of Chapter 1 is based on P, collated with S • **Here Beginneth the First Chapter** S has the general heading "Revelations to one who could not read a letter Anno Domini 1373" and the rubrics "A Particular of the Chapters" and "The first chapter: off the noumber of the Revelations particularly" • 2 **shewinges** S reads "sheweings or revelations particular" • 3 **of thornes** S reads "with thornys" • 4 **comprehended** from S: P reads "conteined," but this verb appears nowhere else in *A Revelation,* whereas "comprehend" makes several appearances, e.g., at 9.12 • 5 **oning** P reads "unithing," S "unite." The implication of the reading in S, that God and the soul are already united, does not form part of the content of the first revelation, and the word "unite" occurs only three times in the work as a whole, always with reference to the Trinity, as at 46.25–26: "his might, his wisdom, his charite, and his unite suffereth him not to be wroth." "Unithing" never occurs elsewhere in *A Revelation*. The passage must refer to 5.16–18: "For till I am substantially oned [from A/S/W: P reads "unyted"] to him I may never have full reste ne very blisse: that is to say, that I be so fastned to him that ther be right nought that is made betweene my God and me" • 5–6 **shewinges and techinges of endelesse wisdom and love** S reads "sheweings of endless wisedome and teacheing of love." Closely related manuscripts even of carefully copied Middle English texts, such as Nicholas Love's *Mirror of the Blessed Life of Jesus Christ,* are full of small variations like this, most of which we do not include in the apparatus • 7 **oned** from S: P reads "joyned," but this word appears nowhere else in the manuscripts of *A Revelation* or *A Vision* • 14 **precious bloud** S, often more laconic, reads "blood" • 16–17 **all his blessed servantes** S reads "his blissed servants," but "all" is important here, as the account of the sixth revelation, in Chapter 14, makes clear • 20 **irkede** from S: P reads "werines." See 15.6, where both read "irkenes" • 21 **sekerly** from S: P reads "verily," a weaker term that does not appear in Chapter 15, to which this sentence refers • 23 **drying** S reads "dyeing," with the *e* struck out. In P, the *r* has been added above the line. "Dying" is locally the more obvious reading, after the phrase "last paines," but the eighth revelation is all about the drying of Christ's skin. See textual notes to 16.24, 17.1, 23.9 • 24 **blisseful** from S: P reads "blessed." Julian did use "blessed"/"blissed" (as in line 17), but on the evidence of A and S very often seems to have opted for "blisseful." Like many early writers, she apparently did not distinguish between the etymologically distinct terms "bliss" and "bless." P has versions of "blisseful" on a few occasions (see 46.15; 51.269; 64.33, 40, 41; 72.18), sometimes in its adverbial form (see 49.24, 28), and sometimes renders it as "blessed"/"blessyd," as here, with the occasional use of the adverbial "blessedly." Much more often, however, P prefers "blessydfulle," with the adverbial form "blessydfully," both to A/S's versions of "blisseful"/"blissefully" and to A/S's "blissed"/"blessed." Partly because P's treatment of the word is so uncertain, partly to preserve the richness that comes of conflating "bliss" and "bless," we here adopt the forms of this word used by A and S and preserved only irregularly in P: "blisseful," "blissed," and "blissefully." On the many occasions when P renders these words "blessydfulle" and "blessydfully," we do so without further comment in the notes (unless the situation in the other manuscripts is ambiguous), marking the use of A/S readings with the symbol used for global emendations: • (see section 4.2a of the Introduction). On the other hand, we allow to stand P's relatively common spelling of "blisse" as "blesse" • 25 **after** S reads "and," simplifying the syntax. P's reading better reflects the contents of the ninth revelation 25–26 **in solace and mirth** S reads "solacid and myrthid" • 26 **fullehede** from S: P reads "glorie," a form not found elsewhere in the manuscripts, although there are examples of "glorious" and "glorified" • 27 **blisseful** from S: P reads "blessed" • 28 **enjoying** adapted from S, which reads "enjoyand": not in P (but see 24.1, 7). Here,

as elsewhere, we adopt the grammatical form usual in P (*-ing*) in emending from S. See page 41 of the Introduction • 30 **all sovereyn being** S reads "most worthy being," but uses the phrase "al sovereyn beyng" in the rubric to Chapter 26, where this revelation is described • 34 **asseeth** from S: P reads "amendes" but in Chapter 29, to which this passage refers, has "asseeth" • 35 **Than meaneth he thus** S reads "where also our lord seith." For "meaneth" in this sense, see 29.12 • 39 **privities, not** S reads "privityes now." Either could be right, but the word "now" does not occur in Chapter 30's account of this revelation • 41 **two fair properties** S reads "two properties" • 41 **seker** from S: P reads "suer." In the first half of *A Revelation* P regularly reads "suer," "suerest," "suerly," and "suernesse" for A/S's "seker"/"siker," "sekerest"/"sikerest," "sekerly"/"sikerly," "sekernesse"/"sikernesse," etc. In this edition, we assume that these readings are a product of scribal translation, and follow A or S without further comment in the notes, marking the use of A/S readings with the symbol used for global emendations: •. Later in the text, "seker" and "sekerly" begin to be used to replace other words, which we indicate in textual notes, while "sekernesse" is adopted into the text itself. See page 41 of the Introduction • 42 **alike** from S: P reads "one lyke," but has "alike" in 42.11, to which this passage refers • 44 **shall** from S: P reads "shuld," in the subjunctive mood, but has "shalte" in 64.9, to which this passage refers • 46 **and, forto, be fulfilled of joy** P reads "and for to be fulfilled with joy," S "and be fullfilled of joy." See 64.11 • 47 **blisseful** from S: P reads "blessed" • 48 **wonneth** from S: P reads "dwelleth," and S and A elsewhere also use this term. However, in 52.31–32, P, referring to this same revelation, has Christ "endlesly wonnyng . . . us" • 48 **yeming** S reads "geveand," P "comannding." The reference is to 68.7–8, where S reads "he ruleth and gemeth hevyn and erth," and P has "yevyth" for S's "gemeth," either a mistranscription or a rationalization of an obscure word. "Gemeth"/"yemeth" is from Middle English "yemen," to rule or nurture, so P's reading here ("comannding") offers a good translation of the word

[CHAPTER 2] The text of Chapter 2 is based on P, collated with A and S • S has the rubric "The Second Chapter. Of the tyme of these revelations, and how she asked three petitions" • 1–2 **This revelation . . . deadly flesh** S reads "These revelations were shewed to a simple creature that cowde no letter." S's version of the whole chapter is briefer than P's, and all three manuscripts show a higher level of variation than in most of the rest of the text • 1 **shewed** from A/S: P reads "made." For the principle of emendation involved here, where A's disagreement with P is often the deciding factor, see page 40 of the Introduction • 2 **thirteenth** S reads "eighth," and May 8 has accordingly become the feast day of Julian of Norwich in the Anglican and Episcopalian Churches. Either could be right: the *x* of "xiii" and the *v* of "viii" could easily be misread for each other • 3 **thre giftes by the grace of God** A reads "thre graces be the gyfte of God," S "three gifts of God." "Gift" and "grace" are theologically synonymous in this context • 4 **bodily sicknes** S reads "bodily sekenesse in youth at thirty yeeres of age." See line 32, where S omits P's similar passage. S's reading here (and again at 3.5, see below) assumes that the term "youth" covers human life at least to the age of thirty, as is the case with the Latin equivalent of the word, *iuventas*. The P scribe or a predecessor appears to have read the reference to youth differently, in relation to the time when Julian made her wishes. This understanding of the word seems the more likely • 5 **For the first** S reads "As in the first" • 5 **come to my minde with devotion** from A: not in P/S. The clause could have been omitted deliberately when Julian wrote *A Revelation,* but it is hard to see why, since "came [P/S "come"] to my mynd with contricion" in line 17 was retained. In general *A Revelation* is more concerned with balance and euphony than *A Vision.* Our inclusion of the clause assumes that it disappeared from the textual tradition of *A Revelation* early enough for both P and S to omit it. Another possibility is that it was already missing in the copy of *A Vision* that was used as the basis for Julian's revision • 7 **Mary** from A/S: not in P • 10 **knowinge** from A: P/S read "knowledge," but this is not the form Julian uses in *A Vision* or elsewhere in *A Revelation.* P and S offer only one other example of the form each: see textual note to 5.20 and S's rubric to Chapter 56 • 11 **paines** added above the line • 12 **that were living that time and saw his paines** A reads "that were belevande his paynes that tyme and sythene"; S shortens to "that seene that time his peynes." The differences between A and P may be the result of textual confusion, rather than authorial revision, the result of a mix-up between "belevande" and a spelling for "lyvyng" such as "levande." If so, it is unclear which is preferable. A's reading is tempting, because denser and more theologically complicated, implying that the group Julian wished to join at the site of the Passion is a mystical company of believers, rather than the historical group of Christ's friends and disciples • 12–13 **For I would have be one of them and have suffered with them** S reads "For I would be one of them and suffer with him" • 14–15 **for I beleved to be saved by the marcy of God** not in S • 15 **This was my meaning . . . shewing** S truncates this to "The cause of this petition was that after the sheweing" • 17 **For the secunde, come** from A: P reads "For the secunde came," S "The second came." P's reading is not grammatical. This is one of several instances in which the P scribe or a predecessor seems not to have understood Julian's use of absolute phrases • 17–18 **frely without any seking: a wilful desire to have of Gods gifte a bodily sicknes. I would that that sicknes** S reads "frely desireing that sekenesse," eliding the passage's account of Julian's request. This is probably not a deliberate omission but the first example in S of eyeskip, where a scribe's eye confuses two occurrences of a similar word or phrase (here "seking" and "sekenes") and as a result

omits the intervening words. There are nearly thirty such lines missing in S. See page 38 of the Introduction • 19 **undertake** A reads "take," S "underfongyn," P "have undertaken." This is one of many instances in which P's tense structure differs from that in A/S, often in the direction of greater complexity. In this edition, we tend to favor the simpler tense structures of A/S. S uses "underfongyn" (accept or receive) for P's "undertake" on four occasions in *A Revelation* (here and at 14.22, 39.31, 41.29), A reading "resayve/d" (receive/d) at 14.22 and 39.31, W agreeing with S's reading at 41.29. At 74.7, P has "undertaken" in the sense of "receive," where S has "understonding." Although "underfong" may go back to the earliest manuscripts, the evidence is complicated enough that we have thought best to retain P's "undertake" • 19–20 **holy church** from A/S: P reads "the holie church." Compare 3.2–3 • 20, 23, 26 **should/shuld die** from A/S or A: P reads "should have died" (× 3) • 21 **fleshly ne** not in S • 22 **this sicknes** from A/S: P reads "that sicknes" • 23 **tempests** from A/S: P offers the more familiar and specific "temptations," and never uses "tempests" as either noun or verb. See, e.g., notes to 47.38, 68.56 • 26 **for I hoped that it might be to me a spede when I shuld die** mostly from A: P reads "for I hoped that it might have ben to my a reward when I shuld have died," S "and that for the more speede in my deth." S reads like an abbreviated version of A, justifying our use of A readings here • 27 **and maker** not in A/S. Terms for God and the Virgin are often given in different forms in the three manuscripts • 28 **that I desired of him was** A reads "I desirede thame," S omits • 29 **For methought this was not the commune use of prayer. Therfor I said** A differs slightly. S reads "seyng thus," again much truncating the passage • 30 **wotest** A reads "woote," S "wotith," P "knowest." Our reading adopts A/S's term (which does occur in P but is often replaced by "know"), but retains the grammatical form favored by P • 30 **If it be thy wille that I have it, grant it me** from A: P reads "if that it be thy wille that I might have it," S "if it be thy will that I have it." "Grant it me" improves the sense of the conditional clause, which is illogical in P/S. Compare line 5 and note • 31–32 **This sicknes I desired in my youth, that I might have it when I ware thirtieth yeare olde** not in S, but see textual note to 3–4. Especially given S's earlier use of the word, P's "yowth" seems preferable to A's "thought" • 36–37 **Right as I asked the other twayne with a condition, so asked I this third mightly without any condition** S shortens to "And all this last petition I asked without any condition"

[CHAPTER 3] The text of Chapter 3 is based on P, collated with A and S • S has the rubric "Of the sekenese opteyned of God be petition. Third Chapter" • 3 **wened** from A/S: P here and often elsewhere reads "went" for this word, probably a "syncopated" spelling, where -*ed* is spelled *t* because the final syllable is elided in speech, a common phenomenon in later Middle English. ("Went" is the manuscript spelling at line 29.) We use the unsyncopated form here and elsewhere (e.g., 8.25) partly to avoid confusion with the past tense of "go," partly to regularize the spelling of a word that **P** spells in three different ways in this single passage: "went" (here), "weenied" (line 4), "wenyd" (line 5), all rendered "wened" in this edition. For a discussion of our policies on the spellings of **P** and **A**, see section 4.1a of the Introduction • 4 **langorid forth** from **A/S**: **P** reads "lay" • 5–6 **felt a great louthsomnes to die**: **A** reads "was ryght sarye and lothe thought for to dye," **S** "in youngith yet, I thought great sweeme to dye." It is hard to adjudicate between the three versions, but **P/S** both use "swemly" below, in 10.8 • 6 **liked** from **A/S**: **P** reads "lyketh," probably not as the result of a deliberate tense switch (see textual note to 2.19) but rather of confusion on the **P** scribe's part between two different letters in her exemplar, the letters _d_ and _ð_ (eth, which would be modernized to _th_). Such confusion is likely also a factor in many other disagreements between **P** and **S** or **A/S**, and is sometimes evident in corrections in **P** itself: for example, in Chapter 23 the **P** scribe repeatedly corrected her own _th_ to _d_ at the ends of words like "shewed," perhaps having initially read "shewed" as "sheweð," while elsewhere she corrected in the opposite direction, e.g., at 80.8, where she crossed out "doo" and substituted "thoo," perhaps having initially read "doo" as "ðoo." The hypothesis of _d/ð_ confusion on the part of the **P** scribe accounts for a number of apparent tense switches and other disagreements through _A Revelation_. For _d_ substitutd in **P** for **S** or **A/S** _th_, see 4.34, 6.26, 10.67, 11.36, 24.20, 35.6, 45.4, 52.26, 53.14, 58.40, 64.16; for _th_ substituted in **P** for **S** or **A/S** _d_, see 6.19, 8.19, 15.12, 23.10, 23.35, 25.8, 37.14, 57.31 • 8–9 **by the grace of that living** not in **S** • 10–11 **in regard of that endlesse blesse. I thought** **S** reads "in reward of that endlesse blisse—I thought nothing. Wherefore I thought." For the "regard"/"reward" variation, see textual note to 7.6. **S**'s addition could be a creative response to an error in the scribe's exemplar, such as a repetition of "I thought." Compare line 13, where for **A/P**'s "with all" **S** reads "with all with all" • 15 **stered** from **A/S**: **P** reads "holpen" (helped), rendering a rather different sense • 15–16 **underlening with helpe** **S** reads "underlenand with helpe," **P** "undersett with helpe." Both do away with the specificity of **A**'s "lenande with clothes to my heede" • 17 **thinke** **P/A/S** all read "thinking," but this may be an error for the infinitive ("thinken"), not the participle. See further textual note to 4.1 for the periodic confusion between the two, although this would be the only instance of such confusion in **A** • 17 **would** from **A/S**: not in **P** • 18 **by then** from **A/S**: **P** reads "before" • 19 **thee the** from **A/S**: **P** reads "the" • 19 **saviour** **S** reads "maker and saviour." See textual note to 2.27 • 20–21 **eyen were** from **A/S**: **P** reads "eyen was" • 21 **uprightward** from **S**: **P** reads "upright," **A** "upwarde," each supporting half of **S**'s reading • 24 **and it was alle darke** from **A/S**: **P** reads "it waxid as

darke" • 25 **night** it is tempting to add the extra phrase "and myrke" from **A**, but Julian may have deleted it in revision, to avoid repetition of synonyms • 25 **wherin held** **S** reads "wherein I beheld" • 26 **and ferful** not in **A/S** • 27 **if** from **A/S**: not in **P** • 27 **mekille** from **A/S**: here and in many parallel situations **P** reads "much," although it does have "mekille" on occasion, e.g., at 42.12, and we take this to have been Julian's preferred form. Elsewhere, we adopt "mekille" from **A/S** without further comment in the notes, indicating these adoptions with the symbol used for global revisions: •. See section 4.2a of the Introduction • 28 **over part** **S** reads "other party" • 29 **My most paine was shortnes of winde and failing of life** "wynde" is from **A**: **P** reads "breth." **S** has the more truncated "with shortness of onde" • 30 **sothly** from **S**: **P**, here and in many similar places, reads "verily." In **A/S**'s use of the two words (and a third, "truly"), "sothly" is always emphatic, while "verily" and "truly" can have some of the lightness of modern "indeed." Moreover, **P**'s preference for "verily" or "trewly" is not consistent: on a number of occasions, "sothly" or its cognates ("soth," "sothnes," "sothfastly") are used instead (see, e.g., 33.3; 50.22; 78.14; 82.6, 25, 26). It seems that the **P** scribe has engaged in a wholesale, but not complete, translation of Julian's "sothly" and its cognates. Here and elsewhere in this edition, we thus generally adopt **A/S**'s readings in situations involving these words • 33 **the** from **A/S**: not in **P** • 35 **for my hart was wilfully set therto** not in **S** • 38 **as I had before prayed** not in **S** • 39–40 **Thus . . . desired** not in **S**: in **P**, the _u_ of "thus" has been altered to an _i_, a change we do not follow • 43–44 **With him . . . give me grace** **S** has the laconic "and therefore I desired to suffer with him"

THE FIRST REVELATION

[CHAPTER 4] The text of Chapter 4 is based on **P**, collated with **A** and **S**. For lines 24–35 we also collate the first of the excerpts in **W** • **S** has the rubric "Here begynnith the first revelation. Of the pretious crownyng of Criste etc., in the first chapter. And how God fullfilleth the herrte with most joy. And of his greate meekenesse. And how the syght of the passion of Criste is sufficient strength ageyn all temptations of the fends. And of the gret excellency and mekenesse of the blissid virgin Mary. The Fourth Chapter" • 1 **trekile** from **A**: **S** has a different form of the infinitive, "trekelyn"; **P** has the participle "rynnyng." This seems to be one of a number of instances where the **P** scribe understands the infinitive or third-person plural -_yn/-en_ ending as -_ing,_ a mistake also occasionally made by **S**. See also textual note to 3.17 • 2 **plentuously and lively, right as it was** **S** reads "ryth plenteously, as it were" • 3–4 **Right so . . . sufferd for me** we see no way of adjudicating whether these clauses belong grammatically with the previous or the next sentence. As a way of evoking the miraculous transformation that is taking place, Julian here adopts a grammatical informality common in much Middle

English prose but relatively rare in *A Revelation* • 9 **the trinity is our endlesse joy and our blisse** S reads "everlasting joy and blisse" • 10 **and in our lord Jesu Christ** not in S • 13 **Benedicite dominus!** S corrects to "Benedicite domine," which is grammatically easier. See sidenote • 15 **will be so homely** A reads "wolde be so homblye." A's use of the conditional better conveys Julian's feeling at the time, but P/S's "will" serves to generalize her experience in a fashion typical of *A Revelation* as a whole • 17–18 **Thus I toke it . . . before the time of my temptation** S has the more truncated "This I tooke for the time of my temptation" • 18–19 **For methought it might well be . . . tempted of fiendes** S reads "for methowte by the sufferance of God, I should be tempted of fends" • 19 **and with his keping** not in S • 20 **died** from A/S: P has the fussier "should die," paralleling "should . . . be tempted" in line 19 • 22 **that should be saved** not in S • 22–23 **and against all ghostely enemies** S reads "and ghostly temptation" • 24 **our lady Saint Mary** A reads "oure ladye," S "our blissid lady," another example of variation in the manuscripts between ways of referring to sacred persons. See textual note to 2.27 • 29 **a** added above the line • 30–31 **For this was her marvayling: that he that was her maker would be borne of her that was made** not in S. The A scribe repeats "a sympille creature of his makynge" for "made," inadvertently recopying the end of the previous sentence, an error known as "dittography." W follows P. See also page 34 of the Introduction, note 86 • 33 **sothly** from A/S: P reads "verily" • 34 **worthines** From A/S/W: P reads "wordines," perhaps mistaking an ð in her exemplar for a *d*. See textual note to 3.6 • 34 **fullhead** S reads "grace"

[CHAPTER 5] The text of Chapter 5 is based on P, collated with A and S. For lines 2–36 we also collate W • S has the rubric "How God is to us everything that is gode, tenderly wrappand us. And all thing that is made, in regard to almighty God, it is nothing. And how man hath no rest till he nowteth himselfe and all thing for the love of God. The Fifth Chapter" • 1 **that I saw this sight of the head bleeding** not in S: A reads "that I sawe this bodyly syght." The greater specificity in the phrasing in P over A is made necessary by the passage describing Julian's sight of Mary, added in *A Revelation* just before this, at 4.24–35 • 3–6 **He is oure clothing, that for love . . . as to my understanding** the absence of the first "that" in A, and other small differences with P, may be scribal. W has further small variations. S is much briefer: "He is our clotheing that for love wrappith us, halseth us and all beclosyth us for tender love, that hee may never leave us, being to us althing that is gode, as to myne understondyng" • 8 **as me semide** not in S: W reads "as it had semed"; A reads "to my undyrstandynge" but does not have "with the eye of my understanding" in the next sentence • 8 **any** from A/W: P/S read "a" • 11 **have fallen** added in the margins • 11 **littlenes** A/S read "little." W reads "lytyllhed," but

"lytillnes" the next time the word occurs, at line 20 • 12–13 **And so hath all thing being** A/S add "the" before "being"; W reads "And so hath all thyng his begynnyng," a remark not wholly relevant in this context • 15 **is** (× 2) from A/W: S has only the first "is," not in P • 15–16 **But what is that to me? Sothly, the maker, the keper, the lover** a composite reading. A reads "Botte whate is that to me? Sothelye, the makere, the lovere, the kepere." W reads "But what is this to me? Sothly, the maker, the keper, and the lover." P reads "But what behyld I therin? Verely, the maker, the keper, the lover," with "I therin" added in the margins and other evidence of correction. S reads "But what is to me sothly the maker, the keper, and the lover I canot tell." S's reading resembles a creative response to a problem in her exemplar, probably the omission of "that" after "what is"; P's response perhaps suggests unease at what the scribe imagined the question, taken out of context, must mean: "But what do I care about it?" rather than "But what does this mean for me?" • 16 **oned** from A/S/W: P reads "unyted" • 17 **full reste** A reads "love, reste" • 19–20 **This little thing . . . for littlenes** not in S, though almost identical in W. Significantly revised from A • 20 **Of this nedeth us to have knowinge** P reads "knowledge." W reads "knowynge" (compare A) and has other small variations. S's reading of this and the next clause ("that us liketh to nought all thing that is made") is "It needyth us to have knoweing of the littlehede of creatures and to nowtyn all thing that is made" • 20 **to nought** from A/S: P reads "nought" • 21 **unmade** *un* added above the line • 26 **rested** from A/S/W: P reads "in reste" • 26, 27 **he** from A/S/W: P reads "she" (× 2). The readings in P often show a preference for feminizing the soul, influenced by the gender of Latin *anima*. However, from the evidence of the other manuscripts it seems that Julian preferred "he" or "it," thinking of both these pronouns as ungendered. At 49.36, the P scribe first wrote "it," then crossed it out and substituted "she," raising the possibility that she was also responsible for silently changing the word elsewhere. Avoidance of "she" is of a piece with *A Revelation*'s overall policies concerning gender-specific language • 29 **nakedly** from S/W: P reads "naked" • 29 **yerning** from S/W: P reads "dwellyng," perhaps a translation of a misreading of "yerning" as "wonyng" • 34 **God, of thy goodnes** from W: not in S. The P scribe first wrote "And these wordes god of the goodnes thei be full lovesum . . . ," almost as in W, then altered this to "And these wordes of the goodnes of God be full lovesum," presumably having understood "the" as a definite article, rather than as a personal pronoun • 34 **touche** from S (in the form "touchen"): P/W read "touchyng," both scribes probably reading the third-person present plural for the present participle. See textual note to 4.1 • 35 **comprehendeth** from S/W: P reads "fulfillith" over an erasure, which could possibly be "comprehendeth" • 36 **and overpasseth** from S/W: P reads "~~over passeth~~," presumably because the omission of "and" made the erased word nonsensical • 36–37 **hath made** from S/W: P reads "made" • 37 **precious**: S reads "blissid"

[CHAPTER 6] The text of Chapter 6 is based on P, collated with S and W, which excerpts almost the entire chapter • S has the rubric "How we shold pray. Of the gret tender love that our lord hath to mannes soule, willing us to be occupied in knowing and loveing of him. The Sixth Chapter" • 1 **as to my understanding** from W: P reads "to my understanding," not in S. The wording in W is common elsewhere in *A Revelation*, and the implication of P's reading, that the "shewing" was given to Julian's faculty of understanding in particular, is inconsistent with what she says about the multiple modes in which she received the revelation • 2 **prayer** S reads "prayeing" • 3 **for unknowing of love** S reads "for lak of understonding and knowing of love." The scribe is perhaps trying to work in words earlier left out, here "understanding." The phrase also occurs at 73.20 • 4 **sothly** from S: P reads "verily" • 4 **that it is more worship** S/W read "that is more worshippe," but P's "it" seems necessary to the sense • 7 **if we make** W reads "though we make" • 8 **right nought** W reads "no thyng" • 11 **worshipful woundes** S reads "wounds" • 11 **and** from S/W: P reads "for," which is syntactically not so clear and disturbs the passage's parallelism • 12 **it is of his goodnes** from S/W: P reads "it is of the goodnes of God" • 13 **him bare** from S/W: P reads "bare him" • 19 **For God of his goodnes hath ordained meanes to help us** from S: W adds "for God of his grete goodnes" after "goodnes," but otherwise follows S. P presents the same idea reordered: "For the meanes that the goodnes of god hath ordeineth to helpe us" • 19 **full faire and fele** S reads "wole faire and fele," P "full faire and many," W "in most lovyng and blessed maner." S's "fele" is likely the correct reading at 36.51, where the phrase is "many and fele"/"full." The level of variation in this sentence suggests some larger textual problem here • 21 **gone** from S: the P scribe or a predecessor, thinking historically, reads "went"; W reads "goeth" • 21 **belong** from S (in the form "belongen"): P reads "be langyng," W "ben longyng," a probable misreading of the third-person plural ending as a participle. See textual note to 4.1 • 26 **quickeneth** from S/W: P reads "quickened," probably confusing the letter ð in her exemplar with d. See textual note to 3.6 • 26 **bringeth it on life** from S/W: P reads "maketh it leve" • 27 **maketh** from S/W: P reads "make" • 29–33 **A man goeth . . . of oure nede** not in S. This omission of a passage apparently referring to excretion could be deliberately delicate, but could also be because the scribe of S found the sentence incomprehensible (see sidenote) • 32 **it is shewed ther wher he seith** W reads "he shewyth that he seeth" • 35 **hath made** from S/W: P reads "made" • 35–36 **For as . . . bowke** W is briefer: "For as the bodi is cladde in the clothe, and the fleshe and the harte in the bouke" •

37 **cladde and enclosedde in the goodnes of God** S reads "cladde in the goodnes of God and inclosyd" • 38 **For all these may waste and were away** from S/W: P reads "For all they vanyssche and wast awey" • 39 **likenes** from S/W: P has "comparison" • 40, 41 **cleve, cleving** W reads "clyme," "clymyng," turning the passage into a meditation on mystical ascent. The scribe probably misread "cleve" for the more familiar word • 42 **presciously** S reads "specially" • 45 **oure maker** from S/W: P reads "that oure maker," which is syntactically less clear • 47 **unmesurable** S reads "onenestimable" • 47–48 **oure lorde** S reads "almitie God" • 50 **blin** from S/W: P reads "sesse" • 50 **loving** S reads "longyng" but has "loving" in line 52 • 51 **we may no more wille** W reads "may we desyre no more"

[CHAPTER 7] The text of Chapter 7 is based on P, collated with S, W in lines 3–8, and for several passages A • S has the rubric "How our lady, beholdyng the gretenes of hir maker, thowte hirselfe leste. And of the great droppys of blode renning from under the garland. And how the most joy to man is that God most hie and mightie is holyest and curtesiest. Seventh Chapter" • 1 **our good lorde** S reads "our lord God" • 3–4 **This wisdom . . . her God** not in S. Probably another example of eyeskip, with the recurring phrase "wisdom and truth" the occasion of error. See page 38 of the Introduction • 4 **and** added above the line • 4 **and so good. This gretnesse** W reads "and so good, that the gretenes" • 6 **regard** S reads "reward." In W, the w of "reward" is scratched out, and a g added above the line. Elsewhere, S usually uses "reward" for P's "regard"; A uses both. Partly to avoid confusion with the other word "reward" (in the sense of "heavenly reward"), this edition treats "reward"/"regard" variation as a matter of spelling and silently retains P's "regard" • 8 **vertues** from S/W: P reads "vertuous" • 8 **overpasseth** from S/W: P reads "passyth" • 10 **plenteous** from A/S: P reads "pituous" • 12–14 **they . . . they . . . they** S reads "it" (× 3). Despite the apparent need for plural pronouns, S's reading is defensible. In lines 11–12 P has just used "it" in the same way, to refer to the drops of blood "as it had comynn oughte of the veynes" • 12 **browne** from S: P reads "brorme" • 15–16 **nevertheles . . . bewty and livelines** instead of this clause, S has a sentence that means much the same thing, but alters the balance of the argument: "The fairehede and the livelyhede is like nothing but the same." This reads like an attempt to reconstruct sense out of words similar to those found in P that had become illegible in S's exemplar • 17–18, 22 **the evesing of an house** S reads "evys" (× 2) • 19 **roundhede** from S: P reads "roundnesse" but "roundhede" in the following lines. Further emendations of P's suffix "-nesse" to A/S/W's "-hede" are made without further comments in the notes and marked in the text by use of the symbol for global emendations: • See section 4.2a of the Introduction • 21–22 **the scale of herring . . . spreding** S reads "the scale of heryng, in the spreadeing in the forehede, for round-hede" • 24 **that I saw** not in **S** • 25 **oure good lorde S** reads "our God and lord" • 30 **in previte and openly S** plausibly reads "prive and partie," "partie" from Middle English "apert," public • 32 **litille S** reads "simple" • 32, 36, 38 **sothly** (× 3) from **S**: **P** reads "verely" • 33 **geftes** from **S**: **P** reads "gestes," although the long *s* for *f* is pre-sumably a mere slip of the pen • 34 **this mannes hart S** reads "manys herete" • 39 **shalle he shew us all, when we shall see him S** reads "shall be shewne us all whan we se him" • 40 **beleve and trowe P** reads "beleve and trust," **S** "willen and trowen." In **P**, "trow" and "trust," which are not really synonyms, are regularly conflated, though **P** has the phrase "beleve or trowe" at 72.30. **A/S** distin-guish the terms • 45 **know in this life S** reads "weten in this tyme of life." **A/P/S** all use both "know" and "wit" as synonyms, though in somewhat different proportions • 48 **made** from **S**: **P** reads "is made," ungrammatically • 51 **in a time** from **S**: **P** reads "for a tyme," a phrase used by **P/S** at 27.24 in a different sense. For "in a tyme" in this sense, see 22.39 • 51–52 **than faith kepeth it, by grace S** reads "than the feith kepyth be grace"

[CHAPTER 8] The text of Chapter 8 is based on **P**, col-lated with **S** and, in some cases, **A** • **S** has the rubric "A recapitulation of what is seid. And how it was shewid to hir generally for all. Eighth Chapter" • 1 **plentuous bleding** from **A/S**: **P** reads "plentuousnesse of bledyng" • 2 **dominus S** reads "domine" (as in 4.13) • 4 **blisseful** from **A**: **S** reads "blissid," **P** "blessydfulle" • 6 **that is his deerwurthy mother A**'s "that sche ys his dereworthy modere" has a subtly different emphasis • 10 **mekille and** from **A/S**: **P** reads "great" • 11 **sheweth A** reads "schewed" (in margin), **S** "is shewid." Any of these read-ings could be correct • 11–12 **him that is the maker S** reads "him that is the maker of all thing" • 12 **For to a soul** from **A**: **P/S** read "For a soul" • 12 **all thing S** reads "all" • 14–15 **The fifth . . . saide S** reads "The fifth is he that made all things for love; be the same love it is kept and shall be withoute end" • 14 **that he has made** from **A**: **P** reads "that he that it made," with "it" added above the line. Perhaps the **P** scribe was confused by the folio break • 15 **as it is** "is" added at the end of the line • 18 **and gave me S** reads "with" • 19 **And P** reads "~~And~~ And" • 19 **dwelled** from **A/S**: **P** reads "dwellth" • 21 **or lengar time the same P** reads "or lengar tyme the same syght," **A** "or the same langer tyme," **S** "or ell lenger time the same" • 23 **might alle see S** reads "might seen" • 25 **todaye** from **A/S**: **P** reads "this daye" • 26 **demede** from **A/S**: **P** reads "demyde particulerly," a reference to the "particular judgment," as distinct from the "general judgment" at the end of time. For **P**'s "theological improvements," see page 42 of the Introduction • 27 **loved** from **A/S**: **P** reads "schulde love" • 29 **sweme** from **S**: **P** reads "wonder," probably a scribal guess at the meaning of a word that had become obscure. However, **P** uses forms of "sweme" at 10.8 and 16.6 • 31 **Alle that I say of me, I mene S** reads "And that I say of me I sey" •

31 **say** *a* added above the line to a word that initially read "sy" • 31 **in the person** from **A/S**: **P** reads "in person" • 35 **God** from **A/S**: **P** reads "in God" • 36–37 **with as grete joy and liking as Jhesu had shewde it to you** from **A**: **P** reads "with a grete joy and lykyng, as Jhesu hath shewid it to yow"

[CHAPTER 9] The text of Chapter 9 is based on **P**, col-lated with **S** and in some passages **A** • **S** has the rubric "Of the mekenes of this woman, kepeing hir alway in the feith of holy church. And how he that lovyth his evyn cristen for God lovith all thing. Ninth Chapter" • 4 **in love S** reads "in comfort," the scribe perhaps recopying "comfort" from the previous line. **A** does not contain the phrase • 4 **sothly** from **A/S**: **P** reads "verely" • 4 **loveth A** reads "loves," **S** "lovid" • 6 **had** from **A/S**: **P** reads "hath" • 7–8 **I hope** not in **A**. The kind of phrase that could have begun life in the margins of a copy of *A Vision* or *A Revelation*, though it appears regularly in *A Revelation*. **S** reads "in hope" • 8 **onehede** from **A/S**: **P** reads "oned," probably a spelling error for the same word • 13 **and in God is alle A** reads "and so in man ys alle," **S** "and God is in al." Although **S**'s seems the least logical of the three readings, in context they all mean much the same • 13–14 **And he that loveth thus, he loveth alle** not in **S**: probably an example of eyeskip • 15 **beholdeth** from **S**: **A** reads "behaldes," **P** "behold" • 18 **precheth and techeth S** reads "levith, preachith, and teachith" • 19 **understonde** from **S**: **P** reads "underston-dyng" • 19 **kept** from **S**: **P**, perhaps reflecting a scribal anxiety to stress Julian's continuing orthodoxy, has the grammatically less satisfactory "kepe it" • 21–22 **and with this meaning** not in **S**. The phrase may seem otiose, but it parallels the earlier use of "meaning" in line 20, just as "with this intent" parallels "willing" • 23 **as one in Gods mening** from **S**: **P** reads "as in Gods menyng" • 26 **may not** from **A/S**: **P** reads "may"

THE SECUNDE REVELATION

[CHAPTER 10] The text of Chapter 10 is based on **P**, col-lated with **S**, **W** for most of lines 56–81, and in some pas-sages **A** • **S** has the rubric "The second revelation is of his discolouryng, etc. Of our redemption and the discolouring of the vernacle. And how it plesith God we seke him besily, abiding him stedfastly and trusting hym mightily. Tenth Chapter" • 5 **overyede S** reads "overrede" • 5 **beclosed** from **S**: **P** reads "closyd," but "beclosyd" in the next line • 6 **therewhiles** from **S**: **P** reads "the whiles" • 6 **it** added above the line • 8 **light S** reads "sight" • 10 **Thee nedeth** from **S**: **P** ungrammat-ically reads "thou nedyth" • 15 **in this life S** reads "in this" • 16 **led downe** from **S**: **P** reads "lett down" • 17 **begrowen** from **S**: **P** reads "begrowyng" • 20 **shoulde** *l* added above the line to a word that originally read "shoude" • 23 **this beleve** from **S**: **P** reads "the beleve" • 27 **in a feer S** reads "in doute" • 28 **understode** from **S**: **P** reads "understonde" • 29 **foule, black, dede hame P** reads "fowle blacke dede," **S** "foule dede hame." See line

49 • 29 **which** P reads "which ~~that~~," S "that." "Which that" is found nowhere in *A Revelation,* although "which" and "that" are both used to introduce relative clauses, "which" regularly elsewhere in this passage • 31 **owne** from S: P reads "one" • 35 **fairhede** from S: P reads "feyerest" • 37 **say** P reads "see" • 42 **he that made man** S reads "that made man" • 45 **gainmaking** from S: P reads "awne makyng" • 49 **foule, blacke, dede hame** from S: P reads "fowle blacke dede." "Hame," skin, is essential to the sense here, since in the next clause Christ's "godhede" is hidden inside this object. Note that in P "dede" is understood as "deed," in S as "dead" • 49–50 **wherein oure fair, bright, blessed lorde hid his godhede** S reads "wherein our faire, bryte, blissid lord God is hid." S's reading may be an attempt to shift the text away from the formally discredited, but still popular, theological theory that Christ's purpose in becoming incarnate in the flesh was to deceive Satan • 50 **full sekerly** from S: P reads "verely" • 51 **trowe** from S: P reads "beleve" • 53 **eighth** taken from the phrase S adds at line 56: P reads "seconnde" • 53 **in the sixteenth chapter** not in S: P reads "xviii chapter," but the passage refers to the eighth revelation, Chapter 16, an account of the gradual drying and discoloration of Jesus' skin as he dies. The sentence may well have made its way in from the margins of an earlier manuscript. Cross-references between revelations are common in this work, but seldom specify chapters • 53 **speketh** S reads "tretith" • 54 **meneth** in both P and S the word could also be "meveth" (moves). However, variations of "there it seyeth . . . it meneth" are formulaic in *A Revelation.* See, e.g., 57.2, 80.22. Like its predecessor, the sentence reads like a marginal gloss that has made its way into the text of *A Revelation,* which the sentence refers to as "it" • 55 **chere** from S: P reads "ether" • 56 **as it may be seen** P adds "here after" in the top margin, S "in the eighth revelation," a phrase that may have some relation to P's earlier "in the xviii chapter". However, we understand the sentence to refer to the discussion of the vernacle just concluded, and read both these phrases as scribal additions intended to make sense of a confusing passage • 57 **continual** from S: P reads "contynually," W "contynuyng" • 58 **full mekille** from S: P reads "moch," W "full meche" • 59 **And this is wrought in every soule** S reads "and this wrought in the soule" • 64 **we seke into** S reads "we seke him to" • 65 **him** from S: P reads "her." See textual note on 5.26, 27 • 67 **the soule** S reads "thyselfe" • 67 **receiveth** from S: P reads "receyved" • 68 **festeneth** from S: P originally read "fustsynyth," but the scribe canceled the first four letters of the word and added *re* in the margin to make "resynyth" • 68 **onto** from S: not in P • 69 **either in seking or in beholding** from W: P reads "eyther in sekyng or beholdyng," S "either be sekyng or in beholdyng" • 69 **may do** S adds "to him" • 73 **by discretion** S reads "that discretion," reflecting an attempt to make sense of the last clause's relation to the sentence as a whole: P reads "dyscrecion." S's "that" results in a very tortuous syntax. A word like

"by" seems to have gone missing here, and we supply it as a stopgap • 74 **of his gifte** not in S • 76 **unskilfulle** from S/W: P reads "unresonable." See 73.40 for P's one use of "unskilfulle" • 76 **is** from S: not in P/W • 77 **gruching** from S/W: P reads "grongyng" • 79 **seker** from S: P reads "and tru," W "sure" • 79 **that we know that he shall aper** S reads "We knowen he shall appere," W "we shall know that he will appere" • 81 **swithe** from S/W: P reads "swete," though elsewhere it reads "soone" for S's "swithe," a word P never uses. See 51.239, 55.14, 61.43 • 81 **trowed** from S: P reads "trustyd," W "belevyd" • 81–82 **hende, homely, and curteise** from W: P reads "homely, curteyse," S "hend and homley"

THE THIRD REVELATION

[CHAPTER 11] The text of Chapter 11 is based on P, collated with S, A, and W, which excerpts lines 1–18 (with omissions in lines 3–4, 8–12), 42–46, and 35–39, in that order • S has the rubric "The third revelation etc. How God doth al thing except synne, never chongyng his purpose without end. For he hath made al thing in fulhede of goodnes. The eleventh Chapter" • 3 /fol. 23ar/ The foliation in P, in the scribes hand, inadvertently gives us a second folio 23, here numbered 23a • 3 **that sight that he doth alle that is done. I merveyled in that** not in S, presumably because of eyeskip between the two occurrences of "that sight" • 5 **truly** from S: P reads "veryly," after reading "truly" in the previous line. W has neither • 6, 8 **foreseing** (× 2) from S: A and W each read respectively "forluke" (× 1) and "foreseeng" (× 1), P "forsayde" (× 2), which gives much less good sense. Compare 27.5 and 53.17, where P's reading seems again to reflect a desire to avoid reference to divine providence • 7 **and our unforsight** from S/W: P reads "and unforsyght" • 8 **bene** not in S • 9 **and** from S: not in P • 10 **ourselfe** P reads "our" • 11 **these thinges be by happes** S reads "these ben happis" • 11–13 **Thus I understonde . . . ne aventure** S reads "but to our lord God thei be not so," W "Wherfor wel I wot that in syght of our lord God is no happe ne adventure" • 14 **Wherfore** W, having read "Wherfor" for P's "Thus" at line 11, now continues the sentence across our paragraph break, reading "and therfor" • 14 **behoved** S reads "behovith" • 16 **the creature** from S/W: P reads "the creatures" • 17 **sothly** from S: P reads "verely" • 24 **as I shall say after, when** S reads "as I shal sey, where" • 27 **domes** S reads "doings" • 28 **bringe** P/S/W all read "bringing," reading the third-person plural "bringen" as a participle. See textual note to 4.1 • 33 **best dede is done** from S: P reads "best dede that is done," which is syntactically confused • 35 **ordained to fro** from S: P reads "ordeynyd tofor." See line 44 • 36 **changeth** from S/W: P reads "channgyd" • 38 **all thinge was** from S: P/W read "all thynges were," but revert to Julian's collective singular for most of the rest of the chapter. Despite S's isolation here, its reading is preferable, preserving the important conceptual parallel between "all thing" and "anything" that governs the sentence • 42 **blissefully** from S: P reads "blessedly" • 43 **thing** from **S/W: P** again reads "thyngs" • 44 **fro** from **S/W: P** reads "for" • 47 **sothly** from **S: P** reads "verely" • 47 **behoved** from **S: P** reads "behovyth," but see line 14 • 48 **enjoying in God** from **S: P** reads "and joy in God"

THE FOURTH REVELATION

[CHAPTER 12] The text of Chapter 12 is based on **P**, collated with **S** and **A** • **S** has the rubric "The fourth revelation etc. How it likith God rather and better to wash us in his blode from synne than in water, fore his blode is most pretious. Twelfth Chapter" • 1 **plentuously** from **A/S: P** reads "plentuous" • 3–4 **The hote blode ranne out so plentuously S** reads "so plenteously the hote blode ran oute" • 5 **ther S** reads "than" • 11 **full holsomly A** reads "fullye," **S** "full homely" • 14 **all** from **S:** not in **P** • 14 **overfloweth S** reads "beflowyth," but "overflowith" at line 20 • 17 **the vertu of this precious plenty S** reads "The pretious plenty" • 17–18 **It descended S** reads "descendid," making what follows part of the previous sentence • 18 **brak S** reads "braste," the only use of this word in the manuscripts • 18–19 **them, all that were there S** reads "deliveryd al that were there" • 19 **belong S** reads "longyd" • 22 **ascendeth S** reads "ascendid," but the present tense here parallels that of "overfloweth" in line 20 • 22 **in the blessed body S** reads "to the blissid body" • 24 **evermore** from **S: P** reads "ovyr more," which occurs at 75.21 with the sense "moreover" • 24 **all heaven S** reads "all hevyns"

THE FIFTH REVELATION

[CHAPTER 13] The text of Chapter 13 is based on **P**, collated with **S** and **A** • **S** has the rubric "The fifth revelation is that the temptation of the fend is overcome be the passion of Criste, to the encres of joy of us, and to his peyne, everlestingly. Thirteenth Chapter" • 1 **or God** from **S: P** reads "or that God," **A** "oure God" • 1 **beholde him S** reads "beholden in him" • 2 **conveniable S** reads "conable" • 2 **the understanding S** reads "intellecte," a word that occurs nowhere else in the manuscripts • 3 **simpilnes S** reads "simplicite" • 4 **formed S** reads "formys" • 4 **these wordes** from **P/S: A** plausibly reads "this worde." See next note • 5 **This worde S** reads "These words," but for Julian "word" often refers to an entire statement, meaning something like "divine utterance." **A** reads "this worde" • 6–7 **a parte of the feendes malice, and fully his unmight, for he shewed** not in **S**, presumably omitted because of eyeskip between "our lord shewed" in line 5 and "he shewed" in line 6 • 9 **all soules of salvation A** reads "alle chosene saules," **S** "all sent of salvation" ("sent" = "saints"?). Predestination was a difficult theological issue in both the fourteenth and the early seventeenth centuries (when **S** and **P** were copied), so the level of variation in allusions to it is not surprising. "Chosen soule" occurs at 39.1, "men/man of salvation" at 20.4 • 10 **his** (1) **S** reads "Cristes" • 11 **attemed** from **S: P** reads "ashamyd." "Attemed" is not found elsewhere in the manuscripts but seems the

stronger reading, attributing fury to the devil at his own powerlessness • 12 **to shame and paine A** reads "to payne and to schame," **S** "to shame and wo" • 14 **lokked S** reads "tokyn." See textual note to 65.19. **A** confirms **P**'s reading on both occasions • 15 **endelessly having regard S** reads "endlesly hath regarde," simplifying the syntax • 18 **contrary S** reads "contriven" • 19 **scorne his malis and nought** from **A/S: P** reads "scornyng hys malys and nowghtyng." See textual note to 4.1 • 22–23 **have laughed** from **A: P** reads "a laughyd" (with "a" a syncopated form of "have"), **S** "lauhyn" • 23 **laugh** from **A/S: P** reads "laghyng" • 23–24 **But wele I wot that sight that he shewed me made me to laugh** not in **A/S**, though **A**, independent at this point, has the words "Neverthelesse him likes that we laugh." **A** *Revelation* is clearly reworking *A Vision* here, and the line was probably omitted in **S** through eyeskip from one "laugh" to the next • 25 **feend S** reads "devil." **P** uses this term three times, all in Chapter 33, but otherwise favors "feend" • 26 **be leding of** from **S: P** reads "beholdyng to." Compare 51.36 • 30–31 **And I se scorne, that God scorneth him** "I" and "God" added above the line. The clause originally read "And se scorne that scorneth him" • 33 **fulle ernest** from **A/S: P** reads "fulle grette ernest" • 34 **ther I saide "he is scorned," I ment that God scorneth him** Julian has not in fact used the expression "he is scorned," but in **P/S** has used "that God scorneth him" (in line 31). It is tempting to think that 30–31 were supposed to read "And I se scorne, that he is scorned, and he schalle be scorned" • 34 **ment S** reads "mene," but "ment" in line 36 • 36 **shalle** from **S: P** reads "schulde," but "shalle" in line 31 • 36–37 **For I saw he shalle be scornede** not in **S**, another example of eyeskip • 37–38 **to whos salvation he hath had gret envye S** reads "to hose consolation he hath gret invye." "Consolation" is not found elsewhere in the manuscripts, which prefer the word "comfort" • 40 **sorow S** reads "tribulation" • 40 **endlesly** from **S: P** reads "forevyr," a word that does not appear elsewhere in the manuscripts

THE SIXTH REVELATION

[CHAPTER 14] The text of Chapter 14 is based on **P**, collated with **S** and **A** • **S** has the rubric "The sixth revelation is of the worshippfull thanke with which he rewardith his servants. And it hath three joyes. Fourteenth Chapter" 1 **our lorde S** reads "our good lord" • 1 **of thy servys** and not in **S** • 1–2 **and namely of** from **S: A** reads "and namely in," **P** reads "of" • 3 **our lorde God S** reads "our lord" • 3–4 **which lorde hath called S** reads "which hath cleped." "Clepe" is unattested in **A/P/W**, but is used several times in **S** where **P** reads "call." It may go back to the earliest manuscripts • 4 **derewurthy frendes S** reads "derworthy servants and freinds" • 5 **and all fulfilleth S** reads "and fulfillid" • 7 **of endelesse love** from **S: P** reads "in endelesse love" • 8–9 **alle heven S** reads "hevyns" • 11 **wilfully** from **A/S: P** reads "wyllyngfully." See also line 16 • 12 **wurshipfulle** from **A/S: P** reads "wurshyppe" • 14 **thinketh** from **A/S: P** reads "thyngkyth that" • 14 **methought that** from A/S: P reads "mythought" • 15 **have deservede** S reads "deserve" • 18 **se that** from A/S: P reads "se the" • 19 **subjettes** S reads "servants" • 20–21 **then ther wurship** S reads "than is his worshippe," but the force of the passage concerns the honor of the "subjettes," not of the "king" • 22 **And for the thurde** S reads "The third is" • 22 **undertaken** A reads "resayvede," S "underfongyn." See textual note to 2.19, where the manuscripts offer the same choices • 26 **wonderly** from A/S: P reads "wonderfully" • 29–30 **the lever he is to serve him all the dayes of his life** from S: P reads "the levyr she ys to serve hym all hyr lyfe." See textual note to 5.26, 27

THE SEVENTH REVELATION

[CHAPTER 15] The text of Chapter 15 is based on P, collated with S and A • S has the rubric "The seventh revelation is of oftentymes felyng of wele and woo etc., and how it is expedient that man sumtymes be left withoute comfort, synne it not causeing. Fifteenth Chapter" • 1 **In this liking** not in S • 2 **fastned** S reads "susteinid" • 3–4 **all in peese, in eese, and in reste** A reads "that I was in peez, in ese, and in ryste," S "in al peace and in reste" • 8 **fulle litille** S reads "litil" • 10 **liking** S reads "in likyng" • 10 **so mighty** from A/S: P reads "so myghtely" • 11 **bodely ne gostely** S reads "bodily" • 12 **shewed** from A/S: P reads "sheweth," probably confusing the *d* in her exemplar for *ð* and modernizing this to *th*. See textual note to 3.6 • 14 **time of joy** S reads "same tyme of joy" • 15 **Saint Peter** S reads "Peter" • 116 **me** added above the line • 17 **shewde me to lerne me at my understanding** first "me" from A: S "shewid me, after myn understodyng" • 18 **some soules** A reads "ylke man," but P/S's readings suggest that Julian retreated from the absoluteness of this assertion • 18–19 **to faile** from A/S: P reads "for to fayle" • 21 **althogh sinne** from S: A reads "towhethere, synne," P "all thogh hys synne" • 27 **paine** from A/S: P reads "paynes" • 28 **in the endlesse liking that is God** A reads "in endelesse lykynge, that es God allemyghtty, oure lovere and kepare," S "in endless likyng"

THE EIGHTH REVELATION

[CHAPTER 16] The text of Chapter 16 is based on P, collated with S and A • S has the rubric "The eighth revelation is of the last petivous peynes of Christe deyeng, and discoloryng of his face and dreyeng of his flesh. Sixteenth Chapter" • 1–2 **the swete face** A reads "that swete faace," S "his swete face" • 2 **sithen more** from A/S: not in P • 2 **deade pale** S reads "pale, dede" • 3 **sithen more browne blew** from S: A reads "sithene mare blewe," P "after in browne blew" • 5 **there I saw** from A/S: P reads "Ther in saw I" • 6 **fresh and rody, lively and liking** S reads "freshe, redy, and likyng" • 6 **a swemfulle change** from S: P reads "a peinfulle chaungyng," A "a hevy change." See textual note to 8.29 • 7 **also the nose clongen togeder and dried** A reads "also the nese changede and dryed," S "also the nose clang and dryed," P "also hys

nose cloeggeran togeder and dryed." "Cloeggeran" is unattested in MED or OED, but might be a genuine form of "clongen," to impede or stick, a form of the word used in P in line 23 and adopted here • 8 **waxid** S reads "was" • 8–9 **alle changed and turned oute of the fair, fresh, and lively coloure** S reads "al turnyd oute of faire lifely colowr" • 9–10 **For that same time . . . wonder colde** S reads "for that eche tyme that our lord and blissid savior deyid upon the rode it was a dry, harre wynde and wond colde." We have adopted S's "harre." P reads "sharp" • 12 **dwellid** from S: P reads "was" • 15 **twain withouten and twain within** from S: not in P • 17 **And the paine** S reads "and peynfully" • 18 **dry in my sight** S reads "dey, in semyng, be" • 19 **sufferde he paine** from S: P reads "sufferde he" • 20 **paining** from S: A reads "pining," P "peyne" • 21 **alwey suffering the gret paine** A reads "allewaye sufferande payne," S "away, sufferand the last peyne" • 21 **to me** from S: not in P • 22 **specifieth** S reads "menyth" • 24 **drying** S reads "deyeng"

[CHAPTER 17] The text of Chapter 17 is based on P, collated with S and A • S has the rubric "Of the grevous bodyly threst of Criste causyd four wysys, and of his petovous coronyng, and of the most payne to a kinde lover. Seventeenth Chapter" • P's opening reads "~~The ix Revelation And~~ the xvii chapter" • 1 **drying** A reads "dryhede," S "deyng." Compare 1.23, 16.24, 23.9 • 1 **this worde that Crist said** S reads "the words of Criste" • 2 **gostly** S reads "gostly the which I shal speke of in the thirty-first chapter" • 3–4 **and for the gostely thurst was shewed as I shalle sey after** not in S • 4 **And I understode by the bodily thurste that the body had failing of moister** A reads "And I undyrstode of bodelye thyrste that the bodye hadde of faylynge of moystere," S "the which I understode was causid of failyng of moysture" • 6 **alle alon** S reads "alone" • 8 **gretenes, hardhede, and grevoushede** from S: P reads "grete hardnes and grevous" • 9 **satilde** S reads "saggid" • 9 **rasing** P reads "ransyng," S "wrangyng," but see line 14 • 11 **drying** S reads "deyande." See line 1 • 12–22 **And in the beginning . . . it fall** this passage is very different in S: "and in the begynnyng, while the flesh was fresh and bledand, the continuant sytyng of the thornys made the wounds wyde. And ferthermore I saw that the swete skyn and the tender flesh, with the heere and the blode, was al rasyd and losyd abov from the bone with the thornys where thowe it were daggyd on many pecys, as a clith that were saggand, as it wold hastely have fallen of for hevy and lose while it had kynde moysture; and that was grete sorow and drede to me, for methowte I wold not for my life a sen it fallen. How it was don I saw not, but understode it was with the sharpe thornys and the boystrous and grevous setting on of the garland onsparably and without pety." The differences could go all the way back to the holograph of *A Revelation* if material was added in the margin at this point and then inserted in different places by copyists. The passage was clearly worked over heavily • 14 **tender** P reads "terdyr," but this must be a simple error • 23 **after** S reads "sone" • 25 **that was round about** S reads "and sette abute" • 25 **so it was environed** S reads "and thus it envyronyd" • 28 **and the fleshe** S reads "of the flesh" • 29 **rumpelde** S reads "ronkyllid" • 29 **aged** S reads "akynned" • 31 **The secunde** S reads "The secund was" • 32 **The thurde is that he was hanging** S reads "The thred, hangyng" • 34 **ministrid to him** S reads "ministred to hym in al his wo and disese" • 34 **that paine** S reads "his peyne" • 36 **two paines** S reads "the paynys" • 36 **blissed** S reads "blissful" • 39 **other paines** from A/S: P reads "all other peynes" • 41 **The shewing** S reads "The which shewing" • 43 **presens** S reads "paynys" • 44 **fulle litille** S reads "but litil" • 46 **For methought my paines passed ony bodely deth** S reads "For methowte it passid bodely dethe, my paynes" • 47 **paine in helle** S reads "payne" • 48 **paines** from S: P reads "peyne" • 48–49 **to se thy love suffer** from S: P reads "to se the lover to suffer" • 49 **more then** S reads "more to me than" • 50 **sothfastly** from A/S: P reads "stedfastly"

[CHAPTER 18] The text of Chapter 18 is based on P, collated with S and A • S has the rubric "Of the spiritual martyrdom of our lady and other lovers of Criste, and how al things suffryd with hym, goode and ylle. Eighteenth Chapter" • 1 **in parte** S reads "a part of" • 1 **our lady** from A/S: P reads "our blessed lady." See textual note to 4.24 • 2 **the gretnes of her love** S reads "the gretnes of his lovyng" • 2 **mekillehede** from A/S: P reads "grettnes" • 3–4 **his creatures** S reads "creatures" • 7 **he loved** S reads "is lovid" • 7–8 **And so alle** S reads "And al" • 8 **paines more** from A/S: P reads "more payne" • 14 **and erth** S reads "the erth" • 15 **lorde** S reads "God" • 20 **two maner of people that knew him not** S reads "two manner of folke" • 22–23 **wonders and merveyles, sorowse and dredes** S reads "wonderous and mervelous sorowes and dreds" • 25 **the** added above the line • 26–27 **to worke in ther kinde** S reads "to werkyn of kynd" • 29 **noughted** (× 2) from S: P reads "payned" and "of payne." S's reading gains some weight from 20.7–8, where A/S agree on the word, and a good deal from 28.19, which refers to "[t]hat ech maner noughting that he shewde in his passion," alluding to this passage. P's "in this maner of payne" seems weak by comparison. See textual note to 27.12

[CHAPTER 19] The text of Chapter 19 is based on P, collated with S and A • S has the rubric "Of the comfortable beholdyng of the crucifyx, and how the desyre of the flesh without consent of the soule is no synne, and the flesh must be in peyne, suffring, til bothe be onyd to Criste. Nineteenth Chapter" • 1 **In this time** S reads "In this" • 1 **fro the crosse** A reads "besyde the crosse," S "up of the crosse" • 2 **behelde the crosse** A reads "lukyd uppon the crosse," S "beheld in the cross" • 3–4 **for ugging of fends** from S: A reads "botte uglynesse of feendes," P "fro drede of fendes" • 4 **reason** *a* added above the line • 7 **and either** from A: S reads "Either," P

"Here" • 9 **have bene** from A: P/S use the syncopated form of "have," reading "a bene" • 18 **sothly** from S: P reads "werely" • 19 **daunger** S reads "daming." The P scribe cancels "daunger" and includes a marginal note substituting "frelte," which reads like a tentative translation of a word the P scribe found meaningless. "Daming" is possible, either in the sense "condemning" or as meaning "judgment" (Middle English "deming"), but "daunger," a word meaning something like "reluctance" or "standoffishness" in its original, courtly and erotic context, seems the best of the available readings • 21 **in one** from S: not in P • 23 **now in wo** S reads "wo" • 24–25 **that repented** from S: P reads "that I repentyd" • 27 **sothly** from S: P reads "truly" • 29 **to our lorde Jhesu** S reads "into our lord Jesus"

[CHAPTER 20] The text of Chapter 20 is based on P, collated with S and A • S has the rubric "Of the onspekabyl passion of Criste, and of three things of the passion alway to be remembrid. Twentieth Chapter" • 2 **men** from A: P/S read "man." See lines 3–4 • 3 **might** S reads "might suffrin" • 3 **only** S reads "allonly" • 3, 4 **men** (× 2) from A/S: P reads "man" • 5–6 **No tongue may telle, or herte fully thinke, the paines that oure saviour suffered for us** from A: P/S read "might telle or fully thinke," attaching this to the previous sentence, so that the entire passage in P reads as follows: "I meene nott oonly more payne than alle man myght suffer but also that he sufferd more payne than all man of salvacion that evyr was, from the furst begynnyng in to the last day, myght telle or fully thynke, havyng regard to the worthynes of the hyghest worshyppful kyng and the shamfulle and dyspyteous peynfull deth." S is almost identical. Emendation is justified by the fact that P/S's reading makes much poorer sense than A's reading. Not only is the form of the inexpressibility topos strange: Jesus suffered more pain than all saved souls, working throughout human history, could collectively describe or think. "Havyng regard to" is meaningless in this context. A, on the other hand, builds a clear account of the extent of Christ's suffering from an explanation of the phrase "alle men" as meaning not just "anyone at all" but "all men put together"—the only useful refinement to this in P/S being the qualification "of salvacion," since the damned souls might be thought to suffer as much as Christ (see 17.47–50). The agreement between P and S in this passage must, according to this theory, be the result of confusion in an early manuscript of *A Revelation*. Perhaps the line was blotted or damaged, and P/S's reading represents a scribe's unsuccessful attempt to reconstruct it • 7 **shamfulle, dispiteous, and painful** from A: P reads "shamfulle and dyspyteous peynfull," S "shamly, dispitous, peynful" • 8 **fulliest noughted** from A/S: P reads "foulest comdempnyd" • 8 **utterliest** from A/S: P reads "utterly" • 9–10 **what he is that suffered** from S: P reads "that he is God that sufferyd," "God" having been added above the line, presumably because the P scribe's copying of "that" rather than "what" a few

words earlier rendered the statement meaningless without it • 10–11 **seeing after these other two pointes . . .
whom that he suffered** not in **S**. Eyeskip between the
two instances of "suffered" may be to blame • 12 **to
mind in parte S** reads "a part in mende" • 12 **hight** from
S: P reads "hygh" • 17 **And every mannes sorow, desolation, and anguish S** reads "every manys sorow and
desolation" • 19 **more over S** reads "more" • 23 **love in
him S** reads "love of him" • 24 **wilfully** from **S: P** reads
"wyllyngfully" • 25 **suffered it with gret joy S** reads "suffrid it with wel payeyng" • 25 **beholdeth thus S** reads
"beholdyth it thus" • 26 **of Cristes passion passe all
paines** added in the margin, after the scribe noticed she
had omitted a line through eyeskip • 27 **everlasting joy
S** reads "everlestyng passyng joyes"

[CHAPTER 21] The text of Chapter 21 is based on **P**, collated with **S** and **A** • **S** has the rubric "Of three behol-
dyngs in the passion of Criste, and how we be now
deyng in the crosse with Criste, but his chere puttyt
away al peyne. Twenty-first Chapter" • **S** and **P** begin
this chapter in different places, **P** in midsentence at
"sodenly" (line 8). This divergence in chapter divisions
between the two manuscripts may represent confusion
in their common source. The preferred chapter division
in **P** is more dramatic, separating Christ's sorrows and
his joys and literally interrupting the syntax. **S**'s makes
better rhetorical sense, respecting what was probably
intended as the peroration of Chapter 20. Here we follow **S**. See Marion Glasscoe, "Changing *Chere* and
Changing Text in the Eighth Revelation of Julian of
Norwich," *Medium Aevum* 66 (1997): 115–21, for a fuller
discussion, and compare the problems in chapter division later in the work, discussed in the textual note to
63.40 • 2 **with contrition** from **S: P** reads "with a contric-
cion" • 5 **mightes S** reads "might" • 8–9 **changed in
blissful chere S** reads "chongyd his blissfull chere" •
9 **blissful** from **A/S: P** reads "blessyd" • 11 **agrefe** from
S: A reads "gref," **P** "anguysse." See line 17 • 12 **we be now**
"be" added above the line • 15 **alle be one time S** reads
"shal be no tyme," which in context means the same •
17 **full blissed** from **S: P** reads "fulle of blysse" • 18 **sothfastly** from **S: P** reads "verely" • 19 **agreve** from **S: P**
reads "trobylle," but see its use of "agrefe" in line 17 •
20–21 **chere of passion, as he bare in this life his crosse S**
reads "time of passion as he bare in this life and his
crosse" • 21 **our kind asketh S** reads "our frelete askyth"

THE NINTH REVELATION

[CHAPTER 22] The text of Chapter 22 is based on **P**, collated with **S**, **A**, and **W**, which excerpts (with some
reordering) lines 1–5 and 12–30 • **S** has the rubric "The
Ninth revelation is of the lekyng etc., of three hevyns
and the infinite love of Criste desiring everyday to suffre
for us if he myght, althow it is not nedeful. Twenty-
Second Chapter" • 1 **good** added above the line. In **S**
the whole phrase reads "our good lord Jesus Christ" •
4–5 **And if I might suffer more, I wolde suffer more**

from **A/S/W: P** has a more complicated tense structure,
reading "And yf I myght have sufferyd more I wolde a
sufferyd more" • 13 **might have liked him better** from
A/S/W: P reads "myght haue ben lykeyd to hym better" •
15 **fulle** from **A/S/W: P** reads "wele" • 20 **all** from **S/W:**
not in **P** • 20 **harde** from **A/S/W:** not in **P** • 22, 25 **sothly**
(×2) from **S:** P reads "truly" • 23 **had** from **A/S/W: P** reads
"hath" • 26 **ne take it** not in **S** • 27 **or shuld** from **S/W:**
P reads "or shuld die" • 39 **noble, precious, and wurshipfulle dede S** reads "nobele, worshipfull dede" • 45 **it
was don as wurshipfully as Crist might do it** not in **S**,
perhaps because of eyeskip • 47 **than it was done** not in **S**

[CHAPTER 23] The text of Chapter 23 is based on **P**, collated with **S**, **A**, and **W**, which excerpts lines 14–34 • **S**
has the rubric "How Criste wil we joyen with hym gretly
in our redemption and to desire grace of hym that we
may so doe. Twenty-Third Chapter" • 1 **an** from **S: P**
reads "and," but see 22.4 • 8 **is** from **S:** not in **P** • 9 **drying S** reads "deyng." See textual note to 17.1 • 10 **was
shewed** from **S: P** reads "was shewyth." The **P** scribe has
repeatedly corrected "sheweth" to "shewed" throughout
this section, but missed this instance and another in line
35. See textual note to 3.6 for a suggested explanation •
14 **and so shall we in him** "in him" added in the margin,
next to an erasure • 15 **hath done for us, and doeth**
from **S/W: P** reads "doyth for us, and hath done" •
16 **that he did S/W** read, respectively, "that he dede" and
"that he dedde": **P** reads "that he dyed." "Dede"/"dedde"
could mean either "died" or "did" in **S/W**, but only "did"
gives good sense. Christ's death does not "begin . . . at
the swete incarnacion," and all his life, not only his
death, is "cost" and "charge" to him • 18 **enjoyeth** from
S/W: P reads "evyr joyeth" • 19 **Jhesu wille we take hede**
from **A/S: P** reads "A! Jhesu wylle we ~~take~~ hede." Presumably the scribe deleted "take" to make the sentence
more exclamatory, after her excited addition of "A!" •
25 **endelessly** from **S/W:** not in **P** • 26 **By that other
worde** from **P/A/W: S** reads "and be that other word."
There is no verb here, but see 25.3–4 for another example
of a similar construction • 26 **that** from **A/S/W:** not in
P • 26–27 **If thou arte apaid, I am apaide** from **A/S/W:**
P reads "Yf thou arte welle apayd, I am welle apayde,"
but this is not what Christ originally says at 22.3. **S** in
turn incorporates "wel" into the phrase "that I myght
apaye the" in line 28 • 28 **for** from **A/S/W: P** reads "of" •
29–30 **A glade gever** from **S/W: P** reads "Evyr a glade
geaver" • 35 **also** from **A/S: P** reads "as" • 35 **shewed**
from **S: P** reads "shewyth" • 38–40 **That other . . . endlesse blisse S** reads "Another, that he browte us up into
hevyn and made us for to be his corone and endles
blisse; another is that he hath therwith bawte us from
endless peynys of helle"

THE TENTH REVELATION

[CHAPTER 24] The text of Chapter 24 is based on **P**, collated with **S**, **A**, and **W**, which excerpts the entire chapter • **S** has the rubric "The Tenth Revelation is that our

lord Jesus shewith in love his blissid herte cloven in two, enjoyand. Twenty-Fourth Chapter" • 1 **With a glad chere** from S/W: P reads "Wyth a good chere" • 1 **enjoyenge** from S/W: P reads "with joy." The scribe seems to have found this absolute use of the participle awkward • 3 **delectable** from S/W: P reads "and delectable" • 4 **to rest** from S/W: P reads "and rest" • 6 **poure all out** from S/W: P reads "poure out" • 7 **even** from S/W: not in P • 7 **this swete enjoyeng** from S/W: P reads "hys enjoyeng" • 8 **blessed** from S/W: P reads "blyssydfulle" • 8 **as farforth as he wolde that time** not in S • 9 **strengthing the pour soule** S reads "steryng than the pure soule" • 11 **full blissefully** from S: W reads "ful blessedly," P "well blessydfully" • 11 **loved** from A/S/W: P reads "love" • 13 **See thin owne brother, thy savioure. My childe, behold and** not in S, probably omitted through eyeskip. W reorders the passage: "My derlynge, beholde and see thyn owne brother, thi sovereyne. My chylde, beholde and se thi lorde God, thy maker and thi endeles joye" • 16 **loved** from S: P/W both read "love," but on the final occasion this statement of Christ's is quoted (at line 23), P agrees with S in reading "loved," though W again reads "love" • 16 **as if he had saide** not in S, a confusing omission • 18 **wilfully** from S/W: P reads "wyllyngfully" • 19 **endlesse** from S/W: P reads "evyrlastyng" • 20 **liketh** from S/W: P reads "lykyd"

THE ELEVENTH REVELATION

[CHAPTER 25] The text of Chapter 25 is based on P, collated with S and A • S has the rubric "The Eleventh Revelation is an hey gostly shewing of his moder. Twenty-Fifth Chapter" • 1 **same chere** from A/S: P reads "chere" • 4 **wilt** S reads "wold" • 8 **shewed** from S: P reads "shewyth" • 8 **highly enjoyeng** from S: P reads "blysse and joy," avoiding the participial phrase. See textual note to 24.1 • 11–12 **speketh in love to** S reads "spekyth to" • 17 **may leern** from S: P reads "am leern" • 19 **gramercy** from A/S: P reads "grannt mercy" • 20 **likenes** from A: P reads "lykyng," S "presens" • 24–25 **and in the liking that he hath in hir and she in him** from A/S: not in P, where a line may have been left out through eyeskip between "hyr" and "hym" • 29–30 **And in this worde that Jesus saide— "Wilte thou see her?"—methought it was the most liken worde that he might have geve me of her** partly from S: P reads "myght geve," than "might have geve." This sentence is syntactically much less fluid than A's "And in that worde that Jhesu saide—'Wille thowe see hire?'—methought I hadde the maste likinge that he might hafe giffen me." In the revision, emphasis is shifted from Julian's reactions to the "worde" itself, a shift so characteristic of *A Revelation* that there can be no question of following A. Still, it is tempting to suggest that the second word, "in," should have been canceled in revising and was not. It is still just possible to read "it was" as "there was" or "there lay," as in the

translation given in the sidenote • 32 **conceived** S has the interesting reading "grevid," but see 4.26 • 33 **was** from A/S: not in P

THE TWELFTH REVELATION

[CHAPTER 26] The text of Chapter 26 is based on P, collated with S and A • S has the rubric "The Twelfth Revelation is that the lord our God is al sovereyn beyng. Twenty-Sixth Chapter" • 1 **shewed** P reads "shweyd," with the final letter altered • 3 **fullhede** from S: P reads "full," although a noun is clearly needed • 3 **homely and curteys** and S reads "homely and curtesly" •4 **Jhesu** added in the left margin • 8 **ere** from A: P reads "before," S "here" • 8 **passeth** so P and S, although "passed" seems as likely • 9 **for they were in the highest** S reads "and it arn the heyest" • 11 **can think** S reads "may willen"

THE THIRTEENTH REVELATION

[CHAPTER 27] The text of Chapter 27 is based on P, collated with S and A • S has the rubric "The Thirteenth Revelation is that our lord God wil that we have grete regard to all his deds that he hav don in the gret noblyth of al things makyng and of etc., how synne is not knowin but by the peyn. Twenty-Seventh Chapter" • 2 **that nothing** from A/S: P reads "nothyng" • 2 **me** from A/S: P reads "my" • 5 **forseeing** from S: A reads "forseande," P "forseyde." See textual note to 11.6, 8 • 9 **neded** S reads "neydyth" • 10 **and alle shalle be wele** P and S agree in adding this clause to the statement as it is reported in A, but it is later omitted in P (line 28), and Julian never alludes to the repetition of "alle shalle be wele" in her exhaustive discussion of Christ's words here, despite the obvious opportunity for developing a trinitarian analogy from the three paratactic clauses formed by inclusion of the clause. It is possible that this famous repetition began life as an excited annotation by an early reader in the margins of P and S's common ancestor • 12 **utter noughting** from A/S: P reads "uttermost trybulation," avoiding the word "noughting," as in 18.29, though it has forms of the word in 5.26–27 and 28.19 • 13–14 **alle the paines and passions of alle his creatures** from A/S: P reads "all hys paynes and passion of alle hys creatures" • 14, 15 **noughted** from A/S: P reads "trobelyd" (× 2) • 15–16 **that is to say, till we be fully noughted** from A/S: not in P, whose scribe may have missed a line in her exemplar • 19 **and with alle this** P reads "with alle thys," S "and with al these" • 22 **hath** from S: A reads "has," P "had" • 23 **that it is cause of** from A/S: P reads "that is caused therof" • 23–24 **And this paine** S reads "And thus payne" • 24 **it is somthing** from A/S: P reads "is somthyng" • 28 **soth** from S: P reads "tru" • 28 **but alle shalle be wele** S adds "and al shall be wele." P's reading is supported by A. See textual note to line 10 • 30 **a gret** from A/S: P reads "grett" • 31 **for my sinne** from S: A reads "for my synnes," P "of my synne" • 34 **make knowen** from S: P reads "opynly make and shalle be knowen," the scribe adding the "en" of "knowen" above the line. Three words may have been omitted in S, but it is hard to make sense of P's "whych pryvyte he shalle opynly make." The P scribe or a predecessor may have wanted to push the revelation of God's secrets more firmly into the future • 35–36 **endlessely have joye** S reads "endlesly joyen in our lord God," which may be right

[CHAPTER 28] The text of Chapter 28 is based on **P**, collated with **S**. **A** is relevant only in the first few lines of the chapter • S has the rubric "How the children of salvation shal be shakyn in sorowis, but Criste enjoyth wyth compassion; and a remedye agayn tribulation. Twenty-Eighth Chapter" • 3–4 **For fulle wele he loveth pepille that shalle be saved** S reads "for that wel, wel belovid people that shal be savid." The emphasis on Christ's love, despite the presence of sin in the world, continues in line 10 • 7 **shewing** not in S • 7 A, **a gret thing** S reads "A gret thing" • 9 **pite** S reads "reuth" • 11 **them** from S: P reads "him" • 11 **lacked** from S: the P scribe or a predecessor, perhaps unable to tolerate "lack" as a verb, has written "lowhyd" (humiliated). "Lacked" is parallel with the phrase "no lacke" earlier in the line • 12 **raped** from S: P reads "mokyd," perhaps to avoid the sexual connotation of "raped" • 13 **and of the pride** not in S • 14 **and heynen them** from S: not in P. This is likely the result of an eyeskip in P because of the similarity between "heynen" and "hevyn" • 16 **togeder gader** from S: P reads "gader." For the importance of "togeder" here, see 31.15 • 19 **That ech maner noughting that he shewde** S reads "That same nowtyng that was shewid" • 23 **it alle shalle be turned us to wurship** P reads "~~it~~ alle shalle ~~be~~ turned us to wurschyp," S "it shal al be turnyd to worshippe." The P scribe seems to have been confused by the phrase "turned us to wurschyp," where "us" is dative ("for us") and "to" means "into" • 24 **suffer** from S: P reads "sufferyd" • 25 **noughting** from S: P reads "trybulacion" • 26–27 **And the well beholding of this wille save us** "well" added above the line, with "doth" canceled before "save us," so that the clause originally read "And the beholdyng of thys wylle doth save us." S reads "And the beholdyng of this will save us" • 27 **sothly** from S: P reads "verely" • 28 **love** added above the line

[CHAPTER 29] The text of Chapter 29 is based on **P**, collated with **S** and **A** • S has the rubric "Adam synne was gretest, but the satisfaction for it is more plesyng to God than ever was the synne harmfull. Twenty-Ninth Chapter" • 4 **durste** P reads "druste," probably a scribal error • 4 **wherwith** from A/S: P reads "wherwith that" • 7 **to** from A/S: P reads "into" • 12 **in this teching** from A/S: P reads "and in thys techyng" • 13 **sithen** from A/S: P reads "sythen that" • 14 **know** added above the line

[CHAPTER 30] The text of Chapter 30 is based on **P**, collated with **S** and **A** • S has the rubric "How we should

joye and trusten in our savior Jesus, not presumyng to know his privy counsell. Thirtieth Chapter" • 1 **He gave me** from A/S: P reads "He gave" • 2 **open and clere and fair** from A/S: P reads "opyn, clere, feyer" • 6 **joyeng** from A/S: P reads "and joyeng" • 9 **thus may we sey, enjoyeng** from A/S: P reads "thus may we see and enjoye," another instance of the scribe's resistance to using the present participle. See textual note to 24.1 • 13 **witte** from A/S: P reads "know," but uses "wytt" in this sense at line 16 • 15 **mekille** from A/S: P reads "gretly that" • 18 **to wille to be like to them** A, P, and S all differ here: A reads "to willene to be lyke to hym," S "to willen like to hem," P "that oure wylle be lyke to them." In P, the verb "wille" is avoided, but P's reading retains the probable sense of the passage best. A's "hym" may be a misreading of "hem," while the omission of "to be" in S simplifies the thought • 20–21 **we shalle onely enjoye . . . and trust in him for alle thing** S truncates this: "we shal trosten and enjoyen only in our savior blisful Jesus for althynge" • 20 **shalle** from A/S: P reads "shulde"

[CHAPTER 31] The text of Chapter 31 is based on **P**, collated with **S** and **A** • S has the rubric "Off the longyng and the spiritual threst of Criste, which lestyth and shall lesten til domysday; and be the reason of his body he is not yet full gloryfyed ne al unpassible. Thirty-First Chapter" • 3 **wille . . . shalle**, from S: P reads "shalle . . . wylle," while A places "wille . . . schalle" before "maye" and "can." It is clear from the exposition of the saying in lines 5–9 that S's readings are to be preferred • 9 **oning** from A/S: P reads "comyng" • 10 **God will be enclosed** from A/S: P reads "God wylle that we be enclosyd," but the next sentence shows that the subject is Christ's need, not human need • 13 **some** from S: not in P, but necessary to the sense • 15 **thurste: a love-longing to have us all togeder, hole in him to his endlesse blisse** from S, with the exception of "endlesse": P reads "thurste and love longyng of us all togeder here in hym to oure endlesse blysse," which makes much less good sense • 19 **which very endlesse blesse** S reads "which endles blis" • 21 **is** added above the line • 25 **the ninth** S reads "the ninth revelation" • 29 **And** originally "A," with *nd* added above the line • 34 **verely** from S: P reads "truly," but "verely" later in the sentence • 38–39 **And though he have longing and pitte, they ben sondry propertees** S plausibly reads "and, thow, longyng and pite arn two sundry properties." See 74.23 for this use of "though"

[CHAPTER 32] The text of Chapter 32 is based on **P**, collated with **S** and, for a few lines only, **A** • S has the rubric "How althyng shal be wele and scripture fulfillid. And we must stedfastly holdyn us in the faith of holy chirch, as is Crists wille. Thirty-Second Chapter" • 1 **Alle maner a thing shalle be wele** S reads "Althyng shal be wele" • 3 **maner of understonding** S reads "understondyng" • 10 **sorowing and morning** from S: P reads "sorow and morne" • 15 **hede** from **S**: not in **P** • 17 **wele** **S** adds "etcetera" • 17–18 **the workes** from **A/S**: **P** reads "workes" • 20 **what the deed shall be S** reads "whan the dede shall be" • 21 **whan it shalle be done S** reads "whan it is don" • 21–24 **The goodnesse . . . how it shalle be done** not in **S**, either left out because of eyeskip between the two occurrences of "shalle be [or perhaps "is"] done" or because the passage is so audacious theologically. **S** and **P** have an unusual number of disagreements in this chapter, and **S** an unusual number of omissions • 25 **peesed** from **S**: **P** reads "peesable," but "esed . . . and peesed" seems preferable. **P** has "peesed" at 49.36, "pesible" at 55.36 • 26 **let us of true enjoyeng S** reads "let us of trewth, enjoyeng" • 31 **mening S** reads "merveland" • 35, 36 **man** (× 2) from **S**: **P** reads "meny," "many" • 38 **ende** from **S**: **P** reads "ande" • 41–42 **That that is unpossible P** has "that is unpossible," with a squiggle above the line after "that," apparently a highly abbreviated attempt to write a second "that." **S** reads "that is impossible." "That that" in the sense "that which" occurs elsewhere in *A Revelation,* and makes better grammatical sense here • 48 **But what the dede shal be** not in **S** • 49 **no** added above the line

[CHAPTER 33] The text of Chapter 33 is based on **P**, collated with **S** • **S** has the rubric "Al dampnyd soule be dispised in the syte of God as the devil. And these revelations withdraw not the feith of holy church, but comfortith. And the more we besy to know Gods privites the less we knowen. Thirty-Third Chapter" • 1 **full** from **S**: **P** more cautiously reads "som" • 2 **take prefe S** interestingly reads "maken privy," to make secret or personal • 6–7 **for ought . . . right nought S** reads "for my desire I coude of this ryte nowte" • 9 **ende P** reads "endyng," **S** "enden." See textual note to 4.1 • 12 **shewde S** reads "made" • 15 **fourth S** reads "fifth" • 15 **and** from **S**: not in **P** • 17 **saw his paines S** reads "sen hym in peyne" • 19 **saving tho that were converted by grace S** reads "savyng those that converten be grace," its use of the present tense here just possibly implying the sinister notion of Jewish blood debt developed from Matt. 27:25: that generations of Jews born after the Crucifixion and not responsible for it might be damned for their surrogate responsibility for Christ's death • 24 **For he wille . . . he shalle do** not in **S**, perhaps omitted through eyeskip • 28 **sothly** from **S**: **P** reads "verely" • 29 **knowing S** reads "knowing therof"

[CHAPTER 34] The text of Chapter 34 is based on **P**, collated with **S** and **A** • **S** has the rubric "God shewyth the privityes necessarye to his lovers, and how they plese God mekyl that receive diligently the prechyng of holy church. Thirty-Fourth Chapter" • 2 **therto belonging S** reads "that longen therto." See 7.50 for this use of "belonging" • 3–4 **which himselfe shewed . . . which** not in **S**, another instance of eyeskip • 6–7 **They are . . . but not only . . . but they are . . .** in **S**, the sentence structure is rendered differently: "It arn . . . not only . . . but it

arn . . ." • 8 **open to us himselfe S** reads "more opyn to us." **P**'s reading better captures the passage's emphasis on revelation • 10 **fulle curtesly oure good lorde wille shew us what it is S** reads "ful curtesly wil our lord will shewen us and that is this." Even if "and that is this" is treated as a separate clause, the passage makes poor sense • 12–13 **mightly and mekely and wisely P** reads "myghtly and wysely," **A** "myghttelye and mekelye and wyrschipfullye," **S** "mytyly and mekely and wilfully." A triad of some sort is likely to be preferable, but at least two of the three choices for the last term are attractive; the least so is "worshipfully," not otherwise recommended as an attitude toward the church anywhere in the manuscripts of *A Revelation.* The grouping "mightely, wisely, and mekely" occurs at 8.34 in a context similar to this, but "mightly, wisely, and wilfully" also occurs at 19.26–27 and 43.13 • 13–14 **For he it is, holy church S** reads "For it is his holy church," but Julian's understanding of the church, as in **A**, is that it literally corresponds to the body of Christ. See especially Chapter 31 • 15 **ende S** reads "leryd" (taught), but this seems to repeat "he is the teching" in line 14 • 16 **and shall be knowen** added in the margin • 17 **sothly** from **S**: **P** reads "truly" • 18 **that** from **A/S**: **P** reads "as"

[CHAPTER 35] The text of Chapter 35 is based on **P**, collated with **S** and **A** • **S** has the rubric "How God doith al that is good, and suffrith worshipfully al by his mercy, the which shal secyn whan synne is no longer suffrid. Thirty-Fifth Chapter" • 4 **not taught P** reads "nott ~~the~~ taught" • 6 **sheweth** from **A/S** (**A** in the form "shewes"): **P** reads "shewyd" • 10 **not be glad** from **A**: **P** reads "nott by glad," **S** "not only be glad" • 10–11 **nothing . . . no manner of thing** from **A/S**: **P** reads "any thyng . . . any manner thyng," without the common Middle English double negative • 17 **rightfulle** from **S**: **P** reads "ryghtfully" • 19 **eville S** reads "ony evil" • 21 **and his mervelous mekenesse S** reads "in his mervelous mekeness" • 26 **hath ordained P** reads "hath ordeyne," **S** "ordeyned" • 28 **blisseful** from **S**: **P** reads "blessyd" • 32–33 **in wurkinge** from **S**: **P** reads "wurkynge" • 37 **joyes** from **S**: **P** reads "joy" • 39 **wele paide S** reads "wel plesyd," but the allusion is to Christ's speech in 22.1–2: "Arte thou well apaid that I suffered for thee?"

[CHAPTER 36] The text of Chapter 36 is based on **P**, collated with **S** • **S** has the rubric "Of another excellent dede that our lord shal don, which be grace may be known a party here. And how we shuld enjoyen in the same. And how God yet doith myracles. Thirty-Sixth Chapter" • 2–4 **and it shall be wurshipfulle . . . God himselfe shall do it** not in **S**, probably as a result of eyeskip, since "hymselfe shalle do it" occurs three times in three sentences • 2 **by me P** reads "by hym," the scribe not realizing that "by me" means "on my behalf," but giving "by me" correctly in line 28 • 6 **hevenly S** reads "heyly" • 9 **alle his lovers S** reads "his lovers" • 12 **holy** from **S**: **P** reads "holy seyntes," apparently reflecting uneasiness with the use of "holy" as a noun. See textual note to 41.28 • **13 understonde** P reads "unstonde" • **15–16 than for to come** S reads "for to come" • **24 shall** from S: P reads "shuld" • **28 this** s added above the line • **30 and by me it shalle be done** not in S • **31–32 And this shalle be the highest joy that may be beholden of the dede: "That God himselfe shalle do it"** first "the" from S, whose version of this sentence reads "And this shal be the heyest joye that may ben, to beholden the dede that God hymselfe shal don." P's reading gives the sentence the structure of a text and accompanying gloss: the same structure as is used in the previous two sentences. S's version may be a rationalization of the sentence after a key word (such as the final "it") had dropped out in the process of transmission, rendering it meaningless • **35 of noughting thiselfe** adapted from S, which reads "to nowten thyself": P reads "of knowyng thyselfe," characteristically avoiding "nought" as a verb. See textual note to 18.29 • **38 calleth** S reads "clepyth." See textual note to 14.3–4 • **39 Let me alone** S cryptically reads "Lete be al thi love," referring, presumably, to love for the damned • **41 perced therwith** S reads "aperceyvid therein" • **46 be knowen soner** S reads "be don sooner," but see lines 47–48 • **49 farthermore** S reads "moreover" • **49–50 and shewing** not in S • **51 fele** from S: P reads "full," but "many and fele" is formulaic • **52 shall do** from S: P reads "shall," which is added in the margin • **53 trobil** S reads "tribulation" • **54–55 make us to drede God, crying for helpe** adapted from S, which reads the infinitive "cryen" for the participle "crying": P reads "make us to cry to God for helpe" • **55 And gret miracles come after** S reads "Myracles commen after that"

[CHAPTER 37] The text of Chapter 37 is based on P, collated with S and A • S has the rubric "God kepyth his chosen ful sekirly althowe thei synne, for in these is a godly will that never assayed to synne. Thirty-Seventh Chapter" • **1 my** from A/S: not in P • **9–10 of gostly keping** S reads "and gostly kepyng," but in Christ's words to Julian, "sekerly" modifes "kepe." The certainty of Christ's preservation of the soul is a major theme in *A Revelation* • **11 sekernesse of keping** S reads "sekirnes and kepyng," P "suernesse of kepyng" • **14 in** P reads "in in" • **14 assented** from A/S: P reads "assentyth." See textual note to 3.6 • **16 will** added above the line

[CHAPTER 38] The text of Chapter 38 is based on P, collated with S and A • S has the rubric "Synne of the chosen shall be turnyd to joye and worship. Exemple of David, Peter, and John of Beverley. Thirty-Eighth Chapter" • **1 Also** from A/S: P reads "And" • **2 right** added in the margin • **3–9 Right . . . worshipes** we have taken the entire passage from S, except that we read "after as the sinne" in line 5 for S's "after their." P reads "Ryght as dyverse synnes be ponysschyd with dyvers paynes after that it be grevous, ryght so shalle they be rewardyd with dyvers joyes in hevyn for theyr victories, after as the

synne have ben paynfulle and sorowfulle to the soule in erth. For the soule that shalle come to hevyn is so precyous to God, and the place so wurshypfulle, that the goodnes of God sufferyth nevyr that soule to synne fynally that shalle come ther. But what synners they are that so shal be rewarded is made knowen in holy church, in erth, and also in heaven by overpassing worshypes." The passage is a major crux, but it seems probable that in P or its exemplar adjustments have been made here out of theological caution. A scribe has perhaps misunderstood "the goodnes of God suffereth never that soule to sinne that shalle come ther" out of context, as an assertion that those who go to heaven are sinless. In S, the whole statement means: "God never allows a soul destined for heaven to sin without rewarding that sin," which is Julian's claim in the chapter as a whole. The earlier addition of the phrase "for theyr victories" equally alters the argument, this time by understanding the "they" that are the subject of the sentence as the saved, not as their sins. P's final sentence skillfully borrows from the rest of the chapter, but is still a relatively pedestrian transition to it, in comparison with the logic and daring of S • **11 merely** added in the margin • **13 Thomas of Inde** from A: P reads "thomas and Jude," S "those of Inde" • **19 hende** from S: P reads "kynd," probably an attempt at translating an obsolete word. See 10.81 for P's one use of the word • **21 full high saint** S adds "in hevyn" • **23 he** from S: not in P • **23 mekille** from S: P reads "gretly" • **28 sinned or fallen** S reads "fallen" • **28 soth** from S: P reads "tru"

[CHAPTER 39] The text of Chapter 39 is based on P, collated with S and A • S has the rubric "Of the sharpnes of synne and the godenes of contrition. And how our kynd lord will not we dispair for often fallyng. Thirty-Ninth Chapter" • **2 forbeteth** from A/S: P reads "to betyth" • **2 and** from A: P reads "or" • **2 forbreketh** from A: P reads "tobrekyth." "And alle forbreketh him" is not in S • **2–3 him . . . him . . . his . . . he . . . himselfe . . . he** A has plural pronouns here • **2 noyeth** from S: A reads "noghtes," P "purgyth." A's reading is plausible, but "noyeth" is used in 76.15, in a passage that may allude to this one, while P's does not elsewhere render "nought" as "purge" • **4 as it were to sinke** S reads "as to synken" • **11 mekille** from S: P reads "gretly" • **11 meekely taken** P reads "meekely takyth"; S omits. This unsupported emendation seems necessary to make grammatical sense of the sentence • **13–14 that we be cast in, gostly and bodely** S reads "that wil be cast in, bodily and gostly" • **15–16 for we se that** S reads "because" • **18 And also . . . grace** not in S, presumably because of eyeskip • **19 that** S reads "Than" • **20 even with saintes** S reads "even hey seynts" • **24 heled** P and S both omit A's "and namlye of synnes that ere dedely in the selfe" • **27 lord** from A/S: not in P • **28 no degre** from S: P's reading, "any degre," rationalizes the characteristic Middle English double negative • **31 undertake** S reads "underfongyn," A "resayfe." Compare the similar divergences in

2.19 • 32 **alle shame turne S** reads "shame be turnyd" •
33 **more from A/S:** not in **P** • 38 **mede P/S** both read
"nede," but "mede" fits the context better, especially if **S**'s
"him," rather than **P**'s "them," is taken as the reading in
the following line (see next note). With "nede," the sentence as it is in **P** makes local sense: we need all the more
to rely on "oure everlasting keper" (line 37) because we
give "oure enmes" (line 38) "occasion" to attack us "by
oure falling"; **S**'s reading of "him" makes more difficult,
but still just plausible sense. But the reading "mede"
makes the sentence into a statement about the relationship between sin and reward, summing up the entire
teaching on this topic in Chapters 38–39, besides making
easier grammatical sense: "And our reward is all the
greater by the extent to which we give him the opportunity to reward us by our falling" • 39 **for we geve him**
from **S:** **P** reads "for we geve thym," with the initial *t*
added in the margin. This suggests the word was "hym"
in **P**'s exemplar

[CHAPTER 40] The text of Chapter 40 is based on **P,** collated with **S, A,** and in one short passage (lines 16–20)
W • **S** has the rubric "Us nedyth to longyn in love with
Jesus, eschewyng synne for love. The vyleness of synne
passith al peynes. And God lovith wol tenderly us while
be in synne, and so us nedyth to doe our neybor. Forti-
eth Chapter" • 2 **oure sinne S** reads "synne" • 5–6 **desyer
to amending** from **S:** **P** reads "desyer amendyng," making "amendyng" begin a new clause. This is possible, but
it leaves "desyer" vague and implies that the soul can
amend itself, without the Holy Spirit's aid • 6 **mightes**
from **S:** **P** reads "myght." See 21.5 and 26.9 for the phrase
"alle my mights" meaning "all the powers of my soul" •
8 **soth** from **S:** **P** reads "true" • 9–10 **frendfulle wellcoming** from **S:** **P** reads "frendfully wellcomyng," but "frendfulle" here needs to be an adjective, not an adverb • 10
seyeng thus: "My dere darling" **S** reads "sayand swetely
thus: 'My derlyng'" • 12 **my loving** from **S:** **P** reads "me
lovyng," but the possessive "my" seems preferable •
16 **understond** from **S/W:** **P** reads "understode." The
shift to the present tense is probably correct, since the
rest of the chapter consists of direct exhortation of the
reader • 16 **sothly** from **S:** **P** reads "verely" • 19 **ever S**
reads "evermore" • 23 **soth** from **S:** **P** reads "tru" •
25 **sothly** from **S:** **P** reads "truly" • 25 **For the same tru
love S** reads "of the same trew love," extending the previous sentence • 26 **techeth us alle this comfort** from **S:** **P**
reads "touchyth us alle by hys blessyd comfort," which
upsets the parallelism of the sentence and looks like a
reconstruction of an illegible passage in the exemplar •
27 **hate** added above the line, which originally read "that
we shalle syn only for love" • 31 **and** from **A/S:** **P** reads
"than," perhaps as a result of an attempt to make sense
of the syntax • 34 **hateth no helle P** reads "hatyth no
payne," **S** "hath no helle." A crux that needs to be read in
the light of a companion passage, 76.6, where the question whether hell is to be hated is clearly at issue, and

which we take to be an allusion to this sentence. **S**'s
reading is possible, but **P**'s "hatyth no payne" looks like
a theologically wary response to an exemplar that contained the stronger "hateth no helle," like the companion passage. A few lines earlier, the work states that "we
shalle hate sin only for love" (lines 26–27), clearly implying that hell is not worthy of hatred. A third passage, at
63.11–12, adds helpfully that "sinne is wurse . . . than hell
without ony liknesse" • 34–35 **for alle . . . but sinne** not
in **S,** presumably omitted as a result of eyeskip between
the two occurrences of the word "sinne" • 40 **be** added
above the line • 44 **this word** from **A/S:** **P** reads "these
wordes"

THE FOURTEENTH REVELATION

[CHAPTER 41] The text of Chapter 41 is edited from **P,**
collated with **S** and **W** (which includes substantial
excerpts of Chapters 41–44) and **A** • **S** has the rubric
"The Fourteenth Revelation is as afornseyd, etc. It is
impossible we shuld pray for mercy and want it. And
how God will we alway pray thow we be drey and bar-
ryn, for that prayer is to him acceptabil and plesante.
Forty-First Chapter" • 1 **prayer** from **P/W: A/S** read
"prayers" • 2 **rightfulle prayer** from **P/W: S** reads "ryt-
fulnes." See 1.41 • 6 **in** from **A/S/W: P** reads "by" •
9–10 **and thou besekest it!** from **S: P** reads "and thou
sekyst it," **A** "And if thowe beseke it," **W** "and thou besekist it," although in a context where the order of two
clauses is reversed. Possible to read as beginning the
next sentence: "If you ask for it"—as do Colledge and
Walsh in *A Book of Showings,* under the influence of **A**'s
"And if thowe beseke." However, the interpretations of
the clause in lines 12–14, where it is linked with Christ's
"full gret plesance and endlesse mede," and in 43.9–11,
where it expresses God's gratitude, make it clear that the
clause is an exclamation. Rather than express a hypothesis ("if"), the conjunction "and" suggests inevitability
("and so"): an inevitability in the relationship between
God's activities in generating prayer and human prayer
itself, with which much of the next few chapters is effectively concerned • 10 **beseking** from **A/S/W: P** reads
"sekyng" • 12 **fifth P/A/S/W** all read "furst," but "reson"
here means "clause," and the clause "and thou besekest
it" is the fifth clause of Christ's speech, the first four having been dealt with in the previous sentence, which
describes "the furst reson, with the thre that folowe."
The unusual joint error may be coincidence: "first" and
"fifth" look similar (the medieval long *s* [ʃ] looks like an
f), and the scribe of **A** and that of the manuscript from
which the Long Text manuscripts ultimately derive
could have made the same mistake. But the error could
go back to the copy of *A Vision* used in the writing of *A
Revelation* • 13 **besekest** from **S/W: A/P** read "beseke" •
15 **unpossible** from **W: S** reads "impossible," **P** "unpossible thyng." See, e.g., 32.42 for **P**'s use of this word •
17 **himselfe hath** from **S/W: P** reads "hymselfe he hath" •
19–20 **the goodnesse and grace that he doeth to us, but**

his **proper goodnesse** S reads "Godis goodness" • 20 **sothfastly** from S/W: P reads "verely" • 24 **trew, gracious** from W: P reads "trew and gracious," S "new, gracious." See line 45 • 28 **holy** from S: P reads "holy seyntes," W "holy company." Disagreement between P and W suggests that both reflect an uneasiness about the use of "holy" as a noun, though see 63.6 ("holy") and 33.10 ("holen") • 29 **undertake** S/W read "underfong," but see textual note to 2.19 • 33 **blissful** from S: P reads "blessyd" • 33 **interly** P reads "interly inwardly," the second word having presumably begun life as a gloss on the first: S reads "inderly" • 35 **Pray interly: though thou fele nought** not in S, probably because of eyeskip • 35 **interly** P again reads "interly inwardly" • 41 **fele** from S: P reads "felle" • 44 **wher he seyth** S reads "aforn this word" • 45 **true, inward knowing** from P/W: S again reads "new inward knowing." See line 24 • 47 **stereth** from S: P/W both read "steryd," but a shift to the past tense seems unlikely here, given the solid use of the present tense elsewhere in the paragraph • 48 **seyth** from S/W: P reads "sey" • 53 **his** added above the line

[CHAPTER 42] The text of Chapter 42 is edited from P, collated with S and W • S has the rubric "Off three thyngs that longyn to prayer. And how we shuld pray. And of the goodnes of God, that supplyeth alway our imperfection and febilnes whan we do that longyth to us to do. Forty-Second Chapter" • 9–10 **he shalle make it so** from P/W: S reads "we shall make it so," which seems to misrepresent the argument here • 12 **mekil** note P's use of this word, for which it generally reads "much," as does W here • 14 **grounde in whom** S reads "ground on whom," W "grounde hymselfe of whom." P's reading is defensible. Compare line 24, where all three manuscripts read "in this grounde" • 17 **but mercy** from S/W: P reads "but yf mercy" • 25 **wonning** from S/W: P reads "dwellyng" • 27 **thre thinges** S reads "the thyngs" • 39, 51 **det** (× 2) from S: P reads "dewte." See 47.1: "Two pointes longe to our soule by det"; also 60.24, 53 • 39 **so** added above the line • 45 **all creatures in this life** S reads "cretures" • 46 **tru longing** S reads "wel longyng" • 47 **Failing of oure blisse** from S: P reads "Saworyng or seyng oure blysse." The alternatives are perhaps two attempts to transcribe a word the scribe could not read. S gives better sense • 48 **mind** from S: P reads "menyng" • 49 **And thus . . . trust** not in S, presumably omitted because of eyeskip between the two occurrences of "trust" • 52 **when we do it** S reads "whan we have don it" • 52 **soth** from S: P reads "true" • 54 **I am grounde** from S: P reads "I am the grounde," "the" added above the line. See 41.8 • 56 **wekenesse** from S: P reads "wyckydnesse"

[CHAPTER 43] The text of Chapter 43 is based on P, collated with S, in some passages A, and for lines 15–47 W • S has the rubric "What prayor doth, ordeynyd to God will. And how the goodnes of God hath gret lekyng in

the deds that he doth be us, as he wer beholden to us, werkyng althyng ful swetely. Forty-Third Chapter" • 11 **beholden** from A/S: P reads "beholdyng" • 14 **wille doen** from A: S reads "shal don," P "wyll have doen." The use of the passive in P here seems inconsistent with Julian's emphasis on the immediacy of God's activity in answering prayers • 17 **alle oure mightes** P is here supported by W: S reads "al our myte," but the reference is to all the powers of the soul • 19 **is oned** from W: P reads "is onyd," with "to be" added in the margin; S reads "it is onyd." The correction in P incorrectly assumes that "onyd" refers to mystical union • 22 **it** from S/W: P reads "she," an example of the preference in P for female pronouns for the soul • 22 **by grace** S reads "be his grace" • 24 **abling** from A/S/W: P reads "unablynes" • 25 **itselfe** from A/W: P reads "herselfe," S "hymself" • 25 **by unrest** from A/S: P reads "by her unrest"; W omits • 25 **himselfe** from A/S/W: P reads "herselfe" • 26 **he** from A/S/W: P reads "she" • 27 **alike** from A/S/W: P reads "oonlyke" • 30 **into** from S/W: P reads "to" • 33 **wene or thinke** from S: P/W read "mene or thynke," but "wene" (imagine) gives better sense here than "mene" (intend). P has "wene" in 40.4 and 61.13. A copyist could easily have mistaken one word for the other • 34 **enjoying** from S: W reads "and enjoyng," P "and enjoye," avoiding this use of the participle. See textual note to 24.1 • 35 **entende to his wonning** adapted from W, which reads either "wonyng" or "wowyng": P reads "entende to his motion," S "entred to his wonyng." There is some confusion here, with the P scribe translating a word something like "movynge." "Wowyng" (wooing) is a plausible reading in this erotic context, even though Julian does not elsewhere use the term. However, 81.9–11 uses a cluster of terms related to lines 33–39 here, among them the word "wonneth": "Mervelous and solempne is the place where the lorde wonneth [P "dwellyth"], and therfore he wille that we redely intend to his gracious touching" • 36 **And thus shalle we** S reads "And then shal we" • 41 **had** from S/W: P reads "hyd" • 41 **him** from S/W: not in P • 43 **than** from S: P reads "ther," W "thus" • 47 **as** from S/W: P reads "and"

[CHAPTER 44] The text of Chapter 44 is based on P, collated with S and, in lines 6–17, W • S has the rubric "Of the properties of the trinite. And how mannys soule, a creature, hath the same properties, doyng that that it was made for: seyng, beholdyng, and mervelyng his God, so by that it semyth as nowte to the selfe. Forty-Fourth Chapter" • 2 **lastingly** from S: P reads "duryngly." Compare 57.4, "lastyngly withoute ony stinting," probably an allusion to this passage. "Duryngly" does not occur elsewhere in any of the manuscripts • 4 **blisseful soule of our lady** S reads "soule of our blisful lady" • 7 **mervelous, holy delight** from W: S reads "holy mervelous delyte," P "mervelous delyght" • 9 **For God is** S reads "for he is" • 10 **mans** from S/W: P reads "a mans" • 15 **the clernesse and clennesse** from W: S reads "the clertye and the clenes," **P** "the bryghtnes and clernesse" • 16 **beknowen** from **S/W**: **P** reads "know"

[CHAPTER 45] The text of Chapter 45 is based on **P**, collated with **S** • **S** has the rubric "Of the ferme and depe jugement of God and the variant jugement of man. Forty-Fifth Chapter" • 3 **demeth S** reads "jugith," after reading "demyth" in line 1 • 4 **sheweth** from **S**: **P** reads "shewed," but a tense switch seems unlikely here • 11–12 **high, endlesse love S** reads "hey, endless life," but it is love that assigns no blame to sinners here • 13 **assigne** from **S**: **P** reads "assignys" • 13–14 **this was** from **S**: **P** reads "theyse were," presumably referring to both "domes." But, as the passage as a whole makes clear, only the "fair, swete dome" of "Goddes rightfulhede" is "swete and delectable" • 15 **understonde P** reads "understondyng," **S** "understond," but the past participle is needed here • 17 **behoveth S** reads "behovyd," but the present tense parallels "be" (**S** "arn") in the next sentence • 19 **advice and desyer S** reads "desir" • 20 **me** from **S**: **P** reads "we" • 24 **herein techeth** from **S**: **P** reads "here in erth." **P**'s scribe may have misunderstood "herein" in her exemplar and then rationalized the sense • 24 **sothly** from **S**: **P** reads "verely" • 25 **wey** added above the line • 27 **mistely S** reads "mytyly." For the "misty" nature of the "example," see 51.60 • 28 **stond** from **S**: **P** reads "stode," perhaps a result of scribal discomfort with the implication that Julian still does not understand her revelation, although the sentence as a whole is in the present and future tenses • 28 **lives ende S** reads "end" • 31 **knowing and understonding S** reads "understondyng" • 32 **failings** from **S**: **P** reads "felynges," but the gesture of humility implied by **S**'s reading seems more probable at the end of this particularly speculative chapter. See also 47.24

[CHAPTER 46] The text of Chapter 46 is based on **P**, collated with **S** • **S** has the rubric "We cannot knowen our self in this life but be feith and grace, but we must know ourself synners. And how God is never wreth, being most nere the soule, it kepyng. Forty-Sixth Chapter" • 2–3 **but in our faith . . . what oureselfe is** not in **S**, presumably because of eyeskip between the two occurrences of "what oureselfe is" • 9 **alle manner of wo and paine S** reads "manner of peyne and wo" • 11–12 **in which . . . oure God** not in **S**, again possibly because of eyeskip • 24 **sothfastly** from **S**: **P** reads "verely" • 25–26 **For he is God, he is good, he is truth, he is love, he is pees. And his might, his wisdom, his charite, and his unite suffereth him not to be wroth S** is somewhat truncated here, reading "For he is God, good, life, trueth, love, peas, his charite, and his unite suffrith hym not to be wroth" • 25 **And** added in the margin • 31 **so** not in **S** • 34 **sothly** from **S**: **P** reads "verely"

[CHAPTER 47] The text of Chapter 47 is based on **P**, collated with **S** • **S** has the rubric "We must reverently

mervelyn and mekly suffren, ever enjoyand in God. And how our blyndhede, in that we se not God, is cause of synne. Forty-Seventh Chapter" • 1 **longe** from **S** (in the form "longen"): **P** reads "longyng" • 3 **witte** from **S**: **P** reads "know" • 6 **should** from **S**: **P** reads "shalle," but in context the statement is conditional • 10 **noughte** from **S**: **P** reads "oughte," characteristically avoiding a Middle English double negative construction • 11 **working of mercy S** reads "werks of mercy" • 13–14 **frailte and uncunning** from **S**: **P** reads "sympylnesse and uncunnyng." The **P** scribe once records "frailte" (62.1) and twice "freelte" (74.2, 79.27), but on another occasion, at 49.27, finds the spelling of the word in its exemplar too opaque and rather desperately translates "pronyte." "Sympylnesse" is a possible reading here, but although the word "simple" has various connotations through *A Revelation*, the state of simplicity is not elsewhere treated as a cause of sin • 17 **stering no sorowing S** reads "steryng the yernyng," perhaps an error for the plausible "steryng ne yernyng" • 24 **failing** from **S**: **P** reads "felyng" • 26 **that that** from **S**: **P** reads "that" • 34 **no** from **S**: not in **P**, again avoiding the double negative (see line 10) • 35 **contrariousnes S** reads "contrariout," **P** "contraryous," but the sentence requires a noun • 36 **continuance S** reads "contrivans," a word that occurs nowhere else in the manuscripts. "Continuance" alludes back to "continuant" in line 33 • 37 **tempested** from **S**: **P** reads "temptyd," but Julian is talking about suffering, not the urge to sin. See textual note to 2.23

[CHAPTER 48] The text of Chapter 48 is based on **P**, collated with **S** • **S** has the rubric "Off mercy and grace and their propertyes. And how we shall enjoy that ever we suffrid wo patiently. Forty-Eighth Chapter" • 1 **wonning** from **S**: **P** reads "dwellyng." See note to 54.3 • 3 **and maketh it buxom, and accordeth it to God S** has these clauses in reverse order • 4 **in this life S** reads "here in this lif" • 5 **on mannes perty S** reads "in mannys partie" • 7 **of** from **S**: **P** reads "ef" • 8 **in oure party S** reads "on our partie" • 9 **wrath S** reads "wretchid," but "wrath" seems the stronger reading in context • 13 **all one in love P** reads "all love in love," **S** "alone in love." Both manuscript readings could derive from the phrase "all one," either by conflation of "all" and "one" or by *n/u* confusion in "one." For examples of similar phrases, see 9.4 ("alle one in love"), 63.8–9 ("one in love"), 76.23–24 ("one in his loving") • 21 **departeth S** reads "cummyth." For "deperte," see, e.g., 54.2 • 24, 25 **moderhode, ryal lordshippe S** adds "the" before both these terms • 27 **with mercy** not in **S** • 29 **plentuouse** from **S**: **P** reads "plentuousnesse" • 31 **wurshippeful S** reads "worship"; **P** adds "full" above the line. "Full" seems necessary to the sense • 32 **blisseful** from **S**: **P** reads "blyssyd" • 34 **wise** the **P** scribe writes this word twice and then deletes the second • 35 **and blisse overpassing** the **P** scribe initially wrote "wurschyp, blysse. And ovyrpassyng," then canceled "And," adding a marginal "and" before "blysse" •

40–41 **is to slake and waste oure wrath** from S: P reads "~~is to~~ slaketh and wastyth oure wrath," the scribe adding the "yth" of "wastyth" above the line. Perhaps the P scribe found her first attempt incomprehensible, having written "slaketh" for "slake," and reconstructed the passage around this mistake

[CHAPTER 49] The text of Chapter 49 is based on P, collated with S • S has the rubric "Our lif is growndid in love, withoute the which we perish. But yet God is never wroth, but in our wreth and synne he mercifully kepith us, and tretith us to peace, rewarding our tribulations. Forty-Ninth Chapter" • 1 **this** from S: P reads "it" • 2 **beholden** from S: P reads "beholdyng," but the past participle is clearly needed here • 4 **grounded** the final letter is written above the line • 6 **and** from S: not in P • 8 **contraries** from S: P reads "contrarioese" • 9 **it behoveth nedes to be** from S: P reads "it behovyth us nedys to beleve." P's reading makes of the unity of God's love a matter of perception, where the chapter as a whole presents it as a matter of fact. For other examples of "behoveth nedes to be" see 46.4, 51.46–47, 56.22 • 10 **in one love** S reads "on in love" • 10 **contrariouse** from S: P reads "contrary," but has "contraryouse" at line 22 • 12 **sothly** from S: P reads "truly" • 13 **touch** from S: P reads "whyle," but the point seems to be that even a moment of God's anger, if it could exist, would undo creation • 17 **mercifully** S reads "manner full" • 19 **sekerly** from S: P reads "truly" • 26 **deseses** added in the margin after a word like "dysses" was crossed out in the text • 26–27 **falleth to oure blindnesse and oure frailte** from S: P reads "fallyng into oure blyndnesse and oure pronyte." Perhaps under the influence of the exemplum of the lord and servant, told in Chapter 51, the P scribe misunderstands the verb "fall" as "fall down" rather than "befall" • 27 **sekerly** from S: P reads "suer and" • 30 **pesible** from S: P reads "plesabil," but S makes better sense, in light of the other references to peace and love as a pair in this passage. P uses "pesible" in 55.36 • 36 **it is truly peesed in the selfe** from S: P reads "she is truly peesyd in herselfe," another example of the preference in P for the feminine gender for the soul. However, "she" here is written in the margin, standing in for an "it" that has been crossed out: a situation that suggests that the P scribe herself, not one of her predecessors, may have been responsible for P's feminizing of the soul • 38 **in no manner** S reads "ne no manner" • 41–42 **then they ar made more swete** the P scribe originally wrote "then be we made swete," before editing the phrase • 43 **very fairnesse** S reads "very faire"

[CHAPTER 50] The text of Chapter 50 is based on P, collated with S • S has the rubric "How the chosen soule was nevere ded in the syte of God. And of a mervel upon the same. And three things boldid hir to aske of God the understondyng of it. Fiftieth Chapter" • 1 **that evermore** S reads "and evermore" • 7 **sothly** from S: P reads

"truly" • 20 **feer** S reads "awer" • 22 **tru** S reads "so" • 24 **sothnes** from S: P reads "truth" • 24 **truth** S reads "trueths"

[CHAPTER 51] The text of Chapter 51 is based on P, collated with S • S has the rubric "The answere to the doute afor by a mervelous example of a lord and a servant. And God will be abidyn. For it was nere twenty yeres after, ere she fully understode this example. And how it is understod that Crist syttith on the ryth hand of the fader. Fifty-First Chapter" • 8 **stondeth before** S reads "standyth by aforn," probably a version of the same phrase • 12 **sore** from S: P reads "sorow," but "sore" at lines 20 and 244 • 13 **walloweth and writheth** P reads "walloweth and wryeth," S "waylith and writheth." The P scribe first wrote something like "walryth" across the line break, perhaps conflating "waloweth" with "wryeth," then added a *w* in the left margin before *ryth* to make "wryth" and *loweth* in the right-hand margin of the previous line, after *wal*, and finally canceled "wryth." For "walloweth and writheth," see lines 250 and 258 • 17 **full febil** S reads "febil" • 21 **felable** from S: P reads "moch," which seems vague by comparison • 28 **thus mekely suffer** S reads "mekely suffren there" • 30 **maner of blame** S reads "blame" • 30 **sothly** from S: P reads "verely" • 35–38 **this was shewed with a leding of my understanding into the lorde, in which I saw him hyely enjoy for the wurshipful restoring and noble that he will and shall bring his servant to by his plentuous grace** P reads "this was shewed with a ledyng of my understandyng in to the lorde in restoryng whych I saw hym hyely enjoy for the wurschypfull restyng and noble that he wyll and shall bryng his servaunt to by his plentuous grace"; S is the same as P, except that it omits "in restoryng" and reads "nobleth" for "noble." We understand P's "restoryng" as a correction of the word "restyng" a few words later, perhaps written in the margin of P's exemplar and mistakenly introduced into the text as a separate word. Compare the repetition of the passage in lines 133–36: "And this was shewed in a touch, wher I sey [S: P has "saw"] that my understanding was led into the lorde, *in which* I saw him heyly enjoye for the *worshipful restoring* that he will and shall bring his servant to by his plentuous grace" (italics added) • 40 **Lo** S reads "Lo, lo" • 41 **had and taken** S reads "takeyn" • 42 **skille** from S: P reads "reson," as at 10.76 ("unresonable"). See 73.40 for its one use of a version of "skille" • 48 **hyely** S reads "verily" • 50 **hye** from S: P reads "the hye" • 54 **went** S reads "cam" • 58 **derecte** S reads "aret" • 59 **unknowinge** from S: P reads "thre knowynges": perhaps the scribe read "onknowynge" as "one knowing" and thought her exemplar had made a mistake. S's reading makes better sense in context, since the point of the passage as a whole is to stress how slowly Julian understood the exemplum • 60 **the privites** S reads "three propertes," which is possible but makes the reference to "thre propertes" in line 63 seem redundant. Compare 46.38–39: "I saw in the same shewing that moch privite is hid" • 66 **fro the beginning to the ende** S adds "that is to sey, of this boke," an addition that may have begun life as a marginal gloss on this difficult passage. As a gloss, the phrases are misleading, however, for Julian is clearly thinking of the revelation itself, not of her written account. See 46.13 for the phrase "fro the beginning to the ende" clearly used to describe the revelation • 76 **assented** S reads "assend" • 78 **wolde** from S: P reads "wylle" • 81, 82 **at** (× 2) from S: P reads "and" • 83 **behaving** "be" added above the line • 87–88 **to make thereby to be understonde** S reads "to maken that thereby understonden" • 88 **alle manne** S reads "a man," but see the repetitions of "alle" in the following sentence • 90–91 **he was turned** S reads "he turnyd," which makes the servant's misery sound like a condition actively sought, not the by-product of zeal • 91 **hole** from S: not in P, though necessary to the argument of the passage. Compare use of the word in, e.g., 45.2, 53.12–14, the second of which alludes to this passage • 100 **paine** S reads "paynys" • 101 **socurreth** S reads "sorowith." No form of "socur" is used elsewhere in the manuscripts, but "sorowith" seems inconsistent with the Lord's "chere" • 103 **the lorde** S reads "our lord" • 106 **fair brown** from S: P reads "feyer brown whyght." This is a possible reading, since *A Revelation* elsewhere has the colors "browne rede" (7.12) and "browne blew" (16.3), where "browne" means "dark"; "browne whight" would then mean something like "tanned." However, see lines 130–32, where "brownhed" is said to be "most according to shew his holy sobernesse" (most appropriate to display his holy sobriety), and thus to be a color in its own right, not a shade • 108 **hevens** from S: P reads "hevynlynes." See line 133 • 114 **and the pity** S reads "in the pite" • 115–16 **The joy and the blisse was of the falling of his deerwurthy son** S omits "the falling of," a daring three-word evocation of the Incarnation as exactly parallel to the Fall • 122 **sothly** from S: P reads "verely" • 127 **wolde adight** from S: P reads "wolde have dyght," the scribe probably reading the initial *a* of "adyten" as the shortened or syncopated Middle English form of "have" • 134 **sey** from S: P reads "saw," but this is a reference back to lines 35–38, which this sentence quotes almost verbatim, as the chapter revisits this fragmentary revelation in moment-by-moment detail • 141 **lefte side** S reads "lift" • 142 **defauted** S reads "defacid." Compare "defauting," line 209, and see line 29 • 143 **fitting** from S: P reads "syttyng," probably a simple transcription error • 153–54 **and an hard traveler** not in S • 164 **delve and dike and swinke and swete and turne** from S (where all the verbs end in *-en*). Besides omitting one verb ("swinke"), the P scribe or a predecessor renders all of them as participles: "delvyng and dykyng and swetyng and turnyng." See textual note to 4.1 • 166–67 **nobille and plentuous fruite** from S: P reads "nobylle plentuousnesse" • 169–70 **take this met with the drinke** S reads

"take this mete, with the drinke in the mete." Perhaps "in the mete" means "as part of the meat" and was added because the gardener's preparation of drink has not been mentioned • 183 **on** from S: P reads "of" • 186 **rightful** from S: P reads "ryght" • 186–87 **be seperath** not in S • 194 **manhode and Adam** from S: P reads "manhode of Adam," although "manhode" here clearly refers to the human nature of Christ • 207 **whit** S reads "which," which makes much less good sense • 209 **straighthede** S reads "steytehede," P "strayghtnesse" • 209 **defauting** S reads "defaceing" • 210 **laborar** S reads "labour" • 213 **don** from S: not in P • 213 **worshippe** P reads "worschppe" • 214 **sothfastly** from S: P reads "truly" • 214 **sholde** S reads "shal" • 217 **blisseful passion** from S: P reads "passion" • 221 **longeth or desireth** S omits the last two words • 225–26 **For Jhesu is all that shall be saved, and all that shall be saved is Jhesu** from S: P's reading, "For Jhesu is in all that shall be saveyd, and all that shall be savyd is in Jhesu," tones down the absolute identification of Jesus and the saved that is part of the logical working-out of the lord-and-servant exemplum at this point • 227 **vertues** from S: P reads "vertuous" • 233 **sheweth** S reads "shewid" • 235 **on side and on the lefte** from S: P reads "on the lyfte syde" • 239 **as swithe** from S ("also swythe"): P reads "as sone" • 245 **mans** the P scribe originally wrote "maners" before crossing out the last four letters and subtituting *ns* • 247 **sweppes and the scorges** from S: P reads "roddys and scorgys" • 248 **renting** P reads "renryntyng" • 251 **moning** from S: P reads "mornyng." See 51.13 • 256 **The body ley** S reads "the body was" • 258 **moning** from S: P again reads "mornyng" • 265–66 **on his riche and nobil seet** S reads "in his noblest sete" • 267 **dredfully, unornely** from S: P reads "dredfully" • 271 **and** P reads "an"

[CHAPTER 52] The text of Chapter 52 is based on P, collated with S • S has the rubric "God enjoyith that he is our fadir, bother [for "mother"], and spouse. And how the chosen have here a medlur of wele and wo, but God is with us in three manner. And how we may eschew synne but never it [*sic*]. Fifty-Second Chapter" • 5 **him** from S: not in P • 9 **lastingly** S reads "stedfastly." See line 28 • 14 **openeth** S plausibly reads "he opynyth" • 16 **are** from S: P reads "be," but "are" in the equivalent place in the following clause • 19 **ech** S reads "ilke" • 26 **sheweth** from S: P reads "shewede" • 32 **yeming** from S (in the form "yemand"): P reads "gydyng." See textual notes to 1.48, 68.8 • 40 **thus** P reads "tus" • 41 **now** from S: not in P • 47–48 **alle holy** S reads "as holy" • 55 **nakidly** from S: P reads "mekely." The allusion is to the topos that confession should be "naked," hiding nothing • 64–66 **wilfully . . . wilfully** from S: P omits this passage, presumably through eyeskip from one "wilfully" to the next, perhaps encouraged by the repetitions of the verbs "see" and "know" • 68–69 **And himselfe wurketh there it is** S reads "and hymselfe wurkith it then it is" • 72 **is** the P scribe originally wrote "was" but then crossed it out • 80 **restorid** from **S**: **P** reads "dystroyed," the scribe perhaps not understanding that "restored" here means "redeemed"

[CHAPTER 53] The text of Chapter 53 is based on **P**, collated with **S** and, from line 44 on, **W** • **S** has the rubric "The kindness of God assigneth no blame to his chosen, for in these is a godly will that never consent to synne. For it behovyth the ruthfulhede of God so to be knitt to these that ther be a substance kept that may never be departid from hym. Fifty-Third Chapter" • 1 **And thus I saw S** reads "And I saw" • 1 **wit P** reads "know," **S** "wetyin." The phrase "will we wit" is formulaic, used several times later in the chapter • 5 **defaute** from **S**: **P** reads "defaute finall," which gives a very different sense • 8 **fere S** reads "awer," as it does in the passage to which this sentence refers, at 50.20 • 11 **continually P** reads "contynnly" • 14 **ech S** reads "ilke" • 14 **behoveth** from **S**: **P** reads "behovyd" • 17 **forseeing** from **S**: **P** reads "forseyde," but "foreseyeng" at line 28. See textual note to 11.6, 8 • 25 **entent and assent S** reads "assent" • 27 **wenden** from **S** ("wyndyn"): **P** reads "goo" • 31 **a love** from **S**: **P** reads "alone" • 34 **understode S** reads "understond" • 36 **slime S** reads "slyppe" • 41 **all the mater S** reads "the matter" • 44 **wit** from **S/W**: **P** reads "know" • 46 **shulde be S** reads "shall be" • 50 **this S** reads "his" • 53 **knit in this knot, and oned W** agrees with **P**: **S** reads "knitt and onyd"

[CHAPTER 54] The text of Chapter 54 is based on **P**, collated with **S** and **W** • **S** has the rubric "We ought to enjoye that God wonyth in our soule and our soule in God, so that atwix God and our soule is nothing, but as it were al God. And how feith is ground of al vertue in our soule be the holy gost. Fifty-Fourth Chapter" • 3 **trowe** from **S/W**: **P** reads "truste" • 3, 6, 7, 8, 10, 11 **wonning** (× 3), **wonneth** (× 4): from **S**: **P/W** both read "dwellyng," "dwellyng place" (line 8, **P** first example only, **W** both examples), and "dwellyth" (× 4). **S** twice reads "dwelleth" in this sense (51.119 and 64.31), and twice "dwelling" (68.23, 41), but elsewhere distinguishes "dwellen" (to remain or await) from "wonnen" (to live or inhabit). "Dwelling" is a temporary, even if long-term, state, more often of mind than body: see, e.g., 2.38, "the third dwellid continually." "Wonning" is a permanent state of rest. **P**'s two uses of "wonning" (at 52.31 and 55.27) suggest that this distinction was established in the **P** tradition, even if it is partly effaced in **P** itself • 4 **sothly** from **S**: **P** reads "truly" • 12 **by God** so **P/W**: **S** reads "God," equating God with the substance in a less nuanced way than the chapter goes on to do • 17, 18, 19 **are all beclosed, are beclosed** (× 4) from **S**, where the form is "arn al beclosid": **P** reads "are closyd," "be closyd" (× 3), and "are closyd"; **W** uses "enclosed" and "closed." **P**'s usual form of "are" is "be," which would turn the phrase "are/arn beclosed" into the clumsy "be beclosed." The scribe or her exemplar might well have wanted to avoid this, as we have wanted to

avoid it here. **P** uses forms of "beclose" at 5.4, 6.29, 10.6, 49.17, etc. • 23 **in which vertu S** reads "in which" • 27 **For Crist marcifully is werking in us S** reads "For Crists mercifull werking is in us"

[CHAPTER 55] The text of Chapter 55 is based on **P**, collated with **S** and, for lines 2–8, with **W** • **S** has the rubric "Christ is our wey, ledand and presenting us to the fader. And forwith as the soule is infusid in the body, mercy and grace werkyn. And how the second person toke our sensualite to deliver us from duble deth. Fifty-Fifth Chapter" • 11 **believe S** reads "feithyn," a word not used elsewhere in the manuscripts • 14 **swithe** from **S**: **P** reads "soone." Compare 10.81, 51.239 • 18 **understode S** reads "understond" • 21 **same** (× 2) **S** twice reads "selfe" • 23 **in which citte S** reads "in which se" • 24 **wonne** from **S**: **P** reads "dwell" • 24 **blissefully** from **S**: **P** reads "blessydly" • 29 **either S** reads "neyther" • 29 **taking** from **S**: **P** reads "take" • 37–38 **behoved . . . shuld S** reads "behovith . . . shal" • 41 **ever S** reads "on" • 46 **party S** reads "parte," **P** "partys" • 46 **And that was shewed S** reads "that I was shewid" • 47 **ech** not in **S**

[CHAPTER 56] The text of Chapter 56 is based on **P**, collated with **S** and with **W** in lines 1–32 • **S** has the rubric "It is esier to know God than our soule. For God is to us nerer than that, and therefore if we will have knowing of it, we must seke into God. And he will we desir to have knowledge of kynde, mercy, and grace. Fifty-Sixth Chapter" • 1 **come** the **P** scribe first wrote a word like "more," perhaps repeating it from a few words earlier, then crossed it out • 7 **them** from **W**: **S** reads "hem," **P** "hym" • 8–9 **it is both good and trew W** reads "it ar bothe good and trewe," **S** "they arn both good and trew." The sense is "either [stirring] is good and true" • 11 **togeder S** reads "to God" • 11 **it S** reads "thai," which is what "it" means here • 12 **seker P** reads "suer," **S** "very," not noticing the sentence's progression from "very" to "seker" to "endles." For the emendation of "suer" to "seker," see textual note to 1.41 • 17–18 **And as anemptis oure substance . . . And anemptis oure sensualite S** reads "And anempts our substance and sensualite," probably missing out a line as a result of eyeskip • 17 **as** added above the line • 17, 18 **called** (× 2): **S** reads "clepid" • 24 **sothly** from **S/W**: **P** reads "suerly" • 26 **that** from **S/W**: not in **P** • 30 **full** from **S/W**: not in **P** • 34, 34–35 **substantial kindhede** (× 2) **P** reads "substanncyally kyndnesse . . . sybstancyall kyndnesse," **S** "substantial heyhede . . . substantial kindhede" • 37 **oure being** not in **S** • 43 **we beginne here S** reads "they ben begun here" • 45 **evenly S** reads "verily" • 47 **coming P/S** both read "connyng," but it is hard to make sense of the sentence without the emendation • 49 **as moch good and as grete good S** reads "as ful goods and also greter godes"

[CHAPTER 57] The text of Chapter 57 is based on **P**, collated with **S** • **S** has the rubric "In our substance we aren full. In our sensualite we faylyn, which God will restore be mercy and grace. And how our kinde, which is the heyer part, is knitt to God in the makyng, and God, Jesus, is knitt to our kind in the lower part in our flesh takyng. And of feith spryngyn other vertues. And Mary is our moder. Fifty-Seventh Chapter" • 3 **sothly** from **S**: **P** reads "truly" • 4 **this grete richesse S** reads "the gret riches" • 8 **owne P** originally read "owne good," but the second word is crossed out • 13 **whom** from **S**: **P** reads "whose" • 14 **shalle be perished S** plausibly reads "shall perishen" • 25 **other goodes** from **S**: **P** reads "oure goddys" • 27–28 **That one is that we owe to understand and know** not in **S**, presumably because of eyeskip • 31 **hath ordained** from **S**: **P** reads "hath ordeyneth" • 35 **same S** reads "ilk" • 44–45 **it saide . . . he seyth S** has "he seith . . . it seith" • 47 **sitte P** reads "syttyth" • 47 **wonne** from **S**: **P** reads "dwell" • 50 **sothly** from **S**: **P** reads "verely"

[CHAPTER 58] The text of Chapter 58 is based on **P**, collated with **S** • **S** has the rubric "God was never displesid with his chosin wif. And of three properties in the trinite: faderhede, moderhede, and lordehede. And how our substance is in every person, but our sensualite is in Criste alone. Fifty-Eighth Chapter" • 6 **ech S** reads "ilke" • 14 **be departed** from **S**: **P** reads "parte." See line 38 • 17 **lordhede** from **S**: **P** reads "lordschyppe" • 18, 20 **as** (× 2) from **S**: **P** reads "and" • 25 **we have** from **S**: not in **P** • 25 **in** added above the line • 31 **substantially S** reads "substantial" • 36 **taking S** reads "takyng flesh," but "taking" here parallels "making" in line 35 • 40 **oneth** from **S**: **P** reads "onyd" • 44 **large geving of trewth** from **S**: **P** reads "a gyfte of trust," but the phrase needs to parallel "curtesse werkyng" in line 45 • 50 **oure substance is in oure fader S** reads "our substance is our fader," and later "is our moder," though "*in* our lord the holy gost" • 52 **ech S** reads "ilke"

[CHAPTER 59] The text of Chapter 59 is based on **P**, collated with **S** and with **W** for lines 10–19 and 32–41 • **S** has the rubric "Wickednes is turnyd to bliss be mercy and grace in the chosyn. For the properte of God is to do good ageyn ille be Jesus our moder in kynd grace. And the heyest soule in vertue is mekest, of which ground we have other vertues. Fifty-Ninth Chapter" • 1 **all** added above the line • 2 **which is God** from **S**: **P** reads "which is in God," "in" added above the line • 5–6 **to all that shall be saved S** reads "to al these that shal be savid" • 12 **the wisdom and the kindnes** from **W**: **S** reads "the wisdam"; **P** adds "and the kyndnes" in the margin • 14–15 **I it am that maketh the to love** from **W/S**: not in **P**, omitted through eyeskip, since it is nearly identical with the following sentence. **S** does not include "it" in several of these sentences, while **W** has no final "I it am," before "the endlesse fulfyllyng" (lines 15–16) • 17 **ther it is lowest** from **W**: **P** reads "yett it is lowest," **S** "when it is lowest," the scribe having read "then the soule is heyest" for

P/W's "ther the soule is hyest" in line 16. We take it that the work is fully identifying the highest and the lowest aspects of the soul • 18 **in oure sensualite S** reads "and our sensualite" • 20 **knew** from **S**: **P** reads "knowyth" • 29 **mekehede** from **S**: not in **P** • 32–33 **oure very moder** from **S/W**: **P** reads "our very surst moder" (for "first") • 35 **godly wille P/S** read "goodly wylle," but the reference is to the "godly wille" of 53.8–10, etc. • 38 **grounde S** reads "groundid" • 38 **taking S** reads "taken," which spoils the parallel with "making" • 41 **And alle is one love S** reads "and al his own luf"

[CHAPTER 60] The text of Chapter 60 is based on **P**, collated with **S** and, for much of the chapter, **W** • **S** has the rubric "How we be bowte ageyn and forthspred be mercy and grace of our swete, kynde, and ever lovyng moder Jesus. And of the propertes of moderhede. But Jesus is our very moder, not fedyng us with mylke but with himselfe, opening his syde onto us and challengyng al our love. Sixtieth Chapter" • 2 **understonde** from **S/W**: **P** reads "understode" • 2 **brought S** reads "bowte" • 3–4 **ware made** from **S/W**: **P** reads "ware in, made" • 5 **holy** from **S/W**: **P** reads "hole" • 9 **the sovereyn S** reads "is sovereyn" • 10 **all S** reads "ful" • 11 **office P** reads "officie" • 12–13 **nerest . . . sekerest** not in **S**, probably omitted through eyeskip • 15 **to paine and to dying S** reads "is us to peyne and to deyeng" • 15 **A S** reads "and" • 16 **very** added above the line • 16 **alone S** reads "al love," despite its earlier transcription of "alone" in line 14 • 17 **within him** the **P** scribe initially wrote "with hym," then crossed out "hy," made the *m* into *in*, and added a new "hym." **S** reads "within himself" • 18 **traveyled** from **S/W**: **P** reads "traveyle," probably taking the word as a noun paralleling "love" • 18–19 **the sharpest throwes and the grevousest paines** from **S/W**: **P** reads "the sharpyst thornes and grevous paynes" • 23 **of** from **S/W**: not in **P** • 23 **fede** from **S** "fedyn," **W** "fede": **P** reads "fynde," but "fede" in line 26 • 25 **sucke** added above the line • 29 **saide** from **P/S**: **W** reads "seyeth," following Julian's more usual practice of referring to Christ's words in the present tense • 36 **tenth S** reads "ninth," **P** reads "ix revelation," but the words are from the tenth revelation, Chapter 24 • 37 **loved** from **W/S**: **P** reads "love," as it often does in recording this saying of Christ's. See textual note to 24.11 • 37 **beholding P** reads "beholde" • 39–41 **This fair . . . of alle P** corresponds to **W**. **S** reads "This fair lovely word moder, it is so swete and so kynd of the self that it may ne verily be seid of none but of him, and to hir that is very moder of hym and of all." **S**'s irrelevant inclusion of Mary in the sentence is an indication of how radical Julian's application of the term "mother" to Jesus could be. But it detracts from the focus of the argument • 42 **God** from **P/W**: **S** reads "good" • 46–47 **And ever as it waxeth in age and in stature S** reads "And as it wexith in age" • 47 **working** from **S/W**: **P** reads "werkes" • 48 **chastised S** has the good Middle English word "bristinid," not found elsewhere in the manuscripts • 49 **to receive** from S/W: P reads "receyve" • 53 **oure** from S/W: not in P • 54 **to faderhod and moderhod** S reads "be faderhede and moderhede," then adds the clause "for Gods faderhede and moderhede." W reads "it is to fadirhed and moderhed." Evidently, the sentence caused confusion, although P's version of it is clear enough

[CHAPTER 61] The text of Chapter 61 is based on P, collated with S and, for much of the chapter, W • S has the rubric "Jesus usith more tenderness in our gostly bringing forth. Thow he suffrith us to ffallyn in knowing of our wretchidness, he hastily reysith us, not brekyng his love for our trespas. For he may not suffre his child to perish. For he will that we have the properte of a child, fleing to him alway in our necessite. Sixty-First Chapter" • 1 **in keping** S reads "of keping" • 2 **likenes** from S: P/W read "comparyson," but see 6.39, where S/W agree against P, and 63.12, where P has "liknesse" • 3 **prepareth** S reads "directith," W "addith" • 7 **us** added above the line • 7–8 **be well apaide** S reads "bend payd" • 9 **be strengthed** S reads "be thus strenthyd" • 10 **by his swete grace** from S: P/W read "by his grace." Parallels "swete werking" in line 9 • 15 **to see it** from P/S: W reads "to know it and to se it" • 17 **so fulsomly know** S reads "fulsomely so knowen" • 19 **verely** not in S • 23 **is** from S: P reads "was," but "is" in the following line • 24 **Another** from S: P reads "And other" • 30 **own** from S: P reads "one." "Her" or "his own" might be easier, but as always *A Revelation* is concerned to avoid gender-specific language • 32 **never suffer** S reads "not suffre" • 38 **adred** from W: S reads "dred," P "afeerd" • 38–39 **And if it may do no more, it cryeth on the mother** not in S, probably omitted through eyeskip between the two instances of "mother" • 43 **swithe** from S: P/W read "sone" • 44 **more** from S/W: P reads "for" • 44 **it** not in P • 52 **flode** from P/W: S reads "foode" • 55 **diligent** S reads "diligently" • 57 **entende** from S ("entendyn"): P reads "entended"

[CHAPTER 62] The text of Chapter 62 is based on P, collated with S • S has the rubric "The love of God suffrith never his chosen to lose tyme. For all their troble is turnyd into endles joye. And how we arn al bownden to God for kindness and for grace. For every kind is in man and us nedyth not to seke out to know sondry kindes, but to holy church. Sixty-Second Chapter" • 2 **outcastings** from S: P reads "chargynges" • 8 **he** not in S • 13 **shall** from S: P reads "shulde" • 21 **wonneth** from S: P reads "dwellyth." See textual note to 54.3, 6, 7, 8, 10, 11 • 21 **shall** from S: P reads "shulde" • 24 **moder** not in S

[CHAPTER 63] The text of Chapter 63 is based on P, collated with S and, for lines 32–34 only, W • S has the rubric "Synne is more peynfull than hell, and vile and hurting kinde. But grace savith kinde and destroyith synne. The children of Jesus be not yet all borne, which

pass not the stature of childhood, livyng in febilnes till thei come to hevyn, where joyes arn ever new begynnand without end. Sixty-Third Chapter" • 2 **itselfe** S reads "the selfe" • 3 **save kinde, and kepe kinde** S reads "saven kind" • 8 **unmade** not in S. See 53.39 • 11 **wurse** S reads "very" • 12, 13 **sothly** (× 2) from S: P reads "verely" and "trewly" • 13 **and thus** P begins a new sentence, with "Al this is," which gives less clear sense • 13 **loving soule** S reads "lovid soule" • 23 **oure very moder** S reads "very moder" • 24–25 **sovereyne goodnesse** S reads "hey sovereyn goodnes" • 28 **wille** not in S • 33 **itselfe** so P/W: S reads "the selfe" • 33 **eche** S reads "ilke" • 34 **Theyse be as fair vertues** S reads "these arn the fair vertues" • 37 **gracious** added above the line • 38 **ther** S reads "than" • 40 **welle** P concludes Chapter 63, and thus the long series of chapters that follow from Chapter 51, with "alle manner thing shall be welle," the great promise first made in Chapter 27. S includes lines 40–44 as part of Chapter 63, beginning Chapter 64 with a return to the material taken from *A Vision*. The confusion, which follows an earlier inconsistency at the start of Chapter 21 (see textual note to Chapter 21), anticipates similar problems later on in *A Revelation*, suggesting that chapter and revelation numbers may have been added to the holograph of *A Revelation* sufficiently late in composition or copying that a chapter division might not always have been clear. A few chapters later, P and S subdivide Chapters 66–68 differently, P treating as two chapters what is given as Chapter 66 in S, and S doing the same to what P gives as Chapter 68 (P 66/67 = S 66; P 68 = S 67/68). There are further disagreements and difficulties until Chapter 73, although they are then resolved, and the two manuscripts run parallel until the end. Both manuscript traditions, that is, usually agree, and both reflect an awareness that the total number of chapters needed to be 86. Here and in Chapters 69–73 we side with S; in Chapters 66–68 we side with P. In this case, the language of the last two sentences is that of Chapter 63 and its predecessors, while Revelation Fifteen is in a different style and advances different arguments. For the other cases, see below • 41 **moderhed** S reads "moder" • 44 **shall** from S: P reads "shulde"

THE FIFTEENTH REVELATION

[CHAPTER 64] The text of Chapter 64 is based on P, collated with A, S, and, in lines 1–15 and 39–40 W • S has the rubric "The Fifteenth Revelation is as it shewid etc. The absense of God in this lif is our ful gret peyne, besyde other travels. But we shal sodenly be taken fro all peyne, having Jesus to our moder. And our patient abyding is gretly plesyng to God. And God wil take our disese lightly, for love, thinkand us alwey at the poynte to be deliverid. Sixty-Fourth Chapter" • P begins the fifteenth revelation and Chapter 64 earlier, at Chapter 63.40. See textual note • 2–3 **the wele and the blessed being that is there** S reads "the wele and the bliss that is beyng there," **W** "the wele and the blessed beynge that is in hevyn" • 3 **ben no paine** from **A/S/W**: **P** reads "no payne ben" • 5–6 **also of my owne wretchednesse, sloth, and werinesse S** has "wekehede" for "werynesse"; **W** reads "also myne owne wretchednesse, slouth and irkenesse halpe therto" • 10 **disese** from **A/S/W**: **P** reads "dyseses" • 10–11 **And thou shalte come up above** this clause is added partly in the margin, partly over the line • 12 **never more have** from **P/W**: **A/S** read "never have" • 12 **no manner of sicknes** not in **S** • 13 **of misliking** from **A/S**: **P** reads "mysselykyng" • 16 **rewardeth** from **A/S**: **P** reads "rewardyd" • 19 **a man** from **A/S**: **P** reads "man" • 21–22 **this life and this langor** from **S**: **A** reads "this lyfe in this langoure," **P** "this lyfe and thys longyng" • 25 **feerfulle S** reads "ogyley," a word elsewhere used only of the devil • 25 **swilge stinking mire S** reads "bolned quave of styngand myre." Both phrases seem to be good Middle English, although **P**'s "swylge" (bog, swelling) is not attested as an adjective in either MED or OED: perhaps "of" has disappeared between "swylge" and "stynkyng" • 28 **swilge S** reads "bolnehede" • 30 **bliveth S** reads "belevith" • 34 **longing S** reads "lovand" • 34 **marvelous** from **S**: **P** reads "mercyfulle" • 37 **the overpassing joy S** reads "the overpassing" • 44 **frailte** from **S**: **P** reads "fragylyte," but elsewhere uses "frailte" (62.1) or an alternate spelling, "freelte" (74.2, 79.27). "Fragilite" was a new word in late Middle English, not attested before the late 1390s, and rare before the late fifteenth century • 46 **in no manner** not in **S** • 48 **agreve** from **S** (in the form "agreven"): **A** reads "greve," **P** "agrevyd" • 53 **the lesse** from **S**: **P** reads "lesse"

[CHAPTER 65] The text of Chapter 65 is based on **P**, collated with **S** and **A** • **S** has the rubric "He that chesith God for love with reverent mekeness is sekir to be savid, which reverent mekenes seith the lord mervelous grete, and the selfe mervelous litil. And it is God will we drede nothing but him. For the power of our enemy is taken in our freinds hand. And therfore al that God doith shall be gret likyng to us. Sixty-Fifth Chapter" • 2–3 **with endlesse love that werketh in him that grace S** plausibly reads "which endless love werkith in him that grace" • 3 **trustly S** reads "trosty," **A** "treulye" • 3 **as S** reads "all," **A** "als" • 4 **sekernesse** from **S**: **P** reads "suerte" • 7 **For, as it was shewed S** reads "as it was shewid," as part of the previous sentence • 9 **the selfe** from **S**: **P** reads "herselfe" • 15 **regard S** reads "reward," **A** "knawynge" • 17 **ought ech soule S** reads "oweth our soule" • 19 **witte** from **A**: **S** reads "weten," **P** "know" • 19 **the** from **A/S**: **P** reads "our" • 19 **loked** from **A** (which has the form "loken"): **P** reads "loketh," **S** "token." See textual note to 13.14 • 20 **hande** from **A/S**: **P** reads "handes" • 20 **wote sekerly this, he** from **S**: **P** reads "knoweth this sekerly she," **A** "wate sekerly this" • 21 **he** from **A/S**: **P** reads "she" • 21 **he setteth** from **S**: **P** reads "she set," **A** "sette" (conditional) • 29 **shewinges S** reads "revelations" •

31 **shewed** from **S**: **P** reads "shewyth" • 32 **processe** the **P** scribe originally wrote "prosse" then corrected the word

THE SIXTEENTH REVELATION

[CHAPTER 66] The text of Chapter 66 is based on **P**, collated with **S** and **A** • **S** has the rubric "The sixteenth revelation, etc. And it is conclusion and confirmation to all fifteen. And of hir frelte and morning in disese, and lyte speking after the gret comfort of Jesus, seying she had ravid. Which, being hir gret sekeness, I suppose was but venial synne. But yet the devil after that had gret power to vexin hir ner to deth. Sixty-Sixth Chapter" • 1 **sixteenth revelation S** reads "the sixteenth" • 4 **wher it seyth** not in **S** • 6 **disesse** from **S**: **P** reads "dysesses" • 6 **in shewing S** reads "folowand" • 7 **soone I felt that I should life longer** added in the lower margin. For "life longer" **S** reads "liven and langiren," **A** "langere lyffe" • 8 **a dinne** from **S**: **P** reads "a noyse" • 10 **morned and heved** a composite reading. **S** reads "moned and hevyed," **P** "mornyd hevyly," **A** "heved and mourned" • 10–11 **for feeling of my bodely paines A** reads "for fallynge to my paynes" • 11 **failing** from **A/S**: **P** reads "fautyng" • 13 **enterly** from **A/S**: **P** reads "inwardly." See textual notes to 41.33, 35 • 17 **that sawe no more therof S** reads "that saw I no mor therof," **A** "that says na mare therto" • 19 **have** from **A/S**: **P** reads "a," a syncopated form of "have." See textual note to 3.3 • 19–20 **But I coulde telle it to no prest S** reads "but at that tyme I cowde tell it no preist" • 20 **I beleved not oure lorde God A** reads "I leved nought oure lorde God," **S** "I leve not our lord God," **P**, somewhat elaborately, "when I, by seaying I raved, I shewed my selfe nott to belyve oure lorde god?" • 21 **This I beleft sothfastly** from **A/S**: **P** reads "Nottwithstanding I beleft hym truly" • 22 **from** from **A/S**: **P** reads "oute of" • 23 **A, lo I, wrech!** from **S**: **A** reads "Loo, I, wrich!" **P** "A, loo, ~~w~~how wrechyd I was!" The struck-out **w** here suggests that the **P** scribe herself may have emended this passage, from "A, loo, wrech!"

[CHAPTER 67] The text of Chapter 67 is taken from **P**, collated with **S** and **A** • **S** treats the whole of Chapter 67 as part of its Chapter 66, and thus has no rubric here. See textual note to 63.40 • 4 **frekness S** reads "blak steknes," the latter word probably a misspelling of "frekness," an East Anglian term, according to MED and OED. **P** reads "frakylles" • 5 **not scored afore S** reads "evisid aforn." "Evisid" means "shorn," while "score" is a Middle English form of the word "shorn." Either is possible. But the most important disagreement between **P** and **S** is over the word "not," which determines whether Julian saw the devil with uncut or cut hair at the front of his head. Here we suppose the devil looked shaggy • 6 **loke S** reads "semelant" • 6 **shewde S** reads "shewing" • 8 **have strangled me** from **A/S**: **P** reads "stoppyd my breth and kylde me." **P**'s reading may be a medieval gloss on a relatively unfamiliar term • 11 **had I my** from **A/S**: **P** reads "had ony" • 14 **Is it S** reads "It is" • 15 **have** burned P/S read "a burnyd." See textual note to 3.3 · 17 **to tempest me** from A/S: P reads "only to tempte me" · 19 **I behelde it as both one** P reads "I behelde it as both in one," A "I holde it as bathe ane," S "I beheld it is bothen one"

[CHAPTER 68] The text of Chapter 68 is based on P, collated with S and A · S, a chapter number behind at this point, divides Chapter 68 into Chapters 67 and 68, with the rubrics "Of the worshipfull syte of the soule, which is so nobly create that it myte no better a be made, in which the trinite joyeth everlastingly. And the soule may have rest in nothing but in God, which sittith therin reuling al things. Sixty-Seventh Chapter," and, after line 35, "Of sothfast knowing that it is Jesus that shewid all this and it was no ravyng. And how we owen to have sekir troste in all our tribulation that we shall not be overcome. Sixty-Eighth Chapter." See note to 63.40 · 2 **warde** S reads "world," but the rest of the language of the passage imagines the soul as a city or city-state · 3 **blisseful** from S: P reads "blessyd" · 4 **sitteth** from A/S (in the form "sits"): not in P, perhaps omitted because it is close in spelling to "cytte" (see "sitte," line 27) · 5 **very God and very man** S reads "God and man" · 6 **solempnest** from S: P reads "most solempne" · 6–7 **solemply in wurshippes** so P/A: S reads "solemnly and worshiply" · 8 **yemeth** P reads "yevyth," S "gemeth," A "yemes." See textual note to 1.48 ("yeming") · 9 **yemeth** P reads "yevyth" · 8–10 **The manhode . . . the blessed godhed: that is** not in S, where at least two lines have here been lost to eyeskip between the two occurrences of the phrase "that is" · 12 **remove it** from A/S: P reads "remove" · 13, 23, 27 (× 2) **wonning/wonneth** from S: P reads "dwellyng"/"dwellyth" · 15 **couth** from S: P reads "myght," which destroys the careful progression of auxiliary verbs for each person of the trinity: "might," "could," "willed" · 17 **blessed** from S: P reads "blessydfulle" · 24 **sothly** from S: P reads "truly" · 25 **itselfe** S reads "the selfe" · 28 **citte** P reads "sytte" · 31 **blisseful** from S: P reads "blessyd" · 31, 32 **have** from S: P reads "a," the syncopated form of the verb again · 33–35 **But for he . . . mannes soule** not in S, probably omitted through eyeskip between two of the three occurrences of "mannes soule" here · 37 **This was a delectable sighte** the opening of Chapter 68 in S · 40 **oneth** from S: P reads "onyd" · 41 **sitte** from A: S reads "sitten," P "syttyng," probably as a result of misreading the -en infinitive ending as a participal · 41 **for the sekernesse of sitting shewde endlesse dwelling** P reads "truth" for "sekernesse"; S reads "for the sekirnes of sitting shewith endles dwelling," A "for the behaldynge of this sittynge schewed to me sikernes of his endelesse dwellynge" · 42 **gave** P reads "gawe" · 42 **sothfastly** from S: P reads "truly" · 43 **lorde** from A/S: P reads "lordes," the final s apparently added as an afterthought · 47 **trust thee therto** P reads "trust therto," A "kepe \the/ therto," S "troste thou therto" · 48 **that it is oure lorde Jhesu**

from A/S: P reads "that is oure lorde Jhesu" · 51 **sekernesse** from A/S: P reads "feytfullnes" · 54 **this worde** S reads "these words" · 56 **tempestid** from A/S: P reads "trobelyd." See textual note to 2.23 · 58 **seker** from S: A reads "sekernesse," P "feytfull" · 60 **And sone after all was close** from A/S: P reads "And sone all was close" · 60 **saw no more** P reads "saw no more afftyr this." See textual note to 69.1

[CHAPTER 69] The text of Chapter 69 is based on P, collated with S and A · S has the rubric "Of the second long temptation of the devill to despeir. But she mytyly trosted to God and to the feith of holy church, rehersing the passion of Christe, be the which she was deliverid. Sixty-Ninth Chapter" · P and S end the chapter at different places: see textual note to line 12 ("My bodely eye") · 1 **After this** from A/S: in P, this is the final phrase of the previous chapter · 2 **the bodely heet** from A: P reads "bodely heet"; S omits the phrase · 3 **jangeling** from A/S: P reads "talkyng" · 4 **jangled** from A/S: P reads "talkyd" · 4 **if** from A/S: not in P · 5 **muttering** from A/S: P has the interesting word "whystryn," a form of "whispering" · 7 **mouth** from S: P reads "moch," which makes poor sense in context · 10 **have done** from S: P reads "a done" · 11 **bisines** from A/S: P reads "lykenesse" · 12 **My bodely eye** P begins Chapter 70 here, eleven lines into the second episode of diabolic temptation. Our chapter division follows S · 12 **there I had seen in comforte** A reads "that I hadde sene comforth in," S "wher I had ben in comfort" · 14–15 **that was in me. And I thought** from A: P reads only "that I thought," S "And I thowte." Although the phrase "was in me" is unique to A, it seems necessary for the sense · 18 **sothly** from A/S: P reads "faythfully" · 20 **morne** from A/S: P reads "morow"

[CHAPTER 70] The text of Chapter 70 is based on P, collated with S and A · S has the rubric "In all tribulation we owe to be stedfast in the feith, trosting mytyly in God. For if our faith had no enimyte, it should deserve no mede. And how all these shewings arn in the faith. Seventieth Chapter" · P and S begin and end this chapter in different places. See textual notes to 69.12 ("My bodely eye") and 70.20 · 6 **that it is in the faith that he shewde** S reads "that it is the feith that he shewid." For other uses of the phrase "in the faith," see 53.12, 69.15–16 · 7 **believe** S reads "leve," P "love." P's reading is probably based on a misreading of "leve" · 7 **ever joyeng** S reads "enjoyand" · 9 **bounde** from S (in the form "bounden"): P reads "beholdyng" · 16 **lost** S reads "lestist" · 16 **couth or might not** S reads "couthest not." P's "or myght" may be a scribal translation of "couth," rather than part of the original text · 18 **where** P reads "where where" · 19 **believe it** S reads "leve," P "lerne." See 68.46 · 20 **not be overcom** P begins Chapter 71 here, awkwardly between Christ's words and their exposition. Our chapter division follows S · 23 **willing** P reads "wyllyng wyllyng" • 23 **seker** from S: P reads "feythfulle" • 24 **behestes** from S: P reads "promyses" • 25 **enemes** S reads "enemy" • 26 **lighte** S reads "syte" • 27 **diverse manner** S reads "sundry manners" • 29 **receive** from S: P reads "receyvyng," unbalancing the sentence • 30 **helth** S reads "helpe" • 32 **throw** S reads "be"

[CHAPTER 71] The text of Chapter 71 is based on P, collated with S • S has the rubric "Jesus will our soules be in glad cher to hym. For his cher is to us mery and lovely. And how he shewith to us three manner cher: of passion, compassion, and blissid cher. Seventy-First Chapter" • 2 **he beholdeth** S reads "be havith," P "he behelde" • 6 **thre** from S: P reads "the" corrected to "ther" • 7 **with us** S reads "here" • 10 **hath nede to his mercy** S reads "have to his mercy" • 17 **meddeling** S reads "medlarid" • 17 **blisseful** from S: P reads "blessyd" • 18–19 **of swete lightening** S reads "and swete lyteyng" • 19 **seker** from S: P reads "true" • 21 **solace** from S: P reads "joyes." For the formula "solace and comfort," see, e.g., 62.6

[CHAPTER 72] The text of Chapter 72 is based on P, collated with S • P has no chapter division here, but numbers the following chapter as Chapter 73. Our chapter-division follows S • S has the rubric "Synne in the chosen soulis is dedly for a time, but thei be not ded in the syght of God. And how we have here matter of joy and moneing, and that for our blindhede and weyte of flesh. And of the most comfortable chere of God. And why these shewings were made. Seventy-Second Chapter" • 2 **shall** from S: P reads "shulde" • 3 **togeder** S reads "to God" • 5 **light** S reads "life" • 5 **peasable** S reads "perfectly" • 6 **perty** S reads "pite" • 7 **that sinne** the P scribe repeats this phrase then crosses out the second instance • 8 **blisseful** from S: P reads "bessyd" • 10 **blisseful** from S: P reads "blessyd" • 14 **sothfastly** from S: P reads "feythfully" • 19 **that is to sey . . . liknes** not in S • 19 **wonneth** from S: P reads "dwellyth" • 20 **halseth** from S: P reads "colleth," but compare 5.4, where P reads "halseth" • 22, 25, 27, 31, 36 **morning** S reads "moning" • 22 **nor of seking** not in S • 23 **that precious sight** S reads "pretious, blisfull syte" • 26 **sekernesse** S reads "sekirne," P "feythfulnesse" • 27 **we be** from S: P reads "we" • 29 **fair** from S: not in P • 30 **darkhede** S reads "myrkehede," P "darknesse" • 30 **unnethes** from S: P reads "scace" • 30 **sekernesse** from S: P reads "feythfulnes" • 31 **stinte** from S: P reads "leve," having "stynte" in line 23 • 34 **solace** from S: P reads "joy" • 36 **stinte of** from S: P again reads "leve" • 39 **fair** from S: not in P • 42 **seyth** S reads "seyd" • 42 **thou lovest** S reads "is lowist" • 43 **knowing** S reads "knowyngs" • 45 **we know mekely what oureselfe is, anemptes oure sinne** from S: P reads "we know mekely that ourselfe is agaynst oure synne" • 46 **anemptes oure febilnes** P reads "agaynst oure febylnes," S "febilnes." In S, the end of the sentence is abbreviated, and the P

scribe probably misreads "anemptes" in her exemplar, as she seems to have done in the previous line. Earlier, P has several times rendered "anemptes" correctly, e.g., at 51.215; 57.1; 58.18, 20

[CHAPTER 73] The text of Chapter 73 is based on P, collated with S and A • S has the rubric "These revelations were shewid three wises. And of two gostly sekenes of which God will we amend us, remembering his passion, knowing also he is al love. For he will we have sekirnes and liking in love, not takyng onskilfull hevyness for our synnes past. Seventy-Third Chapter" • 9 **alle** S reads "that all" • 11 **tempesteth** from A/S: P reads "trobyllyth" • 15 **shall** from A/S: P reads "shulde" • 16 **And for helpe against this** S reads "And full helpe of this" • 18 **esely** so P/A: S reads "wisely" • 25 **stinte** from A: S reads "astynten," P "fayle" • 28 **by** S reads "for" • 30 **covenants** from S: P reads "promyse." See 76.28 • 30 **nor kepe not** from S: P reads "nor kepe," avoiding the Middle English double negative • 31 **say** S reads "seen" • 32 **see** S reads "finde" • 34 **wekenesse** from A/S: P reads "wyckydnesse" • 34–35 **for it cometh of enmite** from S: A reads "for it comes of the enmy," P, more cautiously, "whych comyth thorugh lack of true jugment" • 36 **of** not in P • 37 **sekernesse** from A/S: P reads "feythfulnes" • 38, 39 **forgeteth/forget** so P/A: S reads "forgivith"/"forgiven" • 39 **right** from A/S: not in P • 39 **anemptes** from S: P reads "agaynst." See 72.46

[CHAPTER 74] The text of Chapter 74 is based on P, collated with S and A • S has the rubric "Ther ben four manner of drede. But reverent drede is a lovely true that never is without meke love. And yet thei be not both one. And how we should pray God for the same. Seventy-Fourth Chapter" • 2 **man** A/S both read "a man," and A has "a man" for P/S's "man" several times in this passage • 6 **For man that is harde of slepe of sinne** not in S, presumably omitted through eyeskip. The omission misleadingly makes the "man sterid and waked" from sin the subject of the whole combined sentence • 6 **receive** S reads "perceivyn." This was probably a local adjustment, made because the omission described in the previous note rendered "receive" nonsensical • 7 **hath undertaken** the S scribe, again rewriting to make sense of the sentence, has "have understonding of." A reads "hafe getyn" • 12 **tru knowing** S reads "the knowing" • 16 **full softe** from S: A reads "fulle swete and softe," P "softe" • 23–24 **And, though, this reverent drede and love be not both in one, but they are two** A reads "And yit is this reverente drede and luffe nought bathe ane, bot thay er twa," from which we have taken "they" for P's "it." S reads "And thow this reverent drede and love be not partid asunder, yet thei arn not both one, but thei aren two." "Be not partid asunder" is probably the S scribe's attempt to make sense of "thow," which she understood as meaning "although" rather than "nonetheless." See textual note to 31.38–39, where it is S that uses "though" in the sense here • 30 **barme** from **S**: **P** reads "arme" • 32 **blisseful** from **S**: **P** reads "blessyd" • 33 **seker** from **S**: **P** reads "feythfulle" • 33 **that** the **P** scribe first wrote "and," then crossed it out, substituting "that" in the margin • 37 **properte S** reads "profitt" • 38 **delectabile** from **S**: **P** reads "swete" • 39 **shalle** from **S**: not in **P** • 41 **and to love him** from **S**: **P** reads "and love hym" • 43 **mightilier P** alters the syntax by adding "that we trust," a phrase not in **S**

[CHAPTER 75] The text of Chapter 75 is based on **P**, collated with **S** • **S** has the rubric "Us nedith love, longing, and pite. And of two manner of longing in God which arn in us. And how, in the day of dome, the joy of the blissid shal ben incresid, seing verily the cause of allthyng that God hath don, dredfully tremeland and thankand for joye, mervelyng the gretnes of God, fulhed of all that is made. Seventy-Fifth Chapter" • 1–2 **theyse thre that I shall say us nedeth: love, longing, and pitte. Pitte in love** mostly from **S**, which, however, reads "neden" for "us nedeth." The passage in **P** reads "theyse thre that I shall say: nede, love, longyng. Pytte and love." "Us nedeth," rather than "neden" or "nede," seems necessary for the sense. Perhaps the fact that the phrase "us nedeth" already occurs in the previous sentence, while "nede" as a noun appears alone in the next one, interfered with both scribes' copying of the sentence • 4 **drawen his holy soules S** reads "anwin his holy" • 7–8 **of which we have the same in us, and of the same vertue, and for the same end** from **S**: not in **P**, probably omitted as a result of eyeskip between the two occurrences of "end" • 9–10 **ever more and more P** reads "evyrmore and more," **S** "evermore" • 16 **that soules afore have had in heven** added in the bottom margin • 16–17 **plentuously shalle beflowe P** has the strange reading "flye," **S** "be flowing." Our emendation assumes that in **S** the normal -en infinitive has been mistaken for the participle. See textual note to 4.1. **S** also reads "beflowe" at 12.14 • 20, 21, 23 **shalle** (× 3) from **S**: **P** reads "shulde" • 21 **overmore S** reads "evermore" • 23 **and P** reads "an" • 27 **majeste S** reads "myte" • 28, 29 **mekehede/litilhede** from **S**: **P** has the strange readings "moch more" and "lest parte" • 30 **maketh creature S** reads "makith the creature," but see line 19 • 32 **to wille have knowing S** reads "to witten and knowen" • 35 **grethede** from **S**: **P** reads "grett hyghnesse" • 38 **he** not in **P**

[CHAPTER 76] The text of Chapter 76 is based on **P**, collated with **S** • **S** has the rubric "A loveand soule hatith synne for vilehede more than all the peyn of hell. And how the beholdying of other mannys synne, but if it be with compassion, lettith the beholdyng of God. And the devill, be putting in remembrans our wretchidness, would letten for the same. And of our slawth. Seventy-Sixth Chapter" • 6 **it hateth no helle but sinne** from **S**: **P** reads "it hatyth no helle, but helle is synne." Our reading assumes an allusion to 40.34, and the **P** scribe's

theological nervousness, paralleled in the earlier passage, around the work's reference to hell • 10, 12 **mennes** (× 2) **S** plausibly reads "mannys" • 10 **minde S** reads "my mynde" • 11 **for remedye** from **S**: not in **P** • 15 **tempesteth** from **S**: **P** reads "trobelyth." See 68.56, 73.11 • 16 **understande S** reads "understode" • 22 **fasten us homely to him S** reads "settyn us to hym, homely" • 23 **ever one S** reads "al one" • 25 **are in, in oureselfe** from **S**: **P** reads "are in oureselfe" • 28 **covenant P** reads "convannt," **S** "command." "They" are here quoting 73.29–30 back at the reader, recasting • 28 **behotest** from **S**: **P** reads "promysse" • 29 **anon S** reads "anon after" • 36 **sory S** plausibly reads "wery"

[CHAPTER 77] The text of Chapter 77 is based on **P**, collated with **S** • **S** has the rubric "Off the enmite of the ffend, which lesith more in our uprising than he winnith be our fallyng. And therfore he is scornyd. And how the scorge of God shuld be suffrid with mynde of his passion, for that is specially rewardid aboven penance be ourselfe chosen. And we must nedes have woo, but curtes God is our leder, keper, and bliss. Seventy-Seventh Chapter" • 5 **manyfold** from **S**: **P** reads "many times" • 9 **and shewde that he shalle be skorned** not in **S** • 12 **touch S** reads "neyghen," but see line 40 • 13 **deservede S** reads "a shrewid" • 15 **skillefully** from **S**: **P** reads "wysely." Compare 73.40 and see textual note to 10.76 ("unskilfulle") • 16 **spedfulle to S** reads "necessarye for" • 18 **skorging and the chastising that S** reads "scorge and chastening of" • 19 **paide** from **S**: **P** reads "plesyd" • 21 **upon himselfe S** reads "of himselfe" • 23 **shulde S** reads "shall" • 24, 25 **minde of** (× 2) **S** twice reads "mynde in" • 28 **overdon mekille, deming** adapted from **S**, which reads "over don mekil demandand": not in **P**. "Demandand" (insisting) seems likely to be an error for "demand/deming" (reckoning or judging). See 11.27–29 • 31–32 **whiche thou arte . . . thy penance** not in **S**, presumably omitted because of eyeskip between the two occurrences of "penance" • 32 **this living S** reads "thi living" • 37 (first instance) **in S** reads "is" • 37 **seker** from **S**: **P** reads "feythfulle" • 47 **And to be like** from **S**: **P** reads "and be lyke"

[CHAPTER 78] The text of Chapter 78 is based on **P**, collated with **S** • **S** has the rubric "Our lord will we know three manner of goodnes that he doith to us. And how we neede the lyte of grace to knowen our synne and febilnes, for we arn nothing of ourselfe but writchidnes. And we may not know the horribilnes of synne as it is. And how our enemy would we should never know our synne till the last day, wherfore we arn mekil bowndend to God that shewith it now. Seventy-Eighth Chapter" • 2 **foule S** reads "vile" • 3 **his mercy S** reads "his grace and mercy" • 15 **broken** from **S**: **P** reads "brekyng" • 15 **anemptes** from **S**: **P** reads "agaynst" • 19 **foule S** reads "vile" • 21, 23 **hele/heling** from **S**: **P** reads "cure"/"curying." This word is used in a related sense in 55.15 only, but "hele" is the regular form in both **P** and **S** • 24 **nedy S** reads "nedith" • 28 **oure** from **S**: **P** reads "and oure" • 30 **rested S** reads "stynte." In 37.2, to which this passage alludes, God "abode" • 28 **there S** reads "than"

[CHAPTER 79] The text of Chapter 79 is based on **P**, collated with **S** • **S** has the rubric "We are lernyd to our synne, and not to our neighbors but for their help. And God will we know whatsomever stering we have contrary to this shewing, it comith of our enemy. For the gret love of God knowen, we should not ben the more reckles to fallen. And if we fallen, we must hastely risen or ell we are gretly onkind to God. Seventy-Ninth Chapter" • 3 **in that time S** reads "at that time • 7 **ther S** reads "here" • 9 (first instance) **ther S** reads "where" • 9 (second instance) **ther S** reads "then" • 11 **For that wolde I have wist, dredful S** reads "for that wold I have wist dredfully." **P** has the syncopated form "a" for "have" • 12 **sekerly** from **S**: **P** reads "swetly," but see "unsekernesse" in line 9 • 13–14 **be his grete goodnesse and his grace** from **S**: **P** reads "his grete goodnesse and his gracious," which is just possible but syntactically confusing • 15 **in two** from **S**: **P** reads "unto" • 21 **swetnesse of the homely love S** plausibly reads "swetenes and homley loveing" • 22 **that it is S** plausibly reads simply "is" • 25 **of this stering S** reads "for this stering" • 27 **touching S** reads "touchith" • 29 **that we abide therwith S** reads "we abiden thus" • 31 **alle alone S** reads "al alufe," but see line 34 • 32 **swemefully, and moningly** from **S**: **P** reads "monyng and mornyng"; this reading avoids the use of the word "sweme," as is usual, but not invariable, in **P**. The phrase "the moning and the morning" is used in both **P** and **S** at 82.1, possibly alluding to this passage, and giving **P**'s reading here some support. However, at 29.1, **P** and **S** both read "generally, swemly, and mourningly," while at 71.6–8 the "chere of passion" Christ showed during his sufferings is described as "morning and swemfulle," and these passages, especially the second, seem to us to provide the probable model for the phrasing here • 33 **and** from **S**: **P** reads "of"

[CHAPTER 80] The text of Chapter 80 is based on **P**, collated with **S** • **S** has the rubric "By three thyngs God is worshippid and we be savid. And how our knowing now is but as an ABC. And swete Jhesus doith all, abyding and monyng with us. But whan we arn in synne Christ monyth alone. Than it longith to us, for kindness and reverens, hastely to turne agen to him. Eightieth Chapter" • 2 **kindly reson S** reads "reson naturall" • 6 **accorde P** reads "accordyng," **S** "attenden." We understand this to be a misreading in **P** of the infinitive for the participle. See textual note to 4.1 • 8 **these** from **S**: **P** reads "thoo," the scribe having first written, then crossed out, "doo," an especially clear example of the trouble the **P** scribe had distinguishing *d* and *th* or *ð* in her exemplar. See textual note to 3.6 • 8 **gretnesse S** plausibly reads "gret things" • 14 **wonneth** from **S**: **P** reads

"dwellyth" • 14 **yemeth P** reads "gevyth," which we take to be a misreading of "gemeth," **S** "governith," which we take as a translation of the same term. See textual notes to 1.48 ("yeming"), 68.8 • 16 **in erth** not in **S** • 21–22 **abideth us, swemefully and moningly S** reads "abidith swemefully and monyng," **P** "abydyth us, monyng and mornyng." See 79.31–32 • 23 **sweming and moning** from **S**: **P** reads "monyng and mornyng" • 23 **for S** reads "that" • 28 **bereth S** reads "kepith" • 29 **swemly and moning** from **S**: **P** reads "monyng and mornyng" • 32 **he S** plausibly reads "it" • 35 **kepeth S** plausibly reads "sheildith"

[CHAPTER 81] The text of Chapter 81 is based on **P**, collated with **S** • **S** has the rubric "This blissid woman saw God in divers manners, but she saw him take no resting place but in mannys soule. And he will we enjoyen more in his love then sorowen for often falling, remembring reward everlasting and liveing gladly in penance. And why God suffrith synne. Eighty-First Chapter" • 1 **to his creature** not in **S** • 10 **wonneth** from **S**: **P** reads "dwellyth" • 15 **living here to be penance S** reads "liveing and penance" • 15 **kinde longing in us S** reads "kind loveand" • 19 **this** added in the margin • 20 **shall** from **S**: **P** reads "shulde"

[CHAPTER 82] The text of Chapter 82 is based on **P**, collated with **S** • **S** has the rubric "God beholdith the monyng of the soule with pite and not with blom. And yet we do nowte but synne, in the which we arn kept in solace and in drede. For he will we turne us to him, redy clevand to his love, seand that he is our medicyne. And so we must love, in longing and in enjoyeing. And whatsoever is contrarie to this is not of God but of enmity. Eighty-Second Chapter" • 4–5 **therfore thou arte . . . without sinne** not in **S**, presumably omitted because of eyeskip between the two occurrences of "without sinne" • 5–6 **all the tribulation and disese** from **S**: not in **P** • 8 **behelde S** plausibly reads "beholdith" • 9 **without blame and sinne** from **S**: **P** reads "without synne" • 13 **do nought** from **S**: **P** reads "do." See 36.4 • 18 **saw S** reads "have" • 20 **understonde S** reads "understode" • 20 **this S** reads "us" • 22 **liver S** reads "lover" • 24 **one P** reads "oure" • 26 **higher S** reads "heyest" • 29 **solace** from **S**: **P** reads "joy," leading to the redundant phrase "gostly joy and trew enjoyeng"

[CHAPTER 83] The text of Chapter 83 is based on **P**, collated with **S** • **S** has the rubric "Of three properties in God: life, love, and light. And that our reason is in God, accordand. It is heyest gift. And how our feith is a light commeing of the fader, mesurid to us and in this night us ledand. And the end of our wo: sodenly our eye shall be openid in full light and clerte of syte, which is our maker, fader and holy gost in Jhesus our savior. Eighty-Third Chapter" • 5 **three** not in **S** • 5 **propertees** the **P** scribe initially wrote "lyghte" before this word, and then crossed it out, the word having presumably been reintroduced by mistake from the previous line • 6 **seen** not in **S** • 7 **cleve** from **S**: **P** reads "clevyng" • 7 **mightes S** reads "myte" • 13 **stonding** from **S**: **P** reads "stondyth" • 17–18 **clernes of sight oure light S** reads "clerte of light our sight" • 18 **fader** not in **S**

[CHAPTER 84] The text of Chapter 84 is based on **P**, collated with **S** • **S** has the rubric "Charite is the light, which is not so litil but that it is medefull, with travel, to deserven endles worshipfull thanke of God. For feith and hope leden us to charite, which is in three manners. Eighty-Fourth Chapter" • 2 **clerly** not in **S** • 4 **wurshipful thanke S** reads "endless worship," but see 14.12 • 6 **faith and** not in **S** • 8 **charite** from **S**: **P** has the incomprehensible reading "thacite"

[CHAPTER 85] The text of Chapter 85 is based on **P**, collated with **S** • **S** has the rubric "God lovid his chosen fro without begynnyng. And he never suffrith them to be hurte whereof their bliss might be lessid. And how privities now hidden in hevyn shall be knowen, wherfore we shall bliss our lord that everything is so wele ordeynid. Eighty-Fifth Chapter" • 9 **shalle** not in **S** • 11 **thing S** reads "wise" • 11 **ben** added in the margin • 11 **wele S** reads "full wele" • 11–12 **with one S** reads "without" • 13 **thin ordinance, or S** reads "then ordeynd beforn that"

[CHAPTER 86] The text of Chapter 86 is based on **P**, collated with **S** • **S** has the rubric "The good lord shewid this booke shuld be otherwise performid than at the first writing. And for his werking he will we thus prey, him thankand, trostand, and in him enjoyand. And how he made this shewing because he will have it known, in which knoweing he will give us grace to love him. For fifteen yeere after, it was answerid that the cause of all this shewing was love, which Jhesus mote grant us, Amen. Eighty-Sixth Chapter" • 2 **togeder S** reads "to God" • 3 **thus** from **S**: **P** reads "this" • 8–9 **with so grete**

love . . . more light from **S**: not in **P**, an example of eyeskip • 9 **fro S** reads "for" • 9 **darknesse S** reads "merkness" • 11 **witte** from **S** ("witten"): **P** reads "wytt in" • 14, 15 **shewed** (×2) from **S**: **P** reads "shewyth," despite the use of the past tense in the clause "love was his menyng" • 14–15 **What shewid he the? Love** from **S**: not in **P**, presumably omitted through eyeskip • 15–16 **wit more S** reads "witten and knowen" • 16 **other S** reads "other thing" • 19 **alle his werkes S** reads "all his werke" • 19–20 **and in this love . . . to us** not in **S**, probably omitted as a result of eyeskip between the two instances of "and in this love" • 22 **shalle we see S** reads "shall be seen" • 22–23 **withouten ende S** and adds "which Jhesus mot grant us" • 23–25 **Deo gracias . . . propicietur Deus** not in **S**, which instead has a lengthy final note: "Thus endith the revelation of love of the blissid trinite, shewid by our savior Christ Jesus for our endles comfort and solace, and also to enjoyen in him in this passand jorney of this life. Amen, Jhesu, Amen. I pray almyty God that this booke com not but to the hands of them that will be his faithfull lovers, and to those that will submitt them to the feith of holy church, and obey the holesom understondyng and teching of the men that be of vertuous life, sadde age, and profound lernyng. For this revelation is hey divinitye and hey wisdam, wherfore it may not dwelle with him that is thrall to synne and to the devill. And beware thou take not on thing after thy affection and liking and leve another, for that is the condition of an heretique. But take everything with other. And truly understonden, all is according to holy scripture and growndid in the same; and that Jhesus, our very love, light, and truth shall shew to all clen soules that with mekenes aske perseverantly this wisdom of hym. And thou to whome this booke shall come, thanke heyly and hertely our savior Christ Jhesu that he made these shewings and revelations for the, and to the, of his endles love, mercy, and goodnes, for thine and our save guide and conduct to everlestyng bliss; the which Jhesus mot grant us. Amen"

APPENDIX: RECORDS AND RESPONSES, 1394–1674

A. *The Westminster Revelation (with Hugh Kempster)*[1]

Date and Provenance: On the evidence of the dialect, the compilation from which the Westminster *Revelation* was taken may have been written in the East Midlands in the first half of the fifteenth century.

Description: This set of excerpts from *A Revelation*, the earliest copy of any part of this work, is the final third of an untitled and anonymous compilation of extracts from four Middle English religious works. The other three works are the homiletic psalm commentaries *Qui habitat* and *Bonum est* (Psalms 91 and 92 [Vulgate 90 and 91]), often attributed to Walter Hilton, long excerpts of which make up the first third of the work; and *The Scale of Perfection*, certainly by Hilton, portions of which make up the middle third.[2] The compilation, which is some twenty-five thousand words long, does not give any description of its purpose or contents, although it has a certain thematic integrity, despite the compilation's fidelity to the varied terminologies and arguments of its sources; there is little doubt that this is a single work. Except when excerpting *The Scale,* the compiler moves through the sources in order, cutting much material and adding brief bridging passages where the sense requires it, but not otherwise changing the wording of the texts. None of the excerpts is identified, although those from *A Revelation* assume the reader will recognize the text and its author: one begins, "Also, in the nyneth shewyng, our lord God seyd to her thus" (fol. 83v). This suggests the work was composed and circulated in a milieu (possibly a convent or other institution) in which Julian was a familiar figure.[3]

The compilation is about the contemplative life of a "ryghtwysse man" (a righteous person)—"he that wonyth [dwells] in the helpe of the hyeste," as its opening words put it—and especially how, with a "goostly eye" (spiritual eye)

1. The text of the Westminster manuscript published here was originally taken from Hugh Kempster's edition, "Julian of Norwich: The Westminster Text of *A Revelation of Love*," *Mystics Quarterly* 23 (1997): 177–245, although it has been checked afresh against the manuscript and modified to suit its present context. We are grateful to Father Kempster for his generosity.

2. For detailed description and analysis, see Edmund Colledge and James Walsh, eds., *Of the Knowledge of Ourselves and of God: A Fifteenth-century Florilegium* (London: Mowbrays, 1961), and Marleen Cré, "Westminster Cathedral Treasury MS 4: A Fifteenth-Century Spiritual Compilation" (M.Ph. diss., University of Glasgow, 1997).

3. For further discussion, see Hugh Kempster, "A Question of Audience: The Westminster Text and Fifteenth-Century Reception of Julian of Norwich," in *Julian of Norwich: A Book of Essays,* ed. Sandra J. McEntire (New York: Garland 1998), 257–90.

opened by grace, such a person perceives God, the self, the world, and the unrighteous (Westminster Cathedral Treasury MS 4, fols. 1–12). Persecuted by the worldly, the "ryghtwysse man" is armed by humility and by his intimacy with God's divine, as well as human, nature, lifted above the world to contemplate heaven and hell and his nearness to God: "Ther is no creature so nere ne nether so godly ne so helpely to me as the blessed kynde of God is [there is no created thing so near nor so godly nor so helpful to me as is the blessed nature of God], for he may through his grace enter into the substance of my soule. . . . I wyll seke hym in my soule: he is not ferre from me, for he seyth hym selfe, 'the kyngdomm of heven is within the,' that is hym selfe" (fol. 14). Praising this "ryghtwysse man" (on one occasion through the mouth of Christ, fols. 18v–25r) and making a clear distinction between this person and other types of Christian, the compilation assumes the distinction between ordinary Christians and "contemplatives" Julian's writings tend to avoid. It also assumes a spirituality that is not, in Julian's sense, visionary: "What Jhesu is in hym selfe may no soule know ne see here in this lyfe, but by effecte of his workyng he may be sene," begins one passage, derived from chapter 43 of book 2 of *The Scale* (fol. 65v). It is not surprising, then, that when excerpting from *A Revelation,* the compiler omits all references to Julian's "bodily sights," focusing exclusively on "ghostly sights"; includes none of the passages concerning Julian's "evenchristen"; and omits almost the whole of the theologically speculative Revelation Thirteen, with its doubts on the viability of the doctrine of eternal damnation and insistence that hell is not seen. In general terms, the Westminster *Revelation* can be understood as a version of Julian's thought designed to deepen its connections with the thought of her most prominent orthodox contemporary, Hilton.

Source and Treatment of the Texts: Westminster Cathedral Treasury MS 4, which contains a good, if mechanical, later copy of the original compilation and the only manuscript in which it survives, is usually dated to around 1500 on the basis of its handwriting and orthography. The compilation is the only work in this small, delicate-looking book. Unlike the other texts excerpted in the compilation, *A Revelation* is set off from the excerpts it follows by a blank half-page in the manuscript, so that it begins at the top of a page (on the verso of the folio). In this transcription of the *Revelation* portion of the text, we normalize thorn (þ) and yogh (ȝ), rationalize the scribal variation between *u* and *v*, and *i* and *j*, expand abbreviations, and add punctuation consistent, where possible, with the text of *A Revelation* edited above. Paragraph divisions, which only occasionally correspond to a paragraph marker in the manuscript, are intended as a guide to the compilation's pattern of borrowings from *A Revelation*. Words and phrases added by the compiler, especially at points of transition between passages, are here placed in italics.

* * *

/fol. 72v/ *Oure*[4] *gracious and goode lorde* God shewed me in party the wisdom and the trewthe of the soule of oure blessed lady, Saynt Mary, wherein I understood the reverent beholdynge that she behelde her God, that is her maker, marvelynge with grete reverence that he wolde be borne of her that was a simple creature of his makyng. For this was her mervelyng: that he that was her maker wolde be borne of her that is made. And this wysdom and trowth, knowynge the grettenes of her maker and the lytyllnes of her- /fol. 73r/ selfe that is made,

---

4. The first set of excerpts is taken from *A Revelation,* Chapters 4–7: Revelation 1.

caused her to sey full mekely unto Gabryell: "Lo me here, Goddis handmayden." [*Rev.* 4.26–33]

This wysedom and trewth made her to beholde her God so gret, so hygh, so myghty, and so good, that the gretenes and the nobilte and beholdyng of God fulfylled her of reverent dred. And with thys she sawe herselfe so lytyll and so lowe, so symple and so pore in regarde[5] of her God, that this reverent drede fulfylled her of mekenes. And thus[6] by this ground she was fulfylled of grace, and of all maner of vertues, and overpassyth all creaturys. [*Rev.* 7.3–8]

In this /fol. 73v/ syght I undyrstod sothly that she is more than all that God made beneth her in worthynes and in fulhed. For above her ther is nothyng that is made, but the blessed manhed of Criste, as to my syght. *And this oure good lord shewed to myne undirstondyng in lernyng of us.* [*Rev.* 4.33–35]

Also, I saw that oure good lord is to us all thyng that is good and comfortable to oure helpe. He is oure clothyng, the which for love wrappith us and wyndith us, helpith us and ablyth us, and hangith aboute us for tender love, that he may never /fol. 74r/ leve us. And so in this syght I sawe that he is all thyng that is good, as to my undyrstondyng. [*Rev.* 5.2–6]

And in this, he shewed me a lytil thyng the quantite of a hasylnott, lyeng in the pawme of my hand as it had semed, and it was as rownde as eny ball. I loked therupon with the eye of my understondyng, and I thought: "What may this be?" And it was aunswered generally thus: "It is all that is made." I merveled howe it myght laste, for methought it myght sodenly have fall to nought for lytyllhed. And I was answered in my under- /fol. 74v/ stondyng: "It lastyth and ever shall, for God lovyth it. And so hath

all thyng his begynnyng by the love of God." [*Rev.* 5.7–13]

In this lytyll thyng I sawe thre propertees. The fyrste is that God made it, the secunde is that God lovyth it, and the thrid is that God kepith it. But what is this to me? Sothly, the maker, the keper, and the lover. For tyll I am substancially oned to hym, I may never have full reste ne verey blysse; that is to sey, that I be so fastened to hym that ther be nothynge that is made betwene my God and me. [*Rev.* 5.14–18]

This litil thynge that is made, methought /fol. 75r/ it myght have fall to nought for lytillnes. Of this nedith us to have knowynge, that it is lyke to nought all thyng that is made, for to love and have God that is unmade. For this is the cause why that we be not all in ese of harte and soule: for we seke here reste in this thyng that is so lytyll, where no reste is in, and know not our God, that is all myghty, all wise, and all good. For he is verey reste. God wyll be knowen, and it likith hym that we reste us[7] in hym. For all that is beneth hym sufficith not to us. And this is the cause why that no soule is rested tyll it be /fol. 75v/ noughted of all that is made. And when he is wylfully noughted for love to have hym that is all, then is he able to resceve goostely reste. [*Rev.* 5.19–27]

Also, our lorde shewed that it is full grete pleasance to hym that a sely soule com to hym nakedly, pleynely, and homly. For this is the kynde yernyng of the soule by the touchyng of the holy gooste, as by the undirstondyng that I have in this shewyng:[8] "God, for thi goodnes yeve unto me thyselfe. For thou art inough to me, and I may nothyng aske that is[9] lesse that may be full wurshyppe to thee. And yf I aske eny- /fol. 76r/ thyng that is lesse, ever me wan-tith. But only in the I have all." And thes wordis,

---

5. **regarde** corrected in the manuscript from "rewarde."
6. **thus** from **P/S**: **W** "this."
7. **reste us** "us" added above the line.
8. **shewyng** note in margin reads "oratio."
9. **that is** "is" added above the line.

"God of thy goodnes," it ar full lovesum to the soule, and ful nygh touchyng the wyll of our lorde. For his goodnes comprehendith all his creaturis and all his blessed werkis and overpassith withoute ende. For he is the endeleshed, and he hath made us only to hymselfe and restored us by his precious passion, and ever kepith us in his blessed love. And al this is of his goodnes. [*Rev.* 5.28–38]

This shewyng was yeve, as to my understondynge, to lerne oure soules wiseli to cleve to the goodnes of God. /fol. 76v/ And in that same tyme, the custom of oure prayer was brought to my mynde: how that we use, for unknowyng of love, to make many meanys. Than sawe I sothly that is more worshippe to God, and more very delyte, that we feythfully prey to hym selfe of his goodnes and cleve therto by his grace, with true undirstondyng and stedfast beleve, than yf we made all the meanys that hart may thynke. For though we make all this menys, it is to lytyll and not full worshyp to God. But in his goodnes is all the whole, and there feylith no thyng. [*Rev.* 6.1–8]

For this as I shall sey /fol. 77r/ came to my mynde in the same tyme. We prayde to God for his holy fleshe and for his precious blode, his holy passion and his dereworthi deeth, his worshypfull woundis: and all the blessed kyndenes, the endeles lyf that we have of all this, it is of hys goodnes. And we pray hym for his moder love that hym bare: and all that helpe that we have in her, it is of his goodnes. And we pray for hys holy crosse that he deyd on: and al the helpe and vertue that we have of the crosse, it is of his goodnes. And on the same wyse, all the helpe that we have of speciall /fol. 77v/ sayntis, and all the blessed company in heven, the dereworthy love and the holy, endeles frendeshyp that we have of them, it is all of his goodnes. [*Rev.* 6.9–18]

For God of his goodnes, *for God of his grete goodnes*, hath ordeyned meanys to helpe us in most lovyng and blessed maner. Of whiche the cheyf and principall meane is the blessed kynde that he toke of the mayden Mary, with all the menys that goeth before and commyth aftir, whiche ben longyng to our salvacion and endeles redempcion. Wherefore it pleasith hym that we seke hym and worshyp hym by menys, undirstondyng and knowyng that /fol. 78r/ he is goodnes of all. [*Rev.* 6.19–24]

Forto the goodnes of God is the hygheste prayer, and it commyth downe to us, to the loweste party of our nede. It quycknyth our soule and bryngith it on lyf, and makith it to wax in grace and in vertue. It is neriste in kynde and rediest in grace. For it is the same grace that the soule sekith and ever shall, tyll we know our God vereyly that hath us all in hym beclosed. A man goeth upryght, and the soule of his bodi is sperd as a purse ful feyre. And when it is tyme of his necessary, it is opened and sperd ayen well honestely. And that is /fol. 78v/ he that doth this, he shewyth that he seeth: "He commyth downe to us, to the lowest party of our nede." For he hath no dispyte of that that he hath made, nether he hath no disdeyne to serve us at the symplest office that longith to our body in kynde, for love of the soule that he hath made to hys owne lykenes. For as the bodi is cladde in the clothe, and the fleshe and the harte in the bouke, so be we, soule and body, clad and closed in the goodnes of God. [*Rev.* 6.25–37]

Ye, and more homly! For all thees may were and waste away. But the goodnes of God is ever whole, and nere /fol. 79r/ to us withoute eny lykenes. For truely our lover desyrith that the soule clyme to hym with all the myghtes, and that we be evyr clymyng to his goodnes. For of all thyng that hart may thynk, it pleasyth moste God and soneste spedith. For our soule is so preciously lovyd of hym that is hyghest, that it overpassith the knowlege of all other creaturis: that is to sey, ther ys no creature that is made that may wete how meche and how swetely and how tenderly our maker lovyth us.[10] [*Rev.* 6.38–45]

---

10. **lovyth us** note in margin reads "Amor Dei in nobis" (the love of God in us).

Wherfor we may, with his grace and with his helpe, stonde[11] */fol. 79v/* in goostly behol-dynge, with everlastyng mervelyng in this here overpassyng, unmesurable love that our lorde hath to us of his goodnes. And therfor we may aske of oure lover, with reverence, all that we wyll. For oure kyndely wyll is to have God, and the good wyll of God is to have us, and we may never blyn in wyllyng ne of lovyng tyll we have hym in fulnes of joy. And than may we desyre no more. For he wyll that we be occupied in knowyng and lovyng of hym tyll the tyme com that we shall be fulfilled in */fol. 80r/* heven. For of all thyng, the beholdeng and the lovyng of the maker causith the soule to seme leste in his owne sight, and moste fyllith it with reverent drede and true mekenes, and with plente of charite to his evencristen. [*Rev.* 6.46–53, 55–58]

Ferthermore,[12] we be nowe so blynde and so unwyse that we can never seke God tyll what tyme that he of his goodnes shewyth hymselfe to us. And when we see ought of hym gra-ciously, than ar we stered by the same grace to seke hym with grete desyre to se hym more blis-sefully. And thus I sawe hym and sought hym, */fol. 80v/* and I had hym and wanted hym. And this is and shulde be our common wurkyng in this lyf, as to my syght. [*Rev.* 10.11–15]

For the contynuyng sekyng of the soule pleasyth God full meche, for it may do no[13] more than sekyng, sufferyng, and trustyng. And this is wroght on eche a soule that hath it bi the holy goost. And the clerenes of fyndynge is of a speciall grace of God when it is his wyll. The sekyng with feyth, hope, and charite plesith our lord God, and the fyndyng pleasith the soule, and fulfyllyth it of joyes. And thus was I lerned to my under- */fol. 81r/* stondyng that the sekyng

is as good as beholdyng, for the tyme that he wyll suffer the soule to be in traveyle.[14] It is Goddis wil that we seke into the beholdyng of hym, for by that shall he shewe us hymselfe of his speciall grace when he wyll. And how a soule shall have hym in his beholdyng he shall teche hymselfe. And that is moste wurshyp to hym and most profit to the soule, and it moste resceyvyth of mekenes and vertues, with the grace and ledyng of the holy goost. For a soule that only fasteneth[15] hym to God with very truste, */fol. 81v/* eyther in sekyng or in behol-dyng, that is the moste wurship that he may do, as to my syght. [*Rev.* 10.57–70]

It is Godis wyll that we have thre thynges in our sekyng of his yefte. The fyrste is we seke wyllfully and besyly withoute slouth, as it may be with his grace, gladly and merily without unskylfull hevynes and vayne sorowe. The secunde: that we abide hym stedfastly for his love, withoute grutchyng and stryvynge ayenste hym, into our lyvys ende, for it shall leste but a whyle. The thryd is that we truste in hym myghtily, of full sure feyth. For it is his wyll that */fol. 82r/* we shall know that he will appere sodenly and blessedfully to al his lovers. For his workynge is prevey, and it will be perceyvyd, and his apperyng shal be swith sodene. And he wyll be belevyd, for he is full hende, homly, and curteys. Blessed mutte he be! [*Rev.* 10.73–82]

And aftir this I sawe God in a poynt—that is to sey, in myne understondyng—by whiche sight I sawe that he is all thyng. I behelde with avisement, seyng and knowyng in that sight that he doth all that is done, be it never so litill. And I sawe that nothyng is don by happe ne by adventure, but */fol. 82v/* all by the foreseeng of Goddys wysedom. And yf it be hap or adventur in the syght of man, our blyndenes and our

---

11. **helpe, stonde** from **P/S**: **W** reads "hooly stondynge."
12. The second group of excerpts is taken from *A Revelation,* Chapters 10–11: Revelations 2–3.
13. **do no more** from **P/S**: **W** "do more."
14. **in traveyle** note in margin reads "Seeke God."
15. **fasteneth** corrected in the manuscript from "festeneth."

unbeforesyght is the cause. *Wherfor* wel I wot that in syght of our lord God is no happe ne adventure. And therfor me behovyd nedisly to graunt that all thyng that is done it is well done, for our lord God dothe all. For in this tyme the wurkyng of creature was not shewed, but of oure lord God in creature. For he is in the mydde poynt of all thyng, and all he dothe, and I was sure that he doeth no synne. And /fol. 83r/ here I sawe sothly that synne ys no dede. [*Rev.* 11.1–3, 5–7, 12–18]

Also, amonge other shewynges, was[16] our good *lord* meanyng thus: "Se, I am God. Se, I am in al thyng. Se, I do all thyng. Se, I lefte never myne hande of my wurkes, ne never shall withoute ende. See, I led all thyng to the ende[17] that I ordeyned it to, fro withoute begynnynge, by the same myght, wisedome, and love that I made it with. How shulde than enythyng be amys?" [*Rev.* 11.42–46]

I sawe full surely that he changyth never his purpose in no maner thyng, ne never shall withoute ende. For ther was nothyng unknowyn to hym /fol. 83v/ in his ryghtfull ordynannce fro without begynnynge. And therfor all thynges were sett in order, or enythyng was made, as it shulde withoute ende. [*Rev.* 11.35–39]

Also,[18] *in the nyneth shewyng,* our lord God seyd *to her thus:* "Art thou well payed that I sufferd for thee?" And *she* seyd: "Ye good lord, graunt mercy. Ye good lord, blessed mote thou be!" Than seyd Jhesu, oure good lorde God: "Yf thou be payed, I am payed. It is a joy, a blysse, and an endelesse lykynge to me that I ever sufferde passion for thee. And yf I myght suffer more, I wolde suffer more" [*Rev.* 22.1–5]

And in thees same /fol. 84r/ wordys—"Yf I myght"—I sawe sothly that as often[19] as he might dye, as often he wolde, and love shulde never lett hym have rest tyll he had done it. And I beheld with greate diligence for to wete how ofte[20] he wolde dye yef he myght. And sothly the nombre passed myne understondynge[21] and my wittes so ferre that my reason myght not, ne coude not, comprehende it ne take it. And when he had thus ofte deyed, or shulde, yett he wolde sett it at nought for love. For though the swete manhed of Criste myght suffer but ones, the goodnes of hym may /fol. 84v/ never cesse of profer—every day to the same, yf it myght be. [*Rev.* 22.21–30]

Also, it is Goddis wyll that we have trewe lykynge with hym in oure salvacion, and therin he wyll that we be myghtyli comforted and strengthed, and thus wyll he merely with his grace[22] that our soule be occupied. [*Rev.* 23.11–13] *For* we be his blysse, hys mede and his wurship, and we be his coronn. (And this was a singular mervell and full delectable beholdyng,[23] that we be his coronn!) This that I sey is so grete blysse to oure lorde Jhesu that he settith at nought all his traveyll and his hard pas- /fol. 85r/ sion, and his cruell and shamefull deth. [*Rev.* 22.17–20] *The fader* is full pleasyd with the dedis that Jhesu hath done about oure salvacion, wherefore we be not only his by his byenge, but also by the curteys yefte of his father. For we be his blysse and his mede, *as it is seyd before,* [*Rev.* 22.15–17] and that yefte and that mede is so blyssefull to oure lord Jhesu that his father[24] myght have yeve hym no mede that myght have lykyd hym better. [*Rev.* 22.12–13]

---

16. **was** not in MS. An alternative would be "shewed."
17. **the ende** "the" added above the line.
18. The third group of excerpts is taken from *A Revelation*, Chapters 22–24: Revelations 9–10.
19. **as often** W reads "as ~~of~~ often."
20. **how ofte** "ofte" added above the line.
21. **understondynge** W reads "unstondynge."
22. **with his grace** W reads "with ~~his~~ his grace."
23. **beholdyng** first two letters added above the line.
24. **that his father** W reads "~~that his fade~~ that his father."

For in us he lykyth withoute ende, and so shall we within hym with his grace. All that he hath done for us, and dothe, and /fol. 85v/ ever shall doo, was never coste ne charge to hym ne myght be, but only that he dedde in our man-hed, begynnynge at the swete incarnacion, and lestyng tyl the blessed uprysyng on Ester day in the mornyng. So longe dured the coste and the charge aboute oure redempcion in dede, of whiche dede he enjoyeth endelesly, as it is afore seyd. [*Rev.* 23.14–19]

Also, Jhesu wil that we take hede to this blysse that is in the trynyte of oure salvacion, and that we desyre to have as meche goostely lykynge, with his grace, as is aforeseyde: that is to sey, that the lykyng of /fol. 86r/ oure salvacion be lyke to the joye that Criste hath of our salvacion as it may be whyle we ben here. All the blessed trynyte wrought in the passion of Criste, mynystryng abundaunce of vertues and plente of grace to us by hym. But only the maydenys sone sufferd, wherof all the gloriouse trynyte endelesly enjoyeth. And this was shewed in this worde: "Art thou wel payed?" By that other word that Criste seyd—"Yf thou art payed, I am payed"—as yf he had seyd: "Yt is joy and lykyng inough to me, and I aske not else of the /fol. 86v/ for my traveyle but that I might pay thee." [*Rev.* 23.19–28]

And in this,[25] he broght to my mynde the propertee of a glad yever.[26] A glad yever takyth but lytyll hede at the thyng that he yevyth,[27] but his desyre is, and all his entent, to pleace hym and solace hym to whom he yevith it. And yf the resceyver take the yefte[28] gladly and thanke-fully, then the curteys yever settythe at nought all his coste and all his traveyle, for joye and delyte that he hath for he hath so plesed and solacyd hym that he lovyth. Plenteously and fully was this shewed. [*Rev.* 23.29–34]

Also, with glad chere our /fol. 87r/ lord loked into his syde and beheld, enjoyenge. And with his swete lokynge he ledde furthe the under-stondyng of his creaturys by the same wounde into his syde, withyn. And there he shewed a feyre, delectable place, and large inow for all mankynde that shall be sauf to reste in pees and love. And therwith he brought to mynde his dereworthy blod and his precious water whiche he lett poure all oute for love. And with that swete beholdynge he shewed his blessed harte evyn cloven at twoo. And with this swete enjoyng he shewed in undyrstondyng, in /fol. 87v/ partye, the blessed godhed, as ferfurth as he wolde at that tyme, strengthynge the pore soule for to understonde as yt may be seyed: that is to meane, the endeles love that was withoute begynnyng, and is, and shal be ever. [*Rev.* 24.1–10]

And with this, oure lord God seyd ful bles-sedly, "Loo, how I lovyd thee," as yf he had seyed: "My derlynge, beholde and see thyn owne brother, thi sovereyne. My chylde, beholde and se thi lorde God, thy maker and thi endeles joye. See what lykynge and blysse I have in thy salvacion, and for my love enjoy with me." [*Rev.* 24.11–14]

Also, to more /fol. 88r/ understandynge, this blessed worde was seyed, "Loo how I love the," as yf he had seyed: "Beholde and see that I lovyd the so meche, or I dyed for the, that I wolde dye for the. And now I have deyed for the, and suf-ferde peyne wylfully that I may. And now is all my bitter[29] peyne and all my traveyle turned to endeles joye and blysse bothe to me and to thee. Howe shulde it now be that thou shuldiste eny thyng pray me that lykyth me, but that I shulde full gladly graunt it the? For my lykynge is thi holynes and thy endeles joye and blysse with /fol. 88v/ me." [*Rev.* 24.15–21]

---

25. **And in this** w reads "and it this."
26. **yever** *y* added above the line.
27. **yevyth** note in margin reads "A Gladde Geaver."
28. **yefte** first *e* added above the line.
29. **bitter** corrected from "better."

This is the undirstondyng, symply as I can sey, of thys blessed worde: "Loo how I love thee." All this shewed oure lorde God to make us gladde and mery. [*Rev.* 24.22–23]

Also,[30] I undirstond sothly that all maner thynge is made redy to us by the grete goodnes of God, so ferfurthe that, what tyme we ben oureselfe in peace and in charite, we be vereyly saufe. But for that we may not have this in fulnes while we ben here, therfore it befallyth us evermore to lyve in swete prayer and in lovely longyng with our lorde /*fol. 89r*/ Jhesu. [*Rev.* 40.16–20]

Also, oure lorde shewed for prayer, in whiche shewyng I sawe two condicions in our lordis meanyng. Oon is rightfull prayer, and the other is sure truste. But yet ofte tymis our truste is not full. For we be not sure that God heryth us, as we thynke for oure unworthynes, and for that we fele nothyng. For we be as bareyne and as drye often tymes aftir oure prayer as we were before. And thus, in oure felyng, oure foly is cause of our wekenes. For thus I have felt in myselfe. [*Rev.* 41.1–6]

And all this brought /*fol. 89v*/ oure lorde sodenly to my mynde, and shewed thees wordis and seyed: "I am grounde of thi besekyng. Firste it is my wyll that thou have it, and I make the to wyll it. How shulde it than be that thou shuldiste not have thi besekynge, seeth I make the to besekyng it, and thou besekist it?" And thus in the ferst reson of the thre that folowyth,[31] our lord God shewyth a myghty comfort, as may be seyeng in the same wordis. In the ferste reson— where he seyeth, "and thou besekyst it"—there he shewyth full grete plesance, and endeles mede that he /*fol. 90r*/ wyll yeve us for our besekynges. And in the sexte reson[32]—there he seyeth, "How

shulde it than be?"—this was seyd for a unpossible. For it is the moste unpossible that may be that we shulde beseke mercy and grace and not have it. For of all thyng that our lord makyth us to beseke, hymselfe hath ordeyned it to us fro withoute begynnynge. [*Rev.* 41.7–18]

Here may we see than that oure besekynge is not cause of the goodnes and grace that he dothe unto us, but his[33] owne proper goodnes. And that shewyth he sothfastly in all thees swete wordys, there he seyth: /*fol. 90v*/ "I am grounde of thi prayer and of thy besekynges." And our lorde wyll that this be knowen of all his lovers in erthe. And the more that we knowe it, the more shulde we beseke it, yf it be wysely taken. And so is oure lordis menyng. [*Rev.* 41.19–23]

Wyse sekynge is a trew, gracious, lestyng wyll of the soule, oned and fastened into the wyll of our lorde God hymselfe. He is the fyrste resceyver of our prayer, as to my syght, and he takyth it ryght thankefully and hyghly enjoyeth. He sendyth it up above and settith it in tresory, where it shall never peryshe. It is /*fol. 91r*/ there before God with all his holy company, contynually resceyvyd, ever spedyng oure nedis. And when we shall underfong our blysse, it shall be yeve us for a degree of joye, with endeles, wurshypfull thankynges of hym. [*Rev.* 41.24–30]

Ful glad and mery is our lord God of our prayer. He lokith theraftir, and he wolde have it. For with his grace it makith us lyke to hymselfe in condicion as we be in kynde. Also, he seyeth: "Pray, though thou thynke it savour the not." [*Rev.* 41.31–34]

Also, to prayer langith thankynges. Thankyng is a trewe, inwarde knowyng, with /*fol. 91v*/ grete reverence and lovely drede,[34] turnyng ourselfe

---

30. The fourth group of excerpts is taken from *A Revelation*, Chapters 40–44: Revelations 13–14.

31. **ferst reson of the thre that folowyth** "of" here is "with" in **P/S**.

32. **the ferste reson . . . the sexte reason** "ferste" here is "fifth" in **P/S**, and while "sexte" is the same as **P/S**'s "sixth," the numbering is incorrect in **W**, which has changed the order of clauses in Christ's speech, relocating "reasons" four and five to the end. It may be that the scribe did not realize that "reason" here means "clause."

33. **his W** reads "his ~~his~~."

34. **lovely drede** note in margin (in later hand) reads "graciarum actio" (act of thanksgiving).

with all our myghtis into the wurkynge that oure lorde God steryd us to, injoyeng and thankyng hym inwardely. And somtyme, with plenteous-nes, it brekith owte with voyce and seyth: "Good lord, graunt mercy, blessed mote thou be!" And sometyme, when thy harte is drye and felyth nought, or else by temptacion of our enymye, than it is dryven by reason and by grace to krye upon oure lorde with voyce, rehersynge his blessed passion and his grete goodnes. And so the vertue /fol. 92r/ of our lordis worde turnyth into the soule, and quycknyth the hart, and entrith in by his grace into trewe wurkyng, and makith it to pray full blessedly. To enjoy in our lorde God, it is a lovely thankyng in his syght. [*Rev.* 41.45–55]

Our lord wyll that we have trewe undirston-dyng, and namely in thre thynges that longith to our prayer. The fyrste is by whom and how that our prayer spryngith. By whom, he shewed when he seyd, "I am grounde"; and how, by his goodnes, for he seyeth, "Fyrst it is my wyll." And for the secunde: in what maner and how /fol. 92v/ we shulde pray. That is, that our wyll be turned into the wyll of oure lorde God, enjoyenge. And so meanyth he whan he seyth: "I make the to wyll yt." For the thyrde: that we knowe the fruyt and th'ende of our prayer: that is, to be oned and lyke to our lord in all thyng. And to this menyng and for this ende was all this lovely lesson shewed. And he wyll helpe us, and he shall make it so, as he seyeth hymselfe. Blessed mote he be! [*Rev.* 42.1–10]

For this is oure lordis wyl: that oure prayer and our truste be both alyke large.[35] For yf we truste /fol. 93r/ not as moche as we pray, we do not full wurship to our lorde in oure prayer, and

also we tary and peyne ourselfe. And the cause is, as I beleve, for we know not truely that our lord God is grounde hymselfe of whom our prayer spryngith. And also that we know not that it is yeven us by his grace of his grete and tender love. For yf we knewe this, it wolde make us truste to have, of our lordes yefte, all that we desyre. For I am sure that no man that askyth mercy and grace with true menynge but mercy and grace be fyrst yeve /fol. 93v/ unto hym. [*Rev.* 42.11–18]

But somme tymes it commyth to oure minde[36] that we have prayed long tyme, and yet we thynke that we have not oure askynge. But here-fore shulde not we be hevy, for I am sure by oure lordis menyng that eyther we abyde a better time, or more grace, or else a better yefte. He wyll that we have trewe knowyng in hymselfe that he is beyng. And in thys knowyng, he wyll that our undirstondyng be grounded with all our myghtis, all our entent, and all oure meanyng. And in thys grounde, he wyll that we take our /fol. 94r/ stede and our wonyng. [*Rev.* 42.19–25]

And by the gracious lyght of hymselfe he wyll that we have undyrstandyng of thre thynges. The fyrste is thi noble and excellent makyng. The secunde is the precious and dere-worthy ayen-byeng. The thirde is that all thyng that he hath made beneth us to serve us, he for our love kepith it. Than menyth he thus, as yf he seyed: "Beholde and se that I have done all this before thy prayer, and now thou art, and prayeste me." And this our lord God meanyth: that it longith to us for to wette that the grettist /fol. 94v/ dedis be done, as holy churche techyth. [*Rev.* 42.26–32]

And in thee selfe, to our soulis,[37] we have that we desire. And than we se not for the tyme

---

35. **large** note in margin (in later hand) reads "Spes" (hope).

36. **minde** corrected in the manuscript from "mende."

37. **And in thee selfe, to our soulis** this seems to derive from two words in *Rev.* 42.32 ("And in"), followed by four words in *Rev.* 43.15–16 ("hymselfe to oure soule"), modified. As punctuated, the clauses mean "and in the self, from the point of view of our souls," but this is not lucid. It may be that the manuscript from which **w** was copying had a leaf missing at this point, so that the scribe's omission of *Rev.* 42.33–43.15 and failure to make sense at this point were accidental.

what we shulde more pray, but all our entent with all our myghtis is sett wholi into the beholdyng of hym. And this is an high and unparcevable[38] prayer, as to my sight. For all the cause wherfore we pray is onyd into the sight and the beholdyng of hym to whom we pray, merveylously enjoyenge with reverent drede and so grete swetnes and delite in hym that we cannot pray[39] /fol. 95r/ nothyng but as he steryth us for the tyme. And well I wote, the more the soule seeth of God, the more it desyreth hym by grace. [*Rev.* 43.15–22]

But when we se hym not so, than fele we nede and cause to pray, for faylyng and for ablyng of oureselfe to our lorde Jhesu. For when a soule is tempested and troubled and lefte to itselfe, than ys tyme to pray to make hymselfe souple and buxum to God. But he by no maner of prayer makith God souple to hym. For he is ever alyke in love. And thus I saw that what ty- /fol. 95v/ me we se nedis[40] wherfor we pray, than our lord God folowyth us, helpynge our desyre. And whan we of his speciall grace pleynely beholdith hym, seyng noo other nedis, than we folowith hym and he drawyth us into hym by love. For I saw and felt that his merveylous and his fulsum goodnes fulfyllith all other myghtis. And therwith I sawe that his contynuynge wurkyng in all maner thyng is done so godly, so wysely, and so myghtily that it plesith all our ymagynyng and all that we can meane and thynke. And than /fol. 96r/ we can do no more but behold hym and enjoyng, with a myghti desyre to be all onyd into hym, and entende to his wonyng,[41] and enjoyeng in his love, and delyte in his goodnes. [*Rev.* 43.23–35]

And thus, by his swete grace, shall we in oure owne meke, contynuyng prayer, come[42] unto hym now in this lyf by many prevey touchynges of swete gostly syghtis and felyng, mesured to us as oure symplenes may beer it. And this is wrought and shall be by the grace of the holy goost, so longe tyll we shall deye in longyng for love. /fol. 96v/ And than shall we all come into oure lord God, ourselfe clerely knowyng and God fulsomly havyng; and we endelesly be had all in God, hym vereyly seyng and fulsomly felyng, and hym goostly felynge, and hym goostly heryng, and delytably smellyng, and swetely swalowyng. And thus shall we se God face to face, homly and fulsomly. The creature that is made shall se and endelesly beholde God that is the maker. For thus may no man se God and leve aftir, that is to sey in this dedly lyf. But whan he of his speciall /fol. 97r/ grace wyll shew hym here, he strengthith the creature above the selfe, and he mesuryth the shewynge aftir his owne wil, as it is moste profitable for the tyme. [*Rev.* 43.36–47]

Trewthe seeth God, and wysedom beholdith God. And of thees two commyth the thryd, and that is a merveylous, holi delyte in God, whiche is love. Where trewth and wysdom ys, verely there is love, and veryli commynge of them both, and all of Goddis makyng. For God is endeles sovereyne trowth, endeles sovereyne wysedom, endeles sovereyne love un- /fol. 97v/ made. And mannys soule is a creature in God, the whyche hath the same propertees made, and evermore it dothe that it was made fore: it seeth God, and it beholdith God, and yt lovyth God. Where God enjoyeth in the creature, and the creature enjoyeth in God, endelesly merveylyng, in the which merveylyng he seeth his God, his lorde, his maker, so high, so grete and so good in rewarde of hym that is made, that unethis the creature semyth ought[43] to itselfe.

---

38. **unparcevable** W reads "unparceable."
39. **cannot pray** note at foot of page reads "so great" (repeating this phrase from the previous line).
40. **se nedis** from P/S: W reads "sedis."
41. **wonyng** corrected in the manuscript from "wowynge."
42. **come** corrected in the manuscript from "commyng."
43. **ought** corrected in the manuscript from "nought."

But the clerenes and clennes of trowth and wysedom makith /fol. 98r/ hym to se and to beknowen that he is made for love, in whiche love God endelesly kepith hym. [*Rev.* 44.6–17]

Also,[44] he wyll that we wett that oure soule is a lyf; whiche lyf, of his goodnes and grace, shall leste in heven withoute ende, hym lovyng, hym thankyng, and hym praysyng. *Also,* he wyll that we wett that the nobleste thyng that ever he made is mankynde, and the fulleste substance and the hyeste vertue is the blessed soule of Criste. And ferthermore, he wyll that we know that this dereworthy soule was preciously knytt to hym in the ma- /fol. 98v/ kyng. Whiche knot[45] is so sotyl and so myghty that it is oned into God, in whiche onynge it is made endelesly holy. Ferthermore, he wyll that we wett and understonde that all the soulis that shall be savyd in heven withoute ende be knyt in thys knot, and onyd in this onynge, and made holy in this holynes. [*Rev.* 53.44–46, 48–54]

And for grete endeles love that God hath to all mankynde, he makith no departyng in love betwene the blessed soule of Criste and the leeste soule that shall be savyd. For it is well easy to lyve and to trowe that the dwellyng of the /fol. 99r/ blessed soule of Criste is full high in the glorious godhed. And sothly, as I understand in our lordis menyng, where the blessed soule of Criste is, there is the substance of all the soulis that shal be savyd by Criste. Hyghly ought we to enjoy that God dwellith in oure soule, and meche more hyly we ought to enjoy that oure soule dwellith in God. Our soule is made to be Goddis dwellyng-place; and the dwellyng-place of oure soule is in God, whiche is unmade. A hyghe understondyng it is inwardly to se and to knowe that God, which /fol. 99v/ is oure maker, dwellyth in oure soule; and a hygher undirstondyng it is, and more, inwardly to se and to know

oure soule, that is made, dwellith in God in substance—of whiche substance, by God, we be that we be. [*Rev.* 54.1–12]

Also, the almyghty trouthe of the trynyte is oure fader, for he made us and kepith us in hym. And the deepe wysedome of the trynite is oure moder, in whom we be all enclosed. And the high goodnes of the trynyte is oure lord, and in hym we ar closed, and he is in us: almyghty, all wisedom, and all goodnes; oon God, oon /fol. 100r/ lorde, *and oon goodnes.* [*Rev.* 54.15–18, 21]

Also, I sawe that Criste, all havyng us in hym that shall be savyd by hym, wurshypfully presentyth his fader in hevyn with us. Whiche present well thankefully his father resceyvyth, and curteysly yevyth it to his sonne, Jhesu Criste. Whiche yefte and wurkyng is joye to the father and blysse to the sone and lykyng to the holy gooste. And of all thyng that to us longyth, it is moste lykyng to our lorde that we enjoy in this joye, whiche is in the blessed trynyte of our salvacion. [*Rev.* 55.2–8]

Also, I sawe ful surely that it /fol. 100v/ is redyer to us and more easy to come to the knowyng of God than to knowyng of our owne soule. For oure soule is so depe grounded in God, and so endelesly tresored, that we may not come to the knowyng therof tyll we have fyrste knowyng of God, whiche is the maker to whom it is oned. But notwithstondynge, I sawe that we have kyndely of fulnes to desyre wysely and truely to knowe oure owne soule, wherby we ar lerned to seke it there it is, and that is in God. And thus, by the gracious ledynge of the holy /fol. 101r/ gooste, we shulde knowe them bothe in oon. Whether we be stered to knowe God or our selfe soule, it ar bothe good and trewe. God is nerer to us than owre owne soule. For he is grounde in whom oure soule stondyth, and he

---

44. The fifth group of excerpts is taken from *A Revelation,* Chapters 53–64: Revelations 14–15.
45. **knot** from **P/S: W** reads "knat."

is mene that kepith the substance and the sensualyte togeder, so that it shall never depart. For oure soule syttith in God in verey reste, and oure soule standith in God in sure strength, and oure soule is kyndely rooted in God in endelesse love. [*Rev.* 56.1–13]

And therfore, yf we wyll have knowynge of oure soule, and communyng and da- /*fol. 101v*/ liance therwith, it behovyth to seke into oure lord God in whom it is enclosyd. And annentis oure substance: it may ryghtfully be called our soule. And anentis our sensualite: it may ryghtfully[46] be called our soule, and that is by the onyng that it hath in God. That wurshypfull cite that our lord Jhesu syttith in, it is our sensualite, in whiche he is enclosed. And our kyndely substance is beclosyd in Jhesu Criste, with the blessed soule of Criste syttyng in reste in the godhed. [*Rev.* 56.14–15, 17–21]

And I sawe ful surely that it behovyth nedis /*fol. 102r*/ that we shall be in longynge and in penance, into the tyme that we be led so depe into God that we may verely and truely know oure owne soule. And sothly I saw that into thys high depenes oure lorde hymselfe ledith us, in the same love that he made us and in the same love that he bought us, bi his mercy and grace, through vertue of his blessed passion. [*Rev.* 56.22–27]

And notwithstondyng all this, we may never come to the full knowyng of God tyll we first know clerely oure owne soule. For into the tyme that it be in the /*fol. 102v*/ full myghtis, we may not be all full holy—and that is that oure sensualite, by the vertue of Cristes passion, be brought up into the substance, with all the profitis of oure tribulacion that oure lorde shall make us to gete by mercy and grace. [*Rev.* 56.28–32]

Also, as verely as God is oure fader, so as vereli God is oure moder. And that shewyth he in all, and namely in thees swete wordis there as

he seyeth: "I it am." That is to sey: "I it am, the myght and goodnes of fadirhed. I it am, the wysedome and the kyndenes of moderhed. I it am, the lyght and the grace that /*fol. 103r*/ is all blessed love. I it am, the trinite. I it am, the unite. I it am, the hygh soveryne goodnes of all maner thyng. I it am that makith the to love. I it am that makith the to longe, the endeles fullnes of all trew desyres." For ther the soule is hygheste, nobeleste, and worthyeste, there it is lowyst, mekyste, and mildist.[47] And of this substanciall ground, we have all oure vertues in oure sensualite by ryght of kynde, and by helpyng and spedynge of mercy and grace, withoute the whiche we may not profite. [*Rev.* 59.10–19]

Also, Jhesu, the secunde person in trinite /*fol. 103v*/ in whom is the fader and the holy gooste, he is verely our moder in kynde of our first makyng, and he is oure very moder in grace by takyng of oure kynde made. I understond thre maner of beholdyng of moderhed in God. The fyrste is grounde of oure kynde makyng. The secunde is takyng of oure kynde, and there begynnyth the moderhed of grace. The thyrde is moderhed of werkyng, and therin is a furthespredyng by the same grace, of length and of brede, of heyth and of depenesse without ende. /*fol. 104r*/ And all is oon love. [*Rev.* 58.53–54, 59.32–33, 37–41]

But now me behovyth to sey a litil more of this furthespredyng, as I understonde in the menynge of oure lorde: how that we be brought ayen, by the moderhed of mercy and grace, into our kyndely stede, where that we wer made by the moderhed of kynde love, whiche kynde love that never levith us. [*Rev.* 60.1–4]

Oure kynde moder, our gracious moder, for he wolde all wholy become our moder in all thing, he toke the grounde of his werke full lowe and full myldely in the maydens wombe,

---

46. **ryghtfully** from **P**/**S**: **W** reads "ryghtfull."
47. **mildist** corrected above the line from "meldist."

takyng fleshe of her, redy in /fol. 104v/ oure pore fleshe, hymselfe to do the servyce and the office of moderhed in all thyng. The moders servyce is nereste, redieste, and sureste. It is neriste, for it ys of kynde; redieste, for it is most of love; and sureste, for it is of trewth. This office ne myght, ne coude never non do to the full but Criste Jhesu, God and man, alone. [*Rev.* 60.5–7, 10–14]

We knowe wel that all oure moders bere us with peyne and to deyeng. But our verey moder Jhesu, he alone beryth us to joy and to blysse and endeles lyvyng—blessed moste he be! Thus he sustey- /fol. 105r/ nyth us within hym in love, and traveyled into the full tyme that he wolde suffer the sharpeste throwes and the grevouste peynes that ever were or ever shall be, and deyed at the laste. And when he had done, and so borne us to blysse, yet myght not all this make asythe to his mervelous love. And that shewed he in thees hygh, overpassyng wordis of love: "Yf I myght suffer more, I wolde suffer more." He myght no more dye, but he wolde not stynt of workyng. Wherfor than hym behovyth to fede us, /fol. 105v/ for the derewor-thy love of moderhed hath made hym dettour to us. [*Rev.* 60.15–24]

The moder may yeve[48] her chylde to souke her mylke. But our precious moder Jhesu, he may fede us with hymselfe, and dothe full curteysly and full tenderly with the blessed sacrament of his body and blode that is pre-cious fode of verey lif. And with all the swete sacramentis he susteynyth us well mercyfully and graciously. And soo mente he in thees gra-cious wordys where he seyeth: "I it am that holy churche prechyth the and techyth the." That is to sey: /fol. 106r/ "All the helthe and the lyf of sacramentis, all the vertue and the grace of my worde, all the goodnes that is ordeyned in holy church to the, I it am."[49] [*Rev.* 60.25–32]

The moder may ley her chylde tenderly to her breste. But oure tender lorde Jhesu, he may homly lede us to[50] his blessed breste by his swete, open syde, and shewe us therein party of his godhed and the joyes of heven, with goostly surenesse of endeles blysse. That shewed he in thees swete wordis wher he seyd: "Loo, how I loved the," beholdynge into his syde, enjoyeng. [*Rev.* 60.33–38]

This feyre, lovely worde, "moder," /fol. 106v/ it is so swete and so kynde in itselfe that it ne may vereyly be seyd of noon, ne to noon, but to hym and of hym that is very moder of lyfe and all. To the properte of moderhed belongyth kynde love, wysedom, and knowyng; and it is God. For though it be so that oure bodyly furthbrynging be but lytyll, lowe, and symple in regarde[51] of oure gostely furthbrynger, yet it is he that dothe it in the creature by whom that it is done. [*Rev.* 60.39–44]

The kynde, lovynge moder that wote and knowyth the nede of her chylde, she kepyth it full tenderly as /fol. 107r/ the kynde and condi-cion of moderhed wyll. And ever as it wexith in age and in stature, so she chaungith her wurkyng, but not her love. And whan it is waxen of more age, she sufferith it to be chastisyd in brekyng downe of vicis, to make the chylde to resceyve vertues and grace. This workyng, with all other that be good, our lord doth in them by whom it is done. [*Rev.* 60.45–50]

Thus he is our moder in kynde by the wurkyng of grace in us, lower partith[52] for love of the hygher. And he will[53] that we knowen it, for

---

48. **yeve** note in margin (in later hand) reads "Eucharista" (the Eucharist).
49. **I it am** *I* added in a faint later hand.
50. **to** added above the line.
51. **regarde** corrected in the manuscript from "rewarde."
52. **lower partith** P/S read "in the lower perty."
53. **he will** from P/S: W reads "he whiche."

he wolde /fol. 107v/ have all oure love fastened to hym. And in this I sawe that all oure dettes that we owe by Godis byddynge, it is to fadirhed and moderhed, is fulfilled in trew lovynge of God, whiche blessed love Criste workyth in us. And this was shewed in all, and namely in the high plenteousnes wordis where he seyd: "I it am that thou lovyst." [*Rev.* 60.51–56]

And in oure goostly furthbryngyng he usyth more tendernes in kepynge, withoute comparison, by as meche as oure soule is of more price in his syght. He kendelyth oure undirstondyng, he /fol. 108r/ addith oure weyes, he esyth oure consciens, he comfortith our soule, he lyghtith our hart and yevyth us, in party, knowyng and lovyng in his blessed godhed— with gracious mynde in his manhed and his blessed passion, with curteys merveylyng in his high, overpassyng goodnes—and makyth us to love all that he lovyth for his love, and to be payed with hym and with all that he dothe and in all his werkes. And whan we fall, hastily he reysith us by his lovely beclepping and his gracious touchyng. And when we be strengthed by his /fol. 108v/ swete wurkyng, than we wylfully chose hym, by his grace, to be his servantis and his lovers, lastingly withoute ende. [*Rev.* 61.1–11]

And yet, aftyr this, he sufferith some of us to fall more grevously and more hard than ever we dydde before, as we thynkyth. And then wen we, the whiche be not all wise, that all were nought that we have begonne. But that is not so. For it nedith us to fall, and it nedith us to know it and to se it. For yf we fall not, we shuld not know how feble and how wretched we be of oureselfe. [*Rev.* 61.12–17]

And *also,* it nedith us to see our /fol. 109r/ fallyng, for yf we se it not, though we fall, it shulde not profite us. And commonly, first we fall and

aftir we se it; *and thorough that syght, by* the mercy of God, *we be lowe and meke.*[54] The moder may suffer her child to perishe, but oure hevenly moder Jhesu Criste may never suffer us that be his chyldryn to peryshe; for he is almighty, all wysedomm, and all love, and so is noon but he. Blessed mote he be! [*Rev.* 61.26–33]

Also, oftentymes when oure fallyng and oure wretchednes is shewed us, we be so sore adred and so gretely ashamed of /fol. 109v/ oureselfe that unnethis we wet where that we may holde us. But than wyll not our curteys modir that we flee awey, for hym were nothing lother, but he wyll than that we use the condicion of a chylde. For when it is diseasid or adred, than yt rennynth hastily to the moder. And yf may do no more, it cryeth on the modir for helpe with all the myghtis. So wyll our lorde that we do as a meke chylde, sayeng thus: "My kynd moder, my gracious modyr, my dereworthy moder, have mercy on me. I have made /fol. 110r/ myselfe[55] foule and unlyke to the, and I ne may ne can amende yt, but with thyne helpe and grace." And yf we fele us not eased than as sone, than be we sure that he usyth the condicion of a wyse modir. For yf he se that it be more profite to us for to wepe and moorne, than he wil suffer it with ruyth and pytey into the beste tyme, for love. And he wyll than that we use the properte of a chylde,[56] that evermore kyndly trustith to the love of the moder in well and in wo. [*Rev.* 61.34–46]

And *our lord God* wyll that we take us myghtily to the feyth of holy /fol. 110v/ churche, and fynde there our dereworthy moder in solace of trew undirstondyng with all the blessed commoun. For oon singular person[57] may oftetymes be broken, as it semyth to the selfe. But the whole body of holy churche was never broken,

---

54. **we be lowe and meke** gestures back to the previous paragraph of *A Revelation,* 61.24–27, but also significantly shifts Julian's theology, by omitting her notion that falling, as well as repentance, is "of the mercy of God."
55. **myselfe** from **P/S: W** reads "selfe."
56. **a chylde** "a" added above the line.
57. **oon singular person** note in margin (in later hand) reads "Ecclesia."

ne never shall withoute ende. And therfore a sure thynge it is, and good and gracious, to wyll mekely and myghtyly, fastened and oned to our moder holy churche, that is Criste Jhesu. For the flood of mercy that is his dereworthy blode and preciouse water, it is plenteous to make us feyre and clene. The blessede /fol. 111r/ woundis of oure savyour[58] ben open and enjoye to hele us. The swete gracious handis of our modyr be redy and dilygent about us. [Rev. 61.47–55]

For he, in all this wurkyng, usyth the very office of a kynd norse, that hath nothinge else to do but to attende aboute the salvacion of her chylde. It is the office of oure lorde Jhesu Criste to save us, it is his wurshyp to do it, and it is his wyll we know it. For he wyll that we love hym swetely and truste on hym mekely and myghtyly. And this he shewed in thees graciouse wordis: "I kepe thee full /fol. 111v/ surely." [Rev. 61.56–60]

Ferthermore, a kyndely chylde despeyryth not of the moders love, and kyndely the childe presumyth not of itselfe, kyndly the chylde lovyth the moder, and eche of them both other. [Rev. 63.32–34]

Also, I had grete desyre and longynge of Godis yefte to be delyvered of this worlde and of this lyfe. For oftetymes I beheld the wo that is here in this lyfe and the wele and the blessed beynge that is in hevyn. And methought sometymes, though ther had be no peyne in this lyfe but the absence of our lorde God, it was more than I myght bere. And this made /fol. 112r/ me to moorne and besyly to long. And also myne owne wretchednesse, slouth, and irkenesse halpe therto, so that me lyked not to lyve and to traveyle as me fell to do. [Rev. 64.1–7]

And to all our curteis lord God answered for comforte and pacience, and seyd thees wordis: "Sodeynly thou shalt be taken fro all thi peyne and fro all thy seykenesse, fro all thi

disese and fro all thi woo. And thou shalt cum up above, and thou shalt have me to thi mede and rewarde, and thou shalt be fulfilled of joye and of blysse. And thou shalt never more have no maner of peyne, /fol. 112v/ nether no maner of seykenesse, no maner of myslykyng, ne no wantyng of wyll, but ever in joye and blysse withouten ende. What shulde it than greve the to suffer a whyle, sothen it is my wyll and my wurship?" [Rev. 64.8–15]

It is Godis wyll that we sett the poynt of our thought in this blessed beholdyng as often as we may and as long. [Rev. 64.39–40]

☙

B. Bequests to Julian of Norwich, 1393–1416

Date and Provenance: 1393–1416; Norfolk and Suffolk.

Description: Four wills survive bequeathing money to Julian, one in Anglo-Norman, three in Latin. Three are translated here, all for the first time: those of the chantry priest Thomas Emund from Aylesham in Norfolk, made in 1404, proved in 1406; the Norwich citizen John Plumpton, proved in 1415; and the aristocratic Isabel Ufford, daughter of the earl of Warwick and widow of the earl of Suffolk, proved in 1416. Ufford's will differs from the others not only because it is written in Anglo-Norman but because it details the last public appearance of a truly wealthy and powerful woman; its arrangements are correspondingly more elaborate and its bequests more munificent than those of Emund and Plumpton. The fourth will, that of Roger Reed, rector of St. Michael's, Coslany, Norwich, proved in 1393 or 1394, which provides the earliest evidence of Julian's enclosure as an anchoress, was recently damaged by fire and water and is now illegible. He left two shillings to "Julian ankorite."[59] There

---

58. **savyour** *r* added above the line.
59. See Edmund Colledge and James Walsh, *A Book of Showings to the Anchoress Julian of Norwich,* 2 vols., Studies and Texts 35 (Toronto: Pontifical Institute of Mediaeval Studies, 1978), 33–34.

are also wills bequeathing money to an unnamed anchorite at St. Julian's, Conesford, in 1423 and 1428, but, although it is possible Julian lived into her eighties, these may refer to her successor.

The making of a will in late medieval England was an important spiritual and legal exercise, and many wills were copied into the "registers" (records of activity) of the bishops or archbishops responsible for proving them as permanent records of the manner in which people of consequence disposed of their bodies, souls, and assets. Formulaic though they are, the wills below all bespeak a solemn desire on the part of those making them to leave this life with all earthly debts (financial and emotional) settled—failure to make restitution was a serious sin—and with due preparation completed for death, burial, and prayers for the soul. While the wills even of celibate clergymen reveal deep attachment to family members, carefully passing particular items on to particular people, the wills treat these gifts as only one part of a wider network of giving, comprising both works of charity and implicit or explicit appeals for prayers. Friars, nuns, hospitalers, anchoresses, prisoners, lepers, and the sick are all potential recipients, as are parish churches, favorite altars, and colleagues and friends. Medieval wills are some of the most powerful reminders of the functional reality of the community Julian calls "alle mine evenchristen."[60]

Source: All three wills survive in archiepiscopal registers, those of Emund in the register of Archbishop Arundel (London, Lambeth Palace, Register of Arundel, I.f.540d), those of Plumpton

and Ufford in that of his successor, Archbishop Henry Chichele (ed. Ernest F. Jacob, 4 vols., Oxford: Clarendon Press, 1943–47, 3.413 and 2.94–97).

B.1. Will of Thomas Emund

In the name of God, Amen. I, Thomas Emund, chantry priest of Aylesham, sound in mind, make my will in this fashion at Norwich on the nineteenth day of May, on the feast of Saint Dunstan the archbishop, in the year of our Lord 1404. First, I commend my soul to God almighty, the blessed Virgin Mary, and to all the saints. My body I leave to be buried in the cemetery of the Friars Minor in Norwich.[61] Item: I bequeath twenty shillings to these same friars, for prayers for my soul and the soul of my mother, Margaret, and the souls of all to whom I am obliged, and of all the faithful. Item: I bequeath twenty pence to St. Peter's, Mancroft.[62] Item: I leave ten shillings to be divided equally among the nuns of Carrow. Item: thirty pence to the Preaching Friars of Norwich.[63] Item: thirty pence to the Carmelite Friars. Item: thirty pence to the friars of the order of Saint Augustine. Item: twenty pence to Brother Simon of Aylesham, of the order of the Friars Minor. Item: I leave twenty pence for repairs to the parish church at Aylesham. Item: twenty pence to the high altar at the same church. Item: twelve pence to the high altar of St. Mary's, Carrow. Item: I bequeath twenty pence to Lord Roger, recluse at Carrow.[64] Item: twelve pence to Julian, anchoress at the church of St. Julian in Norwich. Item: eight pence to Sarah, living with her. Item: I bequeath

---

60. For a rich account of the religious and social background, see Norman P. Tanner, *The Church in Late Medieval Norwich, 1370–1532* (Toronto: Pontifical Institute of Mediaeval Studies, 1984), whose maps and index identify most of the places mentioned in these wills. For the relationship between Julian's thought and the death culture evoked in these wills, see Amy Appleford, "Learning to Die: Affectivity, Community, and Death in Late Medieval English Writing" (Ph.D. diss., University of Western Ontario, 2004).

61. I.e., the Franciscans, their friary a few hundred yards north of Julian's cell.

62. Then as now the largest and most important of Norwich's parish churches.

63. I.e., the Dominicans.

64. Not otherwise known.

forty pence to my sister Joanne. Item: my multi-colored bedspread in blue with red and white roses, with its pillow, and a saddle. Item: forty pence for distribution to the poor. Item: I leave twenty pence to each of my executors, if they execute my will.

Apart from these bequests I leave the rest of my goods in the hands of my executors for the discharge of my debts and to pay for my funeral, and for the benefit of my soul and the souls of my mother and brothers and sister, my benefactors and the souls of all the faithful departed, as seems to them best pleasing to God and beneficial to the salvation of my soul. The executors of my will are Robert Emund, my priest, and William Emund, servant, and William Emund [sic], whom I call brothers.

B.2. Will of John Plumpton

The will of John Plumpton. In the name of God, Amen. I, John Plumpton of the city of Norwich, sound in mind, make my will in this fashion at Norwich on the twenty-fourth day of the month of November in the year of our Lord 1415. First I commend my soul to God almighty, the blessed Mary and all the saints, and I bequeath my body to be buried in the cemetery of the church of St. John's, Madermarket in Norwich. Item: I bequeath five shillings to the high altar of the church of the Holy Trinity, Norwich.[65] Item: I bequeath forty pence to each of the orders of friars in Norwich. Item: I bequeath twelve pence to the lepers at every gate of the city of Norwich.[66] Item: I leave twelve pence to every sister, together and separately, in the hospital of St. Paul's, Norwich. Item: I leave six pence to every sick person in the beds of the hospital of St. Giles, Norwich, and twelve pence to every sister there.[67] Item: I leave all my houses

and my tenements, including buildings, gardens, and everything pertaining to them within the liberty of the city of Norwich, for the payment of my debts by my executors and for setting my soul in order, in the construction of an aisle in the south part of the church of St. John's, Madermarket in Norwich, at the direction of my executors. Item: I bequeath six shillings, eight pence, to the prisoners in the castle of Norwich. Item: I bequeath forty pence to the prisoners in the Guildhall, Norwich. Item: I bequeath forty pence to the secular canons of the chapel of the blessed Mary in the fields in Norwich. Item: I bequeath forty pence to the anchoress in the church of St. Julian's, Conesford, in Norwich, and twelve pence to her maid. Item: I bequeath her former maid, Alice, twelve pence.

The rest of my goods and chattels and everything owed me I leave in the hands of my executors for the making of the said aisle and for setting my soul in order.

I appoint and ordain through those present Samson Baxter, mercer, citizen of Norwich, Edmund Alderford, cleric, and Clement Elyngham, chaplain, to be executors of this my testament, and I bequeath forty shillings to each executor for his work. In witness of which I place my seal to this my present will.

B.3. Will of Isabel Ufford

Will of Isabel Ufford, countess of Suffolk. In the name of the Father, of the Son, and of the Holy Spirit, amen. I, Isabel Ufford, countess of Suffolk, sound in mind, ordain and make my last will and testament, the twenty-sixth day of September in the year of our Lord 1416 in the following manner and form: that is to say, first of all I bequeath my soul to our lord God and his

---

65. Norwich cathedral, at the time also a Benedictine priory.
66. There were sick-houses outside five of Norwich's city gates. See Tanner, *Church in Late Medieval Norwich,* xii.
67. St. Paul's and St. Giles' were the two main hospitals within the walls of Norwich.

sweet mother, our lady Saint Mary, and to all the saints of heaven, and my body to be buried in the ground at Campsey,[68] next to my husband.

Item: I leave five square candles and four thick candles[69] to provide light around my body at the vigil and on the day of my burial, and twenty-four torches for poor people, clad in white without flags, to hold around my bier, and I desire that the rest of the torches not used up on the day should be distributed to the poor outside the church at the discretion of my executors and administrators, after a donation has been made to the house. Item: I leave one hundred pounds and no more for all the expenses associated with my burial, the vigil and the day, as well as the giving of alms to the poor and all other expenses associated with the day. And I desire that my funeral service be held within one month of my death as soon as properly possible, without further delay. Item: I desire that after my death, first, my debts be paid and the services of my servants be compensated, and that there be no other shroud around my corpse than a shroud of black.

Item: I leave forty marks to the house at Campsey, and forty shillings to the prioress there, and twenty shillings to each nun; and one hundred shillings in gold to my very dear sister, Maud Ufford, and a silver chalice goblet with a cover. Item: I leave one hundred marks for the restoration of the church at Redlingfield. Item: I leave forty shillings to the prioress of the same

place and twenty shillings to each lady there. Item: because of the great need I know I have both for prayers and for the singing of masses, I desire and pray my executors that they will make provision for me for certain annuary priests,[70] that is to say, thirteen secular annuary priests to sing for the term of three years for my soul and for the soul of the most honorable lord of Suffolk, whom God pardon, and for the souls of my most honored lord's father and mother, and for all the souls of those to whom I am indebted.

Item: five marks to each house of the four orders of friars in Suffolk and Norfolk for annual Masses for my soul and for the souls of the above-named.[71] Item: I leave twenty pounds to the house of Snape. Item: forty pounds to the house of Mendham. Item: forty pounds to the house of Bruisyard. Item: I leave twenty marks to the monks of Thetford. Item: twenty marks to the house of Flixton.[72]

Item: I leave twenty shillings to Julian, recluse at Norwich.[73] Item: forty pounds to my most dear nephew, Thomas Ferris. Item: forty pounds to Esmond Stapleton. Item: a silver goblet with its cover and a silver ewer with its cover to Simon Felbridge, knight. Item: forty pounds in silver and a silver goblet with its cover to Michael Stapleton. Item: a goblet and a silver cover in memory of me to John Staunton. Item: twenty marks to John Lancaster, squire. Item: twenty marks to Esmond Oldhall, esquire. Item:

---

68. An important English convent, in Suffolk, where Ufford spent her last years. For the religious houses named in this will, see David Knowles and R. Neville Hadcock, *Medieval Religious Houses: England and Wales* (London: Longman, 1971).

69. *mortoris.*

70. Priests employed on a yearly basis to sing Masses for the souls of the dead.

71. There were over twenty houses of friars in Norfolk and Suffolk in 1416.

72. Snape and Mendham were houses of Benedictine monks. Thetford had several houses, but the Benedictines may again be the recipients of this bequest. Bruisyard and Flixton were convents, Bruisyard of minoresses, Flixton of canonesses.

73. "Item jeo devys a Julian recluz a Norwich xxs." Mentioned between gifts to religious houses and personal gifts, Julian's relationship with Isobel Ufford, if any, is left unclear. The bequest of twenty shillings, though large by the standards of Plumpton, Emond, and Reed, is in this context a small gift to a social inferior, the same as Ufford leaves the Campsey nuns.

twenty marks to Sir John Bluntesham, clerk. Item: ten marks to Richard Roose. Item: ten marks to Sir William Worstede, master of my lord's chantry, and forty shillings to each of his companions. Item: forty marks to Sir John Jeremouth.[74]

Item: I leave Marion ten [marks]. Item: twenty marks to Simon Bliant. Item: forty shillings to John Leving. Item: forty shillings to the two sisters at Sudbury. Item: I leave to every parochial church within whose parish I have ploughs one of the best ploughs as a mortuary gift.

And for the rest of my goods not bequeathed by me, I desire that my executors and administrators distribute them in works of charity as their great worthiness will see fit, for the salvation of my soul and of those to whom I am attached.

And to carry out this my testament I name, ordain, and make my executors: that is, my lord Simon Felbridge, knight; my lord Miles Stapleton, knight; John Lancaster, esquire; Esmond Oldhall, esquire; Sir John Blunteshorm, clerk; Robert Rouse; and Simon Bliaunt, praying them that they will do what is said above on my behalf in the same way they would want someone to do for them in a similar situation.

In witness of the fact that this is my will, I here place my seal.

Written the 26th day of September in the above-mentioned year. And since I may perhaps leave various works that should be done by way of almsgiving unperformed, therefore I sincerely ask my executors that, whatever is carried out according to my last will, it be carried out principally in the name of the soul of my much honored lord of Suffolk, whom I love and

by whom I feel myself to be so greatly beloved, and afterward for myself and for those to whom I am indebted.

❦

C. *Excerpt from* The Book of Margery Kempe *(chapter 18)*

Date and Provenance: 1430s; King's Lynn, Norfolk (known at the time as Bishop's Lynn).

Description: Apart from the wills included in Item B, *The Book of Margery Kempe* provides the only contemporary literary reference to Julian the historical anchoress, living enclosed in Norwich and meeting with visitors to speak with them about the gifts of God. In or around 1413, Margery Kempe (as the *Book* tells it) journeyed to Norwich from her home in Bishop's Lynn (some forty miles away) to appear before the bishop of Norwich's officers to answer for her faith. Here she was supported and her form of spirituality praised by one of her many advisors and confessors, Richard Caister (d. 1420), the vicar of St. Stephen's (see *Book*, 1.17). While in Norwich she also visited with other religious authorities, including "Jelyan," the "ankres," said to be an "expert" in the matter of visions, or "wondirful revelacyons." The excerpt edited here, describing their meeting and Julian's words to her, constitutes one of the *Book*'s most important discussions of the doctrine of "discretion of spirits," establishing the principle that a loving confidence in the truth of divine revelations is necessary to their proper interpretation. This principle, which the rest of the *Book* shows Margery Kempe trying to follow, has clear parallels in Julian's reflections at the end of *A Vision* and in several passages of *A Revelation:* that special revelations, once duly tested, must

---

74. A roster of names from well-connected East Anglian families. Many of these people or their relatives are named in *The Paston Letters and Papers of the Fifteenth Century,* ed. Norman Davis, 2 vols. (Oxford: Clarendon Press, 1976). See also Colin Richmond, *The Paston Family in the Fifteenth Century* (Cambridge: Cambridge University Press, 1990).

be distrusted no more but require faith if they are be of spiritual value. The excerpt also provides an interesting and, in Middle English, unusual example of a learned woman counseling a less well educated one; the *Book* makes Julian refer to several biblical and patristic passages in a short space.

Given Kempe's well-documented appetite for devotional texts in English (see *Book*, 1.17, 58) and the generic similarity between her *Book* and Julian's writings, it is odd that this account never mentions those writings, either to acknowledge them or to claim them as texts Kempe had read.[75] By 1413, Julian (now seventy) would have long completed her first version, *A Vision,* and very likely also her revision, *A Revelation.* While it is possible that Kempe simply did not know of their existence, several details in her account are close enough to *A Revelation* to suggest otherwise: the image of the soul as the seat of God (see *A Revelation,* Chapter 68); the notion that any vision that leads a visionary away from orthodox belief cannot be from the Holy Spirit, since this would be contrary to his nature ("the worshep of God" and "charite" in the *Book* more or less correspond to "the faith of holy church" in Chapter 9 of *A Revelation*); perhaps the *Book*'s use of terms such as "revelacyons" and "evyncristen." Whether or not these should be treated as allusions to Julian's writings, the account adds a public dimension to what we know about Julian, and confirms her religious authority in Norwich and the surrounding area of East Anglia during her life.

Source and Treatment of Text: *The Book of Margery Kempe* survives in a single manuscript, British Library MS Additional 61823; the following

excerpt is taken from fols. 21r–v. In the excerpt, manuscript spellings are retained, except that thorn (þ) and yogh (ʒ) are normalized to *th* and *y* or *g,* variation between *u* and *v, i* and *j,* are rationalized in accordance with modern spellings, and abbreviations are expanded. Punctuation is editorial. An excellent recent edition of the entire text is by Barry Windeatt (Longmans, 2000).

* * *

The befor-seyd creatur was mech comfortyd bothe in body and in sowle be this good mannys wordys and gretly strengthyd in hir feyth. And than sche was bodyn[76] be owyr lord for to gon to an ankres in the same cyte whych hyte[77] Dame Jelyan. And so sche dede and schewyd hir the grace that God put in hir sowle of compunccyon, contricyon, swetnesse, and devocyon, compassyon wyth holy meditacyon and hy contemplacyon, and ful many holy spechys and dalyawns[78] that owyr lord spak to hir sowle, and many wondirful revelacyons whech sche schewyd to the ankres to wetyn[79] yf ther wer any deceyte in hem, for the ankres was expert in swech thyngys and good cownsel cowd gevyn.[80] The ankres, heryng the mervelyows goodnes of owyr lord, hyly thankyd God wyth al hir hert for hys visitacyon, cownselyng this creatur to be obedyent to the wyl of owyr lord God and fulfyllyn wyth al hir mygthys whatevyr he put in hir sowle yf it wer not ageyn the worshep of God and profyte of hir evyncristen, for, yf it wer, than it wer nowt the mevyng of a good spyryte, but rathar of an evyl spyrit.

"The holy gost mevyth nevyr a thing ageyn charite, and, yf he dede, he wer contraryows to hys owyn self, for he is al charite. Also he

---

75. For a recent discussion of Margery Kempe's reading practices, see Jacqueline Jenkins, "Reading and *The Book of Margery Kempe,*" in *A Companion to the "Book of Margery Kempe,"* ed. John H. Arnold and Katherine J. Lewis (Cambridge: D. S. Brewer, 2004), 113–28.

76. **bodyn** bidden.

77. **which hyte** who was called.

78. **dalywans** dalliance.

79. **wetyn** know.

80. **gevyn** give.

mevyth a sowle to al chastnesse, for chast levars be clepyd[81] the temple of the holy gost, and the holy gost makyth a sowle stabyl and stedfast in the rygth feyth and the rygth beleve. And a dubbyl man in sowle is evyr unstabyl and unstedfast in al hys weys.[82] He that is evyrmor dowtyng is lyke to the flood of the see, the whech is mevyd[83] and born abowte wyth the wynd, and that man is not lyche to receyven the gyftys of God.[84] What creatur that hath thes tokenys he muste /fol. 21v/ stedfastlych belevyn that the holy gost dwellyth in hys sowle. And mech mor, whan God visyteth a creatur wyth terys of contrisyon, devosyon, er compassyon, he may and owyth to levyn that the holy gost is in hys sowle. Seynt Powyl seyth that the holy gost askyth for us wyth mornynggys and wepyngys unspekable:[85] that is to seyn, he makyth us to askyn and preyn wyth mornynggys and wepyngys so plentyuowsly that the terys may not be nowmeryd.[86] Ther may non evyl spyrit gevyn thes tokenys, for Jerom seyth that terys turmentyn mor the devylle than don the peynes of helle.[87] God and the devyl ben evyrmor contraryows, and thei schal nevyr dwellyn togedyr in on place, and the devyl hath no powyr in a mannys sowle. Holy wryt seyth that the sowle of a rytful man is the sete of God,[88] and so I trust, syster, that ye ben. I prey God grawnt yow perseverawns. Settyth al yowr trust in God and feryth not the langage of the world, for the mor despyte, schame, and represf that ye have in the world the mor is yowr meryte in the sygth of God. Pacyens is necessary unto yow, for in that schal ye kepyn yowr sowle."

Mych was the holy dalyawns that the ankres and this creatur haddyn be comownyng[89] in the lofe of owyr lord Jhesu Crist many days that thei were togedyr.

☙

D. The Cambrai Nuns: Margaret Gascoigne and the Upholland Manuscript

Date, Provenance, and Description: The two items that follow originate in the English Benedictine community of Cambrai (in modern Belgium), one of two houses of Benedictine nuns established in France and the Low Countries during the seventeenth century, in exile from England (the other was in Paris). Cambrai (dedicated to Our Lady of Consolation) was founded in 1623 and for the first decade of its existence offered a home to the Benedictine monk and contemplative writer Augustine Baker, a man much interested in his medieval English predecessors, who served as the convent's spiritual director. Like its sister house at Paris (Our Lady of Good Hope, founded from Cambrai in 1651), Cambrai fostered an individualistic environment of highly literate contemplation. Baker and the house's long-serving first abbess, Catharine Gascoigne, encouraged the nuns to read, copy, and compose and to accept their inner impulses as sent by God. The community's two early literary stars were Margaret Gascoigne, younger sister of the abbess, and the celebrated Gertrude More, great-granddaughter of Sir Thomas More. Partly because of Baker, Cambrai was also a center for the study of Middle English devotional

---

81. **clepyd** called.

82. **dubbyl man . . . weys** James 1:8.

83. **mevyd** moved.

84. **He that is . . . God** James 1:6–7.

85. **the Holy Gost . . . unspekable** Rom. 8:26.

86. **nowmeryd** numbered.

87. **terys turmentyn . . . helle** Not traced in Jerome, but attributed to Bernard in the Middle English *Speculum Christiani* and to Peter Damian elsewhere. Probably proverbial.

88. **sowle of a rytful man . . . God** Perhaps an allusion to 2 Cor. 6:6: "We are the temple of the living God." See also *Rev.*, ch. 68.

89. **by comownyng** through communing.

texts, especially Walter Hilton's *Scale of Perfection* but including William Flete's *Remedy Against the Troubles of Temptations* and *The Cloud of Unknowing*. For decades after Baker's departure—precipitated by a disagreement with the convent's official chaplain, Francis Hull, over Baker's attacks on the practice of constant examination of conscience and frequent confession, then much in vogue—the nuns continued to copy his own many sermons and treatises, some of which formed the basis for the posthumous *Holy Wisdom,* compiled by Serenus Cressy.[90]

The first set of excerpts (D.1) is from a "treatise . . . composed by a Religious Virgin of the holy order of St. Benet," edited by Baker— apparently from "loose papers" left in the cell of Margaret Gascoigne after her death (age twenty-nine) in 1637—presumably while he was living at the Benedictine monastery of St. Gregory's, Douai. Baker seems to have transcribed these papers, with occasional comments, for the benefit of his colleagues at Douai, prefacing them with a long and loving account of Gascoigne's life, character, and death, partly designed to justify his own practices as a spiritual director (the two halves of this project, Baker's biography and Gascoigne's writings, have survived as separate texts).[91] Baker thus treats Gascoigne's "loose papers" as a private record of her eight years as a nun, the first four spent in agonizing

uncertainty over his direction that she should refrain from continual and overscrupulous confession of her sins, the last four recording her ascent from the purgative life, through illumination, into the unitive life. But while her "treatise," a series of carefully linked soliloquies to God, indeed shows a movement from fear of damnation to a state of ecstatic love, it is too well crafted and thematically consistent to have the simple relationship with Gascoigne's spiritual autobiography Baker ascribes to it. Drawing on various sources, circling around a number of biblical passages and quotations from writers such as Thomas à Kempis and Gertrude of Helfta, much of the treatise is in fact a recurrent meditation on two linked fragments of Julian's *Revelation:* the clause "For thou art inough to me" in Revelation One (5.31–32); and the clauses attributed to Christ in Revelation Thirteen as an antidote to "the beholding of the reproved": "Let me alone, my derwurdy childe, intende to me, I am inogh to the. And enjoy in thy saviour and in thy salvation" (36.39–40). According to Baker, it was in these latter words that Gascoigne took comfort on her deathbed as she imitated the model of devotion provided by Julian's text:

> She caused one, that was most conversant and familiar with her, to place (written at and underneath the Crucifix, that remained there before

---

90. See Peter Salvin and Serenus Cressy, *The Life of Father Augustine Baker, O.S.B. (1575–1641),* ed. Justin McCann (London: Burns & Oates, 1933), a composite of several early biographies of Baker. See also Augustine Baker, *Holy Wisdom; or, Directions for the Prayer of Contemplation* (Wheathampstead, Hertfordshire: Anthony Clarke Books, 1972).

91. "Gascoigne A" and "Gascoigne B," in the system adopted in "A Descriptive Catalogue of MSS. in English and Foreign Libraries for the Works and Life of Father Augustine Baker, O.S.B.," chap. 6 of *Memorials of Father Augustine Baker and Other Documents Relating to the English Benedictines,* ed. Justin McCann and Hugh Connolly, Catholic Record Society 33 (London: Catholic Record Society, 1933). "Gascoigne B" is the "treatise" in St. Mary's Abbey, Colwich, MS Baker 18. "Gascoigne A" is Downside Abbey MS Baker 42, which begins with a Latin note from the scribe, explaining that he has had only the first part of Baker's work to hand. Gascoigne B entitles the whole work "Certein Devotions of Dame Margaret Gascoigne Late Religious of the English Benedictin Convent of Virgins at Cambrie. Founde upon her death, of her owne hande writing, and according to such that was in loose papers or leaves heere transcribed and coppied. Whereunto is prefixed a Discourse concerning partlie her life, but principallie the maner of her death" (pp. 4–6). Neither half of the work has ever been edited, although sections 42–43 are transcribed on Julia Bolton Holloway's website (www.umilta.net).

her, and which she regarded with her eyes during her sickness and till her death) these holy words that had sometime ben spoken by God to the Holie Virgin Julian the ankresse of Norwich, as appeareth by the old manuscript Booke of her Revelations, and with the which words our Dame had ever formerlie been much delighted: "Intend (or attend) to me, I am enough for thee: rejoice in me thy Saviour, and in thy Salvation." Those words (I say) remained before her eyes beneath the Crucifixe till her death.[92]

This moving tableau, which sums up well the importance of Julian's words in Gascoigne's treatise, shows Gascoigne subsuming her own death in the visionary death described in *A Revelation,* and practicing a form of *imitatio Julianae* in her determination to depend on the image of the dying Christ for her "heven" (*Rev.* 19.12–17).

Nine out of sixty-nine sections of the treatise revolve around Julian's words (an addendum written by Baker to section 18, which gives his understanding of the structure of Gascoigne's treatise, has also been included here). In the first two (sections 17–18), the clause "thou art inough to me" concludes soliloquies in which the meditator confronts her desire to confess and reconfess her sins, out of fear of divine punishment, with her need to learn trust in God's loving sufficiency. According to Baker's addendum, the resolution of this confrontation pushes Gascoigne from the "purgative" into the "illuminative" state. In the third (section 28), "thou art inough to me" is combined with the motto of the Franciscans, *Deus meus et omnia* (my God and my all) to affirm the meditator's final conquest over doubt of divine mercy; again, Baker suggests that the phrase precipitates a transition for Gascoigne, this time into the "Unitive" state. In the fourth

and fifth (sections 30–31), the phrase signifies the meditator's acceptance of whatever God sends and desire to sit at his feet; section 31 links "thou art inough to me" with the first verse of Psalm 23 (Vulgate 22): "The Lord is my shepherd; I shall not want." The sixth and seventh sections (42–43) expound the longer passage of *A Revelation,* culminating in a speech Gascoigne places in Christ's mouth in exactly the way Julian attributes to Christ the words on which Gascoigne is meditating. Now the meditator, imitating *A Revelation,* is creating visionary scenarios of her own. Finally, in the eighth and ninth sections (48–49), "thou art inough for me" returns, in a meditation on God's omnipotence and on Paul's "Who shall separate us from the love of Christ?" (Rom. 8:35), which includes an evocation of Julian's image of God as mother, as the meditator proclaims her final confidence in victory over temptation. From the first to the last phase of Gascoigne's treatise, Julian's words provide a touchstone, talismanically repeated, strenuously reinterpreted.

The second set of excerpts (D.2) is from a small devotional anthology (known as the Upholland manuscript from its residence until recently in St. Joseph's College, Upholland), likely compiled between 1641 and 1651 (or possibly 1641 and 1684) by various nuns, one of whom was the prolific and careful Cambrai scribe Barbara Constable (Cambrai, 1641–84); another may have been Bridget More (Cambrai 1631–51; Paris 1651–65), copyist of the St. Mary's Abbey manuscript of Gascoigne's treatise. Extracting passages of spiritual note seems to have been a regular recreational activity for the Cambrai and Paris nuns. This miscellany, whose general emphasis is on the desirability of the contemplative life, contains excerpts from the Desert

---

92. Downside Abbey MS Baker 42, pp. 232–34. We are grateful to Dame Margaret Truran, OSB, archivist at Stanbrook Abbey, for bringing this passage to our attention. For a discussion, see Margaret Truran, "Spirituality: Fr. Baker's Legacy," in *Lamspringe: An English Abbey in Germany, 1643–1803,* ed. Anselm Cramer (York: Ampleforth Abbey, 2004), 83–96.

Fathers originally made by Baker, passages of Henry Suso, John Tauler, Walter Hilton, Thomas à Kempis, Teresa of Avila, and, near the end, parts of several chapters of *A Revelation* (26–32), edited here. The extracts from Julian have been attributed to Baker and could be by him, but there is no special reason to think that he, rather than one of the nuns, was responsible for them.[93]

The Julian material in the anthology seems originally to derive either from the Paris manuscript or, perhaps, from its now lost medieval precedessor (the "old manuscript Booke of her Revelations" from which Gascoigne read the work, according to Baker), or just possibly (if Bridget More was not one of the scribes) from Cressy's 1670 edition, which in turn likely derives from Paris.[94] The extracts, which are essentially concerned with the meaning of Christ's "alle shalle be wele" (*Rev.* 27.10), keep fairly close to the exemplar, but frequently include glosses or short explanations: for example, adding to the clause "these words . . . be not declared heere" the explanatory "the meaning of them"; or, after the clause "the more plenteously that we take of this," adding the parenthetical expansion "joying in our sallvation." There are also many cuts—for example, of the second half of Chapter 27—which might be suggestive of caution toward some of Julian's more optimistic pronouncements, but also have the affect of emphasizing the prophetic aspect of these chapters. Here, "alle shalle be wele" becomes a direct response to the sufferings of persecuted individuals in a persecuted church: "Holy Church shall be shaked in sorrow and anguish, and tribulation in this world, as a man shaketh a cloath in the wind" (see *Rev.* 28.4–6). This is the freest of the seventeenth-century attempts to render passages of *A Revelation*.

Sources and Treatment of Texts: The selections from Gascoigne's treatise (D.1) are edited from St. Mary's Abbey, Colwich, MS Baker 18, copied by Bridget More and part of the library of the Paris convent until 1793. It is bound with vellum leaves from the same late medieval choir-office book as the Upholland manuscript (D.2), which must have been compiled at Cambrai, so More may well have made the copy before 1651, when the Paris house was founded. Since the dissolution of St. Joseph's College, in 1999, the Upholland manuscript has been in private hands (whose is unknown); the following edition has been made from a photocopy of the Julian excerpts on folios 113r–116v (compared with Owen's thesis edition). In both manuscripts, Christ's words, and a few others, are written in larger script, setting them off from the rest of the text, and represented here as text within quotation marks. In these editions, we have silently expanded abbreviations, rationalized scribal *i* and *j*, and *u* and *v*; all other manuscript spellings have been retained, and capitalization and punctuation have been slightly modified for clarity.

D.1. St. Mary's Abbey, Colwich, MS Baker 18
/p. 94/   17.

Alas my God, how lamentable is this my case; for if I still continue the practise of passing over matters, as I have beene counselled to do, it seemeth to my naturall judgment that my case

---

93. The anthology has been edited by Hywel Wyn Owen, "An Edition of 'The Upholland Anthology'" (B.A. diss., University of Liverpool, 1962), who published his findings in "Another Augustine Baker Manuscript," in *Dr. L. Reypens-Album*, ed. A. Ampe (Antwerp: Uitgave van het Ruusbroec-Genootschap, 1964), 269–80, an article in which Gascoigne's use of *A Revelation* (in sections 42–43 only) in Colwich Abbey, MS Baker 18, was first noticed; and again, this time with an edition of the Julian material, in an article written with Luke Bell, "The Upholland Anthology: An Augustine Baker Manuscript," *Downside Review* 107 (1989): 274–92.

94. Owen, "Another Augustine Baker Manuscript," notes that Upholland often glosses the same words as Cressy in his edition, but that the manuscript more often follows Paris.

is almost damnable. And if on the other side I yeald to satisfie my conscience or minde urging me to do the contrarie of such practice, I plainlie see I thereby fall into such a laborinth of miseries that the world is scarse able to procure to me a greater and more dangerous ruin, and when I shall have done all I can, perhaps be as farre from that which I sought (being satisfaction of soule) as I was before I begunne such doeng. What therfore shall I do? Is there no hope for a sinner?[95] Are the gates of mercie, /p. 95/ which have remained open to receive so manie, shutt against me onlie the most miserable of all creatures? O no, no. Hast thou ever heard or knowen, that our most gratious Lord hath given to anie soule a desire to forsake their sinnefull life, to be converted to him, and trulie to confesse their sinnes, and yet hath left them ignorant or permitted them to be forgettfull of some of those their sinnes for which he woulde damne them? Hath he ever deallt thus with anie? Surelie no? And why then doest thou feare that he will deale so with thee, whome he hath alreadie so much prevented with his grace and mercies? Doth not his divine wisedome see and knowe the secret corners of thy hart, and also by what meanes thou maiest be purged and freed from all those and othere thy feared or reall sinnes and defects? But wilt thou saie perhaps he doth not love thee, and therefore will not helpe thee in the necessitie? Have /p. 96/ not his owne wordes in a thousand places of holie scriptures and to divers holie persons, testified the contrarie? Is that most indulgent hart of his become more harde to thee, then to anie other? Surelie, I will nevere admitte anie such conceipt into my minde, but will alwaies answere those thoughts with this one worde, and with this I will alwaies conclude, that "thou my God art inough to me."[96]

18.

I do undoubtedlie beleeve and confesse, that there is no sinne or defect so little, but shall according to thy justice be punished; so do I also beleeve and confesse, that there is no sinne so great but that thy sweet mercies doe take delight to forgive them, nor sinner so loaded with sinnes, but that thou are both more able and willing to take them quite away, and free the soule from them /p. 97/ all, which I humblie beseech thee to doe with me for thy great mercies sake.

Thou onlie my God, who art all seeing and knoweng wisedome, doest see and know whether my soule be in this dangerous case which my fearefull conscience doth suggest me to be in, or no; Thou also who art all might, canst deliver me from such perillousnes, so farre as thou seest me to be in, and thou who art all love, shall I doubt but that thou wilt do it? O no; lett that never enter into my hart, but in that and all other occasions and cases, lett me ever conclude and satisfie myselfe with this, that "Thou art inough to me."

(Hetherto her devotions
seeme to be chieflie or only
concerning her greater
sinnes and the tentation about
iterating of confession and
they seeme to be as her purgative state; and now next followe her devo- /p. 98/ tions seeming more to be of the state of proficience (as inlightned to it by the precedent purgative) tending to the amending of her lesser dailie faultes and imperfections; and henceforward she speakes little, or rather nothing at all, of the foresaid tentation (and thinges are transcribed by me in the order and succession wherewith they were originallie written by her) wherby it

---

95. This clause is added in the margin.
96. See *Rev.* 5.31–32, and context.

seemeth she was come to be either wholie freed from the said tentation, or but verie litle moved or touched by it, and continued so till her verie expiring out of this life; and it seemeth to me by some good tokens thereof, that the said tentation helde her for the space of the first foure yeares of her religious estate, and no longer, the residue of her life, (being other fowre yeares,) being spent first in the saide exercises now next ensuing, which I said to be of proficiencie or illuminative and afterwardes she came /p. 99/ to good quietnes and peace in soule, exercising her selfe in manner proper to the unitive waie, as you maie discerne heerafter, when I shall come to expresse them, consisting much in suffering in other various matters and manners well knowen onlie to God (and herselfe) for whose love she did undergoe them;

and now I beginne with those
I termed of pro-
ficiencie.)[97]

/p. 125/   28.

The remembrance of my life past with the multitude and greevoysnes of my sinnes, as thou knowest, my Lorde, /p. 126/ doth cause so great an horror and trembling in my afflicted soule, that I can not see what in the world were able to yealde me anie hope or solace in this so great a miserie, but onlie this, "Of having thee for my God,"[98] my soule being encompassed and besett with the pricking thornes of sinnes, which never cesse to sting my guiltie conscience, wherein there is nothing but confusion, allmost voide of hope, not knoweng how by anie meanes to cleere my gaullie[99] conscience, or ease me of the heavie burthen thereof, the weight of it being so great, that it can finde no ease or comforte, but onlie in the bottomlesse sea of thy mercies. But

shall I saie, that thou hast refused to visit, comforte, and upholde me in this lamentable case? O no, my deere Lorde; for then should I do thee an /p. 127/ infinit wrong; for what can be so greevous and painefull to me, as is the sweetnes and comforte great, of this onlie happines of "having thee to be our God." Lett others seeke for what other things they please besides this, but for my parte I neither have or enjoie nor desire to have anie thing but onlie this, for the comforte of my afflicted soule, which doth not cesse out of the satisfaction it hath in thee to crie out; "Deus meus et omnia;[100] thou art inough to me"; and in thy mercies do I more hope then do I feare all my sinnes, which yet do so much terrifie me and afflict me; for though in my owne soule and conscience I can not see how it is allmost possible for me to escape eternall death, yet finallie I cannot doubt of thy mercie and grace without doeng my self verie great wrong, and to thee an infinite wrong, /p. 128/ I meane I cannot but hope that thou willt enlighten me to see and know thy most blessed will in all things concerning me, at least so farre as shall be necessarie for my soules salvation, and wilt enable me through the vertue of thy allmightie grace to fullfill such thy will, according to thy pleasure, thou thereby fullie supplieng my owne infinite debilitie and insufficiencie therein, that doth raise and cause so much feare unto me.

(Thus farre went her devotions
that seeme to be of the second waie
or state, being that of "pro-
ficiencie," or "illuminative"; And now next followe other of hers of the third waie or state, being the "Unitive," consisting more of purer love, and much freed from her former feares, but intermingled with matters of suffering.)

---

97. An editorial addition by Baker, as are most of the parenthetical passages. Purgation, illumination, and union are classically the three stages of the spiritual life.

98. Unidentified: not in *A Revelation*.

99. MS reads "gaulie" or "guullie." Either an error for "guilty," or "gaulie," bitter.

100. "My God and my all," the motto of the Franciscan order.

/p. 131/ 30.

Can I saie that anie thing is wanting to me concerning either corporall necessities or spirituall giftes or graces, whilst in those wants thy most gracious will is founde? O no; for "thou art inough to me," and thy will more desired by me, then all these things beside.

Notwithstanding that which I feele being greevous to my nature, or whatsoevere farthere or other affliction thou maist please to sende me or permitte to fall on me, though it seeme to my blinde senses not to be for my good, yet I will not feare it, or the issue of it, because, "thou art my */p. 132/* God, who alone art inough to me," and never deniest thy selfe to me humbly craving thy gratious descent into my soule, and aboade therein; nor will I be solicitous or carefull concerning such matter of affliction, because thou hast taken the care of me, ("Oure Lorde ruleth me, and nothing shall be wanting to me";)[101] I will not desire to have it otherwise, because thou wouldst have it to be in this manner.

O my beloved, thou knowest my desire, and the longing of my harte and soule, and that I would have nothing but thee, even at this time in which I finde and feele this contradiction and difficultie, as well as in the time of most sweet affection and fervour towards thee.

31.

O how watchfull and attentive */p. 133/* oughtest thou (my soule) to be at all times, and in all places, for to see if happilie thou canst espie anie occasion of performing this noble office, to which thou art assigned, for yealding thy most beloved his pleasure and delight.

O my poore soule, seeing it is the will of thy beloved to permitte me thus to remaine in exile and banishment, and in some sorte seperate from him, who is the onlie desired of thy hart, yet lett us keepe our fidelitie to him, who is in this case no lesse worthie of it to the full, then if we were admitted to his gracious fellt or perceaved presence. Lett us not admitt of anie other love but his, nor have affective correspondence or conversation with anie other. Lett nothing ells be pleasing or gratefull to us; lett us desire nothing ellse; admitte of nothing ells, feare */p. 134/* nothing, whilst we remaine constantlie faithfull to him, but saie; "Dominus regit me, et nihil mihi deerit."[102] Thow alone, O Lorde, "art inough to me." Lette us adhere to him; lett us sitte at his feete watching and expecting his comming into our soule with the greatest joy; yet sometimes bemoaning our miseries, as that through our negligences and defallts we are thus farre seperated from him; for such his distance or abscence from us, is through our fallt, and not his, for our correction and humiliation, not for anie pleasure or delight he therein takes to himselfe, who hath publicklie professed to the contrarie, saieng, that "it is his delight to be with the children of men,"[103] by solacing their soules by his most sweet and gracious perceaved presence and workings. Therefore lett us never cease to love him, praise */p. 135/* him, intende him,[104] honour him, serve him, obey him, ever more and more seeke after him, of whome never inough can be had, and seeke nothing but to demonstrat our most deere affection to him, hope in him, rejoice in him, and ever abide in him.

darknes, ignorance po-
vertie, frailtie and fallings

/p. 155/ 42.

Thou hast saide, O Lorde, to a deere child of thine, "Lette me alone, my deare worthy childe,

---

101. Marginal note: "Psalm 22," i.e., Psalm 23:1. See note 102.

102. Ps. 23:1 (Vulgate 22:1), following here the Septuagint version: "The Lord rules me, and nothing is lacking to me."

103. A marginal note identifies the source: "Proverbs 8.31."

104. "Intende" here is the earliest sign that Gascoigne is thinking not only of "thou art inough to me" but of the wider context of that passage, as she quotes it in full in section 42.

intende (or attende) to me, I am inough to /p. 156/ thee; rejoice in thy Saviour and Salvation"[105] (this was spoken to Julian the Ankress of[106] Norwich, as appeareth by the booke of her revelations.) This o Lorde I reade and thinke on with great joie, and cannot but take it as spoken allso to me. Thou therein biddest me "lette thee alone;" to which I can not but answere and readilie yealde and submitte my selfe, sayeng; "O yes, my Lorde"; for what doe I desire more then to lett thee alone in all things which thou wouldest do or permitte in me, or concerning me, which I am most assured wholie to be intended by thee for the cleansing and salvation of my soule, as yet most uncleane and unworthy of thee; thou wouldest for that end purge me of all impediments in my waie of sincere ten- /p. 157/ dance towards thee and serving of thee, whereby thou mightest allwaies finde me as pliable to thy Blessed will, as waxe before the fire in the hande of the artesman is pliable to the maner of his working. "Intende to me," saiest thou, and thou knowest, that, that is it which I aime at, and seeke to do at all times, both daie and night, and nothing ells, but that I maie continuallie attende to thee,

> (And in her last sicknes, she
> caused those words to be placed
> before her eyes at the crucifixe,
> which she regarded till her death);

Thou saiest allso, "I am inough to thee"; and to this I would willinglie answere with the tongues and voices of all creatures, saieng; "Yes, my deare Lorde," thou alone indeed art inough to me; for if all friends turne into /p. 158/ foes, and all pleasures into paines, yet art thou "inough to me," those other things being all as nothing in regarde of thee, who hast all good in thee, and art and ever shallt be all in all to me. And even but to remember those thy most delicious wordes, "I am inough to thee," is so great a joie to my hart, that all the afflictions, that are, or (as I hope) ever shall fall upon me (at least which I can imagin) do and shall cause me to receave from them so much comforte, solace, and encouradgment, as that I hope by thy grace, they shall be most dearlie welcome unto me. Thou there saiest farther, "rejoice in thy Saviour and in thy Salvation"; But though my love be so colde, that I am farre from doeng this as I /p. 159/ ought, yet I desire that with all the might and powers of my soule, and with all the affection of my harte, I could rejoice in thy infinite happines; and though my soule be never so poore and in never so great miseries, yet I desire according to such abilitie as is in me of thy gift, to joy and rejoy together with thee, "for what thou art and doest possesse in thy immense riches, power and glorie," and in all that is pleasing to thee in all things, in thy selfe and in all thy creatures, in the riches of others, and my owne povertie and miserie (for to them, whom thou art pleasing to, what thing of thine can be displeasing?) And what is wanting in me (through disabilitie) to performe in this matter, I will rejoice and exullt in hart, that in all fullnes and perfection it is supplied /p. 160/ and aboundeth in thee thy self, where I hope my selfe accordinglie in the time which thou hast from eternitie foreordained for it, to finde by experience such supplie and amends for all mine and other creatures insufficiencies in the matter. I farthermore rejoice "in my Salvation" which I confidentlie hope in vertue of thy most free and liberall goodnes, in the end to obtaine at the handes of thy mercie, and in no sorte as if I could expect anie such matter as due to me or merited by me, nor anie other waies to be attained to by me, then by thy free gift[107] and meere mercie (in vertue of the grace and deserts of my most

---

105. See *Rev.* 36.39–40.
106. MS reads "or."
107. MS reads "giuft."

deere Lorde and Saviour Jesu Christ thy onlie and most dearelie beloved sonne) /p. 161/ which mercies and goodnesses of thine I have allreadie in various maners even in my owne most unworthie selfe so greatlie and so frequentlie experienced, that I can not, nor maie heerafter doubt thereof, but ever maie, must, and will to the end confidentlie hope in the same, and thereon onlie and wholie relie.

43.

Thou knowest, o Lord, that since thy sweet goodnes hast admitted my sinnefull soule to make this covenant with thee,[108] that thou first taking on thee, as thou seemedst to me to do, all the care pertaining to my wellfare, I accordinglie leaving that care wholie to thee, would and should take (for my parte) care onlie of thy honor and service and the loving of thee with all the power of my soule /p. 162/ and sences so farre as thy most gracious grace should enable me therein, since the which kinde of covenant or contract so made between us, whensoever I am in my nature frighted with vaine humane feares, or take unnecessarie care concerning my either soule or bodie, thou doest, as it seems to me, thus sweetlie reprehende me for it, and as it were sayeng to my soule in this or the like maner; "What hast thou to do with that? Doth it not belong to me to have care of thee for these points? Why does thou medle with that which doth not belong to thee, but to me? Looke and attende to that which belongeth to thy owne parte, which is to take care of loving, honouring, and serving me, and /p. 163/ therefore cesse thou as to those other points, and (as before) lett me alone; attende thou to me; for I am inough to thee."

/p. 173/ 48.

"Beata gens, cuius est Dominus Deus eius."[109] Thou hast saied by thy prophet; "You shall be my people and I will be your God. O Deus meus et omnia"; this trulie is inough /p. 174/ for me; for what more can be desired? O how happie am I in this one thing, to witt, that thou art my God. This (as I saie) as it seemes to me (and so is the veritie it selfe) is all our happines, being farre in excellencie above all the other good things that could happen to us, and in this point of true and sole hapiness doth my hart exceedinglie rejoice, yea much more then anie tongue is able to expresse; this onlie is that which comforteth me in all afflictions; what joy could be joie to me without this? And what affliction is there which doth not finde comforte in this, or by this is not turned from affliction into the truest and greatest sweetnes? My sinnefull soule being loaded with innumerable sinnes and iniquities hath turned her about on all sides, and could finde no ease, none other to comforte her, none /p. 175/ other to secure her, none other to satisfie her, none other one jotte of thing to abate or lessen the heavie and gallie burthen she fellt, but onlie thee "my God and my all."

49.

"Quis me separabit a charitate Christi?"[110] Whatsoever shall for that end present it selfe to my soule, I hope that through thy holie assistance, it shall never make such seperation, that is most odious and tormenting to my soule so much as to thinke of; for if it come to trouble and disquiet me with greefe, how can it be? For to whom thou my sweet Lorde God art pleasing, what can be displeasing? If it come to fright

---

108. In section 39, Gascoigne offers her heart as a protecting shelter for God when he is wearied by the sinfulness of his creatures, in exchange for the refuge of his heart when she is in need, promising that she will trust his heart, not the words of a confessor, to save her when she faces death and judgment.

109. Marginal note: "Psalm 32.12: Happy nation whose god is our Lord."

110. MS has marginal note: "Rom 8" (Rom. 8:35).

me, I will turne my selfe to thee, as a /p. 176/ childe into the bosome of his mother, crieng out; "responde pro me."[111] And if it come to flatter and please me, thou knoweest I will none but thee; thou onlie suffisest me my God; "Thou art inough to me."

D.2. The Upholland Extracts

/fol. 113r/   SAINT JULIAN

THE 12 REVELATION

And after this our lord shewed himselfe more glorifyed, as to my sight then I had seene him before; wherin I was learned to know that our soule shall never have rest till it come into him; knowing that he is full of joy, homely and curteous, and most blessed and true life. Oftentimes our lord Jesu sayd: "I it am. I it am. I it am that is highest. I it am that thou[112] lovest. I it am that thou likest. I it am that thou servest. I it am that thou longest after. I it am that thou desirest. I it am that thou meanest. I it am that is all. I it am that shewed myself to thee before."

The number of the words passeth my witts and understanding, and all my mights, for they were in the highest, as to my sight; /fol. 113v/ for therein is comprehended I am not able to tell what, so that it cannot be expressed. But the joy that I saw in the shewing of them exceedingly surpasseth all that hart can thinke, or soule may desire. And therefore these words (the meaning of them) be not declared heere; but every one according to the grace God hath given him in understanding and loving, let them receave them in our lords meaning.

THE 13 REVELATION

And after this, our lord brought to my mind the longing desire I had to him before. And I saw that nothing letted or hindred us but sinne. And me thought if sinne had not bin, we should all have bin cleane and pure, and like to our lord as hee made and created us. And thus in my folly before this time I often wondred why, by the foresaid great wisedome of god the beginning of sinne was not hindred or prevented, for then me thought that all should have bin well. This stirring and /fol. 114r/ thought in my mind, I should have forsaken and not have yealded unto it; yet nevethelesse it caused me to mourne and sorrow without discretion, but Jesu who in this vision enformed me of all thinges that were needfull, answered by this word and sayd: "Sinne is behovefull. But all shall be well." In this naked worde, "Sinne," our lord brought to my mind generally all that is not good.

THE 28 CHAPTER

Thus, I saw how Christ hath compassion on us for the cause of sinne, for full well our lord loveth People that shall bee saved. That is to say gods servants; Holy Church shall be shaked in sorrow and anguish, and tribulation in this world, as a man shaketh a cloath in the wind. And as to this, our lord answered showing in this manner: "Ah, A great thing shall I make hereof in heaven, of endles worship and of everlasting joy." Yea so far forth I saw that our lord rejoyceth at the tribulation of his servants with pitty and /fol. 114v/ compassion; that to each person that he loveth and intendeth to bring to his bliss he layeth on him something; that is to say some affliction or tribulation, that is no impediment to the soule in the sight of God, wherby they be humbled and despised in this world, scorned, mocked, and contemned by others. And this he doth to hinder and prevent the harme which they are apt to fall into, and would incurre by the pride, the pompe, and the vaine glory of this wretched life, and for to make their way the more readdy, and better prepare them to come to heaven, and enjoy his blisse without end everlasting; for he sayth, "I

---

111. See Isa. 38:14; also *Rev.* 61.34–46.
112. MS has "yᵒ" for "thou" three times: here, and in "thou servest" and in "thou desirest."

shall all to breake you from your vaine affections, and your vitius pride; and after that I
shall gather you and make you meeke and mild,
cleane and holy by uniting you to mee." And
then I saw that each kind compassion that man
hath on[113] his even Christian with charity, it is
Christ in him, whose love to man made him to
esteeme little of all the paines he suffered in his
passion, which love againe was shewed heere in
this compassion, wherin were two thinges to be
understood in our lords meaning. The on was
the blisse that we be /fol. 115r/ brought unto,
wherin his will is that we rejoyce; the other is,
for our comfort in our paine and tribulation.
For he will that wee know that all shall turne to
his worship and to our profit by the vertue of
his holy passion: and that we know that wee
suffered right nothing alone, but with him, and
that we see him our ground. And that we see his
paines and his tribulations so farre to exceed
and surpasse all that we can suffer, that it cannot be fully thought or imagined. And the well
beholding and considering of this will keepe us
from overmuch trouble and despaire in the
feeling of our paines, and we see verely that our
sinnes deserve it, yet his love excuseth us, and of
his great curtesy he doth away all our blame,
and beholdeth us with ruth and merveilous
pitty as children, Innocents and unspotted.

THE 30 CHAPTER

In this our Lords will is to have us occupied
and exercise, to joy in him, for he joyeth in us.
And the more plenteously that we take of this
(joying in our sallvation) with[114] reverence and
humility, the more thanks /fol. 115v/ we deserve
of him, and the more speedy and expedient it is
to our selves. And thus we may see and enjoy or
rejoyce in, that our part is our Lord. The other
part is hid and shutt up, or concealed from us;
that is to say, all that is besides our sallvation.

For that is our lords privy counsell, and it
belongeth to the Royall Lordship of allmighty
god to have his privy counsels in peace. And it
belongeth to his servants for obedience and reverence to him, not to have a will or desire to
know his counsels. Our lord hath pitty and
compassion on us, for that some creatures do
busy themselves so much therein (seeking and
desiring to know and understand the secrets of
allmighty god). And I am sure if we know how
much we should please him and ease ourselves
to forbear it we would do it.

The saints in heaven, thay have a will to
know nothing, but that which our Lord will
shew them. And also their charity and desire is
ruled according to the will of our Lord. And
thus owght we to have our will like to them;
Then shall we nothing will nor desire, but the
will /fol. 116r/ of our lord like as they do. For we
bee all one in gods meaning. And heer I was
taught that I should only enjoy in our Blessed
Saviour Jesu, and trust in him for all thinges.

THE 32 CHAPTER

One time our good lord sayd, "All manner of
thing shall be well." And another time he sayd,
"Thou shalt see thyselfe that all manner of
things shall be well." And these two sayings the
soule tooke and understood in sundry manners. One was this, that our lord will that wee
know that he not only taketh care of, and hath
regard to noble thinges, and to great, but also to
little and to small, to lowe and to simple, to the
one and to the other. And so meaneth he in that
he sayth, "All manner of thing shall be well." For
he will that we know that the least thing shall
not be forgotten. An other is this, that there be
many deeds evill donne in our sight, and so
great harmes comes, and are taken thereby that
it seemeth to us that it were /fol. 116v/ impossible
that ever they should come to a good end. And

---

113. MS reads "one."
114. MS reads "which."

upon these wee looke sorrowfull and mourne therfore, so that it cannot rest in the blessedfull holding of God as we should doe. And the cause is this, that the use of our reason and understanding is now so blind and lowe that we cannot know nor understand the high mervailous wisedome, and the goodnes of the most blessed Trinity. And thus meaneth he where he sayth, "Thou shalt see thy selfe that all manner of thing shall be welle," as if he had sayd, "Take or beleeve faithfully and trust fully and hearafter thou shalt see it verely and truely in fullnes of joy." And thus in the same five words before sayd, "I may make all thinges well," I understood a mighty comfort (that wee owght to take) of all the workes of our Lord god, that are to come.

❦

E. Serenus Cressy's Edition of A Revelation *and the* Stillingfleet Controversy

Date, Provenance, and Description: This group of excerpts begins with the introductory materials to Serenus Cressy's printed edition of *A Revelation* in 1670 (E1) (described in some detail on pages 16–17 of the Introduction), and continues with the controversy into which this edition was swept as a result of an attack on Cressy, and through him on Roman Catholicism, mysticism, and visionary experience, by the learned and rationalist Anglican bishop of Worcester, Edward Stillingfleet (1635–99). Cressy was born around 1605 and converted to Catholicism at the age of forty, in 1646, becoming spiritual advisor to the Paris nuns for several months in 1651, immediately after his ordination. (He died in 1674.)[115] Sharing his friend Augustine Baker's interest in the Middle English mystics, he published Hilton's *Scale of*

Perfection in 1657, thirteen years before his edition of *A Revelation*. This edition, with its careful transcription of the Paris manuscript (or a manuscript very like it), its respect for the lexis and syntax of Middle English, and its judicious glosses, suggests that his study of Julian may have begun as early as his time in Paris; certainly, the community of nuns reading and contemplating her words, copying, recopying, and sharing the manuscripts between them, would have provided a suitable environment.

Cressy's edition was published in London, during a time of relative tolerance toward Roman Catholicism, and of high Catholic hopes for their eventual reestablishment in England. It was no doubt partly to shatter these hopes that, in 1671, Edward Stillingfleet published his thunderous tract *A discourse Concerning the idolatry Practised in the church of rome and the danger of Salvation in the Communion of it: in an answer to some Papers of a Revolted Protestant: wherein a particular Account is given of the Fanaticism and Divisions of that Church* (London: Printed by Robert White for Henry Mortlock, 1671) (E2). This well-informed attack on the Catholic faith, in the shape of an answer to "a revolted Protestant" (Cressy), attempts to shift charges that the Protestant Churches have encouraged "fanaticism" (a term associated, in the 1670s, with dissident groups such as the Quakers and the Ranters) onto Catholicism, by claiming that it is Catholics, with their tolerance for visions, miracles, and mysticism, that are the true "fanatics." Rather as Baker found himself under attack from within his church by those suspicious of his views on inner illumination, so Cressy, and the visionary with whom he had most recently identified himself, Julian of Norwich, thus became, in Stillingfleet's polemic, symbols of the irrationality and idolatry characterizing Catholicism as a

---

115. For studies of Cressy, see Hilary Steuert, "A Study in Recusant Prose: Dom Serenus Cressy, 1605–74," *Downside Review* 66 (1948): 165–78, 287–301; George H. Tavard, *The Seventeenth-Century Tradition: A Study in Recusant Thought* (Leiden: E. J. Brill, 1978), 109–26.

whole. Stillingfleet's method is simply to quote passages of *A Revelation* in order to hold them up to ridicule, but he has a good eye for what he thinks obscure. As Cressy and others noted, it was the strangeness of Julian's idiom that enraged him most. In a brief later reference to *A Revelation*, part of a long argument that Catholicism regards visionary "novelties" as a part of revealed truth, he returns to the oddity of Julian, insinuating that "the *worthy publisher* of the *sixteen Revelations of Mother Iuliana*" ought to know all about "*new and strange revelations*"; for "if those be not *new* and *strange*, I think none ever ought to be accounted so" (342–43; not edited below).

Cressy and others replied to Stillingfleet's charges against Catholicism (not all of these replies have survived), and both Cressy and a certain O.N. again refer to Julian (E3–4). Cressy's response, which has the same gallantry he brings to his presentation of *A Revelation* in his edition, has the air of something written by a person who feels protective about a pet project. Rather than engage in counterpolemic, his strategy is to expose the mixed motives underlying Stillingfleet's attack, accusing his learned opponent of having approached his reading of Catholic books with a lack of charity and intellectual curiosity, so that the discovery of common ground or shared needs and concerns becomes by definition impossible. O.N.'s brief reference to Julian suggests that Stillingfleet is confusing "fanaticism" with linguistic archaism, and suggests that, if this is so, Chaucer must also "look to himself"; clearly, something real was at stake for Cressy and his Catholic contemporaries in defending the Middle English idiom of the fourteenth-century spiritual writers they admired. Finally, Stillingfleet replied to the replies (E5), reiterating points he had made and refusing to budge from his contempt for Julian and her idiom.

Sources and Treatment of Texts: Cressy's prefatory material to his edition of *A Revelation* is here taken from the copy housed in the British Library (shelfmark: Cup.403.a.36). The ensuing polemical passages are transcribed from the copies made available by Early English Books OnLine. All passages are copied exactly as they appear in the printed text, except that the long "s" ($\int$) is presented as a single "s," and variations between *u* and *v, i* and *j,* are rationalized.

E.1. From XVI REVELATIONS *of Divine Love, Shewed to a Devout Servant of our Lord, called* MOTHER JULIANA, *an Anchorete of* NORWICH: *Who lived in the Dayes of* KING EDWARD *the Third* (probably London: Published by R. F. S. Cressy, 1670), "permissu superiorum."[116]

Accedite ad Deum et illuminamini. Psal. 33. v. 5[117]

/fol. A2r/ **To his most Honoured** *Lady,* **the** *Lady Mary Blount, of Sodington.*

Madam,
The just and grateful Resentment which I have of the unmerited kindness, and friendship of your *late* most Worthy and Noble *Husband* Sir *George Blount,* of your *Ladiship,* and your whole Family, obliged me, impatiently to desire an occasion, to make a publick Acknowledgement thereof. Permit me therefore here, to offer to your *Ladyship* this small *Present,* in which notwithstanding, I can challenge no Interest or Right, but only the Care of publishing it. The Author of it, is a Person of your own Sex, who lived about Three Hundred years since, intended it for *You,* and for such Readers as your self, who will not be induced to the perusing of it by Curiosity, or a desire to learn strange things, which afterward they will at best vainly admire, or perhaps out of incredulity contemn. But

---

116. I.e., "by leave of his spiritual superiors."
117. RSV Psalm 34:6: "Look to him and be radiant."

your *Ladiship* Will, /fol. A2v/ I assure my self, afford *Her* a place in your Closet, where at your Devout Retirements, you will enjoy her Saint-like Conversation, attending to her, whilst with Humility and Joy, She recounts to you the Wonders of our *Lords* Love to *Her,* and of his *Grace* in *Her.* And being thus employed, I make no doubt but you will be sensible of many Beams of her Lights, and much warmth of her Charity, by reflection darted into your own Soul. Now that such may be the effects of this Book, is the desire of (Madam) *Your Ladyships most Humble and most Obliged Servant in our Lord,* H. CRESSY

/fol. A3r/ **To the Reader.**
Devout Reader,
Whatsoever benefit thou mayst reap by this Book, *thou art obliged for it to a more* Venerable Abbot *of our* Nation, *by whose order and liberality it is now published, and by consequence sufficiently* Approved.[118]

I conceived it would have been a prejudice to the agreeable simplicity of the Stile, *to have changed the Dress of it into our* Modern Language, *as some advised. Yet certain more out of* Fashion, Words *or* Phrases, *I thought meet to explain in the* Margine.

I was desirous to have told thee somewhat of the happy Virgin, *the* Compiler *of these* Revelations: *But after all the search I could make, I could not discover any thing touching her, more than what she occasionally sprinkles in the* Book *it self. The* Postscript *acquaints us with her* Name, Juliana: *As likewise her* Profession, *which was of the strictest sort of* Solitary Livers; *being Inclosed all her life (alone) within* four Walls: *whereby, though all* Mortals *were excluded from her dwelling, yet* Saints *and* Angels, *and the* Supream King *of both, could, and did find* Admittance. *Moreover, in the same* Postscript *we find, that the* Place *in a high* /fol. A3v/ *manner*

dignified by her abode, and by the access of her Heavenly Guest, was the City of Norwich. *The* Time *when she lived, and particalarly, when these* Celestial Revelations *were afforded her, she her self in the beginning of the* Book *informes us, was in the year of* Grace MCCCLXXIII. *that is, about three years before the death of the famous* Conquerour, King Edward the Third: *At which time she her self was about* Thirty years *of age. And to conclude, in the last* Chapter *of the* Book *she signifies, that* more than Fifteen years *after these* Revelations *had been shewed her, how for resolution of a certain* Doubt *of hers touching the meaning of one of them,* Our Lord *himself was pleased to* answer her Internally in Ghostly understanding.

As for the Manner *of these* Revelations, *it was the same of which we read innumerable Examples, both among* Ancient *and* Modern Saints. *The* Objects *of some of them were represented to the* Imagination, *and perhaps also to the* outward Sight; *sometimes they were represented in* Sleep, *but most frequently when she was* Awake. *But those which were more* pure, *in time and withall more* certain, *were wrought by a* Divine Illapse *into the* Spiritual part *of the* Soul, *the* Mind *and* Understanding, *which the* Devil *cannot counterfeit, nor the* Patient comprehend, *though withal it excluded all* Doubt *or Suspicion of Illusion.*

But the principal thing *which I desire to recommend to the* Reader's *Consideration, is the* preceding Occasion, *and* Subsequent Effects *of these* /fol. A4r/ Divine Favours *bestowed by* Almighty God *on his* Humble Devout Handmaid.

She was far from expecting, or desiring such unusual Supernatural Gifts. *Matters stood thus with her: She thought her self too much unmortified in her Affection to Creatures, and too unsensible of our Lords Love to her. Therefore to cure the* former, *she requested a* Sickness *in extremity, even*

---

118. Marginal note: The V. R. F. Jo. Guscoyn L. Abbot of Lambspring.

to death, *in her own and others Conceit; a* Sickness *full of bitter pain and anguish, depriving her of all outward Refreshments, and of all inward Comforts also, which might affect the sensual Portion of the Soul. And for a remedy to the* Latter, *she begg'd of our Lord, that he would Imprint in her Soul, by what way he thought best, a deep and vigorous Conception, and Resentment of those most violent Torments, which he in his infinite* Love *suffered for her on the Cross, to the end she might be even forced to return to him a suitable affection.*

Yet in making these Requests, *she expressed a perfect* Resignation (*as to the* manner) *to his Heavenly Will. The only* graces *that she did, and might, and so may we, desire* absolutely, without any Condition, *were a true* Spiritual Hatred *and* Contempt *of her self, and of all worldly, or sensual Contentments; a perfect* Sorrow *and compunction for* Sins *past; and a Cordial* Love, *and* Reverential Fear *of Almighty God. These were the Gifts she desired: And as for the means of procuring these Graces, she proposed the best to her seeming: yet so, as being assured that* God /fol. A4v/ *knew what was best for her, she left them to his* Divine *pleasure.*

It was, no doubt, by Divine Inspiration, *that she at first made such* Petitions, *both for the* Substance *and* Manner, *and therefore* God *granted them as she desired; yea, in a manner more extraordinary than she durst pretend to, as the* Reader *may observe. And how wonderful the* Effects *of them were, the whole contexture of her* Discourses *upon each* Revelation *will excellently demonstrate.*

And now, since she her self professes, that the Lights *and* Torches *which* God *was pleased to give her, were intended not for her self alone, but for the* Universality *of God's* true *Servants, for whose benefit also she wrote them, the* Devout Reader *will, I hope, think himself obliged not to content himself with a fruitless admiring, but will, after her example, aspire to alike affectuous,*

operative Contemplation *of the meer* Nothingness *of* Creatures, *of the inconceivable* ugliness *of* Sin, *of the infinite* tenderness *and* indefectibility *of* God's Love *to his* Elect, *and of the* Omnipotency *of* Divine Grace *working in them; to which* Grace *alone all* Good *in us is to be ascribed.*

E.2. From A DISCOURSE *Concerning the* IDOLATRY *Practised in the* CHURCH OF ROME *and the danger of Salvation in the Communion of it: in an answer to some Papers of a Revolted Protestant: wherein a particular Account is given of the Fanaticism and Divisions of that Church,* **by Edward Stillingfleet (London: Printed by Robert White for Henry Mortlock, 1671).**

/p. 235/ CHAP. IV. *Of the Fanaticism of the* Roman Church.

The unreasonableness of objecting Sects and Fanaticisms to us as the effects of reading the Scriptures. Fanaticism countenanced in the Roman Church, *but condemned by ours. Private revelations made among them the grounds of believing some points of doctrine, proved from their own Authors. Of the Revelations pleaded for the immaculate Conception. The Revelations of S. Brigitt and S. Catharin directly contrary in this point, yet both owned in the Church of* Rome. *The large approbations of S. Brigitts by* Popes *and* Councils; *and both their revelations acknowledged to be divine in the lessons read upon their dayes. S. Catharines wonderful faculty of smelling souls, a gift peculiar to her and* Philip Nerius. *The vain attempts of reconciling those Revelations. The great number of female Revelations approved in the* Roman Church. *Purgatory, Transubstantiation, Auricular Confession proved by Visions and Revelations. Festivals ap-* /p.236/ *pointed upon the credit of Revelations: the Feast of* Corpus Christi *on the Revelation made to* Juliana, *the Story of it related from their own Writers: No such things can be objected to our Church. Revelations still owned by them; proved from the Fanatick Revelations of Mother* Juliana *very lately published by*

Mr. Cressy: *Some instances of the blasphemous Nonsense contained in them.*

/p. 257/ §. 5.[117] And is it not a hard case now, we should be so often told of *Fanaticism* among us, by the members of the *Roman Church?* Where are the Visions and Revelations ever pleaded by us in any matter of *Doctrine?* Did we never discard any of the *Roman opinions* or practices upon */p. 258/* the account of *Revelations* made to Women or to any private persons? Do we resolve the grounds of any doctrine of ours into any Visions and Extasies? have we any *Festivals* kept upon such occasions? Do we collect *Fanatical Revelations,* and set them out with comments upon them, as *Gonsalvus Durantus* hath done those of St. *Bridgitt?*[118] Have we any mother *Juliana*'s among us? or do we publish to the world the *Fanatick Revelations* of *distempered brains* as Mr. *Cressy* hath very lately done, to the great honour and service of the Roman Church, *the sixteen Revelations of Divine Love shewed to a devout servant of our Lord* (and Lady too) *called Mother* Juliana? We have, we thank God, other wayes of imploying our devout retirements,[119] than by reading such fopperies as those are. Excellent men! that debarr the people reading the *Scriptures* in their own tongue, and instead of them put them off with such Fooleries, which deserve no other name at the best than the *efforts* of *Religious madness.* Were we to take an estimate of *Christian Religion* from such Raptures and Extasies, such Visions and Entertainments as those are, how much must we befool our selves to think it *sense?* Did ever *H. N. Jacob*

Behmen,[120] or the highest *Enthusiasts* talk at a more extravagant rate than this *Juliana* doth? */p. 259/* As when she speaks of *our being beclosed in the mid-head of God, and in his meek-head, and in his benignity, and in his buxomness, though we feel in us wrath, debate, and strife:*[121] Of *being substantially united to God;*[122] *and that, God is that goodness which may not be wrath, for God is not but goodness: our soul is oned to him, unchangeable goodness; and between God and our soul is neither wrath nor forgiveness in his sight, for our soul is so fulsomely oned to God of his own goodness, that between God and our soul may be right naught.*[123] That *in mankind that shall be saved is comprehended all; that is to say, all that is made and the maker of all; for in man is God, and God is all, and he that loveth thus he loveth all:*[124] That *our soul is so deep grounded in God, and so endlesly treasured that we may not come to the knowing thereof, till we have first knowing of God; which is the maker to whom it is oned, and therefore if we will have knowing of our soul, and commoning, and dalliance therewith, it behooveth to seek into our Lord God in whom it is inclosed: and that worshipful City that our Lord Jesu sitteth in, it is our sensuality in which he is inclosed; and our kindly substance is beclosed in Jesu with the blessed soul of Christ, resting in the Godhead: and notwithstanding all this we may never come to the full knowing of God till we know first clearly our own soul; for into /p. 260/ the time that it is in the full mights, we may not be all holy; and that is, that our sensuality by the vertue of Christs passion be brought up into the substance, with all the profits of our tribulation,*

---

117. Marginal note: *Revelations still owned by them.*

118. Gonsalvus Durantus: editor of an important seventeenth-century edition of the works of Bridget of Sweden.

119. The phrase alludes to Cressy's prefatory dedication on his edition to Lady Blount: "at your Devout Retirements, you will enjoy her Saint-like Conversation" (see above, Item E.1).

120. *H. N. Jacob Behmen:* Jacob Boehme, seventeenth-century mystic and esotericist.

121. Marginal note: *16 Revelations of divine love.* ch. 49 *p.* 112. See *Rev.* 49.17–18.

122. Marginal note: *Ch.* 5. *p.* 12. See *Rev.* 5.16.

123. Marginal note: *Ch.* 46 *p.* 105. See *Rev.* 46.28–32.

124. Marginal note: *Ch.* 9, *p* 14. See *Rev.* 9.11–14.

that our Lord shall make us to get by mercy and grace. I had in party touching, and it is grounded in kind; that is to say, our reason is grounded in God which is substantially kindness.[125] Afterwards she discourseth *of three properties in the Holy Trinity, of the Fatherhead, of the Motherhood, and of the Lordship, and she further saw that the second person which is our Mother substantially, the same dear worthy person is now become our Mother sensual; for we be double of Gods making, substantial and sensual.*[126] We may justly admire what esteem Mr. *Cressy* had of that *Lady* to whose devout retirements he so gravely commends the blasphemous and senseless tittle tattle of this *Hysterical* Gossip. It were endless to repeat the Canting and Enthusiastick expressions, which signifie nothing in Mother *Juliana*'s Revelations; and one would wonder to what end such a Book were published among us, unless it were to convince us of this great truth, that we have not had so great *Fanaticks* and *Enthusiasts* among us, but they have had greater in the *Roman Church.* And by this means they may think to prevail upon the *Fanaticks* among us, by perswading them, /*p. 261*/ that they have been strangely mistaken concerning the *Church* of *Rome* in these matters; that she is no such enemy to *Enthusiams* and *Revelations* as some believe; but that in truth she hath not only always had such, but given great *approbation* and *encouragement* to them. So that among all their visions they do but mix some that confirm their particular Doctrines; as the *Visions* of *Juliana* concerning *the great Worship of the B. Virgin from her son,* the *holy Vernacle at* Rome, and such like *fopperies*;[127] these make all the rest very acceptable among them.

E.3. From FANATICISM *fanatically imputed to the* CATHOLICK CHURCH *by* DOCTOUR STILLINGFLEET: *and The Imputation refuted and retorted by S[erenus] C[ressy], a Catholick* (probably Douai, 1672).

/*p. 62*/ 64. It is truly a sad thing to consider with what disposition of mind persons qualified, as (it seems) the *Doctour* is, do apply themselves to the reading of *Books* of *Piety* written by *Catholicks*. It is as daggers piercing their hearts when they find no advantage to express their malignity: If in a great volume full of most heavenly *Instructions* for the exercise of all vertues and dutyes to *God* and man, they can find but a line or two into which they think they can make their Venemous teeth to enter, by that line or two they become edified, that is comfortable nourishment to their minds, the whole Book besides being nauseous to them; Would not *damned* soules in *Hell,* if *Spirituall Books* were sent them, thus read and thus descant upon them?

65. Now whether the *Doctour* (and some other of his freinds) has not shewed himself such a *Reader* of *Catholick Books* truly innocent, devout, and in /*p. 63*/ which the breathing of *Gods Spirit* may, as it were, be perceived, let any indifferent *Reader* of his *Book* be judge. How many of such *Books,* from *S. Gregory* to *S. Ignatius* his time, does the *Doctour* shew that he has read, how many *Lives* of *Saints,* how many Treatises of *Devotion,* and among them he will give me leave to name *Sancta Sophia,*[128] and poor *Mother Juliana?* And what account does he give to his *Readers* of the *Spirituall* Benefit reaped by him from his laborious reading? He it seems is not able out of them all to suggest any point of

---

125. Marginal notes: *Ch. 56, p 144; p. 145. See Rev. 56.2–34.*
126. Marginal note: *Ch. 58 p. 151. See Rev. 58.16–17, 30–33.*
127. See *Rev.* 25.1–34, 10.25–37.
128. Augustine Baker's posthumous treatise *Holy Wisdom,* compiled and published by Cressy (see Introduction, page 16, note 42).

Instruction in *Christian Doctrin,* not one good affection to *God,* not the least encouragement to a vertuous holy life. All these things are vanished out of his memory, and evaporated out of his brain, having never affected his heart. What then does he yeild for his *Readers* edification? He teaches him in reading such *Books* to pronounce mimically and Scornfully what he finds there concerning *Miracles,* how wel soever attested, and concerning *Divine Favours* communicated by *God* to his Speciall *Servants:* and this being done, to call them *Fanaticks,* and so doeing to esteem such re- /p. 64/ lations sufficiently confuted, and such *Spirituall Books* sufficiently disparaged. He teaches him to snatch out of a great *Book* three or four passages lamely and imperfectly cited, to give what construction to them he pleases, and whether he does not understand, or overunderstand them, to pronounce them still *Fanaticall,* and there is an end of those Books: By the *Doctours* good will no *Protestant* hereafter must receive the least good from them, unless pride, malice, and contempt of godlines be good things.

66. Now having named in the last place poor *Mother Juliana,* a devout *Anchoret* about three hundred years since living in *Norwich,* I must needs Signify my wonder, what could move his Spleen and choler against her litle *Book.* It is true, her language to the ears of this age, seems exotick: But it is such as was spoken in her time: therefore she may be excused: Her expressions touching *Gods* favours to her are homely, but that surely is no sin. For affections to *God* are sett down with great simplicity indeed, but they are withall cordiall and fervent, and apt to imprint them /p. 65/ selves, in the heart of an unprejudiced *Reader.* The sense and tast she shews to have had of *Gods Speciall love* to his servants, of the omnipotent efficacy of his *Grace,* and his impregnable defence and watchfullnes over his *Elect,* to secure them finally from all dangers of *Tentations,* is indeed admirable.

Yet the *Doctour* has no eyes to see any of these things. But through what glasses he looked when he spied out *blasphemy* in her Writing, I am not able to say: *Blasphemy,* which never hitherto could be observed by so many learned and *Religious* persons as have perused them. But it is no wonder that *Spiders* should suck and digest into *poyson* the most wholesom nourishment.

E.4. *THE ROMAN-CHURCH'S DEVOTIONS VINDICATED From Doctour Stillingfleet's misrepresentation. By O. N. a Catholick* (?, 1672). /p. 112/ If Mother Juliana's Revelations have many things new and strange, yet, if therein be nothing contrary to Faith or *Good manners,* nor words taken in a modern-improper sence will amount to Heresy, I hope this Author will not put her in the List of his Fanaticks, unless he can make good the same of them; or, that he can prove her old English to be Fanaticism, but then let Chaucer also look to himself.

E.5. *AN ANSWER to several late TREATISES, Occasioned by a Book entituled A DISCOURSE Concerning the IDOLATRY Practised in the CHURCH OF ROME, and the Hazard of Salvation in the Communion of it,* by Edward Stillingfleet (London: Printed by R.W. for Henry Mortlock, 1673). /p. 9/ I shall however declare my mind freely to you; if I had no other notion of the Christian doctrine, than what I have from the Doctrines of your Church as contrary to ours; no other measures of *Christian* piety than from your mystical *Theology;* no better way to Worship *God* than what is practised among you; no greater certainty of *Inspiration* from *God* than of the *Visions* and *Revelations* of your late *Saints;* no other *miracles* to confirm the *Christian* doctrine than what are wrought by your *Images* and *Saints,* I should sooner choose to be a *Philosopher,* than a *Christian* upon those terms. [. . .]

/p. 11/ But I would fain know of these men, whether they do in earnest make no difference between the Writings of such as Mother *Juliana* and the Books of *Scripture;* between the Revelations of S. *Brigitt,* S. *Catharine, &c.* and those of the *Prophets;* between the actions of S. *Francis* and *Ignatius Loyola* and those of the *Apostles?* if they do not, I know who they are that expose our *Religion* to purpose; if they do make a difference, how can the representing their visions and practices reflect dishonour upon the other, so infinitely above them, so much more certainly conveyed down to us with the consent of the whole Christian World? Thus much may here suffice to represent the arts our *Adversaries* are driven to, to defend themselves; I cannot blame them that they would engage *Religion* on their side, but so have all *Fanaticks* in the World as well as they; and I cannot for my heart see, but /p. 12/ this heavy charge of *Blasphemy* and undermining Religion does as justly lye on them, who deride the *Fanaticks* among us, as on those who have discovered the *Fanaticism* of the *Church* of *Rome.* [. . .]

BIBLIOGRAPHY
by Amy Appleford

Section 1 provides an annotated list, ordered chronologically, of the extant manuscripts, important editions, and modernizations of *A Vision* and *A Revelation*. The list sketches in broad, rough strokes a history of attempts to address the spirit of Julian's universalism and the complexities of her text; the list also situates the current edition as both a response to and a product of that history. The desire to make Julian's message accessible to all "evencristen" is manifest in the work of glossing or translating—from the notations in margins of the Sloane manuscript to Cressy's glosses, to the many modernizations produced in the twentieth century—while the desire to recollect the historical specificity of Julian's language, thinking, and style similarly underwrites the scholarly editions of her two texts. Section 2 provides an annotated list of late medieval "primary sources," important texts that inform or come out of Julian's intellectual and cultural milieu. The sidenotes of this edition refer extensively to Carl Horstmann's compilation *Yorkshire Writers: Richard Rolle of Hampole and His Followers* because it gathers some of the best-known works of religious prose and poetry in Middle English into two handy volumes and because, lately reprinted, it is comparatively accessible to modern students and scholars. An invaluable resource, Horstmann's compendium provides single manuscript transcriptions, without critical apparatus. Accordingly, readers may wish to refer to the critical editions listed (where available) in the annotations to supplement their reading of Horstmann's edition. Sections 3 and 4 present an overview of important scholarly writing on Julian and on late medieval religious culture; this does not attempt to be exhaustive. Sections 5 and 6 suggest Julian's continuing presence in modern literary, religious, and popular culture: from pastoral works written for a wide audience that continue the early-twentieth-century presentation of Julian as offering "comfortable words for Christ's lovers" to the high modernism of T. S. Eliot's *Four Quartets* and to Julian's latest incarnation as Webmistress in the multimedia forum of the Internet. These can only be a sampling, as at any one time over a hundred titles are available in print alone, dedicated to an idea of Julian's spirituality or of her writing. (A caveat about Web sources: as of yet there is no refereed Web site dedicated to Julian; all the information on the Web about her or her writings should be treated with caution.) In this bibliography EETS stands for Early English Text Society, o.s. for Ordinary Series, and e.s. for Extra Series. TEAMS is the acronym of the Consortium for the Teaching of the Middle Ages.

1. MANUSCRIPTS, LIFE RECORDS, EARLY REACTIONS, EDITIONS, AND MODERNIZATIONS (ARRANGED BY DATE)

London, Lambeth Palace, Register of Arundel (Will of Thomas Emund), I fol. 540d. See section B.1 of the Appendix.

Norwich, Norwich Consistory Court, Register Harsyk (Will of Roger Reed), fol. 198v (made illegible by water damage).

London, Register of Henry Chichele (Will of John Plumpton). In Ernest F. Jacob, *The Register of Henry Chichele, Archbishop of Canterbury, 1414–1443*, 3:413. Oxford: Clarendon Press, 1945. See section B.2 of the Appendix.

London, Register of Henry Chichele (Will of Isabel Ufford). In Ernest F. Jacob, *The Register of Henry Chichele, Archbishop of Canterbury, 1414–1443*, 2.94–97. Oxford: Clarendon Press, 1936–37. See section B.3 of the Appendix.

London, British Library MS Additional 37790, fols. 97–115 (formerly the Amherst MS).
> The unique manuscript copy of *A Vision;* made sometime after 1435 from an exemplar dated 1413.

London, British Library MS Additional 61823, fols. 21r–v.
> The sole surviving manuscript of *The Book of Margery Kempe*, with its account of Margery's meeting with Julian around 1413. See section C of the Appendix.

London, Westminster Cathedral Treasury MS 4, fols. 72v–112v.
> The manuscript is a copy, ca. 1500, of a compilation, made perhaps half a century earlier, in which excerpts from *A Revelation* are combined with selections from works by Walter Hilton. See section A of the Appendix.

Paris, Bibliothèque Nationale MS Fonds Anglais 40.
> *A Revelation,* copied sometime after the 1580s, perhaps by an English Benedictine nun in Paris or Cambrai.

Colwich, St. Mary's Abbey MS Baker 18, pp. 94–176. Ca. 1630.
> A portion of a text written by Margaret Gascoigne, a young nun of the Benedictine house of Cambrai, where the Sloane manuscript of *A Revelation* was probably written. Extemporizes on several passages from *A Revelation.* See section D.2 of the Appendix. (Gascoigne A)

Stratton-on-the-Fosse, Downside Abbey MS Baker 42. Ca. 1650.
> Copy of a biography of Margaret Gascoigne by Augustine Baker. The biography originally formed the first part of a "life and works" of Gascoigne by Baker, of which the text preserved in Colwich formed the second part. (Gascoigne B)

London, British Library MS Sloane 2499. Ca. 1650.
> *A Revelation,* possibly copied by Sister Clementina Cary, an English Benedictine nun at Cambrai, later abbess of the Paris daughter house.

Lancashire, St. Joseph's College MS, fols. 114r–117v (the Upholland Anthology). Ca. 1630.
> Brief selections from *A Revelation,* probably also made by an English Benedictine nun. Currently lost. See section D.2 of the Appendix.

Cressy, R. F. S. [Serenus], ed. 1670. *XVI Revelations of Divine Love, Shewed to a Devout Servant of our Lord, called* MOTHER JULIANA, *an Anchorete of* NORWICH: *Who lived in the Dayes of* KING EDWARD *the Third.* London.
> The first printed edition of *A Revelation,* probably based on the Paris MS. Printed with marginal glosses of difficult words. See section E.1 of the Appendix.

Stillingfleet, Edward. 1671. *A DISCOURSE Concerning the IDOLATRY Practised in the CHURCH OF ROME and the danger of Salvation in the Communion of it: in an answer to some Papers of a Revolted Protestant: wherein a particular Account is given of the Fanaticism and Divisions of that Church.* London: Printed by Robert White for Henry Mortlock. Pp. 235–61.

> An attack on Julian's *Revelation,* as edited by Serenus Cressy, by a prominent Anglican bishop and controversialist. See section E.2 of the Appendix.

Cressy, R. F. S. [Serenus]. 1672. *FANATICISM fanatically imputed to the CATHOLICK CHURCH by DOCTOUR STILLINGFLEET: and The Imputation refuted and retorted by S.C., a Catholick.* [Douai?]. Pp. 62–65.

> Cressy's defense of Julian. See section E.3 of the Appendix.

"O. N." 1672. *THE ROMAN-CHURCH'S DEVOTIONS VINDICATED From Doctour Stillingfleet's misrepresentation. By O. N. a Catholick.* N.p. P. 112.

> An anonymous second defense of Julian. See section E.4 of the Appendix.

Stillingfleet, Edward. 1673. *AN ANSWER to several late TREATISES, Occasioned by a Book entituled A DISCOURSE Concerning the IDOLATRY Practised in the CHURCH of ROME, and the Hazard of Salvation in the Communion of it.* London: Printed by R.W. for Henry Mortlock. Pp. 9–12.

> Stillingfleet's counterattack against Cressy, "O. N.," and others. See section E.5 of the Appendix.

London, British Library MS Sloane 3705. Late 1600s.

> A semi-modernized version of Sloane 2499 collated with either the Paris MS or Cressy's printed edition.

London, British Library MS Stow 42. Late 1600s or early 1700s.

> A handwritten copy of *A Revelation,* based on Cressy's edition.

Poiret, Pierre. 1708. *Petri Poireti Bibliotheca Mysticorum Selecta, tribus constans partibus. . . .* Amsterdam: N.p.

Parker, G. H., ed. 1843. *Sixteen Revelations of Divine Love, Made to a Devout Servant of Our Lord Called Mother Juliana, an Anchorete of Norwich [. . .].* Leicester: Crossley.

> A reissue of Cressy's edition of *A Revelation* with some modernization of format and spelling; includes a select glossary.

Hecker, I. T., ed. 1864. *Sixteen Revelations of Divine Love Made to a Devout Servant of Our Lord Called Mother Juliana.* Boston: Ticknor & Fields.

> A modernization of Cressy's edition of *A Revelation.*

Collins, H., ed. 1877. *Revelations of Divine Love Shewed to a Devout Anchoress by Name Mother Julian of Norwich.* London: T. Richardson & Sons.

> The first printed edition based on the Sloane MS; modernized.

Warrack, Grace, ed. 1901. *Revelations of Divine Love: Recorded by Julian of Norwich at Norwich Anno Domini 1373.* London: Methuen & Co. (13th ed., 1949; reprint, London: Methuen & Co., 1958.)

> The most influential modern translation of *A Revelation.* Based on Sloane 2499, Warrack's version contains an introduction on the manuscript tradition and Julian's life, which establishes that the author of the text is not Juliana Lampit, anchoress at Carrow, but rather Julian, anchoress at St. Julian's.

Tyrrell, G., ed. 1902. *XVI Revelations of Divine Love Shewed to Mother Juliana of Norwich 1373.* London. (2nd ed., London: Kegan Paul, Trench, Trübner & Co, 1920.)

> A reprint of Cressy's version by a leading figure in the Catholic Modernist movement.

[Anon.] 1908. *All Shall Be Well: Selections from the Writings of the Lady Julian of Norwich A.D. 1373.* London.

> An anonymous collection of extracts taken from Warrack's modernization.

Meunier, Gabriel, trans. 1910. *Révélations de l'amour de Dieu.* Paris: H. Oudin. (2nd ed., Tours: A. Mame, 1925.)

Harford, D., ed. 1911. *Comfortable Words for Christ's Lovers.* London: H. R. Allenson. (Reprint, 1912; 3rd ed., 1925, titled *The Shewings of Lady Julian, Recluse of Norwich.*)

> First printed edition of *A Vision;* modernized.

[Anon.] 1915. *The Showings of a Vision Being Extracts from Revelations of Divine Love Shewed to a Devout Anchoress by Name Julian of Norwich.* London.

> A book of selections compiled by an Anglican sister from Warrack's version; with a preface by George Congreve.

Hudleston, R., ed. 1927. *Revelations of Divine Love Shewed to a Devout Ankress by Name Julian of Norwich.* London: Burns, Oates & Washbourne. (Reprint, 1935.)

> A modernization of the Sloane copy of *A Revelation;* includes an introduction to and summary of text, as well as notes and glossary.

Karrer, Otto, ed. 1927. *Offenbarungen der göttlichen Liebe.* Translated by George Gerlach. Paderborn: F. Schöningh.

De Luca, Maria, trans. 1932. *Rivelazioni dell'amore divino.* Turin: Società editrice internazionale.

> An Italian translation of *A Revelation* based on the Sloane text.

Reynolds, Francis [Sister Anna Maria Reynolds], ed. 1956. "A Critical Edition of the Revelations of Julian of Norwich (1342–c.1416), Prepared from All the Known Manuscripts with Introduction, Notes and Select Glossary." Ph.D. thesis, Leeds University.

> First critical edition of *A Vision* and *A Revelation;* extensively consulted for Colledge and Walsh's *Book of Showings* and used as basis for Reynolds and Holloway's *Julian of Norwich: Showing of Love.*

———. 1958. *A Shewing of God's Love.* London. (Reprint, 1974.)

> A semi-modernized version of *A Vision.*

Bottoni, Pietro. 1957. *Rivelazioni dell'amore divine.* Rome: Editrice Studium.

> An Italian translation of *A Revelation,* based on Hudleston's modernization of the Sloane text.

Strakosch, Elisabeth, trans. 1960. *Offenbarungen von göttlicher Liebe.* Einsiedeln: Johannes Verlag.

> A German translation of *A Revelation.*

Colledge, Edmund, and James Walsh, eds. 1961. *Of the Knowledge of Ourselves and of God: A Fifteenth-Century Florilegium.* London: Mowbrays.

> A modernization of the contents of Westminster Cathedral Treasury MS 4, with scholarly introduction.

Walsh, James. 1961. *The Revelations of Divine Love of Julian of Norwich.* London. (Reprinted 1973, 1974, 1975.)

> A modernization of the Sloane text, based on Sister Anna Reynolds's Ph.D.-thesis edition.

Owen, Hywel Wyn. 1962. "An Edition of 'The Upholland Anthology.'" B.A. diss., University of Liverpool.

> Only complete edition of a seventeenth-century manuscript; contains several excerpts from *A Revelation*'s thirteenth revelation.

Wolters, Clifton, trans. 1966. *Julian of Norwich: Revelations of Divine Love.* Penguin Classics. Harmondsworth, Middlesex: Penguin.

> A loose translation of the Sloane text of *A Revelation,* possibly based on Warrack's edition.

Glasscoe, Marion, ed. 1976. *A Revelation of Love.* Exeter Medieval Texts. Exeter: University of Exeter Press.

> First published scholarly edition of *A Revelation,* closely based on the Sloane copy, which includes an introduction to Julian and her milieu, glossary, and bibliography. Most popular student edition before Crampton, and often used for citations to Julian in preference to Colledge and Walsh's 1978 edition (below).

Maisonneuve, Roland, trans. 1976. *Le petit livre des révélations, selon le manuscrit court du British Museum.* Hauteville, Switzerland, and Paris: Editions du Parvis.

> A French translation of *A Vision.*

Reynolds, Anna Maria, and Marie-Etienne Baudry, trans. 1977. *Révélation de l'amour de Dieu, version brève des "Seize révélations de l'amour divin."* Bégrolles: Abbaye de Bellefontaine.

del Mastro, M. L., trans. 1977. *Revelations of Divine Love: Juliana of Norwich.* Garden City, N.Y.: Image Books. (Reprint, 1994. With the title *The Revelation of Divine Love in Sixteen Showings Made to Dame Julian of Norwich.* Liguori, Mo.: Triumph Books.)

> Translation of *A Revelation* based on the Sloane text.

Beer, Frances, ed. 1978. *Julian of Norwich's Revelations of Divine Love: The Shorter Version, from BL Add. MS 37790.* Middle English Texts 8. Heidelberg: Carl Winter Universitätsverlag.

> A scholarly edition of *A Vision,* with an introduction on Julian, the manuscripts, and the textual and thematic relationship of *A Vision* and *A Revelation.* Began as a Ph.D. thesis under the direction of Edmund Colledge.

Colledge, Edmund, and James Walsh, eds. 1978. *A Book of Showings to the Anchoress Julian of Norwich.* 2 vols. Studies and Texts 35. Toronto: Pontifical Institute of Mediaeval Studies.

> Critical edition of *A Vision* and *A Revelation.* Vol. 1 includes arguments regarding Julian's doctrinal and theological sources, a study of the manuscript tradition, and the text of *A Vision,* the last indebted to Frances Beer's thesis edition (see previous item). Vol. 2 contains an annotated edition of *A Revelation* based on the Paris copy, collated with the Sloane manuscripts, the Upholland Anthology, and the Cressy printed edition. Indebted in its early stages to Sister Anna Maria Reynolds's Ph.D. thesis edition, and begun as a collaboration between Reynolds and Walsh, but eventually rethought from the ground up.

———. 1978. *Julian of Norwich: Showings.* Classics of Western Spirituality. New York: Paulist Press.

> The most influential of the English translations of *A Vision* and *A Revelation.*

Pezzini, Domenico, trans. 1984. *Libro delle rivelazioni.* Milan: Ancora.

Rissanen, Paavo, 1985. *Jumalan rakkauden ilmestys äiti Juliana Norwichlainen.* Helsinki: Hki Kirjaneliö.

> A Finnish translation of *A Revelation.*

Moniales bénédictines de Solesmes, trans. 1986. *Révélations de l'amour divin.* Paris, Téqui.

John-Julian [Swanson], Fr., O.J.N., and John Matarazzo, trans. 1988. *A Lesson of Love: The Revelations of Julian of Norwich.* London: Darton, Longman & Todd.

> A translation of *A Revelation* by the founder of the Episcopalian Order of Julian of Norwich.

Leonardi, Claudio, ed. 1992. *Libro delle rivelazioni.* In *Il Cristo: Testi teologici e spirituali da Riccardo di San Vittore a Caterina da Siena,* 5:449–537. Milan: Arnoldo Mondadari.

Crampton, Georgia Ronan, ed. 1994. *The Shewings of Julian of Norwich.* TEAMS Middle English Text Series. Kalamazoo, Mich.: Medieval Institute Publications.

> A student edition, closely based on the Sloane text. Includes an introduction that emphasizes Julian's place in late medieval women's writing, a select glossary, and extensive bibliography.

———, ed. 1994. *The Shewings of Julian of Norwich.* TEAMS Texts Online. Kalamazoo, Mich.: Medieval Institute Publications. http://www.lib.rochester.edu/camelot/teams/Crampton.htm.
> The first web version of *A Revelation.*

Skinner, John, trans. 1996. *Julian of Norwich, A Revelation of Love.* Evesham: Arthur James.
> Annotated edition of *A Revelation.*

Kempster, Hugh, ed. 1997. "Julian of Norwich: The Westminster Text of *A Revelation of Love.*" *Mystics Quarterly* 23:177–245.
> First published Middle English edition of the Julian of Norwich portion of Westminster Cathedral Treasury MS 4.

Cré, Marleen. 1997. "Westminster Cathedral Treasury MS 4: A Fifteenth-Century Spiritual Compilation." M.Ph. diss., University of Glasgow.
> Edition of the complete contents of Westminster Cathedral Treasure MS 4.

Spearing, Elizabeth, and A. C. Spearing, trans. 1998. *Revelations of Divine Love.* Penguin Classics. Harmondsworth, Middlesex: Penguin.
> Translations of *A Vision* and *A Revelation* (the latter based on Glasscoe's edition of the Sloane text), designed to replace Clifton Wolters's translation in the same series.

Reynolds, Sister Anna Maria, and Julia Bolton Holloway, eds. 2001. *Julian of Norwich: Showing of Love.* Biblioteche e archivi 8. Florence: Sismel, Edizioni del Galluzzo.
> Lavish edition of the Westminster, Paris, Sloane 2499, and Additional 37790 MSS with facing-page translation; provides extensive, often highly speculative histories of the process of composition and of the origins of the different manuscript versions.

Holloway, Julia Bolton. 2003. *Julian of Norwich: Showing of Love.* London: Darton, Longman & Todd.
> Translation based on the Sloane text, collated with Westminster, Paris, and Additional MSS.

2. SOURCES AND ANALOGUES

Allen, Hope Emily, ed. *English Writings of Richard Rolle, Hermit of Hampole.* Oxford: Clarendon Press, 1931.

Ancrene Wisse. In Savage and Watson, *Anchoritic Spirituality,* 41–208.
> An influential early-thirteenth-century English guide to living as an anchoress, still widely consulted and copied in Julian's lifetime. For an edition of the Early Middle English original, see *Ancrene Wisse,* edited by Robert Hasenfratz, TEAMS Middle English Texts Series (Kalamazoo, Mich: Medieval Institute Publications, 1998).

Andrew, Malcolm, and Ronald Waldron, eds. *The Poems of the Pearl Manuscript: Pearl, Cleanness, Patience, and Sir Gawain and the Green Knight.* 4th ed. Exeter: University of Exeter Press, 2002.

Anselm. *The Prayers and Meditations with the Proslogion.* Translated by Benedicta Ward. Harmondsworth, Middlesex: Penguin Books, 1973.

The Apocalypse of Paul [*Visio Pauli*]. In *The Apocryphal New Testament,* 525–55.
> One of the earliest and most influential of the otherworld visions that helped to construct medieval Christian notions of the afterlife. Though ascribed to the apostle Paul, this work was probably written in Greek in the fourth century.

The Apocryphal New Testament. Translated and edited by Montague Rhodes James. Oxford: Clarendon Press, 1924.

Augustine. *Confessions.* Translated by Henry Chadwick. Oxford: Oxford University Press, 1998.

Bernard of Clairvaux. *The Book on Loving God* [*De Diligendo Deo*]. Translated by Robert Walton. In *Treatises,* vol. 2, *The Steps of Humility and Pride; On Loving God.* Cistercian Fathers 13. Kalamazoo, Mich.: Cistercian Publications, 1980.

> An influential mid-twelfth-century account of the grades or degrees of love.

Bonaventure, Saint. *Itinerarium mentis in Deum* [The mind's journey into God]. St. Bonaventure, N.Y.: Franciscan Institute, Saint Bonaventure University, 2002.

> The most important mystical work of this mid-thirteenth-century Franciscan theologian.

Bridget of Sweden, Saint. *The "Liber Celestis" of St. Bridget of Sweden: The Middle English Version in British Library MS Claudius B i, Together with a Life of the Saint from the Same Manuscript.* Edited by Roger Ellis. EETS, o.s., 291. Oxford: Oxford University Press, 1987.

> The major collection of Bridget's revelations, organized and introduced by her confessor, Alphonse of Pecha.

The Chastising of God's Children. In *The Chastising of God's Children and the Treatise of Perfection of the Sons of God,* edited by Joyce Bazire and Eric Colledge. Oxford: Blackwell, 1957.

> Late-fourteenth-century compilation on temptation, tribulation, and the possibilities and dangers of visionary experience; draws on a number of Continental sources (most importantly Ruusbroec and Alphonse of Pecha) as well as on *Ancrene Wisse.* Perhaps written for the nuns of Barking Abbey.

Chaucer, Geoffrey. *The Canterbury Tales.* In *The Riverside Chaucer,* edited by Larry D. Benson. 3rd ed. Boston: Houghton Mifflin.

——. *The Consolation of Philosophy.* In *The Riverside Chaucer,* edited by Benson.

——. *Troilus and Criseyde.* In *The Riverside Chaucer,* edited by Benson.

Cicero. *De Inventione.* In *Cicero,* vol. 2, *De Inventione; De optima Genere Oratum; Topica,* translated by H. M. Hubbell. Loeb Classical Library. Cambridge, Mass.: Harvard University Press, 1968.

> One of the most influential of the early Latin manuals of rhetoric.

Cleanness. In Andrew and Waldron, *Poems of the Pearl Manuscript.*

> Fourteenth-century alliterative poem, probably by the author of *Sir Gawain and the Green Knight,* that describes the horrifying effects of God's hatred of impurity, from Noah's flood to the destruction of Sodom, to the fall of King Belshazzar.

The Cloud of Unknowing. In *The Cloud of Unknowing and the Book of Privy Counselling,* edited by Phyllis Hodgson. EETS, o.s., 218. Oxford: Oxford University Press, 1944.

> Late-fourteenth-century account of contemplation written in the East Midlands.

Contemplations of the Dread and Love of God. In Horstmann, *Yorkshire Writers,* 2:72–105.

> Early-fifteenth-century treatise on the life of devotion written for a general audience. Horstmann takes his text from the Wynkyn de Worde edition of 1506. For a critical edition, see Margaret Connolly, ed., *Contemplations of the Dread and Love of God,* EETS, o.s., 303 (Oxford: Oxford University Press, 1993).

The Cyrurgie of Guy de Chauliac. Edited by M. S. Ogden. EETS, o.s., 265. Oxford: Oxford University Press, 1971.

D'Abernon, Pierre. *La lumere as lais.* Edited by Glynn Hesketh. 3 vols. ANTS 58. London: Anglo-Norman Text Society, Birkbeck College, 2000.

> Thirteenth-century Anglo-Norman poetic version of the *Elucidarium,* a theological treatise in dialogue form by Honorius of Autun.

Dante Alighieri. *The Divine Comedy.* Edited and translated by Charles S. Singleton. 6 vols. Princeton: Princeton University Press, 1970–75.

Edmund of Abingdon. *The Mirror of Holy Church.* In Horstmann, *Yorkshire Writers,* 1:240–61.

> An influential early-thirteenth-century exposition of the life of religion by Edmund, archbishop of Canterbury, probably written in Latin but much translated into both Anglo-Norman and English. Horstmann edits MS Vernon. For a critical edition of the Latin text, see *Speculum religiosorum and Speculum ecclesie,* edited by Helen P. Forshaw, British Academy: Auctores Britannici Medii Aevi 3 (London: Oxford University Press, 1973).

Elizabeth of Hungary, Saint. *The Two Middle English Translations of the Revelations of St. Elizabeth of Hungary.* Edited by Sarah McNamer. Middle English Texts 28. Heidelberg: Universitätsverlag C. Winter, 1990.

> An account of the appearances to Elizabeth of the Virgin Mary, who gives the visionary new information about her life and the life of Christ.

Flete, William. *The Remedy Against the Troubles of Temptations.* In Horstmann, *Yorkshire Writers,* 2:106–23.

> An anti-ascetic treatise on comfort in temptation and suffering written in Latin c. 1350 by an English hermit who lived in Italy and was closely associated with Catherine of Siena. Horstmann takes his text from the Wynkyn de Worde edition of 1519, a much-expanded fifteenth-century translation.

Gospel of Nicodemus. In *The Apocryphal New Testament,* 94–146.

> One of the apocryphal Gospels and during the Middle Ages the main source of information about Christ's harrowing of hell between his death and resurrection. For a Middle English version, see *The Middle English Harrowing of Hell and Gospel of Nicodemus,* edited by W. H. Hulme, EETS, e.s., 100 (Oxford: Oxford University Press, 1907).

Grosseteste, Robert. *Le château d'amour de Robert Grosseteste.* Edited by Jessie Murray. Paris: Champion, 1918.

> A widely read early-thirteenth-century poetic exposition of Christian theology and history written in Anglo-Norman French.

Hilton, Walter. *The Scale of Perfection.* Edited by Thomas H. Bestul. TEAMS Middle English Texts Series. Kalamazoo, Mich.: Medieval Institute Publications, 2000.

> A two-book treatise on the contemplative life initially written for an anchoress but quickly circulated to a broad audience. The single most influential Middle English treatise of its kind.

The Holy Boke Gratia Dei. In *Richard Rolle and Þe Holy Boke Gratia Dei: An Edition with Commentary,* edited by Sister Mary Luke Arntz. Elizabethan and Renaissance Studies 92:2. Salzburg: Institut für Anglistik und Amerikanistik Universität Salzburg, 1981.

> A fourteenth-century English adaptation of rules for nuns and recluses directed toward a general audience.

Holy Maidenhood. In Savage and Watson, *Anchoritic Spirituality,* 223–44.

> An early-thirteenth-century treatise, a product of the same milieu as *Ancrene Wisse,* that urges the advantages of virginity on anchoresses and nuns already sworn to it.

Horstmann, Carl, ed. *Yorkshire Writers: Richard Rolle of Hampole, an English Father of the Church, and His Followers.* Swan Sonnenschein & Co., 1895. Reprinted with two volumes bound as one, and new preface by Anne Clark Bartlett, Cambridge: D. S. Brewer, 1999.

Jacobus de Voragine. *The Golden Legend: Readings on Saints* [*Legenda aurea*]. Translated by William Granger Ryan. Princeton, N.J.: Princeton University Press, 1993.

The most important medieval collection of saints' lives, translated into English and printed, late in the fifteenth century, by William Caxton.

John of Morigny. *Liber visionum.* Edited and translated by Claire Fanger and Nicholas Watson. University Park: Pennsylvania State University Press, forthcoming.

Kempe, Margery. *The Book of Margery Kempe.* Edited by Barry Windeatt. New York: Longman, 2000.

The other great East Anglian visionary work by a fifteenth-century woman.

Langland, William. *The Vision of Piers Plowman: A Critical Edition of the B-Text Based on Trinity College Cambridge ms B.15.17.* Edited by A. V. C. Schmidt. 2nd ed. London: Dent, 1995.

An influential late-fourteenth-century allegorical poem about contemporary Christian society and its ills and the relation between social reality, moral ideals, and their theological underpinnings.

Mechtild of Magdeburg. *The Flowing Light of the Godhead.* Translated by Frank Tobin. Classics of Western Spirituality. New York: Paulist Press, 1999.

Ogilvie-Thomson, S. J., ed. *Richard Rolle: Prose and Verse.* EETS, o.s., 293. Oxford: Oxford University Press, 1988.

Patience. In Andrew and Waldron, *Poems of the Pearl Manuscript.*

A fourteenth-century alliterative poem, probably by the author of *Sir Gawain and the Green Knight,* that narrates the story of Jonah as a negative exemplum of the usefulness of patient submission to God's will.

Pearl. In Andrew and Waldron, *Poems of the Pearl Manuscript.*

A fourteenth-century visionary poem, probably also by the author of *Sir Gawain and the Green Knight,* that is concerned with virginity, death, and the nature of heavenly reward.

Pecock, Reginald. *The Reule of Crysten Religioun.* Edited by William Cabell Greet. EETS, o.s., 271. Oxford: Oxford University Press, 1927.

A mid-fifteenth-century English exposition of Christian faith intended to popularize a scholastic approach to doctrine and religious reasoning.

Pety Job. In Horstmann, *Yorkshire Writers,* 2:380–89.

A long fifteenth-century lyric rendering of the nine lessons for the dead used in the liturgical office for the dead and taken form the Book of Job. Horstmann takes his text from ms Harley 1706. For a recent edition, see *Moral Love Songs and Laments,* edited by Susanna Greer Fein, TEAMS Middle English Texts Series (Kalamazoo, Mich.: Medieval Institute Publications, 1998).

"*The Pore Caitif:* Edited from ms Harley 2336 with Introduction and Notes." Edited by Mary Teresa Brady. Ph.D. diss., Fordham University, 1954.

Fourteenth-century treatise of religious instruction compiled from different sources, organized as a "ladder" to heaven, and self-consciously written for the widest possible audience.

The Pricke of Conscience (Stimulus Conscientiae). Edited by Richard Morris. Berlin: A. Asher, 1863. Reprint, New York: AMS, 1973.

A highly influential mid-fourteenth-century poetic treatise on sin, death, the day of Judgment, the other world, and the role of fear in fashioning Christian behavior.

The Prickynge of Love. Edited by Harold Kane. 2 vols. Elizabethan and Renaissance Studies 92:10. Salzburg: Institut für Anglistik und Amerikanistik Universität Salzburg, 1983.

A Middle English version of *Stimulus amoris* by James of Milan, a fourteenth-century treatise on the devotional life organized as a series of affective meditations aimed at stirring the user to a physical, as well as spiritual, love for Christ.

The Privity of the Passion. In Horstmann, *Yorkshire Writers,* 1:198–218.

> A detailed affective account of Christ's sufferings and death translated from the *Meditationes vitae Christi* by Johannes de Caulibus, an influential early-fourteenth-century life of Christ written for a nun. Horstmann takes his text from Lincoln Cathedral Library MS Thornton A.1.17, and reproduces the manuscript's ascription of the work to Bonaventure. See Denise Baker's modern translation in *Cultures of Piety: Medieval English Devotional Literature in Translation,* edited by Anne Clark Bartlett and Thomas Bestul (Ithaca: Cornell University Press, 1999).

The Revelation of the Monk of Eynsham. Edited by Robert Easting. EETS, o.s., 318. Oxford: Oxford University Press, 2002.

Rolle, Richard. *Ego Dormio.* In Ogilvie-Thomson, *Richard Rolle: Prose and Verse.*

> An ecstatic mid-fourteenth-century English exposition of the stages of love written for a nun or anchoress. See also Allen's edition in *English Writings of Richard Rolle.*

———. *Form of Living.* In Horstmann, *Yorkshire Writers,* 1:3–49.

> An exposition of the spiritual life written for the mid-fourteenth-century anchoress Margaret Kirkeby. Horstmann takes his text from MS Cambridge Dd.V.64. For a critical edition, see Ogilvie-Thomson, *Richard Rolle: Prose and Verse,* and Allen, *English Writings of Richard Rolle.*

———. *Meditations on the Passion.* In Horstmann, *Yorkshire Writers,* 1:83–91.

> A meditation on and affective narrative account of Christ's sufferings and death. Horstmann takes his text from MS Cambridge Ll I. 8. For a critical edition also based on this manuscript, see Allen, *English Writings of Richard Rolle.*

Savage, Anne, and Nicholas Watson, trans. and eds. *Anchoritic Spirituality: "Ancrene Wisse" and Associated Works.* Classics of Western Spirituality. New York: Paulist Press, 1991.

Sawles Warde. In Savage and Watson, *Anchoritic Spirituality,* 209–22.

> An allegorical account of the uses of fear, hope, and the cardinal virtues, produced in the same early-thirteenth-century milieu as *Ancrene Wisse.*

South English Legendary. Edited by Charlotte D'Evelyn and Anna J. Mill. 2 vols. EETS, o.s., 235, 236. Oxford: Oxford University Press, 1956.

> A widely circulated thirteenth-century English collection of saints' lives.

"*Speculum devotorum:* An Edition with Commentary." Edited by John P. Banks. Ph.D. diss., Fordham University, 1959.

> A well-researched early-fifteenth-century English life of Christ, based on numerous sources, probably written for a nun of the Bridgettine house of Syon by a Carthusian.

A Treatise of Ghostly Battle. In Horstmann, *Yorkshire Writers,* 2:420–36.

> A fifteenth-century introduction to the religious life written in the form of an allegory. Horstmann takes his text from MS Harley 1706.

"Woefully Arrayed." In *Religious Lyrics of the Fifteenth Century,* edited by Carleton Brown. Oxford: Clarendon Press, 1939.

3. SECONDARY SOURCES: JULIAN OF NORWICH

Abbot, Christopher. *Julian of Norwich: Autobiography and Theology.* Cambridge: D. S. Brewer, 1999.

Aers, David, and Lynn Staley. *Powers of the Holy: Religion, Politics, and Gender in Late Medieval English Culture.* University Park: Pennsylvania State University Press, 1996.

Baker, Denise Nowakowski. "Julian of Norwich and Anchorite Literature." *Mystics Quarterly* 19 (1993): 148–60.

———. *Julian of Norwich's "Showings": From Vision to Book.* Princeton, N.J.: Princeton University Press, 1994.

———. "The Structure of the Soul and the 'Godly Wylle' in Julian of Norwich's *Showings*." In Jones, *Medieval Mystical Tradition,* 37–50.

Barratt, Alexandra. "How Many Children Had Julian of Norwich? Editions, Translations, and Versions of Her Revelations." In *Vox Mystica: Essays on Medieval Mysticism,* edited by Anne Clark Bartlett, Thomas H. Bestul, Janet Goebel, and William F. Pollard. Cambridge: D. S. Brewer, 1995.

Bauerschmidt, Frederick Christian. *Julian of Norwich and the Mystical Body Politic of Christ.* Notre Dame, Ind.: University of Notre Dame Press, 1999.

Bradley, Ritamary. "Julian of Norwich." In vol. 9 of *A Manual of the Writings in Middle English, 1050–1500,* edited by Albert E. Hartung and J. Burke Severs. 9 vols. to date. New Haven: Connecticut Academy of Arts and Sciences, 1967–.

———. "Patristic Background of the Motherhood Similitude in Julian of Norwich." *Christian Scholar's Review* 2 (1978): 101–13.

Cervone, Cristina Maria. "The 'Soule' Crux in Julian of Norwich's *A Revelation of Love.*" *Review of English Studies* 55 (2004): 151–56.

Clark, J. P. H. "Fiducia in Julian of Norwich." *Downside Review* 99 (1981): 97–108.

———. "Fiducia in Julian of Norwich, II." *Downside Review* 99 (1981): 214–29.

———. "Nature, Grace, and the Trinity in Julian of Norwich." *Downside Review* 100 (1982): 203–20.

———. "Predestination in Christ According to Julian of Norwich." *Downside Review* 100 (1982): 79–91.

———. "Time and Eternity in Julian of Norwich." *Downside Review* 109 (1991): 259–76.

Colledge, Edmund, and James Walsh. "Editing Julian of Norwich's Revelations: A Progress Report." *Mediaeval Studies* 38 (1976): 404–2.

Cré, Marleen. "Vernacular Mysticism in the Charterhouse: An Analysis of BL MS Additional 37790 in Its Religious and Literary Context." Diss., University of Fribourg, 2001. (Revised version forthcoming as volume 10 of The Medieval Translator [Turnhout: Brepols].)

Deighton, Alan. "Julian of Norwich's Knowledge of the Life of St John of Beverley." *Notes and Queries* 40 (1993): 4.440–43.

Evasdaughter, Elizabeth N. "Julian of Norwich." In *Medieval, Renaissance, and Enlightenment Women Philosophers, A.D. 500–1600,* vol. 2 of *A History of Women Philosophers,* edited by Mary Ellen Waithe. Dordrecht: Kluwer Academic Publishers, 1989.

Glasscoe, Marion. "Changing *Chere* and Changing Text in the Eighth Revelation of Julian of Norwich." *Medium Aevum* 66 (1997): 115–21.

———. "Visions and Revisions: A Further Look at the Manuscripts of Julian of Norwich." *Studies in Bibliography* 42 (1989): 103–20.

Hide, Kerrie. *Gifted Origins to Graced Fulfilment: The Soteriology of Julian of Norwich.* Collegeville, Minn.: Liturgical Press, 2001.

Hilles, Carroll. "The Sacred Image and the Healing Touch: The Veronica in Julian of Norwich's *Revelation of Love.*" *Journal of Medieval and Early Modern Studies* 28 (1998): 553–80.

Jantzen, Grace M. *Julian of Norwich: Mystic and Theologian.* New York: Paulist Press, 1988.

Johnson, Lynn Staley. "The Trope of the Scribe and the Question of Literary Authority in the Works of Julian of Norwich and Margery Kempe." *Speculum* 66 (1991): 820–38.

Kempster, Hugh. "A Question of Audience: The Westminster Text and Fifteenth-Century Reception of Julian of Norwich." In McEntire, *Julian of Norwich*, 257–90.

Lang, Judith. "'The Godly Wylle' in Julian of Norwich." *Downside Review* 102 (1984): 163–73.

Leech, Kenneth, and Benedicta Ward, eds. *Julian Reconsidered.* Fairacres Publications 106. Oxford: SLG Press, 1988.

McEntire, Sandra J., ed. *Julian of Norwich: A Book of Essays.* Garland Medieval Casebook 21. New York: Garland, 1998.

McInerney, Maud Burnett. "'In the Meydens Womb': Julian of Norwich and the Poetics of Enclosure." In *Medieval Mothering,* edited by John Carmi Parsons and Bonnie Wheeler. New York: Garland, 1996.

Molinari, Paul. *Julian of Norwich: The Teaching of a Fourteenth-Century English Mystic.* London: Longmans, 1958.

Nolcken, Christina von. "Julian of Norwich." In *Middle English Prose,* edited by A. S. G Edwards, 97–108. New Brunswick, N.J.: Rutgers University Press, 1984.

Nuth, Joan M. *Wisdom's Daughter: The Theology of Julian of Norwich.* New York: Crossroad, 1991.

Olsen, Mary. "God's Inappropriate Grace: Images of Courtesy in Julian of Norwich's Showings." *Mystics Quarterly* 20 (1994): 47–59.

Palliser, Margaret Ann. *Christ, Our Mother of Mercy: Divine Mercy and Compassion in the Theology of the Shewings of Julian of Norwich.* Berlin: Walter de Gruyter, 1992.

Peters, Brad. "Julian of Norwich and Her Conceptual Development of Evil." *Mystics Quarterly* 17 (1991): 181–88.

Reichardt, P. F. "'Speciall sainctes': Julian of Norwich, John of Beverley, and the Chronology of the *Shewings.*" *English Studies* 82 (2001): 385–392.

Reynolds, Sister Anna Maria. "Some Literary Influences in the *Revelations* of Julian of Norwich (c. 1342–post 1416)." *Leeds Studies in English* 7–8 (1952): 18–28.

Riddy, Felicity. "Julian of Norwich and Self-Textualization." In *Editing Women,* edited by Ann M. Hutchison, 101–24. Toronto: University of Toronto Press, 1998.

———. "'Women Talking About the Things of God': A Late Medieval Sub-Culture." In *Women and Literature in Britain, 1150–1500,* edited by Carol M. Meale, Cambridge Studies in Medieval Literature 17, 104–27. Cambridge: Cambridge University Press, 1996.

Robertson, Elizabeth. "Medieval Medical Views of Women and Female Spirituality in the *Ancrene Wisse* and Julian of Norwich's *Showings.*" In *Feminist Approaches to the Body in Medieval Literature,* edited by Linda Lomperis and Sarah Stanbury, 142–67. Philadelphia: University of Pennsylvania Press, 1993.

Ruud, Jay. "Nature and Grace in Julian of Norwich." *Mystics Quarterly* 19 (1993): 71–81.

Sprung, Andrew. "The Inverted Metaphor: Earthly Mothering as Figura of Divine Love in Julian of Norwich's *Book of Showings.*" In *Medieval Mothering,* edited by John Carmi Parsons and Bonnie Wheeler. New York: Garland, 1996.

———. "'We Nevyr Shall Come out of Hym': Enclosure and Immanence in Julian of Norwich's Book of Showings." *Mystics Quarterly* 19 (1993): 47–61.

Stone, Robert Karl. *Middle English Prose Style: Margery Kempe and Julian of Norwich.* The Hague: Mouton, 1970.

Sutherland, Annie. "'Oure Feyth Is Groundyd in Goddes Worde'—Julian of Norwich and the Bible." In Jones, *Medieval Mystical Tradition*, 1–20.

Tamburr, Karl. "Mystic Transformation: Julian's Version of the Harrowing of Hell." *Mystics Quarterly* 20 (1994): 60–67.

Watson, Nicholas. "The Composition of Julian of Norwich's *Revelation of Love*." *Speculum* 68 (1993): 637–83.

———. "The Trinitarian Hermeneutic in Julian of Norwich's *Revelation of Love*." In McEntire, *Julian of Norwich*, 61–90.

———. "'Yf Wommen Be Double Naturelly': Remaking 'Woman' in Julian of Norwich's *Revelation of Love*." *Exemplaria* 8 (1995): 1–34.

Windeatt, B. A. "The Art of Mystical Loving: Julian of Norwich." In Glasscoe, *Medieval Mystical Tradition*, 1:55–71.

———. "Julian of Norwich and Her Audience." *Review of English Studies*, n.s., 28 (1977): 1–17.

4. SECONDARY SOURCES: OTHER

Appleford, Amy. "Learning to Die: Affectivity, Community, and Death in Late Medieval English Writing." Ph.D. diss., University of Western Ontario, 2004.

Baker, Augustine. *Holy Wisdom; or, Directions for the Prayer of Contemplation*. Edited by Serenus Cressy. Wheathampstead, Hertfordshire: Anthony Clarke Books, 1972.

Beckwith, Sarah. *Christ's Body: Identity, Culture, and Society in Late Medieval Writing*. London: Routledge, 1993.

Bell, Luke, and Hywel Wyn Owen. "The Upholland Anthology: An Augustine Baker Manuscript." *Downside Review* 107 (1989): 274–92.

Benedictines of Stanbrook. *In a Great Tradition: Tribute to Dame Laurentia McLachlan, Abbess of Stanbrook*. New York: Harper, 1956.

Birrell, T. A. "English Catholic Mystics in Non-Catholic Circles." *Downside Review* 94 (1976): 60–81, 99–117, and 213–31.

Bynum, Caroline Walker. *Holy Feast and Holy Fast: The Religious Significance of Food to Medieval Women*. Berkeley and Los Angeles: University of California Press, 1987.

———. *Jesus as Mother: Studies in the Spirituality of the High Middle Ages*. Berkeley and Los Angeles: University of California Press, 1982.

Clark, John P. H. "Late Fourteenth-Century Cambridge Theology and the English Contemplative Tradition." In Glasscoe, *Medieval Mystical Tradition*, vol. 5.

Coleman, Joyce. *Public Reading and the Reading Public in Late Medieval England and France*. Cambridge Studies in Medieval Literature 26. Cambridge: Cambridge University Press, 1996.

Colledge, Edmund. *The Mediaeval Mystics of England*. New York: Scribner, 1961.

Davis, Norman, ed. *The Paston Letters and Papers of the Fifteenth Century*. 2 vols. Oxford: Clarendon Press, 1976.

de Certeau, Michel. *Mystic Fable* [*Fable mystique*]. Trans. Michael B. Smith. Chicago: University of Chicago Press, 1992.

Dunn, F. I. "Hermits, Anchorites, and Recluses: A Study with Reference to Medieval Norwich." In *Julian and Her Norwich: Commemorative Essays and Handbook to the Exhibition "Revelations of Divine Love,"* edited by Frank Dale Sayer. Norwich: Julian of Norwich 1973 Celebration Committee, 1973.

Ellis, Roger. "'Flores ad Fabricandum . . . Coronam': An Investigation into the Uses of the Revelations of St. Bridget of Sweden in Fifteenth-Century England." *Medium Aevum* 51 (1982): 163–86.

Erler, Mary C. "English Vowed Women at the End of the Middle Ages." *Mediaeval Studies* 57 (1995): 155–205.

———. *Women, Reading, and Piety in Late Medieval England.* Cambridge Studies in Medieval Literature 46. Cambridge: Cambridge University Press, 2002.

Erler, Mary C., and Maryanne Kowaleski, eds. *Gendering the Master Narrative: Women and Power in the Middle Ages.* Ithaca: Cornell University Press, 2003.

Gilchrist, Roberta, and Marilyn Oliva. *Religious Women in Medieval East Anglia: History and Archaeology, c.1100–1540.* Norwich: Centre of East Anglian Studies, University of East Anglia, 1993.

Gillespie, Vincent. *Looking in Holy Books: Essays on Late Medieval Religious Writing in England.* Religion and Culture in the Middle Ages. Cardiff: University of Wales Press, 2005.

Glasscoe, Marion. *English Medieval Mystics: Games of Faith.* New York: Longman, 1993.

———, ed. *The Medieval Mystical Tradition in England.* 6 vols. Exeter: University of Exeter Press, 1980, 1982; Cambridge: D. S. Brewer, 1984, 1987, 1992, 1999.

Hanna, Ralph. "Some Norfolk Women and Their Books, ca. 1390–1440." In *The Cultural Patronage of Medieval Women,* edited by June Hall McCash, 288–305. Athens: University of Georgia Press, 1996.

Heffernan, Thomas J. *The Popular Literature of Medieval England.* Knoxville: University of Tennessee Press, 1985.

L'Hermite-Leclercq, Paulette. "La réclusion volontaire au Moyen Âge: Une institution religieuse spécialement féminine." In *La condición de la mujer en la Edad Media,* 136–54. Madrid: Universidad Complutense, 1986.

Hollywood, Amy. *The Soul as Virgin Wife: Mechtild of Magdeburg, Marguerite Porete, and Meister Eckhart.* Notre Dame, Ind.: University of Notre Dame Press, 1995.

Hudson, Anne. "A Lollard Sect Vocabulary?" In *Lollards and Their Books,* 165–80. London: Hambledon, 1985.

———. *Premature Reformation: Wycliffite Texts and Lollard History.* Oxford: Oxford University Press, 1988.

Inge, William Ralph. *Christian Mysticism.* New York: Meridian Books, 1956.

———. *Studies in English Mystics.* London: Murray, 1905.

James, William. *The Varieties of Religious Experience: A Study in Human Nature.* New York: Longmans, Green, 1902.

Jantzen, Grace. *Power, Gender, and Christian Mysticism.* Cambridge Studies in Ideology and Religion 8. Cambridge: Cambridge University Press, 1995.

Jenkins, Jacqueline. "Reading and *The Book of Margery Kempe.*" In *A Companion to "The Book of Margery Kempe,"* edited by John H. Arnold and Katherine J. Lewis, 113–28. Cambridge: D. S. Brewer, 2004.

Jones, E. A., ed. *The Medieval Mystical Tradition in England: Exeter Symposium 7.* Cambridge: D. S. Brewer, 2004.

Keiser, George R. "Serving the Needs of Readers: Textual Division in Some Late Medieval English Texts." In *New Science out of Old Books: Studies in Manuscripts and Early Printed Books in Honour of A. I. Doyle,* edited by Richard Beadle and A. J. Piper, 207–26. Aldershot: Scolar, 1995.

Knowles, David. *The English Mystical Tradition.* New York: Harper, 1965.

———. *The English Mystics.* London: Burns, Oates & Washbourne, 1927.

Knowles, David, and R. Neville Hadcock. *Medieval Religious Houses: England and Wales.* London: Longman, 1971.

Lagorio, Valerie, and Ritamary Bradley. *The 14th-Century English Mystics: A Comprehensive Annotated Bibliography.* New York: Garland, 1981.

Lagorio, Valerie, and Michael Sargent (with Ritamary Bradley). "English Mystical Writings." In vol. 9 of *A Manual of the Writings in Middle English, 1050–1500,* edited by Albert E. Hartung and J. Burke Severs. 9 vols. to date. New Haven: Connecticut Academy of Arts and Sciences, 1967–.

Mack, Phyllis. *Visionary Women: Ecstatic Prophecy in Seventeenth-Century England.* Berkeley and Los Angeles: University of California Press, 1992.

Marx, C. William. *The Devil's Rights and the Redemption in the Literature of Medieval England.* Cambridge: D. S. Brewer, 1995.

McCann, Justin, and Hugh Connolly, eds. *Memorials of Father Augustine Baker and Other Documents Relating to the English Benedictines.* Catholic Record Society 33. London: Catholic Record Society, 1933.

McGinn, Bernard. *The Presence of God: A History of Western Christian Mysticism.* 3 vols. so far. New York: Crossroad, 1991–.

Meale, Carol M., ed. *Women and Literature in Britain, 1150–1500.* Cambridge: Cambridge University Press, 1993.

Mooney, Catherine M., ed. *Gendered Voices: Medieval Saints and Their Interpreters.* Philadelphia: University of Pennsylvania Press, 1999.

Newman, Barbara. *From Virile Woman to WomanChrist: Studies in Medieval Religion and Literature.* Philadelphia: University of Pennsylvania Press, 1995.

———. *God and the Goddesses: Vision, Poetry, and Belief in the Middle Ages.* Philadelphia: University of Pennsylvania Press, 2003.

Oliva, Marilyn. *The Convent and the Community in Late Medieval England: Female Monasteries in the Diocese of Norwich, 1350–1540.* Woodbridge, Suffolk: Boydell Press, 1998.

Owen, Hywel Wyn. "Another Augustine Baker Manuscript." In *Dr. L. Reypens-Album,* ed. A. Ampe, 269–80. Antwerp: Uitgave van het Ruusbroec-Genootschap, 1964.

Parkes, M. B. "The Literacy of the Laity." In *Literature and Western Civilization,* vol. 2 of *The Mediaeval World,* edited by David Daiches and Anthony Thorlby, 555–78. London: Aldus, 1973.

Pepler, Conrad. *The English Religious Heritage.* London: Blackfriars, 1958.

Poor, Sara S. "Mechthild von Magdeburg: Gender and the 'Unlearned Tongue.'" In Somerset and Watson, *Vulgar Tongue,* 57–80.

Richmond, Colin. *The Paston Family in the Fifteenth Century.* Cambridge: Cambridge University Press, 1990.

Riehle, Wolfgang. *The Middle English Mystics [Studien zur englischen Mystik des Mittelalters].* Translated by Bernard Standring. London: Routledge & Kegan Paul, 1981.

Sagovsky, Nicholas. *"On God's Side": A Life of George Tyrrell.* Oxford: Clarendon Press, 1990.

Salvin, Peter, and Serenus Cressy. *The Life of Father Augustine Baker, O.S.B. (1575–1641).* Edited by Justin McCann. London: Burns & Oates, 1933.

Simpson, James. *Reform and Cultural Revolution: 1350–1547.* Oxford English Literary History 2. Oxford: Oxford University Press, 2002.

Somerset, Fiona, and Nicholas Watson, eds. *The Vulgar Tongue: Medieval and Postmedieval Vernacularity.* University Park: Pennsylvania State University Press, 2003.

Spearitt, Placid. "The Survival of Mediaeval Spirituality Among the English Exiled Black Monks." *American Benedictine Review* 25 (1974): 287–309.

Staley, Lynn. *Margery Kempe's Dissenting Fictions.* University Park: Pennsylvania State University Press, 1994.

Steuert, Hilary. "A Study in Recusant Prose: Dom Serenus Cressy, 1605–74." *Downside Review* 66 (1948): 165–78, 287–301.

Summit, Jennifer. *Lost Property: The Woman Writer and English Literary History, 1380–1589.* Chicago: University of Chicago Press, 2000.

Tanner, Norman P. *The Church in Late Medieval Norwich, 1370–1532.* Studies and Texts 66. Toronto: Pontifical Institute of Mediaeval Studies, 1984.

Tavard, George H. *The Seventeenth-Century Tradition: A Study in Recusant Thought.* Leiden: E. J. Brill, 1978.

Truran, Margaret. "Spirituality: Fr. Baker's Legacy." In *Lamspringe: An English Abbey in Germany, 1643–1803,* edited by Anselm Cramer, O.S.B., 83–96. York: Ampleforth Abbey, 2004.

Tyrrell, George. *Essays on Faith and Immortality.* Edited by Maude Petre. London: Longmans, 1914.

Underhill, Evelyn. *Mysticism: A Study in the Nature and Development of Man's Spiritual Consciousness.* London: Methuen, 1911.

———. *The Mystic Way.* London: Dent, 1913.

———. *The Essentials of Mysticism and Other Essays.* London: Dent, 1920.

Voaden, Rosalynn. *God's Words, Women's Voices: The Discernment of Spirits in the Writing of Late Medieval Women Visionaries.* Cambridge: D. S. Brewer, 1999.

———, ed. *Prophets Abroad: The Reception of Continental Holy Women in Late-Medieval England.* Cambridge: D. S. Brewer, 1996.

Warren, Ann K. *Anchorites and Their Patrons in Medieval England.* Berkeley and Los Angeles: University of California Press, 1985.

Watson, Nicholas. "Censorship and Cultural Change in Late Medieval England: Vernacular Theology, the Oxford Translation Debate, and Arundel's Constitutions of 1409." *Speculum* 70 (1995): 822–64.

———. "Conceptions of the Word: The Mother Tongue and the Incarnation of God." *New Medieval Literatures* 1 (1997): 85–124.

———. "The Middle English Mystics." In *The Cambridge History of Medieval English Literature,* edited by David Wallace, 539–65. Cambridge: Cambridge University Press, 1998.

Watt, Diane. *Secretaries of God: Women Prophets in Late Medieval and Early Modern England.* Cambridge: D. S. Brewer, 1997.

Williams, Rowan. *The Wound of Knowledge: Christian Spirituality from the New Testament to St. John of the Cross.* London: Darton, Longman & Todd, 1979.

Wogan-Browne, Jocelyn, Nicholas Watson, Andrew Taylor, and Ruth Evans, eds. *The Idea of the Vernacular: An Anthology of Middle English Literary Theory, 1280–1520.* University Park: Pennsylvania State University Press, 1999.

5. TEXTUAL CRITICISM

Cerquiglini, Bernard. *In Praise of the Variant: A Critical History of Philology* [*Eloge de la variante*]. Translated by Betsy Wing. Baltimore: Johns Hopkins University Press, 1999.

Greeson, Hoyt S. "Glossary to British Library Sloane 2499." In Sister Anna Maria Reynolds and Julia Bolton Holloway, eds., *Julian of Norwich: Showing of Love,* Biblioteche e archivi 8:627–42. Florence: Sismel, Edizioni del Galluzzo, 2001.

Greetham, D. C. *Textual Scholarship: An Introduction.* New York: Garland, 1994.

Kane, George, E. Talbot Donaldson, George Russell, eds. *Piers Plowman: The Three Versions.* 3 vols. London: Athlone Press, 1960, 1975, 1997.

Laing, Margaret. "Linguistic Profiles and Textual Criticism: The Translations by Richard Misyn of Rolle's *Incendium Amoris* and *Emendatio Vitae.*" In *Middle English Dialectology: Essays on Some Principles and Problems,* edited by Margaret Laing, 188–203. Aberdeen: Aberdeen University Press, 1989.

Machan, Tim. *Textual Criticism and Middle English Texts.* Charlottesville: University Press of Virginia, 1994.

Millett, Bella. "*Mouvance* and the Medieval Author: Re-editing *Ancrene Wisse.*" In *Late-Medieval Religious Texts and Their Transmission,* edited by A. J. Minnis, 9–20. Cambridge: D. S. Brewer, 1994.

Parkes, M. B. *Pause and Effect: An Introduction to the History of Punctuation in the West.* Berkeley and Los Angeles: University of California Press, 1993.

Samuels, M. L. "Spelling and Dialect in the Late and Post–Middle English Periods." In *So Meny People, Longages and Tonges: Philological Essays in Scots and Mediaeval English Presented to Angus McIntosh,* edited by Michael Benskin and M. S. Samuels. Edinburgh: Middle English Dialect Project, 1981.

Zumthor, Paul. *Toward a Medieval Poetics* [*Essai de poétique médiévale*]. Translated by Philip Bennett. Minneapolis: University of Minnesota Press, 1992.

6. DEVOTIONAL AND LITERARY RESPONSES TO JULIAN

Bradley, Sister Ritamary. *Julian's Way: A Practical Commentary on Julian of Norwich.* London: HarperCollins, 1992.

Dillard, Annie. *Holy the Firm.* New York: Harper & Row, 1977. Reprint, 1988.

Eliot, T. S. *Four Quartets.* London: Faber, 2000 [orig. pub. 1935–43].

Hidesley, C. Hugh. *Journeying with Julian.* Harrisburg: Morehouse Publications, 1993.

Lawlor, John. *C. S. Lewis: Memories and Reflections.* Dallas, Tex.: Spence Publishing Co., 1998.

Levertov, Denise. *Breathing the Water.* New York: New Directions, 1987.

Members of the Julian Shrine. *Enfolded in Love: Daily Readings with Julian of Norwich.* London: Darton, Longman & Todd, 1980. Reprint, 1993.

Murdoch, Iris. *Nuns and Soldiers.* London: Chatto & Windus, 1980. Reprint, Harmondsworth, Middlesex: Penguin Books, 1987.

Okulam, Frodo. *The Julian Mystique: Her Life and Teachings.* Mystic, Conn.: Twenty-Third Publications, 1998.

Prescott, H. F. M. *The Man on a Donkey.* Harmondsworth, Middlesex: Penguin Modern Classics in association with Eyre & Spottiswoode, 1969.

Upjohn, Sheila. *Why Julian Now? A Voyage of Discovery.* London: Darton, Longman & Todd, 1997.

Wakeman, Hilary. *Circles of Stillness: Thoughts on Contemplative Prayer from the Julian Meetings.* London: Darton, Longman & Todd, 2002.

Way, Robert E. *The Garden of the Beloved.* New York: Doubleday; London: Sheldon Press, 1975.

Williams, Charles. *The New Christian Year*. London: Oxford University Press, 1941.

————. *The Passion of Christ: Being the Gospel and Narrative of the Passion With Short Passages Taken from the Saints and Doctors of the Church*. London: Oxford University Press, 1939.

————. *War in Heaven*. London: Faber, 1947 [orig. pub. 1930].

7. WEB SITES

The Friends of Julian of Norwich. *Julian of Norwich Shrine*. 2000. http://home.clara.net.

Holloway, Julia Bolton. *The Julian of Norwich~Her 'Showing of Love' and Its Contents~Website*. 1997/2001. http://www.umilta.net/julian.html.

Mellilo, Elizabeth G. "Julian of Norwich." *Gloriana's Court*. 1996–2000. http://www.gloriana.nu/julian.html.

The Order of Julian of Norwich. *Julian of Norwich*. November 2001. http://www.mnsmc.edu/merton/julian.html.